Juvenile Justice

SIXTH EDITION

KÄREN M. HESS, Ph.D.
Normandale Community College

CHRISTINE HESS ORTHMANN

JOHN PAUL WRIGHT
University of Cincinnati

WADSWORTH
CENGAGE Learning·

Australia • Brazil • Japan • Korea • Mexico • Singapore • Spain • United Kingdom • United States

Juvenile Justice, **Sixth Edition**
Kären M. Hess, Christine Hess Orthmann,
John Paul Wright

Senior Publisher: Linda Ganster

Senior Acquisitions Editor: Carolyn
Henderson Meier

Assistant Editor: Virginette Acacio

Editorial Assistant: Casey Lozier

Media Editor: Ting Jian Yap

Senior Marketing Manager: Michelle
Williams

Marketing Coordinator: Jack Ward

Senior Marketing Communications
Manager: Heather Baxley

Senior Content Project Manager:
Christy A. Frame

Senior Art Director: Maria Epes

Senior Manufacturing Planner: Judy Inouye

Rights Acquisitions Specialist: Dean
Dauphinais

Production Service: Sara Dovre Wudali,
Buuji, Inc.

Photo Researcher: Terri Wright

Text Researcher: Sue Howard

Copy Editor: Robin Gold

Text and Cover Designer: Riezebos
Holzbaur/Brie Hattey

Cover Images: Top images, left to right: SW
Productions/Photodisc, John Powell/Getty
Images, © Jeff Greenberg/Alamy; bottom
image: Paul Bradbury/Getty Images

Compositor: Integra

For product information and technology assistance, contact us at
Cengage Learning Customer & Sales Support, 1-800-354-9706.
For permission to use material from this text or product,
submit all requests online at **www.cengage.com/permissions.**
Further permissions questions can be e-mailed to
permissionrequest@cengage.com.

Library of Congress Control Number: 2011945550

Student Edition:

ISBN-13: 978-1-133-04962-3

ISBN-10: 1-133-04962-1

Loose-leaf Edition:

ISBN-13: 978-1-133-52537-0

ISBN-10: 1-133-52537-7

Wadsworth
20 Davis Drive
Belmont, CA 94002-3098
USA

Cengage Learning is a leading provider of customized learning solutions
with office locations around the globe, including Singapore, the United
Kingdom, Australia, Mexico, Brazil, and Japan. Locate your local office at
www.cengage.com/global

Cengage Learning products are represented in Canada by
Nelson Education, Ltd.

To learn more about Wadsworth, visit **www.cengage.com/wadsworth**

Purchase any of our products at your local college store or at our
preferred online store **www.CengageBrain.com.**

Unless otherwise noted, all content is © Cengage Learning 2013

Printed in the United States of America
3 4 5 6 7   18 17 16 15

Brief Contents

Contents

SECTION II

 Our Nation's Youths

Chapter 4:   Youth in Society: Developmental Risks and Protective Factors   91

Chapter 6: Juvenile Offenders   165

Chapter 7: Youth Gangs   199

SECTION III

 The Contemporary Juvenile Justice System

Chapter 8: The Police and Juveniles   235

Chapter 11: Juvenile Corrections   333

SECTION IV

 The Juvenile Justice System in the Twenty-First Century

Foreword

The juvenile justice system—and there are those who would put quotation marks around *system*—has several specialized components. Each component has long been accustomed to autonomy. Each too often has only superficial knowledge of the other components. And the components seldom work together, even though each may be managing the same problem.

The system should be more than this. Our children are entitled to more. Their lives and their parents' lives are greatly affected by the agencies' responses to their problems. Unfortunately the responses often are unintentionally inconsistent and noncomplementary.

For the system to improve it must know itself. And that means that each professional within each component must know the functions and functioning of all other professionals in the system as they relate to the delinquency, misconduct and neglect of children. At the least, the classic function of each component must be recognized:

- *The police*—must protect the safety of children and the public and investigate the behavioral facts.
- *Welfare and probation services*—must investigate the social facts and provide inpatient and outpatient counseling and supervision of children and their parents.
- *Schools*—must educate children academically and, to a great extent, socially and must ensure peace within their walls.
- *Lawyers*—must stand for their clients, advocating the views of each, whatever they may be.
- *Service providers*—must have treatments that can reunite families and prevent a recurrence of the misconduct that initiated the public's intervention.
- *The court*—must arbitrate and insist on rehabilitative and protective dispositions and must use force and power within the confines of statutes and the Constitution to ensure due execution of these dispositions.

Each should perform its function knowledgeable of what the others are or may do and of the impact each may have on the others. There needs to be a coordination, a flow, a focus on the child and the family.

Beyond this primary interagency knowledge and respect, there must exist within families—whether the children's own or families found for the children or provided by the streets—solid values, caring and stability. Youths will reflect the values and stability of their families. Therefore the system cannot focus only on the child. It must look at the affective family for its influence on both the causes and the rehabilitation of misconduct, whether it be delinquency, status offenses or inadequate parental care.

Each component must look at the family as it affects its own particular function, but more, it must share its investigation and consider the investigations of others, moving toward a collaborative disposition involving the family that will be the most effective for the children.

And even this is not enough. Each professional working with children must understand children, their behavioral patterns and psychological development and their changing emotional needs as they mature, seek independence and acquire sexual appetites. Professionals must understand that boys don't become truant just because they don't like school and that they join gangs because gangs can better satisfy emotional needs that their families have not. Children are not small adults. Legally, they lack the maturity to make important judgments under the stress of changing bodies and with the insistent need for independence.

The juvenile justice system must understand itself and become a *system* in the true sense of the word, working together toward the common goal of assisting children in trouble and protecting them and the public. The juvenile justice system must know itself. This book can be its primer.

—Judge Emeritus Lindsay G. Arthur

Preface

Juvenile Justice, Sixth Edition, is a practical, applied text designed to introduce students to the juvenile justice system as it exists today, including the tremendous heterogeneity found among jurisdictions throughout the country. This completely revised edition provides students with an understanding of the complex amalgam of programs, policies, practices and philosophies that, together, constitute "the juvenile justice system" and the myriad challenges the system faces at this critical point in time. Budgets and resources are stretched thin, caseloads and court dockets in some jurisdictions remain unmanageable, and many families are struggling to hold themselves together. Although juvenile crime has steadily tracked downward from 1994, there is tremendous demand from all sides to make the juvenile justice system more efficient and effective. In the midst of these myriad pressures are new revelations regarding adolescent brain development, new data regarding which interventions are effective, new assessment tools to help practitioners better meet the needs of youth who come in contact with the system—new reasons to hope that juvenile justice can, indeed, accomplish the multiple goals of serving youth in need and those who become delinquent, while protecting society and helping restore victims and communities. But a new direction is needed.

The Approach of This Text

A sea change is occurring in juvenile justice. Interestingly, it has less to do with charting new territory than it does with returning to its roots. More than a century ago, a separate justice system for juveniles was established, based on the belief that children were developmentally distinct from adults and deserved to be treated as such by the state. During the past 30 years, however, this system has progressively eroded to become increasingly more similar to the adult criminal justice system. Today it can be said the juvenile justice system has suffered a bit of an identity crisis. But there is reason for optimism.

When the first edition of this text was published in 1990, violent juvenile crime was on an upward trend and the "get tough" movement was taking hold. Across the country, legislators and policymakers, spurred by a fearful public's demands to crack down on juvenile crime, implemented increasingly punitive sanctions for youthful offenders and allowed the relatively well-defined boundaries between the juvenile and criminal justice systems to become progressively more porous. Today, nearly 20 years beyond the mid-1990s peak in violent juvenile crime and armed with decades of research about the effects of "get tough" measures, the juvenile justice system has begun to realize that this response has not achieved what it was set in place to do and that we can no longer afford to maintain many of these measures because of diminishing financial resources.

One of the overriding themes of this text, paralleling a fundamental trend in the field, is the need to refocus on treating juveniles as juveniles. Without question, there are youths who are violent, dangerous predators and who need to be, based on the gravity of their offenses and the priority of public safety, processed in the criminal justice system. However, for many youths who encounter the system, such a response is inappropriate. Research in developmental neurology provides compelling evidence that adolescence is a period of profound brain growth and cognitive maturing, as neural wiring related to impulsivity, risk-and-consequence assessment and decision-making skills is not completed until the average person is in his or her mid-20s. These findings have led many researchers and policymakers to push for system reforms that will reflect recent research in adolescent development.

Another basic theme of this text is the need to take a systemic approach to juvenile justice issues. Problems with children do not occur in isolation; they occur within an environment of many interactive parts. The family, the school, peers and the community as a whole—all influence how a child develops and grows into an adult. Educators, counselors, social workers, law enforcement officers, attorneys, judges, probation officers and correctional service providers—each makes an important contribution in working to achieve the common goals of preventing or reducing juvenile crime and victimization.

Juvenile justice today stands at a critical crossroads. The failures of the past have caused some to declare the system ineffective and obsolete, broken beyond repair and better off dismantled. Others, however, see a system full of potential but in desperate need of reform and a return to its rehabilitative roots. Very few believe juvenile justice should stay "as is," operating to maintain the status quo. The time is ripe for change in this field.

Organization of the Text

Section I of this text provides an overview of juvenile justice from its origins, to its philosophical and theoretical bases. This part begins with definitions of juvenile justice, how delinquency is measured and the juvenile justice process itself (Chapter 1). Next, the history and philosophy behind the juvenile justice evolution is explained (Chapter 2). The section concludes with theories of what causes delinquency and juvenile offending (Chapter 3).

Section II describes the nation's youths in society and the developmental risk and protective factors they may encounter (Chapter 4). This is followed by a discussion of juvenile victims, including those who are neglected, abused and missing (Chapter 5); juvenile offenders (Chapter 6); and youth gangs (Chapter 7).

Section III takes a close look at the contemporary juvenile justice system and its three major components: law enforcement, the juvenile court and juvenile corrections. The first area of discussion focuses on the law enforcement response to abused or neglected children and to offenders (Chapter 8). This is followed by a look at alternatives between arrest and appearing in juvenile court, a stage referred to as *pretrial services and diversion* (Chapter 9). Next the juvenile court process is discussed from intake to disposition (Chapter 10), followed by a look at juvenile corrections (Chapter 11).

Section IV discusses practices and programs being conducted and proposed in the juvenile justice system. Of utmost importance in these turbulent times is finding effective ways to prevent delinquency and recidivism (Chapter 12). Finally is a discussion of the need to rethink current juvenile justice policies and practices and how the juvenile justice system might be retooled in the twenty-first century (Chapter 13).

New to This Edition

The Sixth Edition of *Juvenile Justice* has been thoroughly reviewed and revised, and all statistics are the most recently available at press time. Most importantly, this edition has been updated with the assistance of Dr. John Paul Wright, a nationally recognized and highly respected researcher and author in the field of criminology, whose experience and expertise in juvenile justice has raised the level of scholarship of this text to an unprecedented height. Specific changes within each chapter are as follows.

Chapter 1 Juvenile Justice: Definitions, Measurement and Process

- Added a definition of *juvenile*
- Tightened the section "What Is Justice?"
- Updated tables with most recently available data
- Trimmed descriptive information regarding data sources

Chapter 2 The History and Philosophy behind the Juvenile Justice System

- Tightened and clarified the discussions surrounding several terms: *deserts, deterrence, medical model, net widening*

Chapter 3 Theories of Delinquency and Juvenile Offending

- Added the terms *functionalism, general deterrence, heritability, specific deterrence*
- Tightened discussion of classical and positivist world views
- Significantly reworked the sections on biological theories (biosocial perspectives) and psychological theories
- Added reference to minority scholars' perspective on criminality

Chapter 4 Youths in Society: Developmental Risk and Protective Factors

- Added the term *teratogens*
- Included a discussion of how youth who have "advantages" (two-parent household, high SES, good community support, education, etc.) can still end up in the juvenile justice system
- Reorganized and expanded the section on oppositional defiant disorder and conduct disorder, including antisocial personality disorder
- Updated statistics on trends in teen drug use and teen pregnancy
- Rephrased the section on exposure to violent media as a debate to better reflect the two sides of the argument: The American Academy of Pediatrics provides anecdotal evidence linking violent games to violent kids, but researchers have been unable to produce any empirical data to support a causal relationship
- Added a discussion/study on the link between parenting style and delinquency

Chapter 5 Juvenile Victims

- Updated statistics from the Annie E. Casey Foundation on child maltreatment
- Cited numerous studies linking childhood maltreatment to numerous negative outcomes: emotional/behavioral problems, running away, school problems, substance abuse, dating violence, delinquency
- Included a new section on child pornography and its victims
- Added a brief section on bullying and cyberbullying, as segue to discussion of youth suicides

Chapter 6 Juvenile Offenders

- Updated statistics and data from the FBI and other sources
- Expanded content on curfew laws
- Reworded confusing passage discussing status offenses versus statutory offenses
- Added new data/studies on juvenile firesetting
- Included new data on female and minority offenders
- Updated content and citations for serious, violent offenders
- New "In the News"
- Updated the discussion on juvenile sex offenders (JSOs) and the trend to re-label these youths as adolescents with illegal sexual behavior (AISBs); also enhanced the scholarship and coverage of research

Chapter 7 Youth Gangs

- Added the term *marginalization*
- Updated statistics on gang membership
- Reorganized sections for better flow, moving "gang organization" to earlier in the chapter
- Better balanced discussion on racial/ethnic characteristics of gangs and gang members to dispel the myth or perception that all gang-involved youth are members of racial minorities
- Deleted sections on outlaw motorcycle gangs and prison gangs, as they very rarely contain juvenile members
- Added some new figures on self-reported and court-recorded offending rates among nondelinquents, delinquents and gang members
- New "In the News"
- Moved the section on Boston's Operation Ceasefire from Chapter 8 to this chapter
- Toned down the rhetoric that pervaded this chapter

Chapter 8 The Police and Juveniles

- Moved some of the general content about gun violence to Chapter 6 (Juvenile Offenders) and the gang-related gun content to Chapter 7 (Youth Gangs) to keep the content in this chapter related to police response
- Added content about Safe School Initiative and school attackers
- New "In the News"
- Added a new "Spotlight on Fight Crime: Invest in Kids"

Chapter 9 Pretrial Services and Diversion

- Updated statistics throughout
- Included more scholarly citations to support the data
- New content on teen court
- Added a new "Programs in Practice" example

Chapter 10 The Juvenile Court

- Updated statistics throughout
- Updated the table with lower age of juvenile court jurisdiction
- Moved blended sentencing to end of juvenile transfer options
- Significantly enhanced the discussion on juvenile transfer mechanisms, including more scholarly citations and recent research on consequences of transfer to adult court
- Included a new table on statutory exclusion laws

Chapter 11 Juvenile Corrections

- Added the terms *incapacitation, rehabilitation, retribution*
- Added an essential section on the goals of corrections
- Updated statistics on juvenile residential facilities
- Cut back on the content of boot camps and changed the discussion to a more historical point of view because there are no longer any state or federally operated boot camps—all are private now
- New content on violence, assault and sexual victimization in secure facilities
- Updated statistics on youth gangs in secure facilities
- Deleted inaccurate references to cruel and unusual punishment (conditions of confinement), as well as the term *cruel and unusual punishment*
- Added more content about treatment program needs of females in secure facilities

Chapter 12 Preventing Delinquency and Recidivism

- Added a section on defining *recidivism* and *desistance* (new term) and the various ways recidivism is measured
- Minor updates to Blueprints programs

Chapter 13 Juvenile Justice at a Crossroads: The Continuing Call for Reform (previously called Epilogue)

- Redirected the nature of the "crossroads" issue from the ideology to be more punitive to the financial reality that we can no longer afford to be more punitive, particularly in light of recent evidence that such measures are ineffective (speaks to budget shortfalls)

How to Use This Book

Juvenile Justice is more than a textbook; it is a planned learning experience. The more actively you participate in it, the better your learning will be. You will learn and remember more if you first familiarize yourself with the total scope of the subject. Read and think about the Contents; it outlines the many facets of juvenile justice. Then follow these steps for *triple-strength learning* as you study each chapter:

1. Read the objectives at the beginning of the chapter. These are stated as "Do You Know?" questions. Assess your current knowledge of each question. Examine any preconceptions you may hold. Glance through the terms presented to see if you can currently define them. Watch for them as you read—they are in bold print the first time they are defined in the text. Then skim the outline to get a sense of the flow of the chapter.
2. Read the chapter, underlining, highlighting or taking notes, whichever is your preferred style.

    a. Pay special attention to all information that is graphically highlighted.

    For example:

      Juvenile justice currently consists of a "one-pot" jurisdictional approach.

    The key concepts of the chapter are presented this way.

    b. Look up unfamiliar words in the Glossary at the back of the book.
3. When you have finished reading a chapter, reread the "Do You Know?" questions at the beginning of the chapter to make sure you can give an educated response to each question. If you find yourself stumped by one, find the appropriate section in the chapter and review it. Do the same thing for the "Can You Define?" terms.
4. Finally, read the discussion questions and be prepared to contribute to a class discussion of the ideas presented in the chapter.

By following these steps, you will learn more information, understand it more fully and remember it longer. It's up to you.

Note: The material selected to highlight using the triple-strength learning instructional design includes only the chapter's key concepts. Although this information is certainly important in that it provides a structural foundation for understanding the topic(s) discussed, do not simply glance over the "Do You Know?" questions, highlighted boxes and summaries and expect to master the chapter. You are also responsible for reading and understanding the material that surrounds these basics—the "meat" around the bones, so to speak.

Good learning!

Supplements

Instructor Resources

Instructor's Resource Manual with Test Bank: The Instructor's Resource Manual with Test Bank for this edition has been revised and updated by Nikki Banks of Grand Rapids Community College. The manual includes learning objectives, key terms, a detailed chapter outline, a chapter summary, discussion topics and an updated test bank. Each chapter's test bank contains questions in multiple-choice, true-false, fill-in-the-blank and essay formats, with a full answer key. The test bank is coded to the learning objectives that appear in the main text and includes the page numbers in the main text where the answers can be found.

Finally, each question in the test bank has been carefully reviewed by experienced criminal justice instructors for quality, accuracy and content coverage. Our Instructor Approved seal, which appears on the front cover, is our assurance that you are working with an assessment and grading resource of the highest caliber.

Online Lesson Plans: Revised by Laura Hahn of Towson University to reflect content in the new edition, the Lesson Plans bring accessible, masterful suggestions to every lesson. This supplement includes a sample syllabus, learning objectives, lecture notes, discussion topics, in-class activities, a detailed lecture outline, assignments, media tools and "What if . . . ?" scenarios. Current events and real-life examples in the form of articles, Web sites and video links are incorporated into the class discussion topics, activities and assignments. The lecture outlines are correlated with PowerPoint® slides for ease of classroom use. Lesson Plans are included on the PowerLecture™ resource and are available for download from the password-protected instructor book companion Web site.

ExamView® Computerized Testing: The comprehensive Instructor's Manual described earlier is backed up by ExamView, a computerized test bank available for PC and Macintosh computers. With ExamView you can create, deliver and customize tests and study guides (both print and online) in minutes. You can easily edit and import your own questions and graphics, change test layouts and reorganize questions. And using ExamView's complete word-processing capabilities, you can enter an unlimited number of new questions or edit existing questions.

The Wadsworth Criminal Justice Video Library: So many exciting new videos—so many great ways to enrich your lectures and spark discussion of the material in this text. Your Cengage Learning representative will be happy to provide details on our video policy by adoption size. The library includes these selections and many others:

- *ABC® Videos*. ABC videos feature short, high-interest clips from current news events as well as historic raw footage going back 40 years. Perfect for discussion starters or to enrich your lectures and spark interest in the material in the text, these brief videos provide students with a new lens through which to view the past and present, one that will greatly enhance their knowledge and understanding of significant events and open up to them new dimensions in learning. Clips are drawn from such programs as *World News Tonight, Good Morning America, This Week, PrimeTime Live, 20/20* and *Nightline*, as well as numerous ABC News specials and material from the Associated Press Television News and British Movietone News collections.

- *Cengage Learning's "Introduction to Criminal Justice Video Series"* features videos supplied by the BBC Motion Gallery. These short, high-interest clips from CBS and BBC news programs—everything from nightly news broadcasts and specials to *CBS News Special Reports, CBS Sunday Morning, 60 Minutes* and more—are perfect classroom discussion starters. Designed to enrich your lectures and spark interest in the material in the text, these brief videos provide students with a new lens through which to view the past and present, one that will greatly enhance their knowledge and understanding of significant events and open up to them new dimensions in learning. Clips are drawn from the BBC Motion Gallery.

Criminal Justice Media Library on WebTutor: Cengage Learning's Criminal Justice Media Library includes nearly 300 media assets on the topics you cover in your courses. Available to stream from any Web-enabled computer, the Criminal Justice Media Library's assets include such valuable resources as Career Profile Videos featuring interviews with criminal justice professionals from a range of roles and locations; simulations that allow students to step into various roles and practice their decision-making skills; video clips on current topics from ABC® and other sources; animations that illustrate key concepts; interactive learning modules that help students check their knowledge of important topics; and Reality Check exercises that compare expectations and preconceived notions against the real-life thoughts and experiences of criminal justice professionals. Video assets include assessment questions that can be delivered straight to the grade book. The Criminal Justice Media Library can be uploaded and customized within many popular Learning Management Systems. Please contact your Cengage Learning representative for ordering and pricing information.

Student Resources

Careers in Criminal Justice Web site: *Can be bundled with this text at no additional charge.* Featuring plenty of self-exploration and profiling activities, the interactive Careers in Criminal Justice Web site helps students investigate and focus on the criminal justice career choices that are right for them. The Web site includes interest assessment, video testimonials from career professionals, resumé and interview tips and links for reference.

CLeBook: Cengage Learning's Criminal Justice e-books allow students to access our textbooks in an easy-to-use online format. Highlight, take notes, bookmark, search your text and, for most texts, link directly into multimedia. In short, CLeBooks combine the best features of paper books and ebooks in one package.

Acknowledgments

First we would like to acknowledge the original lead author, **Robert W. Drowns** (d. 1996), whose experiences working with juveniles as a sworn police officer formed the foundation for the first edition of this text. Mr. Drowns was an instructor at Metropolitan State University (Minnesota), a consultant to the Office of Juvenile Justice and Delinquency Prevention (OJJDP) and a conductor of many seminars and workshops throughout the country on various aspects of juvenile justice.

Second, we would like to thank the reviewers for this revision for their constructive feedback. We also wish to thank the reviewers of previous editions of *Juvenile Justice* for their helpful insight and suggestions: T. F. Adams, Del Mar College; Jennifer Allen, Western Illinois University; Kelly J. Asmussen, Peru State College; Steve W. Atchley, Delaware Technical Community College; Pierrette R. Ayotte, Thomas College; Michael G. Bisciglia, Southeastern Louisiana University; John Bolinger, MacMurray College; Jerald C. Burns; Colleen Clark, Minnesota State University–Mankato; Wesley J. Cotter, Fitchburg State University;

James Cunningham, State Fair Community College; Dorinda Dowis, Colorado State University; Peter Dunn, Suffolk Community College; Patrick Dunworth; J. Price Foster, University of Louisville; Tanya M. Grant, Sacred Heart University; Ralph Grunewald, University of Wisconsin–Madison; Burt C. Hagerman; Ray Harrington, Pfeiffer University; Patricia M. Harris; Frederick F. Hawley; James Paul Heuser; Suzanne Hopf, University of Louisville; Robert Ives; James L. Jengeleski, Argosy University Online; Morris Jenkins, University of Toledo; James Jernigan, Troy University; Soraya K. Kawucha, University of North Texas; Daniel Kesler, John Jay College of Criminal Justice; Peter Kratcoski; Richard Kuiters, Bergen Community College; Jason J. Leiker, Utah State University; Matthew C. Leone; Clarence Augustus Martin; Richard H. Martin, Elgin Community College; Barry McCrary, Western Illinois University; Markita McCrimmon, Central Carolina Community College; Jonathan McLister, Slippery Rock University; Roger McNally, SUNY College at Brockport; Jacqueline Mullany, Triton College; Johnnie Dumas Myers, Savannah State University; David Olson, Loyola University, Chicago; Amy Pinero, Baton Rouge Community College; Jennifer Prutsman-Pfeiffer, SUNY College at Brockport; Alfred Reed, Jr., Los Angeles Southwest College; David Rogers, Aims Community College; Michael Roy, Alpena Community College; Chris Schreck, Rochester Institute of Technology; Paul Steele, University of New Mexico; David P. Stumpf, Minnesota School of Business; Matthew Theriot, The University of Tennessee; Sandra M. Todaro, Bossier Parish Community College; James Vardalis, Tarleton State University; Nicholas M. Wade, Los Angeles Valley College; Arnold R. Waggoner, Rose State College; Jason Waller, Tyler Junior College; and Ruth Walsh, Washtenaw Community College.

A heartfelt thank you to Carolyn Henderson Meier, executive editor at Wadsworth Publishing; Christy Frame, project manager at Wadsworth Publishing; Sara Dovre Wudali, production editor at Buuji, Inc.; Robin Gold, copyeditor; and Terri Wright, photo researcher, for their excellent work on producing this text.

Finally, Christine Orthmann wants to express her deep gratitude to John Wright for agreeing to jump into this project despite his already full schedule. And John Wright would like to extend a sincere thank you to Christine Orthmann and Carolyn Henderson Meier for the opportunity to participate in this book.

About the Authors

Kären Matison Hess, PhD (d. 2010) wrote extensively in law enforcement and criminal justice, gaining a respected reputation for the consistent pedagogical style around which she structured each textbook. She developed the original edition of *Juvenile Justice* with Robert Drowns and carried it through four very successful revisions; much of her work and influence remains unchanged in this new edition.

Other texts Dr. Hess authored or coauthored for Cengage Publishing are *Careers in Criminal Justice and Related Fields: From Internship to Promotion* (6th edition); *Community Policing: Partnerships for Problem Solving* (6th edition); *Constitutional Law and the Criminal Justice System* (5th edition); *Corrections for the 21st Century: A Practical Approach; Criminal Investigation* (10th edition); *Criminal Procedure; Introduction to Law Enforcement and Criminal Justice* (10th edition); *Introduction to Private Security* (5th edition); *Management and Supervision in Law Enforcement* (6th edition); and *Police Operations* (5th edition).

Dr. Hess was an instructor in the English department at Normandale Community College (Bloomington, Minnesota), a frequent instructor for report-writing workshops and seminars for law enforcement agencies around the country and president of the Institute for Professional Development. She was a member of the Academy of Criminal Justice Sciences (ACJS), the American Association of University Women (AAUW), the American Society for Industrial Security (ASIS), the International Association of Chiefs of Police (IACP), the International Law Enforcement Educators and Trainers Association (ILEETA), the Justice Research and Statistics Association (JRSA), the National Criminal Justice Association (NCJA), the National Council of Teachers of English (NCTE), the Police Executive Research Forum (PERF) and the Textbook and Academic Author's Association (TAA), of which she was a fellow and a board member (TAA Foundation). In 2006 Dr. Hess was honored by the University of Minnesota College of Education and Human Development at the school's 100-year anniversary as one of 100 alumni who have made a significant contribution to education and human development.

Christine Hess Orthmann, M.S., has been writing and researching in various aspects of criminal justice for more than 20 years. She is a coauthor of numerous Cengage books, including *Criminal Investigation* (10th edition); *Community Policing: Partnerships for Problem Solving* (6th edition); *Constitutional Law and the Criminal Justice System* (5th edition); *Corrections for the Twenty-First Century: A Practical Approach; Introduction to Law Enforcement and Criminal Justice* (10th edition); *Management and Supervision in Law Enforcement* (6th edition); and *Police Operations* (5th edition)—as well as a major contributor to *Introduction to Private Security*

(5th edition) and *Careers in Criminal Justice and Related Fields: From Internship to Promotion* (6th edition). She is a member of the Academy of Criminal Justice Sciences (ACJS), the American Society of Criminology (ASC), the Text and Academic Authors Association (TAA) and the National Criminal Justice Honor Society (Alpha Phi Sigma) and is a reserve officer with the Rosemount (Minnesota) Police Department. Orthmann has a Master of Science degree in criminal justice from the University of Cincinnati.

John Paul Wright, PhD, received his doctorate in 1996 from the University of Cincinnati and has worked as Professor of Criminal Justice in the School of Criminal Justice at the University of Cincinnati since 2001. Dr. Wright has authored or coauthored more than 100 publications, including seven books, and is nationally recognized for his research into biological factors related to crime as well as his work on the development of violence across the life course.

Juvenile Justice

Definitions, Measurements and Process

> **"** The way in which a society treats its children—its young people—says something about the future of that society, its beliefs, and the viability of those beliefs. The way in which a society treats those of its children who break its laws says something about its humanity, its morality, its resilience, and its capacity for self-correction. **"**
>
> —**National Center for Juvenile Justice**

At the New York House of Refuge, children learned various trades and engaged in physical activities.

Stock Montage

DO YOU KNOW?

- What *parens patriae* is and why it is important in juvenile justice?
- What the most common upper age for original juvenile court jurisdiction is?
- How researchers measure the nature and extent of youthful offending?
- What the Federal Bureau of Investigation's Uniform Crime Reports measures?

- How prevalent delinquency is according to self-reports?
- What the terminology of the contemporary juvenile justice system emphasizes?
- What issues the contemporary juvenile justice system faces?
- How the contemporary conservative and liberal approaches to juvenile justice differ?

CAN YOU DEFINE?

adjudicated

dark figure of crime

delinquent

discrimination

disparity

diversion

juvenile

one-pot approach

parens patriae

petitioned

restorative justice

retributive justice

status offense

Uniform Crime Reports

CHAPTER OUTLINE

Introduction

The Scope of the Juvenile Justice System

Who Is a Juvenile?

What Is Justice?

Measuring the Number of Juvenile Victimizations and Offenses

The FBI's Uniform Crime Reports (UCR)

The National Incident-Based Reporting System (NIBRS)

The Bureau of Justice Statistics National Crime Victimization Survey (NCVS)

The UCR and NCVS Compared

Self-Reports

The Media's Effect on Public Perception of Juveniles

Terminology

Organization and Structure of Juvenile Justice

The Juvenile Justice Process

Arrest

Referral

Intake

Diversion

Detention

Petitioning/Charges Filed

Adjudication Hearing/ Delinquency Finding

Dispositional Hearing

Probation

Confinement in a Secure Correctional Facility

Transfer to Adult Court

The Juvenile Justice System and Criminal Justice System Compared

Issues in Juvenile Justice

To Divert or Not?

Which Is More Just: A Conservative or a Liberal Approach to Delinquency?

Confidentiality versus Openness

Disproportionate Minority Contact (DMC)

Introduction

A separate justice system for juveniles began in the United States more than 100 years ago with the establishment of the first juvenile court in 1899. This system was built around several core principles, first and foremost being that juveniles were different from adults and needed to be treated differently by the justice system. Second, it was argued that juveniles were different from each other and, therefore, deserved individualized treatment based on their unique situations and circumstances. In effect, youths who were abused and neglected should be treated differently from youths who committed minor status offenses or youths who engaged in serious, violent crime. Thus, juvenile justice became a system intended to provide a legal setting in which youths could account for their wrongs or receive official protection.

 The underlying premise of the first juvenile court was that of **parens patriae**, the responsibility of the state to protect its children and youth.

Making the states responsible for its children and youth has resulted in not 1, but 51 (50 states plus Washington, DC) distinct juvenile justice systems throughout the United States, each with its own history and set of laws. Even within a single state, the mandates conceived in the state's capitol building must be interpreted and implemented by various local officials, under widely varying conditions and with widely varying effects. Add to these 51 separate systems the federal juvenile justice system and the challenge of understanding what juvenile justice is becomes even greater.

The Scope of the Juvenile Justice System

One challenge facing the juvenile justice system is the **one-pot approach** to children and youth evident throughout history, an approach that places those who are abused and neglected, those who commit status offenses and those who are delinquents into the same judicial system. A **status offense** is an act that would not be considered a crime if committed by an adult, for example, smoking cigarettes or staying out all night. A juvenile **delinquent** is a youth who commits an act that would be a crime were it to be committed by an adult. The term *delinquent* is intended to avoid stigmatizing youths as criminals. The majority of cases processed through the juvenile justice system today are those involving delinquency; relatively few status offense cases are processed, as alternative dispositions have become increasingly available to handle this population. Chapter 5 focuses on youths who have been victimized: battered, neglected, missing or exploited. Chapter 6 focuses on juveniles who break the law, both status offenders and delinquents.

Throughout this text keep in mind that the juvenile justice system must accommodate both children and youths who *have* serious problems and those who *are* problems, some of whom commit serious, violent offenses. In addition to this challenge the states must establish just who falls into the *juvenile* classification.

Who Is a Juvenile?

Being a juvenile means several things. In terms of human development, a juvenile is an individual who is physiologically, emotionally and intellectually immature. This developmental immaturity dictates a sociolegal status for juveniles that is bound by numerous requirements and restrictions—for example, education laws require juveniles to attend school to a certain age, labor laws restrict when and where juveniles can work, driving laws dictate the age at which juveniles are allowed to obtain a driver's license and impose myriad restrictions on driving privileges, and juveniles are not permitted to enter into legal contracts, including marriage.

The age at which a child comes under the juvenile court's jurisdiction is established statutorily by each state. Most states have upper age limits of juvenile jurisdiction in abuse, neglect and dependency cases and in status offenses—typically through age 20. Many states exclude married or otherwise emancipated juveniles from juvenile court jurisdiction.

The youngest age for juvenile court jurisdiction in delinquency matters ranges from age 6 to age 10. The oldest age for original juvenile court jurisdiction in delinquency matters ranges from 15 to 17, with 17 being the most common age, as summarized in Table 1.1. Therefore, within the context of juvenile justice, a **juvenile** is a youth who is at or below the upper age of original jurisdiction in their resident state.

In earlier editions of this text the age range was from 16 to 19, with the most common age being 18. This lowering of the oldest age reflects the nationwide trend that took hold during the 1980s and 1990s to "get tough" on youth in trouble with the law. Some states, however, are beginning to reconsider this upper age of juvenile court jurisdiction, as discussed later in the chapter.

 Seventeen is most commonly recognized as the upper age for original juvenile court jurisdiction in delinquency matters.

Under special circumstances, or through the use of blended sentencing structures, state legislatures can extend the duration of time the juvenile court has jurisdiction over youth for disposition purposes, if doing so is in the best interests of the juveniles and the state. Currently statutes in 35 states extend certain juvenile court jurisdiction in delinquency cases until age 25. These differences in state statutes regarding who falls under juvenile court jurisdiction make it imperative that juvenile justice practitioners and researchers become familiar with their state's statutes.

Another basic difference among the various juvenile justice systems is just how they view justice itself.

Table 1.1 Upper Age of Original Juvenile Court Jurisdiction, 2009

Age	State
15	Connecticut, New York, North Carolina
16	Georgia, Illinois, Louisiana, Massachusetts, Michigan, Missouri, New Hampshire, South Carolina, Texas, Wisconsin
17	Alabama, Alaska, Arizona, Arkansas, California, Colorado, Delaware, District of Columbia, Florida, Hawaii, Idaho, Indiana, Iowa, Kansas, Kentucky, Maine, Maryland, Minnesota, Mississippi, Montana, Nebraska, Nevada, New Jersey, New Mexico, North Dakota, Ohio, Oklahoma, Oregon, Pennsylvania, Rhode Island, South Dakota, Tennessee, Utah, Vermont, Virginia, Washington, West Virginia, Wyoming

SOURCE: Adapted from Howard N. Snyder and Melissa Sickmund. 2006 (March). *Juvenile Offenders and Victims: 2006 National Report*, p. 103. Washington, DC: U.S. Department of Justice, Office of Justice Programs, Office of Juvenile Justice and Delinquency Prevention. Reprinted by permission.

What Is Justice?

Centuries ago Aristotle warned that no government could stand that is not founded on justice. As a nation, America is firmly committed to "liberty and justice for all." But exactly what is justice?

Justice is a multifaceted concept for which there is no singular definition. Aristotle wrote that the *just* is that which is lawful (universal justice) and that which is fair and equal (particular justice). In discussions of crime and punishment, several types of justice garner the most attention. **Retributive justice** seeks revenge or recompense for unlawful behavior and harkens back to the ancient concept of an eye for an eye (*lex talionis*). Retribution has been the traditional response to crime, with the government meting out punishment to those who offend its laws. **Restorative justice**, conversely, focuses on repairing the harm done to victims and to the community and stresses that offenders must contribute to the repair. As such, restorative justice is alternately referred to as *reparative justice*.

Restorative justice has gained momentum and support throughout juvenile justice in recent years, as rather than seeking retribution (punishment), it seeks restitution—to repair the damages as much as possible and to restore the victim, the community and the offender: "Restorative justice suggests that the response to youth crime must strike a balance among the needs of victims, offenders and communities and that each should be actively involved in the justice process to the greatest extent possible" (Bazemore and Umbreit 2001, 1).

Table 1.2 summarizes the differences between the traditional retributive approach to justice and restorative justice. Figure 1.1 illustrates the restorative justice approach. The renewed interest in and focus on restorative justice and using restorative conferencing as a correctional alternative are discussed in Chapter 9.

Throughout the text, the most current information available about who is actually being served by the juvenile justice system will be provided. The following discussion provides background on just how this information is obtained.

Measuring the Number of Juvenile Victimizations and Offenses

Just how serious is the problem of youthful victims and offenders in the United States? Researchers use a variety of tools to address this question. This overview is intended to help familiarize students with how such statistics and other information about youth who are victimized and those who victimize are obtained.

 Researchers commonly use three methods to measure the nature and extent of unlawful acts by juveniles: official data, victim surveys and self-report data.

Official data are information and statistics collected by the police, courts and corrections agencies on the local, regional and national levels. Two of the most frequently consulted official sources of crime data are those compiled by the Federal Bureau of Investigation (FBI) and the Bureau of Justice Statistics (BJS). Other

Table 1.2 Paradigms of Justice—Old and New

Old Paradigm/Retributive Justice	New Paradigm/Restorative Justice
1. Crime defined as violation of the state	1. Crime defined as violation of one person by another
2. Focus on establishing blame, on guilt, on past (did he/she do it?)	2. Focus on problem solving, on liabilities and obligations, on future (what should be done?)
3. Adversarial relationships and process normative	3. Dialogue and negotiation normative
4. Imposition of pain to punish and deter/prevent	4. Restitution as a means of restoring both parties; reconciliation/restoration as goal
5. Justice defined by intent and by process: right rules	5. Justice defined as right relationships; judged by the outcome
6. Interpersonal, conflictual nature of crime obscured, repressed; conflict seen as individual vs. state	6. Crime recognized as interpersonal conflict; value of conflict recognized
7. One social injury replaced by another	7. Focus on repair of social injury
8. Community on sidelines, represented abstractly by state	8. Community as facilitator in restorative process
9. Encouragement of competitive, individualistic values	9. Encouragement of mutuality
10. Action directed from state to offender: • victim ignored • offender passive	10. Victim's and offender's roles recognized in both problem and solution: • victim rights/needs recognized • offender encouraged to take responsibility
11. Offender accountability defined as taking punishment	11. Offender accountability defined as understanding impact of action and helping decide how to make things right
12. Offense defined in purely legal terms, devoid of moral, social, economic, political dimensions	12. Offense understood in whole context—moral, social, economic, political
13. "Debt" owed to state and society in the abstract	13. Debt/liability to victim recognized
14. Response focused on offender's past behavior	14. Response focused on harmful consequences of offender's behavior
15. Stigma of crime unremovable	15. Stigma of crime removable through restorative action
16. No encouragement for repentance and forgiveness	16. Possibilities for repentance and forgiveness
17. Dependence on proxy professionals	17. Direct involvement by participants

SOURCE: Howard Zehr. "Restorative Justice." *IARCA Journal*, March 1991, 7.

sources of official statistics are the Office of Juvenile Justice and Delinquency Prevention (OJJDP) and the National Institute of Justice (NIJ).

The FBI's Uniform Crime Reports (UCR)

Information about crime comes from data gathered from around the country. In 1930 Congress assigned the FBI to serve as a national clearinghouse for crime statistics. The FBI's National Crime Information Center (NCIC) instituted the **Uniform Crime Reports** (UCR) program to collect offense information for the Part I offenses of murder and nonnegligent manslaughter, forcible rape, robbery,

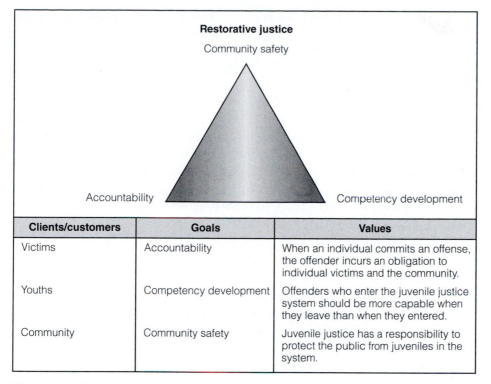

Clients/customers	Goals	Values
Victims	Accountability	When an individual commits an offense, the offender incurs an obligation to individual victims and the community.
Youths	Competency development	Offenders who enter the juvenile justice system should be more capable when they leave than when they entered.
Community	Community safety	Juvenile justice has a responsibility to protect the public from juveniles in the system.

Figure 1.1   Restorative Justice Approach

Adapted from D. Maloney, D. Romig, and T. Armstrong. 1998. *Juvenile Probation: The Balanced Approach*. Reno, NV: National Council of Juvenile and Family Court Judges. Source: Shay Bilchik. 1998 (December). *Guide for Implementing the Balanced and Restorative Justice Model*, p. 6. Washington, DC: Office of Juvenile Justice and Delinquency Prevention.

aggravated assault, burglary, larceny-theft and motor vehicle theft. In 1978 arson was added to the list as a Part I reportable offense.

 The FBI's Uniform Crime Reports contain statistics on violent crimes (murder, aggravated assault causing serious bodily harm, forcible rape and robbery) and property crimes (burglary, larceny-theft, motor vehicle theft and arson).

The UCR program also collects arrest data on 21 other crimes, such as driving under the influence, that constitute the Part II offenses. The annual publication of this program, *Crime in the United States*, reports that in 2009, nearly 18,000 law enforcement agencies representing more than 295 million United States inhabitants, or 96.3 percent of the total population, voluntarily contributed data to the FBI either directly or through state UCR programs.

Over the years the UCR developed into a broad utility for summary-based reporting of crime. The Part I crimes were considered by experts of the time to be the most serious and most commonly reported crimes occurring in the United States, as well as the most likely to occur with sufficient frequency to provide an adequate basis for comparison. Therefore, from 1960 to 2004, the eight Part I crimes served as a collective Crime Index, a general snapshot of offenses occurring throughout the country that was used to gauge fluctuations in the volume and rate of crime reported to law enforcement.

By the late 1970s, however, the law enforcement community saw a need for a more detailed crime reporting program to meet the needs of law enforcement in the 21st century. One of the primary criticisms of the UCR Index program was that it used a hierarchy system in which only the most serious offense in an incident was recorded. For example, if an individual was assaulted and robbed, UCR would record only one offense—the assault. The robbery would go unaccounted. Also, in recent years, the Crime Index has not been a true indicator of the degree of criminality of a locality. For example, larceny-thefts currently account for almost 60 percent of the total crimes reported. Consequently, the volume of larcenies overshadows more serious but less frequently committed crimes.

Because of these numerous shortcomings, in June 2004 the FBI's Criminal Justice Information Services (CJIS) Division, Advisory Policy Board (APB), approved discontinuing the use of the Crime Index in the UCR program and its publications. The CJIS APB recommended that the FBI publish a violent crime total and a property crime total until a more viable index is developed.

A summary of the figures for crimes committed in 2010 is depicted in the Crime Clock (Figure 1.2). The Crime Clock should be viewed with care. This graphic does not imply a regularity in the commission of the Part I offenses; rather it represents the annual ratio of crime to fixed time intervals. The most recent UCR figures are available online at the FBI's Web site. For more information, visit the Criminal Justice Companion Web site at cengagebrain.com, then access the web links for this chapter.

The UCR's statistics give a slight glimpse into delinquency in the United States, but the data must be interpreted cautiously. The UCR Program considers

Figure 1.2 2010 Crime Clock

FBI, 2010. Retrieved from: http://www.fbi.gov/about-us/cjis/ucr/crime-in-the-u.s/2010/crime-in-the-u.s.-2010/offenses-known-to-law-enforcement/crime-clock.

a juvenile to be an individual under 18 years of age regardless of state definition. Also, the data represent only youths who have been arrested. Many are never caught, and many are caught but are diverted and not formally arrested. It has been estimated that 80 to 90 percent of children in the United States younger than 18 commit some offense for which they could be arrested, but only about 3 percent are. In addition, multiple arrests of the same youth for different crimes are counted separately. The total number of arrests does not equal the number of youth who have been arrested because chronic offenders have multiple arrests. Finally, the program does not collect data regarding police contact with a juvenile who has not committed an offense, nor does it collect data on situations in which police take a juvenile into custody for his or her protection, such as neglect cases.

The National Incident-Based Reporting System (NIBRS)

Efforts to redesign and modernize the UCR program resulted in the development of the National Incident-Based Reporting System (NIBRS) in 1988. Intended to supplement or replace the summary data of the UCR, the NIBRS collects detailed incident information on 46 offenses representing 22 categories of crimes. Unlike the UCR, which is bound by the hierarchy rule in counting only the most serious crime committed during a single event, NIBRS counts every offense and, consequently, provides a more complete picture of offending incidents and trends. A complete list of the crime categories included in NIBRS is available on the FBI Web site. For more information, visit the Criminal Justice Companion Web site at cengagebrain.com, then access the web links for this chapter.

In 2007, the most recent year for which data are available, 6,444 agencies contributed NIBRS data to the UCR program, representing 25 percent of the U.S. population and 25 percent of crime statistics collected by the FBI. At that time 31 state UCR programs were certified by the FBI and 15 states were in various stages of planning, developing and testing their NIBRS solutions.

One reason departments may be reluctant to switch to NIBRS is that they will doubtless see a significant increase in crime statistics, while actual crime may, in fact, be decreasing.

The other most commonly referred to official data are those compiled by the Bureau of Justice Statistics.

The Bureau of Justice Statistics National Crime Victimization Survey (NCVS)

The Bureau of Justice Statistics (BJS) National Crime Victimization Survey (NCVS) began in 1973 and gathers information on personal crime experience through interviews with approximately 135,300 people age 12 years and older in 76,000 households nationwide. The survey collects data on crimes against individuals and households, regardless of whether they were reported to law enforcement. The data from this representative sample are then extrapolated to estimate the proportion of each crime type reported to law enforcement and detail reasons given for reporting or not reporting.

The NCVS collects detailed information on the frequency and nature of the crimes of rape, personal robbery, aggravated and simple assault, household burglary, personal and household theft and motor vehicle theft. The survey provides information about victims' age, sex, race, ethnicity, marital status, income and educational level; their offenders' sex, race, approximate age and victim-offender relationship; and the crimes: time and place of occurrence, use of weapons, nature of injury and economic consequences. Questions also cover the victims' experiences with the criminal justice system, self-protective measures used and possible substance abuse by offenders.

The UCR and NCVS Compared

The UCR and NCVS differ significantly. The UCR focuses on arrests of offenders whereas the NCVS focuses on victims of crime. As noted, the NCVS projects crime levels from a selected source of information and reports a substantially higher number of crimes than those reported in the UCR. Some analysts believe neither report is accurate and that crime is two to five times higher than either source reports. The UCR captures crimes reported to law enforcement but excludes simple assaults. The NCVS includes crimes both reported and not reported to law enforcement but excludes homicide, arson, commercial crimes and crimes against children under age 12 (all included in the UCR program). Even when the same crimes are included in the UCR and NCVS, the definitions vary.

Another difference is how rate measures are presented. The UCR crime rates are largely per capita (number of crimes per 100,000 persons), whereas the NCVS rates are per household (number of crimes per 1,000 households). Because the number of households may not grow at the same rate as the total population, trend data for rates measured by the two programs may not be compatible. As might be expected, given the differences in how the data are collected, the rates per 100,000 victims can differ significantly between the two reporting systems. In fact, in every instance when comparisons are made between the FBI's 2007 UCR data and the BJS's 2007 NCVS data, the NCVS shows a much higher incident rate per 100,000 than the UCR shows. Despite these differences, these two official sources are helpful in understanding the extent of crime and victimization.

Self-Reports

Self-report studies let youth personally reveal information about their violations of the law. Self-report formats include one-to-one interviews, surveys and anonymous questionnaires. If truancy, alcohol consumption, smoking marijuana or cigarettes and petty theft are included in self-report scales, low-level or minor delinquency appears to be almost "normal" or universally reported by juveniles.

 According to self-report studies, minor delinquency is almost universal.

When the prevalence and frequency of offending according to court records and self-reports are compared, it is clear that self-report data reveal a greater prevalence and frequency of offending than do court records, as shown in Table 1.3. In comparing self-reports to official crime data, Kirk (2006) found a sizable number of youth self-reported being arrested without having a corresponding official arrest record. In addition, a substantial proportion of youth with an official arrest record failed to self-report they had been arrested.

Table 1.3 Prevalence and Frequency of Offending: Court Records versus Self-Reports

	Prevalence		Frequency	
	Court	Self-Report	Court	Self-Report
Age				
11	1.7	28.4	1.1	2.9
12	2.1	27.9	2.1	4.6
13	8.0	41.5	2.8	11.6
14	10.6	46.4	2.8	13.5
15	13.1	47.6	3.1	16.8
16	13.6	51.3	2.2	18.3
17	12.7	61.1	2.4	21.8
Total	34.0	85.9	4.6	49.2
Offense Type				
Burglary	4.7	22.3	1.6	3.2
Vehicle theft	23.8	33.1	1.8	5.9
Larceny	25.6	66.1	2.0	11.6
Robbery	3.3	8.6	1.2	5.6
Assault	12.7	61.3	2.4	11.4
Vandalism	8.4	47.9	1.9	8.2
Marijuana use	1.8	49.1	1.2	29.9
Drug selling	3.9	21.7	1.6	28.8

Notes: Prevalence = % offending.
Frequency = Average offenses per offender.

SOURCE: David P. Farrington, Darrick Jolliffe, J. David Hawkins, Richard F. Catalano, Karl G. Hill, and Rick Kosterman. 2003. "Comparing Delinquency Careers in Court Records and Self-Reports." *Criminology* (August): 941. Reprinted by permission.

The University of Michigan's Institute for Social Research (ISR) routinely surveys thousands of high school seniors regarding delinquent activities, the results of which are published in *Monitoring the Future*. Anonymous, self-report data are also compiled by PRIDE Surveys, a private organization that works with schools and school districts throughout the country to administer questionnaires designed to elicit information on youth behaviors and other crucial factors that affect learning, such as family issues, discipline, safety, gangs and substance abuse.

Another resource for data on self-reported delinquent and risk-related behaviors is the Centers for Disease Control and Prevention (CDC) Youth Risk Behavior Surveillance System (YRBSS), a national program that monitors six categories of priority health-risk behaviors among youth and young adults: (1) behaviors that contribute to unintentional injuries and violence; (2) tobacco use; (3) alcohol and other drug use; (4) sexual behaviors that contribute to unintended pregnancy and sexually transmitted diseases, including HIV infection; (5) unhealthy dietary behaviors; and (6) physical inactivity. YRBSS synthesizes and summarizes results from national school-based surveys conducted by the CDC and state and local school-based surveys conducted by state and local education and health agencies. Select results from the national survey, 39 state surveys and 22 local surveys conducted among students in grades 9 through 12 during 2009 are given in Table 1.4.

Other sources of self-report data are The National Youth Survey—Family Study, conducted by the University of Colorado's Institute of Behavioral Science;

Table 1.4 High School Students Reporting Victimization or Involvement in Delinquent and Risk-Related Behavior, Including Drug, Alcohol and Cigarette Use, 2009

Delinquent/Risk-Related Behavior	Grade 9	Grade 10	Grade 11	Grade 12	Total
Were involved in a physical fight[1]	37.0%	33.5%	28.6%	24.9%	31.5%
Were injured in a physical fight[1]	4.1	4.1	3.8	2.9	3.8
Carried a weapon on school property[2]	4.9	6.1	5.2	6.0	5.6
Were threatened or injured with a weapon on school property[2]	8.7	8.4	7.9	5.2	7.7
Did not go to school because they felt unsafe at or going to/from school[3]	5.8	5.0	5.3	3.4	5.0
Were offered, sold or given an illegal drug by someone on school property[4]	22.0	23.7	24.3	20.6	22.7
Experienced dating violence[5]	9.2	9.2	10.4	10.4	9.8
Were forced to have sexual intercourse[5]	6.6	7.1	8.2	7.8	7.4
Seriously considered attempting suicide[6]	14.8	13.4	14.5	12.1	13.8
Attempted suicide[7]	7.3	6.9	6.3	4.2	6.3
Rode with a driver who had been drinking alcohol[8]	27.5	28.0	29.4	28.2	28.3
Drove while drinking alcohol[8]	5.0	8.3	11.4	15.4	9.7
Lifetime alcohol use[9]	63.4	71.1	77.8	79.7	72.5
Current alcohol use[9]	31.5	40.6	45.7	51.7	41.8
Episodic heavy drinking (binge drinking = 5+ alcoholic drinks in a row)[10]	15.3	22.3	28.3	33.5	24.2
Drank alcohol before age 13[11]	28.1	22.2	17.9	14.2	21.1
Currently smoke more than 10 cigarettes/day[12]	8.0	6.2	8.1	8.5	7.8
Current marijuana use[13]	15.5	21.1	23.2	24.6	20.8
Current cocaine use[14]	2.3	2.5	3.3	3.0	2.8
Lifetime inhalant use[15]	13.0	12.5	11.5	9.1	11.7
Lifetime prescription drug abuse[16]	15.1	18.2	22.7	25.8	20.2
Lifetime hallucinogen use[16]	5.9	7.4	8.9	10.0	8.0
Lifetime methamphetamine use[17] (T47)	3.3	3.7	5.2	4.1	4.1
Lifetime Ecstasy use[18] (T49)	4.9	5.2	8.7	8.0	6.7

[1] Table 10, p.47; [2] Table 14, p.51; [3] Table 18, p.55; [4] Table 59, p.96; [5] Table 12, p.49; [6] Table 22, p.59; [7] Table 24, p.61; [8] Table 6, p.43; [9] Table 36, p.73; [10] Table 38, p.75; [11] Table 51, p.88; [12] Table 30, p.67; [13] Table 40, p.77; [14] Table 42, p.79; [15] Table 44, p.81; [16] Table 50, p.87; [17] Table 46, p.83; [18] Table 44, p.81.

SOURCE: Adapted from Danice K. Eaton, Laura Kann, Steve Kinchen, Shari Shanklin, James Ross, Joseph Hawkins, William A. Harris, Richard Lowry, Tim McManus, David Chyen, Connie Lim, Lisa Whittle, Nancy D. Brener, and Howell Wechsler. 2010. *Youth Risk Behavior Surveillance—United States, 2009*. Atlanta, GA: Centers for Disease Control and Prevention, Surveillance Summaries, *Morbidity and Mortality Weekly Report* 59(SS-5, June 4).

the Program of Research on the Causes and Correlates of Delinquency (often simply referred to as the Causes and Correlates Survey), which comprises three coordinating longitudinal projects: the Denver Youth Survey compiled by the University of Colorado, the Pittsburgh Youth Survey compiled by the University of Pittsburgh and the Rochester Youth Development Study compiled by the State University of New York at Albany; and the National Survey of Child and Adolescent Well Being, conducted by the U.S. Department of Health and Human Services, Administration for Children and Families.

Official Statistics versus Self-Reports   Just as the findings from the UCR and the NCVS differ significantly, so do those between official statistics and self-reports. The debate about the relative ability of self-report studies and official statistics to describe juvenile crime and victims is ongoing. Official data are a comparatively more reliable source on serious crime than are self-reports, but self-reports do provide more insight into the frequency and diversity of offending patterns. Self-report studies can capture information on activities that never come to juvenile justice agencies' attention. These self-report studies show a much higher proportion of the juvenile population involved in delinquent behavior. However, such studies also have limitations in that youths may not remember incidents or they may choose not to report them.

Both self-report and official statistics, when properly and carefully used, provide insight into crime and victimization. Delbert Elliott, Director of the Center for the Study and Prevention of Violence, argues that to focus solely on either self-reports or official statistics while abandoning the other is "radically shortsighted; to systematically ignore the findings of either is dangerous, particularly when the two measures provide apparently contradictory findings" (Snyder and Sickmund 2006, 64). Elliott stresses that a full understanding of the etiology and development of delinquent behavior is enhanced by using and integrating self-reports and official data.

A Caveat on Using Statistics   Statistics help constitute what can be called the "big picture" of what is really happening in the United States: "Accurate statistics about crimes and victims are vital because they can shed light on a number of important matters":

- Statistics can provide realistic assessments of the threat posed to individuals by criminal activity.
- Statistics reveal patterns of criminal activity.
- Trends reveal how situations change as time goes by.
- Statistics reveal the costs and losses imposed by criminal behavior.
- Statistics can be used to project a rough or "ballpark figure" of how many people are likely to need assistance.
- Statistics also are required to evaluate the effectiveness of recovery efforts and preventive strategies.
- Profiles are statistical portraits that yield an impression of what is usual or typical about the average victim. (Karmen 2007, 43–45)

Karmen (2007, 45) stresses, "As useful and necessary as statistics are, they should always be viewed with a healthy dose of scientific skepticism." He notes,

"Cynics joke that statistics can be used by special interest groups just like a lamppost is used by a drunkard—for support rather than for illumination."

Official statistics are cited throughout this text in various discussions of youth victimization and delinquency, and it is important that the reader be mindful of the following caveats when interpreting crime data. Official statistics reflect only reported crimes, and these reports are voluntary and vary in accuracy and completeness. In addition not all police departments submit crime reports, and federal crimes are not included. Furthermore it is estimated that less than half the crimes committed are reported to the police. The true number of crimes, called the **dark figure of crime**, is unknown and may be substantially greater than official data indicate. Official statistics also do not provide information about the personality, attitudes and behavior of delinquents. This comes from self-reports.

Another caution: Any large-scale data collection program has many possible sources of error. For example, in the UCR program, a police officer may classify a crime incorrectly, and in the NCVS, a Census Bureau interviewer may incorrectly record a victim's response. Crime data are also affected by how victims perceive and recall events. Although both programs have extensive accuracy checks to minimize errors, mistakes may occur at any stage. Despite these difficulties, police departments make frequent use of the information from the UCR program.

In addition to using official data and self-reports, juvenile justice practitioners and the general public may rely on media accounts to understand juveniles and their activities.

The Media's Effect on Public Perception of Juveniles

Crime statistics often stand in stark contrast to media depictions of crime and delinquency. Much of what the public knows about juvenile crime comes from the media, which may overdramatize and distort the true extent and seriousness of the problem. Study after study shows that the media focuses on crime and violence to the neglect of other aspects of law enforcement. Weitzer and Kubrin (2004, 497) found, "Many Americans report that they are fearful of crime. One frequently cited source of this fear is the mass media. The media, and local television news in particular, often report on incidents of crime and do so in a selective and sometimes sensational manner." Naturally, violent crimes committed by young people are often considered more shocking and, thus, "newsworthy" than are those perpetrated by adults. Consequently, this bias in reporting juvenile crime may lead the public to a distorted perception or generalization that our nation's youth are, as a group, more violent than previous generations.

Terminology

Having looked at who is served by the juvenile justice system, the various ages established by state statutes and the various sources of information about children and youth, the focus now is on the terminology, organization and structure of the juvenile justice system. As the juvenile justice system evolved into one separate from the adult system, the terms used were tailored to fit the juvenile system.

 The terminology of the juvenile justice system underscores its emphasis on protecting youth from harmful labels and their stigmatizing effects.

Youth are not *arrested*; they are *taken into custody*. If the allegations against a youth are true, the youth is called a *delinquent* rather than a *criminal*. Youths sentenced to custodial care upon release receive *aftercare* rather than *parole*. Table 1.5 shows other differences between terminology used in the juvenile and criminal justice systems. These differences in terminology will be evident throughout the next section, which examines the organization and structure of the juvenile justice system.

Table 1.5 The Language of the Juvenile and the Criminal Justice Systems

Juvenile Court Term	Adult Court Term
Adjudication: decision by the judge that a child has committed delinquent acts.	*Conviction of guilt*
Adjudicatory hearing: a hearing to determine whether the allegations of a petition are supported by the evidence beyond a reasonable doubt.	*Trial*
Adjustment: the settling of a matter so that parties agree without official intervention by the court.	*Plea bargaining*
Aftercare: the supervision given to a child for a limited period of time after he or she is released from training school but while he or she is still under the control of the juvenile court.	*Parole*
Commitment: a decision by the judge to send a child to training school.	*Sentence to imprisonment*
Delinquent act: an act that if committed by an adult would be called a crime. The term does not include such ambiguities and noncrimes as being ungovernable, truancy, incorrigibility and disobedience.	*Crime*
Delinquent child: a child who is found to have committed an act that would be considered a crime if committed by an adult.	*Criminal*
Detention: temporary care of an allegedly delinquent child who requires secure custody in physically restricting facilities pending court disposition or execution of a court order.	*Holding in jail*
Dispositional hearing: a hearing held subsequent to the adjudicatory hearing to determine what order of disposition should be made for a child adjudicated as delinquent.	*Sentencing hearing*
Hearing: the presentation of evidence to the juvenile court judge, his or her consideration of it and his or her decision on disposition of the case.	*Trial*
Juvenile court: the court that has jurisdiction over children who are alleged to be or found to be delinquent. Juvenile delinquency procedures should not be used for neglected children or for those who need supervision.	*Court of record*
Petition: an application for a court order or some other judicial action. Hence, a delinquency petition is an application for the court to act in a matter involving a juvenile apprehended for a delinquent act.	*Accusation or indictment*
Probation: the supervision of a delinquent child after the court hearing but without commitment to training school.	*Probation* (with the same meaning as the juvenile court term)
Residential child care facility: a dwelling other than a detention or shelter care facility that is licensed to provide living accommodations, care, treatment and maintenance for children and youth. Such facilities include foster homes, group homes and halfway houses.	*Halfway house*
Shelter: temporary care of a child in physically unrestricting facilities pending court disposition or execution of a court order for placement. Shelter care is used for dependent and neglected children and minors in need of supervision. Separate shelter care facilities are also used for children apprehended for delinquency who need temporary shelter but not secure detention.	*Jail*
Take into custody: the act of the police in securing the physical custody of a child engaged in delinquency. The term is used to avoid the stigma of the word *arrest*.	*Arrest*

SOURCE: Harold J. Vetter and Leonard Territo. 1984. *Crime and Justice in America: A Human Perspective*. St. Paul, MN: West. Copyright © 1984 by West Publishing Co. Reprinted by permission of Wadsworth Publishing Co.

Organization and Structure of Juvenile Justice

Although the following discussion is focused on the organization, administration and structure of juvenile *delinquency* services, it applies equally to juveniles who are abused, neglected and dependent and to those who are status offenders. The organization and administration of these services may be centralized (12 states), decentralized (18 states) or a combination (21 states), as shown in Figure 1.3.

Centralized states are characterized by a state executive agency having across-the-board state control of services. *Decentralized states* are characterized, at minimum, by local control of services. Often local authorities run detention centers and some share responsibility for aftercare services with state agencies. *Combination states*, as the name implies, have a mix of state-controlled and locally operated delinquency services. In some instances the state divides responsibility for services between the executive and judicial branches.

Regardless of how the states choose to organize their services, each state has three basic components in its juvenile justice system: law enforcement, courts and corrections. Although schools, child protective services and an abundance of treatment and counseling services are also integral to the functioning and success of juvenile justice, the police, courts and corrections are the three components composing the formal juvenile justice system, and each component acts independently and interdependently.

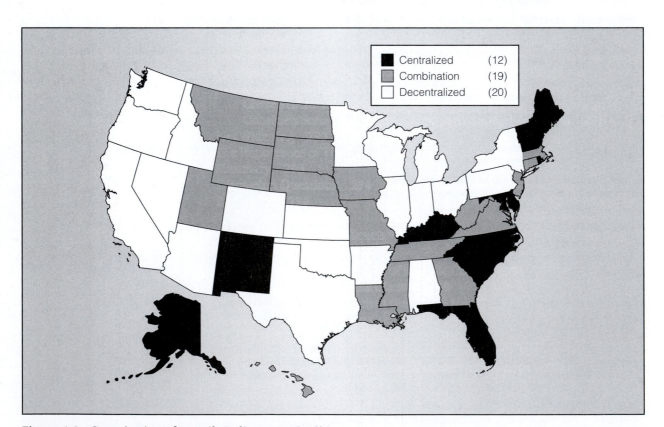

Figure 1.3 Organization of Juvenile Delinquency Services

Retrieved from http://www.ncjj.org/Topic/Delinquency-Services-Summary.aspx

Law enforcement is often the gatekeeper to the system, although juveniles may enter the system by other routes. Within the law enforcement component, juveniles may be assigned to a separate division or may be handled by all officers. In addition, as noted, states vary in the age establishing juvenile status. In many instances, older juveniles may be transferred into the adult system.

What happens in one component directly affects the other two components. When one component attempts to change its policies or procedures with regard to processing juveniles, the change places workload pressure on the other components. For example, if law enforcement arrests and prosecutors elect to process thousands of juveniles, this could create a problem with overcrowded dockets in the courts. Likewise, if the courts sentence thousands of juveniles, the correctional system can become overcrowded, resulting in early release of prisoners and a potential problem for law enforcement. This displacement of workload pressure from one component to the next is a phenomenon often described as the thermodynamics of criminal justice, a concept equally applicable to juvenile justice (Walker 2010). Such pressures meet natural resistance within the system because the tendency is for the system to seek equilibrium, predictability and a return to its "natural" balance. An awareness of this tendency helps one better understand why reform within the juvenile justice system is challenging and why many reform efforts fail. Juvenile justice reform is discussed in Chapter 13.

The Juvenile Justice Process

Case processing of juvenile offenders varies from state to state. Even within a state, juvenile case processing can vary from community to community, reflecting local practice and tradition (Snyder and Sickmund 2006, 104). Any description of juvenile justice processing in the United States must, therefore, be general, outlining a common series of decision points as illustrated in Figure 1.4. The descriptions of each stage are adapted from the *Disproportionate Minority Contact Technical Assistance Manual* (2007, 1-7 to 1-8).

Arrest

Youth are considered arrested when a law enforcement officer takes them into custody for having committed a delinquent act, an act that, if an adult committed it, would be criminal, including crimes against persons, crimes against property, drug offenses and crimes against the public order.

Referral

Referral occurs when a potentially delinquent youth is sent forward for legal processing and is received by a juvenile or family court or juvenile intake agency, either as a result of law enforcement action or a complaint by a citizen or school.

Intake

Youths referred to juvenile court for delinquent acts are often screened by an intake department (within or outside the court). The intake department may dismiss the case for lack of legal sufficiency, resolve the matter informally (without filing charges) or resolve it formally (filing charges).

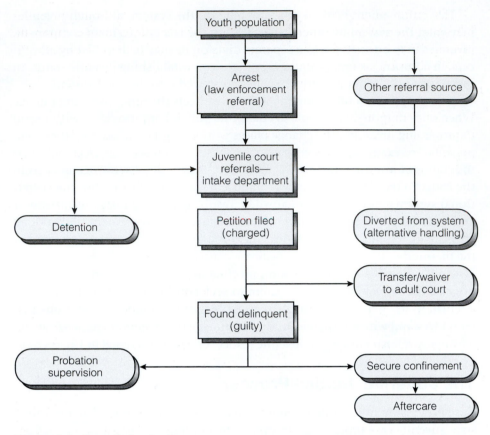

Figure 1.4 Juvenile Justice Process

SOURCE: Adapted from William Feyerherm, Howard N. Snyder, and Francisco Villarruel. "Chapter 1: Identification and Monitoring." In *Disproportionate Minority Contact Technical Assistance Manual.* 2009 (July). 4th ed, pp. 1–5. Washington, DC: Office of Juvenile Justice and Delinquency Prevention.

Diversion

Diversion is a filtering process that removes youths from formal juvenile court jurisdiction and places them on an alternative path that allows the case to proceed with adjudication. The diversion population includes all youth referred for legal processing but handled without filing formal charges. Diversion is a focus of Chapter 9.

Detention

Detention refers to the secure placement of youths into a facility at some point during court processing of their case (i.e., before disposition). In some jurisdictions, this population also includes youths held in secure detention while awaiting placement following a court disposition. It may also include youths held in jails and lockups but not those held in shelters, group homes or other nonsecure facilities.

Petitioning/Charges Filed

Petitioned (formally charged) delinquency cases appear on a court calendar in response to the filing of a petition, complaint or other legal document requesting the court to adjudicate a youth as a delinquent or status offender or to waive jurisdiction and transfer a youth to criminal court. Petitioning occurs when a juvenile court intake officer, prosecutor or other official determines a case should be handled formally. In contrast, informal handling is voluntary and does not include filing charges.

Adjudication Hearing/Delinquency Finding

At the *adjudication hearing* (comparable to the preliminary hearing in the adult system) the youth is questioned about the alleged offense. If the evidence is insufficient, the petition may be dismissed. If enough evidence exists that the child is delinquent, a court date is set for the disposition hearing (comparable to the trial in the adult system). Being **adjudicated** delinquent is roughly equivalent to being convicted in criminal court. It is a formal legal finding of responsibility.

Dispositional Hearing

If found to be delinquent, a youth normally proceeds to a disposition hearing, where the judge has several alternatives. Based on the findings of the investigation, the judge may place the youth on probation or in a foster home, release the child to the parents, commit the child to an institution or make the child a ward of the court. Serious juvenile offenders may be committed to psychiatric care institutions, reformatories, county and state schools for delinquents or other secure facilities.

Probation

In probation cases youth are placed on formal or court-ordered supervision following a juvenile court disposition. Probation is discussed in detail in Chapter 12.

Confinement in a Secure Correctional Facility

In confinement cases youth are placed in secure residential or correctional facilities for delinquent offenders. The confinement population does not include youth placed in any form of out-of-home placement. Group homes, shelter homes and mental health treatment facilities, for example, would usually not be considered confinement. Correctional alternatives are described in Chapter 12.

Transfer to Adult Court

Transferred or waived cases are those in which juveniles have their cases handled not in the juvenile court but in the adult criminal court. Such transfer is typically reserved for exceptional cases involving serious, violent or chronic youthful offenders. Historically, the power to transfer a juvenile to criminal court rested solely with the juvenile court judge, through the mechanism called *judicial waiver*. However, since the 1970s, several other mechanisms have evolved which have removed this transfer decision from judges and placed it with prosecutors (*prosecutorial waiver* or *direct file*) and lawmakers (*legislative waiver* or *statutory exclusion*). When a waiver request is denied, the matter is usually scheduled for an adjudicatory hearing in the juvenile court. If the request is granted, the juvenile is judicially waived

© John Neubauer/PhotoEdit

Arrest and referral are two critical stages in the processing of a juvenile and can lead to diversion and informal handling of the youth (in essence, giving them a "second chance") or to formal processing and a juvenile record.

to criminal court for further action. Waiver to criminal court is discussed more fully in Chapter 10.

The Juvenile Justice System and the Criminal Justice System Compared

The juvenile justice system strives to be an informal, private, non-adversarial system that stresses rehabilitation rather than punishment of youth. This is in direct contrast to the criminal justice systems of most states. Table 1.6 shows the juvenile court process compared to the adult process. In considering the comparing and contrasting of the juvenile and criminal justice systems, the difference in terminology should also be observed.

Note the common ground in operating assumptions, the role of law enforcement and intake/prosecution and other critical stages of the juvenile and criminal justice process. Also bear in mind that youth may move between the juvenile and criminal justice systems, as illustrated in Figure 1.5.

Diversion may occur at numerous points during the processing of a case. Whether such diversion is of benefit is one of several important issues in juvenile justice.

Issues in Juvenile Justice

 Issues in juvenile justice include whether to divert, whether to take a conservative or liberal approach to delinquency, whether to keep juveniles' records confidential or to share information and whether minorities are overrepresented in the juvenile justice system.

Table 1.6   Comparison of the Juvenile and the Criminal Systems

Although the juvenile and criminal justice systems are more alike in some jurisdictions than in others, generalizations can be made about the distinctions between the two systems and about their common ground.

Juvenile Justice System	Common Ground	Criminal Justice System
Operating Assumptions		
Youth behavior is malleable.	Community protection is a primary goal.	Sanctions should be proportionate to the offense.
Rehabilitation is usually a viable goal.	Law violators must be held accountable.	General deterrence works.
Youth are in families and not independent.	Constitutional rights apply.	Rehabilitation is not a primary goal.
Prevention		
Many specific delinquency prevention activities (e.g., school, church, recreation) are used.	Educational approaches are taken to specific behaviors (drunken driving, drug use).	Prevention activities are generalized and are aimed at deterrence (e.g., Crime Watch).
Prevention is intended to change individual behavior and is often focused on reducing risk factors and increasing protective factors in the individual, family and community.		
Law Enforcement		
Specialized juvenile units are used.	Jurisdiction involves the full range of criminal behavior.	Open public access to all information is required.
Some additional behaviors are prohibited (truancy, running away, curfew violations).	Constitutional and procedural safeguards exist.	Law enforcement exercises discretion to divert offenders out of the criminal justice system.
Some limitations are placed on public access to information.	Both reactive and proactive approaches (targeted at offense types, neighborhoods, etc.) are used.	
A significant number of youths are diverted from the juvenile justice system, often into alternative programs.	Community policing strategies are employed.	
Intake—Prosecution		
In many instances, juvenile court intake, not the prosecutor, decides which cases to file.	Probable cause must be established.	Plea bargaining is common.
The decision to file a petition for court action is based on both social and legal factors.	The prosecutor acts on behalf of the state.	The prosecution decision is based largely on legal facts.
A significant portion of cases are diverted from formal case processing.	Prosecution is valuable in building history for subsequent offenses.	
Intake or the prosecutor diverts cases from formal processing to services operated by the juvenile court prosecutor's office or outside agencies.	Prosecution exercises discretion to withhold charges or divert offenders out of the criminal justice system.	
Detention—Jail/Lockup		
Juveniles may be detained for their own protection or the community's protection.	Accused offenders may be held in custody to ensure their appearance in court.	Accused individuals have the right to apply for bond/bail release.
Juveniles may not be confined with adults unless there is "sight and sound separation."	Detention alternatives of home or electronic detention are used.	
Adjudication—Conviction		
Juvenile court proceedings are "quasi-civil" (not criminal) and may be confidential.	Standard of "proof beyond a reasonable doubt" is required.	Defendants have a constitutional right to a jury trial.
If guilt is established the youth is adjudicated delinquent regardless of offense.	Rights to be represented by an attorney, to confront witnesses and to remain silent are afforded.	Guilt must be established on individual offenses charged to conviction.

(*continued*)

Table 1.6   Comparison of the Juvenile and the Criminal Systems (*continued*)

Juvenile Justice System	Common Ground	Criminal Justice System
Right to jury trial is not afforded in all states.	Appeals to a higher court are allowed.	All proceedings are open.
Experimentation with specialized courts (e.g., drug courts, gun courts) is under way.		
Disposition—Sentencing		
Disposition decisions are based on individual and social factors, offense severity and youth's offense history.	Decisions are influenced by current offense, offending history and social factors.	Sentencing decisions are bound primarily by the severity of the current offense and by the offender's criminal history.
Dispositional philosophy includes a significant rehabilitation component.	Decisions hold offenders accountable.	Sentencing philosophy is based largely on proportionality and punishment.
Many dispositional alternatives are operated by the juvenile court.	Decisions may give consideration to victims (e.g., restitution and "no contact" orders).	Sentence is often determinate, based on offense.
Dispositions cover a wide range of community-based and residential services.	Decisions may not be cruel or unusual.	
Disposition orders may be directed to people other than the offender (e.g., parents).		
Disposition may be indeterminate, based on progress demonstrated by the youth.		
Aftercare—Parole		
Function combines surveillance and reintegration activities (e.g., family, school, work).	The behavior of individuals released from correctional settings is monitored.	Function is primarily surveillance and reporting to monitor illicit behavior.
	Violation of conditions can result in reincarceration.	

SOURCE: *Juvenile Justice: A Century of Change.* 1999. Washington, DC: National Report Series. *Juvenile Justice Bulletin* (December): 10–12.

To Divert or Not?

No problem is more troublesome than the delicate balance between protecting children in a free society and protecting society from criminal behavior. Concern over this issue was evident during the conception and birth of juvenile justice more than a century ago. Indeed, throughout the evolution of the juvenile justice system, society's values and attitudes toward crime and those who commit it have swung back and forth, constantly adjusting to suit how society perceives delinquency, as discussed in the next chapter.

The decision to divert youth from the formal juvenile justice process at numerous points along the way results in what some refer to as the funnel effect or the leaky net. Both concepts are used to illustrate how, at each point in the system, fewer and fewer youth pass through. For example, Figure 1.6 shows that for every "typical" 1,000 delinquency cases processed in 2007, 444 (44.4%) were not petitioned and 556 (55.6%) were petitioned (kept in the formal juvenile justice system). Of those petitioned, 5 (< 1%) were waived to criminal court, 199 (35.8%) were not adjudicated delinquent, and 352 (63.3%) were adjudicated delinquent (again, kept in the formal juvenile justice system). Of those adjudicated delinquent, 197 (56%) received probation, 89 (25.3%) were placed in a secure residential facility, and 66 (18.7%) received another sanction. If one considers secure confinement the "ultimate" disposition of a fully processed delinquency case, less than 9 percent of all youth who enter the intake stage are subject to the full weight of the juvenile justice system.

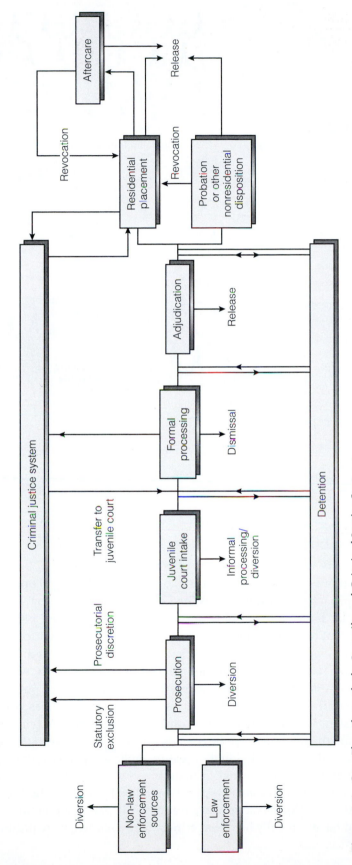

Figure 1.5   Case Flow through the Juvenile and Criminal Justice Systems

SOURCE: Howard N. Snyder and Melissa Sickmund. 2006 (March). *Juvenile Offenders and Victims 2006 National Report*, p. 105. Washington, DC: U.S. Department of Justice, Office of Justice Programs, Office of Juvenile Justice and Delinquency Prevention.

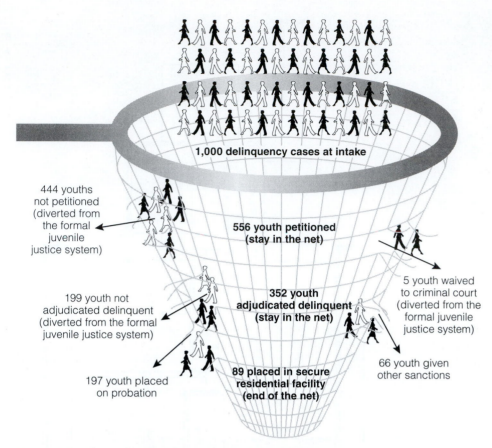

Figure 1.6 The Leaky Net of Juvenile Case Processing

Adapted from Crystal Knoll and Melissa Sickmund. 2010 (June). *Delinquency Cases in Juvenile Court, 2007*, p. 4. Washington, DC: Office of Juvenile Justice and Delinquency Prevention, Fact Sheet. (NCJ 230168)

Which Is More Just: A Conservative or a Liberal Approach to Delinquency?

Closely related to the issues of whether youth should be diverted from the system is the issue of whether society should take a conservative or liberal approach to delinquency. When viewed against the backdrop of prevailing social sentiment and philosophy regarding crime and punishment, citizens' current attitudes remain pivotal in defining the structure and process of the juvenile justice system. Today's justice professionals and, in fact, society as a whole have differing attitudes and opinions regarding how the juvenile justice system *should* address the issues of delinquency. These philosophies are often categorized as either conservative or liberal although, as with many either/or classifications, there exists a continuum from one extreme to the other and, along the line, there can be considerable overlap between the two philosophies. Rarely does any individual or justice application exist at the extreme endpoint, either purely conservative or liberal.

The classical *conservative* attitude has been described as "getting tough" with kids. Conservatives have traditionally placed a premium on crime control and have generally held that crime and delinquency are products of individual choice.

The classical conservative approach to juvenile justice is to "get tough on juveniles"—to punish them.

The conservative philosophy accepts retribution as a purpose of punishment. The conservative view also supports the use of imprisonment to control crime and antisocial behavior. Rehabilitative programs may be provided during incarceration, but correctional treatment is not a necessity. The contemporary conservative perspective advocates working within the system to deal with delinquent youth and has become strongly aligned with "what works," those pragmatic, data-driven approaches to delinquency, not just "get tough" measures. In fact, most conservatives support appropriate decarceration (the opposite of incarceration, or the process of systematically removing people from prisons) and making offenders accountable by providing needed treatment.

In contrast, the classical *liberal* attitude toward juvenile justice is heavily treatment-oriented, advocating rehabilitation, not punishment, for youth who are antisocial and wayward. The liberal perspective emphasizes due process protections and advocates for greater legal rights for juveniles. Liberals assert crime and delinquency are products of environmental factors such as disadvantaged neighborhoods or the lack of social opportunities. As such, liberals believe more resources need to be devoted to improving the environmental conditions that breed antisocial conduct, and they are more inclined to look outside the formal juvenile justice system for solutions and responses to delinquency.

 The traditional liberal approach to juvenile justice stresses treatment and rehabilitation, including community-based programs.

Another issue facing the juvenile justice system is whether juvenile justice proceedings and records should be confidential or open.

Confidentiality versus Openness

Delinquency cases have historically been handled with high degree of confidentially, both in records (juvenile records were sealed or expunged, not to follow a youth into adulthood) and hearings (unlike most criminal trials, delinquency hearings were not open to the public). However, states have begun to de-emphasize traditional confidentiality concerns while emphasizing information sharing. During the early 1990s, states made significant changes in how the juvenile justice system treats information about juvenile offenders, particularly violent juvenile offenders. As juvenile crime became more serious, community protection, the public's right to know and service providers' need to share information displaced the desire to protect minors from the stigma of youthful indiscretions. Legislatures throughout the country have increasingly called for a presumption of open hearings and records, at least for some juvenile offenders. During the past decade, the nationwide trend has been to increase the openness of delinquency hearings, and the most current data indicate that 15 states have statutes or court rules that permit or require juvenile delinquency hearings to be open to the general public, as shown in Figure 1.7 (Szymanski 2010). The trend also extends to the openness of delinquency records:

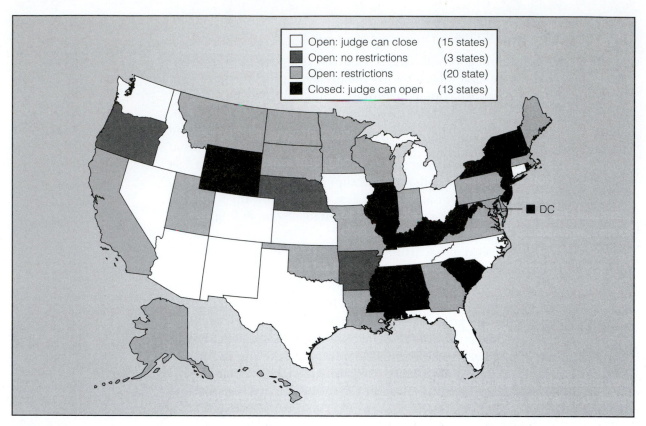

Figure 1.7 What States Allow for Open Juvenile Delinquency Hearings?

L. A. Szymanski 2010. "What States Allow for Open Juvenile Delinquency Hearings?" *NCJJ Snapshot* 15 (10). Pittsburgh, PA: National Center for Juvenile Justice.

Formerly confidential records are now being made available to a wide variety of individuals. Many states open records to schools and youth-serving agencies as well as individuals and agencies within the justice system. . . . As of the end of the 2004 legislative session, juvenile codes in all states allow information contained in juvenile court records to be specifically released to one or more of the following parties: the prosecutor, law enforcement, social service agencies, schools, the victim or the public. . . . In addition the media can access juvenile offenders' identities in most states. (Snyder and Sickmund 2006, 109)

Disproportionate Minority Contact (DMC)

Another issue is whether disproportionate minority contact is the result of racism in the juvenile justice system. The most recent study of disproportionate minority contact in the juvenile justice system looked at longitudinal community studies of delinquency in Pittsburgh, Pennsylvania; Rochester, New York; and Seattle, Washington and found a distinguishable level of disproportionate minority contact (DMC) in the juvenile justice system. Minorities, especially African American and Hispanic youth, are, on the whole, more likely to come into contact with the criminal justice system whether it be at the arrest stage or further along at the stage of confinement (Huizinga et al. 2007). This study found that minority youth, although constituting 34 percent of the juvenile population nationwide, continue to be greatly overrepresented in the juvenile justice system, representing 62 percent of juveniles detained and 67 percent of those committed to secure juvenile facilities, with Black youth overrepresented more than any other group.

DMC will be explored further in later discussions of arrests, diversion, confinement and transfer to criminal court. Although it is clear that minorities are overrepresented in the juvenile justice system, the more salient question is whether this represents racial discrimination. Many discussions of racial discrimination are muddied because of failure to differentiate between *discrimination* and *disparity* (Walker, Spohn, and DeLone 2007, 18). **Discrimination** refers to unfair, differential treatment of a particular group of youth, for example, Hispanics. **Disparity** refers to a difference, but not necessarily involving discrimination. Consider, for example, the fact that most college classes have primarily relatively young students, but this does not indicate age discrimination (Walker et al.). In criminal justice the critical distinction is between legal and extralegal factors: "*Legal factors* include the seriousness of the offense, aggravating or mitigating circumstance or an offender's prior criminal record. These are considered legitimate bases for decisions by most criminal justice officials because they relate to an individual's criminal behavior. *Extralegal factors* include race, ethnicity, gender, social class and lifestyle" (Walker et al.). Walker et al. (412) conclude

> Methodologically sophisticated research reveals that racial and ethnic differences in juvenile victimization and offending rate can be attributed in large part to family and community characteristics. African American and Hispanic youth are more likely than White youth to be the victims of violent crime because they spend more time away from home, and are more likely to live in single-parent households and disadvantaged communities. Similarly, the higher rates of violent offending found among minority youth than White youth reflect the fact that minority youth are more likely to live in disadvantaged neighborhoods, to be members of gangs, and to have weak bonds to social institutions such as schools. The sources of risk of victimization and offending are similar for all teenagers, but the likelihood of experiencing these risk factors is higher for youth of color than for White youth.

The preceding issues are not new; they have their roots in the evolution of the juvenile justice system itself, as discussed in the next chapter.

Summary

- The underlying premise of the first juvenile court was that of *parens patriae*, the responsibility of the state to protect its children and youth.
- Seventeen is most commonly recognized as the upper age for original juvenile court jurisdiction in delinquency matters.
- Researchers commonly use three methods to measure the nature and extent of unlawful acts by juveniles: official data, self-report data and victim surveys.
- The FBI's Uniform Crime Reports contain statistics on violent crimes (murder, aggravated assault causing serious bodily harm, forcible rape and robbery) and property crimes (burglary, larceny-theft, motor vehicle theft and arson).

- According to self-report studies, minor delinquency is almost universal.
- The terminology of the juvenile justice system underscores its emphasis on protecting youth from harmful labels and their stigmatizing effects.
- Issues in juvenile justice include whether to divert, whether to take a conservative or liberal approach to delinquency, whether to keep juveniles' records confidential or to share information and whether minorities are overrepresented in the juvenile justice system.
- The classical conservative approach to juvenile justice is "get tough on juveniles"—to punish them. The traditional liberal approach to juvenile justice stresses treatment and rehabilitation, including community-based programs.

Discussion Questions

1. At what age do people become adults in your state?
2. Do you support a separate justice system for juveniles? Why or why not?
3. Which view of justice do you support?
4. What are some problems with the Uniform Crime Reports? The National Incident-Based Reporting System?
5. How influential is the media in shaping the public's attitudes toward juveniles?
6. How do the components of the juvenile justice system interact?
7. What do you consider the most important issue facing juvenile justice?
8. What are the major differences between the criminal justice system and the juvenile justice system?
9. Do you tend to favor a liberal or a conservative approach to delinquency?
10. Given that minorities are overrepresented in the juvenile justice system, do you believe this is the result of discrimination?

References

Bazemore, Gordon, and M. Umbreit. 2001 (February). *A Comparison of Four Restorative Conferencing Models.* Washington, DC: OJJDP Juvenile Justice Bulletin. (NCJ 184738)

Crime in the United States, 2009. 2009. Uniform Crime Reports. Washington, DC: Federal Bureau of Investigation. Accessed August 30, 2011. http://www2.fbi.gov/ucr/cius2009/index.html.

Disproportionate Minority Contact Technical Assistance Manual. 2007. 3rd ed. Washington, DC: Office of Juvenile Justice Delinquency Prevention.

Huizinga, David, Terrence Thornberry, Kelly Knight, and Peter Lovegrove. 2007 (September). *Disproportionate Minority Contact in the Juvenile Justice System: A Study of Differential Minority Arrest/Referral to Court in Three Cities.* Washington, DC: Department of Justice.

Karmen, Andrew. 2007. *Crime Victims: An Introduction to Victimology.* 6th ed. Belmont, CA: Wadsworth.

Kirk, David S. 2006. "Examining the Divergence across Self-Report and Official Data Sources on Inferences about the Adolescent Life-Course of Crime." *Journal of Quantitative Criminal Criminology* (June): 107–129.

Snyder, Howard N., and Melissa Sickmund. 2006 (March). *Juvenile Offenders and Victims 2006 National Report.* Washington, DC: U.S. Department of Justice, Office of Justice Programs, Office of Juvenile Justice and Delinquency Prevention.

Szymanski, L. A. 2010. "What States Allow for Open Juvenile Delinquency Hearings?" *NCJJ Snapshot* 15 (10). Pittsburgh, PA: National Center for Juvenile Justice.

Walker, Samuel. 2010. *Sense and Nonsense about Crime and Drugs: A Policy Guide.* 7th ed. Belmont, CA: Wadsworth/Cengage Learning.

Walker, Samuel, Cassia Spohn, and Miriam DeLone. 2007. *The Color of Justice: Race, Ethnicity, and Crime in America.* 4th ed. Belmont, CA: Wadsworth.

Weitzer, Ronald, and Charis E. Kubrin. 2004. "Breaking News: How Local TV News and Real-World Conditions Affect Fear of Crime. *Justice Quarterly* (September): 497–520.

Helpful Resource

Bohm, Robert M., and Brenda Vogel. 2011. *A Primer on Crime and Delinquency Theory.* 3rd ed. Belmont, CA: Wadsworth.

The History and Philosophy behind the Juvenile Justice System

2

> " Children are our most valuable natural resource. "
>
> —Herbert C. Hoover

London's Bridewell was similar to a debtor's prison. It confined both children and adult "vagrants."

© Stock Montage

DO YOU KNOW?

- When and where the first house of refuge (reformatory) was opened in the United States?
- Who the child savers were and what their philosophy was?
- When and where the first juvenile court was established?
- How the first juvenile courts functioned?
- What functions probation was to serve within the juvenile court system?
- How Progressive Era proponents viewed crime? What model they refined?
- What resulted from the 1909 White House Conference on Children and Youth?
- What act funded federal programs to aid children and families?

- What the Four Ds of juvenile justice refer to?
- What was established by the following key cases: *Kent v. United States, In re Gault, In re Winship, McKeiver v. Pennsylvania, Breed v. Jones, Schall v. Martin*?
- What effect isolating offenders from their normal environment might have?
- What the Uniform Juvenile Court Act provided?
- What the major impact of the 1970 White House Conference on Youth was?
- What the two main goals of the JJDP Act of 1974 were?
- What juvenile delinquency liability should be limited to according to the American Bar Association?

CAN YOU DEFINE?

Bridewell	deserts	justice model	preventive detention
child savers	deterrence	medical model	youthful offenders
corporal punishment	double jeopardy	net widening	
decriminalization	due process	poor laws	

CHAPTER OUTLINE

Introduction

Social Control in Early Societies

Developments in England: A Brief Overview

The Development of Juvenile Justice in the United States

The Puritan Period (1646–1824)

The Refuge Period (1824–1899)

Houses of Refuge

Reform Schools

Foster Homes

The Child Savers

Other Developments during the Refuge Period

The Juvenile Court Period (1899–1960)

The 1899 Juvenile Court Act

Early Efforts at Diversion: The Chicago Boy's Court and Youth Counsel Bureau

Federal Government Concern and Involvement

The Juvenile Rights Period (1960–1980)

The Four Ds of Juvenile Justice

The Kent Decision

The Gault Decision

The President's Commission on Law Enforcement and Administration of Justice

Youth Service Bureaus

The Uniform Juvenile Court Act

The White House Conference on Children and Youth

The Office of Juvenile Justice and Delinquency Prevention and the Juvenile Justice and Delinquency Prevention Act

A Return to Due Process Issues: Other Landmark Cases

The Issue of Right to Treatment

Decriminalization of Status Offenses

Development of Standards for Juvenile Justice

The Crime Control Period (1980–Present)

Schall v. Martin (1984) and Preventive Detention

Still Evolving

Introduction

A separate justice system for **youthful offenders** (usually under age 18) is, historically speaking, relatively recent. An understanding of how this system evolved is central to understanding the system as it currently exists and the challenges it faces (see Figure 2.1).

It has been said that the historian is a prophet looking backward. History reveals patterns and changes in attitudes toward youths and how they are treated. The emphasis has changed from punishment to protection and back. As one philosophy achieves prominence, problems persist and critics clamor for change. History also reveals mistakes that can be avoided in the future as well as hopes and promises that remain unfulfilled.

Social Control in Early Societies

People have banded together for companionship and protection for tens of thousands of years. As early societies developed, they established rules to maintain social order and protect their members' safety. Everyone was to conform to society's expectations. Those who broke the rules were severely punished. Most early societies treated all wrongdoings and criminal offenses alike. Children and adults were subject to the same rules and laws, were tried under the same legal process and, when convicted, suffered the same penalties.

In early societies men were the heads of their families. In such patriarchal societies rebellion against a father, even by adult sons, was not tolerated. Punishment was swift and severe. The father in ancient Roman culture also exercised unlimited authority over his family, being allowed to administer **corporal punishment** (inflict bodily pain) and even sell his children into slavery. One important concept from the Roman civilization that influenced the development of juvenile justice was *patria postestas*—referring to the absolute control fathers had over their children and the children's absolute responsibility to obey. This concept evolved into the doctrine of *parens patriae*, a basic tenet in our juvenile justice system.

Developments in England: A Brief Overview

Events in England had a great influence on the juvenile justice system that developed in the United States. The earliest legal document written in English contained the laws of King Aethelbert (around 600 AD). These laws made no special allowance for an offender's age. In fact several cases document children as young as 6 being hanged or burned at the stake.

Early in English history, the Roman Catholic Church greatly influenced how children were viewed. Church doctrine stated that children younger than 7 had not yet reached the age of reason and, thus, could not be held liable for sins. English law adopted the same perspective. Under 7 years of age, children were not considered legally able to have the required intent to commit a crime. From ages 7 to 14, it was presumed they did not have such intent, but if evidence proved differently, children could be found guilty of committing crimes. After age 14, individuals were considered adults.

In thirteenth-century England, common law (law of custom and usage) gave kings power of being the "father of his country." The king was perceived as

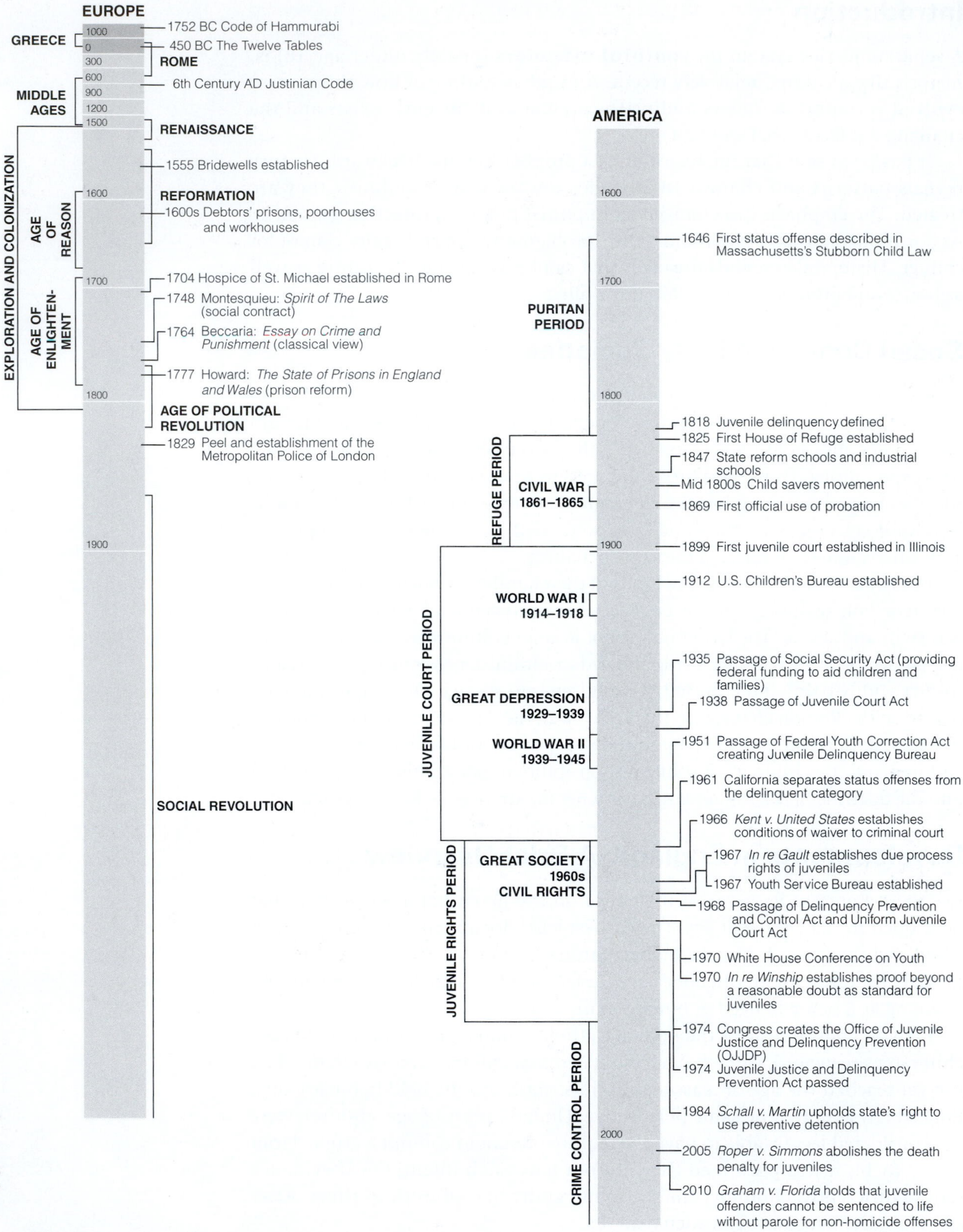

EUROPE

GREECE
- 1000
- 0
- 300

- 1752 BC Code of Hammurabi
- 450 BC The Twelve Tables

ROME
- 600
- 900
- 1200

- 6th Century AD Justinian Code

MIDDLE AGES
- 1500

RENAISSANCE

- 1555 Bridewells established

- 1600

REFORMATION
- 1600s Debtors' prisons, poorhouses and workhouses

AGE OF REASON

AGE OF ENLIGHTEN-MENT
- 1700
- 1704 Hospice of St. Michael established in Rome
- 1748 Montesquieu: *Spirit of The Laws* (social contract)
- 1764 Beccaria: *Essay on Crime and Punishment* (classical view)
- 1777 Howard: *The State of Prisons in England and Wales* (prison reform)
- 1800

AGE OF POLITICAL REVOLUTION
- 1829 Peel and establishment of the Metropolitan Police of London

EXPLORATION AND COLONIZATION

- 1900

SOCIAL REVOLUTION

© Cengage Learning 2013

AMERICA

- 1600

PURITAN PERIOD
- 1646 First status offense described in Massachusetts's Stubborn Child Law
- 1700
- 1800

REFUGE PERIOD
- 1818 Juvenile delinquency defined
- 1825 First House of Refuge established
- 1847 State reform schools and industrial schools
- Mid 1800s Child savers movement
- 1869 First official use of probation

CIVIL WAR 1861–1865

- 1900
- 1899 First juvenile court established in Illinois

JUVENILE COURT PERIOD
- 1912 U.S. Children's Bureau established

WORLD WAR I 1914–1918

GREAT DEPRESSION 1929–1939
- 1935 Passage of Social Security Act (providing federal funding to aid children and families)
- 1938 Passage of Juvenile Court Act

WORLD WAR II 1939–1945
- 1951 Passage of Federal Youth Correction Act creating Juvenile Delinquency Bureau
- 1961 California separates status offenses from the delinquent category
- 1966 *Kent v. United States* establishes conditions of waiver to criminal court

GREAT SOCIETY 1960s CIVIL RIGHTS
- 1967 *In re Gault* establishes due process rights of juveniles
- 1967 Youth Service Bureau established
- 1968 Passage of Delinquency Prevention and Control Act and Uniform Juvenile Court Act

JUVENILE RIGHTS PERIOD
- 1970 White House Conference on Youth
- 1970 *In re Winship* establishes proof beyond a reasonable doubt as standard for juveniles
- 1974 Congress creates the Office of Juvenile Justice and Delinquency Prevention (OJJDP)
- 1974 Juvenile Justice and Delinquency Prevention Act passed
- 1984 *Schall v. Martin* upholds state's right to use preventive detention

CRIME CONTROL PERIOD
- 2000
- 2005 *Roper v. Simmons* abolishes the death penalty for juveniles
- 2010 *Graham v. Florida* holds that juvenile offenders cannot be sentenced to life without parole for non-homicide offenses

Figure 2.1 Timeline of Significant Dates in Juvenile Justice

guardian over the person and property of minors, who were considered wards of the state and, as such, received special protection. The Latin phrase meaning "father of the country" is *parens patriae*, giving the king the right and responsibility to care for children. *Parens patriae* was used to justify the state's intervention in the lives of its feudal lords and their children, and it placed juveniles between the civil and the criminal systems. The chancery courts heard issues involving guardianship but did *not* have jurisdiction over children who committed crimes. Such youths were handled within the criminal court system.

The sixteenth and seventeenth centuries in Europe—a period called the Renaissance—marked the transition from medieval to modern times and were characterized by an emphasis on art and the humanities, as well as a more humanistic approach to criminal justice. In 1555 London's **Bridewell** Prison became the first institution to control youthful beggars and vagrants. Based on an underlying theme of achieving discipline, deterrence and rehabilitation through work and severe punishment, Bridewell's goals were "to make [wayward youths] earn their keep, to reform them by compulsory work and discipline, and to deter others from vagrancy and idleness" (Grunhut 1948, 15). Parliament passed a law in 1576 calling for construction of Bridewell-type institutions in every county to confine both children and adults who were considered idle and disorderly. Some parents voluntarily committed their children to Bridewell believing the emphasis on hard work would benefit the youth.

During Elizabeth I's reign (1558–1603), England passed **poor laws** that established the appointment of overseers to *indenture* poor and neglected children into servitude. Such children were forced to work for wealthy families who, in turn, trained them in a trade, domestic service or farming. Such involuntary apprenticeships were served until the youths were 21 or older. These Elizabethan poor laws were the model for dealing with poor children for the next 200 years.

In 1601 England proposed establishing large workhouses for children who could not be supported by their parents. The children would be placed there and "bred up to labor, principles of virtue implanted in them at an early age, and laziness be discouraged … and, settled in a way serviceable to the public's good and not bred up in all manners of vice" (Webb and Webb 1927, 52). This proposal was finally implemented with the passage of the Gilbert Act of 1782 decreeing that all poor, aged, sick and infirm be placed in *poorhouses* (almshouses). Under the act, poor infants and children who could not go with their mothers were not placed in the poorhouse but with a "proper person" (de Scheveinitz 1943, 20–21).

Another important milestone in the development of juvenile justice was the founding of the London Philanthropic Society in 1817, one purpose of which was to reform juvenile offenders. The Society opened the first English house of refuge for children, a major shift from family-oriented discipline to institutional treatment.

The Development of Juvenile Justice in the United States

Although the English justice system served as the basis for juvenile justice in America, a distinctively American system evolved in response to conditions unique to this country. Juvenile justice in the United States is generally recognized as having progressed through five distinct stages, beginning with the first European settlers to land in the New World, whose philosophies defined and shaped what is now referred to as the Puritan Period.

The Puritan Period (1646–1824)

The American colonists brought with them much of the English criminal justice system, including poor laws and the forced apprenticeship system for poor and neglected children. They also continued the centuries-old philosophy of *patria postestas*, giving fathers absolute authority over all family matters and justifying harsh consequences for children who misbehaved. In fact, early laws prescribed the death penalty for children who disobeyed their parents. The colonial Puritan philosophy regarding juvenile behavior was enacted into law in 1646 when Massachusetts passed the Stubborn Child Law, creating the first status offense, an act considered illegal for minors only. The law stood unrevised for more than 300 years.

Even then, age was a consideration in juvenile justice, as Blackstone (1776, 23) summarized the law regarding youths' responsibility: "Under seven years of age indeed an infant cannot be guilty of a felony; for then a felonious discretion is almost an impossibility in nature; but at eight years old he may be guilty of a felony." Furthermore, according to the common law, although a youth under age 14 may be adjudged incapable of discerning right from wrong, it appeared to the court and the jury that he *could* discern between good and evil (Blackstone). Thus, if accused of a major criminal act, the juvenile would proceed through the justice system as an adult. Trials and punishment were based on age, and anyone older than 7 was subject to the courts. Jails, the only form of incarceration, were primarily used for detention pending trial.

During this period, the fundamental mode of juvenile control was the family, with the church and other social institutions also expected to handle juvenile delinquents. Until the end of the eighteenth century, the family was also the main economic unit, with family members working together farming or in home-based trades. Children were important contributors to these family-based industries. The privileged classes found apprenticeships for their children so they could learn marketable skills. The children of the poor, in contrast, often were bound out as indentured servants.

The end of the eighteenth century brought the Industrial Revolution, which forever changed the face of America. Families left the fields and farms and flocked to the cities to work in factories. Child labor in these factories replaced the apprenticeship system. Increasing industrialization, urbanization and immigration created severe problems for families and their children. The social control once exerted by the family weakened—children in the workforce had to obey their bosses' demands, often in conflict with their parents' demands. In addition, poverty was increasing for many families. This combination of poverty and diminished family control set an "ominous stage," with some Americans fearing a growing "dangerous class" and seeking ways to "control the wayward youth who epitomized this threat to social stability" (Krisberg and Austin 1993, 15).

To counteract the continued breakdown of traditional forms of social control, communities created institutions for children where they could learn

Highlights of Puritan Period Reform

Philosophy Children were inherently sinful and in need of strict control or punishment when necessary. Most nonconforming children were of lower-class parentage.

Treatment Misbehaving children were generally controlled by familial punishment. External, community punishment and control were necessary only when the parents failed.

Policies Communal legal sanctions were guided by the British tradition of common law, allowing children older than 7 to receive public punishment. Children could be punished publicly for several status offenses such as rebelliousness, disobedience and sledding on the Sabbath. Thus, separate systems of justice were set up for children and adults. Institutions created to care for orphaned and neglected children included almshouses and orphanages.

SOURCE: Adapted from materials of the Center for the Assessment of the Juvenile Justice System (Hawkins et al. 1980).

good work and study habits, live in a disciplined and healthy environment and develop character. Five distinct, yet interrelated, institutions evolved to handle poor, abused, neglected, dependent and delinquent children brought before a court: (1) indenture and apprenticeship, (2) mixed almshouses (poorhouses), (3) private orphanages, (4) public facilities for dependent children and (5) jails.

Another significant development during this period was an 1818 committee report linking pauperism, or poverty, with juvenile delinquency—the first public recognition of the term *juvenile delinquency*. This correlation remained an object of focus in juvenile justice throughout the 1800s and 1900s.

The rising concern and social reform that marked the turn of the nineteenth century saw reformers seeking to change laws and public policy as they affected children. During 1820 and 1821, the Society for the Prevention of Pauperism surveyed U.S. prisons and found prevalent a highly punitive approach toward prisoner treatment. The society's report criticized imprisoning individuals regardless of age or the severity of crime. In 1824 the society reorganized to become the Society for the Reformation of Juvenile Delinquents in the City of New York, whose purpose was to establish a reformatory. This development signaled a fundamental shift in the underlying philosophy concerning youths and the justice system and moved American juvenile justice into its next evolutionary stage—the Refuge Period.

The Refuge Period (1824–1899)

During the Refuge Period reformers created separate institutions for youths such as houses of refuge, reform schools and foster homes. However, from the onset, these special institutions for juveniles still housed together delinquent, dependent and neglected children (Krisberg and Austin 1993, 17).

Houses of Refuge

 In 1824 the New York House of Refuge, the first U.S. reformatory, opened to house juvenile delinquents, defined in its charter as "youths convicted of criminal offenses or found in vagrancy."

The House of Refuge was the predecessor of today's training schools. Children were placed there by court order and usually stayed until they reached the age of maturity. Children who misbehaved lost certain rewarded positions or were

© The Bettmann Archive/Corbis

In this engraving from an American newspaper of 1868, a 6-year-old sentenced for vagrancy to the House of Refuge on Blackwell's Island, New York City, pleads unavailingly for mercy for his first offense.

whipped. The labor of the House was contracted out to local businesses. Youths were given apprenticeships and training in practical occupations.

The states' authority to send children to such houses of refuge under the doctrine of *parens patriae* was upheld in 1838 in Pennsylvania in *Ex parte Crouse*. In this case a mother claimed that her daughter was incorrigible and had her committed to the Philadelphia House of Refuge. The girl's father sought her release but was denied by the court, which stated:

> The object of the charity is reformation, by training its inhabitants to industry; by imbuing their minds with principles of morality and religion; by furnishing them with means to earn a living; and above all, by separating them from the corrupting influence of improper associates. To this end, may not the natural parents, when unequal to the task of education, or unworthy of it, be superseded by the *parens patriae*, or common guardian of the community?

However, many houses of refuge were prisons with harsh discipline, including severe whippings and solitary confinement. Despite public disapproval of the harsh discipline and health hazards, 20 such institutions had opened in the United States by 1860.

Krisberg and Austin (1993, 16) suggest, "Although early 19th-century philanthropists relied on religion to justify their good works, their primary motivation was protection of their class privileges. Fear of social unrest and chaos dominated their thinking. The rapid growth of a visible impoverished class, coupled with apparent increases in crime, disease and immorality, worried those in power."

From 1859 to 1890 many houses of refuge were replaced by reform schools, which often were indistinguishable from the houses of refuge.

Reform Schools

By the middle of the nineteenth century, the more progressive states began to develop new institutions—*reform schools*—intended to provide discipline in a "homelike" atmosphere where education was emphasized. Although reform schools emphasized formal schooling, they also retained large workshops and the contract system of labor.

Foster Homes

While many states were building reform schools, New York in 1853 emphasized placing neglected and delinquent children in private *foster homes*, frequently located in rural areas. At the time, the city was viewed as a place of crime and bad influences, in contrast with the clean, healthy, crime-free country.

The foster home was to be the family surrogate used in all stages of the juvenile justice process. This concept faltered for a variety of reasons. Personality conflicts between foster parents and juvenile clients often caused disruption. In addition, accrediting and monitoring foster home licenses was inadequate and sometimes ignored completely.

The Child Savers

Many reforms swept through the United States during the nineteenth century, including the child-saving movement, which began around the middle of the 1800s. The **child savers** believed that children's environments could make them "bad." These wealthy, civic-minded citizens tried to "save" unfortunate children by placing them in houses of refuge and reform schools.

These reformers firmly believed that children should not be tried in a criminal court alongside adults nor be sentenced to jail with hardened criminals. The reformers believed that society owed more to its children.

 The child savers were reformers whose philosophy was that the child was basically good and was to be treated by the state as a young person with a problem.

The reformers thought that children's contact with the justice system should not be a process of arrest and trial, but should seek answers to what the children are, how they have become what they are and what society should do in the children's, as well as society's, best interests to save them from wasted lives. The child savers' motivating principles were (Task Force Report 1976, 6):

- Children should not be held as accountable as adult transgressors.
- The objective of juvenile justice is to help youngsters, to treat and rehabilitate them rather than to punish them.
- Dispositions should be predicated on an analysis of the youth's special circumstances and needs.
- The system should avoid the punitive adversary role and formalized trappings of the adult criminal process.

Highlights of Refuge Period Reform

Children were protected from confinement in jails, prisons and institutions by the opening of houses of refuge. Responsibilities shifted back and forth between the private and public sectors. Between 1878 and 1898 Massachusetts established a statewide system of probation to aid the court in juvenile matters, a method of corrections currently used in every state.

Child labor was regulated, special services for handicapped children were developed and public education grew. Public responsibility for protecting and caring for children became accepted. However, no legal machinery existed to handle juveniles who needed special care, protection and treatment as wards of the state rather than as criminals.

Philosophy Poverty was a crime that could be eliminated by removing children from offending environments and reforming their unacceptable conduct. Youth problems increased as by-products of rapid urbanization: poverty, immigration and unhealthy environments.

Treatment Nonconforming children were controlled by external institutions, such as houses of refuge and reformatories created by paternalistic child savers. Public education was used to "Americanize" foreign and lower-class children. Several private organizations were created to assimilate foreign and lower-class youths into American culture. Private groups were organized to rescue children from poor and unfit environments. Locked facilities were built across the nation. Orphan asylums became popular ways to house and mold the conduct of children left homeless by the Civil War or neglected by unfit parents.

Policies Local and state governments became providers of care and treatment for neglected and delinquent children. The *parens patriae* tradition, correctional policies that separated adult and youthful offenders, and indeterminate sentencing for juvenile inmates were adopted. Statutory definitions of juvenile delinquency were expanded to include new status offenses, such as begging, cheating and gambling.

The child savers were not entirely humanitarian, however. They viewed poor children as a threat to society who needed to be reformed to conform, to value hard work and to become contributing members of society (Platt 1968).

Other Developments during the Refuge Period

By the middle of the refuge period, organizations such as the Young Men's Christian Association (YMCA) and the Young Women's Christian Association (YWCA) had opened chapters within the United States to provide recreation and counseling services to youths, thereby preventing delinquency. The Civil War (1861–1865) was followed by reconstruction and massive industrialization. Many children were left fatherless by the war, and many families moved to urban areas seeking work. Often children were exploited in sweatshops or roamed the streets in gangs while their parents worked in factories.

In 1866 the first specialized institution for male juveniles was authorized in Washington, DC. This House of Corrections consisted of several cottages containing 60 or more beds. At this time state reformatories also came into existence, including the New York State Reformatory at Elmira, which opened in 1877.

By the end of the 1800s, reform schools introduced vocational education, military drill and calisthenics into the institutions' regimens. At the same time, some reform schools changed their names to "industrial schools" and later to "training schools," to emphasize the "treatment" aspect of corrections. For example, the Ohio Reform Farm School opened in 1857, later became the Boy's Industrial School and was renamed again to the Fairfield School for Boys.

Several other significant events occurred during the 1800s that altered the administration of juvenile justice (Griffin and Griffin 1978, 20):

1870—First use of separate trials for juveniles (Massachusetts)
1877—Separate dockets and records established for juveniles (Massachusetts)
1880—First probation system applicable to juveniles instituted (Massachusetts)
1898—Segregation of children under 16 awaiting trial (Rhode Island)
1899—First juvenile court established (Illinois)

A juvenile court movement began during the 1890s that provided citizen participation in community-based corrections. This citizen participation through the Parent Teacher Association (PTA), founded in 1897, induced the Cook County (Illinois) Bar Association to write the law establishing a juvenile court in Chicago (Hunt 1973), the first of its kind, propelling juvenile justice into its third evolutionary phase—the Juvenile Court Period.

The Juvenile Court Period (1899–1960)

The Juvenile Court Period was born at the beginning of what is often referred to as the Progressive Era or the Age of Reform—the first quarter of the twentieth century. According to reformers, children were not inherently bad but were made so by society and their environment. Progressives believed that the family was especially influential and that parents were responsible for bringing their children up to be obedient and to work hard. When parents were unable to fulfill such responsibilities, reformers believed in state intervention. Their vision materialized in the shape of the 1899 Juvenile Court Act, titled an "Act to Regulate the Treatment and Control of Dependent, Neglected and Delinquent Children."

The 1899 Juvenile Court Act

Passed in Illinois, this act represented the U.S. criminal justice system's first formal recognition that it owed a different duty to children than to adults and that impressionable, presumably salvageable youths should not be mixed in prisons with hardened criminals. The law created a public policy based on the **medical model**—that is, a model of individual diagnosis and individual treatment. An underlying philosophy of the medical model was that delinquency was a preventable and treatable condition; in cases where prevention failed and delinquent behavior occurred, the condition could be treated and cured.

The act created the first juvenile court in the United States and provided social reform and a structured way to restore and control children in trouble. It also provided a way to care for children who needed official protection.

 In 1899 the Illinois legislature passed a law establishing a juvenile court that became the cornerstone for juvenile justice throughout the United States.

Key features of this act included:

- Defining a delinquent as any detainee younger than 16.
- Separating children from adults in institutions.
- Setting special, informal procedural rules for juvenile court.
- Providing for use of probation officers.
- Prohibiting detention of children younger than 12 in a jail or police station.

The Juvenile Court Act gave "original jurisdiction in *all* cases coming within the terms of this act," removing those younger than 16 from the criminal court's jurisdiction and placing them in a paternalistic system that viewed juvenile delinquents as victims of their environments not responsible for their offenses. Rehabilitation and the child's welfare were of prime concern. The adjudicative process within the juvenile court was to be special; it was *not* to function as an adult criminal court but more like a social welfare agency. The Juvenile Court Act equated poor and abused children with delinquent and criminal children and provided that they be treated in essentially the same way, establishing the one-pot approach described in Chapter 1.

 The first juvenile courts were administrative agencies of circuit or district courts. They served a social welfare function, embracing the rehabilitative ideal of reforming children rather than punishing them.

Passage of the Illinois Juvenile Court Act marked the first time that probation and probation officers were formally made *specifically* applicable to juveniles. The act stipulated

> The court shall have authority to appoint or designate one or more discreet persons of good character to serve as probation officers during the pleasure of the court ... it shall be the duty of the said probation officer to make such investigation as may be required by the court; to be present in court in order to represent the interests of the child when the case is heard; to furnish to the court such information and assistance as the judge may require; and to take such charge of any child before and after trial as may be directed by the court.

 Probation, according to the 1899 Illinois Juvenile Court Act, was to have both an investigative and a rehabilitative function.

Social workers served the juvenile court as probation officers and held this same philosophy. They collected facts about youths' misbehavior, including the history of their families, school performance, church attendance and neighborhood. Social workers made recommendations for disposition to the judges and provided community supervision and casework services to the vast majority of children adjudicated by the juvenile courts.

Besides providing for probation officers, the Juvenile Court Act also stipulated that juvenile courts were to have separate records and informal procedures. The adversary function of the criminal court was deemed incompatible with the procedural safeguards of the juvenile court, reflecting the basic doctrine of *parens patriae*. Because children were legally wards of the state, they were perceived to be without constitutional rights. The act was construed liberally so that the care, custody and discipline of children would approximate as nearly as possible that given by individual parents. Custody or guardianship was a legal status created by court order giving an adult the right and duty to protect, provide food and shelter, train and discipline a child. To that end, several important parts of a criminal trial, such as the indictment, pleadings and jury, were eliminated. Despite this, juvenile court was initially regarded as far more humane than criminal court.

Some scholars assert the system was set up to take advantage of children. Disputing the benevolent motives of the juvenile court founders, these scholars have suggested that the civil liberties and privacy rights of juveniles diminished in the process. Although reformers of the time were optimistic, college-educated people who believed that individualized treatment based on a juvenile's history was critical, they were also concerned with their own futures.

 The progressives further developed the medical model, viewing crime as a disease to treat and cure by social intervention.

Commonwealth v. Fisher (1905) defended the juvenile court ideal, reminiscent of the holding of the court in the *Crouse* case of 1838:

> To save a child from becoming a criminal, or continuing in a career of crime, to end in maturer years in public punishment and disgrace, the legislatures surely may provide for the salvation of such a child, if its parents or guardians be unwilling or unable to do so, by bringing it into one of the courts of the state without any process at all, for the purpose of subjecting it to the state's guardianship and protection.

Early Efforts at Diversion: The Chicago Boy's Court and Youth Counsel Bureau

Diversion is the official halting of formal juvenile proceedings against a youthful offender and, instead, treating or caring for the youth outside the formal juvenile justice system. In 1914 diversion from juvenile court began in the Chicago Boy's Court, an extralegal form of probation to process and treat young offenders without labeling them as criminals.

The Boy's Court version of diversion used four community service agencies: a Catholic church agency, a predominantly Protestant agency, a Jewish Social Service Bureau and the Colored Big Brothers. The court released juveniles to the supervision and authority of these agencies. After a sufficient time to evaluate each youth's behavior, the agencies reported back to the court. The court took the evaluation and, if satisfactory, the judge officially discharged the individual. No record was made.

Toward the end of the Juvenile Court Period, in the early 1950s, developments in youth diversionary programs included New York City's Youth Counsel Bureau, established to handle delinquents not deemed sufficiently advanced in misbehavior to direct to court. Referrals were made to the bureau from police, parents, schools, courts and other agencies. The bureau provided a counseling service and discharged those whose adjustments appeared promising. No record was kept to label the youths delinquent.

Federal Government Concern and Involvement

The earliest federal interest in delinquency and child dependency was demonstrated by the 1909 White House Conference on Children and Youth, the theme of which centered on the institutionalization of dependent and neglected children:

> Following the 1909 White House Conference on Dependent Children, in which family preservationists won the debate with the children's rights defenders of the charitable private agencies, the foster care population, ironically, increased. Child welfare's policies supported family preservation, but the practice of child removal advanced by the charity workers continued— to the present day (Golden 1997, 120–121).

The 1909 White House Conference on Children and Youth established the U.S. Children's Bureau in 1912.

In addition, in 1912 Congress passed the first child labor laws.

The aftermath of World War I, the Great Depression and World War II occupied much of the federal government's attention from 1920 to 1960 as it sought to help citizens cope with the pressures of the times. Nonetheless, by 1925 all but two states had juvenile court systems, and the U.S. Children's Bureau and the National Probation Association issued a recommendation for *A Standard Juvenile Court Act* in 1925.

 Passage of the Social Security Act in 1935 began major federal funding for programs to aid children and families.

In 1936, the Children's Bureau began administering the first federal subsidy program, providing child welfare grants to states for the care of dependent, neglected, exploited, abused and delinquent youths.

Recognizing the considerable power and influence the juvenile court held over children's lives and the formulation of youth policy, a group of concerned juvenile court judges came together in 1937 to found the National Council of Juvenile and Family Court Judges (NCJFCJ), an assembly that, over the years, has "established itself as an influential and respected organization" (Schwartz 1989, 91).

The federal government passed the Juvenile Court Act in 1938, adopting many features of the original Illinois act. Within 10 years every state had enacted special laws for handling juveniles.

In the 1940s a number of conferences on children and youths were held, but most public support was directed toward the war and reconstructing families after the war. In 1951 Congress passed the Federal Youth Corrections Act and created the Juvenile Delinquency Bureau (JDB), positioned within the Department

Courtesy Colorado Historical Society (Scan 10027289)

Judge Benjamin Lindsay presided in juvenile court in Denver, Colorado, from 1900 to 1927. These first juvenile courts were informal proceedings focusing on rehabilitation rather than on punishment.

Highlights of Juvenile Court Period Reform

Policymakers and practitioners differed regarding the most effective treatment for unacceptable behavior and over who should be responsible for organizing and regulating juvenile justice. Specialized rules of juvenile procedure were being set forth by a growing number of judicial bodies. The juvenile court was perceived to be a means for attaining certain social ends. However, a growing concern was that the juvenile system carried its own stigma harmful to juveniles by procedures that denied due process of law. By the late 1940s, the gap between the theoretical assistance and actual punitive practices became obvious. Legal challenges to the system's informality and lack of safeguards were brought.

Philosophies Adolescence was accepted as a unique period of biological and emotional transition from child to adult requiring careful control and guidance. Misbehavior by middle-class youths was to be expected and controlled by concerned families, but lower-class youths were to be reformed via public efforts.

Controlling and improving societal rather than individual conditions might decrease the incidence of youthful crime. Children were to be gently led back to conformity, not harshly punished.

Treatment Children were primarily treated by public efforts guided by new public policies and research. Children in need were handled primarily by juvenile courts.

Policies The juvenile court system was adopted by every state to adjudicate youths separately from adults, expanding the *parens patriae* precedent. The federal government broadened its role and began providing direction for youth services, sponsoring conferences, passing legislation to improve conditions for families and youths during the Depression, passing child-labor legislation, supporting the protection of children's basic constitutional rights and creating the Children's Bureau as the first national child welfare agency.

of Health, Education and Welfare, which reflected the prevalence of the medical model at that time as well as the emphasis on prevention.

By the end of the Juvenile Court Period, social work and the juvenile justice system movement were flourishing with their combined focus on youths and their families. The movement gradually became more concerned with professionalism in the intake process and correctional supervision. This went unnoticed by outsiders until the early 1960s.

By the end of the Juvenile Court Period, the U.S. Supreme Court had begun to seriously question the use of *parens patriae* as the sole reason for denying children many constitutional rights extended to adults charged with a crime. In 1956 in *Shioutakon v. District of Columbia*, the courts established the role of legal counsel in juvenile court. If juveniles were to have their liberty taken away, such juveniles had the right to a lawyer in court.

The end of this period also marked the beginning of radical societal changes in the United States that would last the next two decades and extend throughout the fourth developmental phase of our juvenile justice system—the Juvenile Rights Period.

The Juvenile Rights Period (1960–1980)

In the 1960s the American family was undergoing significant changes that directly affected social work and its liaison between the juvenile, the family and the court. Divorces increased, with the result that more children lived in single-parent households. Births to unmarried women increased, and more women entered the labor force.

Juvenile crime received increased attention when, in 1960, the U.S. attorney general reported that delinquency and crime were costing the American public more than $20 million per year. In addition, poor, lower-class delinquents were now joined by youths with middle- and upper-class backgrounds and rural youths.

President Lyndon Johnson's Great Society initiative of the 1960s, known for its "War on Poverty," advanced causes for families and children, providing federal money to attack poverty, crime and delinquency. Further, the 1960s saw racial tensions at an all-time high with leaders such as Malcolm X and groups such as the Black Muslims and the Black Panthers demanding "power to the people." As noted by Krisberg and Austin (1993, 44), "The riots of the mid-1960s dramatized the growing gap between people of color in the United States and their more affluent 'benefactors.'"

Civil rights efforts during the 1960s helped broaden concerns for all children, especially those coming under the jurisdiction of juvenile courts: "Juvenile law, perhaps more than any other aspect of law, reflects the stumbling and confused nature of our society as its values and goals evolve. So it was in the 1960s, when American society put itself through an extraordinary period of self-examination, that a great many problems were identified in the way we handle juvenile crime" (Rieffel 1983, 3).

The Four Ds of Juvenile Justice

To deal with problems identified within the juvenile justice system, new policies were established regarding four key concepts—deinstitutionalization, diversion, due process and decriminalization. Although it was not until the end of this period that sociologist LaMar Empey (1978) formally described these as "the Four Ds of juvenile justice," their implementation in and impact on the juvenile justice system began early in the 1960s.

 The Four Ds of juvenile justice are deinstitutionalization, diversion, due process and decriminalization.

Throughout this period, the major developments in juvenile justice focused on one or a combination of these key concepts. For example, **decriminalization**—referring to legislation that makes status offenses noncriminal acts—was first witnessed in 1961, when California became the first state to separate status offenses from the delinquent category. New York followed suit in 1962, when the revised New York Family Court Act created a new classification for noncriminal misconduct—PINS, Person in Need of Supervision. Other states followed as well, adopting such labels as CINS or CHINS (Children in Need of Supervision), MINS (Minors in Need of Supervision), JINS (Juveniles in Need of Supervision) and FINS (Families in Need of Supervision). These new labels were intended to reduce the stigma of being labeled a delinquent. Throughout the juvenile rights period, a broad range of status offenses were decriminalized.

Other policy changes involved the applicability of due process rights to juveniles. Legal challenges to the notion that the juvenile justice system—and the juvenile court in particular—truly was a benign parent, went as far as the U.S. Supreme Court in the 1960s. Society began to demand that children brought before the juvenile court for matters that exposed them to the equivalent of criminal sanctions receive **due process** protection. The Due Process Clause of the U.S. Constitution requires that no person be deprived of life, liberty or property without due process of law. The Supreme Court began protecting juveniles from the court's paternalism. Due process became a clear concern in *Kent v. United States* (1966).

The *Kent* Decision

Morris Kent, a 16-year-old with a police record, was arrested and charged with housebreaking, robbery and rape. Kent admitted the charges and was held at a juvenile detention facility for almost a week. The judge then transferred jurisdiction of the case to an adult criminal court. Kent received no hearing of any kind.

 The procedural requirements for waiver to criminal court were articulated by the Supreme Court in *Kent v. United States*.

In reviewing the case, the Supreme Court decreed, "As a condition to a valid waiver order, petitioner [Kent] was entitled to a hearing, including access by his counsel to the social records and probation or similar reports which are presumably considered by the court, and to a statement of the reasons for the Juvenile Court's decision."

An appendix to the *Kent* decision contained the following criteria established by the Supreme Court for states to use in deciding whether to transfer juveniles to adult criminal court for trial. The juvenile court was to consider:

- The seriousness of the alleged offense and whether community protection requires waiver.
- Whether the alleged offense was committed in an aggressive, violent, premeditated or willful manner.
- Whether the alleged offense was against persons or property, greater weight being given to offenses against persons, especially if personal injury resulted.
- The prospective merit of the complaint.
- The desirability of trial and disposition of the offense in one court when the juvenile's associates in the alleged offense are adults who will be charged with crimes in the adult court.
- The sophistication and maturity of the juvenile as determined by considering his or her home, environmental situation, emotional attitude and pattern of living.
- The juvenile's record and previous history.

The *Kent* decision warned that the juvenile court's traditional lack of concern for procedural and evidentiary standards would no longer be tolerated.

The *Gault* Decision

In re Gault (1967) elevated the juvenile court process to a national issue: "The *Gault* decision is, by far, the single most important event in the history of juvenile justice" (Schwartz 1989, 99). This case changed the adjudication process almost completely into a deliberately adversarial process. *In re Gault* concerned a 15-year-old Arizona boy, already on probation, who was taken into custody at 10:00 A.M. for allegedly making an obscene phone call to a neighbor. No steps were taken to notify his parents. When Mrs. Gault arrived home at about 6:00 P.M. and found her son missing, she went to the detention home and was told that he was there and that a hearing would be held the next day. At the hearing, a petition was filed with the juvenile court charging general allegations of "delinquency." No particular facts were stated, the complaining neighbor was not present, no one was sworn in, no attorney was present and no record of the proceedings was made. Gault admitted to making part of the phone call in question. At the end of the hearing, the judge said he would consider the matter.

Gault was held in detention for two more days and then released. Another hearing was held four days later that also had no complaining witnesses, sworn testimony, counsel or transcript. The probation officer's referral report charging lewd phone calls was filed with the court. The report was not made available to Gault or his parents. The judge committed him to the state industrial school until age 21. Gault received a 6-year sentence for an action for which an adult would have received a fine or a 2-month imprisonment. The U.S. Supreme Court overruled Gault's conviction on the grounds that he was deprived of his due process rights.

 The *Gault* decision requires that the Due Process Clause of the Fourteenth Amendment apply to proceedings in state juvenile courts, including the right of notice, the right to counsel, the right against self-incrimination and the right to confront witnesses.

In delivering the Court's opinion, Justice Fortas stated

> Where a person, infant or adult, can be seized by the State, charged and convicted for violating a state criminal law, and then ordered by the State to be confined for six years, I think the Constitution requires that he be tried in accordance with the guarantees of all provisions of the Bill of Rights made applicable to the States by the Fourteenth Amendment. Undoubtedly this would be true of an adult defendant, and it would be a plain denial of equal protection of the laws—an invidious discrimination—to hold that others subject to heavier punishments could, because they are children, be denied these same constitutional safeguards. I consequently agree with the Court that the Arizona law as applied here denied to the parents and their son the right of notice, right to counsel, right against self-incrimination, and right to confront the witnesses against young Gault. Appellants are entitled to these rights, not because "fairness, impartiality and orderliness—in short the essentials of due process"—require them and not because they are "the procedural rules which have been fashioned from the generality of due process," but because they are specifically and unequivocally granted by provisions of the Fifth and Sixth Amendments which the Fourteenth Amendment makes applicable to the States.

Thus, the Gault decision provided the standard of due process for juveniles.

The remaining two Ds—deinstitutionalization and diversion—surfaced as focal points for policy change following a harsh examination of the juvenile justice system by the 1967 President's Commission on Law Enforcement and Administration of Justice.

The President's Commission on Law Enforcement and Administration of Justice

In 1967 the President's Commission gave evidence of "disenchantment with the experience of the juvenile court" (President's Commission 1967b, 17). It criticized lack of due process, law enforcement's poor relationship to youths and the handling of juveniles and the corrections process of confining status offenders and children "in need" to locked facilities.

According to the President's Commission (1967b, 69): "Institutions tend to isolate offenders from society, both physically and psychologically, cutting them off from schools, jobs, families and other supportive influences and increasing the probability that the label of criminal will be indelibly impressed upon them." The commission, therefore, recommended that community-based correctional alternatives to institutionalization, or deinstitutionalization, should be considered seriously for juvenile offenders.

At the same time, the President's Commission on Law Enforcement and Administration of Justice published *The Challenge of Crime in a Free Society* (1967), also questioning the policy of incarceration for nonviolent juvenile offenders. In this document, Harvard professor and criminologist James Q. Wilson expressed his views on two competing philosophies of juvenile crime deterrence—whether harsh policies deter juvenile delinquency or if arresting youthful offenders, particularly first-time offenders, might actually steer juveniles toward a lifetime of delinquent behavior. Wilson also theorized that juvenile offenders who have endured arrest may actually enjoy greater status among their peers and that the typically light sentences of juvenile offenders might breed contempt for the system.

 Isolating offenders from their normal social environment may encourage the development of a delinquent orientation and, thus, further delinquent behavior.

The issues raised by the President's Commission, Wilson and others studying juvenile justice policy and practice indicated a need to integrate rather than isolate offenders. The resulting community-based correctional programs, such as probation, foster care and group homes, represented attempts to respond to these issues by normalizing social contacts, reducing the stigma attached to being institutionalized and providing opportunities for jobs and schooling.

The President's Commission also strongly endorsed diversion for status offenders and minor delinquent offenses. In addition, the commission recommended establishing a national youth service bureau and local or community youth service bureaus to assist the police and courts in diverting youths from the juvenile justice system.

Youth Service Bureaus

In 1967 the President's Commission established a federal youth service bureau to coordinate community-centered referral programs. Local youth service bureaus were to divert minor offenders whose behavior was rooted in problems at home, in school or in the community. Although a broad range of services and certain mandatory functions were suggested for youth service bureaus, individually tailored work with troublemaking youngsters was a primary goal.

As envisioned by the commission, youth service bureaus were not part of the juvenile justice system. The bureaus would provide necessary services to youths as a substitute for putting them through the juvenile justice process, thus avoiding the stigma of formal court involvement. The three main functions of local youth service bureaus were diversion, resource development and system modification.

Diversion included accepting referrals from the police, courts, schools, parents and other sources, and included working with the youths in a voluntary, noncoercive manner through neighborhood-oriented services. *Resource development* included offering leadership at the neighborhood level to provide and develop a variety of youth assistance programs, as well as seeking funding for new projects. *System modification* included seeking to change attitudes and practices that discriminate against troublesome youths and, thereby, contribute to their antisocial behavior. Finally, the President's Commission advocated *prevention* as the most promising and important method of dealing with crime, a philosophy embodied in the Uniform Juvenile Court Act of 1968.

The Uniform Juvenile Court Act

In 1968 the historic Delinquency Prevention and Control Act was passed. One provision of this act was to reform the juvenile justice system nationally. Although titled a "court" act, the legislation included provisions that affected law enforcement and corrections, illustrating the interconnectedness of the components of the system.

 The Uniform Juvenile Court Act provided for the care, protection and development of youths, without the stigma of a criminal label, by a program of treatment, training and rehabilitation in a family environment when possible. The act also provided simple judicial and interstate procedures.

The act described probation services, referees, venue and transfer, custody and detention, petitions and summons, hearings, children's rights, disposition, court files and records and procedures for fingerprinting and photographing children. These areas are described in detail in the chapters dealing with law enforcement and the courts.

Despite the best intentions of this act, a growing body of empirical evidence was beginning to cast serious doubt upon the ability of social casework, the linchpin of correctional treatment along with probation and parole, to help rehabilitate youths (Hellum 1979). Fortunately, as will be seen in future chapters, much has been learned during the past 30 years, and there is now a growing consensus that treatment and rehabilitation programs possessing certain characteristics can be quite effective with certain juveniles. But at the time, the prevailing sentiment was that not much was working.

And although rehabilitation remained the major premise on which the juvenile justice system rested, research at that time had found that correctional "treatment," especially in institutions, was often unnecessarily punitive and sometimes sadistic. Modern reformers became appalled that noncriminal youths and status offenders could so easily find their way into the same institutions as seriously delinquent youths. This spawned a rapid growth in community-based alternatives to institutionalization, as well as renewed national interest in juvenile justice.

The White House Conference on Children and Youth

The 1970 White House Conference on Children and Youth warned, "Our families and children are in deep trouble. A society that neglects its children and fears its youth cannot care about its future" (*The White House Conference on*

Youth 1972, 346). The message from the conference was interpreted as a call for special federal assistance to identify the needs of families.

 The major impact of the 1970 White House Conference on Children and Youth was that it hit hard at the foundation of the U.S. system for handling youths, including unnecessarily punitive institutions.

Beginning in 1971 a series of federal cases tried to specify minimum environmental conditions for juvenile institutions. By 1972 a cooperative effort among federal administrations focused on programs for *preventing* delinquency and rehabilitating delinquents outside the traditional criminal justice system, prompting adoption of the Juvenile Justice and Delinquency Prevention Act of 1974.

The Office of Juvenile Justice and Delinquency Prevention and the Juvenile Justice and Delinquency Prevention Act

In 1974 Congress created the Office of Juvenile Justice and Delinquency Prevention (OJJDP) and placed it in the Department of Justice. Congress also passed the Juvenile Justice and Delinquency Prevention (JJDP) Act by a vote of 329 to 20 in the House and with only one dissenting vote in the Senate. The landmark JJDP Act required that for states to receive federal funds, incarceration and even temporary detention should be used for young people only as a last resort.

 The Juvenile Justice and Delinquency Prevention Act of 1974 had two key goals: deinstitutionalization of status offenders and separation or removal of juveniles from adult facilities.

The JJDP Act made funds available to states that removed status offenders from prisons and jails and created alternative voluntary services to which status offenders could be diverted. The act was amended in 1976, 1977, 1980, 1992 and 2002. It was due for renewal in 2007 and, as of January 1, 2012, remained overdue for reauthorization. However two new bills had been introduced to Congress, one of which was designed to amend the JJDP Act of 1974 to provide incentive grants to promote alternatives to incarcerating delinquent juveniles (H.R. 3170), and another of which aims to amend the JJDP Act of 1974 with respect to juveniles who have committed crimes and for other purposes (H.R. 3171). Students can follow the progress of these bills online at the govtrack.us Web site.

The 1980 amendment called for the removal of juveniles from adult jails. In 1992 Congress added a disproportionate minority confinement (DMC) mandate requiring that states receiving JJDP Act formula grants provide assurances that they will develop and implement plans to reduce overrepresentation of minorities.

Although the JJDP Act promoted developing diversionary tactics for juvenile offenders through monetary incentives, claiming such practices would benefit both the system and the youths it handled, the policy of diversion soon revealed weaknesses and was met with some criticism.

A Brief Note about Diversion and Net Widening   The juvenile due process requirements from *Kent* and *Gault*, combined with the rising costs of courts and correctional facilities at the end of the 1960s and throughout the 1970s, resulted in wider use of community-based alternatives to treat youths before and after adjudication. Young offenders were diverted into remedial education, drug abuse programs, foster homes and outpatient health care and counseling facilities.

However, diversion does not necessarily mean less state social control over juveniles. It has had the negative effect of transferring state power from juvenile courts to police and probation departments. Many youngsters who earlier would have been simply released were instead referred to the new diversionary programs. This phenomenon, called **net widening**, was the opposite of diversion's original purpose, which was to lessen the states' power to control juveniles.

Diversion has the potential to widen the net and to increase the risk of violating rights of due process and fundamental fairness because referrals usually occur *before* adjudication. Thus, it is often never established that referred youngsters are actually guilty of any offense that might make them properly the subjects of conditional placement. Diversion is discussed in greater depth in Chapter 9.

A Return to Due Process Issues: Other Landmark Cases

As in the first half of the Juvenile Rights Period, the 1970s saw a continuation of cases addressing juveniles' rights and juvenile court becoming more like adult court in several important ways. Three landmark cases during the 1970s addressed juvenile rights regarding the standard of proof, jury trials and double jeopardy. Whether dealing with status offenders, youths who had committed violent crimes or protecting abused or neglected children, the court no longer had free reign.

The *Winship* Decision: Standard of Proof in Juvenile Proceedings

In re Winship (1970) concerned a 12-year-old New York boy charged with taking $112 from a woman's purse. He was adjudicated a delinquent based on a preponderance of the evidence submitted at the juvenile hearing. He was committed to a training school for 18 months, with extension possible until he was 18 years old, a total possible sentence of 6 years. The question raised was whether New York's statute allowing juvenile cases to be decided on the basis of a preponderance of evidence was constitutional.

Gault had already established that due process required fair treatment for juveniles. The Court held, "The Due Process Clause protects the accused against conviction except upon *proof beyond a reasonable doubt* of every fact necessary to constitute the crime with which he is charged" (italics in original). New York argued that its juvenile proceedings were civil, not criminal, but the Supreme Court said the standard of proof beyond a reasonable doubt not only played a vital role in the criminal justice system but also ensured a greater degree of safety for the presumption of innocence of those accused of crimes.

 In re Winship established proof beyond a reasonable doubt as the standard for juvenile adjudication proceedings, eliminating lesser standards such as a preponderance of the evidence, clear and convincing proof and reasonable proof.

The *McKeiver* Decision: No Right to a Jury Trial

The move toward expanding juveniles' civil rights was slowed by the ruling in *McKeiver v. Pennsylvania* (1971), in which the Court ruled that juveniles do not have the right to a jury trial.

This case involved a 16-year-old Pennsylvania boy charged with robbery, larceny and receiving stolen goods, all felonies in Pennsylvania. He was adjudicated a delinquent. The question for the Court to decide was whether the Due Process Clause of the Fourteenth Amendment guaranteeing the right to a jury trial applied to adjudication of a juvenile court case.

In *McKeiver* the Court held that *Gault* and *Winship* demonstrated concern for the fundamental principle of fairness in justice, with the fact-finding elements of due process necessary and present for this fairness. The Court emphasized in *McKeiver*: "One cannot say that in our legal system the jury is a necessary component of accurate fact finding. There is much to be said for it, to be sure, but we have been content to pursue other ways for determining facts."

 McKeiver established that a jury trial is not a required part of due process in adjudicating a youth as delinquent by a juvenile court.

The Court advocated the presence of an interactive juvenile court judge and concluded that juvenile courts should not become fully adversarial like criminal courts. Requiring a jury might put an end to "what has been the idealistic prospect of an intimate informal protective proceeding." Requiring jury trials for juvenile courts could also result in delays, as well as in the possibility of public trials.

The *Breed* Decision: Double Jeopardy

Double jeopardy was the issue in *Breed v. Jones* (1975). The Supreme Court ruled that defendants may not be tried twice for the same offense. Breed was 17 years old when apprehended for committing acts with a deadly weapon. A California juvenile court found the allegation true. A dispositional hearing determined there were not sufficient facilities "amenable to the care, treatment and training programs available through the facilities of the juvenile court," as required by the statute. Breed was transferred to the criminal court where he was again found guilty. Breed argued he had been tried twice for the same offense, constituting double jeopardy. The Supreme Court agreed and reversed the conviction.

 A juvenile cannot be adjudicated in juvenile court and then tried for the same offense in an adult criminal court (*Breed v. Jones*, 1975).

Beginning in 1976 the majority of states enacted legislation that made it easier to transfer youths to adult courts, signaling a change in philosophy that would eventually lead juvenile justice into its next (and current) phase—the Crime Control Period—to be discussed shortly.

Two other Supreme Court decisions in the 1970s dealt with the media's right to publish information regarding juvenile cases. In *Oklahoma Publishing Company v. District Court in and for Oklahoma City* (1977) a court order prohibited the press from publishing the name and photo of a youth involved in a juvenile court proceeding, although the material was obtained legally from a source outside the court. The Supreme Court found the court order to be an unconstitutional infringement on freedom of the press.

In a similar case, *Smith v. Daily Mail Publishing Company* (1979), the Court also held that if information regarding a juvenile case is lawfully obtained by the media, the First Amendment interest in a free press takes precedence over the interests in preserving the anonymity of juvenile defendants.

The Issue of Right to Treatment

Also in the 1970s two conflicting types of cases emerged: one type tried to establish a "right to treatment" and the other to establish the "least restrictive alternative." *Martarella v. Kelley* (1972) established that if juveniles judged to be in need of supervision are not provided with adequate treatment, they are deprived of their rights under the Eighth and Fourteenth Amendments. *Morales v. Turman* (1973) ruled that juveniles in a Texas training school have a statutory right to treatment. And, in *Nelson v. Heyne* (1974), the Seventh U.S. Court of Appeals confirmed juveniles' right to treatment:

> When a state assumes the place of a juvenile's parents, it assumes as well the parental duties, and its treatment of its juveniles should, so far as can be reasonably required, be what proper parental care would provide.... Without a program of individual treatment, the result may be that the juvenile will not be rehabilitated, but warehoused.

Although many state courts have established a right to treatment, including minimum standards, the U.S. Supreme Court has not yet declared that juveniles have a constitutional right to treatment.

Decriminalization of Status Offenses

In line with efforts to deinstitutionalize status offenders, the Joint Commission on Juvenile Justice Standards, which comprised members from both the Institute of Judicial Administration (IJA) and the American Bar Association (ABA), voted in 1977 for the elimination of uniquely juvenile offenses, that is, status offenses, such as cigarette smoking or consuming alcohol.

 According to the American Bar Association, juvenile delinquency liability should include only such conduct as would be designated a crime if committed by an adult.

The referral of status offenses to juvenile court has been viewed by many as a waste of court resources. These critics believe that court resources are best used for serious recidivist delinquents.

Development of Standards for Juvenile Justice

In 1977 a tentative draft of the IJA/ABA Joint Commission's *Juvenile Justice Standards* was published in 23 volumes, and 17 of the 23 volumes were approved in 1979. The *Standards* were published in 1980. In 1978 the state of Washington began extensive legislative revision of its juvenile justice system based, in part, on these working standards. Following implementation of the new legislation it was found that:

- Sentences were considerably more uniform, consistent and proportionate to the seriousness of the offense and the prior criminal record of the youth.
- Although the overall severity level of sanctions was reduced during the first two years, there was an increase in the certainty that a sanction of some kind would be imposed.
- There was a marked increase in the use of incarcerative sanctions for the violent and serious/chronic offender, but nonviolent offenders and chronic minor property offenders were less likely to be incarcerated and more apt to be required to pay restitution, do community service or be on probation.

Highlights of Juvenile Rights Period Reform

The combination of serious, stigmatizing results achieved without due process safeguards led the Supreme Court in the 1960s to impose new requirements in determining when a juvenile could be made a ward of the state.

Since its inception, the juvenile court was guided by a welfare concept. When the Supreme Court took issue with its procedures, the juvenile court environment moved from a simple family atmosphere to a more adversarial system. Treating juveniles changed to a criminal approach, dispensing punishment and placing youths in locked facilities.

Philosophies Dissent arose among professional child welfare workers and policymakers about the causes of and treatment for juvenile delinquency. Consensus arose among the public and policymakers that the traditional agents of control—family, police, schools and courts—could not curb the rise of delinquency.

Treatment The juvenile court system was revised to include due process, deinstitutionalization, decriminalization and diversion programs. Community-based therapy, rather than institutionalization, became the preferred method of treatment.

Policies Large-scale federal financial and programmatic grants-in-aid were made available to states and localities for delinquency prevention and control programs. The juvenile court came under severe criticism because its philosophy of helping all juveniles rather than punishing delinquents led to an indiscriminate mixing of neglected or abused children, status offenders and violent offenders.

- Compliance with the sentencing guidelines was extremely high; nevertheless, differential handling of minorities and females still existed.
- There was a better record of holding juveniles accountable for their offenses.
- Although the new legislation completely eliminated the referral of *status offenses*, it did not eliminate the referral of *status offenders*. Runaways were more likely to be contacted for delinquent acts, for example. (Rieffel 1983, 36–37, italics in original)

In the 1970s the rising fear of youth crime and rebelliousness coincided with a growing disillusionment with the effectiveness of the juvenile justice system. Citizens and lawmakers, amid mounting skepticism of the principles of rehabilitation established by the JJDP Act, began calling for more punitive measures against juvenile offenders, especially those who committed serious or violent felonies. The result was a much harsher attitude toward youth crime and a call to "get tough" with youthful lawbreakers, philosophies characteristic of the current crime control period.

The Crime Control Period (1980–Present)

As mainstream attitudes about the response to and treatment of juvenile offenders swung to more punitive measures, the formerly prevailing medical model of viewing unlawful behavior began to shift to what is often called a **justice model**. The issues involved and how they are viewed in each model are summarized in Table 2.1.

President Jimmy Carter's administration (presidential term 1977–1981) was deeply committed to removing juveniles from adult jails, and the Department of Justice recommended a 34 percent increase in funding for the fiscal year 1981–1982 for the OJJDP, to be targeted at juvenile jail removal. However, when Ronald Reagan became president in 1981, his administration significantly reduced this funding level, claiming that the goal of removing children from adult jails had been largely accomplished and that, even if it had not, it was a state and local problem (Schwartz 1989, 83–84).

Table 2.1 Comparison of the Medical and Justice Models

Issue	Medical Model 1930–1974	Justice Model 1974–Present
Cause of crime	Disease of society or of the individual.	Form of rational adaptation to societal conditions.
Image of offender	Sick; product of socioeconomic or psychological forces beyond control.	Capable of exercising free will, of surviving without resorting to crime.
Object of correction	To cure offender and society; to return both to health; rehabilitation.	Humanely control offender under terms of sentence; offer voluntary treatment.
Agency/institution responsibility	Change offender; reintegrate back into society.	Legally and humanely control offender; adequate care and custody; voluntary treatment; protect society.
Role of treatment and punishment	Voluntary or involuntary treatment as means to change offender. Treatment is mandatory; punishment used to coerce treatment; punishment and treatment viewed as same thing.	Voluntary treatment only; punishment and treatment not the same thing. Punishment is for society's good, treatment is for offender's good.
Object of legal sanctions (sentence)	Determine conditions that are most conducive to rehabilitation of offender.	Determine conditions that are just considering wrong done, best protection for society and deter offender from future crime.
Type of sentence	Indeterminate, flexible; adjust as offender changes.	Fixed sentence (less good time).
Who determines release time?	"Experts" (parole board for adults, institutional staff for juveniles).	Conditions of sentence as interpreted by Presumptive Release Date (PRD) formula.

SOURCE: D. F. Pace, *Community Relations Concepts.* 3rd ed., p. 127. Copyright © 1993. Placerville, CA: Copperhouse. Reprinted by permission.

By the 1980s the "best interests" of society had gained ascendancy over those of youths. In the 1980s the OJJDP became increasingly conservative, with the emphasis shifting to dealing with hard-core, chronic offenders. Also in the 1980s state and federal concerns tended to center on the problems created by procedural informality and the juvenile court's broad discretion. The adversary system of legal process replaced the sedate environment and process of the "family" court that was directed to consider the "best" interest of the child's health, safety and welfare. The courts returned to a focus on what was right according to the law.

In addition, the conservative swing added two more Ds to our juvenile justice system: deterrence and deserts (Krisberg 1992). **Deterrence** uses punishment or the threat of other sanctions, either formal or informal, to prevent future lawbreaking by showing there are consequences to aberrant behavior. This happens in several ways, the most obvious being locking offenders up so they cannot harm society further. Incarceration may deter by (1) serving as a direct lesson to the incarcerated person that crime does not pay (specific deterrence) and (2) sending the same message to others in the public (general deterrence).

Deserts, or *just deserts* as it is often called, is a concept of punishment as a kind of justified revenge—the offending individual gets what is coming to him or her. This is the concept of *lex talionis*, or an eye for an eye, expressed in the Code of Hammurabi centuries ago. However, part of the original meaning of deserts was that the power to administer appropriate sanctions lay not with the aggrieved person, or victim, but with the state. Thus, in some ways just deserts limited individual revenge by removing the emotional angle and giving the duty to sanction to the state.

In 1982, 214 long-term public institutions in the United States were designated either "strict" or "medium" custody training schools. Most schools involved agricultural training, thought to be reformative and requiring location in rural areas. An unanticipated effect of this was to remove the corrections problem from community awareness—out of sight, out of mind.

Throughout the 1980s and 1990s public support increased for tougher policies directed at juvenile offenders, and state legislatures responded by passing laws that cracked down on juvenile crime, signaling a reversal of the juvenile due process trend of the previous two decades (Snyder and Sickmund 2006, 96). Breen (2001, 50) observes

> This policy shift is evidenced by 49 states that now allow juvenile court prosecutors to waive jurisdiction and transfer cases to adult court. In the opinion of some experts, this authority was given to prosecutors because they traditionally did not have the "soft on crime" attitudes of juvenile court judges. In 26 states, the jurisdictions of juvenile courts now exclude certain violent crimes such as murder, rape and armed robbery. A retreat from the due process revolution of the 1960s is also apparent in *Schall v. Martin*.... Here the U.S. Supreme Court, citing the doctrine of *parens patriae*, upheld the constitutionality of New York's law allowing the preventive detention of juveniles.

Schall v. Martin (1984) and Preventive Detention

At 11:30 P.M. on December 13, 1977, juvenile Gregory Martin was arrested on charges of robbery, assault and criminal possession of a weapon. Because of the late hour and because he lied about his address, Martin was kept in detention overnight. The next day he was brought before the family court accompanied by his grandmother. The family court judge noted that he had lied to the police about his address, that he was in possession of a loaded weapon and that he appeared to lack supervision at night. In view of these circumstances, the judge ordered Martin detained until trial. New York law authorized such pretrial or **preventive detention** of accused juvenile delinquents if "there is a substantial probability that they will not appear in court on the return date or there is a serious risk that they may before the return date commit an act which if committed by an adult would constitute a crime."

While Martin was in preventive detention, his attorneys filed a habeas corpus petition demanding his release. The petition charged that his detention denied him due process rights under the Fifth and Fourteenth Amendments. The suit was a class action suit on behalf of all youths held in preventive detention in New York. The New York appellate courts upheld Martin's claim, stating that most delinquents are released or placed on probation; therefore, it was unfair to confine them before trial. Indeed, later at trial, Martin was adjudicated a delinquent and sentenced to two years probation.

The prosecution appealed the decision disallowing pretrial detention to the Supreme Court for final judgment. The Supreme Court reversed the decision, establishing the right of juvenile court judges to deny youths pretrial release if they perceived them to be dangerous.

 In *Schall v. Martin* (1984) the Supreme Court upheld the state's right to place juveniles in preventive detention, fulfilling a legitimate state interest of protecting society and juveniles by detaining those who might be dangerous to society or to themselves.

Pretrial detention need not be considered punishment merely because the juvenile is eventually released or put on probation. In *Schall* the Court reiterated its belief in the fundamental fairness doctrine and the doctrine of *parens patriae*, trying to strike a balance between the juvenile's right to freedom pending trial and the right of society to be protected. All 50 states have similar language allowing preventive detention in their juvenile codes.

Schall also established a due process standard for detention hearings. This standard included procedural safeguards, such as a notice, a hearing and a statement of facts given to juveniles before being placed in detention. The Court further stated that detention based on prediction of future behavior did not violate due process. Many decisions made in the justice system, such as the decision to sentence or grant parole, are based partly on predicting future behavior. These decisions have all been accepted by the Court as legitimate exercises of state power.

Still Evolving

Developments with the evolving juvenile justice system in the United States had a direct effect on the relationships between children and their parents, children and the state and parents and the state. The major developments and influences on these relationships are summarized in Table 2.2. Bear in mind, however, the developments described and neatly categorized in the table are actually fluid, overlapping and ongoing.

In examining the development of juvenile justice, it is clear that the system today is considerably different in philosophy and form than that which existed several centuries ago. This history paved the way for current "innovations" in policy and practice, such as Balanced and Restorative Justice (BARJ) clauses, Juvenile Accountability Incentive Block Grants (JAIBG), peer juries, community mediation, the Blueprints for Violence Prevention program, Targeting Community Action Planning (TCAP) and many other programs—initiatives explored in later chapters.

Also keep in mind that the philosophies, policies, practices and programs that dominate the field today and are the focus of the remainder of this text, will likely pass, at some point, into the history chapters for future juvenile justice practitioners, as the juvenile justice system continues to evolve in response to an ever-changing society and its needs. This fluctuation has been graphically illustrated by the swinging of a pendulum from side to side, often falling somewhere between the two extremes, as illustrated in Figure 2.2. Which direction the juvenile justice system will take in the twenty-first century is unclear.

Table 2.2   Juvenile Justice Developments and Their Impacts

Periods	Major Developments	Precipitating Influences	Child/State	Parent/State	Parent/Child
Puritan 1646–1824	Massachusetts Stubborn Child Law (1646)	A. Christian view of child as evil B. Economically marginal agrarian society	Law provides: A. Symbolic standard of maturity B. Support for family as economic unit	Parents considered responsible and capable of controlling child	Child considered both property and spiritual responsibility of parents
Refuge 1824–1899	Institutionalization of deviants; New York House of Refuge established (1824) for delinquent and dependent children	A. Enlightenment B. Immigration and industrialization	Child seen as helpless, in need of state intervention	Parents supplanted as state assumes responsibility for correcting deviant socialization	Family considered to be a major cause of juvenile delinquency
Juvenile Court 1899–1960	Establishment of separate legal system for juveniles—Illinois Juvenile Court Act (1899)	A. Reformism and rehabilitative ideology B. Increased immigration, urbanization and large-scale industrialization	Juvenile court institutionalizes legal irresponsibility of child	*Parens patriae* doctrine gives legal foundation for state intervention in family	Further abrogation of parents' rights and responsibilities
Juvenile Rights 1960–1980	Increased "legalization" of juvenile law—*Gault* decision (1967); Juvenile Justice and Delinquency Prevention Act (1974) calls for deinstitutionalization of status offenders	A. Criticism of juvenile justice system on humane grounds B. Civil rights movements by disadvantaged groups	Movement to define and protect rights as well as provide services to children	Reassertion of responsibility of parents and community for welfare and behavior of children	Attention given to children's claims against parents; earlier emancipation of children
Crime Control (1980–present)	Shift from medical (treatment) model to justice model and "get tough" attitude; "best interests" of society gained ascendancy over those of youths; Supreme Court approves of preventive detention for youths—*Schall* decision (1984); emphasis on deterrence and just deserts	A. Increase in violent juvenile crime B. Proliferation of gangs C. Spread of drug use	Adversary system of legal process replaces sedate "family" court process; courts return to a focus on what is right according to the law	Parents in some states are held liable for their child's criminal conduct	Unknown

SOURCE: J. David Hawkins, Paul A. Pastor, Jr., Michelle Bell, and Sheila Morrison. 1980. *Reports of the National Juvenile Justice Assessment Center: A Topology of Cause-Focused Strategies of Delinquency Prevention.* Washington, DC: U.S. Government Printing Office. Updated by author.

Krisberg (1992, 157) observes, "Although the conservative revolution in juvenile justice was motivated by the concepts of deterrence and deserts, the emergence of a 'get tough' philosophy also produced another 'D' in the world of juvenile justice—disarray." One reason for this observation may be the conflicting views on the causes of delinquency as discussed in the next chapter.

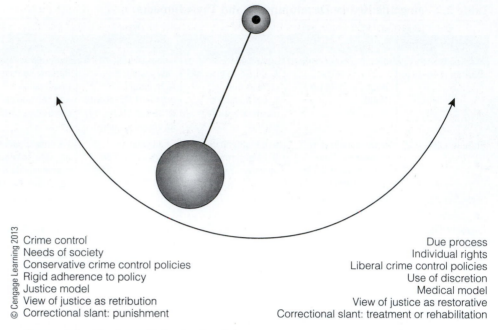

Crime control	Due process
Needs of society	Individual rights
Conservative crime control policies	Liberal crime control policies
Rigid adherence to policy	Use of discretion
Justice model	Medical model
View of justice as retribution	View of justice as restorative
Correctional slant: punishment	Correctional slant: treatment or rehabilitation

Figure 2.2   The Juvenile Justice Pendulum

Summary

- In 1824 the New York House of Refuge, the first U.S. reformatory, opened to house juvenile delinquents, defined in its charter as "youths convicted of criminal offenses or found in vagrancy."

- The child savers were reformers whose philosophy was that the child was basically good and was to be treated by the state as a young person with a problem.

- In 1899 the Illinois legislature passed a law establishing a juvenile court that became the cornerstone for juvenile justice throughout the United States.

- The first juvenile courts were administrative agencies of circuit or district courts. They served a social service function, embracing the rehabilitative ideal of reforming children rather than punishing them.

- Probation, according to the 1899 Illinois Juvenile Court Act, was to have both an investigative and a rehabilitative function.

- The progressives further developed the medical model, viewing crime as a disease to treat and cure by social intervention.

- The 1909 White House Conference on Children and Youth established the U.S. Children's Bureau in 1912.

- Passage of the Social Security Act in 1935 began major federal funding for programs to aid children and families.

- The Four Ds of juvenile justice are deinstitutionalization, diversion, due process and decriminalization.

- The procedural requirements for waiver to criminal court were articulated by the Supreme Court in *Kent v. United States*.

- The *Gault* decision requires that the Due Process Clause of the Fourteenth Amendment apply to proceedings in state juvenile courts, including the right of notice, the right to counsel, the right against self-incrimination and the right to confront witnesses.

- Isolating offenders from their normal social environment may encourage the development of a delinquent orientation and, thus, further delinquent behavior.
- The Uniform Juvenile Court Act provided for the care, protection and development of youths, without the stigma of a criminal label, by a program of treatment, training and rehabilitation in a family environment when possible. The act also provided simple judicial and interstate procedures.
- The major impact of the 1970 White House Conference on Youth was that it hit hard at the foundation of our system for handling youths, including unnecessarily punitive institutions.
- The Juvenile Justice and Delinquency Prevention Act of 1974 had two key goals: deinstitutionalization of status offenders and separation or removal of juveniles from adult facilities.
- *In re Winship* established proof beyond a reasonable doubt as the standard for juvenile adjudication proceedings, eliminating lesser standards such as a preponderance of the evidence, clear and convincing proof and reasonable proof.
- *McKeiver* established that a jury trial is not a required part of due process in adjudicating a youth as delinquent by a juvenile court.
- A juvenile cannot be adjudicated in juvenile court and then tried for the same offense in an adult criminal court (*Breed v. Jones,* 1975).
- According to the American Bar Association, juvenile delinquency liability should include only such conduct as would be designated a crime if committed by an adult.
- In *Schall v. Martin* (1984) the Supreme Court upheld the state's right to place juveniles in preventive detention, fulfilling a legitimate state interest of protecting society and juveniles by detaining those who might be dangerous to society or to themselves.

Discussion Questions

1. The juvenile justice system has been defined as "justice that applies to children and adolescents with concern for their health, safety and welfare under sociolegal standards and procedures." Is this definition adequate? Why or why not?

2. Under the principle of *parens patriae*, how does the state (or the court) accept the role of "parent"? Are all households administered and managed alike?

3. Who are the current "child savers"? What states, associations and individuals have contributed to the present child-saver philosophy?

4. What do you consider the major milestones in the evolution of juvenile justice?

5. Is it possible for one system to effectively and fairly serve both children who need correction and those who need protection?

6. How may diversion result in "widening the net" of juvenile justice processing?

7. What are the rationales on which police diversion of juveniles is based in your community and state?

8. What are the major types of police diversion programs in your area and state?

9. What evidence suggests that diversion programs are effective in reducing juvenile recidivism?

What findings, if any, contradict this evidence? Do you know of a diversion program that is working or one that has failed? Why did it succeed or fail?

10. What are the advantages and disadvantages of diversion?

References

Blackstone, William. 1776. *Commentaries on the Laws of England,* Vol. 4. Oxford, UK: Clarendon.

Breen, Michael D. 2001. "A Renewed Commitment to Juvenile Justice." *The Police Chief* (March): 47–52.

The Challenge of Crime in a Free Society. 1967. Washington, DC: U.S. Department of Justice, U.S. Government Printing Office, 1967.

de Scheveinitz, Karl. 1943. *England's Road to Social Security.* Philadelphia: University of Pennsylvania.

Empey, LaMar. 1978. *American Delinquency: Its Meaning and Construction.* Homewood, IL: Dorsey.

Golden, Renny. 1997. *Disposable Children: America's Child Welfare System.* Belmont, CA: Wadsworth.

Griffin, Brenda S., and Charles T. Griffin. 1978. *Juvenile Delinquency in Perspective.* New York: Harper & Row.

Grunhut, Max. 1948. *Penal Reform.* New York: Clarendon.

Hawkins, J. David, Paul A. Pastor, Jr., Michelle Bell, and Sheila Morrison. 1980. *Reports of the National*

Juvenile Justice Assessment Center: A Topology of Cause-Focused Strategies of Delinquency Prevention. Washington, DC: National Institute for Juvenile Justice and Delinquency Prevention, U.S. Government Printing Office.

Hellum, F. 1979. "Juvenile Justice: The Second Revolution." *Crime and Delinquency* 3(25): 299–317.

Hunt, G. Bowdon. 1973 (February). "Foreword." In *A Handbook for Volunteers in Juvenile Court*, edited by Vernon Fox. Special issue, *Juvenile Justice*. Reno, NV: National Council of Juvenile Court Judges.

Institute of Judicial Administration (IJA) and the American Bar Association (ABA). 1980. *Juvenile Justice Standards.* Cambridge, MA: Ballinger.

Krisberg, Barry. 1992. "The Evolution of the Juvenile Justice System." Appeared in *The World & I,* April 1990, 487–503. Reprinted in *Criminal Justice 92/93,* 16th ed., edited by John J. Sullivan and Joseph L. Victor, 152–159. Guilford, CT: Dushkin Publishing Group.

Krisberg, Barry, and James F. Austin. 1993. *Reinventing Juvenile Justice.* Newbury Park, CA: Sage.

Platt, Anthony M. 1968. *The Child Savers: The Invention of Delinquency.* Chicago: University of Chicago Press.

The President's Commission on Law Enforcement and Administration of Justice. 1967a. *The Challenge of Crime in a Free Society.* Washington, DC: U.S. Government Printing Office.

The President's Commission on Law Enforcement and Administration of Justice. 1967b. *The Task Force Report: Juvenile Delinquency and Youth Crime.* Washington, DC: U.S. Government Printing Office.

Rieffel, Alaire Bretz. 1983. *The Juvenile Justice Standards Handbook.* Washington, DC: American Bar Association.

Schwartz, Ira M. 1989. *(In)Justice for Juveniles: Rethinking the Best Interests of the Child.* Lexington, MA: D.C. Heath.

Snyder, Howard N., and Melissa Sickmund. 2006 (March). *Juvenile Offenders and Victims 2006 National Report.* Washington, DC: U.S. Department of Justice, Office of Justice Programs, Office of Juvenile Justice and Delinquency Prevention.

Task Force Report on Juvenile Justice and Delinquency Prevention. 1976. *Juvenile Justice and Delinquency Prevention.* Washington, DC: U.S. Government Printing Office.

Webb, Sidney, and Beatrice Webb. 1927. *English Local Government: English Poor Law History,* Part I. New York: Longmans, Green.

The White House Conference on Youth. Washington, DC: U.S. Government Printing Office, 1972.

Cases Cited

Breed v. Jones, 421 U.S. 519 (1975)

Commonwealth v. Fisher, 213 Pa. 48, 62 A. 198, 199, 200 (1905)

Ex parte Crouse, 4 Whart. 9 (Pa. 1838)

In re Gault, 387 U.S. 1 (1967)

Kent v. United States, 383 U.S. 541 (1966)

Martarella v. Kelley, 349 F. Supp. 575 (S.D.N.Y. 1972)

McKeiver v. Pennsylvania, 403 U.S. 528 (1971)

Morales v. Turman, 364 F. Supp. 166 (E.D. Tex. 1973)

Nelson v. Heyne, 491 F.2d 352 (7th Cir. 1974)

Oklahoma Publishing Company v. District Court in and for Oklahoma City, 430 U.S. 308 (1977)

Schall v. Martin, 467 U.S. 253 (1984)

Shioutakon v. District of Columbia, 236 F.2d 666 (1956)

Smith v. Daily Mail Publishing Company, 443 U.S. 97, 99 (1979)

In re Winship, 397 U.S. 358 (1970)

Theories of Delinquency and Juvenile Offending

3

> "There are two great injustices that can befall a child. One is to punish him for something he didn't do. The other is to let him get away with doing something he knows is wrong.

—**Robert Gardner**

© Marilynn Humphries/Newscom

Hundreds of youth march to the Massachusetts State House to support funding for youth jobs. There has been a steep deterioration in teen employment opportunities in Massachusetts and the rest of the country. Providing opportunities for youths to earn money through legitimate means is viewed as one way to stem the problem of juvenile delinquency, crime and violence.

DO YOU KNOW?

- How crimes were originally differentiated?
- What function is served by punishment according to the Durkheimian perspective? The Marxist perspective?
- What two competing views have existed over the centuries and the concepts important to each view?

- What proponents of the classical view and those of the positivist view advocate for offenders?
- What primary theories have been developed to explain the cause of crime and delinquency and the major premises of each?
- Whether any single theory provides a complete explanation?

CAN YOU DEFINE?

anomie
anomie theory
classical view of
    criminality
concordance
conflict theory
consensus theory
critical theory

determinism
deterrence
differential association
    theory
ecological model
functionalism
general deterrence
heritability

incapacitation
labeling theory
natural law
positivist view of
    criminality
primary deviance
radical theory
routine activity theory

secondary deviance
social contract
social disorganization
    theory
social ecology theory
specific deterrence
strain theory

CHAPTER OUTLINE

Introduction
Justice and the Law
Purposes of Law
Consensus Theory
Conflict Theory
Two Competing Views on Crime
    and Criminality
The Classical View

The Positivist View
**Theoretical Causes of Crime
    and Delinquency: A Brief
    Overview**
Rational Choice Theory
Biosocial Perspective
Psychological Theories
Sociological Theories

Learning Theories
Critical Theories
A Summary of Theories on
    the Causes of Crime and
    Delinquency
General Theories of Crime

Introduction

Philosophy, theory and history are intertwined—they simultaneously affect and, in turn, are affected by each other. The separation of discussions involving these elements into various chapters is artificial. Therefore, be mindful of information already presented in Chapter 2 while proceeding through this chapter because these concepts wrap around and support those already covered. It may, at times, appear as if this chapter is backtracking. Indeed, in many cases, the theories discussed will have coincided with particular historical events or philosophical eras that prevailed at various times during the evolution of juvenile justice. In other instances, no such specific correlation exists. In either case, the material presented is intended to fill in some of the "why" and "how" gaps left from the preceding chapter.

As seen in Chapter 2, the juvenile justice system has evolved slowly, influenced by many circumstances. In addition to its historical evolution, the system has deep roots in theories about justice, delinquency, crime and punishment. The previous chapter focused on historical events with specific relevance to juveniles, but this chapter takes a step back to look at broader issues that apply to both youths and adults, such as justice, law and theories of criminality, in an effort to better understand why the paths of juvenile and adult justice diverged.

Justice and the Law

Every society has norms, that is, rules or laws governing the actions and interactions of its people. These are usually of two types: folkways and mores. Folkways describe how people are expected to dress, eat and show respect for one another. They encourage certain behaviors. Mores, in contrast, are the *critical* norms vital to a society's safety and survival. Mores are often referred to as **natural law**—the rules of conduct that are the same everywhere because they are basic to human behavior. The doctrine of natural law states that certain acts—for example, murder—are wrong by their very nature, and behavior that disregards the common decency one human owes to another is morally and legally wrong. Each society has a general idea of what constitutes natural law. Our founding fathers were informed by natural law and identified such principles when they wrote of the "inalienable rights to life, liberty and the pursuit of happiness" and of "truths held to be self-evident." This concept, however, is not shared worldwide. Furthermore, it is it important to realize that differences exist across societies regarding what they consider normative juvenile behavior.

Acts considered immoral or wrong in themselves, such as murder and rape, are called *mala in se*. Acts that are prohibited because they infringe on others' rights, not because they are necessarily considered evil by nature, such as having more than one wife, are called *mala prohibita*.

 Crimes were originally differentiated as

mala in se	mala prohibita
wrong in and of itself	a prohibited wrong
origin in mores	origin in folkways
natural law	human-made law
common law	statutory law
stable over time	changes over time

Natural laws may be declared to be criminal acts by human-made laws. Natural laws have remained relatively unchanged over the years, but human-made laws are altered nearly every legislative session.

Purposes of Law

According to sociologist Max Weber (1864–1920), the primary purpose of law is to regulate human interactions—that is, to support social order. Throughout history, law has served many other "secondary" functions, including to protect the interests of society, govern behavior, deter antisocial behavior, enforce moral beliefs, support those in power, uphold individual rights, identify lawbreakers, punish lawbreakers and seek retribution for wrongdoing. These various secondary functions highlight two distinct theories about the underlying purpose of law in society: Laws can serve a social solidarity purpose, a purpose explained by consensus theory, or they can function to keep social control in the hands of the dominant class, a perspective explained by conflict theory.

Consensus Theory

 Consensus theory holds that individuals within a society agree on basic values—on what is inherently right and wrong. Laws express these values.

This theory dates back at least as far as Plato 429/428–348/347 BC) and Aristotle (384–322 BC). Deviant acts are deviant because society, in general, feels they are abnormal and unacceptable behavior. Consensus theory was expanded by the French historian and philosopher Charles de Montesquieu (1689–1755), a founder of political science. Montesquieu's philosophy centered around the **social contract** theory developed by the seventeenth-century English philosopher Thomas Hobbes (1588–1679), whereby free, independent individuals agree to form a community and give up a portion of their individual freedom to benefit the security of the group.

This social contract applied to minors as well as adults. Youths were expected to obey the rules established by society and to suffer the consequences if they did not. A century later the concept of the social contract was expanded by Émile Durkheim.

Punishment and Social Solidarity—The Durkheimian Perspective

Durkheim (1858–1917), a pioneer in sociology, argued that punishment is a moral process to preserve the shared values of a society, that is, its collective conscience. When individuals deviate from this collective conscience, society is outraged and seeks to restore the moral order: "Punishment thus transforms a threat to social order into a triumph of social solidarity" (Garland 1991, 123). Punishment also reinforces the notions that "authorities are in control, that crime is an aberration, and that the conventions that govern social life retain their force and vitality" (Garland, 127).

 The Durkheimian perspective sees punishment as a way to restore and solidify the social order.

Two key elements of Durkheim's perspective are (1) that the general population is involved in the act of punishing, giving it legitimacy, and (2) it is marked by deeply emotional, passionate reactions to crime. Durkheim (1933, 73–80) believed:

- Crime is conduct "universally disapproved of by members of each society."
- "An act is criminal when it offends strong and defined states of the collective conscience."

According to Durkheim, criminal law synthesizes society's essential morality and establishes boundaries that cannot be crossed without threatening the society's very existence. Durkheim ([1897] 1951, 252) developed a concept known as **anomie**, meaning normlessness, detachment and an ambiguity in understanding relationships within the state and society.

Although laws usually reflect the majority values of a society, which is important in a democracy, they rarely represent the views of everyone. This may result in conflict.

Conflict Theory

Law is sometimes used as a tool against certain groups (e.g., the nonmajority groups) in society. This is the perspective of conflict theory.

 Conflict theory suggests that laws are established to keep the dominant class in power.

Conflict theory shifts the focus from lawbreaking to lawmaking and law enforcing and how laws protect the interests and values of the dominant groups within a society. Under this theory, crime will be more likely to flourish in heterogeneous societies where consensus over society's values is lacking: "Conflict theory holds that the administration of criminal justice reflects the unequal distribution of power in society. The more powerful groups use the criminal justice system to maintain their dominant position and to repress groups or social movements that threaten it" (Walker, Spohn, and DeLone 2007, 95). Examples of conflict theory include the segregation laws prevalent throughout the South from the 1890s through the 1960s and vagrancy laws today, which apply to the poor and other populations that "threaten" the social order (Walker, Spohn, and DeLone 2007). Conflict theory, as manifested in criminal laws aimed at behavior engaged in primarily by the socioeconomically disadvantaged, also explains disproportionate minority contact (DMC) and the overrepresentation of racial and ethnic minorities throughout the criminal justice system (Walker, Spohn, and DeLone, 96). For example, local law enforcement generally focuses more effort and resources on, and receives greater public demand and support for, combating "street crimes," which are committed predominantly by racial and ethnic minorities, but white-collar crimes tend to not be as vigorously targeted.

The roots of this theory can be found in the writings of Karl Marx (1818–1883) and Friedrich Engels (1820–1895) who wrote in the *Manifesto of the Communist Party* (1848, 419):

> The history of all hitherto existing society is the history of class struggles. Freeman and slave, patrician and plebeian, lord and serf, guild-master and journeyman, in a word, oppressor and oppressed stood in constant opposition to one another, carried on an interrupted, now hidden, now open fight, a fight that each time ended in either a revolutionary reconstruction of society at large, or in the common ruin of the contending classes.

Punishment and Class Power—The Marxist Perspective   Rather than viewing punishment as a means of providing social solidarity, Marx saw punishment as a way to enhance the power of the upper class and an inevitable result of capitalism. Marx referred to the lower class as a "slum proletariat" made up of vagrants, prostitutes and criminals. "In effect, penal policy is taken to be one element within a wider strategy of controlling the poor; punishment should be understood not as a social response to the criminality of individuals but as a mechanism operating in the struggle between social classes" (Garland 1991, 128).

The Marxist perspective sees punishment as a way to control the lower class and preserve the power of the upper class.

This rationale was doubtless operating throughout the Middle Ages, the Renaissance, the Reformation and into the nineteenth century. Society was divided into a small ruling class, a somewhat larger class of artisans and a vastly larger class of peasants. Intimidation through brutal criminal law was an important form of social control. Flicker (1990, 38) sees this rationale operating in the development of our juvenile justice system:

> The unfortunate historical fact is that the juvenile justice system . . . began with the right observation and the wrong conclusion. Manifestly, poor people are more likely to beg, steal, and commit certain other crimes related to their social and economic status than affluent people. Although socially unaccept-able, crime could be seen as a response to poverty. It was a way to get money. The preferred solutions—jobs, vocational training, financial assistance for the unemployable—required a constructive community attitude toward the disadvantaged. But a combination of Calvinism, prejudice, and social Darwinism confused cause and effect—idleness, inferiority, and criminal-ity were seen as causing poverty, rather than the reverse. Therefore progres-sive elements in the community, the social reformers, felt justified in saving impoverished children from the inexorable path of crime by investigating their homes and families, attempting to imbue them with principles of Chris-tian morality, and, if unsuccessful, removing them to a better environment.

The theoretical roots of these two perspectives on crime and punishment can be found in centuries-old competing views.

Two Competing Views on Crime and Criminality

Two distinct and opposing views exist regarding who or what is responsible for crime—the classical view and the positivist view.

The Classical View

A leader of the classical school of criminology was Cesare Beccaria (1738–1794), whose seminal treatise *On Crimes and Punishment* was published in 1764. Like all classical theorists, Beccaria believed that individuals possess free will and choose to act on that free will. And like Durkheim, Beccaria believed that society functions under a social contract, with free-willed, rational individuals giving up certain personal liberties to live peacefully together within a society.

 The classical view holds that humans have free will and are responsible for their own actions.

Other important principles of the classical theory, also called the **classical view of criminality**, include:

- Individuals have free will. Some choose to commit crime or engage in delinquency.
- Laws should bring the greatest measure of happiness to the largest number of people.

- Those who break the law should be punished according to penalties established in the law.
- The focus is on crime.

The contemporary version of the classical view is rational choice theory, discussed shortly, the major premise of which is that crime is the product of a conscious decision by the offender.

One tenet of classicism espoused by Beccaria was that the certainty and celerity (swiftness) of punishment were more important than its severity. Another tenet of the classical viewpoint concerned *proportionality* in punishment—that punishment must be of just the right amount, neither too harsh nor too lenient, to mitigate any personal gains accrued through criminal behavior. Such proportional punishment would lead offenders to become "unwilling" to commit future crimes.

 Proponents of the classical view advocate certain, swift and proportional punishment for offenders.

And although proportional punishment is deemed important by those who espouse a classical viewpoint, what is even more important is to hold juveniles accountable for their behavior. How this accountability is exacted is of negligible importance.

Several aspects of the classical view are found in the juvenile justice system. Classical theory suggests that the threat of punishment will lower youths' tendency toward delinquency. If the punishment is severe enough, youths will avoid delinquent activity, a process known as **deterrence**. As first mentioned in Chapter 2, deterrence aimed at a particular offender, such as sentencing a juvenile shoplifter to probation or community service, is called **specific deterrence**; the sanction is intended to dissuade that juvenile from further delinquency. When such a sanction influences other juveniles' behavior and turns them away from delinquency by demonstrating the consequences of aberrant conduct, it is called **general deterrence**.

However, the effectiveness of deterrence is uncertain. The concept of deterrence requires the actor to make a rational decision *before* acting that weighs the costs and consequences of the action against the anticipated benefits, a task some, if not many, juveniles are ill-equipped to perform. Many law violators believe they will never be caught, and if they are caught, they believe they can "beat the rap." Those who violate the law under the influence of drugs may think they are invincible. Punishment is no threat to them.

Juveniles may also resist the threat of punishment because of peer pressure. For example, being rejected by the gang would be worse than getting caught by the police. Indeed, being arrested and serving time are often seen as rites of passage, endowing a sort of higher status on those who make the journey. Also, many juveniles know the differences between juvenile and adult court and believe they will receive less severe punishment because of their age.

Classical theory also advocates **incapacitation** as a consequence for criminal activity. Institutionalization is intended not to rehabilitate offenders, but to keep them away from law-abiding society. Classical theory holds that criminal offenders should be sanctioned because they deserve punishment. Critics, however, say this "just-deserts" approach is merely a desire for revenge. Since the first juvenile court in 1899, the juvenile justice system has opposed deserts-based punishment. Incarcerated juveniles were usually given short sentences (one to three years at most) and sent to a nonpunitive, rehabilitation-oriented institution.

 Classical-view theorists suggest that deterrence, incapacitation and, in some cases, just-deserts punishment are the way to deal with delinquency.

Classical theorists' views conflict with those adhering to the *parens patriae* philosophy, which advocates reform as a more appropriate way to deal with delinquency. During the nineteenth century another view of criminality developed in reaction to the classical theory, when criminologists began to apply the scientific method to explore the causes of crime. This marked the beginning of the positivist viewpoint of crime and criminality.

The Positivist View

The positivist view of criminality transfers emphasis from the crime itself to the criminal behavior. A leader of the positivist view was Cesare Lombroso (1835–1909), an Italian physician who studied, among other things, the brains of criminals and the physical or physiological attributes of certain individuals that might be correlated to deviant behavior. Lombroso's position was that some criminals were born with a biological predisposition to crime and, because of these biological factors, such individuals needed exceptionally favorable conditions in life to avoid criminal behavior. In other words, although most crime was the result of environmental conditions, for a core group of individuals, their biological predispositions outweighed any environmental influences.

Lombroso, who has been called the father of modern criminology, was writing at the same time that Charles Darwin's (1809–1882) theory of evolution was becoming widely circulated, and Lombroso was probably greatly influenced by Darwin's ideas. Although some of Lombroso's work was later found to be flawed, he had started people thinking about causes for criminal behavior other than free will.

 The positivist view holds that humans are shaped by their society and are the products of environmental and cultural influences.

Other important principles of the positivist theory, also called the **positivist view of criminality**, include:

- Individuals' actions are determined not by free will but by biological and cultural factors.
- The purpose of law is to avert revolution and convince the masses to accept the social order.
- The focus is on the criminal.

Positivists take a multifactorial approach, attacking the notion of free will promoted by the classical school, and examine the various factors that are potentially outside the person's control and that may also contribute to criminal behavior. The positivist-view theorists, who believe delinquent behavior is the result of a youth's biological makeup and life experiences, think treatment should include altering one or more of the factors that contributed to the unlawful behavior.

Proponents of the positivist view advocate rehabilitation for offenders.

Positivist theorists stress community treatment and rehabilitation rather than incapacitation. For years the *parens patriae* attitude prevailed, with youths shielded from being labeled and punished as criminals.

Building on Lombroso's idea that environmental influences affect criminal behavior, some scholars developed the positivist view of criminality based on the concept of determinism. **Determinism** views human behavior as the product of multiple environmental and cultural influences rather than a single factor. Determinism also includes an element of choice in that a person's life course is determined by whatever factors they choose to emphasize, rather than being simply the product of free will.

Throughout the ages societies have embraced one view or the other, with many people taking a middle position but tending toward one view. And these two views have profoundly affected the various theories about the causes of crime and delinquency that have been set forth over the years.

Theoretical Causes of Crime and Delinquency: A Brief Overview

Delinquency is a focal point for the juvenile justice system. More energy and effort are spent by those within the system on delinquency than on any other responsibility. The United States generates more aftercare programs than any other country. But delinquency, its causes and effects are usually examined *after the fact*, with research on preventing delinquency getting relatively little attention, which leaves the question: What leads youths to become delinquent?

Do children often grow up to be like their parents because they have inherited something from them or because of the way their parents have raised them? This "nature versus nurture" question is especially relevant for children who become delinquents. Many researchers have tried to answer this question, and the vast array of theories that have resulted range from the very conservative to what some may consider outlandish.

The various theories that have developed over time are of two basic kinds: those that attempt to explain why people fail to obey society's laws—why do they become criminals?—and those that approach the issue from the other side and try to explain why people obey the laws—why do they *not* become criminals? As you explore the following theories, keep these two approaches in mind.

During the first half of the twentieth century, several interpretations of the cause of delinquency gained prominence. The earliest theories explored biological and psychological factors. In fact, physical and psychological examinations of children who were brought before the court were standard orders in the juvenile court process. Judicial disposition often included individual counseling and psychological therapy. In the 1950s, under the influence of therapists such as Carl Rogers (1902–1987), group counseling became common in most juvenile institutions.

Slowly, this approach was replaced with social milieu and environmental explanations for delinquency. Delinquency prevention attempts focused on reorganizing the social environment—both physically, through housing renewal, and socioeconomically, through social welfare. There was a significant philosophical shift of the blame for delinquency from personal to social factors. Consequently, the federal government was increasingly drawn into the process of juvenile delinquency prevention.

 Early efforts to explain crime and delinquency were set forth in the classical theory and the positivist theory. Later theories focused on biological, psychological or sociological causes of crime and delinquency. Most recently, critical theories of the causes of crime and delinquency have been developed.

As mentioned earlier, a modern incarnation of classical theory is rational choice theory. In general, however, all of the other contemporary theories— biosocial, psychological, social learning and social structure— have taken a decidedly positivist slant, a distinction to be aware of while reading this section.

Rational Choice Theory

Rational choice theory, as the name implies, holds that crime and delinquency are the results of a thought process in which the benefits of breaking the law outweigh the threat of punishment. In other words, criminals and delinquents exercise free will when choosing their course of action.

 Rational choice theory argues that crime and delinquency are products of conscious decisions made by individuals who rationally weigh, in advance, the costs and benefits of their illegal behavior.

Two variants of rational choice theory are lifestyle theory and routine activities theory.

Lifestyle Theory   Lifestyle theory basically contends that crime is one part of a lifestyle that involves other reckless behaviors. Thus, delinquency is a likely product when a youth chooses an antisocial way of life. An alternate view of lifestyle theory is used to explain victimization and how people who live a high-risk lifestyle choose greater exposure to crime and violence.

Routine Activity Theory   Cohen and Felson's (1979) **routine activity theory**, sometimes referred to as a victimization theory because it includes in it an element of victim culpability, is also premised on the idea that crime is the result of a conscious choice made possible when three factors intersect: (1) availability of a suitable target, (2) absence of a capable guardian and (3) presence of a motivated offender. For example, choosing to leave a wallet (the target) in the console of an unlocked and unattended parked car (lack of guardianship) invites the motivated delinquent or criminal to steal that wallet. This theory, which is an extension of the human ecology analysis, posits that changes in everyday routine activities can influence crime through any one of these factors. As such, it also suggests that victims make themselves targets by choosing to place themselves in positions that include motivated offenders and lack of guardians.

Biosocial Perspective

A large and growing number of studies confirm that biology plays a role in human behavior, including criminal behavior. At the most basic level, it is recognized that males engage in crime and delinquency at higher rates and frequencies than females do. The neuroandrogenic theory posits that observed differences between the sexes in crime involvement is caused by hormonal differences. For example, high testosterone has been associated with aggressive physical and sexual behavior. Testosterone injected into female rats causes them to adopt the male characteristics of aggressive physical and sexual behavior.

The biological/genetic theory of criminality is premised on the idea that brain-based differences between individuals cause a variety of problem behaviors and that genetic influences cause differences in traits related to crime. Key to any biosocial theory of criminality is the concept of **heritability**, the degree to which genetic factors influence traits or behaviors. Heritability exists at a group level and refers to the proportion of variance, across an entire population, in a trait. For instance, evidence indicates that self-control, IQ, aggression and negative emotionality, all moderately to highly heritable traits, are also correlated to antisocial and criminal behavior (Beaver et al. 2009). Heritability should not be confused with traits that are *inherited* from one generation to the next, such as a daughter who inherits her mother's blue eyes or her father's predisposition to heart disease.

 The biosocial perspective of crime and delinquency holds that the propensity for criminal behavior is heritable and interacts with the environment, a theory supported by evidence derived from a variety of studies.

Biosocial criminologists can point to empirical evidence from five primary sources that support a crime–biology link: family studies, twin studies, adoption studies, molecular genetics studies and brain research and imaging.

Family Studies   Crime runs in families, a phenomenon recognized by criminologists since the early 1900s. Some families produce an above-average number of juvenile delinquents, and they do so over many generations (Farrington 2003; Farrington and Welsh 2007). In this sense, crime is similar to other problem behaviors, such as alcoholism and drug addiction, in that it tends to be concentrated in some families more than others.

Twin Studies   The study of twins gives researchers insight into the extent to which a trait or behavior is heritable. If identical twins, known as monozygotic (MZ) twins because they come from a single fertilized egg and, consequently, share identical genetic material, are more similar physically or behaviorally than fraternal, dizygotic (DZ) twins, who come from two separate fertilized eggs, then genetic influences are suspected. More than a half-century of research has revealed that MZ twins were more likely to demonstrate **concordance**, or a similarity in trait possession (e.g., where both twins have criminal records) than were DZ twins, a finding that supports the heritability of antisocial or criminal behavior. Modern studies show that MZ twins raised apart are still more similar than DZ twins raised together on a range of outcomes. Thousands of twin studies have converged to demonstrate that delinquency and crime are moderately to highly heritable (Arseneault et al. 2003; Kim-Cohen et al. 2004; Mason and Frick 1994; Rhee and Waldman 2002).

A problem with twin studies, however, at least for those children reared together, is the potential confounding of genetic and environmental influences. Adoption studies, including those where twins have been placed in different families and reared apart, have helped disentangle the influences of biological and environmental factors.

Adoption Studies   Children raised in the same environment may turn out similar because of similar child rearing practices. Adoption studies, however, allow researchers to test the degree to which environmental influences affect biologically related children raised in diverse settings. In general, adoption studies show that adopted children often turn out to be more like their biological parents than like their adoptive parents. This is especially true for criminal behavior, where studies show that having a criminal father significantly elevates the likelihood that the son will commit crime—even if the son never met his biological father or was ever made aware of the father's criminality (Mason and Frick 1994).

Molecular Genetics Studies   Twin studies are used to assess the degree to which a behavior or trait is influenced by genes. Such studies cannot, however, tell us which genes are important. For this, biosocial criminologists have turned to molecular genetics studies, which examine actual measured genes for evidence of an association between particular variants of a gene and problem behaviors. Scientists have identified several candidate genes that are likely associated with delinquency, crime and drug addiction (Caspi et al. 2002).

Brain Research and Imaging   For several decades, brain research has been illuminating the way specific chemicals or elements in the body contribute to aggression and perhaps criminality. For example, abnormal levels of manganese, zinc, copper, chromium or lead may cause or contribute to antisocial behavior. Serotonin, a neurotransmitter that helps regulate emotions, has been found to play a role in violent behavior (Davidson, Putnam, and Larson 2000).

Modern technology allows scientists to measure and assess the functioning of the brains of offenders. These assessments can then be compared with the brains of a control group to see if there are important differences. Imaging techniques, although very complex, have allowed scientists new insights into how the brain develops and how it is linked to aggressive, delinquent and criminal behavior.

Current studies using functional magnetic resonance imaging (fMRI) allow researchers to actively view brain activity while a subject is exposed to specific stimuli, such as violent video games or people experiencing pain. One highly progressive group of researchers at the University of Chicago's Center for Cognitive and Social Neuroscience is exploring the biological underpinnings of, among other things, adolescents' perception of and desire to inflict pain. In a study group of conduct disordered (CD) juveniles (conduct disorder is discussed in greater detail in Chapter 4), Decety et al. (2009) found evidence that youth with highly aggressive CD show an atypical neural response pattern when viewing others in pain. Such results suggest the brains of asocial youth may be hardwired differently than are those of youth considered to develop "normally." Although such revolutionary research is still in its infancy, preliminary findings of studies such as this indicate a complex but undeniably biological basis to aggressive behavior in adolescents (Raine 2002; Raine et al. 1998).

The relationship between genetics and crime causation remains highly controversial. And although no credible biosocial criminologist would suggest the existence of a "crime gene," the nature versus nurture debate remains a focal point among those searching for a biological basis for deviant behavior.

Psychological Theories

Adolescents who act out, engage in status offenses or commit serious crime come from all socioeconomic levels and are not psychopathic according to conventional classifications. They may have a clear sense of conscience and be capable of strong feelings, such as intense loyalty to a gang. But their impulses are frequently stronger than their self-control. Exploring psychological causes of crime has produced a number of explanations, including:

- Criminals are morally insane; what they do criminally they do not perceive as wrong.
- Personality is developed in early childhood. Future behavior is determined in early childhood. Subsequent sociological and environmental associations do not change this early behavior development.
- Certain people have personalities so deviant that they have little or no control over their impulses.
- There are criminal families in which succeeding generations gravitate toward criminality.
- Mental and moral degeneration cause crime.

 Psychological theories explaining crime contend that individual differences in thinking or emotion regulation can explain why some people commit crime and others do not.

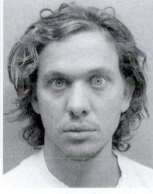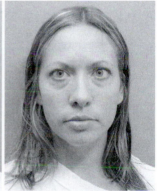

© AP Images/Pueblo County Sheriff's Office, File

The "Dougherty Gang," from left, Ryan Edward Dougherty, 21, Dylan Dougherty Stanley, 26, and Lee Grace Dougherty, 29. In August 2011, the three siblings went on a cross-country crime spree that began in Florida and ended with their capture in Colorado. The event that allegedly sparked their flight: Ryan Dougherty had recently been put on court probation and was forced to register as a sex offender in Florida after sending explicit text messages to an 11-year-old girl. Ryan's fatherless childhood was spent taking risks—doing drugs, breaking into cars, sleeping around. But as he neared the end of his teens, he had tried to change his ways and lead a more responsible life. Things were going fairly well until his bad decision to text a girl he thought was older than she turned out to be. Certain that his conviction would keep him from seeing the son his girlfriend was about to give birth to, and that his sex offender status would prevent him from ever being able to go places with his child where other children were present, Ryan decided to take one more major risk. The three siblings hatched a plan to flee to Mexico, and Ryan would send for his girlfriend and son later. The Dougherty trio robbed a bank in Georgia to fund their trip, and other crimes ensued.

Psychological theories draw attention to the variety of individual factors that help differentiate delinquents from nondelinquents. These factors may be temperamental traits, such as low impulse control, intelligence or callousness; or they may be learned attitudes, values and behaviors. Psychological theories attempt to understand delinquent behavior as well as the cognitive mechanisms that support problem behavior and are generally categorized into personality or trait theory, cognitive theory, psychodynamic theory and learning theory.

Personality and Trait Theories   Psychology has a long history of personality theorizing and research. The essential question is whether, and to what degree, certain personality characteristics or traits are associated with juvenile offending. Research shows, for instance, that chronic delinquents sometimes have personalities that are taxing or difficult for others to understand and interact with. Serious delinquents sometimes lack empathy, are callous in their views of other people and are more likely to have certain personality disorders.

One trait that has captured the interest of researchers is intelligence and its potential correlation to deviance. H. H. Goddard (1866–1957) was one of the earliest psychologists to link intelligence and criminality. Goddard believed that criminals are not necessarily biologically inferior, although they might be intellectually inferior. This correlation was again brought to public attention by Richard Hernstein and Charles Murray (1994), who used the bell-shaped normal curve from statistical studies to promote the idea that individuals' intelligence falls within this curve and may also account for criminality. Modern studies show a modest relationship between intelligence and crime.

Cognitive Theories   The ideas, values and ways of thinking that differ between people form the basis of cognitive theories. Cognition refers to how one interprets one's surroundings, and in general, cognitive theories sensitize us to the manner in which offenders see the world. A large body of empirical evidence has shown that serious delinquents tend to process environmental cues through an aggressive "lens." This lens acts as a filter that biases environmental information in a way that supports an aggressive worldview.

Psychodynamic Theories   The psychodynamic perspective, alternately called the psychoanalytic perspective, emphasizes the connection between early life experiences and personality development. Sigmund Freud (1856–1939), the original psychodynamic theorist, linked early life experiences with the development of the id, ego and super ego, which few people apply to understanding delinquency today. However, Freud also described a series of psychological processes that he described as defense mechanisms. These mechanisms, such as denial or rationalization, are thought to help people make sense of their reality and are regularly identified by counselors who try to help delinquents.

Of most importance to the study of criminality is Freud's explanation of problems that arise from fixation at or regression to the phallic stage (3 to 6 years of age). Fixation or regression to this stage may result in sexual assault, rape or prostitution. It may also result in unresolved Oedipal or Electra conflicts:

> Individuals who do not successfully resolve the Oedipal or Electra complex, and thus do not develop a strong superego capable of controlling the id, were called psychopaths by Freud. (Sociologists call them sociopaths.)

Many criminal offenders are presumed to be psychopaths, sociopaths, or antisocial personalities and are characterized by no sense of guilt, no subjective conscience, and no sense of right and wrong. (Bohm 2001, 53)

Learning Theories   Human beings have a remarkable ability to learn from their experiences and to learn by observation. At its most basic level, learning is a biological process that occurs in the brain, but the content of what is learned is largely environmental. Learning occurs when individuals make cognitive or emotional connections between a stimulus and a response, it occurs when moral values are reinforced or when behavior is rewarded or punished, and it occurs through the observations of others' behaviors. Therefore, according to learning theory, criminal behavior, like any other behavior, is learned either through experience or observation. Learning theories cross many academic disciplines and often serve as a bridge between the disciplines of psychology and sociology in discussions of criminality.

Sociological Theories

Sociology is the study of human social structures and human relationships. Most people start life as members of families and learn, as they grow and mature, how to live with other work and social groups. Sociological theories of criminality hold that delinquents and criminals are molded by social conditions and the broader social environment in which they develop.

Pioneering research by Sheldon and Eleanor Glueck (1896–1980 and 1898–1872, respectively) supports a sociological causation for delinquency. The husband-wife team at Harvard University studied former inmates from the Massachusetts Reformatory and published their initial findings in *500 Criminal Careers* (1930). Results from two follow-up studies were reported in *Later Criminal Careers* (1937) and *Criminal Careers in Retrospect* (1943). These extensive studies of delinquent boys enabled the Gluecks to create a controversial *social predictive index*. The accuracy of this index was tested in the 1950s, and of 220 predictions, 209 were accurate. The social factors in their index included how children were

© Katherine McGlynn/The Image Works

Youths in Brooklyn, New York, play with toy guns. Unfortunately, for some of these youths, such play is a prelude to later delinquency and crime, when real guns will replace these toys.

disciplined and supervised, how much affection was shown in the home and family cohesiveness. In their classic work, *Unraveling Juvenile Delinquency*, the Gluecks (1950) reported that 85 percent of the delinquents released from a Massachusetts correctional institution were from families in which other members were delinquent. In 45 percent of the delinquent cases the mother of the offender had a criminal record; in 66 percent the father had a criminal record.

There are several opinions about the relationship of sociological theories and crime occurrence, including:

- Lack of education, poverty-level income, poor housing, slum conditions and conflict within home and family probably increase crime commission. Achievement expectations are low. If all these conditions disappeared, crime would decrease.
- Continual lawbreaking causes an individual to become part of a subculture that advocates crime and violence as a way to achieve goals or solve problems. It operates outside of society's rules. Crimes committed within the subculture are rarely reported to police.
- Behavior is learned. There is good and bad, right and wrong behavior. Identical pressures affect criminals and noncriminals alike.

Sociological theories are implicated in discussions that contrast white-collar crimes of the wealthy and powerful against street crimes committed by America's underclass, which tend to be the types of offenses that come to mind when many people think of "crime." Sociological theories are also prevalent in discussions of DMC that postulate that minorities are differentially exposed to environmental and socioeconomic factors that are identified as criminogenic. Minority scholars' perspectives in the literature take a decidedly sociological stance when it comes to issues of race and delinquency, adhering to the premise that "social structural inequities produce variations in opportunity structures which cause differential pressures for criminal conduct. Thus, the incidence of illegal behavior in African American neighborhoods is significantly related to and affected by those social structures that substantially influence the life experiences and are outside the immediate control of the individuals involved in such behavior" (Young and Sulton 1996, 3).

 Sociological theories include social disorganization, functionalism, anomie or strain theory and social control theories.

Before exploring these various sociological theories of crime, however, consider briefly the ecological model, by which many sociological criminologists were informed and influenced.

The Ecological Model   Ecology is the study of the relationships between organisms and their environment. Findings from ecology were the basis for the **ecological model**, first described by sociologist Robert E. Park at the University of Chicago (1864–1944). Park, Ernest Burgess and Roderick McKenzie (1928) compared the growth of a city and its attendant crime problems with growth in nature. They found that cities were environments like those found in nature, governed by the same forces that affect natural ecosystems.

Ecologists explain that the plant life in an area of land goes through several stages of growth. First is an invasion period when a new species of plant attempts to gain a foothold. Next the new plant may take over the area or dominate it. Finally the environment stabilizes, accepting the presence of its new dominant organism. A *biotic balance* occurs when the relationships between the different species of plants and their necessary conditions for survival maintain equilibrium. All of the organisms are then able to survive and prosper. Ecologists also describe how two different organisms can live together in a mutually beneficial relationship known as *symbiosis*.

Park encouraged his colleagues and students to study the dynamics of urban life using this ecological model to explain many of the conditions that existed and the problems that plagued cities. Communities could be studied in part by analyzing the invasion, domination and succession of different ethnic and racial groups. Problems within the community could perhaps be alleviated by studying the presence or absence of a biotic balance and symbiosis in a neighborhood.

In addition, according to Park et al., researchers can demarcate a city based on its outwardly moving growth pattern of concentric zones, with each zone representing a particular form of development and community life, as illustrated in Figure 3.1. The ecological model stressed that any explanation of criminal behavior cannot be taken out of its social context.

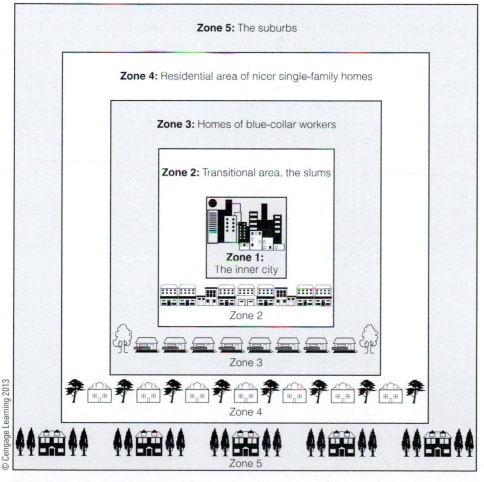

Zone 5: The suburbs

Zone 4: Residential area of nicer single-family homes

Zone 3: Homes of blue-collar workers

Zone 2: Transitional area, the slums

Zone 1: The inner city

Zone 2

Zone 3

Zone 4

Zone 5

© Cengage Learning 2013

Figure 3.1   The Ecological Model

Social Disorganization Theory   Two other Chicago sociologists, Clifford Shaw and Henry McKay (1942), applied the ecological model to a study of delinquency and gang formation. Their **social ecology theory** suggested that ecological conditions predicted delinquency and that gang membership is a normal response to social conditions.

Their area studies involved 25,000 delinquents from the Juvenile Court of Cook County from 1900 to 1933. They, too, found concentric zones within an area, with transitional inner-city zones (Zone 2) having the highest crime rates. This higher rate of delinquency occurred despite an almost complete turnover in ethnic composition. They also found that even in the worst neighborhoods in Zone 2, only about 20 percent of the youths had police or court records.

Shaw and McKay's **social disorganization theory** contended that urban areas produced delinquency directly by weakening community controls and generating a subculture of delinquency passed from one generation to the next. They defined social disorganization as a condition lacking the usual controls over delinquents, with delinquent behavior often approved of by parents and neighbors, and having many opportunities available for delinquent behavior and little opportunity or encouragement for legitimate employment. Shaw and McKay used five indicators of social disorganization: (1) residents of low economic status, (2) many different ethnic groups (high racial heterogeneity), (3) high residential turnover (high mobility), (4) dysfunctional families and (5) urbanization. Their social disorganization theory was built upon by other sociologists, including Robert Sampson and W. Byron Groves (1989), who developed the social disorganization model shown in Figure 3.2.

Functionalism   Functionalism, sometimes called structural functionalism, is one of two grand sociological paradigms (the other being conflict theory). Durkheim, discussed previously under consensus theory, theorized that large, modern, heterogeneous societies are held together by a functional interdependence—every element in society serves a purpose and function. One of the primary assumptions of this theory is that social structure is based on an agreement by the majority of society's members regarding what is important and valued (hence the "consensus of values" referred to in consensus theory). But if the majority of society values adherence to the law, what purpose is served by crime? According to **functionalism**, crime and deviance serve several "greater" purposes for society including:

- Promoting social solidarity—when someone breaks the law, society comes together to reject the deviant and impose punishment, thereby increasing the sense of cohesion and shared values among the law abiding (the *collective conscience*).
- Clarifying and maintaining social boundaries—crime and the ensuing punishment serves as a reminder to people of where the acceptable boundaries lie for behavior.

Furthermore, crime creates a variety of job opportunities for those who must respond to this social problem, such as law enforcement, lawyers and other court personnel, correctional staff, treatment staff and so on. The functionalist perspective also explains how crime may work to lead social change over time as certain laws come to be perceived as unjust, for example, the Jim Crow laws.

Figure 3.2   Social Disorganization Model

SOURCE: Constructed by Robert J. Sampson and W. Byron Groves. 1989. "Community Structure and Crime: Testing Social-Disorganization Theory." *American Journal of Sociology* 94: 783. Printed in S. Giora Shoham and John Hoffman, 1991. *A Primer in the Sociology of Crime*, p. 51. New York: Harrow and Heston Publishers. Reprinted by permission.

Anomie or Strain Theory   American sociologist Robert K. Merton (1910–2003) perceived that a basic conflict exists between cultural goals in the United States and the social structures in place to allow people to achieve these goals. He adopted Durkheim's concept of anomie—the breakdown of social norms, individuals dissociating themselves from the collective conscience of the group—as the basis for his strain theory. According to **strain** or **anomie theory**, people who believe in and strive for the American dream (that is, through hard work anyone can become rich) but fall short of achieving it experience a strain (Merton 1938). This strain can manifest as crime, caused by the frustration felt by people in the lower socioeconomic levels of an affluent society that denies them legal access to social status and material goods (Merton 1957). Mertonian strain theory is a sociological paradigm that explains crime as the result of economic stressors that degrade normal institutions of social control, including the family. When such strain is examined at the level of the individual, as a cause of crime, it is referred to simply as *general strain theory*. In both paradigms, the blockage of opportunities and lack of avenues to legitimate income are seen as the motivations for delinquency and crime.

Anomie or strain theory is explored by Steven Messner and Richard Rosenfeld in *Crime and the American Dream* (2007, x–xi), in which they accept and expand Merton's underlying premise that crime is driven not simply by internal factors and the free will of individuals but, rather, reflects the pressures felt by individuals from their surrounding sociocultural environment:

> The essence of our argument is that the distinctive patterns and levels of crime in the United States are produced by the cultural and structural organizations of American society. American culture is characterized by a strong emphasis on the goal of monetary success and a weak emphasis on the importance of the legitimate means for the pursuit of success. This combination of strong pressures to succeed monetarily and weak restraints on the selection of means is intrinsic to the dominant cultural ethos: the American Dream. The American Dream contributes to crime directly by encouraging people to employ illegal means to achieve goals that are culturally approved. It also exerts an indirect effect on crime through its interconnections with the institutional balance of power in society.

In Messner and Rosenfeld's *institutional anomie theory*, the American dream promotes and sustains an institutional structure in which one institution—the economy—assumes dominance over all others. The resulting imbalance in the institutional structure diminishes the capacity of other institutions, such as the family, education and the political system, to curb crime-causing cultural pressures and to impose controls over and provide support for the members of society. In these ways, the distinctive cultural commitments of the American dream and its companion institutional arrangements contribute to high levels of crime.

Albert Cohen (1955) also built upon Merton's work, adapting his anomie/strain theory in an attempt to explain gang delinquency. Cohen replaced Merton's social goals of wealth with acceptance and status. Youths abandoned the middle-class values for their own values—attaining status among their peers. Cohen's study of delinquent subculture, set forth in *Delinquent Boys* (1955), found that delinquency was caused by social and economic limitations, inadequate family support, developmental handicaps and status frustration. The result: short-run hedonism and group autonomy.

Closely related to strain theorists are those who look at the correlation between unemployment and crime. For example, Susan Carlson and Raymond Michalowski (1997, 210–11) note

> The proposition that increases in unemployment will generate increases in crime has long been accepted as a basic tenet of the macro-sociology of crime and delinquency. A number of otherwise competing models of crime causation such as conflict theory, Marxian theories, social disorganization theories and strain theory share the assumption that economic distress generated by rises in unemployment will increase crimes against both persons and property.

Another strain theorist is Robert Agnew (1992), who believed that instead of pursuing specific goals such as the American dream, most people are more interested in being treated fairly in whatever goals they pursue. He identified three sources of strain: (1) failure to achieve positively valued goals, (2) the removal of positively valued stimuli and (3) the presentation of negative stimuli. Agnew suggested that a major goal of many adolescents is autonomy from adults. He contends that denial of autonomy may lead to delinquency as a way of asserting autonomy—for example, disorderly conduct, obtaining money (stealing) to gain financial independence from parents or venting frustration against those who deny them autonomy (e.g., by imposing curfews). Agnew also points out that strain-inducing events and conditions may cause youths to feel bad, creating pressure to take action that will correct the situation or to take revenge.

Social Control Theories

Social control exists in two dimensions: formal (i.e., the criminal justice system) and informal (e.g., family, neighbors, work, school, peers, the community at large). Social control theorists, instead of focusing on why people commit crime, ask why people do *not* act unlawfully. An influential contemporary social control theorist is Travis Hirschi, whose text *Causes of Delinquency* (1969) greatly influenced current thinking. Hirschi's social control theory traces delinquency to the bond that individuals maintain with society. Social controls rather than moral values are what maintain law and order. A lack of attachment to parents and school can result in delinquency. Hirschi believed that delinquency resulted from a lack of proper socialization and particularly ineffective child-rearing practices: "For Hirschi, proper socialization involves the establishment of a strong moral bond between the juvenile and society. This *bond to society* consists of (1) *attachment* to others, (2) *commitment* to conventional lines of action, (3) *involvement* in conventional activities, and (4) *belief* in the moral order and law" (Bohm 2001, 90). Attachment to others includes respect for significant others as well as an internalization of their norms and values. Commitment involves a commitment to conformity and an understanding of the potential results of nonconformity. Involvement includes using time and energy wisely in school, work and outside activities.

Sociologists Robert Sampson and John Laub developed a model of age-graded informal social control to explain the persistence and desistence of crime and deviance over the life course (1990). According to their theory, the institutions and social bonds that influence behavior or impart an element of social control change during the course of an individual's life. In childhood, the family, school and peers are important sources of social control. As a person grows older, those earlier influences give way to other forces of social control, including employment, marriage, parenthood and civic involvement. Sampson and Laub's social control theory, which takes a community-level perspective, posits that the stronger one's social bonds are, the less likely a person is to engage in juvenile delinquency or adult crime. And although Sampson and Laub acknowledge the concept of *continuity*, in that youths who display stable patterns of antisocial or delinquent behavior and resistance to informal social control are likely to remain on a trajectory that finds them engaged in crime and deviance as adults, the theory also recognizes that life events during adulthood do matter. Adults who are able to form prosocial bonds are more likely to change trajectory and desist from antisocial behavior.

Learning Theories

Learning theories are discussed as both psychological and sociological theories of crime. In the 1930s and 1940s Edwin H. Sutherland (1883–1950) set forth the proposition that criminal behavior is learned through imitation or modeling.

 Learning theory contends that criminal behavior, like any other behavior, must be learned. It can be learned in small groups or by watching others.

In *Principles of Criminology* (1939) with Donald R. Cressey (1919–1987), Sutherland proposed the principles of differential association. Among their propositions are the following (Sutherland and Cressey 1974, 75–77):

- Criminal behavior is learned in interaction with other persons in a process of communication.
- The principal part of the learning of criminal behavior occurs within intimate personal groups.
- The process of learning criminal behavior by association with criminal and anti-criminal patterns involves all the mechanisms involved in any other type of learning.
- A person becomes delinquent because of an excess of definitions favorable to the violation of law over definitions unfavorable to the violation of law. This is the principle of differential association.

Sutherland's **differential association theory** is still an important theory of crime causation: "Learning theory explains criminal behavior and its prevention with the concepts of positive reinforcement, negative reinforcement, extinction, punishment, and modeling or imitation. In learning theory crime is committed because it is positively reinforced, negatively reinforced or imitated" (Bohm 2001, 86). Bohm (86–87) explains these terms:

- Positive reinforcement presents a stimulus that increases or maintains a response. The stimulus (reward) may be material or psychological.
- Negative reinforcement removes or reduces a stimulus that increases or maintains a response (often referred to as aversion stimulus, such as fear of pain or poverty).
- Extinction is a procedure in which behavior that was positively reinforced is no longer reinforced.
- Punishment presents an aversive stimulus to reduce a response.

According to learning theory, criminal behavior is reduced through extinction or punishment.

Many of these factors were explored thoroughly during the 1960s and 1970s based on the behavior modification studies initiated by B. F. Skinner (1904–1990).

Critical Theories

As the name suggests, some theorists became disenchanted with the failure of existing theories to satisfactorily explain the causes of crime. **Critical theory** combines the classical free will and positivist determinism views of crime, suggesting that humans are both self-determined and society-determined: "Critical theories assume that human beings are the creators of the institutions and structures that ultimately dominate and constrain them" (Bohm 2001, 104).

 Critical theories include labeling theory, conflict theory and radical theory.

Labeling Theory   **Labeling theory** has its roots in the work of George Herbert Mead (1863–1931), whose ideas can be summarized in three propositions (Bohm 2001, 105–106):

- Humans act toward things on the basis of the meanings the things have for them.
- The meaning of things arises from social interaction.
- These meanings are handled in, and modified through, an interpretative process people use to deal with things they encounter.

Messner and Rosenfeld (2007, 50) suggest, "Labeling theory makes its principal contribution by calling attention to the interplay between social control and personal identity." Ironically, labeling theory suggests that official efforts to control crime may actually increase it. When individuals are labeled as delinquents, others may treat them as such. This increases the likelihood of those so-identified individuals having difficulty associating with "nondelinquents," which may steer them toward associations with others labeled as delinquents to "fit in" and feel like they belong.

Research on the social processes that might translate labeling into subsequent deviance found that formally labeled juvenile offenders may become aware of stereotypical beliefs existing in their schools and communities and, fearing rejection, may withdraw from conventional peers (Bernburg, Krohn, and Rivera 2006). After observing a sample of 1,000 students, Bernburg, Krohn and Rivera noted that the labeled and non-labeled adolescents often avoided one another to reduce uncomfortable interactions, a process that may result in labeled youths seeking out deviant peer groups to be with those in a similarly disadvantaged social position. The researchers concluded, "Juvenile justice intervention [resulting in labeling a youth as delinquent] increased the likelihood of gang membership more than fivefold . . . and was also significantly related to an increased likelihood of subsequent delinquency."

In labeling theory, it is important to differentiate between primary deviance and secondary deviance. **Primary deviance** is the initial criminal act. **Secondary deviance** is accepting the criminal label and consequently committing other crimes. A youth labeled as delinquent may come to believe this—a self-fulfilling prophecy—and begin to take on the role. The influence of labeling theory was especially strong in the 1960s and 1970s and was obvious in the creation of separate terminology for juvenile and adult court, as seen in Chapter 1. Even the term *delinquent* was an attempt to avoid labeling a youthful offender as a criminal.

Conflict Theory   Conflict theory was explained at the beginning of the chapter, but to briefly review: "Conflict theories emphasize the political nature of crime production, posing the question of how the norms of particular groups are encoded into law and how, in turn, law is used as a means by which certain groups dominate others" (Messner and Rosenfeld 2007, 50). More specifically, "For conflict theorists, the amount of crime in a society is a function of the extent of conflict generated by *stratification*, *hierarchical relationships*, *power differentials*, or the ability of some groups to dominate other groups in that society. Crime, in short, is caused by *relative powerlessness*" (Bohm 2001, 111). Closely related to conflict theory is radical theory.

Radical Theory   Radical theory has its roots in the writings of Marx and the conflict between those in power and the powerless. Bohm (2001, 114–15) describes **radical theory** as a way to explain crime:

> Radical criminologists focus their attention on the social arrangements of society, especially on political and economic structures and institutions (the "political economy") of *capitalism*. . . .

> Crime is a product of the political economy that, in capitalist societies, encourages an individualistic competition among wealthy people and among poor people and between rich and poor people (the intra- and inter*class* struggle) and the practice of taking advantage of other people (*exploitation*).

A Summary of Theories on the Causes of Crime and Delinquency

As noted by Lloyd Ohlin (1998, 143):

> One of the most striking developments in juvenile justice over the past 20 years has been the increasing rapidity and the widening scope of change in theories, goals, and knowledge about delinquency and its prevention or

control. Many competing biological, psychological, social, and cultural theories of delinquency have emerged in the past two decades, yet none is sufficient to account for the rate and forms of delinquency today.

 No single theory is sufficient to explain why delinquency exists. A reasonable combination of theories must be considered.

Table 3.1 presents a review of the major theories on the causation of crime and delinquency.

General Theories of Crime

Criminologist Agnew (2005, 11–12) draws on the writings and research of numerous individuals who have studied the causes of crime and integrates them into a general theory of crime: "The general theory focuses on the major, direct causes of crime and groups these causes into a few well-defined clusters, organized by life domain (self, family, school, peer group and work)."

Table 3.1 Review of the Major Theories on the Causes of Crime

Theory	Major Premise
Rational Choice	Crime is the product of a conscious decision. Offenders are rational actors who weigh the costs and benefits.
Lifestyle	Crime is one part of a lifestyle that involves other reckless behaviors.
Routine Activities	Criminal events occur when motivated offenders come into contact with desirable targets that lack guardianship.
Biosocial Perspective	The propensity for criminal behavior is heritable and interacts with the environment.
Neuroandrogenic	Differences between sexes in crime is caused by hormonal differences.
Biological/Genetic	Brain-based differences between individuals cause a variety of problem behaviors. Genetic influences cause differences in traits related to crime.
Psychological	Individual differences in thinking or emotional regulation explain why some people commit crime and others do not.
Personality or Trait	Temperamental differences between individuals increase their chance of committing crime.
Cognitive	The manner in which offenders see the world, and their tendency to process environmental cues through an aggressive "lens," explains the violent and other antisocial behavior of delinquents and criminals.
Psychodynamic	Early personality development influences the ability of a person to control ego impulses.
Psychopathy	A unique constellation of personality and behavioral characteristics, including a lack of remorse, a lack of conscience and a parasitic lifestyle, increase risk of engaging in crime or delinquency.
General Strain Theory	Youth commit crime when they feel strain, when opportunities are blocked or when things they value are taken away.
Social Structure	Points to unique aspects of the broader social environment that may be crime-producing.
Social Disorganization	Neighborhoods characterized by racial heterogeneity, mobility and female-headed households are criminogenic.
Functionalism	Crime is "normal" and inevitable and serves a purpose in society.
Institutional Anomie	Economic stressors degrade normal institutions of social control, including the family.
Informal Social Control	Rates of crime across neighborhoods reflect differences in collective efficacy, or the ability of communities to informally regulate crime.
Social Learning	Like any other behavior, criminal behavior has to be learned. It can be learned in small groups or learned by watching others.

SOURCE: Dr. John P. Wright. Rendered for this text, 2011.

His integration of theories and research into why people commit crime consists of eight basic propositions:

1. Crime is most likely when the constraints against crime are low and the motivations for crime are high (see Figure 3.3).
2. Several individual traits and features of the individual's immediate social environment directly influence the constraints against and the motivations for crime. Many of these traits and environmental variables are strongly associated with one another and can be grouped into the clusters organized by life domain. These life domains include the self (comprising personality traits of irritability and low self-control), the family (poor parenting practices, no/bad marriages), the school (negative school experiences, limited education), peers (peer delinquency) and work (unemployment, bad jobs).
3. The life domains have reciprocal effects on one another, although some effects are stronger than others.
4. Crime sometimes affects the life domains in ways that increase the likelihood of subsequent crime. For example, crime sometimes contributes to irritability and to poor parenting practices, negative school experiences and association with delinquent peers. Further, prior crime sometimes directly increases the likelihood of subsequent crime. These effects are most likely when individuals already possess traits conducive to crime and are in environments conducive to crime.
5. The life domains interact with one another in affecting crime. Each life domain has a greater effect on crime when the other life domains are conducive to crime (e.g., the individual is already at risk for crime). For example, traits such as irritability and low self-control have a larger effect on crime among individuals in "negative" family, school, peer and work environments.
6. The life domains have largely contemporaneous effects on one another and on crime, although each life domain has a large lagged (delayed) effect on itself. For example, *current* levels of crime are largely a function of *current* personality traits and family, school, peer and work experiences, rather than *prior* traits and family, school, peer and work experiences.
7. The life domains have nonlinear effects on crime, such that as a life domain increases in size it has an increasingly large effect on crime. For example, the effect of negative school experiences on crime becomes progressively larger as school experiences become progressively worse.
8. Certain biological factors and features of the larger social environment affect the level and operation of the life domains. The key factors affecting the life domains are age, sex, race/ethnicity, socioeconomic status and the characteristics of the community in which the individual lives—especially the socioeconomic status of the community.[1]

Michael Gottfredson and Travis Hirschi (1990) have also proposed a general theory of crime centered around the concepts of self-control and opportunity. According to their theory, individuals with low self-control are more likely, when given the opportunity, to engage in crime and delinquency than are individuals who possess high levels of self-control. The key elements of low

---

[1]From Robert Agnew, "Foundation for a General Strain Theory of Crime and Delinquency," *Criminology*, 30 (1992). 2005. Reprinted by permission of the American Society of Criminology.

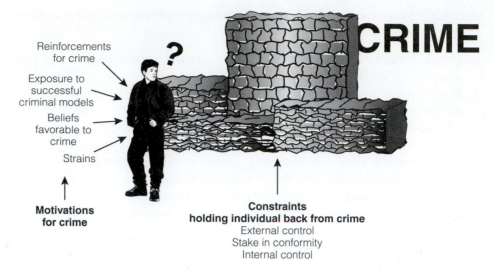

Figure 3.3   The Constraints against and Motivations for Crime

Robert Agnew. 2005. *Why Do Criminals Offend? A General Theory of Crime and Delinquency*, p. 14. Los Angeles, CA: Roxbury.

self-control are the inability to defer or delay gratification; a lack of diligence and tenacity; a tendency to engage in risky, thrill-seeking activity; impulsivity; disinterest in long-term pursuits or the long-term consequences of their behavior; a tendency to be self-centered; and insensitivity to the needs or feelings of others (Gottfredson and Hirschi 1990, 89). As such, people with low self-control are more prone to crime and delinquency and are more likely to engage in a spectrum of analogous antisocial behaviors that provide short-term gratification, such as drug abuse, excessive drinking, gambling, irresponsible sex, reckless driving and so on.

Having examined the primary theories and philosophies that have prevailed throughout the evolution of the juvenile justice system, you should better understand now the ideologies that led juvenile justice to diverge from the path of adult criminal justice. You should also be able to better understand the population the juvenile justice system is responsible for and why some youths become delinquent and others do not.

 ## Summary

- Unlawful behaviors or crimes were originally differentiated in two ways: (1) *mala in se*, an act considered wrong in and of itself based on mores, natural law and common law, and stable over time, or (2) *mala prohibita*, a prohibited wrong, originating in folkways and human-made statutory law and changeable over time.
- Consensus theory holds that individuals within a society agree on basic values—on what is inherently right and wrong. Laws express these values. Consensus theory includes the Durkheimian perspective, which sees punishment as a way to restore and solidify the social order.
- Conflict theory suggests that laws are established to keep the dominant class in power. It includes the Marxist perspective, which sees punishment as a way to control the lower class and preserve the power of the upper class.

- The classical view holds that humans have free will and are responsible for their own actions. Proponents of the classical view advocate certain, swift and proportional punishment for offenders. They suggest that deterrence, incapacitation and, in some cases, just-deserts punishment are the way to deal with delinquency.
- The positivist view holds that humans are shaped by their society and are the products of environmental and cultural influences. Proponents of the positivist view advocate rehabilitation for offenders.
- Early efforts to explain crime and delinquency were set forth in the classical theory and the positivist theory. Later theories focused on biological, psychological or sociological causes of crime and delinquency. Most recently, critical theories of the causes of crime and delinquency have been developed.
- Rational choice theory argues that crime and delinquency are products of conscious decisions made by individuals who rationally weigh, in advance, the costs and benefits of their illegal behavior.
- The biosocial perspective of crime and delinquency holds that the propensity for criminal behavior is heritable and interacts with the environment, a theory supported by evidence derived from a variety of studies.
- Psychological theories explaining crime contend that individual differences in thinking or emotion regulation can explain why some people commit crime and others do not.
- Sociological theories include social disorganization, functionalism, anomie or strain theory and social control theories.
- Learning theory contends that criminal behavior, like any other behavior, must be learned. It can be learned in small groups or by watching others.
- Critical theories include labeling theory, conflict theory and radical theory.
- No single theory is sufficient to explain why delinquency exists. A reasonable combination of theories must be considered.

Discussion Questions

1. Do you take the position of those who hold a classical view or those who hold a positivist view? Do you hold the same view for children as you do for adults?

2. What instances of the Durkheimian or Marxist perspective of punishment can you cite from the historical overview of juvenile justice?

3. Which of the theories of the causation of crime and delinquency seem most logical?

4. Diagram the ecological model as it might look for a major city.

5. How is labeling theory of importance to parents? Teachers? You?

6. Have you ever been labeled? Was it a positive or negative label, and how did you feel about it?

7. Do you believe you can make the American dream a reality for yourself? Why or why not?

8. Do you support a separate justice system for juveniles? Why or why not?

9. What sources of strain (stress) are there in your life? Might they lead you into a criminal act?

10. Why is it important to know how the juvenile justice system evolved and the theories that have been set forth for the causes of crime and delinquency?

References

Agnew, Robert. 1992. "Foundation for a General Strain Theory of Crime and Delinquency." *Criminology* 30: 47–87.

———. 2005. *Why Do Criminals Offend? A General Theory of Crime and Delinquency.* Los Angeles, CA: Roxbury.

Arseneault, Louise, Terrie E. Moffitt, Avshalom Caspi, Alan Taylor, Fruhling V. Rijsdijk, Sara R. Jaffee, Jennifer C. Ablow, and Jeffrey R. Measelle. 2003. "Strong Genetic Effects on Cross-Situational Antisocial Behaviour among 5-year-old Children according to Mothers, Teachers, Examiner-observers, and Twins' Self-reports." *Journal of Child Psychology and Psychiatry* 44 (6): 832–848.

Beaver, Kevin M., J. Eagle Schutt, Brian B. Boutwell, Marie Ratchford, Kathleen Roberts, and J. C. Barnes. 2009. "Genetic and Environmental Influences on

Levels of Self-Control and Delinquent Peer Affiliation." *Criminal Justice and Behavior* 36 (1): 41–60.

Bernburg, Jon Gunnar, Marvin D. Krohn, and Craig Rivera. 2006. "Official Labeling, Criminal Embeddedness and Subsequent Delinquency: A Longitudinal Test of Labeling Theory." *Journal of Research in Crime and Delinquency* 67: 431.

Bohm, R. M. 2001. *A Primer on Crime and Delinquency Theory.* 2nd ed. Belmont, CA: Wadsworth.

Carlson, Susan M., and R. J. Michalowski. 1997. "Crime, Unemployment, and Social Structures of Accumulation: An Inquiry into Historical Contingency." *Justice Quarterly* (June): 210–241.

Caspi, Avshalom, Joseph McClay, Terrie E. Moffit, Jonathan Mill, Judy Martin, Ian W. Craig, Alan Taylor, and Richie Poulton. 2002. "Role of Genotype in the Cycle of Violence in Maltreated Children." *Science* 297 (August): 851–854.

Cohen, Albert K. 1955. *Delinquent Boys: The Culture of the Gang.* New York: Free Press.

Cohen, Lawrence E., and Marcus Felson. 1979. "Social Change and Crime Rate Trends: A Routine Activity Approach." *American Sociological Review* 44: 588–608.

Davidson, Richard J., Katherine M. Putnam, and Christine L. Larson. 2000. "Dysfunction in the Neural Circuitry of Emotion Regulation—A Possible Prelude to Violence." *Science* 289 (July 28): 591–594.

Decety, Jean, Kalina J. Michalska, Yuko Akitsuki, and Benjamin B. Lahey. 2009. "Atypical Empathic Responses in Adolescents with Aggressive Conduct Disorder: A Functional MRI Investigation." *Biological Psychology* 80: 203–211.

Durkheim, Émile. 1933. *The Division of Labor in Society.* New York: Free Press.

———. (1897) 1951. *Suicide.* Glencoe, IL: Free Press.

Farrington, David P. 2003. "Key Results from the First Forty Years of the Cambridge Study in Delinquent Development." In *Taking Stock of Delinquency: An Overview of Findings from Contemporary Longitudinal Studies,* edited by Terrence P. Thornberry and Marvin D. Krohn, 137–183. New York: Kluwer Academic/Plenum.

Farrington, David P., and Brandon C. Welsh. 2007. *Saving Children from a Life of Crime: Early Risk Factors and Effective Interventions.* New York: Oxford University Press.

Flicker, Barbara Danziger. 1990. *Standards for Juvenile Justice: A Summary and Analysis.* 2nd ed. New York: Institute for Judicial Administration.

Garland, David. 1991. "Sociological Perspectives on Punishment." In *Crime and Justice: A Review of Research,* Vol. 14, edited by Michael Tonry, 115–165. Chicago: University of Chicago Press.

Glueck, Sheldon, and Eleanor Glueck. 1930. *500 Criminal Careers.* New York: Knopf.

———. 1937. *Later Criminal Careers.* New York: Commonwealth Fund.

———. 1943. *Criminal Careers in Retrospect.* New York: Commonwealth Fund.

———. 1950. *Unraveling Juvenile Delinquency.* Cambridge, MA: Harvard University Press.

Gottfredson, Michael, and Travis Hirschi. 1990. *A General Theory of Crime.* Palo Alto, CA: Stanford University Press.

Hernstein, Richard J., and Charles Murray. 1994. *The Bell Curve: Intelligence and Class Structure in American Life.* New York: Free Press.

Hirschi, Travis. 1969. *Causes of Delinquency.* Berkeley: University of California Press.

Kim-Cohen, Julia, Terrie E. Moffitt, Avshalom Caspi, and Alan Taylor. 2004. "Genetic and Environmental Processes in Young Children's Resilience and Vulnerability to Socioeconomic Deprivation." *Child Development* 75 (3): 651–668.

Lombroso, Cesare. (1911) 1968. *Crime: Its Causes and Remedies.* Montclair, NJ: Patterson Smith.

Marx, Karl, and Friedrich Engels. 1848. *Manifesto of the Communist Party.* Chicago: Encyclopedia Britannica.

Mason, D. A., and P. J. Frick. 1994. "The Heritability of Antisocial Behavior: A Meta-Analysis of Twin and Adoption Studies." *Journal of Psychopathology and Behavioral Assessment* 16 (4): 301–323.

Merton, Robert K. 1938. "Social Structure and Anomie." *American Sociological Review* 3: 672–682.

———. 1957. *Social Theory and Social Structure.* Rev. ed. New York: Free Press.

Messner, Steven F., and Richard Rosenfeld. 2007. *Crime and the American Dream.* 4th ed. Belmont, CA: Wadsworth.

Ohlin, Lloyd E. 1998. "The Future of Juvenile Justice Policy and Research." *Crime & Delinquency* 44, no. 1 (January): 143–153.

Park, Robert E., Ernest W. Burgess, and Roderick D. McKenzie. 1928. *The City.* Chicago: University of Chicago Press.

Raine, Adrian. 2002. "Biosocial Studies of Antisocial and Violent Behavior in Children and Adults: A Review." *Journal of Abnormal Child Psychology* 30, no. 4 (August): 311–326.

Raine, Adrian, J. Reid Meloy, Susan Bihrle, Jackie Stoddard, Lori Lacasse, and Monte S. Buchsbaum. 1998. "Reduced Prefrontal and Increased Subcortical Brain Functioning Assessed Using Positron Emission Tomography in Predatory and Affective Murderers." *Behavioral Sciences & the Law* 16, no. 3 (Summer): 319–332.

Rhee, S. H., and I. D. Waldman. 2002. "Genetic and Environmental Influences on Antisocial Behavior: A Meta-Analysis of Twin and Adoption Studies." *Psychological Bulletin* 128: 490–529.

Sampson, Robert J., and W. Byron Groves. 1989. "Community Structure and Crime: Testing Social-Disorganization Theory." *American Journal of Sociology* 94: 774–802.

Sampson, Robert J., and John H. Laub. 1990. "Crime and Deviance over the Life Course: The Salience of

Adult Social Bonds." *American Sociological Review* 55: 609–627.

Shaw, Clifford R., and Henry D. McKay. 1942. *Juvenile Delinquency and Urban Areas*. Chicago: University of Chicago Press.

Sutherland, Edwin H., and Donald R. Cressey. 1939. *Principles of Criminology*. Philadelphia: J. B. Lippincott.

———. 1974. *Criminology*. 9th ed. Philadelphia: Lippincott.

Walker, Samuel, Cassia Spohn, and Miriam DeLone. 2007. *The Color of Justice: Race, Ethnicity and Crime in America*. 4th ed. Belmont, CA: Wadsworth.

Young, Vernetta, and Anne Thomas Sulton. 1996. "Excluded: The Current Status of African American Scholars in the Field of Criminology and Criminal Justice." In *African-American Perspectives: On Crime Causation, Criminal Justice Administration, and Crime Prevention*, edited by Anne T. Sulton, 1–16. Boston: Butterworth-Heinemann.

Helpful Resources

Bohm, Robert M. 2001. *A Primer on Crime and Delinquency Theory*. 2nd ed. Belmont, CA: Wadsworth.

Sulton, Anne T., ed. 1996. *African American Perspectives: On Crime Causation, Criminal Justice Administration and Crime Prevention*. Boston, MA: Butterworth-Heinemann.

Youth in Society: Developmental Risks and Protective Factors

4

> "Life affords no greater responsibility, no greater privilege, than the raising of the next generation.
>
> —C. Everett Koop, former U.S. Surgeon General

© Spencer Grant/Getty Images

Peers can have a powerful influence on a youth's behavior, leading children to engage in a group activity that they may not consider doing alone.

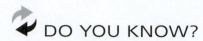
DO YOU KNOW?

- Why the early years of life are important in child development?
- What characteristics of a healthy family are?
- What common moral values might be passed on to children by their parents?
- How many risk factors there are for delinquency?
- What the most significant individual risk factor is for predicting later delinquency?

- What three developmental pathways to delinquency have been identified and the behaviors associated with each?
- What the hazards of labeling a youth a psychopath are?
- What two of the most serious consequences of poverty are?
- What two major peer influences can lead adolescents to delinquency?
- What protective factors are?

CAN YOU DEFINE?

adult supremacy

antisocial personality disorder (APD)

attention deficit hyperactivity disorder (ADHD)

conduct disorder (CD)

developmental pathway

emotional/behavioral disorder (EBD)

fetal alcohol spectrum disorder (FASD)

parental efficacy

protective factor

psychopath

radial concept

risk factor

teratogens

truancy

CHAPTER OUTLINE

Introduction

Before examining our contemporary juvenile justice system, it is important to understand those served by this system—our youths—and the environments from which they come. According to *America's Children* (2011), in 2010 there were 74.2 million children under age 18 in the United States, or 24 percent of the population. This was down from a peak of 36 percent at the end of the "baby boom" in 1964. The report also notes that racial and ethnic diversity continues to increase. In 2010, 54 percent of children under age 18 were White, non-Hispanic; 23 percent were Hispanic; 14 percent were Black; 4 percent were Asian; and 5 percent were all other races. The number of Hispanic children has increased faster than that of any other racial and ethnic group, growing from 9 percent of the child population in 1980 to 23 percent in 2010.

The National Center for Juvenile Justice (*Annual Report 2003*, 4) stresses, "No aspect of national interest is more significant than what happens to young people when they are troubled, particularly those we label as 'abused children,' 'dependent children,' 'neglected children,' 'status offenders' and 'juvenile delinquents.' No problem is more troublesome than the delicate balance between protecting children in a free society and protecting society from criminal behavior." Preventing our children and youths from becoming "problems" of the justice system is a logical first step.

This chapter takes a broad look at the pool of American citizens from which the juvenile justice system draws its clients and focuses on normal patterns of growth and development and special challenges to anticipate. Understanding the general process of child development is important because during this time the seeds of juvenile delinquency and later adult criminality can germinate.

Normal Child Development—A Brief Overview

The study of child development usually deals with children from birth to adolescence and concerns their physical, intellectual, emotional and social growth as they adjust to the demands of society. Although the prenatal period is certainly an important stage, the following discussion on child development will focus on the postnatal period through the late teen years, with various prenatal risk factors discussed later in the chapter.

Growth and development do not occur in isolation. They involve a complex interaction of family, school and community, with the family being the first and most vital influence. As children grow, the school becomes an important influence, be it preschool, kindergarten, public or private school. As youths approach adolescence, the influence of parents and teachers wanes and that of peers becomes stronger. All of this occurs within the broader community in which children live. This **radial concept** of the influences on growth and development is illustrated in Figure 4.1.

The Importance of Infancy and Childhood

Child development experts contend that the early years of life lay the foundation for all that follows. Human brain development occurs at a phenomenal rate in the first three years of life, with neural connections being formed, broken down and reformed faster than at any other time in a person's life. Children

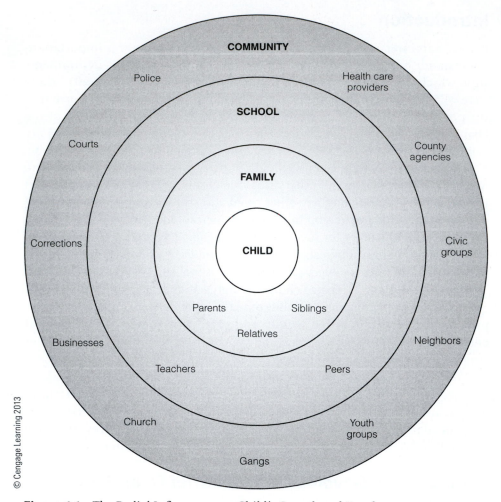

© Cengage Learning 2013

Figure 4.1   The Radial Influences on a Child's Growth and Development

who are nurtured, spoken to and touched in caring, positive ways during these formative years respond with increased brain development, whereas children who experience abuse or neglect suffer diminished brain growth. Dr. Frank Putnam, an expert on the biological and psychological effects of stress and trauma on child development and former researcher at the National Institute of Mental Health (NIMH), reports, "The abused kids we studied at NIMH had smaller brains, even when you control for body size, because they don't have rich connections among the nerve cells. … [That is why] intervention from ages zero to three is so crucial" (Cass and Curry 2007, 100).

It is during this time, with attentive parents or older siblings, that children learn the concept of consequences—rewards and punishments. They also begin to distinguish right from wrong and to develop what is commonly called a *conscience*. This stage is fundamentally important with regard to later delinquency and criminality.

Between the ages of one and three, normal conflicts arise between parents and their children: toilet training, eating certain vegetables, going to bed at a set time, staying within prescribed boundaries and the like. Social conflicts are also common between children at this age in the form of sharing issues and, occasionally, dominance and authority issues (who gets to decide what we play), although the latter typically becomes more prominent at slightly older ages. How these conflicts are resolved will establish the pattern for how the child will deal with conflict later in life. Research suggests that the most aggressive age in humans is two years old. Unfortunately, many parents, relatives and friends attribute hitting, biting and throwing tantrums to the "terrible twos."

Building on the foundation of the first three critical years, children continue to grow and develop physically, mentally and emotionally over the next decade of their lives. During this time they are continuously learning, and brain development is still occurring rapidly. In fact, "Every researcher of early childhood emphasizes the importance of early childhood nurturing and stimulation for putting a child on a positive path toward adulthood because they literally help the brain grow, especially between birth and age seven" (Cass and Curry 2007, 100).

 Infancy and early childhood are important stages in a child's development because brain growth is most rapid during this time.

Brain growth begins to taper off around age 9 or 10, a period sometimes linked to a phenomenon known as "the fourth grade plunge," when schools begin identifying significant academic deficits and failures among students (Cass and Curry 2007, 100).

Most youths get through this phase fairly well, without being negatively influenced by peers. Family influence still usually prevails at this stage. However, during this 10-year or so period of preadolescence those youth who start to push limits and commit offenses turn into the harder-core delinquents. These youngsters are considered to have experienced an "early age of onset" of delinquency, as discussed later in the chapter.

Adolescence

Adolescence generally refers to the teen years, the period from age 12 or 13 to age 18 or 19: "Adolescence is a period of transition from childhood to adulthood, with adolescents preparing for adult family and work roles. Reflecting this fact, adolescents are given *some, but not all* of the privileges and responsibilities of adulthood. They are also expected to assume greater responsibility for their behavior, devote more effort to their schoolwork and expand their social relationships, including romantic relationships" (Agnew 2005, 158–59).

Adolescence is often characterized by rapid physical growth and sexual maturity, self-consciousness, peer pressure and the shift of the primary support system from parents to friends, mood swings, experimentation, reevaluation of values and a search for identity. Adolescents seek increasing levels of independence but can also be very much influenced by their peers. Each generation produces a distinct adolescent subculture with a common language, clothing, music and standards. The result is what is often referred to as a *generation gap*. Table 4.1 summarizes some of the key changes that occur as adolescents develop. Such information can help guide adult expectations regarding "typical" adolescent behavior and attitudes.

Table 4.1 Key Aspects of Adolescent Development

Development Domain	Early Adolescence (10–12 years)	Middle Adolescence (13–15 years)	Late Adolescence (16+ years)
Physical Development	• Puberty starts (usually 2 years earlier for girls than boys)—period of rapid growth • Fidget, squirm, have trouble sitting still • Bodily changes begin to show	• Puberty continues • Clumsiness due to rapid physical development • Extremely aware of and sensitive to own development and that of peers • At-risk habits start (smoking, drinking, drugs)	• Boys' growth has doubled since age 12—they are taller and heavier (on average) than girls • Eating disorders may appear (bulimia, anorexia)
Cognitive Development	• Inconsistent thoughts • Shift from immature to mature thinking • Logic and reasoning discovered • Able to imagine beyond immediate environment • Is important to feel that their opinions count • Thoughts lead to feelings of self-consciousness • Girls are more communicative than boys	• Abstract thinking begins • Problem solving, analytical thinking and writing may be deficient • Greater separation in school between those who succeed and those who fail • Parents have less influence • Decreased evidence of creativity and flexibility • Peer conformity is critically important ("belongingness")	• Critical-thinking and reasoning skills begin • Want to think out their own decisions • Concerned about the purpose and meaning of life • Develop beliefs, values, career choices and identity • Increased peer conformity • New challenges and experiences are required
Emotional Development	• Seek independence, establish individuality • Want some control in decisions affecting life • Propensity toward awkwardness, self-consciousness and bouts with low self-esteem • Need praise and approval from adults to demonstrate concern and care about their welfare	• Crave freedom • Adept at masking true feelings and state of mind • Intense desire and need for privacy • Rapid hormonal and body changes often lead to low self-esteem and lack of confidence • Seek independence from, but still need structure and limits from, parents and adults • Increased sexual desires and experimentation • Need praise and approval from adults to demonstrate concern and care about their welfare	• Develop sense of personal identity • Self-esteem continues to develop and improve • Competencies such as decision making, stress management and coping with problems develop • Friendships are based on mature intimacy and sharing thoughts and feelings—rather than just hanging out and doing things together • Strong sexual feelings are experienced • Generally, strong ties with the family are maintained with increased need for parental love, care and respect
Social Development	• Have a desire to "fit in," to be well-liked is important • Cliques are formed with others • Want to be with friends without adult supervision • Feel that peer pressure is constantly present • Begin experimenting with smoking, alcohol and sex • Appreciate conversations that lead to an exchange of ideas to better understand other people's points of view	• Friendship and romance become increasingly important • Realize that others have different points of view • Begin to define themselves and develop more concrete self-concept • Show increased communication and negotiation skills • Explore rights and responsibilities • Want to hang out with older teens • Parents start to have less influence	• Independence is developed and demonstrated • Susceptibility to peer pressure declines • Parent-teen conflicts decrease • Cooperation and communication increase • Identity formation experienced through exploration and experimentation • Want to distinguish themselves from the crowd • Have large circle of acquaintances and small circle of friends • After-school work prevalent

SOURCE: Adapted from Barry Glick. 1998. "Kids in Adult Correctional Systems." *Corrections Today* (August): 97. Reprinted by permission.

Juveniles often pretend to be adults in various ways, but becoming emotionally mature, socially accepted adults requires a struggle. From a social standpoint, many never succeed. Adolescents may try to look like adults, talk like adults or take on what they believe to be adult ways, but in general they remain quite immature. At the same time that they imitate adult behavior, juveniles also strive for individuality, independence and freedom, which they believe they can achieve by disassociating themselves from society and their parents. Such a position between imitation and disassociation can generate a great deal of internal conflict and psychological stress.

A Summary of Social Cognition and Moral Development

Understanding the typical progression of cognitive and moral development in youth is, without doubt, highly germane to those working in juvenile justice because children's behavior is a direct result of these processes. These developmental stages provide a basis for numerous legislation and policy initiatives dealing with crime and delinquency by setting forth scientifically determined age ranges at which a person typically knows right from wrong and at what age offenders are deemed reasonably capable of understanding the consequence of their actions. These stages also play a role in determining suitable sanctions or treatment options for delinquent youth.

The development of social cognition, based on the theory of cognitive development set forth by Swiss philosopher Jean Piaget, is outlined in Table 4.2. Piaget theorized that children progress through four main periods as they attempt to make sense of the world around them and understand their

Table 4.2   Development of Social Cognition

	Understanding Self	*Understanding Others*	*Understanding Friends*	*Understanding Social Roles*	*Understanding Society*
Preoperational Period (about ages 2–7)	Understands concrete attributes. Understands major emotions, but relies on situation.	Understands concrete attributes, including stability of behavior.	One-way assistance (ages 4–9).	Can generalize role (age 4). Understands person can change role and remain same person.	Feels no need to explain system (ages 5–6).
Concrete Operational Period (about ages 7–12)	Understands personal qualities. Relies on inner feelings as guide to emotions. Understands shame and pride.	Understands personal qualities.	Fair-weather cooperation (ages 6–12).	Understands that people can occupy two roles simultaneously.	Understands social functions observed or experienced (ages 7–8). Provides fanciful explanations of distant functions (ages 9–10). Has acquired concrete knowledge of society.
Formal Operational Period (after about age 12)	Capable of complex, flexible, precise description. Understands abstract traits. Establishes identity.	Capable of complex, flexible, precise description.	Intimate sharing (ages 9–15).	Can deal with abstract conception of society, government and politics (by age 15).	

SOURCE: Elizabeth Hall, Michael E. Lamb, and Marion Perlmutter. 1986. *Child Psychology Today*, 2nd ed., p. 562. New York: Random House. Reprinted with permission of the McGraw-Hill Companies.

place within it. These four periods, or cognitive schemes, are roughly correlated with age and become increasingly sophisticated with maturity: the sensorimotor period (ages 0–2), the preoperational period (ages 2–7), the concrete operational period (ages 7–12) and the formal operational period (ages 12 and up). It is important to be aware of individual differences that may occur and to recognize that development may not always progress in a smooth, continuous manner.

A large part of the responsibility for ensuring that our children successfully navigate the growing-up process, develop a moral conscience and avoid offending behaviors rests with the family.

The Influence of the Family

The family is the foundation for the protection, care and training of our children. It is the first institution to affect children's behavior and to provide knowledge of and access to society's goals, values and expectations. Because the family is usually the first teacher and model for behavior and misbehavior, the structure and interaction patterns of the home can sometimes influence whether children learn social or delinquent behavior. In general, the family can have a positive impact on insulating children from antisocial and criminal patterns, providing it can control rewards and effectively maintain positive relationships within itself. Children develop their sense of being worthwhile, capable, important and unique from the attention and love given to them by their parents. They can develop a sense of worthlessness, incapability, unimportance and facelessness from a lack of attention and love or from physical or sexual abuse. Delinquency is highest when family interaction and controls are weak.

Moral Reasoning and Dilemmas

Inspired by the work of Piaget, psychologist Lawrence Kohlberg sought to understand how children react to moral dilemmas and subsequently devised a six-stage theory of moral development. His study of moral reasoning led to the conclusion that the process of moral development, which continues to evolve throughout one's life, is principally concerned with justice (Kohlberg 1981). In brief, Kohlberg's six stages are organized into three levels:

- Level 1 (*Pre-Conventional*)
    Stage 1—Obedience and punishment orientation (*How can I avoid punishment?*)
    Stage 2—Self-interest orientation (*What's in it for me?*)

- Level 2 (*Conventional*)
    Stage 3—Interpersonal accord and conformity (*The good boy/good girl attitude*)
    Stage 4—Authority and social-order maintaining orientation (*Law and order morality*)

- Level 3 (*Post-Conventional*)
    Stage 5—Social contract orientation
    Stage 6—Universal ethical principles (*Principled conscience*)

The classic example of a Kohlberg dilemma is the following Heinz dilemma: A woman was near death from a special kind of cancer. There was only one drug that doctors thought might save her—a form of radium that a druggist in the same town had recently discovered. The drug was expensive to make, but the druggist was charging 10 times what the drug cost him to produce. He paid $200 for the radium and charged $2,000 for a small dose of the drug. The sick woman's husband, Heinz, went to everyone he knew to borrow the money, but he could only get together about $1,000. He told the druggist that his wife was dying and begged him to either sell it cheaper or let him pay the balance later. But the druggist said, "No. I discovered the drug, and I'm going to make money from it." So Heinz became desperate and broke into the man's store to steal the drug for his wife.

Should Heinz have broken into the laboratory to steal the drug for his wife? Why or why not?

In healthy families, communication is direct and honest, rules are flexible and reasonable and members' attitudes toward the outside world are trusting and optimistic.

However, even children from so-called "good" families can and do become delinquent. Sometimes having all of the "advantages," such as being raised in a two-parent household with a high socioeconomic status, strong community support and good educational system, is not able to thwart delinquency because misbehavior is part of a normal cycle of adolescent development. Research has shown that kids from "good" families who get involved in delinquency sometimes have personality traits (e.g., low impulse control) that predispose such youth to misbehavior; they may become involved with delinquent peers; or they may get involved with drugs and alcohol, which often leads to delinquent acts.

In November 1989 the General Assembly of the United Nations adopted several articles outlining the "rights of the child" (United Nations 1989). The importance of the family was stressed in the preamble to this declaration of rights. The United Nations recognized:

- The family, as the fundamental group of society and the natural environment for the growth and well-being of all its members and particularly children, should receive the protection and assistance that it needs to fully assume its responsibilities within the community.
- The child, for the full and harmonious development of his or her personality, should grow up in a family environment, in an atmosphere of happiness, love and understanding.
- The child should be fully prepared to live an individual life in society and be brought up in the spirit of the ideals proclaimed in the Charter of the United Nations, and in particular in the spirit of peace, dignity, tolerance, freedom, equality and solidarity.

These powerful statements convey the importance of the family and the values the family is to instill in children as it nurtures them and teaches them to be individuals as well as contributing members of society.

Socialization and Values

Children should learn in the home that others have rights that children must respect. They should learn about social and moral values; to be considerate of others' property, possessions and individual selves; to manage their own affairs and to take responsibility for their actions.

Values are extremely important in any society. Values reflect the nature of the society, indicate what is most important and describe how people are expected to behave. Throughout the ages societies have embraced certain values, taught these values to their children and punished those who did not adhere to them. When youths do not accept the values of society, conflict is inevitable.

 Common moral values that might be passed on to children include fairness, honesty, promise-keeping, respect, responsibility and self-control.

Unfortunately, in many families, negative values, such as the use of violence to resolve disputes, or no values are passed on.

© Joel Gordon

The family is, for most children, the strongest socializing force in their lives. To thrive, children need the love and support of their parents.

American Child-Rearing Rights and Parenting Practices

Historically, physical punishment of misbehaving children has received general support in the United States. The familiar adage, "Spare the rod, and spoil the child," attests to the traditional American view that it is parents' responsibility to teach their children right from wrong.

Force and violence toward children, including physical punishment, has been characterized as **adult supremacy**, which has its roots in a common law concept of status derived from a feudal order that denied children legal identity and treated them as objects. In the United States until about 1900, the only person in the family who had any legal rights was the father. Adult supremacy subordinates children to the absolute and arbitrary authority of parents, a relationship whereby power is sanctioned by legal rules. Indeed, courts today give parents wide latitude in disciplining their children so they learn to respect authority.

Parental efficacy examines how parental support and control of youth are associated with delinquency. One area of parental control that has received increasing scrutiny is the use of corporal punishment.

The Debate: To Spank or Not to Spank?   "Spanking and harsher forms of physical discipline have been part of American culture for centuries. The debate over whether adults should have the right to strike a child has created tension between those who firmly believe in the benefits and those who consider it abuse" (Glanton 2001). Currently, spanking of children is expressly permitted by law in 49 states (Minnesota being the exception). Nearly half of all states still allow the use of corporal punishment in schools.

Before children can reason, which is often at a fairly young age, physical measures are commonly relied on. The question often becomes not so much whether such physical coercion is appropriate, but rather what *degree* of physical coercion is appropriate. When does punishment become abuse? Is a slap on the hand the same as a slap to the face? Is a "paddling" through clothing with a bare hand the same as a beating with a belt on a bare bottom?

A meta-analysis of 88 studies conducted over six decades on parental use of corporal punishment led to the conclusion that parents who spank their children risk causing long-term harm that outweighs the short-term benefit of instant obedience: "Parental corporal punishment is associated significantly with a range of child behaviors and experiences, including both short- and long-term, individual- and relationship-level and direct (physical abuse) and indirect (e.g., delinquency and antisocial behavior) constructs" (Gershoff 2002, 549).

Several major national organizations, including the American Academy of Pediatrics (AAP), have taken an official stand against parental use of corporal punishment. An AAP policy statement, originally issued in 1998 and reaffirmed in 2004, asserts, "The more children are spanked, the more anger they report as adults, the more likely they are to spank their own children, the more likely they are to approve of hitting a spouse, and the more marital conflict they experience as adults. Spanking has been associated with higher rates of physical aggression, more substance abuse, and increased risk of crime and violence when used with older children and adolescents" ("Policy Statement: Guidelines for Effective Discipline" 1998, 726).

Other experts have taken a slightly different position. Robert Larzelere, a psychology professor at the Nebraska Medical Center, contends that mild, nonabusive spanking can be an effective reinforcement of nonphysical disciplinary methods, especially in dealing with defiant 2- to 6-year-olds. Larzelere, concerned with the global trend to adopt increasingly extreme anti-spanking bans that lack scientific basis, stresses the need to balance advocacy with science. Larzelere and Kuhn (2005, 1) reviewed 50 years of research on child discipline and selected 26 qualifying studies for meta-analysis in what has become the first scientific review comparing child outcomes of physical punishment versus alternative tactics available to parents. Their results indicated effects that significantly favored conditional spanking over 10 of 13 alternative disciplinary tactics for reducing child noncompliance or antisocial behavior. Their analysis demonstrated that the following alternative disciplinary measures had significantly *worse* outcomes than conditional spanking for either noncompliance (N) or antisocial aggression (A) or both: reasoning (N & A), threats or verbal power assertion (N), privilege removal (N), time out or isolation (A), ignoring (N), love withdrawal (A), restraint or physical power assertion (N), child-determined end to time out (N), scolding (A) and diverting (A). These researchers stress, "Spanking should only be used when children respond defiantly to milder disciplinary tactics, such as time out, or to stop harmful misbehavior (e.g., running

At Issue: Parent Rights vs. Child Rights

Adults have a legally protected right to bodily integrity, free from assault, but children do not, except in extreme circumstances. Parents are authorized to use force against their children because society believes adults are older and presumably wiser and because the right to rear one's child as one chooses is held to be fundamental.

The USA and Somalia are the only countries that have not ratified the UN's 1989 Convention on the Rights of the Child (CRC), mentioned earlier in this chapter. Critics contend the CRC intrudes too much into the parent-child relationship and usurps parents' role and authority in determining how to raise their own child:

"The Convention on the Rights of the Child may be a positive tool for promoting child welfare for those countries that

have adopted it. But we believe the text goes too far when it asserts entitlements based on economic, social and cultural rights.... The human rights-based approach ... poses significant problems as used in this text."—President George W. Bush, 2001

"Americans need to reevaluate why we believe it is reasonable to hit young, vulnerable children when it is against the law to hit other adults, prisoners, and even animals."—Elizabeth Thompson Gershoff, psychologist Columbia University

Should the freedom to spank one's child be dictated by legislation? At what level should this issue be addressed: local, state, federal or international?

into the street)." They also recommend that conditional spanking should always be used in a way that reduces the need to use it in the future and should never be used in a child's first 12 months.

For children to have the best chance to reach their full potential, certain needs must be met. They must be given choices and challenges, healthy and safe surroundings, love, respect and recognition, encouragement, nurturing, direction and independence. Unfortunately, for many of our nation's children, this is *not* the reality. Their healthy development is hindered by inadequate prenatal and childhood medical care, poverty, serious abuse and neglect, violence and disintegrating families, factors that place youth at risk for numerous problems throughout life. Having considered the "normal" pathway people take as they develop from child to adolescent to adult, consider next some of the characteristics, behaviors and circumstances that increase the chances a child may veer off the law-abiding course and onto the track for delinquency.

The Path to Victimization and Delinquency: At-Risk Behaviors and Circumstances

Despite the numerous theories on why children become delinquent, researchers are able to agree on one point: There is no single path to delinquency. The presence of multiple risk factors and how they interact to increase a youth's chance of offending create countless ways for a child to go from obedient to delinquent. Conversely, the existence of certain protective factors can work to offset the risk factors and keep a child headed toward a law-abiding adulthood (Shader 2002, 1).

Various definitions of risk factors exist, but in the context of juvenile justice, a working definition of a **risk factor** is a condition, characteristic or variable that increases the likelihood that a child will become delinquent. Exposure to multiple risk factors can have a cumulative effect, and the relative impact any risk factor has on a child may be either augmented or diminished by the developmental state of that child (Shader 2002, 2).

Researchers have identified hundreds, if not thousands, of risk factors related to delinquency and have grouped them into five basic domains: individual, family, school, peers and community.

A caution on risk factors: Keep in mind that this chapter deals with the general youth population—before they become either victims or offenders—and the circumstances that increase the likelihood that such children will enter the juvenile justice system, either as victims or offenders: "Although researchers use risk factors to detect the likelihood of later offending, many youth with multiple risk factors never commit delinquent or violent acts. A risk factor may increase the probability of offending, but it does not make offending a certainty" (Shader 2002, 2).

Individual Risk Factors

Numerous individual risk factors have been identified as increasing the likelihood that a youth will come in contact with the juvenile justice system, either as a victim or an offender. The following list of risk factors was compiled from several sources, including Shader (2002), Wasserman et al. (2003), Helping America's Youth (2007) and Zahn et al. (2010):

- Early antisocial behavior
- Early onset of aggression
- Conduct disorders, mental illness, other mental health issues
- Developmental disabilities and disorders
- Emotional factors (such as high behavioral activation and low behavioral inhibition)
- Poor refusal skills
- Hyperactivity (ADHD)
- Cognitive and neurological deficits and disorders
- Low intelligence (low IQ), mental retardation
- Lack of guilt and empathy
- Chronic medical or physical conditions
- Prenatal exposure to cigarette smoking, drugs, alcohol or HIV
- Favorable attitudes toward drug use
- Early onset of alcohol or drug use
- Illegal gun possession
- Early sexual involvement
- Teen parenthood
- Exposure to television or media violence
- Victimization (abuse, neglect)
- Gender: Being male
- Race: Being African American or Hispanic
- For girls: early puberty, coupled with stressors such as conflict with parents and involvement with delinquent (and often older) male peers

Although space limitations preclude an in-depth discussion of every listed risk factor, certain select factors will be examined in greater detail. (Victimization is the topic of Chapter 5 and, thus, will not be covered more here.) Be aware that many of these risk factors also tend to co-occur, such as hyperactivity, emotional factors and poor refusal skills.

Early Antisocial Behavior and Aggression

Antisocial behavior, as with any type of behavior, can be highly stable and persist over a person's life course. In fact, juvenile justice experts agree that the best predictor of future behavior is past behavior. All available evidence indicates that children who show the earliest onset of problem behavior generally demonstrate the most chronic and serious delinquent and criminal behavior later in life: "Early antisocial behavior may be the best predictor of later delinquency. Antisocial behaviors generally include various forms of oppositional rule violation and aggression, such as theft, physical fighting, and vandalism. In fact, early aggression appears to be the most significant social behavior characteristic to predict delinquent behavior before age 13" (Wasserman et al. 2003, 2).

 The most significant individual risk factor for predicting later delinquency is early antisocial behavior, specifically aggression.

Developmental Pathways Longitudinal research has revealed that the development of disruptive and delinquent behavior in boys typically occurs in an orderly, progressive manner known as a **developmental pathway**: "A pathway is identified when a group of individuals experience a behavioral development that is distinct from the behavioral development of other groups of individuals. In a developmental pathway, stages of behavior unfold over time in an orderly fashion" (Kelley et al. 1997, 2). Figure 4.2 illustrates a common sequence of the manifestations of disruptive and antisocial behaviors as a child gets older. As indicated, a difficult temperament is generally the earliest problem noted in infants, with hyperactivity becoming more apparent once a child begins to walk and so on.

Kelley et al. (1997, 4) explain that this figure "highlights the fact that a child can exhibit considerable continuity in disruptive and antisocial behaviors, even though the behaviors are manifested differently with increasing age. Children's development toward serious deviant behavior can be thought of as leading to diversification of behaviors, rather than replacement of one problem behavior with another. Few children progress to the most serious behaviors or accumulate the largest

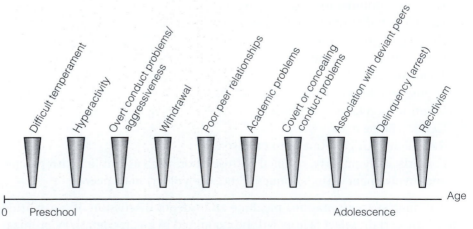

Figure 4.2 Approximate Ordering of the Different Manifestations of Disruptive and Antisocial Behaviors in Childhood and Adolescence

SOURCE: Barbara Tatem Kelley et al. 1997 (December). *Developmental Pathways in Boys' Disruptive and Delinquent Behavior*, p. 4. Washington, DC: OJJDP Juvenile Justice Bulletin. (NCJ 165692)

variety of such problems. It is more common for children to penetrate the deviancy continuum to a lesser degree, reach a plateau, or reverse to a less serious level."

Disruptive and delinquent behavior typically manifests in a predictable sequence, although the age of onset can show great variation among individuals (see Figure 4.3):

> [Conduct such as stubborn behavior] tended to occur earliest at median age 9, with a wide range of onset—the 25th percentile at age 3 and the 75th percentile at age 13. This was followed by minor covert acts, such as lying and shoplifting, at median age 10. Defiance, which involves doing tasks in one's own way, refusing to follow directions and disobeying, emerged next at median age 11. Aggressive behaviors, such as bullying and annoying others, followed at age 12, along with property damage, such as vandalism and firesetting. More seriously aggressive acts, such as physical fighting and violence, came last at median age of 13. (Kelley et al. 1997, 6)

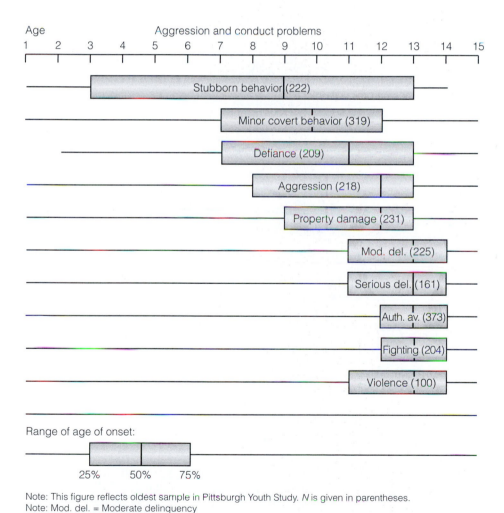

Figure 4.3   Sequence of Age of Onset of Disruptive and Delinquent Child Behavior

SOURCE: Barbara Tatem Kelley et al. 1997 (December). *Developmental Pathways in Boys' Disruptive and Delinquent Behavior*, p. 8. Washington, DC: OJJDP Juvenile Justice Bulletin. (NCJ 165692)

Figure 4.4 shows how these problem behaviors can be sequenced into three distinct developmental pathways to delinquency, each with progressively more serious problem behaviors.

- The *authority conflict path* includes stubbornness, doing things one's own way, refusing to do things and disobedience. It may culminate in authority avoidance by staying out late, truancy or running away.
- The *covert behavior path* includes lying, shoplifting, setting fires, damaging property, joyriding, pickpocketing, stealing from cars, fencing stolen goods, writing illegal checks and using illegal credit cards. It may culminate in serious delinquency such as stealing a car, selling drugs or breaking and entering.
- The *overt behavior path* includes annoying others, bullying and fighting. It may culminate in violence, including attacking someone, strong-arming or forcing sex.

Kelley et al. (1997, 4) see "children's failures to master developmental tasks and to acquire other prosocial skills reflected in these tasks as breeding grounds

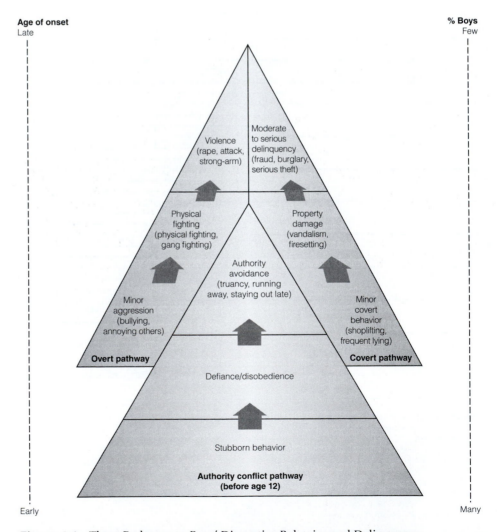

Figure 4.4 Three Pathways to Boys' Disruptive Behavior and Delinquency

SOURCE: Barbara Tatem Kelley et al. 1997 (December). *Developmental Pathways in Boys' Disruptive and Delinquent Behavior*, p. 9. Washington, DC: OJJDP Juvenile Justice Bulletin. (NCJ 165692)

for the development of disruptive and delinquent behavior. Therefore, many youths who eventually become seriously and chronically delinquent somewhere during childhood and adolescence probably missed opportunities to learn one or more key prosocial behaviors."

Oppositional Defiant Disorder and Conduct Disorder

Although a certain level of defiance and uncooperative behavior is common among young children and adolescents, when such behavior exceeds what is considered "typical" conduct, relative to one's peer group, and is not accounted for by a child's developmental stage, it becomes classified as oppositional defiant disorder (ODD). ODD is a diagnosis given to children who demonstrate persistent negativity, disobedience and hostility toward authority. No age limits are set for a diagnosis of ODD, but it typically emerges in childhood, often during the preschool years, and affects boys more frequently than girls. Although youth with ODD are likely to be in trouble with their parents, they are not engaged in behavior that brings them into trouble with the law. If their behavior does escalate to that of lawbreaking, the diagnosis is likely to become conduct disorder (CD). And although ODD is a recognized precursor to conduct disorder, the majority of youths with ODD do not progress to a diagnosis of CD.

Conduct disorder (CD) is a serious childhood psychiatric condition that manifests itself in aggression, lying, stealing and other chronic breaches of socially acceptable behavior. The *Diagnostic and Statistical Manual of Mental Disorders* (*DSM-IV*, 2000) classifies two major subtypes of CD as childhood-onset type and adolescent-onset type. Childhood-onset CD can be diagnosed when at least one of the following criterion antisocial behaviors is exhibited by a child younger than 10 years of age: (1) aggression toward people and animals; (2) nonaggressive destruction of property; (3) deceitfulness, lying and theft; and (4) serious violations of rules. Diagnosis of CD after 10 years of age requires the presence of three of the preceding criteria behaviors. Adolescent-onset CD is defined by the absence of any of the previously listed criterion characteristics before an individual is aged 10 years.

Youths diagnosed with CD pose serious problems for parents, schools and the juvenile justice system, and such youths are likely to have ongoing problems if they and their families do not receive early and comprehensive treatment.

Antisocial Personality Disorder   If a conduct disorder persists, it may develop into **antisocial personality disorder (APD)**, which the American Psychiatric Association (APA) defines as a disorder that exists in individuals age 18 or older who show evidence of a conduct disorder before age 15 as well as a pattern of irresponsible and antisocial behavior since age 15 (*Diagnostic and Statistical Manual of Mental Disorders* 2000). It occurs in about 3 percent of American males and fewer than 1 percent of American females.

People with APD are often referred to as sociopaths or psychopaths, and although psychopathy and APD are related concepts, they are clinically distinct diagnoses. A person can be a psychopath and not have APD and vice versa. Occasionally a person has both, with an estimated 20 percent of those diagnosed with APD also being psychopaths. Psychopathic behavior refers to chronic asocial behavior rooted in severe deficiencies in developing a conscience during childhood. A **psychopath** is regarded as virtually lacking in conscience, displaying remarkable emotional blandness, particularly about actions that profoundly shock "normal" people. A psychopath cares not between right and wrong. They may claim to recognize, and even speak smoothly about, devotion to accepted values and societal norms, and they can be charming in casual personal contacts. Meanwhile, they may be stealing from someone they call a "friend," or harboring malicious intentions toward someone they profess to care about. Psychopaths often make glib promises and resolutions. They are profoundly egocentric and never see their own responsibility for anything that goes wrong. Although most psychopaths have normal intelligence, their thinking is essentially superficial. Despite an ability to learn, they do not profit by the lessons of their own experience, so their behavior is out of step with what they abstractly know. They seem indifferent to the consequences for other people of what they do, and they seem unconcerned about the almost certain negative consequences for themselves.

It is important to note that the APA prohibits psychiatrists from rendering a diagnosis of APD, or psychopathy, in someone younger than 18, recognizing that many youths display callous or detached behavior during adolescence: "Sometimes persistent traits and tendencies of this sort and inadequate emotional responses indicate the picture of the psychopath early in his career. Sometimes, however, the child or the adolescent will for a while behave in a way that would seem scarcely possible to anyone but the true psychopath and later change, becoming a normal and useful member of society" (Cleckley 1988, 270).

Aside from being proscribed by the APA, there is an inherent danger of labeling a youth as psychopathic.

 Labeling a youth as a psychopath may reduce the youth's likelihood of receiving treatment and may increase the youth's likelihood of being transferred to the criminal justice system and treated as an adult.

The salient point to be made here is that there are often points in children's lives where intervention with mental health professionals can help divert youths from a path that leads to the juvenile justice system.

Developmental and Cognitive Disabilities

A broad spectrum of developmental, behavioral, intellectual/cognitive and learning disabilities place youth at increased risk for delinquent behavior. Compounding the problem for youth and those tasked with helping them, many of these disabilities and disorders commonly co-occur.

Emotional and Behavioral Disorders

One challenging segment of youths are those labeled as having an **emotional/behavioral disorder (EBD)**. These youths usually have one or more of the following behavior patterns: severely aggressive or impulsive behavior; severely withdrawn or anxious behaviors, pervasive unhappiness, depression or wide mood swings; severely disordered thought processes that show up in unusual behavior patterns, atypical communication styles and distorted interpersonal relationships. EBD is a broad category that often co-occurs with autism, Asperger's syndrome and ADHD.

Reality Check

An unfortunate truth for many youths with developmental and cognitive disabilities is that, even absent any actual delinquent behavior, they may still be funneled into the juvenile justice system:

> "Increasingly, it is not as much the criminality of the behavior but the lack of alternatives for children with

severe emotional and behavior problems, children who have been expelled from school, and children whose families cannot provide adequate care that brings them into the juvenile justice system."—American Bar Association 2003 report on juvenile justice in Ohio (Brooks, Kamine, and Weitzenhof 2003)

Hyperactivity and ADHD   As seen in Figure 4.2, hyperactivity is a frequently observed predelinquent behavior in young children. **Attention deficit hyperactivity disorder (ADHD)** is a common childhood disruptive behavior disorder characterized by heightened motor activity (fidgeting and squirming), a short attention span, distractibility, impulsiveness and lack of self-control. ADHD is often accompanied by a learning disability.

Learning Disabilities   Five to 10 million children in the United States experience some form of learning disability: "A learning disabled person is an individual who has one or more significant deficits in the essential learning processes" (Association for Children with Learning Disabilities [ACLD] n.d., 4). The most commonly observed symptoms are short attention span; poor memory; difficulty following directions; hand-eye coordination problems; inadequate ability to discriminate between and among letters, numerals or sounds; poor reading ability; difficulties with sequencing; and disorganization (ACLD, 3). Not surprisingly, such children often have discipline problems, are labeled underachievers and are at great risk of becoming dropouts.

Although usually associated with education, the consequences of learning disabilities go well beyond school. Behaviors that may be problematic include responding inappropriately, saying one thing but meaning another, forgetting easily, acting impulsively, demanding immediate gratification and becoming easily frustrated and then engaging in disruptive behavior. Youths with learning disabilities often have experienced failure after failure and lack self-esteem.

Increasing amounts of evidence indicate that a potential cause of developmental disorders and deficiencies in children can be traced to prenatal exposure to various toxins, such as cigarette smoke, alcohol and other drugs. Prenatal exposure to viruses, including human immunodeficiency virus (HIV), can also have devastating consequences to children.

Prenatal Exposure to Cigarette Smoking, Drugs, Alcohol and HIV

Maternal drug use during pregnancy has been linked to a broad array of problem behaviors in the developing children later in life, including reduced intelligence, hyperactivity and impulse-control issues. Even so, many children exposed to such **teratogens**, or agents that interfere with the normal development of a fetus, do not grow up to show these types of deficits. The susceptibility of an embryo or fetus to the detrimental effects of drugs and other teratogens is a result of several factors, including how well the mother's placenta filters out teratogens to keep them from reaching the developing fetus, how well the fetus's blood-brain barrier keeps such agents from reaching the child's developing brain and other genetically determined individual differences that account for variation in a child's ability to be resistant to or to process out potentially damaging agents.

Recognizing the variation in outcomes across children, researchers have begun to examine the possible mechanisms that link maternal drug use to problem behaviors in some children but not others. For example, research from a variety of disciplines indicates that maternal cigarette smoking (MCS) during pregnancy is related to an array of problematic outcomes, including various measures of criminal offending (McGloin, Pratt, and Piquero 2006, 412). Although MCS is a significant precursor to neuropsychological deficit, and such a deficit significantly predicts life-course persistent (LCP) offending, McGloin, Pratt and Piquero contend that this is not the mediating mechanism at work in the relationship between MCS and LCP offending. Instead, these researchers suggest two potential mediators that might explain the relationship between MCS and offending. First, a mother who smokes cigarettes during pregnancy may reflect her hedonistic tendencies to put her needs ahead of her child's health. The second potential mediator is that MCS is a known risk for temperamental and conduct problems in childhood, making these children more likely to be subjected to poor parenting. These two mediating factors could also be at work in situations where a pregnant woman abuses drugs.

In utero exposure to cocaine is also a general risk factor and can cause a variety of problems in children, such as premature birth and low birth weight, small head circumference and later social, emotional and cognitive problems. Research by Bendersky, Bennett and Lewis (2006) found evidence that prenatal exposure to cocaine constituted a risk factor for aggressive behavior problems in school-age children and that the group at greatest risk appeared to be exposed boys living in difficult environmental circumstances.

Another serious problem is **fetal alcohol spectrum disorder (FASD)**, which includes but is not limited to fetal alcohol syndrome (FAS), now the leading known preventable cause of mental retardation in the Western world. When a pregnant woman drinks large amounts of alcohol (beer, wine, liquor) over a long period during the pregnancy, she risks giving birth to a child who may pay a price in mental and physical deficiencies for his or her entire life. Among the characteristics of the syndrome are low birth weight, failure to thrive, developmental delay, organ dysfunction, facial abnormalities, epilepsy and poor coordination. According to the Mayo Clinic, as many as 40,000 babies are born with some type of alcohol-related damage each year in the United States, affecting one to two out of every 1,000 births (Mayo Clinic Staff 2011).

Another group of children that may suffer increased risk of delinquency or other problem behaviors are those prenatally exposed to HIV. Such children may experience deficits in both gross and fine motor skills; reduced flexibility and muscle strength; cognitive impairment including decreased intellectual levels, specific learning disabilities, mental retardation, visual/spatial deficits and decreased alertness; and language delays.

Substance Abuse

During adolescence teens try new things, including experimenting with alcohol and other drugs. This may be out of curiosity, because it feels good, to feel grown up or to fit in. Most teens only experiment, but some develop serious alcohol and drug problems. Those at greatest risk are those with a family history of substance abuse or who are depressed, have low self-esteem or feel like they don't fit in ("Teens: Alcohol and Other Drugs" 2004).

Child Health USA 2010 reported that in 2008, 9.3 percent of adolescents aged 12 to 17 years reported using illicit drugs during the month preceding the survey, with use increasing with age. Alcohol was the most commonly used drug, with 14.6 percent reporting past-month use. Marijuana was the most commonly used illicit drug (6.7 percent). *Monitoring the Future*, a study conducted by the University of Michigan Institute for Social Research of 50,000 students in grades 8, 10 and 12 from 400 schools, was begun in 1975 and has released reports since that time. According to the report, following a sharp rise from 1992 to 1996, teen drug use in 1997 had begun to decline. From 1998 to 2008, a fairly steady downward trend in juvenile drug use was observed, particularly among older teens. However, in 2008, the decade-long decline came to a halt, and by 2010, the overall rate of illicit drug use was again increasing for all grades, although only the increase among 8th graders was significant (Johnston et al. 2011). Figure 4.5 illustrates the trends in illicit drug use among 8th-, 10th- and 12th graders from 1990 to 2010.

Hunter Hurst, Director of the National Center for Juvenile Justice, offers a caution on the offender–drug use link and warns against assuming a cause-effect relationship, noting that while many offenders do use drugs, drugs do not

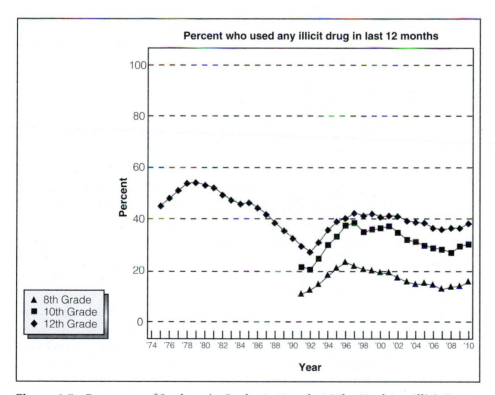

Figure 4.5 Percentage of Students in Grades 8, 10 and 12 Who Used Any Illicit Drug in Last 12 Months

SOURCE: Johnston, L. D., P. M. O'Malley, J. G. Bachman, and J. E. Schulenberg. 2011. *Monitoring the Future: National Results on Adolescent Drug Use: Overview of Key Findings, 2010.* (Ann Arbor, MI: Institute for Social Research, University of Michigan). Reprinted by permission.

reciprocally cause crime: "Everyone from federal judges on down will tell you they do, but from a research standpoint, it's more true that if you are an offender, you will be a drug user" (Cass and Curry 2007, 144). The relationship does not necessarily work in the reverse: that if you are a drug user, you will also be an offender. In fact, although approximately 80 percent of juvenile offenders have substance abuse disorders, only 20 percent of drug users commit crimes (144).

Nonetheless, youths who persistently abuse illegal substances often experience an array of problems including academic difficulties, health-related problems, poor peer relationships and involvement with the juvenile justice system.

Early Sexual Activity and Teen Pregnancy

Early sexual involvement and teen parenthood have also been identified as risk factors for victimization and delinquency. In 2009, 46.0 percent of high school students reported ever having had sexual intercourse (*Child Health USA* 2010). Early sexual activity is an obvious precursor to teen pregnancy, another risk factor for youths.

The 2009 national teen birth rate was 39.1 births per 1,000 females, a 37% decrease from the 1991 rate of 61.8 births per 1,000 females and the lowest rate ever recorded. Yet, the U.S. teen birth rate remains higher than that of any other developed country, with approximately 410,000 teens between 15 and 19 years old giving birth in this country in 2009 (Centers for Disease Control and Prevention 2011). Teen birth rates varied by geography and were highest among southern states. Birth rates for Hispanic and Black teens were 70.1 and 59.0 births per 1,000 females, respectively, compared with 25.6 for White teens. Teen mothers are less likely to complete high school and more likely to end up on welfare. Children of teen mothers are at increased risk of low birth weight and prematurity, mental retardation, poverty, poor school performance, inadequate health care, inadequate parenting and abuse and neglect.

A Debate: Does Exposure to Violence on Television, in Films and in Video Games Cause Violence in Youth?

Violence has been an integral part of American society since its inception, when the country won its independence through war. Hollywood and the general media industry have continued to glamorize the violence that persists in American culture. Few would argue that our youth are exposed to much violence in movies and on television. The question, which has been debated for decades, is whether such viewing is detrimental to those who are growing up.

According to a report by the American Academy of Pediatrics: "Research has associated exposure to media violence with a variety of physical and mental health problems for children and adolescents, including aggressive behavior, desensitization to violence, fear, depression, nightmares, and sleep disturbances. More than 3,500 research studies have examined the association between media violence and violent behavior; all but 18 have shown a positive relationship" ("Policy Statement: Media Violence" 2001). Similarly, results from a 15-year longitudinal study by psychologists at the University of Michigan found that children, both males and females, who are exposed to media violence, who identify with aggressive television characters and who perceive the violence to be realistic are most at risk for later aggression.

Similar arguments and concerns surround the impact on children who play violent video games. Some researchers argue that playing violent video games may actually be more harmful than watching violent television or movies because of the interactive nature of the games. Research has found strong links between violent games, aggressive behavior and delinquency, as constantly improving technology makes virtual gore more realistic than ever (Anderson and Dill 2000, 772).

However, and this cannot be emphasized enough, correlation is *not* the same as causation, and to date, there is no empirical data to support the argument that exposure to violence, per se, does inalterably cause a child to become violent. We are aware of no studies that empirically prove such a causative effect, and there is much speculation that children who have an interest in violent video games or other violent media content are violence-prone to begin with. The debate on this circular cause-and-effect dilemma is sure to continue for some time.

Race

Disproportionate minority contact (DMC) was first introduced in Chapter 1. Considering the fact that minority youth are greatly overrepresented in the juvenile justice system, it is fairly apparent that race presents a significant risk factor. The Children's Defense Fund (*America's Cradle to Prison Pipeline* 2007, 34) stresses, "Racial disparity runs through every major system impacting children's life chance: limited access to health care; lack of early Head Start and quality preschool experiences; children waiting in foster care for permanent families; and failing schools with harsh discipline policies that suspend, expel and discourage children who drop out and don't graduate and push more children into juvenile detention and adult prison." This report notes that a Black boy faces a 1-in-3 chance of going to prison in his lifetime; a Latino boy, a 1-in-6 chance; and a White boy, a 1-in-17 chance (37).

The race risk factor is compounded by many other co-occurring risk factors found throughout the other major domains of family, community, school and peers: unstable families, poverty, poor health care, lack of early education and enrichment opportunities, incarcerated parents, unsafe neighborhoods, substance abuse and availability of guns and drugs.

Family Risk Factors

Unquestionably, the American family has undergone great changes over the years. What began as an extended family, with two or three generations of a family living together, gradually became a nuclear family consisting of parents and their children. When the children grew up, they moved out and started their own families. Changes that have occurred in contemporary American society have been more complex and problematic, including more single-parent families, blended families, adoptive families and dysfunctional families. To be sure, there is more diversity today in what constitutes a "family," but the majority of children still grow up in two-parent households.

In many American families, the traditional bonds of discipline and respect between parent and child have loosened considerably, if not unraveled completely. If the integration process between parents and children is deficient, the children may fail to learn appropriate behaviors: "Ask a guidance counselor, teacher or law enforcement officer the greatest problem they face when it comes to juvenile crime, and the answer is unanimous—parents" (Garrett 2005, 6).

Because of the family's central role in child development and socialization, a constellation of risk factors are present for those youths whose families are fragmented, dysfunctional or otherwise unable to provide adequately for the child's needs. Following are some of the most commonly recognized family risk factors for victimization and delinquency:

- Divorce/broken home
- Transitions/moving frequently/unstable residential patterns
- Poverty/low socioeconomic status
- Parent criminality
- Incarceration of a parent
- Separation from parents
- Poor parent-child relationships/poor family attachment or bonding
- Family management problems/poor parental supervision and lack of monitoring
- Harsh, lax or inconsistent discipline
- Parental psychopathology
- Familial antisocial behaviors
- Sibling antisocial behavior
- Maternal depression
- Low parent education/illiteracy
- Having a young mother
- Family violence
- Domestic abuse
- Child victimization, maltreatment and neglect

As with individual risk factors, many of these family risk factors tend to co-occur, such as family violence, divorce and unstable residential patterns, which effectively multiply the negative impacts these factors have on the children involved.

Divorce and Broken Homes

Family structure is often cited as a significant risk factor for delinquency and other antisocial problem behaviors. According to *America's Children* (2011), in 2010 two thirds (66 percent) of children ages 0 to 17 lived with two married parents, down from 77 percent in 1980. A study of single-father and single-mother families found, "Mean levels of delinquency are highest among adolescents residing in single-father families and lowest among adolescents in two-biological-parent married families. Adolescents in single-mother and stepfamilies fall in the middle" (Demuth and Brown 2004, 77). However, their research also found that parental absence is not a statistically significant predictor of adolescent delinquency.

Although it is clear that divorce has a shattering effect on families with young children, what is less apparent is how much of the stress derives directly from the dissolution of a marriage and how much results from the myriad co-occurring circumstances: "As with many family factors, establishing the exact effects of divorce on children is difficult because of other co-occurring risks, such as the loss of a parent, other related negative life events (e.g., predivorce child behavior problems, family conflict, decrease in family income), and a parent's subsequent remarriage" (Wasserman et al. 2003, 5).

Although the complex dynamics of divorce would require a greater depth of discussion than this text allows, certain basic points can be made. Rarely does divorce happen quickly and quietly. Often there are months or years of conflict, tension and fighting—verbal and physical—that precede the split. Children may witness hurtful behavior and hear hurtful statements, made by and directed at people who are supposed to love and care for each other. Children may also be used as leverage or weapons by one parent against another and may perceive the manipulation as an acceptable way to get what you want from someone else.

Once a divorce happens, children frequently are made to go live with one of the parents, either on a full-time or part-time basis. In cases of full custody, the loss of access to the other parent can have devastating consequences for youth. In cases of joint custody, youth commonly face a future of shuffling between residences and may feel like neither place seems like "home." Such transient residential status has also been identified as a risk factor for delinquency.

Poverty

In 2009, 15.5 million children under 18 years of age—21.0 percent of all children in this country—lived in households with incomes below the federal poverty threshold, up from the low of 16 percent in 2000 and 2001 (*America's Children* 2011). And although there are more poor White children in this country in raw numbers, minority youth are disproportionately poor: 36.0 percent of Black children and 33.0 percent of Hispanic children live in poverty, compared with 12.0 percent of White, non-Hispanic children (*America's Children* 2011). Indeed, "The most dangerous place for a child to try to grow up in America is at the intersection of poverty and race" (*America's Cradle to Prison Pipeline* 2007, 4). In addition, children living in single-parent families are at higher risk of poverty, with the poverty rate for related children living in female-headed households (with no spouse present) at 44 percent in 2009, an increase from the low of 39 percent in 2001 (*America's Children* 2011).

Home conditions of economic deprivation or uncertainty can expose children to myriad negative outcomes, including malnutrition, stress and anxiety. However, it takes more than economic relief to lift families from a pattern of irresponsibility or depravity. Social agencies in every community know certain families that can be counted on to produce more than their share of school failures, truancy, sexual deviation, alcoholism, disorderliness and disease. It must be remembered, however, that poverty alone cannot be blamed for delinquency. Many children raised in extreme poverty grow up just fine.

 Two of the most serious consequences of poverty for children are homelessness and increased risk of lead poisoning.

Homelessness The National Law Center on Homelessness and Poverty reports that families with young children account for 40 percent of the nation's homeless population and that, in any given year, more than 1.35 million children are homeless (*Education of Homeless Children and Youth* 2011). The National Coalition for the Homeless notes the problem of varying definitions used to measure the extent of homelessness, but most include the circumstance of living in a shelter or on the street ("NCH Fact Sheet #2" 2007). The coalition estimates that of the total homeless population, 51 percent are single men, 30 percent are families with children, 17 percent are women and 2 percent are unaccompanied youths. The coalition suggests two trends responsible for the rise in homelessness over the past 20 to 25 years: a growing shortage of affordable rental housing and a simultaneous increase in poverty ("NCH Fact Sheet #1" 2007). This increase is the result of eroding work opportunities and a decline in public assistance.

In 2005, one third of requests for shelter by homeless families were denied. Homeless children have less chance of succeeding in school, with one half of homeless children attending three different schools in one year and 75 percent of homeless children performing below grade level in reading. In addition, one half of homeless women and children fled domestic violence and 47 percent of homeless children have anxiety, depression or withdrawal problems.

Some homeless youths are entirely on their own, including runaways and thrownaways (i.e., their families have kicked them out). Difficulties facing such youths are discussed in Chapter 5.

Lead Exposure   A new study spanning more than 20 years has added fresh evidence to what many researchers have known for decades: "Prenatal and postnatal blood lead concentrations are associated with higher rates of total arrests and/or arrests for offenses involving violence" (Wright et al. 2008, 101). Lead exposure has detrimental neurodevelopmental consequences and has been linked to lower IQ, diminished tolerance for frustration and attention deficit and hyperactivity, all of which are known individual risk factors for delinquent and criminal behaviors. According to the principal investigator for the study: "We need to be thinking about lead as a drug and a fairly strong one.... These kids have been exposed to this drug, chronically, since before birth."

Children who live in poverty are much more likely than others to be exposed to lead from old paint and old plumbing fixtures and from the lead in household dust. Other sources of lead are old water systems, lead crystal and some imported cans and ceramics. Babies exposed to low doses of lead before birth often are born underweight and underdeveloped. Even if they overcome these handicaps, when they go to school they face more obstacles such as behavioral problems, low IQ and deficiencies in speech and language.

Parent Criminality and Incarceration

Not surprisingly, parents who espouse a lawbreaking way of life will likely pass on their antisocial values and attitudes to their children. An estimated 1.5 million children have a parent in prison, a number that does not include those youths whose parent is in jail ("Adolescents with Incarcerated Parents" 2006). Another 3.5 million children have parents on probation or parole (Rowland and Watts 2007, 34). The number of children who have mothers in prison has doubled since 1990 (35). Typically incarcerated mothers are unmarried and the sole support of their children, who may end up with "reluctant relatives" or in foster care.

The cohort of children whose parents are incarcerated is often considered one of the country's largest at-risk populations (Miller 2006; Whitaker and Buell 2007).

Research has shown that children of incarcerated parents are five to six times more likely to become involved in criminal activity than the average child and usually possess most, if not all, of the known factors thwarting normal childhood development: "trauma from witnessing a parent's arrest and distrust of law enforcement; the potential of multiple housing changes; dealing with parental abandonment and related guilt and anger; high probability of change in schools; living in poverty conditions of caregivers; witnessing or learning criminal behavior from a parent prior to arrest; and the experience of stigma, which may create a 'conspiracy of silence' or shunning by schoolmates" (Rowland and Watts 2007, 35).

A co-occurring risk for children with incarcerated parents is the potential to be removed from the home and placed in foster care. Some research has shown that nearly 75 percent of the children who were placed in foster care were actually removed from the home before their mother's first incarceration, not as a direct result of their parents' incarceration (Moses 2006).

Separation from Parents and Foster Care

Separation from parents is a family risk factor for delinquency. This risk factor is present for any children in abusive or neglectful home environments who may, at some point, become clients of the child welfare system. Many juvenile justice experts contend that entry into the child welfare system is often a precursor to involvement with the juvenile justice system: "'In my experience, foster care is just one of those preparatory steps before the kid commits a crime,' one juvenile court judge asserts. 'The vast majority of kids in foster care will do something—trespass, shoplift, assault, smoke marijuana, whatever. If you get in foster care, the risk factors go up, and you'll probably see the kid in the delinquency system'" (Morris 2004, 1).

An added complication is that once a child enters the juvenile justice system, it becomes increasingly more difficult to divert that child back out of the system. According to University of Illinois professor Joseph Ryan, "We know once child-welfare youth are in the juvenile-justice system, they're less likely to get probation and more likely to get pushed deeper into the juvenile-justice system" (Chamberlain 2008). Researchers have found that youth with at least one foster care placement are significantly more likely to receive a delinquency petition at some point, compared with children who have never entered foster care (Morris 2004, 1).

The relationship between foster care and delinquency may not necessarily be causal. Children go into foster care for a variety of reasons and do not leave behind preexisting risk factors for crime and delinquency after they are placed. And many youth who enter foster care have already had contact with the juvenile justice system.

Poor Family Management and Parenting Styles

Under the general theory of crime and delinquency, high levels of delinquency may stem from high levels of poor parenting. Recent research has found evidence to support this theory, finding that parenting styles may, indeed, be differentially linked to delinquency trajectories. A study by Hoeve et al. (2008) identified five distinct delinquency trajectories based on both the level and seriousness of offending over time: nondelinquent, minor persisting, moderate desisting, serious persisting and serious desisting trajectory. Similarly, three distinct parenting styles were identified: authoritative, authoritarian and neglectful. Using data from the 14-year longitudinal Pittsburg Youth Study, and controlling for demographic characteristics (socioeconomic status, ethnicity) and childhood delinquency, Hoeve et al. (2008) found that a neglectful parenting style, characterized by harsh punishment, inadequate discipline and low levels of supportive parenting and supervision, did, in fact, distinguish the moderate and serious trajectories from the nondelinquent and minor trajectories.

Poor Family Attachment or Bonding

Lack of parent-child attachment and bonding has long been recognized as a source of long-term social problems in youths as they age. Emotionally detached parents, with tenuous bonds to their children, are raising a generation of maladjusted children, and the problems extend well beyond the family into the schools and community. The quality and quantity of supervision provided to youth by these parents is low, affording such children more opportunities to find trouble and lessening the probability that any type of corrective discipline or consequences will befall wayward youth.

A survey of educators found that "emotionally immature" parents were reported as being the most crucial problem schools faced: "Discipline and violence problems in schools can be directly traced back to parenting problems in our society" (Yeager et al. 2006). Such parents detach from their children academically and developmentally and defend their children's bad behavior. What begins as a family problem becomes a school and community problem as these children become older.

School Risk Factors

The preschool, kindergarten and elementary school years are extremely important windows in the socialization and development of young children. In fact, many children spend more waking hours each day in the school setting, under the care and supervision of their teachers, than with any other adult, including parents. Unfortunately many children enter school ill equipped to handle the demands of this new environment. Life-course criminologist Wright states, "Think about what school requires: discipline, the ability to acquire and process information and regurgitate it, self-control, the ability to move from one social clique to another, and follow directions from an authority figure. These are complex skills" (Cass and Curry 2007, 99).

The following circumstances have been identified as possible school risk factors for juvenile victimization and delinquency:

- Truancy/frequent absences
- Dropping out of school
- Negative attitude toward school/low bonding and school attachment
- Low academic aspirations or commitment to school
- Low academic achievement
- Identified as learning disabled
- Negative labeling by teachers
- Inadequate school climate (poorly organized and functioning schools)

- Low parent college expectations for child
- Frequent school transitions
- School suspensions

Truancy and Frequent Absences

Perhaps one of the greatest risk factors in regard to school is truancy. **Truancy**, which is loosely defined as habitual unexcused absence from school, is considered a status offense because, although compulsory attendance laws vary somewhat from state to state, every state requires children between certain ages to be in school during the academic year absent a valid excuse. If children are not in school, they are not learning or gaining the knowledge and problem-solving skills required to move successfully into the adult world of employment and self-sufficiency. At the same time, if they are not in school, youth are very likely to be engaged in proscribed activities such as drug use, property crimes or even more serious offenses: "In several jurisdictions, law enforcement officials have linked high rates of truancy to daytime burglary and vandalism" (Baker, Sigmon, and Nugent 2001, 2). Research has clearly identified truancy as a precursor to myriad negative outcomes: "A lack of commitment to school has been established by several studies as a risk factor for substance abuse, delinquency, teen pregnancy, and school dropout" (Gonzales, Richards, and Seeley 2002, 3).

Dropping Out of School

According to the U.S. Department of Education, the *status dropout rate* is the percentage of 16- through 24-year-olds who are not enrolled in high school and have not earned a high school credential (either a diploma or an equivalency credential such as a General Educational Development [GED] certificate). The status dropout rate includes all dropouts regardless of when they last attended school, as well as individuals who may never have attended school in the United States. In 2009 the number of status dropouts was 3,167,000 (*American*

© Monkey Business Images/Shutterstock

Children who experience success in school are more likely to experience success in life; those who experience failure in school are at higher risk of experiencing failure in life.

Community Survey 2009). During the 2008–2009 school year alone, the number of public high school dropouts (grades 9–12) nationwide was a reported 607,789 (Stillwell, Sable, and Plotts 2011). During that school year, the dropout rate was highest for Black students (6.6 percent), followed by American Indian/Alaska Natives (6.3 percent) and Hispanics (6.0 percent). The dropout rate for Whites was 2.7 percent, and the lowest national dropout rate occurred among Asian/Pacific Islanders (2.4 percent) (Stillwell, Sable, and Plotts 2011, 16).

Numerous negative outcomes have been linked to dropping out of high school. According to the U.S. Department of Commerce, high school dropouts are more likely to be unemployed and, if employed, to earn less than those who complete high school. Furthermore, dropouts report being in worse health than do adults who are high school graduates or have otherwise completed their GEDs, regardless of income level, and a disproportionate number of the nation's prison and death row inmates are dropouts (Cataldi, Laird, and Kewal-Ramani 2009).

Peer Risk Factors

Peer risk factors commonly come into play at the same time as school risk factors, as the school environment is the most likely place for youth to be in contact with their peers. As children age, the influence of parents wanes while that of peers increases. To many youths, how their peers perceive them is of paramount importance. Peer risk factors commonly associated with delinquency include:

- Peer rejection
- Peer alcohol, tobacco or other drug use
- Association with delinquent or aggressive peers
- Gang involvement or membership

Gangs are discussed in depth in Chapter 7.

Figure 4.6 illustrates the development of early offending behavior and peer influences in the context of the school environment.

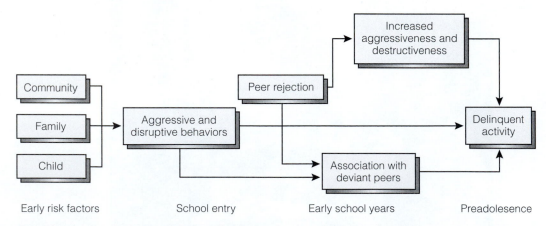

Figure 4.6　Development of Early Offending Behavior and Peer Influences

SOURCE: J. D. Coie and S. Miller-Johnson. 2001. "Peer Factors and Interventions." In *Serious and Violent Juvenile Offenders: Risk Factors and Successful Interventions*, edited by R. Loeber and D. P. Farrington, p. 191–209. Copyright © 2001 Sage Publications. Reprinted by permission of SAGE Publications.

Note in Figure 4.6 the boxes identifying aggressive and disruptive behaviors and peer rejection. An element linking aggressive or disruptive behavior and peer rejection is a child's degree of self-control, which, according to John Wright, a developmental criminologist at the University of Cincinnati, is the key development factor with regard to a child's risks for later delinquency and incarceration. Wright asserts that a child who lacks basic self-control "will be ostracized because children are very perceptive about whom they like and don't like, and this may make him more aggressive.... Most kids have this skill [of self-control] at a fairly early age; those who don't—name the problems. Failure to navigate the social landscape in elementary school places a kid at really high risk of bad outcomes later in life—chronic unemployment, relationship problems, incarceration" (Cass and Curry 2007, 100). In studying the "cause" of low self-control in children, some research has offered evidence that maternal self-control, through its influence on how a mother both punishes and supervises her child, influences the development of self-control in children (Nofziger 2008, 218).

 A strong case can be made that during adolescence deviant peers or peer rejection can influence nondelinquent juveniles to become delinquent.

Community Risk Factors

Of course, children do not exist in bubbles. As they age and gain independence, they venture more into the broader community, where numerous other risk factors present themselves:

- Availability of alcohol and other drugs
- Availability of firearms
- High-crime neighborhood
- Community instability and disorganization
- Social and physical discord
- Living in an economically disadvantaged neighborhood with high poverty
- Safety concerns and feeling unsafe in the neighborhood
- Low community attachment
- Neighborhood youth in trouble

Guns and drugs are discussed in greater detail in Chapter 7. The role of the broader community in juvenile justice and delinquency prevention is the focus of Chapter 8.

Protective Factors

Numerous behaviors and circumstances related to individual characteristics, family, school, peers and the community have been identified that may protect youths from becoming victims or offenders. Often a **protective factor** is the opposite of an identified risk factor. For example, if poor parental supervision is a risk factor, then a high degree of parental monitoring is a protective factor. Low IQ is a risk factor; high IQ is a protective factor.

 Protective factors also relate to individual characteristics, family, school, peers and the community.

Individual Protective Factors

- Healthy, conventional beliefs and clear standards
- High expectations for self
- High IQ
- Perception of social support from adults and peers
- Positive, resilient temperament
- Positive expectations and optimism for the future
- Religiosity and involvement in organized religious activities
- Self-efficacy
- Social competencies and problem-solving skills
- Intolerant attitude toward deviance
- Gender: Being female

Family Protective Factors

- Effective parenting
- Good relationships with parents and attachment/bonding to family
- Having a stable family
- Having parents who set high expectations
- Opportunities for prosocial family involvement
- Rewards for prosocial family involvement

School Protective Factors

- Above-average academic achievement
- Strong school motivation and positive attitude toward school
- Sufficient reading and math skills
- High expectations of students
- High-quality schools
- Clear standards and rules
- Opportunities for prosocial school involvement
- Rewards for prosocial school involvement
- Presence and involvement of caring, supportive adults
- Student bonding (attachment to teacher, belief, commitment)

Peer Protective Factors

- Good relationships with prosocial peers
- Involvement with positive peer group activities

Community Protective Factors

- Clear social norms against misbehavior
- High expectations
- Nondisadvantaged neighborhood
- Safe environment
- Low neighborhood crime

- Presence and involvement of caring, supportive adults
- Prosocial opportunities for participation
- Rewards for prosocial community involvement
- Availability of neighborhood resources

Early Work Experiences: A Risk or Protective Factor?

As youths attain legal working age and go into the community to find employment, the question becomes: Is work a positive or negative influence in these young people's lives? Results of numerous studies are contradictory.

According to Apel et al. (2006), "Research has repeatedly found various negative consequences associated with youth employment, including detachment from parents, poor school performance and dropout, and an increased risk of delinquency and substance use."

A study by Wu, Schlenger and Galvin (2003) found that adolescent employment is positively associated with drug and alcohol use among both males and females. These researchers contend that the mere fact that a youth has a job does not appear to be sufficient in deterring drug or alcohol use; instead, stable employment that reflects a strong commitment or stake in conformity seems to be required.

Other research has examined how job quality might be a detrimental influence on behavior: "Our findings suggest that low-wage, service sector employment opportunity directly increases the likelihood of violent delinquency"

The Cradle-to-Prison Pipeline: A Life-Course Perspective

Many children are born into certain life circumstances with the odds already stacked against them. The Children's Defense Fund has issued a compelling report examining how accumulated and convergent risks form a cradle-to-prison pipeline that traps these children "in a trajectory that leads to marginalized lives, imprisonment and often premature death" (*America's Cradle to Prison Pipeline* 2007, 16). According to this report,

> The United States of America is not a level playing field for all children and our nation does not value and protect all children's lives equally. . . . Countless children, especially poor children of color . . . are already in the Pipeline to Prison before taking a single step or uttering a word, and many youths in juvenile justice facilities never were in the pipeline to college or success. They were not derailed from the right track; they never got on it. (3)

Although the report presents an abundance of sobering facts and bleak scenarios, it also offers hope that, with a firm resolve and true commitment, there can be positive change made in the lives of our nation's youth:

> The Pipeline is not an act of God or inevitable; it is a series of human choices at each stage of our children's development. We created it, we can change it. We know what to do. We can predict need. We can identify risk. We can prevent damage. We can target interventions. We can monitor progress. In doing so, we can guarantee returns on public investments and control costs to children and society. (4)

To effect permanent change, it is necessary to change our response to this issue from reactive to proactive: "Education costs less than ignorance, preventive health care far less than emergency rooms, preventive family services less than out-of-home care, and Head Start much less than prisons" (20). This mind-set is perhaps our greatest challenge, for as a society, we seem content to spend our efforts and dollars on the back end of the pipeline instead of the front end, with states currently spending, on average, nearly three times more per prisoner as per public school student (20).

SOURCE: *America's Cradle to Prison Pipeline.* 2007 (October). Washington, DC: Children's Defense Fund. © October 2007 corrected printing by the Children's Defense Fund. All rights reserved. Reprinted by permission.

(Bellair, Roscigno, and McNulty 2003, 6). Brame et al. (2004) came to similar conclusions, with their research identifying adolescent employment as a risk factor based on its association with increased involvement in criminal activity.

Opposite conclusions, however, have been reached by other researchers regarding the effects of early employment on youth. Studies by Wright and Cullen (2004) found that employment can build social capital that then bonds young people to social institutions: "The results demonstrate that prosocial coworkers disrupt previously established delinquent peer networks and are associated with reductions in adult criminal behavior" (183). They contend, "Stable employment appears to be a key transition in the life course that is associated with reductions in criminal behavior and drug use" (198).

Prevention and Early Intervention Efforts

Prevention is often heralded as the preferred approach to the problems of victimization and delinquency. Ignoring prevention efforts has been likened to "providing expensive ambulances at the bottom of a cliff to pick up the youngsters who fall off, rather than building a fence at the top of the cliff to keep them from falling in the first place" (Hawkins and Catalano 1993).

Early intervention that focuses on the most at-risk youth has been shown, through myriad studies, to be a valid prevention tool. For example, the *Chicago Longitudinal Study* (2000) examined 1,539 children enrolled in the Chicago Public Schools who received services from one or more of 20 child–parent centers (CPCs) while in preschool from 1983 to 1985 or during kindergarten from 1985 to 1986. Ninety-three percent of the children in the sample group were African American. The study followed these children through their years in the public education system and gathered comparable data for a control group of youths who did not receive CPC services. Data from the study showed that the children who participated in the CPC preschool program significantly academically outperformed those who did not, were retained less often and had lower rates of special education placement (*Chicago Longitudinal Study* 2000, 6). The results of this study are not unique in substantiating the benefits of early intervention: "Minority preschoolers from low-income families who participated in school-based intervention programs fared better decades later educationally, socially and economically than peers who did not have the benefit of such programs" (Scott 2007, 13).

Numerous cost-benefit analyses have been done to show how much (or, rather, how little) *preventing* crime and delinquency costs compared with dealing with the law enforcement, court and correctional costs associated with offenders, not to mention the much larger cost to society in terms of lost work productivity, collateral family impacts, medical and counseling treatment for addictions and so on. For example, the CPC study showed that for every dollar invested in the preschool program, $4.71 is saved in reduced costs of remedial education and justice system expenditures and in increased earning capacity and tax revenues (Scott 2007, 14).

Helping America's Youth (HAY)

Helping America's Youth (HAY) is a nationwide effort to raise awareness about the challenges facing our youths, especially youth boys, and to motivate caring adults to connect with youths in three areas: family, school and community.

This initiative brought together a comprehensive array of 10 collaborating federal agencies to produce a guide to make these connections: the U.S. Departments of Health and Human Services, Justice, Agriculture, Education, Labor, Housing and Urban Development, the Interior and Commerce; the Office of National Drug Control Policy; and the Corporation for National and Community Services.

The *Community Guide to Helping America's Youth* (HAY 2007) includes suggestions for forming community partnerships, developing youth-adult partnerships and making the partnerships work. It also includes information on assessing a community and connecting its resources as well as an extensive listing of proven programs for youths that can be searched by risk factor, protective factor or keyword and by age.

In addition HAY has held regional conferences throughout the country to increase public awareness and encourage adults to connect with youths in their communities.

 ## Summary

- Infancy and early childhood are important stages in a child's development because brain growth is most rapid during this time.
- In healthy families, communication is direct and honest, rules are flexible and reasonable and members' attitudes toward the outside world are trusting and optimistic.
- Common moral values that might be passed on to youths include fairness, honesty, promise-keeping, respect, responsibility and self-control.
- Researchers have identified hundreds, if not thousands, of risk factors related to delinquency and have grouped them into five basic domains: individual, family, school, peers and community.
- The most significant individual risk factor for predicting later delinquency is early antisocial behavior, specifically aggression.
- The *authority conflict path* includes stubbornness, doing things one's own way, refusing to do things and disobedience. It may culminate in authority avoidance by staying out late, truancy or running away. The *covert behavior path* includes lying, shoplifting, setting fires, damaging property, joyriding, pickpocketing, stealing from cars, fencing stolen goods, writing illegal checks and using illegal credit cards. It may culminate in serious delinquency such as stealing a car, selling drugs or breaking and entering. The *overt behavior path* includes annoying others, bullying and fighting. It may culminate in violence, including attacking someone, strong-arming or forcing sex.
- Labeling a youth as a psychopath may reduce the youth's likelihood of receiving treatment and may increase the youth's likelihood of being transferred to the criminal justice system and treated as an adult.
- Two of the most serious consequences of poverty for children are homelessness and increased risk of lead poisoning.
- A strong case can be made that during adolescence deviant peers or peer rejection can influence nondelinquent juveniles to become delinquent.
- Protective factors also relate to individual characteristics, family, school, peers and the community.

Discussion Questions

1. The adult world stresses material and financial gain, social status and winning at any cost. Can children adjust to or understand this attitude? What values should adults communicate to children about these attitudes?

2. Does your community have any ghettos or areas where poverty exists? What are some visible signs of such conditions?

3. How does your community handle homeless people, particularly youths? Are there special programs for homeless families with children?

4. Is controlled spanking in certain cases justified? Were you spanked as a child?

5. What values should be passed to the next generation?

6. Do you believe adolescents should be employed?

7. How much of an impact do you think violence on television and in the movies (fictional violence) has on aggressive behavior in youths?

8. How do you think the news industry (reporting on factual or real-world violence) affects the way our society in general, and children in particular, view crime and delinquency?

9. Which of the risk factors are most significant in terms of victimization and delinquency? Least significant?

10. Which of the protective factors are most significant? Least significant?

References

"Adolescents with Incarcerated Parents." 2006. *The Prevention Researcher* 13 (2).

Agnew, Robert. 2005. *Why Do Criminals Offend? A General Theory of Crime and Delinquency*. Los Angeles, CA: Roxbury.

American Community Survey. 2009. Washington, DC: Department of Commerce, Census Bureau.

America's Children: Key National Indicators of Well-Being 2011. 2011. Washington, DC: Federal Interagency Forum on Child and Family Statistics.

America's Cradle to Prison Pipeline. 2007 (October). Washington, DC: Children's Defense Fund.

Anderson, Craig A., and Karen E. Dill. 2000. "Video Games and Aggressive Thoughts, Feelings, and Behavior in the Laboratory and in Life." *Journal of Personality and Social Psychology* 78 (4): 772–790.

Annual Report 2003. 2003. Pittsburgh, PA: National Center for Juvenile Justice.

Apel, Robert, Raymond Paternoster, Shawn D. Bushway, and Robert Brame. 2006. "A Job Isn't Just a Job: The Differential Impact of Formal versus Informal Work on Adolescent Problem Behavior." *Crime and Delinquency* 52 (2): 333–369.

Association for Children with Learning Disabilities (ACLD). n.d. "Taking the First Step to Solving Learning Problems." Pittsburgh, PA: Association for Children with Learning Disabilities.

Baker, Myriam L., Jane Nady Sigmon, and M. Elaine Nugent. 2001 (September). *Truancy Reduction: Keeping Students in School*. Washington, DC: Office of Juvenile Justice and Delinquency Prevention, Juvenile Justice Bulletin. (NCJ 188947)

Bellair, Paul E., Vincent J. Roscigno, and Thomas L. McNulty. 2003. "Linking Local Labor Market Opportunity to Violent Adolescent Delinquency." *Journal of Research in Crime and Delinquency* (February): 6–33.

Bendersky, Margaret, David Bennett, and Michael Lewis. 2006. "Aggression at Age 5 as a Function of Prenatal Exposure to Cocaine, Gender, and Environmental Risk." *Journal of Pediatric Psychology* 31 (1): 71–84.

Brame, Robert, Shawn D. Bushway, Raymond Paternoster, and Robert Apel. 2004. "Assessing the Effect of Adolescent Employment on Involvement in Criminal Activity." *Journal of Contemporary Criminal Justice* (August): 236–256.

Brooks, Kim, Darlene Kamine, and Sharon Weitzenhof. 2003. *Justice Cut Short: An Assessment of Access to Counsel and Quality of Representation in Delinquency Proceedings in Ohio*, p. 1. Washington, DC: American Bar Association, Juvenile Justice Center, National Juvenile Defender Center. http://www.njdc.info/pdf/Ohio_Assessment.pdf

Cass, Julia, and Connie Curry. 2007 (October). "Part II: Case Studies of Children in or at Risk of the Pipeline in Ohio and Mississippi." In *America's Cradle to Prison Pipeline*. Washington, DC: Children's Defense Fund.

Cataldi, Emily Forrest, Jennifer Laird, and Angelina Kewal-Ramani. 2009. *High School Dropout and Completion Rates in the United States: 2007*. Washington, DC: U.S. Department of Education, Institute of Education Sciences, National Center for Education Statistics.

Centers for Disease Control and Prevention. 2011. "Vital Signs: Teen Pregnancy—United States, 1991–2009." *Morbidity and Mortality Weekly Report* 60 (13, April 8): 414–420. http://www.cdc.gov/mmwr/preview/mmwrhtml/mm6013a5.htm?s_cid=mm6013a5_w (accessed September 27, 2011).

Chamberlain, Craig. 2008 (February 28). "Group Homes Appear to Double Delinquency Risk for Foster Kids, Study Says." Urbana: News Bureau, University of Illinois at Urbana–Champaign. http://www.news.uiuc.edu/news/08/0228grouphomes.html (accessed July 23, 2008).

Chicago Longitudinal Study. 2000 (August). Madison: University of Wisconsin–Madison.

Child Health USA 2010. 2010. Washington, DC: Health Resources and Services Administration.

Cleckley, Hervey. 1988. *The Mask of Sanity*, 5th ed. Augusta, GA: Emily S. Cleckley, private printing.

Demuth, Stephen, and Susan L. Brown. 2004. "Family Structure, Family Processes, Adolescent Delinquency: The Significance of Parental Absence versus Parental Gender." *Journal of Research in Crime and Delinquency* (February): 58–81.

Diagnostic and Statistical Manual of Mental Disorders. 2000. 4th ed., Text Revision (*DSM-IV-TR*). Arlington, VA: American Psychiatric Association.

Education of Homeless Children and Youth: The Guide to Their Rights. 2011 (June). Washington, DC: National Law Center on Homelessness and Poverty.

Garrett, Ronnie. 2005. "Kids Today …" *Law Enforcement Technology* (May): 6.

Gershoff, Elizabeth T. 2002. "Corporal Punishment by Parents and Associated Child Behaviors and Experiences: A Meta-Analytic and Theoretical Review." *Psychological Bulletin* 128 (4): 539–579.

Glanton, Dahleen. 2001. "Discipline or Abuse?" *Chicago Tribune*, April 1, 2001.

Gonzales, Ramona, Kinette Richards, and Ken Seeley. 2002. *Youth Out of School: Linking Absence to Delinquency.* 2nd ed. Denver: Colorado Foundation for Families and Children.

Hawkins, J. David, and Richard Catalano. 1993. *Communities That Care: Risk-Focused Prevention Using the Social Development Strategy.* Seattle, WA: Developmental Research and Programs.

Helping America's Youth (HAY). 2007. *The Community Guide to Helping America's Youth.* Washington, DC: The White House. http://guide.helpingamericasyouth. gov/programtool-factors.cfm (accessed July 23, 2008).

Hoeve, Machteld, Arjan Blokland, Judith Semon Dubas, Rolf Loeber, Jan R. M. Gerris, and Peter H. van der Laan. 2008. "Trajectories of Delinquency and Parenting Styles." *Journal of Abnormal Child Psychology* (36): 223–235.

Johnston, Lloyd D., Patrick M. O'Malley, Jerald G. Bachman, and John E. Schulenberg. 2011. *Monitoring the Future: National Results on Adolescent Drug Use: Overview of Key Findings, 2010.* Ann Arbor: University of Michigan Institute for Social Research.

Kelley, Barbara T., Rolf Loeber, Kate Keenan, and Mary DeLamatre. 1997 (December). *Developmental Pathways in Boys' Disruptive and Delinquent Behavior.* Washington, DC: OJJDP Juvenile Justice Bulletin. (NCJ 165692)

Kohlberg, Lawrence. 1981. *The Philosophy of Moral Development: Moral Stages and the Idea of Justice* (Essays on Moral Development, Vol. 1). New York: Harper & Row.

Larzelere, Robert E., and Brett R. Kuhn. 2005. "Comparing Child Outcomes of Physical Punishment and Alternative Discipline Tactics: A Meta-Analysis." *Clinical Child and Family Psychology Review* (March): 1–37.

Mayo Clinic Staff. 2011. "Fetal Alcohol Syndrome." Rochester, MN: Mayo Clinic. http://www.mayoclinic .com/health/fetal-alcohol-syndrome/DS00184

McGloin, Jean M., Travis C. Pratt, and Alex R. Piquero. 2006. "A Life-Course Analysis of the Criminogenic Effects of Maternal Cigarette Smoking during Pregnancy: A Research Note on the Mediating Impact of Neuropsychological Deficit." *Journal of Research in Crime and Delinquency* (November): 412–426.

Miller, Keva M. 2006. "The Impact of Parental Incarceration on Children: An Emerging Need for Effective Intervention." *Child and Adolescent Social Work Journal* (August): 472–486.

Morris, Leslee. 2004. "Youth in Foster Care Who Commit Delinquent Acts: Study Findings and Recommendations." *The Link: Connecting Juvenile Justice and Child Welfare* (Child Welfare League of America) (Summer/Fall): 1, 4.

Moses, Marilyn C. 2006. "Does Parental Incarceration Increase a Child's Risk for Foster Care Placement?" *NIJ Journal* 255 (November): 12–14.

"NCH Fact Sheet #1." 2007 (June). Washington, DC: National Coalition for the Homeless.

"NCH Fact Sheet #2." 2007 (August). Washington, DC: National Coalition for the Homeless.

Nofziger, Stacey. 2008. "The 'Cause' of Low Self-Control." *Journal of Research in Crime and Delinquency* (May): 191–224.

"Policy Statement: Guidance for Effective Discipline." 1998. *Pediatrics* (April): 723–728.

"Policy Statement: Media Violence." 2001. *Pediatrics* (November): 1222–1226.

Rowland, Melissa, and Alice Watts. 2007 "Washington State's Effort to Reduce the Generational Impact on Crime." *Corrections Today* (August): 34–42.

Scott, Cynthia. 2007. "Preschool Programs Pay Off." *Minnesota* (November/December): 13–14.

Shader, Michael. 2002. *Risk Factors for Delinquency: An Overview.* Washington, DC: Office of Juvenile Justice and Delinquency Prevention. http://ojjdp.ncjrs.org/ ccd/ pubsrfd.html

Stillwell, Robert, Jennifer Sable, and Chris Plotts. 2011 (May). *Public School Graduates and Dropouts from the Common Core of Data: School Year 2008–09.* Washington, DC: U.S. Department of Education, Institute of Education Sciences, National Center for Education Statistics.

"Teens: Alcohol and Other Drugs." 2004 (July). Washington, DC: American Academy of Child and Adolescent Psychiatry.

United Nations. *Convention on the Rights of the Child.* Adopted by the General Assembly of the United Nations, November 20, 1989.

Wasserman, Gail A., Kate Keenan, Richard E. Tremblay, John D. Coie, Todd I. Herrenkohl, Rolf Loeber, and David Petechuk. 2003 (April). *Risk and Protective Factors of Child Delinquency.* Washington, DC: Office of Juvenile Justice and Delinquency Prevention, Child Delinquency Bulletin Series. (NCJ 193409)

Whitaker, Mary Scully, and Maureen Buell. 2007. "Children with Incarcerated Parents: Everyone Has a Role." *Corrections Today* (August): 91.

Wright, John Paul, and Francis T. Cullen. 2004. "Employment, Peers and Life-Course Transitions." *Justice Quarterly* (March): 183–202.

Wright, John Paul, Kim N. Dietrich, M. Douglas Ris, Richard W. Hornung, Stephanie D. Wessel, Bruce P. Lanphear, Mona Ho, and Mary N. Rae. 2008. "Association of Prenatal and Childhood Blood Lead Concentrations with Criminal Arrests in Early Adulthood." *Public Library of Science Medicine* 5 (May 27): 101. doi:10.1371/journal.pmed.0050101 (accessed July 23, 2008).

Wu, Li-Tzy, William E. Schlenger, and Deborah Galvin. 2003. "The Relationship between Employment and Substance Use among Students Aged 12 to 17." *Journal of Adolescent Health* 32 (1): 5.

Yeager, Dale, Sam Sulliman, Andreas Demidont, and Dane Brandenberger. 2006. *The State of School Safety in American Schools 2004–2006* [publicly released version of a report prepared for Congress]. Southeastern, PA: SERAPH Research Team.

Zahn, Margaret A., Robert Agnew, Diana Fishbein, Shari Miller, Donna-Marie Winn, Gayle Dakoff, Candace Kruttschnitt, Peggy Giordano, Denise C. Gottfredson, Allison A. Payne, Barry C. Feld, and Meda Chesney-Lind. 2010 (April). *Causes and Correlates of Girls' Delinquency*. Washington, DC: Office of Juvenile Justice and Delinquency Prevention. (NCJ 226358)

Juvenile Victims

> " The cycle of abused and neglected children who have become abusing and neglecting parents with their children in turn being abused, neglected, running away, acting out and often ending up before the courts has not been broken. "
>
> **—Metropolitan Court Judges Committee**

Child victimization takes many forms (neglect, physical assault, psychological or emotional abuse, sexual abuse or bullying), can occur in any setting (home, school, the community) and is not bound by socioeconomic status, religious affiliation or racial identity. Exposure to violence and victimization can cause significant physical, mental and emotional harm in youth, with long-term effects that carry into adulthood.

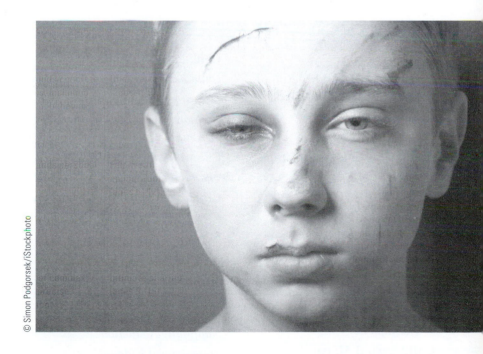

© Simon Podgorsek/iStockphoto

DO YOU KNOW?

- What risks maltreated children and youths face?
- What the major cause of death of young children is?
- What the most common form of child maltreatment is and how serious it is?
- What often characterizes the homes of neglected children?
- What the three components of child abuse and neglect laws typically are?
- What are three of the primary risk factors for child abuse?
- What the likely result of violence is for children?

- Whether child abuse is directly linked to delinquency?
- Which age group has the highest victimization rate?
- What six episode types of missing children are identified in the NISMART–2 study?
- What two federal agencies have concurrent jurisdiction for missing and exploited children? What approach each takes toward missing children?
- What the leading cause of youth suicide is?
- What common warning signs of potential youth suicide are?

CAN YOU DEFINE?

anticipated
    strain
dependency
extrafamilial sexual
    abuse

intrafamilial sexual
    abuse
maltreatment
maximalist alarmist
    perspective

minimalist skeptical
    perspective
neglect
osteogenesis
    imperfecta (OI)

runaway
stereotypical
    kidnapping
thrownaway
vicarious strain

CHAPTER OUTLINE

Introduction
Defining Child Maltreatment
    and Rating Its Severity
Child Neglect
Indicators of Neglect
Physical or Emotional Child
    Abuse
Child Abuse and Neglect Laws
Indicators of Physical Abuse
Indicators of Emotional Abuse
*Causes of or Risk Factors for Child
    Abuse*
Domestic and Family Violence
*Child Abuse and the Link with
    Delinquency*
Child Sexual Abuse

Child Pornography
Child Sexual Abuse and the Internet
Indicators of Sexual Abuse
*Consequences of Being Sexually
    Abused*
Cultural Values and Sexual Abuse
The Issue of Credibility
Children and Youths as Victims
    of Crime and Violence
Missing and Exploited
    Children
Missing Benign Explanation
Missing Involuntary, Lost or Injured
Runaway/Thrownaway
Nonfamily Abduction
Stereotypical Kidnapping

Family Abduction
*A Child Abduction Response Team
    (CART)*
AMBER Alert
*Responsibility for Investigating
    Missing and Exploited Children*
Bullying
Youths and Suicide
Exemplary Programs to
    Prevent or Reduce Child
    Victimization
Nurse-Family Partnership
Building Peaceful Families
Safe Kids/Safe Streets
The Juvenile Victim Justice
    System

Introduction

The juvenile justice system is one entity charged with handling our nation's youngest victims. Child victimization takes many forms. Some children are casualties of traditional forms of crime and violence, some are missing from home because they run away or are "thrown away," some are abducted, others are sexually exploited and still others succumb to untreated mental illness or other pressures and become victims of suicide. However, the most common way our nation's youths are victimized is through child maltreatment.

Defining Child Maltreatment and Rating Its Severity

Maltreatment refers to an act or omission by a parent or other caregiver that results in harm or serious risk of harm to a child. It includes neglect, medical neglect, physical abuse, sexual abuse and psychological maltreatment. Emotional and behavior disorders, running away from home, teen pregnancy, prostitution, dating violence, substance abuse and delinquency and criminality are some of the negative outcomes a child may face as a result of childhood maltreatment (Cullerton-Sen et al. 2008; Conroy et al. 2009; Kim et al. 2009; Maas et al. 2010; Thompson and Tabone 2010; Tyler, Allison, and Winsler 2006; Widom and Maxfield 2001; Wolfe et al. 2009).

 Maltreated youths are at an increased risk for performing poorly in school and displaying symptoms of mental illness; girls are at increased risk of becoming pregnant, using drugs and engaging in serious and violent delinquency.

Most maltreatment cases enter the child welfare system through child protective services (CPS) agencies, which are generally agencies authorized to act on behalf of a child when parents are unable or unwilling to do so. All states require these agencies to assess or investigate reports of child abuse and neglect and to offer rehabilitative services to families where maltreatment has or is likely to occur.

According to the National Child Abuse and Neglect Data System (NCANDS) Child File, nearly 3 million children were subject to an investigated report of child maltreatment in 2009, and 690,869 children were confirmed by state CPS agencies as victims of maltreatment, a rate of 9 out of every 1,000 persons under age 18 (National KIDS COUNT Program 2011).

Rates of child maltreatment vary across demographic groups. Girls' victimization rate is typically higher than the rate for boys. Reported child maltreatment varies by race, with 43 percent of children confirmed by CPS agencies as victims of maltreatment in 2009 being non-Hispanic White (43 percent), 22 percent being non-Hispanic Black and 22 percent being Hispanic. The victimization rate is also inversely related to age, with the youngest children (birth to age 4) having the highest rate; 39 percent of children confirmed by CPS agencies as victims of maltreatment in 2009 were 4 years old or younger (National KIDS COUNT Program 2011).

Neglect was the most common type of maltreatment. Other types of abuse included physical abuse, sexual abuse, psychological maltreatment, medical neglect and categories of abuse based on specific state laws as shown in Figure 5.1.

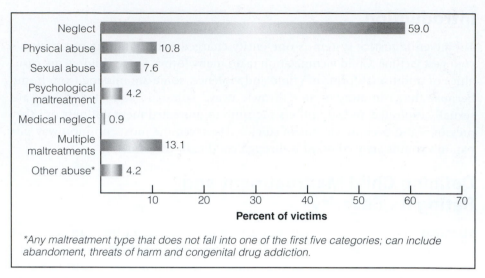

Figure 5.1   Abuse and Neglect among Children under Age 18, by Type of Maltreatment, 2007

U.S. Department of Health and Human Services, Administration on Children, Youth, and Families. 2009. *Child Maltreatment 2007.* Washington, DC: U.S. Government Printing Office.

An important caveat to this data is that it does not include victimized children who have never been made known to the system through a maltreatment report (recall the *dark figure of crime* concept discussed in Chapter 1).

Maltreatment exists in many forms. Definitions of the various types of maltreatment vary from state to state and even locality to locality. The most common subtypes of child maltreatment and their severity are described in Table 5.1.

Most perpetrators of maltreatment (80 percent) are parents—birth parents, adoptive parents and stepparents. Women are overrepresented among both caregivers and maltreatment perpetrators. Nonparental relatives, unmarried partners of parents and daycare providers each made up small proportions of child maltreatment perpetrators. Foster parents, residential facility staff and legal guardians each made up less than 1 percent of maltreatment perpetrators (Snyder and Sickmund 2006, 55).

An Associated Press article ("Children at Higher Risk in Nontraditional Homes" 2007) reports, "Many scholars and social workers who monitor America's families see the abusive-boyfriend syndrome as part of a broader, deeply worrisome trend" that many refer to as "the dark underbelly of cohabitation."

The most serious consequence of maltreatment is death, and those most vulnerable to this fatal outcome are the youngest children. In 2009, 1,676 child fatalities caused by abuse or neglect were reported, more than 80 percent of which involved children younger than the age of 4 (*Child Maltreatment 2009* 2010). Three fourths (75.8 percent) of child fatalities were caused by one or both parents, with 27.3 percent of child fatalities caused by mothers acting alone. Of the children who died, two thirds (66.7 percent) suffered neglect either exclusively or in combination with another type of maltreatment. The second most commonly reported cause of child fatalities was physical abuse (44.8 percent), either alone or in combination with other types of neglect and abuse.

Table 5. 1   Defining Child Maltreatment and Rating Its Severity

Subtype of Maltreatment	Brief Definition	Examples of Least and Most Severe Cases
Physical Abuse	A caregiver inflicts a physical injury upon a child by other than accidental means.	*Least*—Spanking results in minor bruises on arm. *Most*—Injuries require hospitalization, cause permanent disfigurement or lead to a fatality.
Sexual Abuse	Any sexual contact or attempt at sexual contact that occurs between a caretaker or responsible adult and a child for the purposes of the caretaker's sexual gratification or financial benefit.	*Least*—A child is exposed to pornographic materials. *Most*—A caretaker uses force to make a child engage in sexual relations or prostitution.
Physical Neglect	A caretaker fails to exercise a minimum degree of care in meeting a child's physical needs.	*Least*—Food is not available for regular meals, clothing is too small, child is not kept clean. *Most*—A child suffers from severe malnutrition or severe dehydration because of gross inattention to his or her medical needs.
Lack of Supervision	A caretaker does not take adequate precautions (given a child's particular emotional and developmental needs) to ensure his or her safety in and out of the home.	*Least*—An 8-year-old is left alone for short periods (i.e., less than 3 hours) with no immediate source of danger in the environment. *Most*—A child is placed in a life-threatening situation without adequate supervision.
Emotional Maltreatment	Persistent or extreme thwarting of a child's basic emotional needs (such as the need to feel safe and accepted).	*Least*—A caretaker often belittles or ridicules a child. *Most*—A caretaker uses extremely restrictive methods to bind a child or places a child in close confinement such as a closet or trunk for 2 or more hours.
Educational Maltreatment	A caretaker fails to ensure that a child receives adequate education.	*Least*—A caretaker allows a child to miss school up to 15 percent of the time (when he or she is not ill and there is no family emergency). *Most*—A caretaker does not enroll a child in school or provide any educational instruction.
Moral-Legal Maltreatment	A caretaker exposes or involves a child in illegal or other activities that may foster delinquency or antisocial behavior.	*Least*—A child is permitted to be present for adult activities, such as drunken parties. *Most*—A caretaker causes a child to participate in felonies such as armed robbery.

SOURCE: Adapted from Douglas Barnett, Jody Todd Manly, and Dante Cicchetti. 1993. "Defining Child Maltreatment: The Interface between Policy and Research." In *Child Abuse, Child Development and Social Policy*, edited by D. Cicchetti and S. L. Toth, pp. 7–73. Norwood, NJ: Ablex Publishing.

Reality Check: The Dark Underbelly of Cohabitation

Several studies support the concern over maltreatment of children in "nontraditional" living situations:

- A study published in 2005 in the journal of the American Academy of Pediatrics found that children living in households with unrelated adults are nearly 50 times as likely to die of inflicted injuries as are children living with two biological parents.
- Several studies coauthored by David Finkelhor, director of the University of New Hampshire's Crimes against Children Research Center, concluded that children living in stepfamilies or with single parents are at higher risk of physical or sexual assault than are children living with two biological or adoptive parents.
- Research by Robin Wilson, a family law professor at Washington and Lee University, revealed that girls whose parents divorce face significantly higher risk of sexual assault, whether they live with their mother or father.

SOURCE: "Children at Higher Risk in Nontraditional Homes." 2007. Associated Press, November 18, 2007. http://www.msnbc.msn.com/id/21838575/ (accessed October 21, 2008).

 Child neglect has been identified as the biggest single cause of death of young children, followed by physical abuse.

Fatal child abuse may involve repeated abuse over time (e.g., battered child syndrome) or may involve a single, impulsive incident such as shaking a baby. Fatal neglect cases usually result not from anything a caregiver *does* but from what a caregiver *does not* do—the caregiver's *failure to act*. The neglect may be chronic (e.g., extended malnourishment) or acute (e.g., an infant who drowns because of being left unsupervised in a bathtub) (Child Welfare Information Gateway 2008).

Before looking more closely at the various forms of maltreatment, consider the big picture, the stages of child maltreatment case processing through CPS and the juvenile/family court system as illustrated in Figure 5.2. Notice that CPS may provide protective custody of a child outside the home or provide protective supervision of the child within the family unit at any point that a case is closed or dismissed. The specific options once a case enters formal court processing are the focus of Chapter 11.

Child Neglect

 Neglect is the most common form of child maltreatment and may be fatal.

Broadly defined, child **neglect** is inattention to the basic needs of a child, including appropriate supervision, adequate clothing and proper nutrition. Often the families from which neglected children come are poor, disorganized and dysfunctional. They have no set routine for family activity. The children roam the streets at all hours. They are continually petitioned to juvenile court for loitering and curfew violations. The family unit is often fragmented by death, divorce or the incarceration or desertion of parents.

Dysfunctional families often deprive children of affection, recognition and a sense of belonging. The broken and dysfunctional home, in and of itself, does not cause delinquency, but it can nullify or even destroy the resources youths need to handle emotional problems constructively. Children from such families

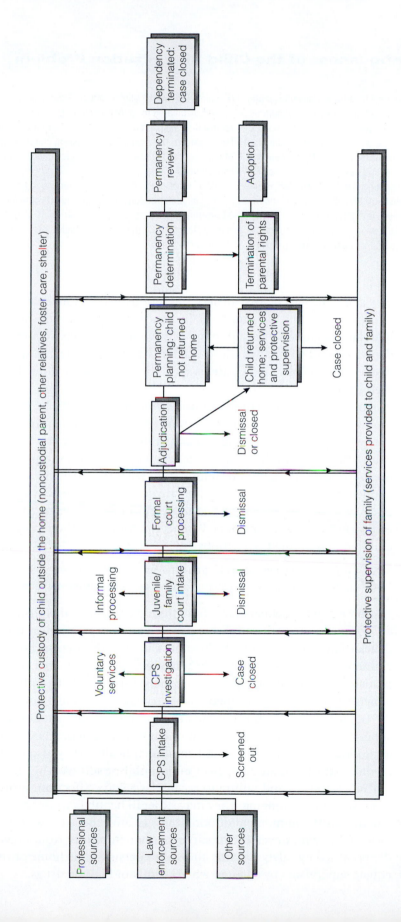

Figure 5.2   Stages of Child Maltreatment Case Processing

SOURCE: Howard N. Snyder and Melissa Sickmund. 2006 (March). *Juvenile Offenders and Victims: 2006 National Report*, p. 48. Washington, DC: Office of Juvenile Justice Delinquency Prevention.

A Debate: The Seriousness of the Child Victimization Problem

Child abuse and neglect is, without doubt, a tragic and unfortunate reality. But disagreement exists about how prevalent or serious the problem of child victimization is. Karmen (2007, 180) describes two conflicting views: the maximalist alarmist and minimalist skeptical perspectives. The **maximalist alarmist perspective** contends that the problem of child and sexual abuse is reaching epidemic proportions: "Dire consequences will follow unless drastic steps are taken. . . . Maximalists try to mobilize people and resources to combat what they believe is a growing crisis."

These claims have resulted in a predictable opposite position—that of the **minimalist skeptical perspective** (Karmen 2007, 180): "Minimalists consider maximalist estimates to be grossly inflated for either a well-intentioned reason or perhaps for a self-serving purpose." Karmen notes that the most heated debates concern the actual fate of missing children, the true extent of physical child abuse and the true prevalence of incest and child molestation.

Which side of the debate do you tend to favor?

As you read through the chapter, see if your views change. For a better informed perspective, consult *Crime Victims: An Introduction to Victimology*, 5th edition, by Andrew Karmen (Belmont, CA: Wadsworth, 2007).

may suffer feelings of loss, anxiety and serious stress. Some may develop aggressive attitudes and strike out, thinking that punishment for misbehavior is better than no recognition or being completely ignored. Conversely, some may become depressed and withdrawn. Even when marriages are intact, both parents often work. Consequently, many parents spend little time in the home interacting with their children.

Some children are stunted in their emotional growth by being raised in a moral vacuum in which parents ignore them. Even more problematic are parents who do not adhere to moral and ethical standards or who have different values than the dominant moral order; they set poor examples for their children. Children's behavior develops from what they see and understand to be happening around them. If children are exposed to excessive drinking, the use of drugs, illicit sex, gambling and related vices by parents or adult role models, they may copy these behaviors. Parents cannot ignore the probability that their children may model their actions.

 The homes of neglected children often are disorganized and dysfunctional, with parents who ignore the children or who set bad examples for them.

Some parents deliberately refrain from discipline in the mistaken belief that authoritative restrictions inhibit children's self-expression or unbalance their delicate emotional systems. At the other extreme are parents who discipline their children injudiciously, excessively and often, weighing neither transgression nor punishment. Family policies that are inconsistent or that emphasize too much leniency or excessive punishment may encourage or allow delinquency to develop.

Neglected children often lack the food, clothing, shelter, medical care, supervision, education, protection or emotional support they need to develop appropriate physical, mental and emotional health. They also may suffer emotional harm through disrespect and denial of self-worth, unreasonable or chronic rejection and failure to receive necessary affection, protection and a sense of family belonging. They may suffer ill health because they are not vaccinated against common childhood illness or are exposed to secondhand smoke or lead. They may even die or suffer permanent injury from preventable accidents caused by safety hazards allowed to persist in the home or through inadequate supervision by a parent who is drunk or high on drugs.

Certainly not all neglect is intentional. It may be the result of parental immaturity or a lack of parenting skills. It may also be the result of a parent's physical, psychological or mental deficiencies. Some parents who neglect their children may do so because they cannot tolerate stress, they cannot adequately express anger or they have no sense of responsibility.

Indicators of Neglect

Among the *physical indicators* of child neglect are frequent hunger, poor hygiene, inappropriate dress, consistent lack of supervision (especially in dangerous activities or for long time periods), unattended physical problems or medical needs and abandonment. The *behavioral indicators* of neglect may include begging, stealing food, extending school days by arriving early or leaving late, constant fatigue, listlessness or falling asleep in school, alcohol or drug abuse, delinquency, stealing and reporting that no one is at home to care for them (Hess and Orthmann 2012).

Physical or Emotional Child Abuse

The problem of child abuse is serious. Such abuse may be physical or emotional. Abuse can also be indirect or "secondhand," as in cases where children are allowed to witness domestic violence between partners. Many states now consider such exposure to violence to be a form of child abuse.

Physical child abuse covers a wide spectrum of behavior. Sometimes the abuse is discipline carried too far. Controversy exists among child development scholars and parents about where the line between discipline and abuse should be drawn, and many parents who cause physical harm to their children while administering disciplinary measures claim they never *intended* to injure their children. The definition of physical abuse, however, leaves less room for interpretation and addresses the issue of intent, stating it is the *nonaccidental*, or intentional, physical injury of a child caused by the child's caretaker.

Injury to a child need not be limited to physical attacks and external wounds. Children may also be damaged through emotional abuse, the chronic failure of a child's caretaker to provide affection and support. Emotional abuse includes any treatment that seriously damages a child's emotional development. For example, Charles Manson was raised by an uncle who constantly called him derogatory names and sent him to school dressed in girl's clothing.

Unfortunately the physical and emotional abuse of children is nothing new in this country or elsewhere throughout the world. In fact, many times throughout history such abuse was widely and openly practiced.

Child Abuse and Neglect Laws

Before the creation of the first juvenile court in the United States, the Society for the Prevention of Cruelty to Children was formed in 1871 after church workers removed a severely beaten and neglected child from her home under a law that protected *animals*. The first Child Protection Service was founded in 1875. Fifty years later the Social Security Act authorized public funds for child welfare.

During the 1940s advances in diagnostic X-ray technology allowed physicians to detect patterns of healed fractures in their young patients. In 1946

Dr. John Caffey, a pediatric radiologist, suggested that multiple fractures in the long bones of infants had "traumatic origin," perhaps willfully inflicted by parents. Two decades later Dr. C. H. Kempe and his associates coined the phrase *battered child syndrome* based on clinical evidence of maltreatment. Karmen (2007, 190) notes, "In the typical case, the victim was younger than 3 years old and suffered traumatic injuries to the head and to limbs; and the caretakers claimed that the wounds were caused by an accident and not a beating." In 1964 individual states began enacting mandatory child abuse laws using Dr. Kempe's definition of a battered child, and by 1966 all 50 states had enacted such legislation.

Laws regarding child abuse and neglect have been passed at both federal and state levels.

 Typically child abuse/neglect laws have three components: (1) criminal definitions and penalties, (2) a mandate to report suspected cases and (3) a civil process for removing the child from the abusive or neglectful environment.

Federal Legislation   In 1974 the federal government passed Public Law (Pub. L.) 93-247, the federal Child Abuse Prevention and Treatment Act. It was amended in 1978 under Pub. L. 95-266. The law states in part that any of the following elements constitutes a crime:

> The physical or mental injury, sexual abuse or exploitation, negligent treatment, or maltreatment of a child under the age of 18, by a person who is responsible for the child's welfare under circumstances that indicate the child's health or welfare is harmed or threatened.

Nonetheless federal courts have also ruled that parents are free to strike children because "the custody, care and nurture of the child resides first in the parents" (*Prince v. Massachusetts* 1944). This fundamental right to "nurture" has been supplanted by the Supreme Court with the "care, custody and management" of one's child (*Santosky v. Kramer* 1982). This shift from "nurture" to "management" could herald a return to older laws, such as the one expressed in *People v. Green* (1909): "The parent is the sole judge of the necessity for the exercise of disciplinary right and of the nature of the correction to be given." The court need only determine whether "the punishment inflicted went beyond the legitimate exercise of parental authority."

To the present, the courts' role has been to decide what, when and to what degree physical punishment steps beyond "the legitimate exercise of parental authority" or what is "excessive punishment." The courts always begin with the presumption that parents have a legal right to use force and violence against their own children. In *Green*, 70 marks from a whipping were held to be excessive and unreasonable, even though the parent claimed he was not criminally liable because there was no permanent injury and he had acted in good faith. But the assumption remained that the parent had an unquestionable right "to administer such reasonable and timely punishment as may be necessary to correct growing faults in young children."

Current laws often protect parents, and convictions for child abuse are difficult to obtain because of circumstantial evidence, the lack of witnesses, the husband-wife privilege and the fact that an adult's testimony often is enough to establish reasonable doubt. All too often the court determines punishment to be reasonable, never reexamining the age-old presumption that hitting children is permissible.

In 2000 Congress passed the Child Abuse Prevention and Enforcement Act, making more funds available for child abuse and neglect enforcement and prevention initiatives. In 2006 the Adam Walsh Child Protection and Safety Act, named for the 6-year-old son of John and Reve Walsh who was abducted and murdered in Florida in 1981, was signed into law and was aimed at tracking sex crime offenders and subjecting them to stiff, mandatory minimum sentences ("Adam Walsh Act Signed" 2006, 5). The act expands previous sex registry requirements, setting forth strict guidelines for states, territories and tribal nations to develop and maintain a jurisdiction-wide sex offender registry. Failure to comply with the guidelines can result in a 10 percent reduction in federal Byrne grant funding. Title I of the act is the Sex Offender Registration and Notification Act (SORNA), which details a comprehensive set of minimum standards for sex offender registration and notification in the United States and seeks to close the loopholes that existed under prior laws. The act also established the Office of Sex Offender Sentencing, Monitoring, Apprehending, Registering and Tracking (the SMART Office), housed in the Office of Justice Programs at the U.S. Department of Justice. This office is responsible for directing the sex offender registration and notification program, administering grant programs and providing technical assistance, coordination and support to other entities ("Closer Look" 2006, 3).

State Laws   Since the 1960s every state has enacted child abuse and neglect laws. On the whole, states offer a bit more protection to children by statute than does the federal government. Legal definitions vary from state to state. California, for example, declares it illegal for anyone to willfully cause or permit any child to suffer or for any person to inflict unjustifiable physical or mental suffering on a child or to cause the child to "be placed in such situations that its person or health is endangered" (California Penal Codes section 273A).

Alaska defines abuse broadly: "The infliction, by other than accidental means, of physical harm upon the body of a child." Other state statutes are much less broad. For example, Maryland's statute states that a person is not guilty of child abuse if the defendant's intentions were good, but his or her judgment was bad. The defendant in *Worthen v. State* (1979) admitted he had punished his 2-year-old stepdaughter because she was throwing a temper tantrum, "but sought to explain it as not having exceeded the bounds of parental propriety." The jury found him guilty of assault and battery for the multiple contusions about the girl's face, ribs, buttocks and legs, but the appellate court ordered a new trial because the trial court in its jury instructions had omitted the defense of good intentions and also the defense that the stepfather had not exceeded the bounds of parental authority. What is "reasonable" varies from state to state, from one judge or court to another and from jury to jury.

Indicators of Physical Abuse

Among the *physical indicators* of physical abuse to a child are unexplained bruises or welts, burns, fractures, lacerations and abrasions. Such physical injuries may be in various stages of healing. Among the *behavioral indicators* of physical abuse are children who are wary of adults, apprehensive when other children cry, show extreme aggressiveness or extreme withdrawal, are frightened of parents or are afraid to go home (Hess and Orthmann 2012).

Some common physical conditions have been mistaken for physical abuse; for example, hemophiliacs bruise easily, and inflammation of the nose's mucous membrane can cause black eyes. The condition of **osteogenesis imperfecta (OI)**, which is characterized by bones that break easily, can also be mistaken for child abuse. According to the Osteogenesis Imperfecta Foundation (n.d.): "A minor accident may result in a fracture; some fractures may occur while a child is being diapered, lifted or dressed."

Parents' behavior can also provide clues to physical abuse. This can include contradictory explanations for a child's injury; attempts to conceal a child's injury or to protect the identity of the person responsible; the routine use of harsh, unreasonable discipline inappropriate to the child's age or behavior; and poor impulse control.

Indicators of Emotional Abuse

Physical indicators of emotional abuse may include speech disorders, lags in physical development and a general failure to thrive. *Behavioral indicators* of emotional abuse may include such habit disorders as sucking, biting and rocking back and forth, as well as conduct disorders such as antisocial or destructive behavior. Other possible indicators are sleep disorders, inhibitions in play, obsessions, compulsions, phobias, hypochondria, behavioral extremes and attempted suicide (Hess and Orthmann 2012).

Causes of or Risk Factors for Child Abuse

Parents or caretakers commit most emotional and physical child abuse. The causes of such abuse often center on a cycle of abuse passed from one generation to the next. Other risk factors that correlate to child abuse include low income, social isolation and parental expectations that exceed a child's abilities. Temperamental characteristics of a child may also increase the risk for neglect and abuse.

 Three of the primary risk factors for child abuse are domestic violence, poverty and individual temperamental factors and characteristics of a child.

The American Medical Association (1985, 797) has identified characteristics of children that increase their risk of being abused: premature birth; birth of a child to adolescent parents; colic, which makes infants difficult to soothe; congenital deficiencies or abnormalities; hospitalization of the newborn resulting in a lack of parental contact; and presence of any condition that interferes with parent-child bonding—many of the same risk factors that were identified in Chapter 4 as being correlated with delinquency.

Domestic and Family Violence

One of the most frequently experienced or observed types of violence is domestic violence, and children who live in a home where intimate partner violence occurs are at increased risk of becoming abuse victims themselves. According to published studies, there is a 30 percent to 60 percent overlap between violence against children and violence against women in the same families (Kelleher et al. 2006, 4). Although the studies on which these ranges are based employ different methods and different populations, they consistently report a significant level of co-occurrence.

Family violence, abuse and neglect can be found in families of all social and economic backgrounds. Children are lied to and lied about, mutilated, shot, stabbed, burned, beaten, bitten, sodomized, raped and hanged. Figure 5.3 illustrates a model of intrafamily violence, the variables affecting it, individual

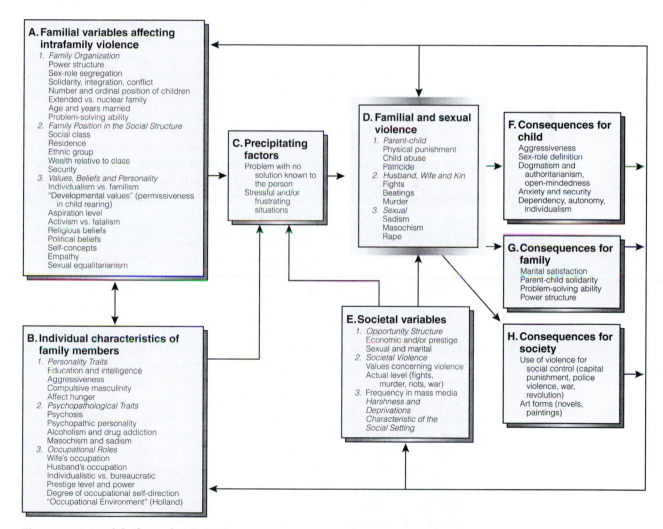

Figure 5.3 Model of Intrafamily Violence

SOURCE: Suzanne K. Steinmetz and Murray A. Straus. 1974. *Violence in the Family*, pp. 18–19. New York: Dodd, Mead.

characteristics of family members, precipitating factors, social variables and the consequences for the child, the family and society.

Witnessing Violence—Secondary Victimization   Violence does not have to be directed specifically at an individual for it to affect that individual. Witnessing actual violence or fearing its potential occurrence can strain and, thus victimize, a person. **Vicarious strain** refers to real-life strains experienced by others around the individual; **anticipated strain** refers to the individual's expectation that current strains will continue into the future or that new strains will be experienced. Agnew (2002) studied the relationship between vicarious and anticipated strain and concluded, "Delinquency is related not only to experienced victimization, but also to certain types of anticipated and vicarious physical victimization" (603).

McGee and Baker (2002) studied the impact of violence on problem behavior among adolescents and found a strong association between youths exposed to violence through direct victimization, witnessing violence, and association with delinquent peers and adjustment outcomes, including internalizing (self-rejection, depression) and externalizing (offenses) problem behavior. They also found a link between victimization and avoidance as a coping strategy. Furthermore, their research revealed a greater influence of victimization on offenses, self-rejection and avoidance among men and a stronger influence of victimization on depression among women in the sample (McGee and Baker 2002, 74). Results of one meta-analysis provide robust empirical evidence that children who witness interparental violence are at risk for a range of psychological, emotional, behavioral, social and academic problems and that exposure to this type of violence may have greater negative effects on children than does the effects of witnessing other forms of destructive conflict (Kitzmann et al. 2003).

The Cycle of Violence   The cycle of violence has been used to describe the phenomenon whereby a victim is transformed into a victimizer over time: "A group of picked-upon students may band together to ambush their bullying tormentors; a battered wife may launch a vengeful attack against her brutal husband; or a child subjected to periodic beatings might grow up to parent his sons in the same excessively punitive way he was raised" (Karmen 2007, 6). The "cycle of violence" model has also been applied by some scholars to explain how violence, as one part of an intergenerational set of problems, can be passed from one generation to the next. Some theories argue that this is a learned way of interacting and that violence, as a learned behavior, can become self-perpetuating. When adults teach children by example that those who are bigger and stronger can use violence to force their wishes on others who are smaller, the lesson is remembered. Children who witness domestic abuse may learn that it is okay to hurt the people you care about and it is acceptable to use violence to get what you want. Other children exposed to domestic violence, however, may learn a contrary lesson—that it is not acceptable to beat or belittle those you care about because the damage caused can be substantial. This type of reaction explains why most children who are abused do not grow up to become abusers themselves. Nonetheless, witnessing violence, particular between parents, has been identified as a risk factor for children, and family violence has been directly linked with delinquency, especially violent offenses.

 Violence may lead to more violence. Children who are abused are more likely to be delinquents and violent themselves.

Child Abuse and the Link with Delinquency

The connection between children's histories of neglect or abuse and subsequent delinquency, crime and other problems has been increasingly reaffirmed by a growing body of evidence (Widom and Maxfield 2001, 2):

- Being abused or neglected as a child increased the likelihood of arrest as a juvenile by 59 percent, as an adult by 28 percent, and for a violent crime by 30 percent.
- Maltreated children were younger at the time of their first arrest, committed nearly twice as many offenses, and were arrested more frequently.
- Physically abused and neglected (versus sexually abused) children were the most likely to be arrested later for a violent crime.

These results have been replicated in numerous other studies. English, Widom and Brandford (2002) found that abused and neglected children were nearly five times more likely to be arrested as juveniles, two times more likely to be arrested as an adult, and more than three times more likely to be arrested for a violent crime than matched controls. Research by Cohen, Smailes and Brown (2004) found that victims of officially identified abuse were more likely to be arrested as adults and more likely to be arrested for a variety of crimes. Lemmon (2006) studied the relationship between childhood maltreatment recurrence and various dimensions of delinquency and found that repeated child maltreatment significantly predicted the initiation, continuation and severity of delinquency, controlling for other risk factors. Rebellion and Van Gundy (2005) also found that longitudinal studies suggest that abuse experienced in childhood contributed to violent offending as well as property offending.

 Child abuse has been directly linked with delinquency.

Loeber, Kalb and Huizinga (2001, 1) assert, "Delinquency and victimization are often intertwined and mutually stimulate each other." They note that many victims are prone to engage in illegal activities, associate with delinquents, victimize other delinquents and avoid legal recourse to resolve conflicts. When delinquent behavior occurs, it may bring about further abuse, resulting in a vicious cycle and ever-worsening behavior.

Children and adolescents who have patterns of delinquency that emanate from the home are imitating the behavior of parents or other family members. In extreme cases, children have been taught how to commit crimes.

Many studies have amplified the link between child abuse and criminal behavior, and many criminal justice professionals on the front lines with juvenile delinquents believe the war on crime will be won only when the focus shifts from building more prison cells to investing more in children—through early childhood programs such as health care for children and pregnant women, Head Start for infants and toddlers, parenting training for high-risk families, programs aimed at preventing child abuse, recreational programs, after-school programs and mentoring programs.

Child Sexual Abuse

Every year roughly 100,000 cases of child sexual abuse are reported. Couple this with experts' estimates that more than 90 percent of child molestations are *not* reported to the criminal justice system and the magnitude of the problem becomes apparent.

Sexual abuse can be classified as intrafamilial or extrafamilial. **Intrafamilial sexual abuse** is sexual abuse by a parent or other family member. **Extrafamilial sexual abuse** involves a friend or stranger. Babysitters are responsible for a relatively small portion of the reported criminal offenses against children: 4.2 percent of all offenses for children under age 6. Among the reported offenses that babysitters commit, sex crimes outnumber physical assaults nearly two to one.

Child Pornography

Child pornography, defined as the possession, trade, advertising and production of images that depict the sexual abuse of children, is a real and growing threat to our nation's children. In 2006 U.S. attorneys handled 82.8 percent more child pornography cases than they had in 1994. State and local law enforcement departments involved in Internet Crimes against Children (ICAC) Task Force agencies reported a 230 percent increase in the number of documented complaints of online enticement of children from 2004 to 2008 and, during that same time period, noted a more than one thousand percent increase in complaints of child prostitution (*National Strategy* 2010). According to a threat assessment undertaken by the Department of Justice, "there has been a dramatic increase in cases of sexual exploitation of children, including the possession, distribution and manufacture of child pornography; the online enticement of children for sexual acts; commercial sexual exploitation of children; child sex tourism; and child sexual molestation, since the 1990s" (*National Strategy* 2010, 8). Notable facts and trends identified by this assessment include:

- The thriving market for child pornography promotes the fresh abuse of children (17).
- Child pornography offenses often are linked to contact offenses (19).
- The children most vulnerable and at risk are those the offenders can easily access and manipulate (21).
- Law enforcement officers are seeing more prepubescent children and infants in child pornography images and more images depicting violent, sadistic acts (22).
- There is steady demand and profit in the prostitution of children (32).

Perhaps the single biggest factor behind the rapid increase in volume of child pornography is the Internet and the ease with which offenders can both find victims through this medium and exchange images with other pedophiles.

Child Sexual Abuse and the Internet

Another identified source of child sexual abuse is the Internet. An estimated 30 million youths go online each year to do homework or explore cyberspace. Geraghty (2007, 30) cautions: "The Internet provides a child predator with access to children on a scale that makes the world his local playground. It is a medium through which digital images and movies documenting the most horrific crimes against children are distributed to a worldwide audience." He notes that all the services the Internet provides—e-mail, the World Wide Web, instant messaging—can be used to facilitate crimes against children. Examples of how this occurs are provided by Collins (2007, 40):

> A fourth-grade student was frequently pulled out of lunch by her teacher, who sexually abused her in the class coatroom and took explicit photographs to memorialize the moment. He demanded her silence by threatening to flunk her and post the pictures on the Internet if she told anyone. Another child, a prepubescent boy, was violently sexually assaulted for several years by a man who acted as his live-in babysitter. While the boy never disclosed his abuse to anyone, thousands of photographs depicting his horrific abuse were circulated around the globe. In another location, a man with no previous criminal record filmed himself sodomizing his 10-month-old granddaughter. He did not need to convince the child to keep the secret; in fact, he said he selected that particular victim because she was preverbal.

The Child Protection and Sexual Predator Punishment Act, passed in 1998, imposes tougher penalties for sex crimes against children, particularly those facilitated by the use of the Internet. The act prohibits contacting a minor via the Internet to engage in illegal sexual activity and punishes those who knowingly send obscenity to children.

In addition to child pornography, the Internet facilitates child sexual abuse in other ways, such as:

- Allowing networking among child abuse perpetrators.
- Enabling perpetrators to seek out and groom victims.
- Facilitating cyberstalking.
- Promoting child sexual tourism.
- Assisting in the trafficking of children. (Wortley and Smallbone 2006, 21)

Human trafficking can involve young children, particularly those not living with their parents because these youth are vulnerable to coerced labor exploitation, domestic servitude or commercial sexual exploitation. Sex traffickers target children because the youths are gullible and there is a market demand for young victims. The average age of entry into prostitution through human trafficking is 12 to 14 years old (*Human Trafficking of Children* 2007).

Numerous challenges exist in controlling Internet child pornography: the decentralized structure of the Internet (a network of networks), uncertainties surrounding jurisdiction, the lack of Internet regulation, differences in legislation among jurisdictions throughout the world, the expertise of offenders, the sophistication and adaptation of Internet technology and the sheer and growing volume of Internet activity (Wortley and Smallbone 2006, 26–27).

Several initiatives are aimed at protecting children in cyberspace. The Office of Juvenile Justice and Delinquency Prevention (OJJDP) funds the ICAC Task Force, which seeks to protect children online. This program helps state and local law enforcement agencies develop effective responses to online enticement and child pornography cases, including community education, forensic, investigative and victim service components. The National Center for Missing and Exploited Children (NCMEC) has a congressionally mandated CyberTipline, a reporting mechanism for child sexual exploitation, which has handled more than 440,000 leads and serves as the national clearinghouse for child pornography cases across the country (Collins 2007, 40).

Project Safe Childhood (PSC) is designed and sponsored by the U.S. Department of Justice to empower federal, state and local law enforcement officers with tools needed to investigate cybercrimes against children. Forty-six federally funded ICAC task forces, consisting of more than 1,000 affiliated state and local organizations, have been created across the country since 1998 (McNulty 2007, 36). Since 2000, these task forces have completed investigations that have resulted in 7,328 arrests. In addition, the FBI made 1,648 arrests in 2005 as part of its Innocent Images National Initiative (IINI).

Indicators of Sexual Abuse

Rarely are the *physical indicators* of sexual abuse seen. Two possible indicators, especially in preteens, are venereal disease and pregnancy.

Among the possible *behavioral indicators* of sexual abuse are being unwilling to change clothes for or to participate in physical education classes; withdrawal, fantasy or infantile behavior; bizarre sexual behavior; sexual sophistication beyond one's age or unusual behavior or knowledge of sex; poor peer relationships; delinquent or runaway behavior; and reports of being sexually assaulted (Hess and Orthmann 2012).

As with physical abuse, the parents' behavior may also provide indicators of sexual abuse. Such behaviors may include jealousy and being overprotective of a child. A parent may hesitate to report a spouse who is sexually abusing their child for fear of destroying the marriage or for fear of retaliation. Intrafamilial sex may be preferred to extramarital sex.

Consequences of Being Sexually Abused

Sexual abuse can have many adverse effects on its young victims, including guilt, shame, anxiety, fear, depression, anger, low self-esteem, concerns about secrecy, feelings of helplessness and an inordinate need to please others (Karmen 2007, 192). In addition, victims of sexual abuse have higher levels of school absenteeism, less participation in extracurricular activities and lower grades.

Research by Siegel and Williams (2003, 84) found, "Sexual abuse victims were significantly more likely to have been arrested as adults than their matched counterparts even controlling for a childhood history characterized by family problems serious enough to have resulted in a dependency hearing." In this case **dependency** refers to the legal status of children over whom a juvenile court has assumed jurisdiction because the court has found their care to fall short of legal standards of proper care by parents, guardians or custodians.

Cultural Values and Sexual Abuse

Cultural values play a role in determining what constitutes abuse. Some practices regarded as normal and acceptable within one culture may be considered sexual abuse by mainstream society or by those from other cultures. For example, in Somalia and other parts of Africa, female circumcision or female genital mutilation (FGM) is a rite of passage performed on infants and young girls. In the United States, however, this practice is considered abuse and is illegal, a situation that causes significant conflict for Somali women who have immigrated to this country.

According to the U.S. Department of Health and Human Resources, an estimated 160,000 girls and women in the U.S. immigrant community have submitted to FGM. Some contend it is hypocritical of the United States to censure another culture for doing to its young girls what America routinely does to its boys.

Another example of how different cultures regard the issue of sexual abuse is seen in the practice of polygamy involving juvenile girls. Within certain areas of the United States, most notably in Utah, polygamy was an acceptable Mormon practice, accompanied by the cultural value that very young girls, some as young as 10, may be forced into arranged marriages. Although the church disavowed polygamy in 1890 in exchange for statehood, an estimated 300,000 families are headed by men with more than one spouse.

Polygamist Tom Green made headlines when he was charged with child rape for having sex with a 13-year-old girl he had married in 1986. Green had 5 wives and 30 children. In 2002 the high-profile case of teenager Elizabeth Smart, kidnapped by Brian David Mitchell, a self-styled prophet, brought the practice of polygamy back to national attention. Mitchell supposedly kidnapped Smart to make her his second wife. Mitchell was convicted in 2010 of kidnapping and sexual assault and sentenced in 2011 to two life terms in prison.

The Issue of Credibility

Because physical indicators of sexual abuse are often not present, allegations of sexual abuse can be difficult to prove. Investigators must also weed out false accusations.

Sometimes allegations of child sexual abuse are made in the context of divorce and custody cases. Unfortunately, the warlike atmosphere inherent in divorce often discredits valid claims. Although rare, false allegations of abuse do occur. Karmen (2007, 196) notes, "When allegations surface during the height of a divorce and tug-of-war over a child, two camps quickly emerge. One side argues that since there are no outsiders who witness violations of the incest taboo within the home, these 'family secrets' usually are not exposed unless the parents break up. The other side contends that baseless allegations are being taken too seriously, and the resulting investigations ruin the lives of innocent parents, usually fathers."

Coercing a child to lie about abuse that never occurred is a form of abuse all its own. Unfortunately, many youths become victims of this type of abuse when they are caught in the middle of custody battles. As parents fight to prove they are better equipped to raise the children, they unwittingly inflict a great deal of emotional and psychological damage on the very people they say they are trying to protect.

Children and Youths as Victims of Crime and Violence

One of the most obvious ways youths are victimized is by becoming a victim of crime. This may occur under the umbrella of ongoing abuse, as already discussed, or it may be an isolated episode by a nonfamily member, as in the case of robbery. Make no mistake; child abuse is violent crime. But the official crime statistics collected by government agencies often lump child abuse events into the general category of violent crime. Thus, keep in mind as you consider such data that an unknown, perhaps considerable, portion of these victimizations are the result of child abuse and not simply single-episode acts of violent crime. According to Snyder and Sickmund (2006), of all offenses reported to law enforcement:

- One of every four violent crime victims is a juvenile, and most are female (31).
- More than one third of juvenile victims of violent crime are under age 12 (32).
- About two thirds of violent crimes with juvenile victims occur in a residence (36).
- Few statutory rapes involve both juvenile victims and juvenile offenders, with the majority of victims being females (95 percent), most of whom were ages 14 or 15. Male offenders were generally much older than their female victims (37).
- In the 10 years from 1993 to 2002, the number of juveniles murdered in the United States fell 44 percent, to the lowest level since the mid-1980s (20).
- On an average day in 2002, about four juveniles were murdered, roughly two White and two Black youth. Adjusting for the differences in their numbers in the general population, this means that in 2002 the risk of a Black youth being murdered was four times that of a White youth (22).

 Youths are victims of crime twice as often as are those over age 25.

Baum (2005) reports that from 1993 to 2003 juveniles ages 12 to 14 and juveniles ages 15 to 17 experienced average annual rates of nonfatal violence about two and a half times higher than the rate for adults (83 and 84 per 1,000, respectively, versus 32 per 1,000). Four in five victims of nonfatal violent crime, ages 12 to 14, perceived the offender to be a juvenile. Juveniles experienced declines for all nonfatal crimes measured—rape/sexual assault, robbery, aggravated assault and simple assault. Victimization rates for overall violence declined more for younger teens than for older teens.

Teplin et al. (2005, 1586) studied mortality rates among 1,829 delinquent youths and compared them to the mortality rates of the general population of Cook County, Illinois. They found the overall mortality rate for the delinquents was more than four times greater than that of the general population and nearly eight times as high among female offenders.

Schreck et al. (2007, 381) researched the validity of the social interactionist (SI) perspective as an explanation of violent victimization. They theorized that early puberty creates unusually high levels of distress for adolescents, causing them to behave in ways that annoy others and provoke victimization. Schreck et al. found that such measures of distress significantly increased violent victimization among youths in the sample and concluded, "Adolescents who experienced emotional distress, performed poorly in school and violated minor rules were more likely to become victims of violent crime" (2007, 397).

Missing and Exploited Children

Another category of victimized youths is children who are missing and exploited. Oftentimes, these children are "missing" by choice because of intolerable conditions in the home, including abuse and violence. The NCMEC is a private, non-profit organization established in 1984 to spearhead national efforts to locate and recover missing children and raise public awareness about ways to prevent child abduction, molestation and sexual exploitation. Since its creation through September 2010, NCMEC has helped law enforcement with more than 171,600 missing child cases, played a role in the recovery of more than 157,700 children, handled more than 2.5 million phone calls through its nationwide hotline and received more than 952,500 reports of child sexual exploitation on its CyberTipline (NCMEC n.d.).

According to the NCMEC, 800,000 children are reported missing every year in the United States, approximately 2,000 every day (NCMEC 2009, 13). FBI data indicate 38,505 active juvenile (under age 18) missing person cases in the FBI's National Crime Information Center (NCIC) database (*NCIC Missing Person Statistics* 2010). Snyder and Sickmund (2006) report:

- Annually about 19 in 1,000 children below the age of 18 are missing from caretakers. Only a small fraction of missing children were abducted (about 10 in 100), most by family members (8 in 10). Runaway youth account for nearly half of all missing children (43).
- Teens ages 15 to 17 accounted for 68 percent of the estimated 1.7 million youths who were gone from their homes either because they had run away or because their caretakers threw them out. Fewer than 4 in 10 of all runaway/thrownaway youths were truly missing—their parents knew where the rest were staying. Most youths who ran away or were thrown out of their homes were gone less than a week (77 percent) (45).

The Missing Children's Act was passed in 1982 and the Missing Children's Assistance Act in 1984. The Missing Children's Assistance Act of 1984 defines a *missing child* as

> Any individual, less than 18 years of age, whose whereabouts are unknown to such individual's legal custodian—if the circumstances surrounding the disappearance indicate that [the child] may possibly have been removed by another person from the control of his/her legal custodian without the custodian's consent; or the circumstances of the case strongly indicate that [the child] is likely to be abused or sexually exploited.

This act requires the OJJDP to conduct periodic national incidence studies to determine the actual number of children reported missing and the number of missing children recovered for a given year. This requirement is being met through the National Incidence Studies of Missing, Abducted, Runaway, and

Thrownaway Children in America (NISMART). NISMART has completed its second in-depth study of this population and has identified six episode types of missing children.

 The six episode types of missing children included in the NISMART-2 study are: missing benign explanation; missing involuntary, lost or injured; runaway/thrownaway; nonfamily abduction; stereotypical kidnapping; and family abduction.

The latest available data from NISMART is from 2002. Comparisons of NISMART-1 and NISMART-2 find no evidence of an increase in the incidence of missing children (Snyder and Sickmund 2006, 46). This report also states that one third of all kidnap victims were younger than 18. The kidnappings of children younger than 12 were most likely to be committed by a family member, primarily a parent. Among female victims ages 15 to 17, about two thirds were kidnapped by an acquaintance and one quarter were kidnapped by a stranger (Snyder and Sickmund 2006, 40). Frequently the greatest challenge with missing children cases is determining the cause.

NISMART-2 defines a missing child in two ways: those who are missing from their caretakers (caretaker missing) and those who are missing from their caretakers and reported to an agency for help in locating them (reported missing) (Sedlak et al. 2002, 3). According to NISMART-2 (Sedlak et al. 2002), in 1999 an estimated 1,315,600 were caretaker missing children; 797,500 were reported missing children. Table 5.2 summarizes statistics for these two types of missing children and the episode type involved.

Missing Benign Explanation

A missing benign explanation episode occurs when a child's whereabouts are unknown to the child's caretaker and this causes the caretaker to (1) be alarmed, (2) try to locate the child and (3) contact the police about the episode for any reason, as long as the child was not lost, injured, abducted, victimized or classified as runaway/thrownaway (Sedlak et al. 2002, 4).

Missing Involuntary, Lost or Injured

A one-year count revealed an estimated 198,300 children were involuntarily missing, lost or injured (Sedlak et al. 2002, 10). A missing involuntary, lost or injured episode occurs when a child's whereabouts are unknown to the child's caretaker and this causes the caretaker to be alarmed for at least one hour and tries to locate the child under one of two conditions: (1) the child was trying to get home or make contact with the caretaker but was unable to do so because the child was lost, stranded or injured; or (2) the child was too young to know how to return home or make contact with the caretaker (Sedlak et al. 2002, 4).

Runaway/Thrownaway

A one-year count indicated an estimated 1,682,900 children either ran away or were thrown away (Sedlak et al. 2002, 10). "A **runaway** incident occurs when a child leaves home without permission and stays away overnight, or a child 14 years old or younger (or older and mentally incompetent) who is away from home chooses not to return when supposed to and stays away overnight; or

Table 5.2   Reasons Children Become Missing

Episode Type	Estimated Total*	95% Confidence Interval[†]	Percent[‡]	Rate per 1,000 Children in U.S. Population (N = 70,172,700)
Caretaker Missing Children (n = 1,315,600)				
Nonfamily abduction	33,000[§]	(2,000–64,000)	3[§]	0.47[§]
Family abduction	117,200	(79,000–155,400)	9	1.67
Runaway/thrownaway	628,900	(48,000–776,900)	48	8.96
Missing involuntary, lost or injured	198,300	(124,800–271,800)	15	2.83
Missing benign explanation	374,700	(289,900–459,500)	28	5.34
Reported Missing Children (n = 797,500)				
Nonfamily abduction	12,100[§]	(< 100–31,000)	2[§]	0.17[§]
Family abduction	56,500	(22,600–90,400)	7	0.81
Runaway/thrownaway	357,600	(238,000–477,200)	45	5.10
Missing involuntary, lost or injured	61,900	(19,700–104,100)	8	0.88
Missing benign explanation	340,500	(256,000–425,000)	43	4.85

NOTE: All estimates are rounded to the nearest 100.

*Estimates total more than 1,135,600, and percents total more than 100 because children who had multiple episodes are included in every row that applies to them.

[†]The 95 percent confidence interval indicates that if the study were repeated 100 times, 95 of the replications would produce estimates within the ranges noted.

[‡]Nonfamily abduction includes stereotypical kidnapping.

[§]Estimate is based on an extremely small sample of cases; therefore, its precision and confidence interval are unreliable.

SOURCE: Andrea J. Sedlak, David Finkelhor, Heather Hammer, and Dana J. Schultz. 2006 (October). *National Estimates of Missing Children: An Overview*, p. 6. Washington, DC: OJJDP, National Incidence Studies of Missing, Abducted, Runaway and Thrownaway Children (NISMART).

when a child 15 years old or older who is away from home chooses not to return and stays away two nights" (Sedlak et al. 2002, 4).

When adolescents cannot cope with a relationship in a family, they may perceive their only recourse to be running away. Historically, running away has been considered a behavioral manifestation of psychopathology. In fact, the American Psychiatric Association has classified the "runaway reaction" as a specific disorder.

Many runaways are insecure, depressed, unhappy and impulsive with low self-esteem. Typical runaways report conflict with parents, alienation from them, rejection and hostile control, and lack of warmth, affection and parental support. Running away may compound their problems. Many become streetwise and turn to drugs, crime, prostitution or other illegal activities.

Problems reported by youths seeking services from runaway and homeless youth centers included such family problems as emotional conflict at home, parents who were too strict and physical abuse and neglect. The National Council of Juvenile and Family Court Judges has stated: "We know that many [youths] who are on the streets are there as a result of sound rational choices they have made for their own safety and welfare, such as avoiding physical abuse, sexual abuse, or extreme neglect at home." For 21 percent of the 1.7 million runaway/thrownaway youths, their episode involved physical or sexual

© Joel Gordon

Running away from home is seen by many youths as a solution to problems at home or school.

abuse at home before leaving or fear of such abuse upon their return (Snyder and Sickmund 2006, 45). Other problems reported included parental drug or alcohol abuse, mental health problems within the family and domestic violence between the parents.

The two most frequently mentioned personal problems were a poor self-image and depression. Other problems included issues at school such as truancy, poor grades and not getting along with teachers; drug or alcohol abuse; and being in trouble with the justice system.

A **thrownaway** incident occurs when a child is asked or told to leave home by a parent or other household adult, no adequate alternative care is arranged for the child by a household adult and the child is out of the household overnight; or when a child who is away from home is prevented from returning home by a parent or other household adult, no adequate alternative care is arranged for the child by a household adult and the child is out of the household overnight (Sedlak et al. 2002, 4).

Very few runaways are homeless and living on the street, and most do not go far: "Survival and safety issues are fairly minimal for the large majority of juveniles who stay with friends or relatives. However a minority face serious risks, such as exploitation by predatory adults, involvement in criminal activity, drug abuse or unsafe sex; health problems stemming from exposure to the elements, poor nutrition and other effects of living on the street; and a higher risk of depression and suicide" (Dedel 2006, 3).

Nonfamily Abduction

A one-year estimate shows approximately 58,200 children were abducted by nonfamily members (Sedlak et al. 2002, 10). A nonfamily abduction occurs when a nonfamily perpetrator takes a child by physical force or threat of bodily harm or detains a child for at least one hour in an isolated place by physical force or threat of bodily harm without lawful authority or parental permission; or when a child who is younger than 15 years old or is mentally incompetent, without lawful authority or parental permission, is taken or detained by or voluntarily accompanies a nonfamily perpetrator who conceals the child's whereabouts, demands ransom or expresses the intention to keep the child permanently (Sedlak et al. 2002, 4).

Stereotypical Kidnapping

A **stereotypical kidnapping** occurs when a stranger or slight acquaintance perpetrates a nonfamily abduction in which the child is detained overnight, transported at least 50 miles, held for ransom, abducted with intent to keep the child permanently or killed (Sedlak et al. 2002, 4). One third of all kidnap victims known to law enforcement are under age 18, and the risk of kidnapping increases substantially for female juveniles after age 9 (Snyder and Sickmund 2006, 40).

Family Abduction

One-year estimates from NISMART-2 indicate that approximately 203,900 children are abducted by family members. A family abduction occurs when, in violation of a custody order, a decree or other legitimate custodial rights, a member of the child's family, or someone acting on behalf of a family member, takes or fails to return a child, and the child is concealed or transported out of state with the intent to prevent contact or deprive the caretaker of custodial rights indefinitely or permanently. For a child 15 or older, unless mentally incompetent, there must be evidence that the perpetrator used physical force or threat of bodily harm to take or detain the child (Sedlak et al. 2002, 4).

Sedlak et al. (2002, 10) note, "Contrary to the common assumption that abduction is a principal reason why children become missing, the NISMART-2 findings indicate that only a small minority of missing children were abducted, and most of these children were abducted by family members (9 percent of all caretaker missing children)."

International Parental Kidnapping   If a child is abducted from this country to another, the laws, policies and procedures of the foreign country determine whether and how the child will be returned (*A Family Resource Guide* 2007, 4). The following warning signs may indicate the threat of an international kidnapping: previously abducted or threatened to abduct the child; citizenship in another country and strong emotional or cultural ties to that country; friends or family living in another country; no strong ties to the child's home state; a strong support network; and no financial reason to stay in the country.

All 50 states and the District of Columbia have laws that treat parental kidnapping as a felony under specified circumstances: "Generally, abductions and retentions that involve crossing state lines or leaving the country are felonies"

(*A Family Resource Guide* 2007, 77). Friends, relatives and others who assist the abduction or who retain or conceal the child can often be criminally charged as accomplices or co-conspirators. In addition, two federal criminal statutes apply in international family abduction cases: the Fugitive Felon Act and the International Parental Kidnapping Crime Act (*A Family Resource Guide*, 78).

A Child Abduction Response Team (CART)

Several compelling reasons exist for having a Child Abduction Response Team (CART): "Most abductions are short term and involve sexual assault; 44 percent of abducted children who are killed are killed in less than one hour of being abducted; 75 percent are killed within 3 hours of being abducted; 91 percent are killed within 24 hours of being abducted; 99 percent of those murdered are killed within 7 days of being abducted" (Swager 2007, 137). Because of the time-sensitive nature of child abductions, the mission of a CART is to bring expert resources to child abduction cases quickly. Such a team typically consists of seasoned, experienced officers from around the region, each with a preplanned response related to that officer's field of expertise, and may include mounted patrol, all-terrain vehicles (ATVs), helicopters, and K9s—whatever resources are readily available. A CART might also include a family coordinator, a media coordinator, a crime scene coordinator, a street patrol coordinator, an interview team coordinator, a research coordinator, a search coordinator and a coordinator of other agencies involved (Moore 2006, 130).

AMBER Alert

Another approach to a missing child report is the AMBER Alert. The AMBER (America's Missing: Broadcast Emergency Response) Alert network was established in 1996 in response to the death of Amber Hagerman, who was abducted while riding her bicycle in Arlington, Texas, and then brutally murdered. AMBER Alerts are emergency messages broadcast when a law enforcement agency determines that a child has been abducted and is in imminent danger. The broadcasts include information that could assist in the child's recovery, including a physical description about the child and abductor. All 50 states now have statewide AMBER Alert plans ("Department of Justice Marks 11th Anniversary" 2007, 1). These alerts may be put on television and radio stations, electronic message systems on highways and other media. In most law enforcement departments, the public information officer is the communication cornerstone of this network: "The public information officer (PIO) should be the primary point of contact for the media. This means that the PIO should be responsible for conveying all information from the law enforcement agency to the public via the media and for fielding inquiries from journalists and the public" (*AMBER Alert: Best Practices Guide* 2006).

According to AMBER Alert's home page, the program is a proven success and has helped rescue more than 426 children nationwide. In several jurisdictions throughout the country, the AMBER Alert system is being expanded to cell phone customers, with subscribers able to register through their participating carriers' Web sites to receive text messages (Kallestad 2005). The program is also being expanded to include tribal law enforcement agencies. For more information, visit the Criminal Justice Companion Web site at cengagebrain.com, then access the web links for this chapter.

An AMBER Alert sign engages the driving public as vital partners to law enforcement in the search for abducted children. Such advisories have met with considerable success in retrieving children alive.

Responsibility for Investigating Missing and Exploited Children

The primary responsibility for investigating missing and exploited children falls at the local and state levels, but the federal government is also involved. Two federal agencies in particular have responsibilities in the area but approach the problem from very different perspectives.

> The Department of Health and Human Services through its Administration for Children and Families (ACF) and the Justice Department through OJJDP have concurrent jurisdiction for missing and exploited children.

Both agencies' authority comes from the 1974 Juvenile Justice and Delinquency Prevention (JJDP) Act, amended in 1978 by the Runaway and Homeless Youth (RHY) Act. The RHY Act took a "social welfare, emergency care" approach to the problem of runaways, playing down law enforcement solutions. This approach is the focus of the ACF, which emphasizes facilitating counseling and communication efforts between the runaway and the family.

The OJJDP approach is very different, focusing on the challenges that runaways present to law enforcement and the juvenile justice system. This approach acknowledges that secure custodial care is often the only practical response to runaway juveniles and the dangers they pose—to themselves and to the community.

The ACF takes a social welfare, emergency care approach to missing children; the OJJDP focuses on the challenges that missing children present to law enforcement and the juvenile justice system.

Clearly, these two approaches are often at odds with each other. Therefore, coordination between the two agencies is vital if the runaway problem is to be effectively addressed.

Bullying

Bullying or being bullied are often considered fairly normal rites of passage for children: "Bullying, a form of violence among children, is common on school playgrounds, in neighborhoods, and in homes throughout the United States and around the world. Often occurring out of the presence of adults or in front of adults who fail to intercede, bullying has long been considered an inevitable and, in some ways, uncontrollable part of growing up" (Ericson 2001, 1). Most people can recall from their own childhood either being teased and taunted at school or being the one who picked on other kids.

Bullying, like other forms of behavior, occurs along a continuum from very mild, relatively benign deeds to more serious, even life-threatening acts. To the question, "What is bullying?" Ericson (2001, 1) responds, "Bullying among children encompasses a variety of negative acts carried out repeatedly over time. It involves a real or perceived imbalance of power, with the more powerful child or group attacking those who are less powerful. Bullying can take three forms: physical (hitting, kicking, spitting, pushing, taking personal belongings); verbal (taunting, malicious teasing, name calling, making threats); and psychological (spreading rumors, manipulating social relationships, or engaging in social exclusion, extortion, or intimidation)." The spread of technology and social media has led to a fourth variant known as cyberbullying, or bullying through electronic means such as cell phones or computers.

Results of a recent study revealed that verbal bullying was the most prevalent form of bullying (53.6 percent), followed by relational (51.4 percent), physical (20.8 percent) and electronic (13.6 percent) (Wang, Iannotti, and Nansel 2009). Gender differences in bullying involvement were also noted, with boys more involved in the physical and verbal forms of bullying and girls more involved in the relational form. Regarding cyberbullying, boys were more likely to be perpetrators and girls more like to be victims. A rather expected result of this study was the association between higher parental support and lower juvenile involvement across all forms and classifications of bullying. An interesting finding was the relationship between the number of friends a juvenile has and their involvement in bullying: "Having more friends was associated with more bullying and less victimization for the physical, verbal, and relational forms but was not associated with cyberbullying" (Wang, Iannotti, and Nansel 2009, 368).

The negative effects of bullying are widespread and include fear of going to school, interference with school achievement, loneliness, humiliation, insecurity, hindered ability to develop prosocial skills or make friends, difficulty making emotional or social adjustments and diminishing overall psychological well-being of both victims and perpetrators (Ericson 2001; Wang, Iannotti, and Nansel 2009). Types of antisocial behavior linked to bullying behavior include vandalism, shoplifting, truancy, dropping out of school and substance abuse (Ericson 2001).

Depression has also been associated with all four forms of bullying; however, recent research has revealed a unique association between cyberbullying and depression, one that is distinct from the patterns discerned among perpetrators and victims involved in the traditional forms of bullying. Results of past studies have indicated that the highest rate of depression occurs among bully-victims or those youth who both bully others and are bullied themselves. However, according to new research, victims of cyberbullying are at a greater risk of developing depression than are those who bully them (Wang, Nansel, and Iannotti 2011). The researchers note that their results highlight the need for further study on the effects of cyberbullying.

Some assert that the anonymity afforded to cyberbullies through such technology has allowed for an increase in the viciousness of verbal and psychological attacks, although research to date has yet to substantiate these claims with any empirical evidence. Cyberbullying has also been implicated as a contributing factor in several highly publicized incidents of suicide involving youth, a provocative proposition given the aforementioned research regarding cyberbullying and depression.

Youths and Suicide

One final and devastating way in which youths become victims is by the taking of their own lives. Youths ages 7 to 17 are about as likely to be victims of suicide as they are to be victims of homicide (Snyder and Sickmund 2006, 25). In most states, juvenile suicides are more common than juvenile homicides (26).

 The leading cause of youth suicide is untreated depression.

About 5 percent of children and adolescents in the general population suffer from depression at any given point in time. Major signs of depression in adolescents include frequent sadness, tearfulness or crying; hopelessness; decreased interest in activities or inability to enjoy previously favorite activities; persistent boredom; low energy; social isolation and poor communication; low self-esteem and guilt; extreme sensitivity to rejection or failure; increased irritability, anger or hostility; difficulty with relationships; frequent complaints of physical illnesses such as headaches and stomachaches; frequent absences from school or poor performance in school; poor concentration; a major change in eating or sleeping patterns; talk of or efforts to run away from home; and thoughts or expressions of suicide or self-destruction (*The Depressed Child* 2004, 1).

Sometimes depression may not be readily apparent. The person may try to cover it up with overactivity, preoccupation with trivia or acting-out behavior such as delinquency, the use of drugs or sexual promiscuity. With or without overt signs of depressions, the possibility of suicide must be considered.

Adolescent suicide is the third leading cause of death among 14- to 24-year-olds and the sixth leading cause of death for 5- to 14-year-olds in the United States (*Teen Suicide* 2004, 1). It is estimated that 500,000 teens attempt suicide every year with 5,000 succeeding. According to the *Sourcebook of Criminal Justice Statistics*, the suicide rate in 2007 for youths 10 to 14 years old was 0.89

per 100,000, down from the peak rate of 1.72 in 1995, and the suicide rate of 15- to 19-year-olds was 6.91 per 100,000, down from a peak rate of 11.14 in 1990. According to the *Youth Risk Behavior Surveillance System* (Eaton et al. 2010), 13.8 percent of high school students seriously considered committing suicide in 2009, 10.9 percent made a suicide plan, and 6.3 percent actually attempted suicide.

 Warning signs of suicide include threatening to kill oneself; preparing for death by giving away favorite possessions, writing good-bye letters or making a will; expressing hopelessness for the future and giving up on oneself; and talking as if no one else cares.

Given the dire consequences that might result from child maltreatment, efforts to prevent or reduce victimization of children and youth are critical.

Exemplary Programs to Prevent or Reduce Child Victimization

Numerous programs are aimed at preventing or reducing victimization of the nation's children and youths. Project Safe Childhood (PSC), the program to safeguard the nation's children and youths from exploitation via the Internet, was discussed earlier in the chapter. One extremely successful early intervention program is the Nurse-Family Partnership.

Nurse-Family Partnership

The Nurse-Family Partnership (NFP) is a program that targets low-income, unmarried, first-time mothers. It connects specially trained nurse practitioners with expectant mothers before their babies are born in an effort to achieve healthy pregnancies and, consequently, healthy babies, with the expectation that this intervention will help achieve long-term improvements in the lives of at-risk families. The intervention process is effective because it concentrates on developing therapeutic relationships within the family and works across five broad domains of family functioning: parental roles, family and friend support, health (physical and mental), home and neighborhood environment and major life events (e.g., pregnancy planning, education, employment).

The program, founded by Dr. David Olds, seeks to help new mothers become better parents, build a strong network of support for mother and child, make homes safe places for babies to live and play, obtain referrals for health care and child care, find ways to continue their education and develop job skills and set family goals for both mother and baby. Although the primary client is the first-time mother, ultimately her baby and all the members of her support system (e.g., friends, parents, boyfriend, child's father) become involved in the program. Nurses begin visiting first-time mothers during pregnancy and continue with weekly or biweekly visits until the child is 2 years old. During home visits, nurses promote the physical, cognitive and social-emotional development of the children and provide general support and instruction in parenting skills.

The NFP currently serves 20,000 families annually and is expanding. The program has undergone extensive testing and evaluation through nearly 30 years of ongoing, longitudinal, randomized trials. Meta-analysis of these scientifically controlled studies has found consistent, dramatic benefits for first-time, low-income mothers and their children, including improved prenatal health, fewer childhood injuries, fewer subsequent pregnancies, increased intervals between births, increased maternal employment and improved school readiness. NFP has been nationally recognized by the Prevention Research Center for the Promotion of Human Development, the Brookings Institute, the Partnership for America's Economic Success, the RAND Corporation, Helping America's Youth (HAY), Blueprints for Violence Prevention, the Coalition for Evidence-Based Policy and the Office of Juvenile Justice and Delinquency Prevention.

Specific program effects when the child reaches age 15 include benefits to mothers (61 percent fewer arrests, 72 percent fewer convictions and 978 fewer days in jail), benefits to children (48 percent reduction in child abuse and neglect, 59 percent reduction in arrests and 90 percent reduction in adjudication as a person in need of supervision for incorrigible behavior) and benefits to society ($17,180 lifetime cost savings for every NFP mother and child and $5.70 saved for every $1 invested in high-risk families) (Lee, Aos, and Miller 2008).

Building Peaceful Families

Building Peaceful Families (BPF) is a Silicon Valley, California, organization devoted to helping families build violence-free homes through training and through events celebrating the value of responsible, positive parenting, with a focus on fathers: "BPF operates from the philosophy that while the desire to be a father may be innate, what a responsible father does is learned; key to this learning is understanding that a responsible father is not abusive to his children or to the mother of his children" ("Building Peaceful Families" 2007, 13). A key initiative of BPF is the Bay Area Fatherhood Conference, designed both for fathers who are parenting or attempting to parent their children and for fathers who have little or no contact with their children. The 2006 conference brought together nearly 650 people for a daylong celebration of the importance of fatherhood. Participants included fathers on probation or parole; fathers with cases in family court, dependency court and juvenile court; and fathers in special programs run by the Department of Corrections.

Safe Kids/Safe Streets

Safe Kids/Safe Streets (SK/SS) is an initiative funded by the OJJDP within the Department of Justice to help communities reduce child abuse and neglect and the aftereffects of such treatment through collaborative, communitywide efforts. These strategies are grounded in research about the causes and correlates of juvenile delinquency in addition to principles of effective prevention and intervention techniques (Cronin et al. 2006, 1). This foundation allows SK/SS to effectively pursue the goals of broadening access to available resources, strengthening primary prevention efforts, improving services for families through empowerment and maintaining accountability for actions. Advisory committees identify and prioritize needs in the planning stages. They then restructure and strengthen the existing system because SK/SS wants

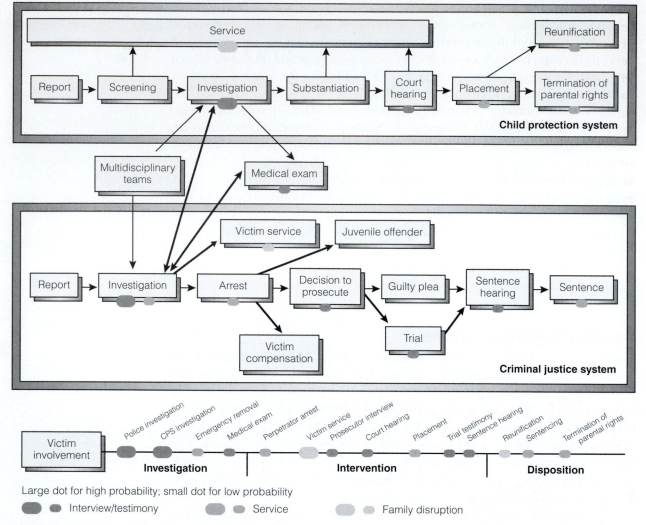

Figure 5.4 The Juvenile Victim Justice System

SOURCE: David Finkelhor, Theodore P. Cross, and Elise N. Cantor. 2005 (December). *How the Justice System Responds to Juvenile Victims: A Comprehensive Model*, p. 3. Washington, DC: OJJDP Juvenile Justice Bulletin. (NCJ 210951)

communities to build on their existing resources. SK/SS promotes community ownership and responsibility.

SK/SS encourages a proactive rather than reactive strategy. By establishing an integrated system with an emphasis on prevention efforts, the community should improve its response to the abuse and neglect of children and adolescents with the goal of breaking the cycle of childhood victimization and subsequent delinquent and criminal behavior.

The Juvenile Victim Justice System

In addition to programs to help prevent or reduce the victimization of the country's children and youths, the justice system has responded to juvenile victims by developing a comprehensive juvenile victim justice system. Finkelhor, Cross and Cantor (2005) describe the juvenile victim justice system as a complex set of agencies and institutions that include police, prosecutors, criminal and civil courts, child protection agencies, children's advocacy centers and victim services and mental health agencies. The system has a structure and sequence, but its operation, despite the thousands of cases it handles every year, is not as widely recognized and understood as is the operation of the more familiar juvenile offender justice system. Figure 5.4 depicts the juvenile victim justice system.

According to Finkelhor, Cross and Cantor (2005, 2), one central complexity of the juvenile victim justice system is it encompasses two distinct subsystems, the criminal justice system and the child protection system. These systems are typically considered separate, but the interaction between cases involving juvenile victims is considerable and increasing.

 ## Summary

- Maltreated youths are at an increased risk for performing poorly in school and displaying symptoms of mental illness; girls are at increased risk of becoming pregnant, using drugs and engaging in serious and violent delinquency.
- Child neglect has been identified as the biggest single cause of death of young children, followed by physical abuse.
- Neglect is the most common form of child maltreatment and may be fatal.
- The homes of neglected children are often disorganized and dysfunctional, with parents who ignore their children or who set bad examples for them.
- Typically child abuse/neglect laws have three components: (1) criminal definitions and penalties, (2) a mandate to report suspected cases and (3) a civil process for removing a child from the abusive or neglectful environment.
- Three of the primary risk factors for child abuse are domestic violence, poverty and individual temperamental factors and characteristics of a child.
- Violence may lead to more violence. Children who are abused are more likely to be delinquent and violent themselves.
- Child abuse has been directly linked with delinquency.
- Youths are victims of crime twice as often as are those over age 25.
- The six episode types of missing children included in the NISMART-2 study are: missing benign explanation; missing involuntary, lost or injured; runaway/thrownaway; nonfamily abduction; stereotypical kidnapping; and family abduction.
- The Department of Health and Human Services through its Administration for Children and Families (ACF) and the Justice Department through OJJDP have concurrent jurisdiction for missing and exploited children. The ACF takes a social welfare, emergency care approach to missing children; the OJJDP focuses on the challenges that missing children present to law enforcement and the juvenile justice system.
- The leading cause of youth suicide is untreated depression.
- Warning signs of suicide include threatening to kill oneself; preparing for death by giving away favorite possessions, writing good-bye letters or making a will; expressing hopelessness for the future and giving up on oneself; and talking as if no one else cares.

Discussion Questions

1. What causes parents or caretakers of children to abuse them?
2. Do your state laws against child abuse and neglect contain two or more of these components: nonaccidental physical injury, physical neglect, emotional abuse or neglect, sexual abuse, abandonment?
3. Of all abuses, which has the most lasting effect? Why?
4. How can a society cope with child abuse and strive to control it?
5. What protection does a child have against abuse? Should the courts rescind parental rights in abuse cases?
6. Do courts act in the best interests of children when they allow abused children to remain with the family?
7. What are the strongest predictors of future delinquent or violent behavior?
8. Are the definitions of *child abuse* and *child neglect* the key elements in determining the volume of child abuse cases in various jurisdictions? How is the volume of cases determined?
9. In your area, how are children protected from abuse? Can the system be improved? How?
10. Are the six episode types of missing children identified by NISMART-2 helpful?

References

"Adam Walsh Act Signed into Law." 2006. *The JRSA Forum* (December): 5.

Agnew, Robert. 2002. "Experienced, Vicarious, and Anticipated Strain: An Exploratory Study on Physical Victimization and Delinquency." *Justice Quarterly* (December): 603–632.

AMBER Alert: Best Practices Guide for Public Information Officers. 2006 (July). Washington, DC: Department of Justice. (NCJ 212703)

American Medical Association. 1985. "AMA Diagnostic and Treatment Guidelines Concerning Child Abuse and Neglect." *Journal of the American Medical Association* 254 (6): 796–800.

America's Children, America's Challenge: Promoting Opportunity for the Next Generation. 2011. The 2011 KIDS COUNT Data Book. Baltimore: Annie E. Casey Foundation.

Baum, Katrina. 2005 (August). *Juvenile Victimization and Offending, 1993–2003*. Washington, DC: Bureau of Justice Statistics Special Report. (NCJ 209468)

"Building Peaceful Families." 2007. *Synergy* (Winter): 13–14.

Child Maltreatment 2009. 2010. Washington, DC: U.S. Department of Health and Human Services, Administration for Children and Families, Administration on Children, Youth and Families, Children's Bureau.

Child Welfare Information Gateway. 2008. *Child Abuse and Neglect Fatalities: Statistics and Interventions*. Washington, DC: U.S. Department of Health and Human Services, Administration on Children, Youth and Families. http://www.childwelfare.gov/pubs/factsheets/fatality.cfm (accessed October 21, 2008).

"Children at Higher Risk in Nontraditional Homes." 2007. Associated Press, November 18, 2007. http://www.msnbc.msn.com/id/21838575/ (accessed October 21, 2008).

"A Closer Look at the Adam Walsh Child Protection and Safety Act." 2006. *NCJA Justice Bulletin* (October): 3.

Cohen, Patricia, Elizabeth Smailes, and Jocelyn Brown. 2004. *Effects of Childhood Maltreatment on Adult Arrests in a General Population Sample*. Washington, DC: Department of Justice. (NCJ 199707)

Collins, Michelle K. 2007. "Child Pornography: A Closer Look." *The Police Chief* (March): 40–47.

Conroy, Elizabeth, Louisa Degenhardt, Richard P. Mattick, and Elliot C. Nelson. 2009. "Child Maltreatment as a Risk Factor for Opiod Dependence: Comparison of Family Characteristics and Type and Severity of Child Maltreatment with a Matched Control Group." *Child Abuse & Neglect* 33 (6): 343–352.

Cronin, Roberta, Francis Gragg, Dana Schultz, and Karla Eisen. 2006 (November). *Lessons Learned from Safe Kids/Safe Streets*. Washington, DC: U.S. Department of Justice, Office of Juvenile Justice and Delinquency Prevention. (NCJ 213682)

Cullerton-Sen, Crystal, Adam R. Cassidy, Dianna Murray-Close, Danta Cicchetti, Nicki R. Crick, and Fred A. Rogosch. 2008. "Childhood Maltreatment and the Development of Relational and Physical Aggression: The Importance of a Gender-Informed Approach." *Child Development* 79 (6): 1736–1752.

Dedel, Kelly. 2006 (February). *Juvenile Runaways*. Washington, DC: Office of Community Oriented Policing Services.

"Department of Justice Marks 11th Anniversary of AMBER Alert." 2007. *OJJDP News @ a Glance* (January/February): 1.

The Depressed Child. 2004 (July). Washington, DC: American Academy of Child and Adolescent Psychiatry.

Eaton, Danice K., Laura Kann, Steve Kinchen, Shari Shanklin, James Toss, Joseph Hawkins, William A. Harris, Richard Lowry, Tim McManus, David Chyen, et al. 2010. *Youth Risk Behavior Surveillance— United States, 2009*. Atlanta, GA: Centers for Disease Control and Prevention, Morbidity and Mortality Weekly Report, Surveillance Summaries, 59 (SS-5, June 4).

English, Diana J., Cathy Spatz Widom, and Carol Brandford. 2002 (February 1). *Childhood Victimization and Delinquency, Adult Criminality, and Violent Criminal Behavior: A Replication and Extension*. Washington, DC: National Institute of Justice. (NCJ 192291)

Ericson, Nils. *Addressing the Problem of Juvenile Bullying.* 2001 (June). Washington, DC: Office of Juvenile Justice and Delinquency Prevention, Fact Sheet #27.

A Family Resource Guide on International Parental Kidnapping. 2007 (January). Washington, DC: Office of Juvenile Justice and Delinquency Prevention. (NCJ 215476)

Finkelhor, David, Theodore P. Cross, and Elise N. Cantor. 2005 (December). *How the Justice System Responds to Juvenile Victims: A Comprehensive Model.* Washington, DC: OJJDP Juvenile Justice Bulletin.

Geraghty, Michael. 2007. "The Technical Aspects of Computer-Facilitated Crimes against Children." *The Police Chief* (March): 30–33.

Hess, Kären M., and Christine H. Orthmann. 2012. *Criminal Investigation.* 10th ed. Clifton Park, NY: Delmar.

Human Trafficking of Children in the United States. 2007 (August 6). Washington, DC: Office of Safe and Drug-Free Schools. http://www.ed.gov/about/offices/list/osdfs/factsheet.html (accessed October 23, 2008).

Kallestad, Brent. 2005. "Cellphone Users to Get AMBER Alert." *The Miami Health Herald,* August 5.

Karmen, Andrew. 2007. *Crime Victims: An Introduction to Victimology.* 5th ed. Belmont, CA: Wadsworth.

Kelleher, Kelly, William Gardner, Jeff Coben, Rick Barth, Jeff Edleson, and Andrea Hazen. 2006 (March). *Co-Occurring Intimate Partner Violence and Child Maltreatment: Local Policies/Practices and Relationships to Child Placement, Family Services and Residence.* Washington, DC: U.S. Department of Justice, unpublished report, Document No. 213503, Award No. 2002-WG-BX-0014.

Kim, Min Jung, Emiko A. Tajima, Todd I. Herrenkohl, and Bu Huang. 2009. "Early Childhood Maltreatment, Runaway Youths, and Risk of Delinquency and Victimization in Adolescence: A Mediational Model." *Social Work Research* 33 (1, March 1): 19–28.

Kitzmann, Katherine M., Noni K. Gaylord, Aimee R. Holt, and Erin D. Kenny. 2003. "Child Witnesses to Domestic Violence: A Meta-Analytic Review." *Journal of Consulting and Clinical Psychology* 71 (2): 339–352.

Lee, Stephanie, Steve Aos, and Marna Miller. 2008 (July). *Evidence-Based Programs to Prevent Children from Entering and Remaining in the Child Welfare System: Benefits and Costs for Washington.* Olympia: Washington State Institute for Public Policy, Document No. 08-07-3901.

Lemmon, John H. 2006. "The Effects of Maltreatment Recurrence and Child Welfare Services on Dimensions of Delinquency." *Criminal Justice Review* (March): 5–32.

Loeber, Rolf, Larry Kalb, and David Huizinga. 2001 (August). *Juvenile Delinquency and Serious Injury Victimization.* Washington, DC: OJJDP Juvenile Justice Bulletin. (NCJ 188676)

Maas, Carl D., Charles B. Fleming, Todd I. Herrenkohl, and Richard F. Catalano. 2010. "Childhood Predictors of Teen Dating Violence Victimization." *Violence & Victims* 25 (2):131–149.

McGee, Zina T., and Spencer R. Baker. 2002. "Impact of Violence on Problem Behavior among Adolescents." *Journal of Contemporary Criminal Justice* (February): 74–93.

McNulty, Paul J. 2007. "Project Safe Childhood." *The Police Chief* (March): 36–39.

Moore, Carole. 2006. "Missing Children Coordination." *Law Enforcement Technology* (July): 130.

National Center for Missing and Exploited Children. 2009. *2009 Annual Report.* http://www.ncmec.org/en_US/publications/NC171.pdf (accessed October 2, 2011).

National Center for Missing and Exploited Children. n.d. "General Information and Publications." n.d. http://www.ncmec.org/en_US/publications/NC21.pdf (accessed October 2, 2011).

National KIDS COUNT Program. 2011. Baltimore: Annie E. Casey Foundation. http://datacenter.kidscount.org/data/acrossstates/ (accessed September 30, 2011).

The National Strategy for Child Exploitation Prevention and Interdiction: A Report to Congress. 2010 (August). Washington, DC: U.S. Department of Justice.

NCIC Missing Person and Unidentified Person Statistics for 2010. 2010. Washington, DC: Federal Bureau of Investigation. http://www.fbi.gov/about-us/cjis/ncic/ncic-missing-person-and-unidentified-person-statistics-for-2010 (accessed October 2, 2011).

Nurse-Family Partnerships: Helping First-Time Parents. 2008. Denver, CO: Nurse-Family Partnership National Service Office Information Packet. http://www.nursefamilypartnership.org/ (accessed October 24, 2008).

Osteogenesis Imperfecta Foundation. n.d. *Child Abuse Issues.* http://www.oif.org/site/DocServer/_Child_Abuse__Child_Abuse_Issues.pdf?docID=7188 (accessed January 21, 2010).

Rebellion, Cesar J., and Karen Van Gundy. 2005. "Can Control Theory Explain the Link between Parental Physical Abuse and Delinquency? A Longitudinal Analysis." *Journal of Research in Crime and Delinquency* (August): 247–274.

Schreck, Christopher, Melissa W. Burek, Eric A. Stewart, and J. Mitchell Miller. 2007. "Distress and Violent Victimization among Young Adolescents: Early Puberty and the Social Interactionist Explanation." *Journal of Research in Crime and Delinquency* (November): 381–405.

Sedlak, Andrea J., David Finkelhor, Heather Hammer, and Dana J. Schultz. 2002 (October). *National Estimates of Missing Children: An Overview.* Washington, DC: Office of Juvenile Justice and Delinquency Prevention. (NCJ 196465)

Siegel, Jane A., and Linda M. Williams. 2003. "The Relationship between Child Sexual Abuse and Female

Delinquency and Crime: A Prospective Study." *Journal of Research in Crime and Delinquency* (February): 71–94.

Snyder, Howard N., and Melissa Sickmund. 2006 (March). *Juvenile Offenders and Victims: 2006 National Report.* Washington, DC: Office of Juvenile Justice Delinquency Prevention.

Sourcebook of Criminal Justice Statistics Online. http://www.albany.edu/sourcebook (accessed October 2, 2011).

Swager, Brent. 2007. "Tampa's Child Abduction Response Team." *Law and Order* (September): 134–138.

Teen Suicide. 2004 (July). Washington, DC: American Academy of Child and Adolescent Psychiatry.

Teplin, Linda A., Gary M. McClelland, Karen M. Abram, and Darinka Mileusnic. 2005. "Early Violent Death among Delinquent Youth: A Prospective Longitudinal Study." *Pediatrics* 115 (6): 1586.

Thompson, Richard, and Jiyoung K. Tabone. 2010. "The Impact of Early Alleged Maltreatment on Behavioral Trajectories." *Child Abuse & Neglect* 34, no. 12 (December): 907–916.

Tyler, Shannon, Kelly Allison, and Adam Winsler. 2006. "Child Neglect: Developmental Consequences, Intervention, and Policy Implications." *Child & Youth Care Forum* 35, no. 1 (February): 1–20.

Wang, Jing, Ronald J. Iannotti, and Tonja R. Nansel. 2009. "School Bullying among U.S. Adolescents: Physical, Verbal, Relational and Cyber." *Journal of Adolescent Health* 45, no. 4 (October): 368–375.

Wang, Jing, Tonja R. Nansel, and Ronald J. Iannotti. 2011. "Cyber and Traditional Bullying: Differential Association with Depression." *Journal of Adolescent Health* 48, no. 4 (April): 415–417.

Widom, Cathy S., and Michael G. Maxfield. 2001 (February). *An Update on the "Cycle of Violence."* Washington, DC: National Institute of Justice, Research in Brief. (NCJ 184894)

Wolfe, David A., Claire C. Crooks, Debbie Chiodo, and Peter Jaffe. 2009. "Child Maltreatment, Bullying, Gender-Based Harassment, and Adolescent Dating Violence: Making the Connections." *Psychology of Women Quarterly* (33): 21–24.

Wortley, Richard, and Stephen Smallbone. 2006 (May). *Child Pornography on the Internet.* Washington, DC: Office of Community Oriented Policing Services.

Cases Cited

People v. Green, 155 Mich. 524, 532, 119 N.W. 1087 (1909)

Prince v. Massachusetts, 321 U.S. 158 (1944)

Santosky v. Kramer, 455 U.S. 745 (1982)

Worthen v. State, 42 Md. App. 20, 399 A.2d 272 (1979)

Juvenile Offenders

6

Property crimes are the most common types of delinquency offenses, with data indicating that more than 25 percent of all arrests for property crimes are of juveniles.

© Ole Graf/zefa/Corbis RF

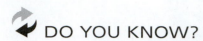
DO YOU KNOW?

- What acts are classified as status offenses in most states?
- Whether the trend for status offense arrests is increasing or decreasing?
- Which delinquency offenses result in the highest number of juvenile arrests?
- Whether the trend for juvenile arrests for property crimes is increasing or decreasing?
- Whether violent juvenile crime is increasing or decreasing?

- What two general trajectories for youth violence are identified by the surgeon general?
- When most youth violence begins and ends?
- How boys who own guns for protection differ from those who do not or who own guns for sport relative to delinquent activity?
- How public health and juvenile justice view violence?

CAN YOU DEFINE?

binge drinking

chronic juvenile offender

contagion delinquent

deviance

expressive violence

instrumental violence

rave

recidivism

serious child delinquent

serious juvenile offender

violent juvenile offender

CHAPTER OUTLINE

Introduction

The juvenile justice system is charged with handling a broad spectrum of youths labeled as "offenders," from those who smoke cigarettes and stay out too late at night (status offenses), to those who vandalize and steal others' property, to those who commit violent crimes against others but are too young to transfer to adult criminal court. An unfortunate reality is that many of these offenders first had contact with "the system" as victims, as discussed in the previous chapter. In some cases, the prevalence and accumulation of risk factors (Chapter 4) place children on a path of antisocial behavior and delinquency, where they become ensnared in the system as a juvenile offender.

An Overview of Juvenile Offenses

Juvenile "offenders" is a broad category that encompasses youth engaged in a wide range of activities, from status offenses, such as liquor law and curfew violations, to property crimes, to serious violent offenses. These three general offense types provide a natural division in which to discuss juvenile misbehavior. And, as will be seen, the number of youths engaged in the various types of offending varies considerably.

According to Federal Bureau of Investigation (FBI) data, 1,288,615 arrests involving juveniles (persons under age 18) were made in 2010, 349,695 of which involved persons under age 15 (*Crime in the United States, 2010*, 2011). The number of juveniles arrested in 2010 was nearly 10 percent lower than the number arrested in 2009, 22 percent lower than the number arrested in 2006 and 23.5 percent lower than the number of juveniles arrested in 2001, reflecting the continued downward trend in juvenile crime after peaking in 1994. Table 6.1 shows the total number of arrests in 2010, by age, including those involving juveniles. Property crimes continue to head the list in terms of the number of juvenile arrests. Note, however, in Table 6.1 that arrests may be made for conduct that falls outside the parameters of *delinquency*; that is, status offenses are often included in juvenile arrest data.

Status Offenders and Offenses

The origin of status offenses in the United States predates the Constitution by more than a century. One of the first such laws—the Massachusetts Stubborn Child Law, enacted in 1646—addressed incorrigibility and allowed parents to bring disobedient children before the court. Execution was a permissible sentence for those children judged to be unrepentant and beyond parental control (Tyler and Segady 2000). Reformers in the early nineteenth century criticized the harsh sanctions placed on wayward, yet noncriminal, children and began advocating for a system that treated such youth with rehabilitation instead of punishment. However, a clear separation was not made between serious offenses committed by juveniles (delinquent acts) and noncriminal conduct indicative of a child being beyond parental control (status offenses) until the middle of the twentieth century (McNamara 2008; Steinhart 1996).

A *status offense* is formally defined as "a minor's violation of the juvenile code by doing some act that would not be considered illegal if an adult did it, but that indicates that the minor is beyond parental control" (Garner 2006, 506). Although states differ in their specific legislation regarding status offenses, this category of youthful misbehavior generally includes incorrigibility (also called ungovernability), running away from home, truancy, curfew violations and underage drinking. The upper age limit for status offenses ranges from 16 to 19, but is 17 in most states. Anyone above the legal age who engages in the same behaviors would not be committing an offense. Historically, girls have been disproportionately sanctioned for status offenses, meaning they tend to be brought into the juvenile justice system more readily for committing these acts than do boys (Davis 2007).

Table 6.1 Number of Arrests in 2010, by Age

Offense charged	Total all ages	Ages under 15	Ages under 18	Ages 18 and over	Under 10	10-12	13-14	15	16	17	18	19	20	21
TOTAL	10,223,558	349,695	1,288,615	8,934,943	8,205	75,408	266,082	244,042	317,280	377,598	468,670	499,103	478,530	437,741
Total percent distribution[1]	100.0	3.4	12.6	87.4	0.1	0.7	2.6	2.4	3.1	3.7	4.6	4.9	4.7	4.3
Murder and nonnegligent manslaughter	8,667	73	784	7,883	0	7	66	119	239	353	543	581	515	523
Forcible rape	15,586	717	2,198	13,388	7	195	515	393	505	583	730	787	692	686
Robbery	87,771	3,936	21,110	66,661	36	558	3,342	4,179	6,052	6,943	7,724	6,938	5,769	4,751
Aggravated assault	318,340	10,917	35,001	283,339	302	2,849	7,766	6,355	8,245	9,484	11,378	12,065	12,199	12,710
Burglary	226,325	14,019	51,298	175,027	438	3,024	10,557	9,832	12,539	14,908	17,244	15,315	12,597	10,622
Larceny-theft	1,002,466	63,254	223,207	779,259	1,097	14,001	48,156	43,189	54,510	62,254	66,064	56,984	47,531	39,961
Motor vehicle theft	55,426	2,465	12,268	43,158	20	273	2,172	2,707	3,443	3,653	3,798	3,176	2,605	2,269
Arson	8,806	2,105	3,578	5,228	204	726	1,175	588	452	433	355	295	283	243
Violent crime[2]	430,364	15,643	59,093	371,271	345	3,609	11,689	11,046	15,041	17,363	20,375	20,371	19,175	18,670
Violent crime percent distribution[1]	100.0	3.6	13.7	86.3	0.1	0.8	2.7	2.6	3.5	4.0	4.7	4.7	4.5	4.3
Property crime[2]	1,293,023	81,843	290,351	1,002,672	1,759	18,024	62,060	56,316	70,944	81,248	87,461	75,770	63,016	53,095
Property crime percent distribution[1]	100.0	6.3	22.5	77.5	0.1	1.4	4.8	4.4	5.5	6.3	6.8	5.9	4.9	4.1
Other assaults	1,008,509	61,754	163,370	845,139	1,750	16,329	43,675	31,534	35,546	34,536	32,388	33,398	34,214	37,215
Forgery and counterfeiting	60,841	163	1,314	59,527	5	31	127	173	304	674	1,663	2,358	2,807	2,540
Fraud	144,956	756	4,585	140,371	20	117	619	690	1,203	1,936	3,403	4,725	5,173	4,764
Embezzlement	13,020	19	349	12,671	0	1	18	20	80	230	584	804	828	730
Stolen property; buying, receiving, possessing	74,313	2,561	11,608	62,705	46	414	2,101	2,335	3,069	3,643	4,973	4,621	3,935	3,602
Vandalism	197,850	23,470	60,591	137,259	1,091	6,369	16,010	11,416	12,822	12,883	12,098	10,397	9,180	8,684
Weapons; carrying, possessing, etc.	123,719	8,170	24,518	99,201	418	2,202	5,550	4,331	5,434	6,583	7,550	7,411	6,345	5,934
Prostitution and commercialized vice	48,281	91	804	47,477	1	5	85	112	208	393	1,392	1,885	2,159	2,068
Sex offenses (except forcible rape and prostitution)	56,332	4,896	10,147	46,185	181	1,392	3,323	1,738	1,767	1,746	2,303	2,110	1,843	1,854
Drug abuse violations	1,273,963	23,016	132,921	1,141,042	152	2,799	20,065	23,223	35,320	51,362	78,870	81,842	75,454	66,334

Offense													
Gambling	7,533	118	1,040	6,493	1	5	112	161	305	456	501	507	463	371
Offenses against the family and children	85,213	964	2,982	82,231	50	222	692	556	717	745	1,483	1,698	1,887	2,290
Driving under the influence	1,087,987	171	9,352	1,078,635	25	20	126	335	2,141	6,705	19,764	29,313	34,499	50,104
Liquor laws	400,608	7,451	75,889	324,719	54	653	6,744	11,353	21,337	35,748	65,538	73,739	62,188	10,469
Drunkenness	442,392	1,231	10,030	432,362	19	88	1,124	1,659	2,357	4,783	11,511	13,333	13,572	20,295
Disorderly conduct	482,991	44,481	121,276	361,715	616	10,720	33,145	24,762	26,675	25,358	21,257	19,305	18,748	22,141
Vagrancy	24,839	474	1,690	23,149	6	66	402	404	474	338	1,162	1,134	948	765
All other offenses (except traffic)	2,892,023	54,165	232,702	2,659,321	1,422	9,477	43,266	45,685	60,060	72,792	94,346	114,338	122,037	125,767
Suspicion	904	25	106	798	1	23	33	15	33	48	44	59	49	
Curfew and loitering law violations	73,897	18,233	73,897	—	243	2,864	15,126	16,178	21,443	18,043	—	—	—	—

[1] Because of rounding, the percentages may not add to 100.0.

[2] Violent crimes are offenses of murder and nonnegligent manslaughter, forcible rape, robbery and aggravated assault. Property crimes are offenses of burglary, larceny-theft, motor vehicle theft and arson.

DATA SOURCE: *Crime in the United States, 2010.* 2011. Washington, DC: Federal Bureau of Investigation, table 38.

Status offenses include actions such as running away, habitual truancy, violating curfew and underage drinking.

We will only briefly mention these offenses here because many were already discussed in previous chapters.

Running Away

The runaway problem was discussed in Chapter 5. However, running away is a status offense in most communities, so the juvenile justice system has jurisdiction in the matter and can act "in the best interest of the child." In 2008 the runaway arrest rate was 327 per 100,000 youth ages 10 to 17, which was 35 percent lower than the 1980 rate and 49 percent lower than the 1997 rate (*OJJDP Statistical Briefing Book* 2009). Fifty-six percent of the runaway arrests in 2008 involved females, and 32 percent involved juveniles under age 15.

Truancy

Truancy was first discussed in Chapter 4 as a risk factor for delinquency and has been identified as one of the top 10 problems in our nation's schools, with absentee rates as high as 30 percent in some cities. Truancy, which is defined by compulsory education laws passed at the state level, is the most frequent status offense for those under age 15. Although national data regarding truancy rates and numbers are limited, some data indicate that truancy peaks around grade 9 (ages 14–15), with the number of truants declining after age 16 (Heilbrunn 2007, 3). Most states have set the upper age of mandatory school attendance at 15, meaning once children turn 16 they may voluntarily withdraw from or "drop out" of school, so some researchers hypothesize that the decline in truancy rates for 16 to 18 year olds is likely partially attributable to the fact that those students most prone to truancy are more apt to drop out completely once they reach the mandatory attendance age (Heilbrunn 2007, 3). Students who have withdrawn from school cannot be counted as truant.

Curfew Violations

One of the most common status offenses is curfew violation. In 2010 an estimated 73,897 juvenile arrests were made for curfew and loitering violations (*Crime in the United States, 2010*, 2011). Twenty-five percent of curfew arrests in 2010 involved juveniles under age 15, and 30 percent involved females.

Our country's first "modern" curfew law was enacted in 1880 in Omaha, Nebraska, and other jurisdictions across the nation soon followed, spurred by the belief that such laws helped prevent juvenile crime and victimization (Fried 2001). The validity of such laws was cemented in public consciousness when President Benjamin Harrison declared juvenile curfews to be "the most important municipal regulation for the protection of the children of American homes, from the vices of the street" (Collins and Kearns 2001, 390; "Juvenile Curfews" 2005, 2402).

Support for curfew laws fluctuated throughout the twentieth century, tapering off during the first three decades, rebounding during the 1940s as World War II disrupted family life and waning again in the 1950s (Collins and Kearns 2001). Then, during the mid-1980s and into the 1990s, as the juvenile violent crime rate began climbing and a "moral panic" swept across the nation, curfews enjoyed renewed status as lawmakers vowed to "get tough" on juvenile crime and rein in a younger generation that was perceived as having become increasingly disobedient and disrespectful of authority (Collins and Kearns 2001; Fried 2001; McNamara 2008). Between 1990 and 1995 more than half of the 200 largest cities in the country enacted a new curfew law or revised an existing one (McDowall, Loftin, and Wiersema 2000), and by the end of the twentieth century, an estimated 80 percent of American cities with populations greater than 30,000 had some type of juvenile curfew statute in place (McNamara 2008; Steinhart 1996).

The effectiveness of curfew laws is controversial. A press release by the National League of Cities states, "The overwhelming majority of cities with curfews say the curfews are effective in improving safety in several areas: combating juvenile crime (effectiveness reported by 97 percent of respondents), fighting truancy (96 percent of respondents), making streets safer (95 percent of respondents) and reducing gang violence (98 percent of respondents) ("Cities Say Curfews Help" 2001, 1).

However, results of numerous studies examining the effects of curfew laws on levels of offending have failed to find a positive correlation between such laws and reduced juvenile crime and delinquency (Adams 2003, 2007; Cole 2003; Fried 2001; Reynolds, Seydlitz, and Jenkins 2000). One of the primary reasons is that juvenile crime activity normally peaks between 3 and 4 P.M. on school days, with similar midday and early evening peaks on nonschool days and, thus, is unlikely to be significantly reduced by nighttime restrictions on movement (Reynolds, Seydlitz, and Jenkins 2000; Snyder and Sickmund 2006). Some research has found temporal displacement of crime in areas where curfews are in effect. Offense data gathered before and after curfew implementation in these jurisdictions show that although nighttime offending and victimization might decrease after a curfew goes into effect, a concurrent increase in offending and victimization is commonly observed during non-curfew hours, offsetting any overall net effect the curfew may have (Adams 2003; Reynolds, Seydlitz, and Jenkins 2000). Such findings suggest that juveniles who are inclined toward delinquency will not simply stop offending because a curfew keeps them home at night—they will very likely adjust the time of their offending to occur during non-curfew hours.

Additional reasons cited for the failure of juvenile curfew laws to translate into significant reductions in delinquency include the finding that officers often enforce such laws haphazardly (Adams 2007; Cole 2003) and that the punishment commonly imposed for curfew violations is perceived by juveniles as being too minor to ineffectively deter such activity (McNamara 2008).

A few studies did find temporary decreases in crime when juvenile curfews were in effect, and some studies reported *increases* in crime following implementation of a nighttime juvenile curfew, possibly because of more increased attention to and detection of crime than because of any real increase in juvenile offending activity (Adams 2003). But overall, the evidence does not support the argument that juvenile curfew laws significantly reduce levels of juvenile offending.

Some parents and organizations such as the American Civil Liberties Union have taken curfew ordinances to court, claiming that they violate students' and parents' constitutional rights. It is claimed that curfews are age discrimination in its purest form and that curfews undermine parental authority, are ineffective and punish law-abiding teenagers. In October 1998 a U.S. Fourth Circuit Court of Appeals held in *Schleifer v. City of Charlottesville* that the Charlottesville, Virginia, curfew was not a violation of the child's or the parents' rights. This case was appealed all the way to the Supreme Court, which in 1999 denied the request to review the case.

Underage Drinking

Alcohol use continues to be a major source of arrests of juveniles. In 2010 an estimated 75,889 juvenile arrests were made for liquor law violations, 10,030 juvenile arrests were made for drunkenness and 2,982 arrests were made involving juveniles driving under the influence (*Crime in the United States, 2010*, 2011).

The most frequent self-reported offense for those 16 and older is liquor law violations. Table 6.2 summarizes students' reported use of alcohol and drugs. Beer consumption held a slight edge over liquor and wine cooler consumption, and marijuana was clearly the most popular illicit drug. Reported use in 2009–2010 of alcohol and most of the drugs is down across the board from the 1996–1997 levels.

Table 6.2   Percentage of Students Who Report Using Alcohol and Drugs by Grade Level of Respondent, 1996–1997, 2001–2002, 2006–2007 and 2009–2010

Annual Use[a]	*1996–1997[d]*	*2001–2002[d]*	*2006–2007[d]*	*2009–2010[e]*
Any alcohol	58.3%	50.4%	43.5%	40.3%
Grades 6 to 8	44.7	34.0	30.6	25.3
Grades 9 to 12	71.0	65.0	59.8	54.8
12th grade	76.5	72.3	68.8	64.1
Beer	46.9	37.2	34.0	31.0
Grades 6 to 8	33.2	22.5	22.8	18.5
Grades 9 to 12	59.6	50.3	48.3	43.1
12th grade	65.3	57.6	56.5	52.3
Wine coolers, breezers	43.6	37.9	32.4	28.8
Grades 6 to 8	33.6	25.7	21.1	16.6
Grades 9 to 12	52.9	48.8	46.7	40.8
12th grade	55.4	53.6	54.6	48.7
Liquor	39.9	32.7	30.1	30.6
Grades 6 to 8	23.7	15.4	16.8	15.5
Grades 9 to 12	54.9	48.1	46.9	45.3
12th grade	62.3	59.4	57.4	55.5
Any illicit drugs	30.1	22.3	19.2	21.4
Grades 6 to 8	20.7	11.9	12.0	12.3
Grades 9 to 12	38.9	31.6	28.3	30.2
12th grade	41.6	37.4	33.1	35.9
Marijuana	25.6	19.5	15.2	17.0
Grades 6 to 8	14.7	8.3	7.3	7.3
Grades 9 to 12	35.8	29.4	25.2	26.4
12th grade	39.4	35.7	30.5	32.8

Annual Use[a]	1996–1997[d]	2001–2002[d]	2006–2007[d]	2009–2010[e]
Cocaine[b]	4.5%	3.7%	4.0%	3.6%
Grades 6 to 8	3.0	2.1	2.3	1.9
Grades 9 to 12	5.9	5.1	6.2	5.2
12th grade	7.0	7.1	8.2	7.2
Uppers (stimulants)	7.7	4.8	5.0	4.9
Grades 6 to 8	4.9	2.4	2.6	2.2
Grades 9 to 12	10.3	7.0	8.0	7.5
12th grade	10.7	8.5%	9.1	10.0
Downers (depressants)	5.7	4.8	5.1	4.8
Grades 6 to 8	4.0	2.4	2.8	2.3
Grades 9 to 12	7.2	6.9	8.0	7.3
12th grade	7.4	8.1	9.1	9.4
Inhalants	8.0	4.8	5.5	5.3
Grades 6 to 8	8.9	4.9	5.1	4.7
Grades 9 to 12	7.1	4.6	6.0	5.8
12th grade	5.8	4.3	5.6	5.9
Hallucinogens[c]	6.6	4.0	3.4	3.8
Grades 6 to 8	3.6	1.9	1.9	1.7
Grades 9 to 12	9.5	5.9	5.2	5.7
12th grade	11.7	8.3	6.4	7.9
Heroin	2.7	2.2	2.6	2.7
Grades 6 to 8	2.4	1.5	1.7	1.6
Grades 9 to 12	3.1	2.9	3.7	3.7
12th grade	3.4	3.7	4.3	4.9
Steroids	NA	2.5	2.7	2.7
Grades 6 to 8	NA	1.9	1.9	1.9
Grades 9 to 12	NA	3.0	3.6	3.5
12th grade	NA	3.4	4.1	4.3
Ecstasy	NA	NA	3.6	3.9
Grades 6 to 8	NA	NA	2.0	1.7
Grades 9 to 12	NA	NA	5.6	5.9
12th grade	NA	NA	6.8	8.2
OxyContin	NA	NA	3.9	NA
Grades 6 to 8	NA	NA	2.1	NA
Grades 9 to 12	NA	NA	6.2	NA
12th grade	NA	NA	7.1	NA
Crystal methamphetamine	NA	NA	3.0	2.7
Grades 6 to 8	NA	NA	2.1	1.8
Grades 9 to 12	NA	NA	4.1	3.7
12th grade	NA	NA	4.8	4.7

NA= data not available
[a] Used one or more times in the past year. [b] Includes crack. [c] Includes LSD and PCP.
SOURCES: Adapted from PRIDE Surveys:
[d] *2006–2007 PRIDE Surveys National Summary, Grades 6 through 12.* 2008. Bowling Green, KY: PRIDE Surveys, pp. 288–289. Table adapted by SOURCEBOOK staff.
[e] *Questionnaire Report for Grades 6 to 12: National Summary Statistics for 2009–2010.* Bowling Green, KY: PRIDE Surveys, September 27, 2010, pp.20–22.

One concern with underage drinking involves the growing body of evidence linking alcohol with adolescent violence. Although studies demonstrating a relationship between alcohol use by juveniles and adolescent violence are not new, recent data have confirmed that youth who often engage in underage drinking are significantly more likely to commit violence even while sober than are nondrinking youth (Felson, Teasdale, and Burchfield 2008, 119).

A growing concern is **binge drinking**, which is the consumption of large quantities of alcohol within a short period. Such rapid ingestion of alcohol causes fast intoxication and can lead to alcohol poisoning, in which the body's breathing and gag reflexes become severely impaired. Although no standard definition exists regarding how much alcohol over how long a time constitutes a "binge," a common amount used in the United States is five drinks for adult males and four drinks for adult females within a 2- to 3-hour time span. These amounts can be particularly dangerous to younger people, as blood alcohol content (BAC) is influenced by body mass. A binge can quickly raise a person's BAC to 0.20, which can prove fatal for first-time drinkers. According to the Centers for Disease Control and Prevention (2008), approximately 90 percent of all alcohol consumed by Americans under the legal drinking age of 21 is in the form of binge drinking, with some reports of children as young as 13 engaged in binge drinking.

One problem associated with alcohol and drugs is the **rave**, an all-night party generally with loud techno music, dancing, drinking and doing drugs. Ecstasy (MDMA) is the drug of choice at raves, but LSD is making a comeback and is often used in combination with Ecstasy.

The National Center for Juvenile Justice (Griffin and Torbet 2002, 109) cautions, "Drug users between the ages of 12 and 17 are more than 5 times as likely to shoplift, steal or vandalize property as non-users in that age range, 9 times as likely to steal cars or commit armed robbery, and 19 times as likely to break and enter or burglarize." A study of the proximal effects of alcohol and drug use on adolescent illegal activity, which used four years of longitudinal data involving 506 adolescent males from the Pittsburgh Youth Study, revealed that participants reported committing offenses against persons more often than general theft under the influence of alcohol or drugs: "Aggressive acts were more often related to self-reported acute alcohol use than to marijuana use. Those who reported committing illegal acts under the influence reported committing offenses with other people and being arrested more often than those who did not. Offenses under the influence were more prevalent among heavier alcohol and drug users, more serious offenders, more impulsive youth, and youth with more deviant peers" (White et al. 2002, 131).

 The trend for status offense arrests, including the offenses of running away, violating curfew and underage drinking, is decreasing.

Other Problem Behaviors

Disorderly youths may be engaged in status offenses as just discussed, or they may be involved in other types of public nuisance behavior such as reckless bicycle riding and skateboarding, street cruising or playing loud car stereos. Such problem behaviors often occur at shopping malls, at plazas in business districts, at video arcades, in public parks, on school grounds, in apartment complex common areas, at public libraries and at convenience stores and fast-food restaurants. Scott (2001, 3) suggests, "Whether the conduct is deemed disorderly depends on many factors, including the youths' specific objectionable behavior, the youths' ages, the complainants' tolerance levels, the community norms, and the specific times and places where the problem occurs."

A recent phenomenon known as a *flash mob* is posing considerable challenges to communities and law enforcement. A flash mob is a group of individuals, often juveniles, who use social media to organize a variety of activities that they carry out en masse. Although such mobs often engage in generalized civil disobedience and rioting where no injuries, damages or loss occur, there are instances where their conduct is criminal, such as mass looting of retail establishments (called a flash rob or mob rob) and public beatings. The larger the group, the

© Laurence Kesterson/Philadelphia Inquirer/MCT/ZUMAPRESS.com

People, many of them juveniles, fill South Street during a flash mob incident that involved thousands and closed the street to traffic from Front Street to Broad in Philadelphia, Pennsylvania.

A Key Issue

Disagreement exists regarding how much emphasis should be placed on the formal handling of status offenders. The Juvenile Justice and Delinquency Prevention (JJDP) Act of 1974 officially decriminalized status offenses and mandated the deinstitutionalization of status offenders (DSO), requiring the removal from correctional or other detention facilities of youths being held for status offenses. One argument behind this stance was that the labeling effect on such youths, by being identified and treated as "offenders," was so stigmatizing that the result of the system's response did more harm than good to these juveniles.

The other side of the issue, however, is that these status offenses are, technically and legally, violations of the law and that a formal response by the system is warranted and justified, particularly given evidence that such behaviors have been found to be precursors for more serious offending.

How much discretion should be allowed when dealing with status offenders? Should status offenders be handled within the juvenile justice system? What should be done with chronic status offenders?

greater the sense of anonymity felt by the perpetrators. However, some police departments around the country are implementing social media units to tackle these types of incidents, using YouTube postings, Twitter hashtags and other electronic evidence to locate and identify flash mob participants. Facial recognition software has also been used to match mob members with images contained in drivers' license databases. To date, however, the most common and effective strategies for preventing flash mobs are the tightening and enforcement of curfew statutes and enhanced police presence in areas most vulnerable to such activity.

Juvenile Delinquents and Delinquency

A juvenile **delinquent** is a youth who commits an act that would be a crime were it to be committed by an adult. Reflecting the rehabilitative philosophy of juvenile justice and the hope that many, if not most, wayward youth can be redirected away from a life of offending, the term *delinquent* is intended to avoid stigmatizing youths as criminals and should *not* be applied to status offenders. Thus *delinquency* is the term used in juvenile justice to replace *criminality*. Table 6.3 summarizes high school seniors' self-reported involvement in certain delinquent activities. The exact phrasing used in the questionnaire is given in *italics*, and the activities are grouped according to their adult (criminal) equivalent, labeled in **boldface**. As noted, the most frequently engaged in delinquent behaviors by self-report are theft of items worth less than $50 and shoplifting.

Table 6.3 High School Seniors Reporting Involvement in Selected Delinquent Activities in Past 12 Months, United States, Selected Classes 1991–2010

Delinquent Activity	Class of 1991	Class of 1997	Class of 2003	Class of 2010
Assault				
Hit an instructor or supervisor?				
Not at all	97.0	96.4	96.8	96.7
Once	1.6	1.8	1.1	1.3
Twice	0.7	0.8	0.9	0.6
3 or 4 times	0.2	0.3	0.2	0.6
5 or more times	0.6	0.8	1.0	0.8
Hurt someone badly enough to need bandages or a doctor?				
Not at all	87.1	85.4	88.0	87.1
Once	8.2	8.9	5.6	6.7
Twice	2.3	2.7	3.1	3.2
3 or 4 times	1.1	1.6	1.7	1.3
5 or more times	1.3	1.6	1.6	1.8
Used a knife or gun or some other thing (like a club) to get something from a person?				
Not at all	96.6	95.5	96.1	96.6
Once	1.6	1.5	1.5	1.6
Twice	0.6	1.2	0.9	0.7
3 or 4 times	0.3	1.0	0.8	0.2
5 or more times	0.9	0.8	0.7	0.9

Delinquent Activity	Class of 1991	Class of 1997	Class of 2003	Class of 2010
Larceny-Theft				
Taken something not belonging to you worth under $50?				
Not at all	68.1	65.8	72.3	72.4
Once	13.7	12.5	13.4	12.1
Twice	7.7	9.3	5.8	6.7
3 or 4 times	4.1	5.9	4.0	3.7
5 or more times	6.5	6.4	4.4	5.0
Taken something not belonging to you worth over $50?				
Not at all	89.9	87.2	90.4	89.4
Once	4.6	6.3	4.3	5.5
Twice	2.1	2.6	1.6	1.8
3 or 4 times	1.7	1.6	1.3	1.2
5 or more times	1.8	2.3	2.4	2.1
Shoplifting				
Taken something from a store without paying for it?				
Not at all	68.9	66.6	73.2	73.2
Once	11.9	11.4	12.1	11.1
Twice	7.4	7.3	5.4	5.0
3 or 4 times	5.3	7.4	4.0	4.9
5 or more times	6.5	7.2	5.2	5.7
Auto Theft				
Taken a car that didn't belong to someone in your family without permission of the owner?				
Not at all	93.8	93.9	94.7	95.3
Once	3.3	3.4	2.3	1.9
Twice	1.2	1.2	1.1	1.4
3 or 4 times	1.0	0.6	0.7	0.7
5 or more times	0.7	0.9	1.2	0.8
Taken part of a car without permission of the owner?				
Not at all	93.7	94.6	94.5	95.4
Once	3.3	2.2	2.8	2.0
Twice	1.3	1.4	1.1	1.5
3 or 4 times	0.6	0.9	0.7	0.2
5 or more times	1.0	0.9	0.8	1.0
Trespass				
Gone into some house or building when you weren't supposed to be there?				
Not at all	75.7	75.3	77.0	75.5
Once	10.8	10.5	10.5	11.4
Twice	6.7	7.0	6.8	6.8
3 or 4 times	3.4	3.8	3.2	3.0
5 or more times	3.6	3.5	2.5	3.3
Arson				
Set fire to someone's property on purpose?				
Not at all	97.9	96.9	96.2	97.0
Once	1.1	1.7	1.6	1.6

(continued)

Table 6.3 High School Seniors Reporting Involvement in Selected Delinquent Activities in Past 12 Months, United States, Selected Classes 1991–2010 (*continued*)

Delinquent Activity	Class of 1991	Class of 1997	Class of 2003	Class of 2010
Twice	0.4	0.4	0.9	0.4
3 or 4 times	0.1	0.2	0.3	0.3
5 or more times	0.5	0.7	1.1	0.7
Vandalism				
Damaged school property on purpose?				
Not at all	87.2	84.8	86.8	90.3
Once	6.5	7.7	6.3	5.2
Twice	3.0	3.1	3.9	2.7
3 or 4 times	1.3	2.2	1.4	0.7
5 or more times	2.0	2.2	1.6	1.0
Damaged property at work on purpose?				
Not at all	93.4	93.3	93.2	95.9
Once	3.2	2.8	3.3	2.0
Twice	1.3	1.7	1.5	1.0
3 or 4 times	0.8	1.0	1.1	0.3
5 or more times	1.3	1.1	1.0	0.8
Arrest				
Been arrested and taken to a police station?				
Not at all	X	90.6	92.0	91.8
Once	X	5.6	4.5	5.4
Twice	X	1.9	1.9	1.5
3 or 4 times	X	1.1	0.7	0.4
5 or more times	X	0.9	0.9	0.9

SOURCE: Lloyd D. Johnston, Jerald G. Bachman, and Patrick M. O'Malley. 1993. *Monitoring the Future: Questionnaire Responses from the Nation's High School Seniors, 1991*, pp.106–109; 2001. *1997*, pp.105–107; 2005. *2003*, pp.112–114 (Ann Arbor, MI: Institute for Social Research, University of Michigan); Jerald G. Bachman, Lloyd D. Johnston, and Patrick M. O'Malley. 2011. *Monitoring the Future: Questionnaire Responses from the Nation's High School Seniors, 2010*, pp.113–115 (Ann Arbor, MI: Institute for Social Research, University of Michigan). Reprinted by permission.

Although violent juvenile crime is certainly a valid concern to society and generates sensational media headlines, by far the most common acts of delinquency are in the form of property crime.

Property Offenses Committed by Juveniles

Both official statistics and self-reports indicate juveniles are heavily involved in property offenses, with 22.5 percent of all arrests for property crimes in 2010 involving offenders younger than 18 (*Crime in the United States, 2010*, 2011).

 The most frequent juvenile arrests are for property crimes, with larceny-theft being the most common (see Table 6.1).

Larceny-Theft   Larceny-theft is the most frequent offense for which juveniles are arrested. Shoplifting accounts for much of the larceny-theft figures. In 2010 an estimated 223,207 juvenile arrests were made for larceny-theft.

A Caution about Statistics and Juvenile Co-Offending

Although it is tempting, almost comforting, to place a high degree of faith in statistics—indeed, this chapter presents an ample amount of them—students are well advised to be cognizant of some potential limitations of these numbers, particularly as applied to juvenile offending:

> Juveniles who commit crimes typically commit them in the company of their peers. This basic fact has been regularly reported in the literature since the late 1920s. Nevertheless, with rare exceptions, contemporary research focuses almost exclusively on juvenile delinquents as individual actors. Indeed, police records tend to undercount co-offending, and published crime rates rarely take co-offending into account. . . . Yet co-offenders provide a basis of multiple reports of single crime events. Not only are those who first offended before age 13 most likely to be co-offenders, but also the sizes of their offending groups (from 2 to 30 in the current study) tend to further exaggerate the contributions of youthful offenders to crimes. This exaggeration seems to contribute to a fear of youths that may be counterproductive. (McCord and Conway 2005, 1)

So what does this mean? If four youths team up to commit a single burglary and all four are taken into custody and entered into the system as "four juvenile arrests" in the category of burglary, this co-offending event has resulted in a significantly skewed statistic. Yes, four juveniles were involved, and four arrests were made, but the offense was a single event, not four separate and distinct delinquent offenses. Thus, looking solely at number of arrests, particularly when it pertains to juvenile offenders, can present a very different picture from what the true level of crime and victimization is in society. In the example just provided, one could assume (incorrectly) that the crime rate was four times higher than it actually is, based solely on the number of arrests. In other words, when looking at the number of juvenile arrests made, consider how such co-offending can relate to the number of actual offenses committed and the likelihood that actual crime levels are different than those implied by the "single offender" arrest statistic.

Forty-six percent of those arrested were female, and 28 percent were under age 15 (*Crime in the United States, 2010*, 2011). Time-of-day analysis shows that shoplifting incidents peak between 3 P.M. and 6 P.M., for both male and female juvenile offenders, regardless of whether it is a school or nonschool day (Snyder and Sickmund 2006, 89).

Burglary Burglary is a crime of opportunity usually committed for quick financial gain, often to support a drug habit. It is the most accessible route to money for unemployed juveniles. In 2010 an estimated 51,298 juvenile arrests were made for burglary. Snyder (2008, 7) observes, "Unique in the set of Property Crime Index offenses, the juvenile arrest rate for burglary declined almost consistently and fell substantially between 1980 and 2006, down 69%."

Motor Vehicle Theft In 2010 an estimated 12,268 juvenile arrests were made for motor vehicle theft. More than one fourth (27.3 percent) of juvenile arrests involved persons under age 15; less than 4 percent were female (*Crime in the United States, 2010*, 2011). According to Snyder (2008, 7), "The juvenile arrest rate for motor vehicle theft more than doubled between 1983 and 1990, up 137%. After the peak years of 1990 and 1991, the juvenile arrest rate for motor vehicle theft declined substantially and consistently through 2006." Arrest data show that this trend continued through 2010.

Vandalism Vandalism is usually a mischievous, destructive act done to get attention, to get revenge or to vent hostility. Children sometimes send messages of personal problems by acting out through vandalism. Destructive behavior can occur because children lack ways of communicating a need for help. Graffiti and tagging are prevalent forms of vandalism in many areas and

© Steven Puetzer/Getty Images

Shoplifting is a common form of delinquent behavior. Some youths shoplift because they have no money to purchase wanted items. Others shoplift for the thrill of it.

are often associated with, but not always related to, gang activity. In 2010 an estimated 60,591 juvenile arrests were made for vandalism, nearly half the number of similar arrests made in 2006.

Arson   Arson, like vandalism, sends a message through a delinquent act. For many children setting fires is a symbolic act, often a symptom of underlying emotional or physical stress. Data from the FBI show that, of all arrests made for arson in 2010, 40.1 percent involved juveniles, and among those juveniles, 59 percent were under age 15 (*Crime in the United States, 2010*, 2011). However, as with many aspects of juvenile justice, terminology is different when the age of the firesetter is factored in, with "child firesetter" used to refer to persons age 12 or younger, "adolescent firesetter" used for those age 13 to the age of majority and "arsonist" for anyone older than the legal age (Putnam and Kirkpatrick 2005, 2).

A distinction is made in the literature between *fireplay*, the term used to describe the relatively normal curiosity and fascination young children have with fire that carries a low level of intent to inflict harm and an absence of malice, and *firesetting*, which is associated with a higher level of intent and degree of malice and in which the youths are viewed "as willful actors who consistently use fire as an instrument of purposeful action" (Putnam and Kirkpatrick 2005, 2). According to the U.S. Fire Administration (2006, 1), "For fires coded as child play and not intentional, 84 percent involved firesetters under the age of 10." An estimated 13,900 such fireplay events were reported in 2002, which caused 210 deaths, 1,250 injuries and $339 million in direct damage (U.S. Fire Administration 2006, 1).

Children who do not abandon normal childhood experiments with fire often may be showing early signs of psychopathy, using fire as an expression of their stress, anxiety and anger. The U.S. Fire Administration (2006, 1) reports that delinquent firesetters are teens who commonly have a history of truancy, gang membership, antisocial behavior or substance abuse. Research similarly indicates that juvenile firesetting is strongly correlated with childhood maltreatment; family dysfunction; school problems; antisocial personality traits such as low impulse control, hostility and aggression; and other co-occurring delinquent behaviors (Lambie and Randall 2011; Root et al. 2008; Vaughn et al. 2010). In fact, "Along with enuresis and animal cruelty, firesetting forms the 'MacDonald Triad,' which is a conceptual model of violence risk that has been linked to multiple homicide, homicide, and sexual offending" (Vaughn et al. 2010, 218).

The National Fire Academy (NFA) conducts a Juvenile Firesetter Intervention Specialist (JFIS) training program for any practitioner who interacts with children involved in firesetting or arson behaviors. Information on the curriculum is available through the U.S. Fire Administration's Web site. For more information, visit the Criminal Justice Companion Web site at cengagebrain. com, then access the web links for this chapter.

 Similar to arrests pertaining to the status offense categories, arrests of juveniles for property crimes have decreased during the past decade, in some cases by a significant margin.

Violent Crime Committed by Juveniles

The FBI's Violent Crime Index includes murder and nonnegligent manslaughter, forcible rape, robbery and aggravated assault. Arrests of persons under age 18 for violent crime was a reported 13.7 percent of all violent crime arrests made in 2010, a figure that has remained fairly constant in recent years (*Crime in the United States, 2010*, 2011). "Clearance data show that the proportion of violent crimes that law enforcement attributes to juveniles has … [held] between 12% and 13% from 1996 through 2006" (Snyder 2008, 4). The Federal Interagency Forum on Child and Family Statistics (2008) reports, "One measure of youth violence in society is the rate of serious crimes by youth perpetrators. In 2005, the rate of serious violent crime offenses was 17 crimes per 1,000 juveniles ages 12–17, totaling 437,000 such crimes involving juveniles. While this is somewhat higher than the 2004 rate of 14 crimes per 1,000 juveniles, it is significantly lower than the rate of 52 crimes per 1,000 juveniles in 1993."

The daily pattern of juvenile violent crime varies between school and non-school days, with violent crime by juveniles peaking between 3 P.M. and 4 P.M. on school days and then gradually tapering off to the low point at 6 A.M. (Snyder and Sickmund 2006, 85). Not to diminish the importance of curfew laws, but this finding has important policy implications for communities looking for ways to lower their incidents of juvenile violent crime, suggesting that after-school programs hold a higher crime reduction potential than do juvenile curfews (Snyder and Sickmund 2006, 86).

Murder Murder is the most serious, yet least often committed, violent crime. In 2010, 784 juvenile arrests were made for murder and nonnegligent manslaughter, a number that accounted for 9 percent of all arrests made for murder that year

(*Crime in the United States, 2010*, 2011). As part of the upward trend in overall violence that occurred throughout the nation during the 1980s and into the 1990s, the juvenile arrest rate for murder more than doubled from 1980 to 1993. Since the mid-1990s murders by juveniles have mostly declined, but from 2004 to 2006 arrest rates increased slightly. Snyder (2008, 6) notes, "The growth in the juvenile murder arrest rate between 2004 and 2006 returned to near its 2002 level; but even with this increase, the rate in 2006 was 73% below its 1993 peak." And the juvenile murder arrest rate in 2010 indicated continuation of the previous downward trend.

Forcible Rape   The juvenile forcible rape rate has continued to decline during the past decade. In 2010 a reported 2,198 juvenile arrests were made for forcible rape, a number comprising 14 percent of all persons arrested for this offense that year (*Crime in the United States, 2010*, 2011). Only 2 percent of juveniles arrested for forcible rape were female. As with other violent crimes, the juvenile arrest rate for this offense has been steadily declining during the past two decades.

According to Snyder and Sickmund (2006, 87), "Sexual assaults by juvenile offenders spike at 8 A.M. and 3 P.M. on both school and nonschool days and [also] at noon on nonschool days." In other words, school days show two spikes in juvenile sexual assault activity, whereas nonschool days show three. However, violent sexual assaults by juveniles are most likely to occur between 2 P.M. and 5 P.M., particularly on school days (Snyder and Sickmund 2006, 87). Juvenile sex offenders will be discussed in more detail later in the chapter.

Robbery   The juvenile arrest rate for robbery declined during much of the 1980s, but then began increasing again in 1988, peaking in the years of 1994 and 1995. Although the overall juvenile robbery arrest rate dropped 16 percent between 1997 and 2006, data show the arrest rates for this violent crime by juveniles rose slightly from 2006 to 2008 before returning to a downward trend. In 2010 a reported 21,110 juvenile arrests were made for robbery, 24 percent of all arrests made for robbery that year (*Crime in the United States, 2010*, 2011). The time-of-day pattern for juvenile robberies closely follows the adult robbery pattern, peaking at 9 P.M. on both school and nonschool days (Snyder and Sickmund 2006, 87).

Aggravated Assault   As with juvenile arrests for murder and rape, arrests of juveniles for aggravated assault increased significantly during the 1980s and into the early 1990s, peaking in 1994, at which time they began a fairly steady, consistent descent. In 2010 a reported 35,001 juvenile arrests were made for aggravated assault, accounting for 11 percent of all arrests made that year for aggravated assault (*Crime in the United States, 2010*, 2011). Juvenile aggravated assault peaks at 3 P.M. on school days and at 8 P.M. on nonschool days (Snyder and Sickmund 2006, 87).

 Arrests for violent juvenile crime dropped from the mid-1990s to the mid-2000s, showed a slight upward trend in 2005 and 2006 and have since returned to a downward trend.

Profile of Delinquency

No single type of personality is associated with delinquency. However, some characteristics are common among delinquents. Those who become delinquent are more likely to be socially assertive, defiant, ambivalent about authority, resentful, hostile, suspicious, destructive, impulsive and lacking in self-control.

They typically are doing poorly in school, skip classes often or have dropped out altogether. In short, they possess many of the risk factors and few of the protective factors discussed in Chapter 4.

Age Trends

Crime is often said to be a young person's activity. Indeed, arrest statistics show most offenders eventually "age out" of crime. Delinquency rates tend to increase dramatically during adolescence, peaking in the mid to late teens. Arrest data show that the intensity of criminal behavior slackens after the teenage years and continues to decline with age. Return for a moment to Table 6.1, which summarizes the arrest data for 2010 by age through 21. Note the arrest figures in the columns for 17-, 18- and 19-year-olds and how, for many offenses, these are the ages for which the greatest number of arrests were made during 2010. Also, if you check the *Crime in the United States* Web site for 2010 arrest data and scroll to the right on Table 38, you see decreasing numbers of arrests in nearly every offense categories for all age groups beyond 19. Note that the ages above 25 are grouped into 5-year cohorts, so although the raw numbers exceed those of the teenage columns, these values (e.g., 25–29, 30–34, etc.) combine five distinct ages into one number. Assuming the arrests were distributed fairly evenly across the five ages in each batch (which, of course, they aren't, but consider they are for comparison purposes), if one divides those values by 5, it becomes evident that the peak arrest numbers for most offenses occur for those persons in their late teens.

Female Delinquents

The profile of delinquency has changed in the past decade to include more females. According to Snyder (2008, 8), 29 percent of juvenile arrests in 2006 involved females, a figure that held steady according to the 2010 data (*Crime in the United States, 2010*, 2011).

Delinquency: A Passing Phase or a Pathway to Adult Criminality?

Research shows most youthful offending is best defined as "adolescent limited" (AL), meaning the participation in low levels of delinquent activity is a relatively normal behavior for teens, and society can expect these "offenders" to grow out of their delinquent behavior as they mature (Moffitt 1993). It is hypothesized that those youth on the AL trajectory come into delinquency more as a function of the natural transitions that occur during puberty. As such, AL offenders are highly likely to desist in their delinquent behavior as they mature—hence the label "adolescent limited" (Wright, Tibbits, and Daigle 2008).

The trajectory that is more concerning is the "life-course persistent" (LCP) pathway, which involves a relatively small percentage of youth who, in early childhood, show a tendency toward antisocial behavior. These youth demonstrate an extremely stable pattern of maladaptive behavior by the time they enter adolescence. Although the delinquent activity of both AL and LCP offenders may be quite similar during adolescence, the underlying causes of their behavior are notably different:

Life-course-persistent offenders show longstanding patterns of antisocial behavior that appear to be rooted, at least in part, in relatively stable psychological attributes that are present early in development and that are attributable to psychopathology, deficient socialization or neurobiological anomalies. Adolescence-limited offending, in contrast, is driven by forces that are inherent features of adolescence as a developmental period, including susceptibility to peer pressure . . ., sensation-seeking, experimentation with risk, a tendency to discount the future, and impulsivity. All of these developmentally driven forces abate as individuals mature into adulthood. (Scott and Steinberg 2008, 54)

Girls have traditionally entered the juvenile justice system through their involvement in status offenses. Violence by adolescent girls often results from a combination of victimization, substance abuse, economic conditions and dysfunctional family systems (Zahn et al. 2010). Researchers have linked the violence perpetuated against females to these girls' increased involvement in violent crime; that is, females are becoming offenders in response to their own victimization. Such research supports the theory that violence perpetuates violence (Herrera and McClosky 2001; Margolin and Gordis 2000; Molnar et al. 2005).

Some researchers contend that the recent increase in arrests is not so much a reflection of an actual increase in delinquent activity by girls as it is an indication of a change in response to female delinquency by the system (Steffensmeier et al. 2005). Zahn et al. (2008, 15), in studying trends in violence by teenage girls, found, "Available evidence based on arrest, victimization, and self-report data suggests that although girls are currently arrested more for simple assaults than previously, the actual incidence of their being seriously violent has not changed much over the last two decades. This suggests that increases in arrests may be attributable more to changes in enforcement policies than to changes in girls' behavior. Juvenile female involvement in violence has not increased relative to juvenile male violence. There is no burgeoning national crisis of increasing serious violence among adolescent girls."

Minority Offenders

A concern throughout the justice system—for both adults and juveniles—is the percentage of minorities involved relative to their proportions in the general population. The issue of disproportionate minority contact (DMC) was introduced in Chapter 1. A large and growing number of studies have found that minority youth, particularly Black youth, are over-involved in crime, particularly violent crime, relative to their percentage of the population at large. This finding is borne out in official data sources and in victimization surveys and self-reports of offending (Ellis, Beaver, and Wright 2009; Felson, Deane, and Armstrong 2008; Williams et al. 2007). In many statistical analyses, the other "major" minority group in the United States—Hispanics—is included in counts of White offenders, and still these combined numbers generally indicate lower rates of delinquency and criminal offending when compared with rates for Black youth.

Reality Check

Despite the ostensible belief that we should strive for gender equality, our society still retains different standards and expectations regarding acceptable behavior for boys and girls. In the early 1990s, a meta-analysis of 172 studies, all of which examined whether parents differentially socialized their children based on the child's gender, found small to negligible effect sizes in how parents rear boys and girls (Lytton and Romney 1991). More recently, however, Zahn et al. (2008, 7) have noted how family dynamics may play a role in the gender differences in juvenile arrests for assault: "Parents have different expectations about their sons' and daughters' obedience to parental authority, and these expectations may affect how the justice system responds to a girl's behavior when she 'acts out' within the home. Research indicates that girls fight with family members or siblings more frequently than boys, who more often fight with friends or strangers."

Thus, one might presume that official arrest data may be a reflection of both actual involvement in crime and how our society, through the justice system, responds to that involvement. Such disparities are observed between genders and between racial and ethnic groups.

According to 2010 U.S. Census data, Black youth constitute approximately 14.5 percent of all citizens under age 18, yet in 2008, the most recent year for which such data is available, Black youth accounted for 52 percent of juvenile violent crime index arrests and 33 percent of juvenile property crime index arrests (Puzzanchera 2009). In 2008 the violent crime index arrest rate for Black juveniles was approximately 5 times higher than the rate for White juveniles. In 2010, of all juveniles arrested for homicide, 62 percent were Black (*Crime in the United States, 2010,* 2011). A study on race differences in delinquency initiation, based on self-report data, found that although Black youths were no more likely than White youth were to initiate minor delinquent acts or major nonviolent delinquent acts, Black youths were more likely than Whites to initiate violent acts (Williams et al. 2007).

Considering the self-reported and officially documented over-involvement of Black youths in delinquent and criminal activities, and that this involvement tends to be of a more serious nature, it should come as little surprise that minority youth are overrepresented in the justice system, from arrest through disposition. Reasons set forth for these observed racial disparities in offending rates include higher exposure of Black youth to risk factors such as low parental supervision, a lack of clarity of rules in the home, association with delinquent peers and the stress of living in poor and violent environments (Stewart and Simons 2010; Williams et al. 2007).

Co-Offending

Much juvenile crime involves co-offending, meaning more than one offender is engaged in a single offense event: "Offenders age 13 and under are more likely to commit crimes in pairs and groups than are 16- and 17-year-old offenders.

© Lannis Waters/Zuma Press

Seventeen-year-old Avion Lewis looks around after pleading guilty in the gang rape of a woman and her son. Lewis faces as many as 11 life sentences for his involvement in the attack. He was also the prosecution's star witness against three other defendants, one of whom Lewis used to call "brother," all of whom were sentenced to life in prison for their involvement in the rape.

About 40 percent of juvenile offenders commit most of their crimes with others. Co-offenders are also more likely than solo offenders to be recidivists.... Co-offending actually may increase the likelihood that offenders will commit violent crimes. When young offenders affiliate with offenders who have previously used violence, the result appears to be an increase in the likelihood that they will subsequently commit a violent crime" (McCord and Conway 2005, ii).

Serious, Chronic and Violent Juvenile Offenders

Serious, chronic or violent juvenile offenders are often transferred out of the juvenile justice system to the criminal justice system. The likelihood of such transfers increases with increased frequency of offending, increased severity of offending and increased offender age. However, it is still important for those working in juvenile justice to be familiar with this population.

- A **serious juvenile offender** has been convicted of a Part I offense as defined by the FBI Uniform Crime Reports, excluding auto theft, petty theft/larceny or distribution of a controlled dangerous substance.
- A **serious child delinquent** is between the ages of 7 and 12 and has committed one or more homicides, aggravated assaults, robberies, rapes or serious arsons.
- A **chronic juvenile offender** has a record of five or more separate charges of delinquency, regardless of the offenses' gravity.
- A **violent juvenile offender** has been convicted of a violent Part I offense, one against a person rather than property, and has a prior adjudication of such an offense or is a youth who has been convicted of murder.

Serious or chronic offenders are typically from low-income families, are rated troublesome by teachers and peers between the ages of 8 and 10, have poor school performance by age 10, are adjudicated a delinquent before age 13 and have a sibling convicted of a crime.

Two general onset trajectories for youth violence have been identified: (1) those who start early, before adolescence, and offend often, who are referred to as early onset or life-course-persistent (LCP) offenders, and (2) those whose offending is limited to a few years during adolescence and who "age out" of delinquency as they mature, referred to as experimenters or adolescence-limited (AL) offenders (Loeber 1982; Moffitt 1993). Echoing the findings of many studies, *Youth Violence: A Report of the Surgeon General* (2001, 4) states, "Youths who become violent before about age 13 generally commit more crimes, and more serious crimes, for a longer time. These young people exhibit a pattern of escalating violence through childhood, and they sometimes continue their violence into adulthood." These youth are the *serious child delinquents*.

 The two general onset trajectories for youth violence are *early*, in which violence begins before puberty, and *late*, in which violence begins in adolescence.

Most serious offenders are also chronic or violent offenders, and some are both chronic and violent (Loeber, Farrington, and Petechuk 2003). As illustrated in the Venn diagrams in Figure 6.1, the pool of early onset delinquents produces a greater percentage of serious, violent and chronic career offenders than does the pool of older onset (adolescence-limited) offenders.

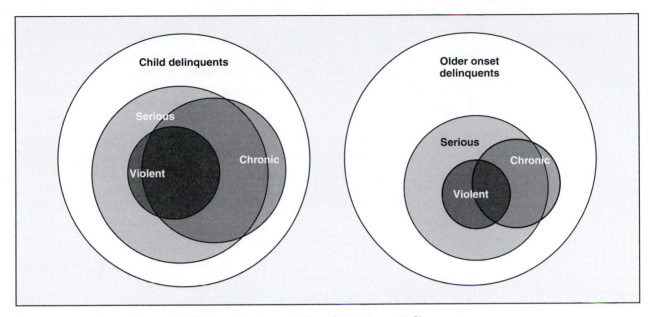

Figure 6.1   Criminal Career Differences between Early and Late Onset Delinquents

SOURCE: H. N. Snyder. 2001. "Epidemiology of Official Offending." In *Child Delinquents: Development, Intervention, and Service Needs*, edited by R. Loeber and D. P. Farrington, pp.25–46. Copyright © 2001 Sage Publications. Reprinted by permission of SAGE Publications.

Serious Child Delinquents

A key finding of the Office of Juvenile Justice and Delinquency Prevention (OJJDP) Study Group on Serious and Violent Offenders—that most chronic juvenile offenders begin their delinquency careers before age 12 and some as early as age 10—led OJJDP in 1998 to establish its Study Group on Very Young Offenders. This study group found that for very young offenders, the most important risk factors are likely individual (e.g., birth complications, hyperactivity and impulsivity) or family related (e.g., parental substance abuse and poor childrearing practices).

This study group also observed that increasing numbers of very young offenders—those ages 7 to 12—are becoming involved with the juvenile justice system, with data indicating that youths under age 13 constitute nearly 10 percent of juvenile arrests: "Compared with juveniles who become delinquent in adolescence, very young delinquents are at greater risk of becoming serious, violent and chronic offenders. They are also more likely than older delinquents to continue their delinquency for extended periods of time" (Snyder et al. 2003, 1).

The study group also notes however, "The good news is that prevention and intervention efforts focused on very young offenders could yield significant benefits. For these benefits to be realized, however, the unique challenges posed by these offenders must be addressed before their delinquency escalates" (Snyder et al. 2003, 1).

Chronic Juvenile Offenders and Recidivism

Chronicity is a factor of both frequency and duration. Thus, *chronic* offenders are those who engage in numerous delinquent acts over time. A review of studies of chronic offenders reveals several conclusions: "First, the proportions of chronic offenders vary considerably from study to study (from 7 percent to 25 percent). Second, the amount of crime accounted for by chronic offenders varies by ethnicity: non-White male chronic offenders account for a greater proportion of official serious delinquency. Third, there are large gender differences: chronic offending is lower in females than in males" (Kempf-Leonard, Tracy, and Howell 2001, 454).

The classic long-term study by Wolfgang, Figlio and Sellin (1972) of delinquents in a Philadelphia birth cohort found that 6 to 8 percent of male juveniles were responsible for more than 60 percent of the serious juvenile offenses. This study also showed that by the third arrest, a delinquent was almost guaranteed a life of crime.

When analyzing chronic offending and trying to "predict" which youth are more likely to continue on a trajectory of delinquency, an important distinction to make is between the *number* of arrests and the *rate* of arrests, with rate incorporating a frequency metric. Noting that arrest *rates* are much more predictive of future arrests than are simple arrest *numbers*, Visher (1987, 532) observes, "Juveniles in the Philadelphia study whose prior arrest rates were high were likely to continue to accumulate arrests (and by inference, to commit crime) at high rates. In other studies, high-rate adult offenders have histories of serious criminal activity, particularly violence, as juveniles."

Chronic juvenile offending is also referred to as juvenile **recidivism**. Identified risk factors for juvenile recidivism include low socioeconomic status; offense history such as earlier contact with the law, greater numbers of prior arrests and more serious prior crimes; family factors such as being physically or sexually abused, raised in a single-parent household or high number of prior out-of-home placements; and social risk factors such as associating with delinquent peers (Cottle, Lee, and Heilbrun 2001). Indeed, as McCord and Conway (2005, 1) found, "Analyses that consider both co-offending and age at first arrest show that youthful offenders are most at risk for subsequent crimes if they commit their crimes with accomplices." This same study revealed, "Violence appears to be learned in the company of others. Those who commit crimes with violent offenders, even if the group does not commit violent crimes, are likely to subsequently commit violent crimes" (McCord and Conway 2005, 1).

Violent Juvenile Offenders

A violent delinquent offender is a juvenile who commits a Part I offense against a person and who has a prior adjudication of such an offense or a youth who has been convicted of murder. Violent youth crime increased significantly during the 1980s and early 1990s and decreased after 1994. *Youth Violence* (2001, 1) notes, "Youth violence is a high-visibility, high-priority concern in every sector of U.S. society. No community, whether affluent or poor, urban, suburban or rural, is immune from its devastating effects.... Since 1993, when the epidemic peaked, youth violence has declined significantly nationwide, as signaled by downward trends in arrest records, victimization data and hospital emergency room records. But the problem has not been resolved."

Surveys consistently find about 30 to 40 percent of male youths and 15 to 30 percent of female youths report having committed a serious violent offense by age 17. Violence can be classified as instrumental or expressive. **Instrumental violence** uses violence as a way to obtain material possessions, for example, forcefully robbing another youth to take a team jacket. **Expressive violence**, in contrast, is a way to vent emotions. Serious violence is part of a lifestyle that includes drugs, guns, precocious sex and other risky behaviors (*Youth Violence* 2001).

 Most youth violence begins in adolescence and ends with the transition into adulthood.

Adolescents with Illegal Sexual Behavior

A particularly challenging problem in juvenile justice concerns how to deal with juvenile sex offenders (JSOs), alternately called adolescent sex offenders (ASOs) or adolescents with illegal sexual behavior (AISBs), which is the preferred term among professionals who deal with this population (Bonner 2008). Youthful sex offenders often begin sexual **deviance**—that is, behavior that departs from the social norm—at a young age and have committed multiple sex offenses and other delinquent acts. Their victims are usually younger children the offenders know. In most cases, offenders did not resort to physical force in committing their offenses.

JSOs or AISBs are differentiated in the literature from child sex offenders (CSOs) or children with sexual behavior problems, with CSOs generally 12 years old or younger. An AISB is boy or girl, 13 to 18 years old, who has been charged with, convicted of or has disclosed involvement as a perpetrator of illegal sexual conduct, as statutorily defined by the jurisdiction in which the offense occurred (Bonner 2008). It is difficult to ascribe a profile to "typical" AISBs because they are a fairly heterogeneous population, demonstrating broad diversity in their own personal abuse history, victim preference, propensity to use violence, risk level for recidivism, current functioning and responsiveness to treatment (Chaffin, Letourneau, and Silovsky 2002; Hunter, Hazelwood, and Slesinger 2000; Kemper and Kistner 2007; Parks and Bard 2006). Perhaps the only consistent finding among studies of AISBs is that the vast majority are males rather than females (Bonner 2008).

A quality that can be assigned to AISBs, however, is that most do not share the common central case characteristics of adult sex offenders. Studies have revealed that AISBs differ significantly from adult sex offenders in that adolescents have fewer victims and generally engage in less aggressive behavior (Miranda and Corcoran 2000); are less driven by deviant sexual compulsivity, sexual arousal or the sexual fantasies reported by many adult sex offenders, the motivation for juveniles' behavior tending instead to be curiosity and experimentation (Becker et al. 1989; Hunter, Goodwin, and Becker 1994); do not generally meet the diagnostic criteria for pedophilia set forth by the American Psychiatric Association and, thus, are not considered sexual predators (APA 2000); and typically demonstrate a shorter duration of criminal behavior, with most AISBs desisting from the long-term re-offending tendencies seen with adult sex offenders (Caldwell 2007). No evidence has been found to suggest the majority of AISBs have a lifelong incurable sexual disorder, and most youthful sex offenders respond well to appropriate treatment and intervention (Bonner 2008).

A subset of AISBs is the female juvenile sex offender. The average age of a female AISB is 14 years, slightly younger than the typical male AISB, and the majority have sustained more extensive and severe physical and sexual abuse as children relative to their male counterparts (Schmidt 2008).

Juvenile Gun Violence

Data analysis of juvenile crime trends during the past two decades shows an interesting and undeniable correlation between the rise in youth violence (most notably a spike in youths committing homicides against youth) and a spike in youth possession of guns. Firearms are used in the majority (86 percent) of homicides committed by juveniles (Sheppard et al. 2000). However, "research also consistently finds that illegal firearm use among juveniles is a relatively small and localized problem" (Lizotte and Sheppard 2001, 10).

A handful of legislation has been passed at the federal level in an effort to keep guns out of the hands of juveniles. The Gun Control Act of 1968 made it illegal for federally licensed firearms dealers to sell handguns to anyone under age 21. The 1994 Youth Safety Handgun Act prohibits the possession of a handgun by anyone under age 18. Nonetheless, state laws vary widely in the minimum age of unrestricted purchase and possession of firearms, with some states seemingly in violation of federal law by setting minimum age limits for purchases from licensed dealers below age 18 for long guns and under 21 for handguns. For example, Montana allows 14-year-olds to legally purchase long guns, and Vermont has set 16 as the minimum age for legally purchasing both long guns and handguns (*Regulating Guns in America* 2008, 83). Wyoming is the only state that does not restrict, through any legislation, access to firearms by juveniles (76). And although federal law does not restrict juvenile offenders from purchasing or possessing firearms, 27 states do have such legislative restrictions.

Despite the legal restrictions imposed on juvenile gun use, youths seem to have little difficulty getting their hands on firearms if they want to. According to the Youth Risk Behavior Survey (YRBS), a national survey conducted every two years by the Centers for Disease Control and Prevention (CDC), in 2009, 5.9 percent of youth respondents admitted having carried a gun at least one day during the 30 days preceding the survey (Eaton et al. 2010). The reported prevalence of having carried a gun in the previous 30 days ranged from 1.8 percent to 11.5 percent across state surveys, with a median rate of 6.5 percent, and from 2.8 percent to 8.5 percent across local surveys, with a median of 5.3 percent (Eaton et al. 2010).

Although some youths, particularly those living in rural areas, use guns for sport and have grown up in families with long-standing traditions of gun use for hunting, other youths report carrying guns for protection. Youths, particularly males, who carry firearms for protection have been found to be significantly more likely to be involved in delinquent activity, as shown in Table 6.4.

 Boys who own guns for protection are significantly and substantially more likely to be involved in delinquent behavior than are either those who do not own guns or those who own guns for sport.

Table 6.4   Percentage of Boys Involved in Delinquency by Gun Ownership Status

Type of Delinquency	Gun Ownership Status (%)		
	No Gun Owned (n = 548)	Gun Owned for Sport (n = 27)	Gun Owned for Protection (n = 40)
Gun carrying	3.2	11.1	70.0
Gun crime	1.3	3.7	30.0
Street crime	14.8	18.5	67.5
Gang membership	7.2	11.1	55.0
Drug selling	3.5	7.4	32.5

SOURCE: Alan Lizotte and David Sheppard. 2001 (July). *Gun Use by Male Juveniles: Research and Prevention*, p. 2. Washington, DC: OJJDP Juvenile Justice Bulletin. (NCJ 188992)

Predictors of Youth Violence

Recall from Chapter 4 the myriad risk factors for delinquency and adult criminality, such as early aggressive behavior and exposure to violence. Other predictors of violence are described by the American Psychological Association (n.d., 6): "Social forces such as prejudice, economic inequality and attitudes toward violence in the mainstream American culture interact with the influences of early childhood to foster the expression of violence." The APA describes several developmental experiences that violent youths frequently share (n.d., 21):

> Youths at greatest risk of becoming extremely aggressive and violent tend to share common experiences that appear to place them on a "trajectory toward violence." These youths tend to have experienced weak bonding to caretakers in infancy and ineffective parenting techniques, including lack of supervision, inconsistent discipline, highly punitive or abusive treatment, and failure to reinforce positive, pro-social behavior. These developmental deficits, in turn, appear to lead to poor peer relations and high levels of aggressiveness.
>
> Additionally, these youths have learned attitudes accepting aggressive behavior as normative and as an effective way to solve interpersonal problems. Aggressive children tend to be rejected by their more conforming peers and do poorly in school, including having a history of problems such as poor school attendance and numerous suspensions. These children often band together with others like themselves, forming deviant peer groups that reinforce antisocial behaviors. The more such children are exposed to violence in their homes, in their neighborhoods and in the media, the greater their risk for aggressive and violent behaviors.

Researchers have begun to look more closely at how neighborhoods and the microsocial conditions therein influence violence levels in youth growing up in those environments. An extensive, 6-year longitudinal study of more than 6,000 children in various Chicago neighborhoods yielded some interesting results. Called the Project on Human Development in Chicago Neighborhoods (PHDCN), this study found (Liberman 2007, 3):

- Neighborhood conditions differ markedly for youth of different race and ethnicity, and those differing conditions in turn account for much of the racial and ethnic difference in youth violence rates.
- Youths in disadvantaged and unsafe neighborhoods are more likely to carry firearms illegally; exposure to firearms violence increases the risk that youths will themselves commit violence.
- Girls who mature early in disadvantaged neighborhoods are at greater risk for being involved in adolescent violence.

IN THE NEWS | "Youth is charged as adult: 17-year-old sentenced to 40 years in prison"
by Edward Marshall, *The Journal*, December 16, 2011

MARTINSBURG—A 17-year-old juvenile who pleaded no contest last month to taking part in an armed home invasion robbery at a Berkeley County kennel last year was sentenced to 40 years in prison Thursday during a sentencing hearing in Berkeley County Circuit Court.

Ronald "Georgie" Whetzel Jr., who is currently incarcerated at a juvenile detention facility in Salem, W.Va., was sentenced by West Virginia 23rd Judicial Circuit Court Judge Gina Groh to a concurrent 1- to 15-year prison sentence on a separate burglary charge related to the Dec. 9, 2010, armed robbery at Beck's Kennel in Inwood, which the victim of the robbery operates out of her residence.

Whetzel, who was indicted as an adult by a Berkeley County grand jury in May, previously pleaded no contest to the burglary charge and one count of first-degree robbery on Nov. 17 as part of a plea agreement that saw a third count of conspiracy dismissed.

Groh also ordered that Whetzel, who was just 16 years old at the time of the robbery, pay $8,000 in restitution to the victim in the case. . . .

Whetzel was represented at Thursday's sentencing hearing by public defender John Lehman, who argued that his client should be sent to the Anthony Center, a correctional facility for youthful offenders. Those sent to the Anthony Center can remain incarcerated for six months to two years, during which time they are required to undergo a strenuous rehabilitation program. Those who successfully complete the program earn the right to be sentenced to probation.

"We have an opportunity to reform this man and make something out of his life," Lehman said. "A place like the Anthony Center can do him a lot of good."

Thursday Lehman argued that there were reasons and circumstances why Whetzel was in the position he was in. Whetzel's father is currently serving a prison sentence for armed robbery, and his mother is serving a prison sentence for forgery and uttering-related offenses. Whetzel's upbringing was described as "disastrous," as his parents had severe issues with drug and alcohol abuse. Whetzel, the defense argued, was also subjected to physical abuse and a culture of criminality by those who surrounded him. Whetzel was ultimately removed from the home by the state Department of Health and Human Resources.

"We have an opportunity with a young man at this age to stop the cycle and break this chain," Lehman said.

Whetzel himself, who was bound in restraints, also made a brief statement to the court prior to sentencing.

"I'm really sorry for what I've done," Whetzel said. "It will never happen again. I just need this one chance to prove myself."

Before the sentence was pronounced, both Deborah Beckman, the victim in the case, and Berkeley County Prosecuting Attorney Pamela Games-Neely addressed Groh. Beck read from a prepared victim impact statement.

"I think I will be forever impacted by this," she said.

The robbery, which occurred shortly after her husband's death, led to significant financial and emotional difficulties for Beckman throughout this past year and she said she is now afraid to be alone.

"I don't know if I'll ever be able to trust anyone like I did," she said.

Games-Neely argued that Whetzel should be sentenced to the penitentiary based on the severity of the crime.

"I have prosecuted his mother and his father and his relatives," she said. "I heard the same speech from his dad and I heard the same speech from his mother."

Not matter what the court did, she said it would never make Beckman feel safe again, and she argued it was unlikely Whetzel would ever be able to pay back the restitution ordered by the court.

"This isn't about haves and have nots. I'm sorry for the way he grew up," Games-Neely said. "Georgie made a choice. He made a choice when he walked into that home with a gun in his hand."

When it came time for Groh to pronounce her sentence, she said the court was not unsympathetic to Whetzel or his upbringing, but said the court's primary concern in the case was public safety and not Whetzel's family "track record."

"What the court finds significant, despite his age and despite his upbringing, is . . . the fact that he made a choice to rob with a handgun folks that were known to him. He started his adult criminal record at the very top with first-degree robbery," Groh said.

SOURCE: (http://journal-news.net/page/content.detail/id/572272/Youth-is-charged-as-adult.html?nav=5006)

A Significant Finding of the PHDCN

It is commonly thought that neighborhoods comprising mainly of racial or ethnic minorities experience higher levels of violence than do those that are primarily White. However, this stereotype does not always prove true, once data are collected and analyzed. The following excerpt from a report summary of the Project on Human Development in Chicago Neighborhoods (PHDCN) provides insight into youth violence in different types of neighborhoods (Liberman 2007, 6–7):

> Youth from different racial and ethnic groups reported committing violence at different rates. African American youth reported the most violence; Mexican American youth reported the least, slightly below Whites. Puerto Rican and "other" youths reported rates in between. Involvement in self-reported violence showed the familiar age-crime curve for all groups, peaking at about age 17....

Why did youth of different ethnic groups commit more or less violence? Their neighborhood conditions, parents' marital status, and immigrant generation accounted for most of the difference. These factors accounted for more than 60 percent of the gap between African American and White violence, and the entire gap between Mexican Americans and Whites.

Among these factors, neighborhood conditions had the strongest influence on youth violence, accounting for about 30 percent of the difference in violence between African Americans and Whites. Less violence was committed by youths living in neighborhoods with more first-generation immigrants and where more residents were employed in professional and managerial occupations.

System Response to Violent Juvenile Offenders

In response to the mounting evidence documenting how a large number of crimes are committed by a small number of repeat offenders, many of whom are also violent, the OJJDP, in the 1990s, instituted a Serious Habitual Offender Comprehensive Action Program (SHOCAP) aimed at youth violence. Although no longer a federally applied OJJDP program, many states have implemented their own versions of SHOCAP using recommendations of the original program because many of the guidelines are still applicable for today's violent juvenile offenders.

The recommendations for *detention* are to establish a policy of separate and secure holding of all designated habitual offenders, to provide a special close custody classification for all designated violent offenders to protect staff and other correctional clients and to monitor and record all activities and transactions of these offenders.

The recommendations at *intake* are mandatory holding of all identified violent offenders brought in on new charges, immediate notification of the prosecutor of the intake and special follow-up and records preparation for the detention hearings.

The recommendations for *prosecution* of violent offenders are to file a petition (charges) with the court based on the highest provable offense, resist any pretrial release, seek a guilty plea on all offenses charged and vertically prosecute all cases (assign only one deputy district attorney to each case). Other recommendations include providing an immediate response to police and detention officials upon notification of the arrest, participating in interagency working groups and on individual case management teams and sharing appropriate information with the crime analyst or official designated to develop and maintain profiles on violent offenders. A formal policy of seeking the maximum penalty for each conviction or adjudication should be established.

All too often chronic, serious violent juvenile offenders "fall through the cracks" of the juvenile justice system because efforts are not coordinated. In response to rising numbers of habitually violent youths, the Colorado

Springs Police Department instituted the Serious Habitual Offender/Directed Intervention (SHO/DI) Program aimed at this group of juvenile offenders. The program had three goals:

- To develop trust and cooperation between agencies serving juveniles
- To identify and overcome real and perceived legal obstacles to cooperative efforts
- To build a credible interagency information process to identify and track habitual juvenile offenders

The ultimate goal was to *incapacitate* repeat offenders, whether through detention, incarceration, probation or other means. One important program component was a court order signed by a juvenile judge allowing the police department to share information with other agencies in the juvenile justice system. Another important outcome of the program was a change in how the juvenile portion of the justice system was viewed. Traditionally juvenile matters received low priority. "Kiddy Court" was not taken seriously, and beginning lawyers were assigned to prosecute juveniles. This practice was changed with the institution of the SHO/DI Program.

The Public Health Model and the Juvenile Justice Perspective

One approach to youth violence is to view it not just as a problem to be dealt with by the juvenile justice system but as a threat to our national health. When violence is viewed in this way, it makes sense to adopt the approach used in our public health system. A basic principle of the public health response to problems is to focus resources on the areas of greatest need.

Another contribution from the public health model is the metaphor of **contagion** as a way to explain the spread of violence. Acts of violence tend to spread rapidly within high-risk areas or hot spots and within groups. Some criminologists find the source of high rates of violence in a subculture of violence that encourages people—young males in particular—to use physical force to command respect and settle conflicts. Others view violence as spreading through cycles of revenge and retaliation among perpetrators and victims. McCord and Conway (2005, 10–11) illuminated some of the uncertainties surrounding a possible contagion effect among juvenile peers with respect to violent offending: "Committing a first offense with violent accomplices contributed to the likelihood that violent crimes would be committed, regardless of age at first arrest. That is, violent peers increase the likelihood that nonviolent offenders will commit violent offenses."

A barrier to implementing a public health approach is the distinct and opposing philosophical traditions of the two approaches. From the juvenile justice perspective, the most important fact about the social reality of violence in our society is that those who perpetrate violence are criminal offenders. The juvenile justice system has its roots in the adult criminal justice system, which is part of the classical tradition that conceives human action as a product of rational and moral choice. Public health is rooted in positivist conceptions of human behavior as "caused" by external forces that, in principle, are subject to modification.

The juvenile justice perspective on juvenile violence is that it is the result of youths' free choice and is to be punished as criminal. The public health perspective is that youths are victims of social forces and they are to be treated.

Are Delinquency and Youth Violence Inevitable?

Many people believe juvenile violence will be an unavoidable part of life in American society unless significant changes are made in how such youths are identified *before* they become seriously delinquent. Reasons for the increase in the seriousness of the offenses and the decrease in the offenders' age range from the problems of increasing gang activity and drug use in the elementary schools to the heightened level of violence in society in general and to increasing stress on families, especially in economically deprived areas.

The juvenile justice system recognizes that some youthful offenders are simply criminals who happen to be young. Every experienced law enforcement officer has dealt with criminally hardened 13- or 14-year-olds. Although this group represents only a small fraction of our youths, they commit a large percentage of all violent crimes. Public safety demands that law enforcement recognize and respond to this criminal element. The challenge for the juvenile justice system is to identify this group of hard-core offenders and to treat them as adults, including providing for the use of juvenile offense records in adult sentencing. This group of hard-core offenders often is responsible for the crime and violence found in the nation's schools and for the violence perpetrated by gangs. Gangs are the topic of the next chapter.

There is reason for hope, however, as the report by the surgeon general stresses: "Youth violence is not an intractable problem. We now have the knowledge and tools needed to reduce or even prevent much of the most serious youth violence" (*Youth Violence* 2001, p.6).

Summary

- Status offenses include actions such as running away, habitual truancy, violating curfew and underage drinking.
- The trend for status offense arrests, including the offenses of running away, violating curfew and underage drinking, is decreasing.
- The most frequent delinquency offenses are property crimes, with larceny-theft being the most common.
- Similar to arrests pertaining to the status offense categories, arrests of juveniles for property crimes have decreased during the past decade, in some cases by a significant margin.
- Arrests for violent juvenile crime dropped from the mid-1990s to the mid-2000s, showed a slight upward trend in 2005 and 2006 and have since returned to a downward trend.
- The two general onset trajectories for youth violence are *early*, in which violence begins before puberty, and *late*, in which violence begins in adolescence.
- Most youth violence begins in adolescence and ends with the transition into adulthood.

■ Boys who own guns for protection are significantly and substantially more likely to be involved in delinquent behavior than are either those who do not own guns or those who own guns for sport.

■ The juvenile justice perspective on juvenile violence is that it is the result of youths' free choice and is to be punished as criminal. The public health perspective is that youths are victims of social forces and they are to be treated.

Discussion Questions

1. What are the most common status offenses in your community?

2. Do other countries have status offenses?

3. Do you believe status offenders should be treated the same as youths involved in serious, violent crimes?

4. Should the term *juvenile delinquency* encompass both those youths who commit status offenses and those who commit nonviolent crimes? Violent crimes?

5. How do you account for the decrease in arrests for status offenses? For property crimes?

6. To what do you attribute the racial disparity in youths arrested?

7. Based on the information provided in this chapter, do you think the developmental pathways identified in Chapter 4 have validity?

8. Have there been any instances of youths involved in serious, violent crime in your community during the past year?

9. Should parents and guardians be held legally responsible when a juvenile commits a violent crime? Why or why not?

10. For serious, violent crimes, such as armed robbery and murder, should the age of the offender be an issue?

References

Adams, Kenneth. 2003. "The Effectiveness of Juvenile Curfews at Crime Prevention." *Annals of the American Academy of Political and Social Science* 587(1): 136–159.

———. 2007. "Abolish Juvenile Curfews." *Criminology & Public Policy* 6 (4): 663–670.

American Psychiatric Association. 2000. *Diagnostic and Statistical Manual of Mental Disorders (DSM-IV-TR)*. 4th ed. Washington, DC: American Psychiatric Association.

———. n.d. *Violence & Youth: Psychology's Response*, Vol. 1. Summary Report of the American Psychological Association Commission on Violence and Youth. Washington, DC: American Psychiatric Association.

Becker, Judith V., John A. Hunter, Robert M. Stein, and Meg S. Kaplan. 1989. "Factors Associated with Erection in Adolescent Sex Offenders." *Journal of Psychopathology and Behavioral Assessment* 11 (4): 353–362.

Bonner, Barbara L. 2008 (Spring). "Adolescents with Illegal Sexual Behavior: Current Knowledge." *The APSAC Advisor* 20 (2): 5–8.

Caldwell, Michael F. 2007 (June). "Sexual Offense Adjudication and Sexual Recidivism among Juvenile Offenders." *Sexual Abuse: A Journal of Research and Treatment* 19 (3): 107–113.

Centers for Disease Control and Prevention. 2008 (August 6). "Quick Stats: Binge Drinking." http://www.cdc.gov/alcohol/quickstats/binge_drinking.htm (accessed November 18, 2008).

Chaffin, Mark, Elizabeth Letourneau, and Jane F. Silovsky. 2002. "Adults, Adolescents, and Children Who Sexually Abuse Children." In *The APSAC Handbook on Child Maltreatment*, edited by John E. B. Myers, Lucy Berliner, John Briere, C. Terry. Hendrix, Carole Jenny, and Theresa A. Reid, 2nd. ed., 205–232. Thousand Oaks, CA: Sage.

"Cities Say Curfews Help Reduce Gang Activity and Violent Crime." 2001 (October 25). Washington, DC: National League of Cities News Fax.

Cole, Danny. 2003. "The Effect of a Curfew Law on Juvenile Crime in Washington, D" *American Journal of Criminal Justice* 27 (2): 217–232.

Collins, Damian C. A., and Robin A. Kearns. 2001 (August). "Under Curfew and Under Siege? Legal Geographies of Young People." *Geoforum* 32 (3): 389–403.

Cottle, Cindy C., Ria J. Lee, and Kirk Heilbrun. 2001. "Identifying Risk Factors for Juvenile Recidivism: A Meta-Analysis." *Criminal Justice and Behavior* 28 (3): 367.

Crime in the United States, 2010. 2011. Washington, DC: U.S. Department of Justice, Federal Bureau of Investigation.

Davis, Carla P. 2007 (July). "At-Risk Girls and Delinquency." *Crime & Delinquency* 53 (3): 408–435.

Eaton, Danice K., Laura Kann, Steve Kinchen, Shari Shanklin, James Ross, Joseph Hawkins, William A. Harris, Richard Lowry, Tim McManus, David Chyen, et al. 2010 (June). *Youth Risk Behavior Surveillance—United States, 2009*. Surveillance Summaries, Vol. 59, No. SS-5. Atlanta, GA: Centers for Disease Control and Prevention.

Ellis, Lee, Kevin Beaver, and John Wright, John. 2009. *Handbook of Crime Correlates*. Oxford, UK: Academic Press/Elsevier.

Federal Interagency Forum on Child and Family Statistics. 2008 (July). *America's Children in Brief: Key National Indicators of Well-Being, 2008*. Washington, DC: U.S. Government Printing Office.

Felson, Richard B., Glenn Deane, and David P. Armstrong. 2008. "Do Theories of Crime or Violence Explain Race Differences in Delinquency?" *Social Science Research* 37 (2): 624–641.

Felson, Richard B., Brent Teasdale, and Keri B. Burchfield. 2008 (May). "The Influence of Being under the Influence: Alcohol Effects on Adolescent Violence." *Journal of Research in Crime and Delinquency* 45 (2): 119–141.

Fried, Carrie S. 2001 (February). "Juvenile Curfews: Are They an Effective and Constitutional Means of Combating Juvenile Violence?" *Behavioral Sciences and the Law* 19: 127–141.

Garner, Bryan A. (Ed.) 2006. *Black's Law Dictionary*. 3rd pocket ed. St. Paul, MN: Thomson/West.

Griffin, Patrick, and Patricia Torbet, eds. 2002 (June). *Desktop Guide to Good Juvenile Probation Practice*. Washington, DC: National Center for Juvenile Justice.

Heilbrunn, Joanna Zorn. 2007 (January). *Pieces of the Truancy Jigsaw: A Literature Review*. Denver, CO: National Center for School Engagement.

Herrera, Veronica M., and Laura Ann McCloskey. 2001. "Gender Differences in the Risk for Delinquency among Youth Exposed to Family Violence." *Child Abuse and Neglect* 25 (8): 1037–1052.

Hunter, John A., Dennis W. Goodwin, and Judith V. Becker. 1994 (June). "The Relationship between Phallometrically Measured Deviant Sexual Arousal and Clinical Characteristics in Juvenile Sex Offenders." *Behavioral Research and Therapy* 32 (5): 533–538.

Hunter, John A., Roy R. Hazelwood, and David Slesinger. 2000 (March). "Juvenile-Perpetrated Sex Crimes: Patterns of Offending and Predictors of Violence." *Journal of Family Violence* 15 (1): 81–93.

"Juvenile Curfews and the Major Confusion over Minor Rights." 2005 (May). *Harvard Law Review* 118 (7): 2400–2421.

Kemper, Therese S., and Janet A. Kistner. 2007 (December). "Offense History and Recidivism in Three Victim-Age-Based Groups of Juvenile Sex Offenders." *Sexual Abuse: A Journal of Research and Treatment* 19 (4): 409–423.

Kempf-Leonard, Kimberly, Paul E. Tracy, and James C. Howell. 2001 (September). "Serious, Violent and Chronic Juvenile Offenders: The Relationship of Delinquency Career Types to Adult Criminality." *Justice Quarterly* 18 (3): 449–478.

Lambie, Ian, and Isabel Randall. 2011. "Creating a Firestorm: A Review of Children Who Deliberately Light Fires." *Clinical Psychological Review* 31 (2): 307–327.

Liberman, Akiva. 2007 (September). *Adolescents, Neighborhoods, and Violence: Recent Findings from the Project on Human Development in Chicago Neighborhoods*. Washington, DC: U.S. Department of Justice, National Institute of Justice. (NCJ 217397)

Lizotte, Alan, and David Sheppard. 2001 (July). *Gun Use by Male Juveniles: Research and Prevention*. Washington, DC: Office of Juvenile Justice and Delinquency Prevention. (NCJ188992)

Loeber, Rolf. 1982 (December). "The Stability of Antisocial and Delinquent Child Behavior: A Review." *Child Development* 53 (6): 1431–1446.

Loeber, Rolf, David P. Farrington, and David Petechuk, David. 2003 (May). *Child Delinquency: Early Intervention and Prevention*. Washington, DC: Office of Juvenile Justice and Delinquency Prevention. (NCJ 186162)

Lytton, Hugh, and David M. Romney. 1991 (March). "Parents' Differential Socialization of Boys and Girls: A Meta-Analysis." *Psychological Bulletin* 109 (2): 267–296.

Margolin, Gayla, and Elana B. Gordis. 2000 (January). "The Effects of Family and Community Violence on Children." *Annual Review of Psychology* 51: 445–479.

McCord, Joan, and Kevin P. Conway. 2005 (December). *Co-Offending and Patterns of Juvenile Crime*. Research in Brief. Washington, DC: U.S. Department of Justice, National Institute of Justice. (NCJ 210360)

McDowall, David, Colin Loftin, and Brian Wiersema. 2000 (January). "The Impact of Youth Curfew Laws on Juvenile Crime Rates." *Crime & Delinquency* 46 (1): 76–91.

McNamara, Robert H. 2008. *The Lost Population: Status Offenders in America*. Durham, NC: Carolina Academic Press.

Miranda, Alexis O., and Colette L. Corcoran. 2000 (July). "Comparison of Perpetration Characteristics between Male Juvenile and Adult Sexual Offenders: Preliminary Results." *Sexual Abuse: A Journal of Research and Treatment* 12 (3): 179–188.

Moffitt, Terrie. 1993. "Adolescence-Limited and Life Course Persistent Antisocial Behavior: A Developmental Taxonomy." *Psychology Review* 100: 674–701.

Molnar, Beth E., Angela Browne, Magdalena Cerda, and Stephen L. Buka. 2005 (August). "Violent Behavior by Girls Reporting Violent Victimization." *Archives of Pediatric and Adolescent Medicine* 159 (8): 731–739.

OJJDP Statistical Briefing Book. 2009 (October 31). http://www.ojjdp.gov/ojstatbb/crime/JAR_Display.asp?ID=qa05220 (accessed October 12, 2011).

Parks, Gregory A., and David E. Bard. 2006 (October). "Risk Factors for Adolescent Sex Offender Recidivism: Evaluation of Predictive Factors and Comparison of Three Groups Based upon Victim Type." *Sexual Abuse: A Journal of Research and Treatment* 18 (4): 319–339.

Putnam, Charles T., and John T. Kirkpatrick. 2005 (May). *Juvenile Firesetting: A Research Overview*. Washington, DC: U.S. Department of Justice, Office of Juvenile Justice and Delinquency Prevention. (NCJ 207606)

Puzzanchera, Charles. 2009 (December). *Juvenile Arrests 2008*. Washington, DC: Office of Juvenile Justice and Delinquency Prevention. (NCJ 228479)

Regulating Guns in America: An Evaluation and Comparative Analysis of Federal, State and Selected Local Gun Laws, 2008 Edition. 2008 (February). San Francisco: Legal Community against Violence.

Reynolds, K. Michael, Ruth Seydlitz, and Pamela Jenkins. 2000 (March). "Do Juvenile Curfew Laws Work? A Time-Series Analysis of the New Orleans Law." *Justice Quarterly* 17 (1): 205–230.

Root, Carol, Sherri MacKay, Joanna Henderson, Giannette Del Bove, and Diana Warling. 2008 (February). "The Link between Maltreatment and Juvenile Firesetting: Correlates and Underlying Mechanisms." *Child Abuse and Neglect* 32 (2): 161–176.

Schmidt, Susan R. 2008 (Spring). "Adolescent Girls with Illegal Sexual Behavior." *The APSAC Advisor* 20 (2): 12–13.

Scott, Elizabeth S., and Laurence Steinberg. 2008. *Rethinking Juvenile Justice*. Cambridge, MA: Harvard University Press.

Scott, Michael S. 2001 (September). *Disorderly Youth in Public Places*. Problem-Oriented Guides for Police Series, No. 6. Washington, DC: Office of Community Oriented Policing Services.

Sheppard, David, Heath Grant, Wendy Rowe, and Nancy Jacobs. 2000 (September). *Fighting Juvenile Gun Violence*. Washington, DC: Office of Juvenile Justice and Delinquency Prevention. (NCJ 182679)

Snyder, Howard N. 2008 (November). *Juvenile Arrests 2006*. Washington, DC: OJJDP Juvenile Justice Bulletin. (NCJ 221338)

Snyder, Howard N., Rachele C. Espiritu, David Huizinga, Rolf Loeber, and David Petechuk. 2003 (March). *Prevalence and Development of Child Delinquency*. Washington, DC: Office of Juvenile Justice and Delinquency Prevention, Bulletin Series. (NCJ 193411)

Snyder, Howard N., and Melissa Sickmund. 2006 (March). *Juvenile Offenders and Victims 2006 National Report*. Washington, DC: U.S. Department of Justice, Office of Justice Programs, Office of Juvenile Justice and Delinquency Prevention.

Steffensmeier, Darrell, Jennifer Schwartz, Hua Zhong, and Jeff Ackerman. 2005. "An Assessment of Recent Trends in Girls' Violence using Diverse Longitudinal Sources: Is the Gender Gap Closing?" *Criminology* 43 (2): 355–406.

Steinhart, David J. 1996 (Winter). "Status Offenses." *The Juvenile Court* 6 (3): 86–99.

Stewart, Eric A., and Ronald L. Simons. 2010 (May). "Race, Code of the Street, and Violent Delinquency: A Multilevel Investigation of Neighborhood Street Culture and Individual Norms of Violence." *Criminology* 48 (2): 569–606.

Tyler, Jerry E., and Thomas W. Segady. 2000. "Parental Liability Laws: Rationale, Theory and Effectiveness." *The Social Science Journal* 37 (1): 79–96.

U.S. Census Bureau. 2010. *2010 Census*. Washington, DC: U.S. Census Bureau.

U.S. Fire Administration. 2006 (July). *Juvenile Firesetting: A Growing Concern*. Washington, DC: Department of Homeland Security. (FA-307)

Vaughn, Michael G., Qiang Fu, Matt DeLisi, John Paul Wright, Kevin M. Beaver, Brian E. Perron, and Matthew O. Howard. 2010. "Prevalence and Correlates of Fire-Setting in the United States: Results from the National Epidemiologic Survey on Alcohol and Related Conditions." *Comprehensive Psychiatry* 51 (3): 217–223.

Visher, Christy. 1987 (December). "Incapacitation and Crime Control: Does a 'Lock 'Em Up' Strategy Reduce Crime?" *Justice Quarterly* 4 (4): 513–43.

White, Helene Raskin, Peter C. Tice, Rolf Loeber, and Magda Strouthamer-Loeber. 2002 (May). "Illegal Acts Committed by Adolescents under the Influence of Alcohol and Drugs." *Journal of Research in Crime and Delinquency* 39 (2): 131–152.

Williams, James Herbert, Richard A. Van Dorn, Charles D. Ayers, Charlotte L. Bright, Robert D. Abbott, and J. David Hawkins. 2007 (June). "Understanding Race and Gender Differences in Delinquent Acts and Alcohol and Marijuana Use: A Developmental Analysis of Initiation." *Social Work Research* 31 (2): 71–81.

Wolfgang, Marvin, Robert Figlio, and Thorsten Sellin. 1972. *Delinquency in a Birth Cohort*. Chicago: University of Chicago Press.

Wright, John Paul, Stephen G. Tibbetts, and Leah E. Daigle. 2008. *Criminals in the Making: Criminality across the Life Course*. Thousand Oaks, CA: Sage.

Youth Violence: A Report of the Surgeon General. 2001. Rockville, MD: U.S. Department of Health and Human Services, Office of the Surgeon General.

Zahn, Margaret A., Robert Agnew, Donna Fishbein, Shari Miller, Donna-Marie Winn, Gayle Dakoff, Candace Kruttschnitt, Peggy Giordano, Denise C. Gottfredson, Allison A. Payne, et al. 2010 (April). *Causes and Correlates of Girls' Delinquency*. Washington, DC: Office of Juvenile Justice and Delinquency Prevention, Girls Study Group. (NCJ 226358)

Zahn, Margaret A., Susan Brumbaugh, Darrell Steffensmeier, Barry C. Feld, Merry Morash, Meda Chesney-Lind, Jody Miller, Allison A. Payne, Denise C. Gottfredson, and Candace Kruttschnitt. 2008 (May). *Violence by Teenage Girls: Trends and Context*. Washington, DC: U.S. Department of Justice, Office of Juvenile Justice and Delinquency Prevention. (NCJ218905)

Case Cited

Schleifer v. City of Charlottesville, 159 F.3d 843, 853 (4th Cir. 1998)

Helpful Resource

Chesney-Lind, Meda, and Randall G. Shelden. 2003. *Girls, Delinquency and Juvenile Justice*. 3rd ed. Belmont, CA: Wadsworth.

Youth Gangs

> **The observation that gang members, as compared with other youths, are more extensively involved with delinquency—especially serious and violent delinquency—is perhaps the most robust and consistent observation in criminological research.**
>
> —Thornberry et al. 2003, 1

Members of the Latin Kings gang display their gang signs during a rally in New York for racial justice.

© Frances M. Roberts/UPPA/ZUMAPRESS.com

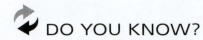

DO YOU KNOW?

- How organized, durable and "dangerous" most youth gangs are?
- How long most juveniles' gang "careers" last?
- Where the biggest gang problems and most violent gangs tend to occur?

- What risk factor categories have been identified for gang involvement and the predictive nature associated with them?
- What population is at greatest risk of becoming victims of gang violence?

CAN YOU DEFINE?

civil gang injunction

crew

gang

graffiti

horizontal
  prosecution

marginalization

moniker

pulling levers

representing

street gang

tagging

turf

vertical prosecution

youth gang

CHAPTER OUTLINE

Introduction

Definitions

Organization and Classification
  of Youth Gangs

Gang Leadership and Membership

*Classifications of Gangs and Gang
  Members*

The Extent and Migration
  of Youth Gangs

Gang Formation: Risk Factors
  and Reasons Why Youths
  Join Gangs

Identifying Characteristics
  of Gangs

Gang Names

Symbols

Clothing

Communication Styles

Tattoos

Illegal Activities of Youth Gangs

Youth Gang Violence and
  Victimization

Youth Gangs and Drugs

The Gangs–Drugs–Violence
  Nexus

Recognizing a Youth Gang
  Problem

Identifying Gang Members

Gangs in Schools

Responding to an Existing
  Youth Gang Problem

*Suppression and Law Enforcement
  Efforts*

*Arresting and Prosecuting Gang
  Members*

*Pulling Levers: The Boston
  Gun Project and Operation
  Ceasefire*

Youth Gang Prevention
  Efforts

Introduction

Belonging to a gang is *not* illegal in this country; however, many of the activities that gangs participate in are illegal. Gangs commit shootings, assaults, robberies and other violent crimes; engage in extortion and other felonies; traffic in drugs; and generally terrorize neighborhoods. Previously loose-knit groups of juveniles and young adults who once engaged in petty crimes may, over time, evolve into powerful, organized gangs, representing a form of domestic terrorism.

The most current data available indicates that approximately 1.4 million gang members, composing more than 33,000 gangs, are criminally active throughout the 50 United States, the District of Columbia and Puerto Rico, a figure representing a 40 percent increase from the one million gang members estimated to have been active in 2009 (National Youth Gang Center 2011). Data from the *National Youth Gang Survey* (NYGS) show that adults (persons age 18 and older) consistently outnumber juveniles in annual national surveys of gang membership, with the most recent data indicating approximately 40 percent of gang members in the United States are under age 18 (National Youth Gang Center 2011). Thus, according to these estimates, there are roughly 560,000 juvenile gang members in this country. Many gangs, especially those that are criminally involved, contain a mix of juvenile and young adult members. Although this is a juvenile justice text, discussion of the topic of gangs necessitates traveling beyond the age boundaries set by conventional standards regarding juveniles to include some broader issues of gangs, irrespective of the age of their members.

Definitions

Everyone has a sense of what a gang is, yet no single, agreed-upon definition has been developed to apply to gangs. Some definitions emphasize criminal activity whereas others stress territoriality. Adding to the challenge of defining a gang is the diversity observed among such groups: "There is no *one* form of street gang. Gangs can be large or small, long term or short term, more or less territorial, more or less criminally involved, and so on. If one treats all gangs as being the same, then the treatment will often be wrong, perhaps even making things worse. … It is the fact of gang diversity itself that should make us cautious about generalizing too quickly about their nature" (Klein 2007, 54–55).

A working group of American and European gang researchers, the assembly of which has come to be known as the *Eurogang program*, defines a street gang as "any durable, street-oriented youth group whose own identity includes involvement in illegal activity" (Klein 2007, 18). The National Youth Gang Center (NYGC) defines a youth gang as "a self-formed association of peers having the following characteristics: three or more members, generally ages 12 to 24; a name and some sense of identity, generally indicated by such symbols as style of clothing, graffiti, and hand signs; some degree of permanence and organization; and an elevated level of involvement in delinquent or criminal activity" (Howell and Egley 2008, 1).

The National Alliance of Gang Investigators' Associations (NAGIA) defines a gang as "a group or association of three or more persons with a common identifying sign, symbol, or name who individually or collectively engage in criminal activity that creates an atmosphere of fear and intimidation" (*National Gang Threat Assessment* 2009, 3). The current federal law (18 U.S.C. § 521 (a)) defines a criminal street gang as "an ongoing group, club, organization, or association of five or more persons: (A) that has as one of its primary purposes the commission of one or more of the criminal offenses described in subsection (c); (B) the members of which engage, or have engaged within the past five years, in a continuing series of offenses described in subsection (c); and (C) the activities of which affect interstate or foreign commerce." And Klein and Maxson (2006, 4) state succinctly, "A street gang is any durable, street-oriented youth group whose involvement in illegal activity is part of its group identity." Clearly, consensus as to how to define a *gang* has yet to be reached.

A Key Issue: The Importance of Definitions

Before a problem can be addressed and tackled, it must be defined. A key issue in combating youth gangs hinges on how they are defined. If they are broadly defined, the gang problem may appear to be gigantic. If narrowly defined, the problem may not seem significant. What constitutes a gang is not always clear, and if a definition cannot be agreed on, it is difficult for communities to quantify the size of their gang problem. When various agents within a community are allowed latitude and subjectivity in defining gangs, the influence of differing agendas can be observed. For example, police departments seeking federal funding earmarked for gang suppression efforts may take a broad approach in defining gangs to maximize the number of gangs and gang members and, hence, the magnitude of the problem, in their jurisdiction. City leaders, school administrators and other individuals in the political arena may prefer a more conservative approach, opting to define more narrowly what constitutes a gang in an effort to downplay the issue and mitigate any negative public perception regarding the quality of life in the community or safety levels within the schools. Thus, a uniform definition used by law enforcement, schools, parents, social workers and city administrators would be of great benefit in efforts to understand the gang problem.

In general, a **gang** is an ongoing group of people that have a common name or common identifying sign or symbol, form an allegiance for a common purpose and engage in unlawful or criminal activity. A **street gang** is a group of individuals who meet over time, have identifiable leadership, claim control over a specific territory in the community and engage in criminal behavior, either individually or collectively. They frequently create an atmosphere of fear and intimidation in a community. The term **youth gang** is often used interchangeably with *street gang* and, in the context of juvenile justice, is preferred because it helps avoid any confusion between this type of gang and the adult criminal street gang.

Before leaving the discussion of definitions, consider briefly the distinction between *youth gangs* and *delinquent peer groups*. Although some of the literature uses these two terms interchangeably, other authors contend a difference exists, the primary distinguishing characteristic being the willingness of youth gangs to use violence at a level not observed with other delinquent peer groups (Battin-Pearson et al. 1998; Howell 1998; Klein 1995; Spergel, Wa, and Sosa 2005). Furthermore, research has shown that, when compared with members of delinquent peer groups, gang members engage in significantly more criminal behavior and drug-related offenses, and they have higher rates of police contact and more arrests (Bureau of Justice Assistance 1998; Delaney 2006).

Organization and Classification of Youth Gangs

There is no such thing as a "typical" gang, and the degree of organization seen among different gangs is extremely varied. However, the overall national youth gang problem can be visualized as a pyramid, with the level of gang organization, sophistication and criminal involvement increasing as one moves toward the apex. The vast majority of youth gangs exist at the base of the pyramid as unsophisticated, loosely organized groups of kids who band together for a while and then disband without any major harm done. The middle layer of the pyramid consists of fewer numbers of gangs that are more organized, and the top echelon of the pyramid is inhabited by a relatively small number of highly sophisticated, organized, criminally involved gangs (Mueller 2007).

 Most youth gangs are loosely organized, short-lived and pose little threat to public safety. Most crime and violence attributed to gangs is caused by a relatively small number of organized groups.

A gang's degree of organization influences the behavior observed among its members, and even incremental increases in structural organization have been found to be related to increased involvement in offending and victimization (Decker, Katz, and Webb 2008). Keep this relationship in mind as you read through the chapter,

Gang Leadership and Membership

Gang organization encompasses the structure of its leadership and subordinate members. Varying levels of member involvement can be found, but most gangs contain leaders, hard-core members, regular members and fringe members or wannabes.

Gang leadership tends to be better defined and more clearly identifiable than does leadership in other types of delinquent groups. The leaders are usually the oldest gang members and have extensive criminal records. They may surround themselves with hard-core members, giving orders and expecting unquestioned obedience. The hard-core members usually commit the crimes and are the most violent. Some have had to earn the right to become true gang members through some sort of initiation.

On the fringes of most gangs are youths who aspire to become gang members, frequently referred to as *wannabes*. They dress and talk like the hard-core members, but they have not yet been formally accepted into the gang. Figure 7.1 shows one common type of gang organization and illustrates how kids who start in the outer ring (potentials or "could-bes") can "progress" inward to become hardened gang members.

Gangs usually adopt specific criteria for membership eligibility, and many gangs employ initiation rituals, often involving one or more criminal acts, as a prerequisite to membership. Once youths reach an age at which they can prove themselves to peer leaders within the gang, they may perform some sort of rite of passage or ceremony called "turning," "quoting" or "jumping in." Or they may be "courted in," simply accepted into the gang without having to prove themselves in any particular way. According to Shelden, Tracy and Brown (2004, 69), "Most youth are informally socialized into the gang subculture from a very early age so that they do not so much join a gang, but rather evolve into the gang naturally. Actually turning or being jumped is little more than a rite of passage." Incidentally, some states have toughened their criminal statutes to make it a stronger felony for an adult to recruit a juvenile into a gang.

It is important to recognize that, even among high-risk youth, gang membership for most individuals tends to be short-lived (Melde and Esbensen 2011; Snyder and Sickmund 2006). Of the studies done on the typical length of gang membership, most confirm the transient nature of such membership and conclude that the majority of youths spend a year or less in a gang, with very few

Hard-Core

These youths comprise approximately 5 to 10 percent of the gang. They have been in the gang the longest and frequently are in and out of jail, unemployed and involved with drugs (distribution or use). The average age is early to mid–20s, but some hard-cores could be older or younger. Very influential in the gang.

Regular Members

Youths whose average age is 14 to 17 years, but they could be older or younger. They have already been initiated into the gang and tend to back up the hard-core members. If they stay in the gang long enough, they could become hard-core.

Claimers, Associates or "Wannabes"

Youngsters whose average age is 11 to 13 years, but age may vary. These are the youngsters who are not officially members of the gang, but they act like they are or claim to be from the gang. They may begin to dress in gang attire, hang around with the gang or write the graffiti of the gang.

Potentials or "Could-Bes"

Youngsters who are getting close to an age at which they might decide to join a gang. They live in or live close to an area where there are gangs or have a family member who is involved with gangs. The potentials do not have to join gangs; they can choose alternatives and avoid gang affiliation completely. Generally, the further into a gang someone is, the harder it is to get out.

Figure 7.1 One Common Type of Gang Organization
© Cengage Learning 2013

juveniles spending the bulk of their adolescent years as members of a gang (Esbensen, Huizinga, and Weiher 1993; Hill, Lui, and Hawkins 2001; Thornberry et al. 1993). Furthermore, although much has been made of how difficult it is for youths to avoid the lure of gangs or to break free from them once they have joined, findings from numerous studies have failed to support these scenarios as reality (Decker and Lauritsen 1996; Huff 1998; Thornberry et al. 2003).

 For most juveniles, gang membership is a short-term event, with most youth desisting from gang involvement after one year or less.

Compared with other types of law-violating youth groups, gangs tend to have closer relational bonds and more continuous affiliation between members. Gang members also demonstrate associational patterns and bonds through certain identifying characteristics such as their names, symbols and communication styles.

Classifications of Gangs and Gang Members

Just as gangs can be defined in a variety of ways, they can also be classified in different ways. Some criminologists classify gangs as either cultural or instrumental. *Cultural gangs* are neighborhood centered and exist independently of criminal activity. *Instrumental gangs*, in contrast, are formed for the express purpose of criminal activity, primarily drug trafficking. Klein and colleagues have identified five gang typologies (2007, 54–55):

> "Traditional" and "nontraditional" gangs are the largest, longest-enduring, and most crime-producing gangs. They are not the most common form, but they best fit the media stereotype of large inner-city gangs with strong intergang rivalries and violent tendencies.
>
> "Compressed" gangs, primarily adolescent groups of 50 to 100 members and less than ten years' duration, are the most common, found in both large and small cities. Least common are "collective" gangs, rather amorphous, but large collections with little internal structure, sometimes held together by loose neighborhood ties and extensive drug dealing. The smallest in size of our five types, but the most tightly structured, is the "specialty" gang, which is not versatile like the other four types, but rather manifests a narrow pattern of criminal behavior. Drug gangs, robbery or burglary gangs, car theft gangs and skinheads are common examples.

Other variables used to classify and differentiate gangs and gang members include (Delaney 2006):

- Race and ethnicity—Caucasian, African American, Hispanic, Asian, Native American, hybrid/heterogeneous/mixed
- Gender composition—all males, all females, mixed gender
- Age—baby, posse, veteranos
- Setting—street, prison, motorcycle
- Type of activity—drug sales, protection, violence, turf defense
- Degree of criminality—minor, serious

Racial/Ethnic Gangs   The majority of gangs in the United States are racially or ethnically homogeneous and, thus, are frequently discussed and studied in the context of this classification (Delaney 2006; Pyrooz, Fox, and Decker 2010). The most well-known racially or ethnically organized gangs are African American gangs (Bloods, Crips, Vice Lords, Disciples), Hispanic or Latin American gangs (Latin Kings, Mara Salvatrucha 13), Asian gangs (Chinese, Japanese, Korean, Filipino, Cambodian/Laotian, Vietnamese, Hmong), Caucasian gangs (skinheads, Aryan Brotherhood, Ku Klux Klan). Emerging gangs have been seen in Indian Country and in communities experiencing a large influx of immigrants from East Africa (Somalia, Sudan) and the Caribbean (Dominican Republic, Jamaica, Haiti) (*2011 National Gang Threat Assessment* 2011).

Not surprisingly, the racial or ethnic composition of a community's gangs highly reflect community-level demographics, with gang members being predominantly Caucasian in predominantly Caucasian communities, mainly Hispanic in Hispanic communities and so on (Howell 2007). It follows that areas with a highly heterogeneous population, such as large urban areas, are most likely to contain a greater mix of gangs of differing ethnicities.

A common misconception about gang demographics has been that they comprise racial or ethnic minorities almost exclusively (Esbensen 2000; Howell 2007). The leading explanation for the perpetuation of the myth that all gang members are racial or ethnic minorities is that most gang research has focused on high-risk neighborhoods in large cities—areas characterized by high rates of poverty, welfare dependency, single-parent households and residential mobility. These highly socially disorganized communities, which tend to draw the attention of researchers, are also disproportionately inhabited by racial and ethnic minorities. Consequently, the assessment of the overall ethnic or racial composition of youth gangs becomes skewed (Esbensen 2000; Howell 2007).

However, according to one study, 25 percent of all gang-involved youth are Caucasian, 31 percent are African American, 25 percent are Hispanic and the remaining 20 percent are of other races or ethnicities (Esbensen and Lynskey 2001). Results of another survey indicate as many as 40 percent of gang members are Caucasian (Howell, Egley, and Gleason 2002). In fact, some data demonstrate a growing involvement of Caucasian/White youth in gang activity in communities where gangs have not previously been reported. In jurisdictions reporting a "late onset" of gang activity, Caucasians were identified as the predominant racial group within the newly emerging gangs (Howell, Egley, and Gleason 2002).

© Mark Allen Johnson/ZUMAPRESS.com

A female member of the Bloods, a Los Angeles street gang, displays her pistol.

Hybrid Gangs   Although many, if not most, gangs are organized around race or ethnicity and are highly homogeneous with respect to this variable, some street gangs are more racially or ethnically heterogeneous in their membership. Such mixed-race or mixed-ethnicity gangs are known as hybrid gangs, a term that originally referred to a gang's ethnic or racial composition. More recently, however, hybrid gangs have come to include a more diverse group of gangs:

> "Hybrid gang culture" is characterized by members of different racial/ethnic groups participating in a single gang, individuals participating in multiple gangs, unclear rules or codes of conduct, symbolic associations with more than one well-established gang (e.g., use of colors and graffiti from different gangs), cooperation of rival gangs in criminal activity, and frequent mergers of small gangs. (Starbuck, Howell, and Lindquist 2001, 1)

Hybrid gangs also include gangs in which membership comprises both males and females.

Female Gangs   Gangs and gang membership remain, on the whole, predominantly male, but the number of gang-involved females has increased over the years (Delaney 2006; Esbensen 2000; Howell 2007). Lack of consensus exists among researchers about how many gang members are female, with estimates ranging from 8 percent (National Youth Gang Center 2011; Schmalleger 2004) to as many as 50 percent in some locations (Esbensen and Lynskey 2001; Gottfredson and Gottfredson 2001), with other estimates falling somewhere in between (Delaney 2006; Esbensen 2000).

Early constructs of female gang membership treated girls as primarily satellites or auxiliary members of male gangs, whose participation in gang activities was minimal and whose function was often restricted to serving in a sexual role or as a weapon carrier for male gang members (Delaney 2006; Moore and Hagedorn 2001; Thrasher 1927). More recent research, however, has found the nature of female gang involvement to be more complex, and although many females do exist on the periphery of male gangs as auxiliary members, many others belong to autonomous female gangs or exist as full-fledged members of gender-integrated gangs (Moore and Hagedorn 2001).

The most common age at which girls enter gangs is 11 or 12, with the prime age of initiation occurring between ages 13 and 14, but Eghigian and Kirby (2006, 48) note, "It is not unheard of for girls to slide into gang involvement as early as age 8. Those who enter at this age and up to 10 years of age often have relatives who are gang members or have experienced a strong gang presence in their neighborhoods."

The Extent and Migration of Youth Gangs

Gangs have been part of American culture since the country began, particularly within the urban landscape. However, youth gangs did not became a source of nationwide social concern until the 1980s and the sudden spike in violent juvenile offending. Before that time, the gang problem had remained fairly isolated to only a handful of the country's largest cities, particularly Chicago, Los Angeles and Detroit. However, by the end of the 1980s, a gang presence was being felt in large and medium-sized cities throughout the nation, as well as in many rural areas: "Since 1980, no single aspect of street gang existence has captured more attention than the emergence of gangs in literally thousands of previously unaffected communities" (Klein and Maxson 2006, 19).

The last quarter of the twentieth century saw significant growth in gangs and gang problems across the country. In the 1970s less than half the states reported youth gang problems, but by the late 1990s every state and the District of Columbia reported gang activity. During that same period, the number of cities reporting youth gang problems mushroomed nearly tenfold: "Gangs are so prevalent today that they have reached institutional status. ... By the end of the twentieth century, gangs had proliferated in nearly all geographic areas of the United States. Gangs can be found in the suburbs, in small cities, and on Native American reservations" (Delaney 2006, 65).

Part of the reason for this apparent "explosion" in the number of gangs was that people—communities, law enforcement agencies, researchers—had started to systematically define and count them. The availability of federal funds for those jurisdictions able to document a gang "problem" provided the incentive for communities to start keeping track of gangs. In all likelihood, many of the gangs identified during this period of "significant growth" had been present for quite some time but, until the spotlight had been turned on them, had existed with relative obscurity as little effort had been made to quantify them.

Gangs range in size from small groups of three to five up to several thousand. Although specific counts are difficult to come by, nationally known gangs such as the Crips and Bloods have memberships numbering in the tens of thousands. The Los Angeles-based Crips, considered to be the largest of all of the gangs within the United States, has been estimated to have 30,000 to 35,000 members, outnumbering the Bloods by as much as 3 to 1 (Delaney 2006; *National Gang Threat Assessment* 2009). Large gangs are normally broken down into smaller groups, called *sets* or *cliques*, but may still be known collectively under one name. More than 90 percent of gangs have between 3 and 100 members, and only 4 percent have more than 100 members. The number of members in gangs in large cities ranges from 1,200 to 1,500.

The percentage of law enforcement agencies reporting gang problems in 2009 was 17.0 percent in rural counties, 32.9 percent in smaller cities, 51.8 percent in suburban counties and 86.3 percent in larger cities (Egley and Howell 2011). These percentages have remained fairly stable from those reported in 2006, indicating the gang problems have neither increased nor decreased substantially in the past few years. However, gang prevalence trend data collected by the National Gang Center (NGC), which tracks the distribution and level of the gang problem across the United States, shows that gang prevalence rates in 2009 were "significantly elevated" compared with the rates reported in 2000 and 2001 (Howell et al. 2011). As in previous years, the majority of gang problems in 2009 were reported in large cities, defined by the NGC as those with populations of 50,000 or more. In fact, research indicates that American communities fall into one of three general categories with respect to youth gangs (Howell 2007, 39):

- Those that have never had a youth gang problem or have had only intermittent episodes with minor gangs that pose no threat to public safety (typically rural areas and small towns with populations less than 25,000)

- Those that experience a youth gang problem, but the conditions are neither permanent nor serious (generally smaller cities and suburban communities with populations of 25,000 to 100,000)
- Those with a chronic, intractable youth gang problem, in which many of the resident gangs are violent and present serious threats to public safety (cities and suburban areas with populations exceeding 100,000)

Figure 7.2 illustrates the reported gang presence, by county, in 2010; from this map it easy to visualize the "hot spots" of heightened gang activity in specific geographic areas of the country.

 Although youth gangs can exist in communities of any size, the most serious, persistent gang problems, and the largest, most violent gangs, are found in major cities and metropolitan areas with populations greater than 250,000.

The gang problem is not restricted to metropolitan areas. As society in general has become more mobile, gangs and gang members have also increased their mobility, contributing to gang migration. Researchers, however, have pointed out that the notion of massive nationwide gang migration, fueled by a desire to expand drug trafficking operations, is largely a myth, and that if any group migration does occur, the resettlement is generally close to, and often within 100 miles of, the gang's city of origin (Howell 2007; Maxson 1998). The greater tendency is for individual gang members, not entire gangs, to migrate, and the reason most often cited is that the gang member's family chose to relocate to another part of the country for social reasons—usually seeking a better quality of life or to be near friends and relatives (Howell 2007; Maxson 1998; Starbuck, Howell, and Lindquist 2001).

Gang Formation: Risk Factors and Reasons Why Youths Join Gangs

Since Thrasher's pioneering work, *The Gang: A Study of 1,313 Gangs in Chicago* (1927), in which he posited that gangs result from a breakdown in social controls and create a social order where none exist, myriad theories have been proposed to explain gang formation, and hundreds of studies have attempted to identify the causes of gangs and what attracts youths to join them. Recently, studies have begun to look at why youths chose to *not* become involved in gangs and the processes involved in gang desistance (Melde and Esbensen 2011).

The perception that countless youths are pressured into joining gangs is largely a myth: "As unlikely as it may seem, many youths very much want to belong to gangs. Gangs often are at the center of appealing social action—parties, hanging out, music, dancing, drugs, and opportunities to participate in social activities with members of the opposite sex" (Howell 2007, 43). The reasons youth seek out gang membership are varied and numerous. In addition to serving as a recreational outlet (Moore 1991; Sanchez-Jankowski 1991), gangs offer their members a feeling of belonging and importance (Howell 2007; Miller, Barnes, and Hartley 2011), a source of self-esteem and self-identity (Krohn et al. 2011); emotional and psychological support that they may not get from their own parents or families (Howell 2007; Miller, Barnes, and Hartley 2011); a way to express defiance and rebel against parents, other authority figures and those who

Figure 7.2 Map of Nationwide Gang Presence, by County, 2010

SOURCE: NGIC and NDIC 2010 National Drug Survey Data FBI

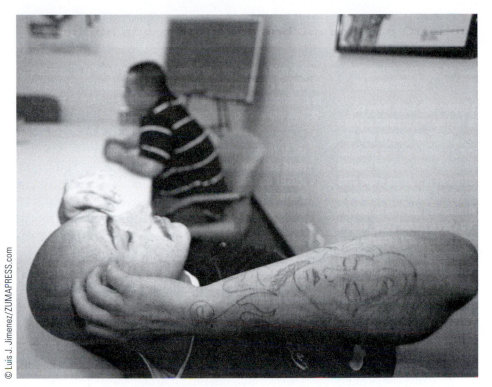

© Luis J. Jimenez/ZUMAPRESS.com

This youth (foreground) is the third generation in his family to become a gang member. He belongs to the Mara Salvatrucha 13 gang.

make them feel "marginalized" (Klein 1995; Miller, Barnes, and Hartley 2011; Moore 1991; Moore and Hagedorn 2001); a place of refuge away from an abusive home life (Moore and Hagedorn 2001); protection from other youths (Sanchez-Jankowski 1991); and economic support and security (Miller, Barnes, and Hartley 2011; Moore and Hagedorn 2001).

Researchers have sought to find and understand the underlying causal mechanisms of gang formation and the risk factors that lead some youths to join gangs while others resist. Similar to the risk factors for generalized delinquency, risk factors for gang involvement are grouped into five domains (Curry and Spergel 1992; Esbensen, Huizinga, and Weiher 1993; Hill et al. 1999; Katz and Schnebly 2011; Snyder and Sickmund 2006; Vigil 1988):

- Individual—early delinquency, deviant attitudes, aggression, substance use and abuse, precocious sexual activity
- Family—single-parent households or other non-two-parent family structures, family dysfunction, incest or other sexual abuse, family violence, parental drug or alcohol abuse, poverty or low socioeconomic status, gang-involved family members, poor family management, problematic parent-child relations, sibling antisocial behavior
- School—low academic achievement, low commitment to school, truancy, negative labeling by teachers, feeling unsafe at school
- Peer—association with and high commitment to delinquent or antisocial peers, low commitment to prosocial peers; gang members in class, friends who are gang members, friends who use or distribute drugs

■ Community—poverty, organized lower-class or underclass communities, neighborhood disadvantage and disorganization, drug availability, firearm availability, gang presence in the neighborhood, low sense of attachment to the neighborhood, lack of a sense of safety, high crime rate, barriers to and lack of social/economic opportunities

It is important to recognize that risk factors are not *causes*, per se, and do not preordain a youth to certain gang membership, but they are highly predictive of gang involvement. Evidence indicates that risk factors are cumulative in the effects, meaning the more risk factors a youth possesses, the greater is the likelihood of gang involvement (Hill et al. 1999; Hill, Lui, and Hawkins 2001). A longitudinal study of youth in Seattle found that those between the ages of 10 and 12 who had two or three identified risk factors were 3 times more likely to join a gang than were youths with one or no risk factors. Those with seven or more risk factors were 13 times more likely to become gang involved (Hill, Lui, and Hawkins 2001). Furthermore, having risk factors across numerous domains increased the likelihood of gang membership more than did a simple accumulation of risk factors in one area.

 As with risk factors for generalized delinquency, risk factors for gang involvement are grouped into the five domains of individual, family, school, peer and community. The greater the number of risk factors a youth experiences, particularly if they occur across numerous domains, the more likely that youth is to become gang-involved.

Table 7.1 presents childhood predictors of youths joining and remaining in a gang.

Some research has examined whether the same or different risk factors explain gang involvement for all racial/ethnic groups or for males and females alike. A key concept in such studies is that of marginality or **marginalization**—the sense that an individual or specific demographic group (e.g., females, Hispanics) feels inferior or subordinate to mainstream society, socially disenfranchised and excluded from full participation in that society. Marginalization can occur across a variety of domains (e.g., economic, sociocultural) and demographic variables (ethnic, gender) and is hypothesized to play a role in gang formation (Krohn et al. 2011; Miller, Barnes, and Hartley 2011; Moore and Hagedorn 2001; Pyrooz, Fox, and Decker 2010; Vigil 1988, 2002).

Vigil's multiple marginality perspective (1988)—in which numerous economic and social disadvantages converge to negatively affect family functioning, diminish the role of education in adolescents' lives and push youths toward street life and "street socialization"—has informed several studies seeking insight about whether and how different factors explain why youth of different ethnicities join gangs (Krohn et al. 2011; Miller, Barnes, and Hartley 2011; Pyrooz, Fox, and Decker 201).

Using a multiple marginality framework, Freng and Esbensen (2007) studied race and gang affiliation, focusing on the following variables: male, Black, Hispanic, single parent, highest parental education, ethnic identity, social isolation, parental attachment, parental monitoring, limited educational opportunities, school commitment, attitudes toward police, neutralization and street socialization. Their research found that many of these multiple marginality

Table 7.1   Childhood Predictors of Joining and Remaining in a Gang

Risk Factor	Odds Ratio*
Neighborhood	
Availability of marijuana	3.6
Neighborhood youth in trouble	3.0
Low neighborhood attachment	1.5
Family	
Family structure[†]	
One parent only	2.4
One parent plus other adults	3.0
Parental attitudes favoring violence	2.3
Low bonding with parents	ns[‡]
Low household income	2.1
Sibling antisocial behavior	1.9
Poor family management	1.7
School	
Learning disabled	3.6
Low academic achievement	3.1
Low school attachment	2.0
Low school commitment	1.8
Low academic aspirations	1.6
Peer group	
Association with friends who engage in problem behaviors[§]	2.0 (2.3)
Individual	
Low religious service attendance	ns[‡]
Early marijuana use	3.7
Early violence[§]	3.1 (2.4)
Antisocial beliefs	2.0
Early drinking	1.6
Externalizing behaviors[§]	2.6 (2.6)
Poor refusal skills	1.8

*Odds of joining a gang between the ages of 13 and 18 for youth who scored in the worst quartile on each factor at ages 10 to 12 (fifth and sixth grades), compared with all other youth in the sample. For example, the odds ratio for "availability of marijuana" is 3.6. This means that youth from neighborhoods where marijuana was most available were 3.6 times more likely to join a gang, compared with other youth.
[†]Compared with two-parent households
[‡]ns = not a significant predictor
[§]These factors also distinguished sustained gang membership (more than one year) from transient membership (one year or less). For each factor, the number in parentheses indicates the odds of being a sustained gang member (compared with the odds of being a transient member) for youth at risk on that factor

SOURCE: Karl G. Hill, Christina Lui, and J. David Hawkins. 2001 (December). *Early Precursors of Gang Membership: A Study of Seattle Youth*, p. 4. Washington, DC: OJJDP Juvenile Justice Bulletin.

variables—specifically highest parental education, limited educational opportunities, school commitment, attitudes towards police, neutralization and street socialization— were important predictors of gang membership.

Identifying Characteristics of Gangs

Gangs maintain their cohesion and sense of identity through their names, symbols, clothing, tattoos and communication styles, including hand signals and graffiti.

Gang Names

Gang names vary from colorful and imaginative to straightforward. They commonly refer to localities, rebellion, animals, royalty and religion. Localities are typically streets (e.g., the Seventeenth Streeters), cities or towns (the Center City Boys), neighborhoods (the Westsiders) and housing projects (the Tiburon Courts). Names denoting rebellion, revolution or lawlessness include the Gangsters, Outlaws, Hustlers, Savages, Warlords and Assassins. Common animal names include the Tigers, Cougars, Panthers, Cobras, Ravens and Eagles. Royal titles include the Kings, Emperors, Lords, Imperials, Knights, Dukes and even Royals. Religious names include the Popes and Disciples. Gangs may also be designated by the leader's name such as "Garcia's Boys." Often, a locality is coupled with another category, for example, the South Side Savages.

Symbols

Gangs use symbols or logos to identify themselves. Often these symbols are taken from professional or college sports teams (e.g., the Latin Kings use the L.A. Kings logo as an identifying symbol), religion and the occult (crosses and pentagrams) and other universally recognized symbols, including the Playboy bunny.

Clothing

It is important for gang members to reinforce their sense of belonging by adopting a gang style of dress. Gang symbols are common. Clothing, in particular, can distinguish a particular gang. Sometimes "colors" are used to distinguish a gang. Gang members also use jerseys, T-shirts and jackets with emblems.

Representing also signifies gang allegiance. **Representing** is a manner of dressing that uses an imaginary line drawn vertically through the body. Anything to the left of the line is representing left, anything to the right is representing right: for example, a hat cocked to the right, right pant leg rolled up and a cloth or bandana tied around the right arm.

Also important may be certain hairstyles, gold jewelry in gang symbols and certain cars. The following list itemizes some identifying symbols of some better-known gangs:

- *Black Gangster Disciples* wear blue and black colors, represent to the right and have as symbols a six-point star, flaming heart and crossed pitchfork.
- *Vice Lords* wear red and black colors, represent to the left and have as symbols a five-point star, a circle surrounded by fire, a half-crescent moon, a pyramid, top hat, cane, white gloves and martini glass.
- *Latin Kings* wear gold and black colors, represent to the left and have as a symbol a three- or five-point crown.

- *Asian gangs* usually wear no colors and show no representation. They are often deadly and violent.
- *Skinheads* wear black boots and leather jackets and have as a symbol the swastika. Their heads are shaved or very nearly bald.

Communication Styles

Street gangs communicate primarily through their actions. Youth gangs need and seek recognition—from their community and from rival gangs. A variety of verbal and nonverbal gang communication is ever present. Clothing, tattoos and symbols can be powerful and effective communication tools. Other avenues of gang communication include slang, hand signals and graffiti.

Hand Signals   A common method of gang communication is that of flashing gang signs or hand signals, the purpose of which is to identify the user with a specific gang. Hand signs communicate allegiance or opposition to another group. Most hand signs duplicate or modify signing used by the deaf and hearing impaired.

Graffiti   Certainly the most observable gang communication is wall writings or **graffiti**, an important part of the Hispanic and Black gang traditions. It proclaims to the world the status of the gang, delineates the boundaries of their turf and offers a challenge to rivals. Graffiti may show opposition for a rival gang by displaying the rival gang's symbols upside down, backward or crossed out—a serious insult to the rival.

In the broken windows crime model, graffiti is a foothold crime leading to a neighborhood's decay: "Neighborhoods plagued with graffiti often become breeding grounds for loitering, littering, loud music, and public urination. . . . As 'good' citizens begin to avoid 'that side of town,' the criminal

© Sven Martson/The Image Works

Graffiti has been called the "newspaper of the street" for gangs. Often abbreviations such as R.I.P. (rest in peace) are found, as in the upper left corner of this graffiti.

element becomes more comfortable and these small public disorder crimes snowball into more serious criminal behaviors. When these more serious crimes flourish, it becomes difficult to assess the true cost of the graffiti offense: expenses mount in terms of prevention, arrests, incarceration, and lost revenue" (Petrocelli 2008, 18).

Many youth gangs characteristically claim identification with and control over specific domains—geographic locations, facilities or enterprises. The best-known manifestation of gang domain identification is the "turf " phenomenon. Gangs establish **turf**, or territorial boundaries, within which they operate and which they protect at all costs from invasion by rival gangs. Gang graffiti usually appears throughout the turf and defines boundaries. Such graffiti usually includes the gang name and the writer's name. It may also assert the gang's power by such words as *rifa*, meaning "to rule," or *P/V*, meaning "por vida" (for life). In other words, the gang rules this neighborhood for life. The number 13 has traditionally meant that the writer used marijuana, but now it also can mean that the gang is from Southern California.

The center of a gang's turf will have the most graffiti. It may name members of the gang, often in order of authority, listed in neat rows under the gang's logo. However, with the increasing mobility of society, graffiti no longer has to necessarily remain within a gang's turf.

Hispanic graffiti is highly artistic and very detailed. It frequently refers to group or gang power. In contrast, graffiti of Black gangs shows less flair and attention to detail and often is filled with profanity as well as expressions of individual power. The symbolism is more obvious and often includes weapons.

Figure 7.3 illustrates a variety of gang communication, including hand signals and symbols used in graffiti.

Tagging is a type of graffiti that mimics gang graffiti, but often those doing the tagging are not members of gangs or involved in illegal activity (other than vandalism). According to Shelden et al. (2004, 52), "Such graffiti is not done to mark turf. Rather it is a way these mostly White middle-class youths call attention to themselves." In some instances, taggers band together into a **crew**. Sometimes the tagging becomes very serious and may even turn deadly. Differences between tagging and gang graffiti are listed in Table 7.2.

Tattoos

Some gangs, particularly outlaw motorcycle gangs and Hispanic gangs, use tattoos as a method of communication and identification. The traditional Hispanic gang uses tattoos extensively, usually visible on arms, hands or shoulders. By contrast, Black gang members seldom use tattoos to identify their members. However, branding—basically the same process used to identify livestock in which a hot iron is held against the skin so as to leave a permanent distinctive "brand"—is becoming somewhat popular among Black and Asian gangs.

Gang tattoos are meant to intimidate, to show gang affiliation and to indicate rank, and they are a gang member's permanent record, telling who he is, what he believes, what he's done, where he's been, where he did time and for how many years, and how many people he's killed. An officer trained to read

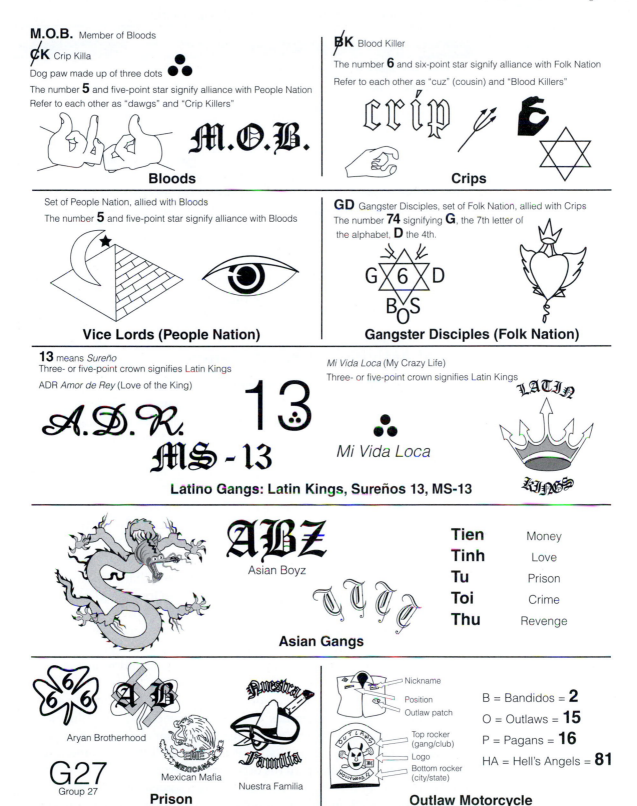

M.O.B. Member of Bloods

C̸K Crip Killa

Dog paw made up of three dots

The number **5** and five-point star signify alliance with People Nation

Refer to each other as "dawgs" and "Crip Killers"

Bloods

M.O.B.

B̸K Blood Killer

The number **6** and six-point star signify alliance with Folk Nation

Refer to each other as "cuz" (cousin) and "Blood Killers"

crip

Crips

Set of People Nation, allied with Bloods

The number **5** and five-point star signify alliance with Bloods

Vice Lords (People Nation)

GD Gangster Disciples, set of Folk Nation, allied with Crips

The number **74** signifying **G**, the 7th letter of the alphabet, **D** the 4th.

G 6 D
B S

Gangster Disciples (Folk Nation)

13 means *Sureño*

Three- or five-point crown signifies Latin Kings

ADR *Amor de Rey* (Love of the King)

A.D.R.

13

MS-13

Mi Vida Loca (My Crazy Life)

Three- or five-point crown signifies Latin Kings

Mi Vida Loca

LATIN KINGS

Latino Gangs: Latin Kings, Sureños 13, MS-13

ABZ
Asian Boyz

Tien	Money
Tinh	Love
Tu	Prison
Toi	Crime
Thu	Revenge

Asian Gangs

Aryan Brotherhood

G27
Group 27

Mexicana EME
Mexican Mafia

Nuestra Familia
Nuestra Familia

Prison

Nickname

Position

Outlaw patch

Top rocker (gang/club)

Logo

Bottom rocker (city/state)

B = Bandidos = **2**

O = Outlaws = **15**

P = Pagans = **16**

HA = Hell's Angels = **81**

Outlaw Motorcycle

Figure 7.3 Gang Communication—Signs and Symbols

SOURCE: From Kären M. Hess and Christine Hess Orthmann. 2010. *Criminal Investigation*, 9th ed., p. 588. Clifton Park, NY: Delmar Publishing Company.

Table 7.2 Differences between Tagging and Gang Graffiti

Tagger Graffiti	Gang Graffiti
Communication secondary, if present at all	Intent made to communicate
Artistic effort a major consideration	Artistic effort secondary, if present at all
Territorial claims infrequent	Territorial claims prominent
Explicit threats rare	Explicit threats made
Explicit boasts about tagger common	Explicit boasts made about gang
Pictures and symbols dominant, letters and numbers secondary	Letters, numbers and symbols dominant
Police intelligence value limited	Intelligence to police provided

SOURCE: *Addressing Community Gang Problems: A Practical Guide.* 1998 (May). Washington, DC: Bureau of Justice Assistance, p. 37. (NCJ 164273)

gang tattoos can discern a suspect's history: "If gang graffiti is the newspaper of the street, then gang tattoos are the 'signposts to the soul'" (Valdemar 2006, 30).

Illegal Activities of Youth Gangs

The primary characteristic distinguishing gangs from lawful groups is the illegal activity of the former. Youth gang members commit a full range of street crimes, although the most distinctive form of gang offense is gang fighting, in which two or more gangs engage in violent combat. Youth gang activity ranges from property crimes to violent crimes against persons and includes graffiti painting, vandalism, arson, student extortion, teacher intimidation, drug dealing, rape, stabbings and shootings.

Ample research offers evidence that gang membership exacerbates delinquency and criminal offending (Battin-Pearson et al. 1998; Decker, Katzy, and Webb 2008; Eghigian and Kirby 2006; Hill, Lui, and Hawkins 2001; Huff 1998; Melde and Esbensen 2011; Thornberry et al. 2003). Tita and Ridgeway (2007, 208) report, "Research has demonstrated that even after controlling for individual level attributes, individuals who join gangs commit more crimes than do nongang members. Furthermore, the offending level of gang members is higher when they report being active members of the gang. Therefore, gang membership clearly facilitates offending above and beyond individual level characteristics." Figure 7.4 compares gang and nongang criminal behavior.

Self-reported and court-recorded offending rates among a sample of 15-year-olds are shown in Figures 7.5 and 7.6, respectively, and illustrate how gang membership contributes to delinquent behavior above and beyond associating with delinquent peers (Battin-Pearson et al. 1998). It is interesting to note that while the general patterns between the two data sets are, visually, very similar, in that both self-report rates and court-recorded rates are lowest among nondelinquent peers and highest among gang members across all categories of offending, the official data reflect only a small percentage of the offenses captured in the self-reports.

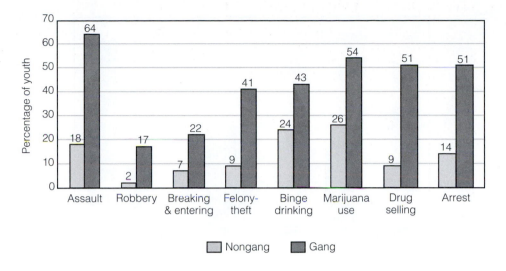

Note: Youth were interviewed at ages 13 to 16 and 18. In each interview, youth reported activities for the past month (except for drug selling and arrest, which were reported for the past year). For gang members, prevalence reflects only the year(s) of membership.

Figure 7.4   Prevalence of Delinquency among Gang and Nongang Youth, Ages 13 to 18

SOURCE: Karl G. Hill, Christina Lui, and J. David Hawkins. 2001 (December). *Early Precursors of Gang Membership: A Study of Seattle Youth*, p. 2, Figure 1. Washington, DC: Office of Juvenile Justice and Delinquency Prevention. (NCJ 190106)

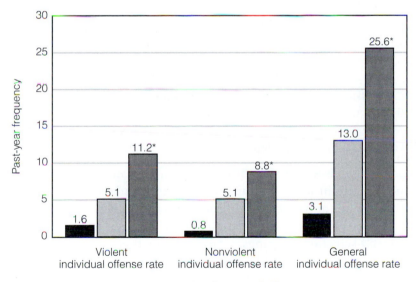

*An asterisk indicates that the rates for gang members are significantly higher than those for youth with delinquent peers (*t*-test, $p < 0.05$).

Figure 7.5   Self-Reported Individual Offense Rates (IOR) at Age 15 (Seattle Social Development Project)

SOURCE: Sara R. Battin-Pearson, Terence P. Thornberry, J. David Hawkins, and Marvin D. Krohn. 1998 (October). *Gang Membership, Delinquent Peers, and Delinquent Behavior*, p. 3, Figure 1. Washington, DC: Office of Juvenile Justice and Delinquency Prevention. (NCJ 171119)

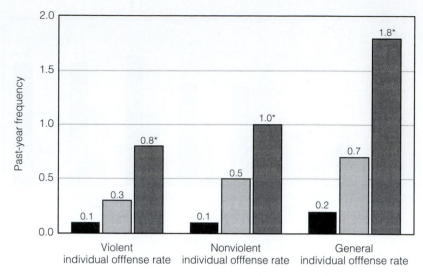

Figure 7.6 Court-Recorded Individual Offense Rates (IOR) at Age 15 (Seattle Social Development Project)

SOURCE: Sara R. Battin-Pearson, Terence P. Thornberry, J. David Hawkins, and Marvin D. Krohn. 1998 (October). *Gang Membership, Delinquent Peers, and Delinquent Behavior*, p. 3, Figure 2. Washington, DC: Office of Juvenile Justice and Delinquency Prevention. (NCJ 171119)

Research seeking to better understand the relationship between delinquency and gang involvement and whether gang membership causes delinquency (or vice versa), has generally produced results that support one of three general theoretical frameworks (Melde and Esbensen 2011, 515):

- The *selection* model, which asserts that delinquents' antisocial propensities stem from certain stable personality traits that nondelinquents lack. As such, delinquent or at-risk youth self-select into gang involvement because the lifestyle suits their already existing antisocial traits, whereas prosocial youth self-select out of gangs. Consequently, there is no causal role ascribed to gang membership in explaining delinquency—the relationship is spurious.

- The *facilitation* model, which holds that delinquent predispositions may exist but are largely dormant until gang involvement "activates" them. According to this model, the gang context assists in developing delinquency by influencing a youth's attitudes, emotions and behaviors in a way that increases criminal involvement. This model assigns causality to gang membership as a force that shapes delinquency.

- The *enhancement* model, which combines the selection and enhancement models by positing that gang members are more antisocial than nongang members to begin with, even before joining a gang, but that the gang involvement intensifies these differences.

Thornberry et al. (2003, 186) assert, "The young men and women who join gangs have multiple deficits in many developmental domains and being a member of a street gang further impedes their prosocial development."

Youth Gang Violence and Victimization

Data indicate that, despite the national drop in violent crime during the past decade, gang violence has remained at "exceptional levels" (Howell et al. 2011, 13). And although the willingness to use violence is considered a defining trait of youth gangs, researchers caution that violence is not an inevitability for all gangs but remains a variable, the use of which varies between different gangs and may fluctuate over time within a gang (Howell 1998; Moore 1988).

Anderson's (1999) thesis is that the code of the streets is an informal system governing the use of violence, especially among young, male African Americans, that stresses maintaining respect through a violent, tough identity: "An important part of the code is not to allow others to chump you, to let them know that you are 'about serious business,' and not to be trifled with" (130). And although noninvolved third parties (i.e., innocent bystanders) are occasionally caught in the crossfire, the majority of victims of gang violence are, themselves, gang-involved (Howell 1998; Shelden, Tracy, and Brown 2004).

 Most victims of gang violence are other gang members.

For many gang members, violence is simply a way of life. For example, if one gang member disrespects another gang member, even within the same gang, violent retaliation may occur. Indeed, one of the hazards of being involved as a perpetrator of gang violence is that the violence usually cycles back to be served on the originator, thus forming an endless loop of offending and victimization, with youth gang members alternately being on the giving and receiving ends of the violence.

Research has consistently demonstrated that youth gang members are more likely to experience violent victimization, and a greater frequency of victimization, than are nongang members (Decker, Katz, and Webb 2008; Gibson et al. 2009; Howell 1998; Taylor et al. 2007). For example, one study found that 70 percent of gang-involved youths reported being the victim of general violence (assault, aggravated assault or robbery) compared with 46 percent of nongang-involved youths (Taylor 2008). However, research by Decker, Katz and Webb (2008) suggests that victimization rates are correlated to organizational levels of gangs, with those who are members of more organized gangs reporting higher victimization rates than do those belonging to less organized gangs (recall the pyramid structure described at the beginning of the chapter and how the degree of gang organization influences member behavior).

Youth Gangs and Drugs

Gangs' involvement with drugs comprises two dimensions: using and selling. Although it is well known that many youth gang members abuse certain drugs, such as alcohol, marijuana, phencyclidine (PCP) and cocaine, what is less agreed on is the extent to which youth gangs deal in drugs. Until the early 1980s when crack, or rock cocaine, hit the market, gangs engaged primarily in burglary, robbery, extortion and car theft. Although drug trafficking existed, it was nowhere near current levels. The reason for the spike in drug sales is, quite simply, profit.

Economic gain is indeed the reason some youths join gangs. However, many studies have found that drug dealing is not a profitable enterprise for the multitude of gang members at the low end of the hierarchy; drug trafficking by youth gangs is not as rampant as others might claim; and most youth gangs lack the discipline, organization and crime skills necessary to sustain a successful drug operation (Bjerregaard 2010; Howell 1998; Klein 1995). When gang members do deal drugs, it is more often on their own initiative rather than as part of an organized enterprise guided by the gang: "Drug trafficking is the province of organized crime syndicates. Gang member involvement at the level of street sales brings gangs into the mix because their members very often use drugs and need to procure them" (Howell 2007, 42). Nonetheless, data from gang units operating in some of the nation's largest local law enforcement agencies indicate that many of the country's gangs are engaged in street-level drug sales and drug trafficking as methods to finance gang operations (Langton 2010).

Table 7.3 identifies some common differences between street gangs and drug gangs.

Huebner, Varano and Bynum (2007) studied the effect of gang members' drug use on recidivism and reported that those who were affiliated with a gang or were drug dependent before prison had higher reconviction rates and recidivated more quickly, compared with those who were not involved with gangs or drug use. Individuals dealing with juveniles must maintain objectivity and refrain from stereotyping gang members as drug users and pushers, keeping in mind that not all gangs deal with drugs and not all who use drugs commit other crimes.

Gangs often purposely exploit the difference between juvenile and adult law in their drug dealing, using younger gang members whenever possible to avoid adult sanctions. Most states will not allow youths under age 15 to be certified as

Table 7.3 Common Differences between Street Gangs and Drug Gangs

Characteristic	Street Gangs	Drug Gangs
Crime focus	Versatile ("cafeteria-style")	Drug business exclusively
Structure	Larger organizations	Smaller organizations
Level of cohesion	Less cohesive	More cohesive
Leadership	Looser	More centralized
Roles	Ill-defined	Market-defined
Nature of loyalty	Code of loyalty	Requirement of loyalty
Territories	Residential	Sales market
Degree of drug selling	Members may sell	Members do sell
Rivalries	Intergang	Competition controlled
Age of members	Younger on average, but wider age range	Older on average, but narrower age range

SOURCE: James C. Howell. 1998 (August). *Youth Gangs Overview*, pp. 6–7. Washington, DC: Office of Juvenile Justice and Delinquency Prevention (NCJ 167249)

adults, and most have statutory restrictions on placing youths under age 18 into adult correctional facilities.

The Gangs–Drugs–Violence Nexus

It is generally agreed that gangs organize along one of two basic lines: violence-oriented (expressive) gangs who exist to fight or entrepreneurially focused (instrumental) gangs structured to make money. Among those gangs for whom drug trafficking is a primary activity, however, violence may accompany their entrepreneurial activities. Research has been divided on whether gang member involvement in drug dealing leads to increased violence. Some studies suggest an increase in violent behavior does not necessarily accompany the gang member–drug seller connection (Fagan 1989; Howell and Decker 1999), but other research contradicts those findings with evidence that drug selling is a major facilitator of violence among gang members (Bellair and McNulty 2009). Perhaps the critical factor in the Bellair and McNulty study is that neighborhood disadvantage was also included as a variable and, as seen in Figure 7.7, was highly positively correlated with violence among gang members who sold drugs.

Recognizing a Youth Gang Problem

Youth gang activity manifests itself in a variety of ways, with gang indicators including graffiti, intimidation assaults, open sale of drugs, drive-by shootings and murders. If a gang problem is recognized, one of the first steps is to identify the gang members.

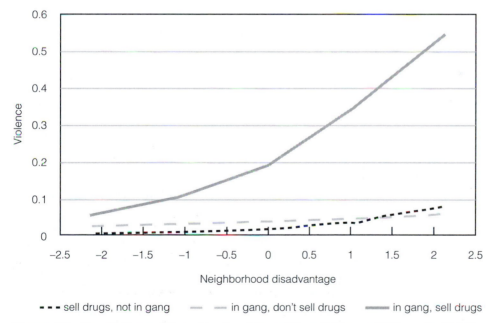

Figure 7.7 Simple Slope of Gang Membership and Drug Selling on Violence by Neighborhood Disadvantage

SOURCE: Paul E. Bellair and Thomas L. McNulty. 2009 (December). "Gang Membership, Drug Selling, and Violence in Neighborhood Context." *Justice Quarterly* 26 (4): © Academy of Criminal Justice Sciences, reprinted by permission of Taylor & Francis Ltd, www.tandfonline.com on behalf of Academy of Criminal Justice Sciences.

Identifying Gang Members

Gang members take pride in belonging to their specific gangs and will make their membership known in various ways. Many gang members have a street name, or a **moniker**. Often more than one gang member has the same moniker. The color and type of clothing can also indicate gang membership. For example, Bloods are identified by red or green colors. Crips are associated with blue or purple bandanas or scarves.

Gang affiliation might also be verified in the following ways: body tattoos of gang symbols, jewelry or apparel associated with gangs, written communications such as doodling on notebooks, hand-signing, vocabulary and use of monikers, group photos that include known gang members, known gang associates and reliable informants. Other signs that an individual may be involved in a gang include abrupt changes in personality and behavior, newly acquired and unexplained money or, conversely, requests to borrow money, and "hanging around" behavior.

Gangs in Schools

Recognizing the presence of gangs in school is a continuous challenge for administrators and juvenile justice professionals throughout the country, particularly in certain inner-city districts. In 2007 approximately 23 percent of students reported the presence of gangs in their schools (Robers et al. 2010). Schools are a prime recruiting ground for gangs. Schools are also a market for illicit drugs and for extorting money from other students. Often gangs will stake out certain areas of a school as their turf. They may engage in vandalism, arson and graffiti painting; stabbings and shootings between rival gangs; and student extortion and teacher intimidation.

Indications that youth gangs may be operating in a school include groups of students congregating by race and naming their group to solidify their identity; an increase in the number of violent, racially based incidents; a rise in the rate of absenteeism or truancy; and a greater number of crimes in the community being committed by truants. Other indicators include graffiti and crossed-out graffiti visible on or near the school, colors worn symbolically by various groups who also use hand signals and unique symbols on T-shirts or in jewelry. Crime and violence in our schools is discussed in Chapter 8.

Responding to an Existing Youth Gang Problem

Responding to gangs requires a systematic, comprehensive, collaborative approach that incorporates prevention, intervention and suppression strategies. The prevention component, discussed in more detail shortly, includes conflict resolution skills and peer counseling. The intervention component includes giving youth gang members the chance to finish high school or obtain a General Education Development (GED) certificate, to have tattoos removed, to obtain gainful employment and legal assistance. The suppression component involves collaboration among police, probation and prosecution, targeting the most active gang members and gang leaders.

The Office of Juvenile Justice and Delinquency Prevention's (OJJDP) Comprehensive Gang Model, developed in the early 1990s by Dr. Irving Spergel and colleagues at the University of Chicago, is based on five strategies: community mobilization, opportunities provision, social intervention, suppression and organizational change and development, that is, implementing policies and procedures that result in the most effective use of available and potential resources (National Gang Center 2010, 3). The most effective approaches use a combination of these efforts.

Suppression and Law Enforcement Efforts

Suppression tactics include street sweeps, intensified surveillance, hot spot targeting, directed patrol, saturation patrol, aggressive curfew and truancy enforcement and caravanning (cruising neighborhoods in a caravan of patrol cars). Table 7.4 shows the law enforcement strategies being used, with what frequency and with what perceived effectiveness when used. Although in-state information exchange was the most-used strategy, it was also among those judged least effective. Street sweeps and other suppression tactics were used by fewer than half the departments, but their effectiveness was judged high.

Table 7.4 Law Enforcement Strategies and Perceived Effectiveness*

Strategy	Used (Percent)	Judged Effective If Used (Percent)
Some or a lot of use		
Targeting entry points	14	17
Gang laws	40	19
Selected violations	76	42
Out-of-state information exchange	53	16
In-state information exchange	90	17
In-city information exchange	55	18
Federal agency operational coordination	40	16
State agency operational coordination	50	13
Local agency operational coordination	78	16
Community collaboration	64	54
Any use		
Street sweeps	40	62
Other suppression tactics	44	63
Crime prevention activities	15	56

*Percentage of cities $n = 211$. The number of cities responding to each question varied slightly.

SOURCE: James C. Howell. 2000 (August). *Youth Gang Programs and Strategies*, p. 46. Washington, DC: OJJDP. (NCJ 171154)

The Richmond, Virginia, directed patrol program used crime statistics and crime logs to determine high-crime days and times in the target area. Additional foot, bicycle, motorcycle and walking officers were added during those times, which resulted in a significant decrease in crime. During the funded periods, Richmond dropped from being the 5th most dangerous city to the 15th. More recently, it has dropped to 29th (National Gang Center 2010).

Gang Units and Task Forces   As early as the 1970s the Los Angeles Police Department saw the need for specialized units to deal with the gang problem. The department's first such program was called Community Resources Against Street Hoodlums (CRASH) and consisted of several specially trained units of patrol officers and detectives organized on a bureau or area level. CRASH put tremendous pressure on the Los Angeles gangs and resulted in many gang members being arrested. In 1988 the department instituted another program to focus specifically on the problem of narcotics and Black street gangs. This program was called Gang-Related Active Trafficker Suppression (GRATS). By year-end 2007, 365 specialized gang units staffed by more than 4,300 sworn officers were operating in 365 of the nation's largest police departments and sheriffs' offices (Langton 2010). Virtually all of these units (98 percent) shared criminal intelligence information with neighboring law enforcement agencies.

Collaboration and communication among law enforcement agencies can greatly enhance efforts to cope with the youth gang problem. Task forces are formed as a coalition of differing perspectives and focus humanpower and resources on a common goal. At the federal level, the Federal Bureau of Investigation (FBI) currently administers 160 Violent Gang Safe Streets Task Forces across the nation. The FBI had previously developed the National Gang Intelligence Center (NGIC) to provide a way for local, state and federal law enforcement to share gang data across jurisdictions and to identify trends related to violent gang activity and migration. Such collaboration is also vital at the local level.

Civil Gang Ordinances and Injunctions   One measure being used to combat existing gang problems is the **civil gang injunction** (CGI) a court-issued order designed to disrupt a gang's routine activities by prohibiting specific gangs or gang members from gathering in a particular public location and engaging in nuisance behaviors, such as loitering, playing loud music, cursing and using certain hand gestures (Langton 2010). Obtaining a CGI varies from jurisdiction to jurisdiction but usually involves gathering evidence that gang members are creating a public nuisance at a specific location and applying to a civil court to require these individuals to refrain from nuisance behavior. After the injunction is issued, the targeted individuals are notified and can be arrested for violating the terms of the injunction, even if the activity does not involve criminal conduct.

A hazard of using CGIs is the potential to cross constitutional boundaries if they are not worded appropriately. Injunctions and ordinances may be challenged as unconstitutional violations of the freedom of speech, the right of association and due process rights if they do not clearly delineate how officers may apply such orders. For example, Chicago passed a gang congregation ordinance to combat the problems created by the city's street gangs. During the three years following passage of the ordinance, Chicago police officers issued more than

89,000 dispersal orders and arrested more than 42,000 people. However, in *City of Chicago v. Morales* (1999), the Supreme Court struck down the ordinance as unconstitutional because its vague wording failed to provide adequate standards to guide police discretion. The lesson here is that any civil injunctions a city passes must be clear in what officers can and cannot do when they observe what they believe to be gang members congregating in public places. Of the 365 documented gang units operating in 2007, 337 of them had used CGIs in response to local gang problems (Langton 2010).

Tougher legislation is also being used as a gang control approach. Because some gangs use their younger members to commit serious crimes, relying on the more lenient juvenile sentencing laws, some jurisdictions have allowed courts to raise the penalties for teenagers convicted of gang-related offenses.

Arresting and Prosecuting Gang Members

The justice system should view gangs as criminal organizations and capitalize on laws against organized crime; for example, money-laundering and asset forfeiture laws help in efforts to arrest and prosecute gang members and thereby weaken the street gang structure. As Lyddane (2006, 1) points out, "It is critical to know your adversary. Understanding the gang mentality and anticipating gang behaviors will aid investigators and prosecutors in acquiring physical evidence and securing testimony that will 'connect the dots' in gang conspiracy investigations. Presenting evidence of the defendant gang affiliation through

---

IN THE NEWS | "NYPD Arrests 43 in Brooklyn Gang Bust, Says They Boasted about Shootings on Twitter: The Charges Include Murder, Assault, Robbery and Conspiracy"

Authorities have arrested 43 alleged members of two feuding gangs in Brownsville, Brooklyn—some of whom police say boasted about their shootings on Twitter.

Police Commissioner Ray Kelly said Thursday that police used social media messages to link alleged gang members to six killings, 32 shootings, 36 robberies and numerous other crimes. There [sic] average age of those arrested was 17 [and ranged in age from 15 to 21].

"Gang members made the mistake of boasting on Twitter, which NYPD officers used to help establish their complicity in murder and other crimes," Kelly said.

Police learned the lexicon of the rival gangs, the Hood Starz and the Waves, and tracked it on social media.

When Hood Starz members shot a rival, they would say they "clapped him off the surfboard," and going into Wave territory was described as "going to the beach." Wave members called Hood Starz "actors" and shooting them was "lining you out."

"Woo" meant you were a Wave and "chew" meant being a Hood Starz, police said. Last summer, a 21-year-old man was visiting Brownsville and was asked by a Wave member if he was "chewing." He did not understand and was shot in the face.

Prosecutors say the bloodshed resulted in the deaths of other innocent bystanders, including a child and his father shot in a courtyard in August.

The crimes date back to 2010 and continued as late as this month.

The indictments follow a widespread investigation by several agencies. The charges include murder, assault, robbery and conspiracy.

Arraignments are being held this week. Some defendants are still at large.

SOURCE: by Shimon Prokupecz, Jonathan Dienst and Joe Valiquette, January 19, 2012 (http://www.nbcnewyork.com/news/local/Brownsville-Gang-Arrests-Brooklyn-NYPD--137668133.html)

exhibits of graffiti, written gang communications, videos and photographs, and video surveillance footage of the defendants at gang events is the adhesive that joins seemingly unrelated criminal offenses into the predicate acts of a gang conspiracy."

Shelden, Tracy and Brown (2004, 263) note, "Prosecutors—key agents of the state—have a tremendous amount of discretionary power and can be quite political in dealing with gang members. As elected officials, prosecutors have a political agenda driven by a combination of public perceptions and fears (which can be and have been manipulated by zealous media) and self-interest (getting reelected or running for higher office)."

Many prosecutors' offices have adopted vertical prosecution strategies to handle gang-related crimes. **Vertical prosecution** involves one assistant prosecutor or small group of assistant prosecutors handling one criminal complaint from start to finish through the entire court process. In contrast, **horizontal prosecution** is an organizational structure strategy whereby individual assistant prosecutors or a small group of assistant prosecutors are responsible for certain phases of the court process.

Pulling Levers: The Boston Gun Project and Operation Ceasefire

Gang membership is one of the principle drivers behind juvenile gun behavior and gun crime (Watkins, Huebner, and Decker 2008). An approach found to effectively reduce juvenile gun crime associated with gang activity was used by the Boston Gun Project in Operation Ceasefire, a widely publicized and replicated initiative that coupled the use of new gun-tracing technologies to interrupt the flow of illegal firearms to youths with a deterrence approach to inform juveniles of the severe criminal consequences they would face if caught with an illegal firearm.

The Boston Police Department implemented Operation Ceasefire by applying the technique of **pulling levers**—a deterrence strategy in which targeted gang members are arrested for the slightest infraction, even jaywalking—in an effort to stop the gang-perpetrated violence (Kennedy, Braga, and Piehl 2001). The impetus behind Operation Ceasefire was the sharp increase in gang-related gun violence and homicides involving members from several dozen gangs in the Boston area, including the Vamp Hill Kings and Intervale Posse. As part of the crackdown on gun violence, Freddie Cardoza, notorious leader of the Intervale Posse, had been arrested for possession of a single bullet, which he had flipped into the air to taunt several nearby police officers. In the aftermath of three King-on-King homicides and hoping to use Cardoza's recent conviction to spread a message to other gang members, the Gun Project called its first forum and invited members of the Kings to attend:

> [Local probation officer] Billy Stewart was master of ceremonies, as he would generally be at subsequent forums. "Thanks for coming," he told the audience. "This isn't a sting; everybody's going to be home for dinner, we just wanted you to know a few things. And this is nothing personal either; this is how we're going to be dealing with violence in the future, and you just happened to be first. So go home and tell your friends about what you hear today."

The forum was dramatic. In essence, the Working Group's message to the Kings was that they and their activities were known, and although the group could not stop every instance of offending, violence would no longer be tolerated in Boston.. . . .

Many gang members in the audience smiled and scoffed. They stopped when the Assistant U.S. Attorney assigned to the group spoke:

"This kind of street crime used to be a local matter. Not anymore. [The] Attorney General cares more about youth violence than almost anything else. ... We can bring in the DEA, we can bring in the FBI, we can bring in the ATF; we can prosecute you federally, which means you go to Lompoc, not stateside, and there's no parole in the federal system any more. You serve your time." ...

The room became more silent when the panel turned to Freddie Cardoza, who was featured on his own flyer used as a handout [See Figure 7.8]. (Kennedy et al. 2001, 35–37)

FREDDIE CARDOZA

PROBLEM: VIOLENT GANG MEMBER

"Given his extensive criminal record,
if there was a federal law against
jaywalking we'd indict him for that."

—Don Stern, U.S. Attorney

SOLUTION: ARMED CAREER
CRIMINAL CONVICTION

Arrested with one bullet
Sentence: 19 years, 7 months
No possibility of parole

ADDRESS:

OTISVILLE FEDERAL
CORRECTIONAL INSTITUTE

Maximum Security Facility, New York

Figure 7.8   Cardoza Flyer Created by the Gun Project Working Group

SOURCE: David M. Kennedy, Anthony A. Braga, and Anne M. Piehl. 2001 (September). "Developing and Implementing Operation Ceasefire." *Reducing Gun Violence: The Boston Gun Project's Operation Ceasefire*, p. 38. Washington, DC: U.S. Department of Justice, Office of Justice Programs. (NCJ 188741)

A study of the effect of the pulling levers deterrence strategy, in which criminal justice and social service attention was focused on a small number of chronically offending gang members responsible for the bulk of urban gun violence problems, found that the strategy was associated with a statistically significant decrease in the monthly number of gun homicides and gun-associated assault incidents (Braga et al. 2008, 132). In fact, as a result of Operation Ceasefire and other strategies, youth firearm-related homicides in the Boston area dropped 75 percent from 1990 to 1998. And although the national crime rate fell during the 1990s, Boston's decrease during this timeframe was six times the national average.

Youth Gang Prevention Efforts

Traditional efforts to deal with the youth gang problem have been reactive. And despite research that suggests that juvenile justice intervention increases subsequent gang involvement and delinquency, consistent with labeling theory (Bemburg, Krohn, and Rivera 2006), many have advocated youth gang *prevention* as a better use of resources and efforts. A two-pronged prevention approach has proven effective, with primary prevention strategies aimed at the community's general population and secondary prevention strategies targeting youth between the ages of 7 and 14 who are at high risk of joining gangs (National Gang Center 2010). Prevention efforts undertaken by law enforcement departments around the country include:

- Participating in community awareness campaigns (e.g., developing public service announcements and poster campaigns).
- Contacting parents of peripheral gang members (through the mail or during personal visits) to alert them that their children are involved with a gang.
- Sponsoring gang hotlines to gather information and facilitate a quick response to gang-related issues.
- Organizing athletic events with teams of law enforcement officers and gang members.
- Establishing working relationships with local social service agencies.
- Making presentations about gangs to schools and community groups as a combined effort at prevention and information gathering.
- Sponsoring school-based gang and drug prevention programs (e.g., DARE and GREAT).

The Gang Resistance Education and Training (GREAT) program was developed by the Bureau of Alcohol, Tobacco and Firearms, the Federal Law Enforcement Training Center and the Phoenix (Arizona) Police Department. This program, similar to the Drug Abuse Resistance Education (DARE) program, helps students say no, but in this case to gangs. The audience is older; GREAT focuses on seventh-graders. McGloin (n.d., 4) explains, "The program's primary objective is prevention and is intended as an immunization against delinquency, youth violence and gang membership." Students are taught to set goals, resolve conflicts nonviolently, resist peer pressures and understand the negative impact gangs can have on their lives and on their community.

 **Summary**

- Most youth gangs are loosely organized, short-lived and pose little threat to public safety. Most crime and violence attributed to gangs is caused by a relatively small number of organized groups.

- For most juveniles, gang membership is a short-term event, with most youth desisting from gang involvement after one year or less.

- Although youth gangs can exist in communities of any size, the most serious, persistent gang problems, and the largest, most violent gangs, are found in major cities and metropolitan areas with populations greater than 250,000.

- As with risk factors for generalized delinquency, risk factors for gang involvement are grouped into the five domains of individual, family, school, peer and community. The greater the number of risk factors a youth experiences, particularly if they occur across numerous domains, the more likely that youth is to become gang-involved.

- Most victims of gang violence are other gang members.

Discussion Questions

1. Are there gangs in your community? Are they youth gangs? If so, what problems do they cause?

2. Have you seen any movies or TV programs about gangs? How are gang activities depicted?

3. What do you think are the main reasons people join gangs?

4. How does a youth gang member differ from other juveniles?

5. How strong do you believe the link is between drugs, violence and gang membership?

6. Should convicted youth gang members be treated like other juvenile delinquents, including status offenders?

7. What might influence you to become a gang member? To not become a gang member?

8. Do you believe the juvenile justice system should support gang summits that claim to be working toward peaceful, lawful ways to improve the situation of gang members?

9. How much, if any, do gangs today differ from those of the 1960s and 1970s?

10. Do you think the youth gang problem will increase or decrease over the next decade?

References

Anderson, Elijah. 1999. *The Code of the Street: Decency, Violence, and the Moral Life of the Inner City.* New York: Norton.

Battin-Pearson, Sara R., Terence P. Thornberry, J. David Hawkins, and Marvin D. Krohn. 1998 (October). *Gang Membership, Delinquent Peers, and Delinquent Behavior.* Washington, DC: Office of Juvenile Justice and Delinquency Prevention. (NCJ 171119)

Bellair, Paul E., and Thomas L. McNulty. 2009 (December). "Gang Membership, Drug Selling, and Violence in Neighborhood Context." *Justice Quarterly* 26 (4): 643–669.

Bemburg, Jon Gummer, Marvin D. Krohn, and Craig Rivera. 2006. "Official Labeling: Criminal Embededness and Subsequent Delinquency: A Longitudinal Test of Labeling Theory." *Journal of Research in Crime and Delinquency* 43 (1): 67–88.

Bjerregaard, Beth. 2010 (January). "Gang Membership and Drug Involvement: Untangling the Complex Relationship." *Crime and Delinquency* 56 (1): 3–34.

Braga, Anthony A., Glenn L. Pierce, Jack McDevitt, Brenda J. Bond, and Shea Cronin. 2008 (March). "The Strategic Prevention of Gun Violence among Gang-Involved Offenders." *Justice Quarterly* 25 (1): 132–162.

Bureau of Justice Assistance. 1998 (May). *Addressing Community Gang Problems: A Practical Guide.* Washington, DC: Bureau of Justice Assistance. (NCJ 164273)

Curry, G. David, and Irving A. Spergel. 1992 (August). "Gang Involvement and Delinquency among Hispanic and African-American Adolescent Males." *Journal of Research in Crime and Delinquency* 29 (3): 273–291.

Decker, Scott H., Charles M. Katz, and Vincent J. Webb. 2008 (January). "Understanding the Black Box of Gang Organization." *Crime & Delinquency* 54 (1): 153–172.

Decker, Scott H., and Janet L. Lauritsen. 1996. "Breaking the Bonds of Membership: Leaving the Gang." In *Gangs in America,* edited by C. Ronald Huff, 103–122. Thousand Oaks, CA: Sage.

Delaney, Tim. 2006. *American Street Gangs*. Upper Saddle River, NJ: Pearson/Prentice Hall.

Eghigian, Mars, and Katherine Kirby. 2006 (April). "Girls in Gangs: On the Rise in America." *Corrections Today* 68 (2): 48–50.

Egley, Arlen, Jr., and James C. Howell. 2011 (June). *Highlights of the 2009 National Youth Gang Survey*. Washington, DC: Office of Juvenile Justice Delinquency Prevention. (NCJ 233581)

Esbensen, Finn-Aage. 2000 (September). *Preventing Adolescent Gang Involvement*. Washington, DC: Office of Juvenile Justice and Delinquency Prevention. (NCJ 182210)

Esbensen, Finn-Aage, David Huizinga, and Anne W. Weiher. 1993 (May). "Gang and Non-Gang Youth: Differences in Explanatory Variables." *Journal of Contemporary Criminal Justice* 9 (2): 94–116.

Esbensen, Finn-Aage, and Dana P. Lynskey. 2001. "Youth Gang Members in a School Survey." In *The Eurogang Paradox: Street Gangs and Youth Groups in the U.S. and Europe*, edited by Malcolm W. Klein, Hans-Jürgen Kerner, Cheryl L. Maxson, and Elmar G. M. Weitekampf, 93–114. Amsterdam: Kluwer Academic.

Fagan, Jeffrey. 1989 (November). "The Social Organization of Drug Use and Drug Dealing among Urban Gangs." *Criminology* 27 (4): 633–669.

Freng, Adrienne, and Finn-Aage Esbensen. 2007 (December). "Race and Gang Affiliation: An Examination of Multiple Marginality." *Justice Quarterly* 24 (4): 600–628.

Gibson, Chris L., J. Mitchell Miller, Wesley G. Jennings, Marc Swatt, and Angela Gover. 2009 (December). "Using Propensity Score Matching to Understand the Relationship between Gang Membership and Violent Victimization: A Research Note." *Justice Quarterly* 26 (4): 625–643.

Gottfredson, Gary D., and Denise C. Gottfredson. 2001. *Gang Problems and Gang Programs in a National Sample of Schools*. Ellicott City, MD: Gottfredson Associates.

Hill, Karl G., James C. Howell, J. David Hawkins, and Sara R. Battin-Pearson. 1999. "Childhood Risk Factors for Adolescent Gang Membership: Results from the Seattle Social Development Project." *Journal of Research in Crime and Delinquency* 36 (3, August): 300–322.

Hill, Karl G., Christina Lui, and J. David Hawkins. 2001 (December). *Early Precursors of Gang Membership: A Study of Seattle Youth*. Washington, DC: Office of Juvenile Justice and Delinquency Prevention. (NCJ 190106)

Howell, James C. 1998 (August). *Youth Gangs: An Overview*. Washington, DC: Office of Juvenile Justice Delinquency Prevention. (NCJ 167249)

———. 2007 (Spring). "Menacing or Mimicking? Realities of Youth Gangs." *Juvenile and Family Court Journal* 58 (2): 39–50.

Howell, James C., and Scott H. Decker. 1999 (January). *The Youth Gangs, Drugs, and Violence Connection*. Washington, DC: Office of Juvenile Justice and Delinquency Prevention. (NCJ 171152)

Howell, James C., and Arlen Egley, Jr. 2008. *Frequently Asked Questions regarding Gangs*. Tallahassee, FL: Institute for Intergovernmental Research.

Howell, James C., Arlen Egley, Jr., and Debra K. Gleason. 2002 (June). *Modern Day Youth Gangs*. Washington, DC: Office of Juvenile Justice and Delinquency Prevention. (NCJ 191524)

Howell, James C., Arlen Egley, Jr., George E. Tita, and Elizabeth Griffiths. 2011 (May). *U.S. Gang Problem Trends and Seriousness, 1996–2009*. Washington, DC: Institute for Intergovernmental Research (IIR) on behalf of the National Gang Center, National Gang Center Bulletin, No.6.

Huebner, Beth M., Sean P. Varano, and Timothy S. Bynum. 2007 (May). "Gangs, Guns, and Drugs: Recidivism among Serious, Young Offenders." *Criminology & Public Policy* 6 (2): 187–221.

Huff, C. Ronald. 1998 (October). *Comparing the Criminal Behavior of Youth Gangs and At-Risk Youths*. Washington, DC: National Institute of Justice, Research in Brief. (NCJ 172852)

Katz, Charles M., and Stephen M. Schnebly. 2011 (May). "Neighborhood Variation in Gang Membership Concentration." *Crime and Delinquency* 57 (3): 377–407.

Kennedy, David M., Anthony A. Braga, and Anne M. Piehl. 2001 (September). "Developing and Implementing Operation Ceasefire." In *Reducing Gun Violence: The Boston Gun Project's Operation Ceasefire*, pp. 5–53. Washington, DC: U.S. Department of Justice, Office of Justice Programs. (NCJ 188741)

Klein, Malcolm W. 1995. *The American Street Gang: Its Nature, Prevalence and Control*. New York: Oxford University Press.

———. 2007. *Chasing after Street Gangs: A Forty-Year Journey*. Upper Saddle River, NJ: Pearson/Prentice Hall.

Klein, Malcolm W., and Cheryl L. Maxson. 2006. *Street Gang Patterns and Policies*. New York: Oxford University Press.

Krohn, Marvin D., Nicole M. Schmidt, Alan J. Lizotte, and Julie M. Baldwin. 2011 (February). "The Impact of Multiple Marginality on Gang Membership and Delinquent Behavior for Hispanic, African American, and White Male Adolescents." *Journal of Contemporary Criminal Justice* 27 (1): 18–42.

Langton, Lynn. 2010 (October). *Gang Units in Large Local Law Enforcement Agencies, 2007*. Washington, DC: Bureau of Justice Statistics. (NCJ 230071)

Lyddane, Donald. 2006 (May). "Understanding Gangs and Gang Mentality: Acquiring Evidence of the Gang Conspiracy." *United States Attorneys' Bulletin* 54 (3): 1–14.

Maxson, Cheryl L. 1998 (October). *Gang Members on the Move*. Washington, DC: Office of Juvenile Justice and Delinquency Prevention. (NCJ 171153)

McGloin, Jean M. n.d. *Street Gangs and Interventions: Innovative Problem Solving with Network Analysis*. Washington, DC: Office of Community Oriented Policing Services. (NCJ211993)

The Police and Juveniles

8

> "Police officers play a crucial role in the juvenile justice system, one that extends beyond enforcing the law. The police officer on the beat has first-hand knowledge of the community and its youth—knowledge that can prove a valuable asset in efforts to prevent delinquency.

—**John J. Wison**

Former Acting Administrator, Office of Juvenile Justice and Delinquency Prevention

Positive face-to-face contacts between police officers and children can help promote the idea of the police officer as a friend and helper.

© UpperCut Images/Photolibrary

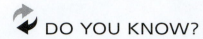

DO YOU KNOW?

- What greatly influences youths' attitudes toward law and law enforcement?
- What primary responsibility officers assigned a child abuse or neglect case have?
- What challenges are involved in investigating crimes against children?
- What the majority of police dispositions involve?
- What factors affect how police officers respond to status offenders?

- Whether the police have discretionary power when dealing with juveniles?
- What the four-pronged threat assessment approach is?
- What the role of the first responder to a school shooting situation should be?
- What an effective approach to school security should include?
- What controversial measures have been taken to make schools safer?

CAN YOU DEFINE?

beyond a reasonable doubt

detention

lockdown

school resource officer (SRO)

station adjustment

taken into custody

temporary custody without hearing

CHAPTER OUTLINE

Introduction

The Police Response to Neglected and Abused Children

Challenges to Investigation

Evidence

A Protocol for Responding to Child Abuse and Neglect

Law Enforcement's Disposition of Status Offenders

The Police Response to Delinquency

Police Discretion and the Initial Contact

Taken into Custody

The Juvenile Holdover

Detention

Prosecution

The Police Response to Juvenile Gun Crime

Youth Firearms Violence Initiative

Project Safe Neighborhoods

The Police Response to Youth Crime and Violence in Our Schools

The School Resource Officer (SRO) Program

Bullying

School Shootings

In Search of Safer Schools

Other Efforts to Prevent School Violence

Partnerships and Community Policing

Police as Mentors to At-Risk Youths

Introduction

The juvenile justice system, as already discussed, is basically concerned with three distinct populations of youths: those who are victims of abuse or neglect, those who commit status offenses and those who commit serious crimes. Law enforcement is commonly the first contact young victims and victimizers have with the juvenile justice system, serving as the gatekeeper to the rest of the system. The police are charged with protecting youths, both victims and offenders, and dealing fairly with them. A balance is sought between what is in the best interest of the youth and what is best for the community. Also, the crime-fighting philosophy must be balanced with the service ideal.

The importance of the officer on the street cannot be overlooked. Every law enforcement officer, no matter at what level, has an opportunity to be a positive influence on youths. Ultimately youths' perceptions about the law and law enforcement will be based on one-on-one interactions with law enforcement officers.

 Youths' attitudes toward law and law enforcement are tremendously influenced by personal contacts with law enforcement officers. Positive interactions are critical to delinquency prevention.

The Police Response to Neglected and Abused Children

Law enforcement agencies are charged with investigating all crimes, but their responsibility is especially great where crimes against children are involved. Children need the protection of the law to a greater degree than do other members of society because children are so vulnerable, particularly if the offense is committed by one or both parents. Even after the offense is committed, the child may still be in danger of further victimization.

In most states, action must be taken on a report within a specified time, frequently three days. If, in the judgment of the person receiving the report, it is necessary to remove the child from present custody, this is discussed with the responsible agency, such as the welfare department or the juvenile court. If the situation is deemed life threatening, the police may temporarily remove the child.

 The primary responsibility of police officers assigned to child neglect or abuse cases is the immediate protection of the child.

Under welfare regulations and codes, an officer may take a child into temporary custody without a warrant if there is an emergency or if the officer has reason to believe that leaving the child in the present situation would subject the child to further abuse or harm. **Temporary custody without hearing** usually refers to a period of 48 hours. Conditions that would justify placing a child in protective custody include:

- Maltreatment in the home that might cause the child permanent physical or emotional damage.
- A parent's refusal to provide needed medical or psychiatric care for a child.
- The child is physically or mentally incapable of self-protection.
- The home's physical environment poses an immediate threat.
- The parents cannot or will not provide for the child's basic needs.
- The parents abandon the child.

Among the service providers mandated to report incidents of suspected child abuse or neglect are child care providers, clergy, educators, hospital administrators, nurses, physicians, psychologists and those in the social services. No matter who receives the report or whether the child must be removed from the situation, it is the responsibility of the law enforcement agency to investigate the charge.

© becky rockwood RF/Getty Images

Responding to cases of child abuse can be very challenging. Not only might such victimization evoke strong emotional reactions in officers called on to help these children, but interviewing young victims takes particular skill and patience. Many child victims are reluctant to "tell on" their abusers, especially if the perpetrator is a parent.

Challenges to Investigation

Many prosecutors at all levels of the judiciary perceive crimes against children as among the most difficult to prosecute and obtain convictions. Therefore, officers interviewing child witnesses and victims should have specialized training to help convict the guilty and to protect the innocent. Regardless of whether crimes against children are handled by generalists or specialists within the department, certain challenges are unique to these investigations.

 Challenges in investigating crimes against children include the need to protect the child from further harm, the possibility of parental involvement, the difficulty of interviewing children, credibility concerns and the need to collaborate with other agencies.

Consultation with local welfare authorities is sometimes needed before asking the court for a hearing to remove a child from the parents' custody or for protective custody in an authorized facility because police rarely have such facilities. As soon as possible the child should be taken to the nearest welfare facility or to a foster home, as stipulated by the juvenile court. The parents or legal guardians of the child must be notified as soon as possible.

Evidence

All the officer's observations pertaining to the physical and emotional condition of the victim must be recorded in detail. Evidence in child neglect or abuse cases includes the surroundings, the home conditions, clothing, bruises or other bodily injuries, the medical examination report and other observations. Photographs may be the best way to document child abuse and neglect where it is necessary to show injury to the child or the conditions of the home environment. Pictures should be taken immediately because children's injuries heal quickly and home conditions can be changed rapidly.

A Protocol for Responding to Child Abuse and Neglect

An effective police response to reports of child abuse and neglect should include:

- A written, agency-wide child abuse policy.
- Written interagency protocols and interagency teams to handle child abuse investigations.
- Immediate telephone notification of the police by protective service agency workers regarding all sexual abuse cases and all cases of serious physical injury or danger.
- Initial interviews conducted jointly with child protective agency workers, especially in sexual abuse cases.
- Patrol officers trained in the identification of abuse.
- Child abuse specialists, skilled as investigators and comfortable interviewing young children.
- Child-friendly interview settings.
- Limited and selective use of videotaping and anatomical dolls by properly trained individuals.

Law Enforcement's Disposition of Status Offenders

In making dispositions on juvenile matters, the police have found that neglectful parents are often so absorbed with their own desires and problems that they have little time to consider their children's needs. Such parents often tend to rely on extrafamilial entities such as church, school or civic groups to guide their children and frequently pursue a policy of appeasement in the home rather than maintaining family discipline. Partly because of this lack of parental guidance, law enforcement agencies are faced with the constant problem of taking youths into custody on relatively minor charges such as curfew violations and loitering.

 The majority of police dispositions involve status offenses (violating curfew, truancy, loitering, underage smoking and drinking of alcoholic beverages and running away).

Police dispositions range from taking no action to referring status offenders to social service agencies or to the juvenile court. The police alternatives are guided by the community, the local juvenile justice system and individual officer discretion. Whether the police actually arrest a juvenile usually depends on several factors, the most important being the seriousness of the offense. Other factors affecting the decision include the juvenile's character, age, gender, race, prior record, family situation and attitude. The decision may also be influenced by public opinion, the media, available referral agencies and the officer's experience.

 In the disposition of status offenders, how police resolve matters often depends on the officers' discretion, the specific incident and the resources available.

Officers' actions usually reflect community interests. For example, conflict may occur between the public's demand for order and a group of young people wanting to "hang around." How police respond to such hanging around is influenced by the officer's attitude and the standards of the neighborhood or community, rather than rules of the state. Each neighborhood or community and the officer's own feelings dictate how the police perform in such matters.

The Police Response to Delinquency

Some localities may handle a delinquent act very differently from others. For example, police investigating an auto theft in the suburbs and finding a youth responsible will often simply send the youth home for parental discipline. The youth will receive a notice of when to appear in court. In contrast, urban juveniles—especially minority youths—caught stealing an automobile are often detained in a locked facility. Sometimes, however, urban youths are at an advantage.

Local standards of appropriate or "normal" youthful behavior influence how police respond to and dispose of delinquency cases. Youths cannot "get away with" as much in some areas as they do in others. What rural law enforcement officers may perceive as criminal behavior is often viewed as a prank by that officer's urban counterpart. Justice for juveniles is not a neatly structured, impartial decision-making process by which the rule of law always prevails and each person is treated fairly and impartially.

Police Discretion and the Initial Contact

Between 80 and 90 percent of youths commit some offense for which they could be arrested, yet only about 3 percent of them are. This is largely because they do not get caught. Further, those who are caught usually have engaged in some minor status offense that can be better handled by counseling and releasing in many instances. Although the "counsel and dismiss" alternative may be criticized as being soft on juveniles, this approach is often the most efficient and effective way to process the case.

 Police officers have considerable discretionary power when dealing with juveniles.

Law enforcement officers have a range of alternatives to take:

- Release the youth, with or without a warning, but without making an official record or taking further action.
- Release the youth, but write up a brief contact or field report to juvenile authorities, describing the contact.
- Release the youth, but file a more formal report referring the matter to a juvenile bureau or an intake unit for possible action.

- Turn the youth over to juvenile authorities immediately.
- Refer the case directly to the court through the district or county attorney.

In some instances youths engaging in delinquent acts are simply counseled. In other instances they are returned to their families, who are expected to deal with their children's deviant behavior. Sometimes youths are referred to social services agencies for help. And sometimes they are charged and processed by the juvenile justice system.

Parents, schools and the police are the main sources for the referral of youths into the juvenile justice system. Of these three sources, the police are, by far, the most common source of referrals.

In a few jurisdictions, if the child is not released without official record, he or she is automatically turned over to the juvenile authorities, who make all further decisions in the matter. If the child is referred to court, another decision is whether police personnel should release or detain the child. Officers try to dispose of juvenile cases in a way that considers the best interests of both the juvenile and the community.

Taken into Custody

Police contact with children may result either from a complaint received or from observing questionable behavior. In their initial contact with juveniles, the police are indirectly guided by the language of the Juvenile Court Act of 1899, which states that juveniles are "**taken into custody**," not arrested. This is interpreted to mean the police's role is to salvage and rehabilitate youth, a role indirectly sanctioned by many judges who encourage settling disputes and complaints without referral to the court. Despite this preferred terminology, many criminal justice professionals still refer to the action as a juvenile *arrest*.

If a youth is detained, the officers must be aware that the Supreme Court has emphasized that persons under legal age do have certain constitutional rights, albeit not the full complement of rights afforded adults. The protection, critical to the juvenile offender, is twofold:

1. At no point in any criminal investigation may the rights of the juvenile be infringed upon.
2. A crime by a juvenile must be proven beyond a reasonable doubt. **Beyond a reasonable doubt** is less than absolute certainty, but more than high probability.

Juveniles also have the right to remain silent, the right to counsel, the right to know the specific charge and the right to confront witnesses. According to the Federal Bureau of Investigation's (FBI's) annual *Crime in the United States* report, of the juvenile offenders taken into custody in 2010, two thirds (67.7 percent) were referred to juvenile court jurisdiction and nearly 8 percent (7.9%) were referred to criminal or adult court (*Crime in the United States 2010* 2011). Approximately one fifth (22.6 percent) were handled within the department and released—called **station adjustment**. The remaining few cases were referred to a welfare agency or other police agency. Table 8.1 shows the police dispositions of juvenile offenders taken into custody in 2010, broken down by the size of the jurisdiction and whether the custody occurred within a metropolitan or nonmetropolitan county.

Table 8.1 Police Disposition of Juvenile Offenders Taken into Custody, 2010 (2010 estimated population)

Population Group	Total[1]	Handled within Department and Released	Referred to Juvenile Court Jurisdiction	Referred to Welfare Agency	Referred to Other Police Agency	Referred to Criminal or Adult Court	Number of Agencies	2010 Estimated Population
Total Agencies								
Number	495,453	111,876	335,279	2,365	6,856	39,077	5,209	121,215,136
Percent[2]	100.0	22.6	67.7	0.5	1.4	7.9		
Total Cities								
Number	423,659	100,313	284,961	2,019	5,688	30,678	3,960	88,280,366
Percent[2]	100.0	23.7	67.3	0.5	1.3	7.2		
Group I (250,000 and over)								
Number	112,738	36,606	72,666	146	1,161	2,159	36	26,155,247
Percent[2]	100.0	32.5	64.5	0.1	1.0	1.9		
Group II (100,000 to 249,999)								
Number	58,916	12,823	43,703	453	783	1,154	83	12,315,412
Percent[2]	100.0	21.8	74.2	0.8	1.3	2.0		
Group III (50,000 to 99,999)								
Number	82,159	16,782	58,634	476	1,317	4,950	238	16,101,572
Percent[2]	100.0	20.4	71.4	0.6	1.6	6.0		
Group IV (25,000 to 49,999)								
Number	55,665	10,247	38,421	166	1,135	5,696	348	12,006,184
Percent[2]	100.0	18.4	69.0	0.3	2.0	10.2		
Group V (10,000 to 24,999)								
Number	63,086	13,113	40,264	404	741	8,564	808	12,877,732
Percent[2]	100.0	20.8	63.8	0.6	1.2	13.6		
Group VI (under 10,000)								
Number	51,095	10,742	31,273	374	551	8,155	2,447	8,824,219
Percent[2]	100.0	21.0	61.2	0.7	1.1	16.0		
Metropolitan Counties								
Number	56,598	9,259	40,317	232	999	5,791	655	24,543,709
Percent[2]	100.0	16.4	71.2	0.4	1.8	10.2		
Nonmetropolitan Counties								
Number	15,196	2,304	10,001	114	169	2,608	594	8,391,061
Percent[2]	100.0	15.2	65.8	0.8	1.1	17.2		
Suburban Area[3]								
Number	209,287	43,383	137,399	1,193	2,714	24,598	3,337	59,279,363
Percent[2]	100.0	20.7	65.7	0.6	1.3	11.8		

[1]Includes all offenses except traffic and neglect cases.
[2]Because of rounding, the percentages may not add to 100.0.
[3]Suburban area includes law enforcement agencies in cities with less than 50,000 inhabitants and county law enforcement agencies that are within a Metropolitan Statistical Area. Suburban area excludes all metropolitan agencies associated with a principal city. The agencies associated with suburban areas also appear in other groups within this table.
SOURCE: *Crime in the United States 2010*. 2011. Washington, DC: U.S. Department of Justice, Federal Bureau of Investigation, Table 68.
http://www.fbi.gov/about-us/cjis/ucr/crime-in-the-u.s/2010/crime-in-the-u.s.-2010/tables/10tbl68.xls

One problem of referral for juvenile authorities and the court, especially in a metropolitan area, is that it may be difficult to determine by appearance alone if a person is a juvenile. Youths may lie about or try to manipulate their age for practical reasons. For example, a youth detained on a status offense may claim to be over the age limit and, consequently, *not* an offender. Or youths taken into custody for minor offenses such as disorderly conduct or prostitution often claim to be over the age limit, reasoning that if treated as adults they will simply be forced to spend a night in jail, hear a lecture by a judge and accept whatever penalty is disposed. If they identify themselves as juveniles, their detention usually is extended, and interference with their freedom and liberty may well be more substantial.

The Juvenile Holdover

An Implementation Guide for Juvenile Holdover Programs (Mowatt and Chezem 2001) cites the following scenario:

> It was early Saturday morning. David, a 15-year-old who lives in a small town with a population of about 1,500, was driving his father's car and was stopped by the only police officer on duty. The headlights on David's car were not turned on and he was driving erratically. The officer suspected that David had been drinking. When tested with the officer's preliminary breath tester, David blew a 0.07. His blood alcohol content (BAC) was below the legal level of 0.08 for driving under the influence (DUI) in this state, but it is a zero-tolerance jurisdiction, meaning that the presence of any alcohol in the system of a 15-year-old was a violation.
>
> In addition, David did not have a valid driver's license and he was out after curfew. He was cited for all three violations, the car was secured, and a tow was ordered. David, now seated in the rear of the squad car, told the officer that he had been at a party and acknowledged that he had been drinking beer. David revealed that he had been drinking a lot lately. He stated that his parents were out of town for the weekend and could not be reached by phone. He was to be alone at home until late Sunday night and had no other relatives living in this community.
>
> The officer had no on-duty backup and there were five more hours left on his shift. There was no safe place to drop David off, and department policy prohibited having the youth ride in the squad car for the remainder of the shift. The nearest emergency shelter facility for youths would be a three-hour round trip. Driving there would take up most of the time left on the officer's shift. The only option was to return to police headquarters and wait with David until morning. Then, arrangements could be made to locate his parents or to find a place for David to stay for the rest of the weekend. It was Friday night and because of one juvenile who was drinking alcohol and driving while impaired police coverage was not available for the community for the rest of the night.

The *Implementation Guide* (Mowatt and Chezem 2001, 1) notes, "When viewed from a national perspective, juvenile holdover programs are multifaceted. In general, however, they are short-term, temporary holding programs for youths that can be located in either a secure, nonsecure or a combination secure/nonsecure setting." The guide (7–8) describes key elements of a successful holdover program as being easily accessible, integrated into a network of services for youths, with a trained staff able to respond to a youth's immediate needs, able to provide comfortable facilities with minimum services for an overnight stay and able to respond to and de-escalate the immediate situation if necessary (crisis intervention). An effective holdover program also has screening and assessment capacity, has referral expertise and is able to coordinate post-release services to the youth and family and evaluate its effectiveness.

Detention

In some instances, law enforcement officers may determine that the most appropriate disposition is detention. **Detention** is the period during which a youth is taken into custody by police and probation before a petition is filed. Detention is governed by two requirements of the Juvenile Justice and Delinquency Prevention (JJDP) Act of 1974: (1) removing all juveniles from adult jails and lockups and (2) separating juvenile and adult offenders. The act states that

> [J]uveniles alleged to be or found to be delinquent and youths within the purview of paragraph (12) (i.e., status offenders and non-offenders) shall not be detained or confined in any institution in which they have regular contact with adult persons incarcerated because they have been convicted of a crime or are awaiting trial on criminal charges.

In addition state laws and department policies may affect who is detained and under what conditions. Most state statutes governing the detention of juveniles are quite general. Among the criteria used by states are these:

- For the juvenile's or society's protection
- Lack of parental care available
- To ensure a juvenile's presence at a juvenile court hearing
- The seriousness of the offense and the juvenile's record

Juvenile court statutes often require that once children have been taken into custody, they may be released only to their parents, guardians or custodians. Where such a law exists, a decision to detain automatically follows if the parents, guardians or custodians cannot be found. The child is placed in detention and must be referred to court. Thus the police are removed from the referral process.

In most states police may take a child into custody for the child's own protection until appropriate placement can be made. Standards to guide police personnel in the decision whether to release or detain may be formally prepared in written instructions by police administrators and court authorities. In some states *mandatory referral* to juvenile authorities or even directly to court may be required for all crimes of violence, felonies and serious misdemeanors. Similarly all juveniles on parole or probation may be referred. Some jurisdictions refer if the juvenile has had previous contact with the police.

Prosecution

When the prosecutor receives a recommendation for petition (trial), at least three options are available: dismiss the case, file the petition or determine that the charges are so serious that the case should be heard in adult court, waiving jurisdiction. If a petition is filed, this begins the formal adjudication process.

Based on police reports, the county attorney may refer a juvenile to the screening unit of the juvenile court. The formal processing of juvenile cases is discussed in greater depth in Chapters 9 and 10.

The Police Response to Juvenile Gun Crime

The changing nature of youth crime during the 1980s and 1990s caused a shift in the justice system to a more punitive, "get tough" approach to dealing with violent juvenile offenders. This is a change that, despite declines in gun violence and homicides in recent years, persists in many jurisdictions: "In response to the surge in violent crime and the public's demand for quick, impressive action, many police departments have moved away from community policing, relying instead on traditional law enforcement strategies to fight crime. Tactical enforcement teams, 'stop and frisk' initiatives, neighborhood sweeps, gang injunctions, and public housing 'bar out' (a 'no-trespass' policy used by public housing authorities to reduce drug activity and other crimes) have been used to target and reduce violent crime" (Straub 2008, 1).

Youth Firearms Violence Initiative

One approach to juvenile gun crime was the Youth Firearms Violence Initiative (YFVI) launched in 1995 by the U.S. Department of Justice's Office of Community Oriented Policing Services (COPS). COPS provided up to $1 million to police departments in 10 cities[1] to fund interventions directed at combating the rise of youth firearms violence. Among the key findings of this initiative, according to Dunworth (2000, 1–2), were these:

- A dedicated unit may exert a greater effect on gun-related crime than a unit that applies traditional tactics and uses patrol officers on a rotating basis.
- When employed as part of YFVI, traditional enforcement tactics did not produce significant changes in firearms violence levels.
- Cooperating with other law enforcement agencies and community organizations and representatives was a key factor in effective implementation of firearms violence control and prevention strategies.
- Proactive arrest policies focused on gun-related offenses were shown to have a consistent measurable association with subsequent gun-related crime.
- Most of the participating departments returned to traditional policing approaches when federal funding ended.

Table 8.2 summarizes the strategies and tactics used at five of the sites. It is of interest that only Baltimore implemented school-based activities.

Project Safe Neighborhoods

Another gun reduction initiative is Project Safe Neighborhoods (PSN), a nationwide commitment to reduce gun crime by networking existing local programs that target gun crime and providing those programs with additional tools necessary to be successful. The goal is to take a hard line against gun criminals through every

---

[1] The 10 cities in the YFVI were Baltimore, Maryland; Birmingham, Alabama; Bridgeport, Connecticut; Cleveland, Ohio; Inglewood, California; Milwaukee, Wisconsin; Richmond, Virginia; Salinas, California; San Antonio, Texas; and Seattle, Washington.

Table 8.2 Police Department Strategies and Tactics of the Youth Firearms Violence Initiative (YFVI)

Site	Total Budget and Configuration	Street-Based Activities	School-Based Activities	Community-Based Activities	GIS*/Crime Analysis
Baltimore	$999,906 • Cherry Hill: 9 officers • Park Heights: 15 officers	• Juvenile Violent Crime Flex Team: surveillance, intelligence gathering and targeted enforcement • Curfew Enforcement Team: focused on chronically truant students	• In Park Heights, two city police officers worked with middle and high schools • Supported the Magnet School for Law Enforcement, a criminal justice curriculum for high school students • Three officers implemented the Straight Talk About Risk (STAR) Program	• Community resource centers (Kobans) in schools provided a police presence and liaison with community groups • Curfew enforcement officers provided information, counseling and housing to truant students and families	• Department had GIS capability prior to YFVI
Cleveland	$685,342 • 27 officers, 2 sergeants	• Residential Area Policing Program (RAPP) Houses: located in neighborhoods with high violence, staffed around the clock for 90 days	None	• RAPP House officers coordinated cleanup and youth activities • RAPP House used for neighborhood meetings	• Department had GIS capability prior to YFVI
Inglewood	$787,201 • Strategy Against Gang Environments (SAGE) Gang Enforcement Task Force: 1 sergeant, 6 officers • Strengthened the Street Terrorist Enforcement and Prevention (STEP) Task Force: 6 officers, 1 probation officer, 1 district attorney	• SAGE program: civil remedies against gang members; task force focused on weapons violations • STEP: act with criminal sanctions against street gangs and a task force that conducted street enforcement • Probation officer targeted gang members on probation	None	• Rites-of-Passage Mentoring Program used police officers, firefighters and community leaders to teach youths civic values, self-esteem and conflict mediation • Gun and Weapons Buy-Back Program • KIDSAFE campaign taught parents about the dangers of handgun use and possession • Media and poster campaign addressed youth firearm violence prevention	• Juvenile records computerized for YFVI • Internally developed a GIS system (with minimal YFVI funding)
Salinas	$999,524 • Violence Suppression Unit (VSU): 1 lieutenant, 2 sergeants, 16 officers	• VSU: dedicated to work full time on suppressing youth handgun violence • Crime tip hotline • Intensified efforts to locate firearms and track down their origins	None	None	• An outside contractor implemented an ArcView/ArcInfo system
San Antonio	$999,963 • Rotation: 9 officers deployed nightly	• Weapons Recovery and Tracking Team • Street Crime Arrest Team	None	None	• Researched the youth firearm violence problem • Computer linkup with trauma centers throughout the city

*Geographic information systems

SOURCE: Terence Dunworth. 2000 (November). *National Evaluation of the Youth Firearms Violence Initiative*, p. 5. Washington, DC: National Institute of Justice Research in Brief. (NCJ 184482)

available means to create safer neighborhoods. PSN seeks to achieve heightened coordination among federal, state and local law enforcement, with an emphasis on tactical intelligence gathering, more aggressive prosecutions and enhanced accountability through performance measures. The philosophy of PSN as applied to youth is based on the previously mentioned corresponding spikes in juvenile violent crime and juvenile gun possession, with the anticipation that a reduction in youths carrying firearms would also result in a reduction in violent juvenile crime. For more information, visit the Criminal Justice Companion Web site at cengagebrain.com, then access the web links for this chapter.

Of special concern to law enforcement are youths who carry guns in our schools. Although the 1994 Gun Free Schools Act requires schools receiving federal education funds to have a policy mandating the expulsion of students who bring firearms to school, some youths still manage to bring guns onto school property, as discussed shortly.

The Police Response to Youth Crime and Violence in Our Schools

Property crimes are nothing new for schools. A favorite target of youth out to commit vandalism has often been their local school, with such offenses ranging from spray-painted walls and broken windows to complete destruction of interior classrooms and other school property. Particularly when the offense is perceived as minor, such as graffiti or a few stolen items from a science classroom, these acts are unlikely to be reported to the police, making dealing with the problem that much more difficult (Petrocelli 2007, 32).

What has become of increasing concern to educational institutions and law enforcement agencies across the country is the prevalence of violent crime in our nation's schools. Some youths are demonstrating an increased capacity for violence, which has crept into the schools and made students fearful of victimization by their classmates. Although schools are, by and large, one of the safest places for children, some campuses have reacted to the threat of violence by installing metal detectors and surveillance cameras, and a few have employed the use of drug- and weapons-detector dogs.

Noonan and Vavra (2007) highlight the critical importance in understanding the dynamics of criminal acts in educational settings to allow law enforcement, school administrators, policymakers and the public to construct adequate, effective responses: "Schools and colleges are valued institutions that help build upon the nation's foundations and serve as an arena where the growth and stability of future generations begin. Crime in schools and colleges is therefore one of the most troublesome social problems in the nation today. Not only does it affect those involved in the criminal incident, but it also hinders societal growth and stability" (Noonan and Vavra 2007, 1).

In their five-year study, Noonan and Vavra (2007) found that 3.3 percent of all incidents reported via the National Incident-Based Reporting System (NIBRS) involved school locations. Offense records indicate that such incidents were most likely to include the use of personal weapons (the offender's hands, fists, feet, etc.), but reports of the offender's use of alcohol, computers or drugs were minimal. Reported offenders of crime in schools were most likely to be 13- to 15-year-old

White males who were known to the victims; however, there was nearly an equally large number of 16- to 18-year-old reported offenders. More than half of the arrestees associated with crime at school locations were arrested for simple assault or drug/narcotic violations. Arrestees had similar characteristics to the reported offenders, most likely being reported as 13- to 15-year-old White non-Hispanic males who were residents of the community of the school location where the incident was reported. Interestingly, across all five years of the study, the highest number of offenses reported consistently occurred during October each year.

Robers, Zhang and Truman (2010) report the following key findings related to indicators of school crime and safety:

- Overall victimization at school has continued to decline from 1992 to 2008.
- One out of 21 students are victims of crime at school—mostly thefts.
- Reports of gang presence at schools have remained fairly steady since 2005, with 23 percent of students ages 12 to 18 reporting gangs at their schools.
- Incidents of fighting at school decreased overall between 1993 and 2009, although the percentage of students being involved in physical fights did not change significantly from 2007 to 2009. Generally, the peak grade level for fighting occurred in ninth grade.
- Incidents of weapon carrying at and away from school have declined over the past several years.
- The percentage of students who fear attack or harm at school decreased substantially between 1995 and 2007.
- Violent deaths at school remain rare. Between July 1, 2008 and June 30, 2009 there were 15 homicides and 7 suicides of youth ages 5 to 18 at school.
- The percentage of students ages 12 to 18 who reported being bullied at school increased, from 28 percent in 2005 to 32 percent in 2007.

Several states have passed laws requiring school officials to report certain types of offenses to local police. In many states failure to report violent incidents to a law enforcement agency is a criminal offense—usually a misdemeanor.

Educators commonly detect and report incidents of suspected child abuse or family violence. Educators may also, however, be firsthand witnesses to and, on occasion, victims of violence, as the aggression experienced at home by some children finds its way onto school grounds. A variety of elements may lead police in a certain jurisdiction to respond to incidents of school violence.

A trend, particularly among smaller departments, in tailoring a more effective response to school violence is to provide more cross-training and pooling of resources. A comprehensive, step-by-step discussion of police response to school violence is beyond the scope of this text; however, several publications focus entirely on this subject. A particularly useful document addressing school violence is the *Guide for Preventing and Responding to School Violence* published by the International Association of Chiefs of Police (IACP). It is based on the input of more than 500 experts and 15 focus groups with a diverse range of disciplines.

The School Resource Officer (SRO) Program

A much publicized delinquency prevention plan, the police–school liaison program, was developed in 1958 in Flint, Michigan, with the cooperation of school authorities, parents, social agencies, juvenile court officials, businesses and the police department. The foundation for the police–school liaison program established a workable relationship with the police department and the public school system. This program gradually evolved into what is today the **school resource officer (SRO)** program.

Part Q of Title I of the Omnibus Crime Control and Safe Streets Act of 1968 defines the SRO as "a career law enforcement officer, with sworn authority, deployed in community-oriented policing, and assigned by the employing police department or agency to work in collaboration with school and community-based organizations." According to the National Association of School Resource Officers, school-based policing is the fastest growing area of law enforcement.

SROs do not enforce school regulations, which are left to the school superintendent and staff. Instead the officers work with students, parents and school authorities to apply preventive techniques to problems created by antisocial youths who have not or will not conform to the community's laws and ordinances. The techniques used by school resource officers involve counseling children and their parents, referring them to social agencies to treat the root problems, referring them to drug and alcohol abuse agencies and being in daily contact in the school to check their progress. Often SROs deal with predelinquent and early delinquent youths with whom law enforcement would not have been involved under traditional programs.

SROs frequently patrol the elementary school areas until school starts in the morning, and also during the noon hour and after school. They watch for any suspicious people or automobiles and for infractions of safety rules regarding routes to and from school. They also check the middle-school areas for anyone loitering around the building or grounds trying to pick up students in the area. The appendix at the end of this book provides a detailed job description for an SRO.

Many aspects of the SRO program benefit students, the school and the community. The communication developed between the law enforcement agency and school personnel provides information to guide young people. Respect for law enforcement agencies is built up in the minds of the youths. The SRO becomes their friend. The effective preventive work of the SRO program may be a considerable part of the answer to the problem of juvenile antisocial behavior.

The goals of the SRO program fall into two general categories: preventing juvenile delinquency and improving community relations.

In seeking to prevent delinquency, officers focus on both preventive actions and the official investigation of criminal activity, apprehension and court referral. Officers assigned to schools approach delinquency prevention through a variety of activities:

- Acting as instructors for various school groups and classes
- Acting as counselors to students, separately or with school personnel
- Maintaining contacts with parents or guardians of students who exhibit antisocial behavior
- Making public appearances
- Maintaining files of information on students contacted
- Investigating complaints of criminal activity occurring within the school complex and the surrounding area
- Maintaining close contact with other police agencies

The second general goal of SRO programs focuses on community relations, projecting and maintaining an image of the police as serving the community,

© Augusta Chronicle/ZUMAPRESS.com

A school resource officer speaks with students as she patrols the halls at a middle school in Augusta, Georgia. Positive contacts with individual youth help foster an image of the police as the "good guys" and influence the attitudes of students, as well as of their friends and families. Many popular myths about laws and law enforcement officers are dispelled through this type of interaction.

rather than simply enforcing laws. Enhancing community relations is accomplished in several ways.

Public appearances are a key technique. Officers speak and present films or slide programs to many types of groups, such as Parent Teacher Associations (PTAs), service groups, church fellowships, civic gatherings, youth clubs and civil rights groups. There usually is an interplay of ideas at such gatherings, and the officers sell the idea of community service.

Another focus is *parent contacts.* Behavioral problems are often apparent in the school before they develop into more serious delinquent activity. Officers in the school know about such problems and can contact parents, working together with them to avoid any progression into serious delinquent behavior.

Possibly the most effective community relations technique at officers' disposal is *individual contact.* Officers have contact with many young people of all ages. In projecting an image of the "good guys," they influence the attitudes of those students counseled as well as of their friends and families. Many popular myths about laws and law enforcement officers are dispelled through this type of interaction.

Another important area is *liaison work with other interested agencies*, including juvenile courts, social agencies, mental health agencies, other schools and private organizations. Officers gain operational knowledge of each and learn to coordinate their efforts with these other agencies to better treat children.

Displaying interest indicates to these agencies that police are concerned with more than simply apprehension and detention in dealing with delinquency.

Undoubtedly teachers have a definite effect on their students' attitudes. Officers who help teachers with problem students improve teachers' images of the police. This, along with personally knowing a police officer, does much in long-range police-community relations and, as any preventive program must be, this preventive program is long range.

Finally, *recreational participation* is a type of interaction with youths that breaks down many walls of resentment. Officers who participate in organized athletics with youngsters build a rapport that is carried over into their other contacts with those youths.

SROs have traditionally educated students about topics such as pedestrian safety and the dangers of substance abuse. That role has broadened as local law enforcement agencies attempt to defuse potentially violent student situations. Among such situations is bullying.

Bullying

It has been said that bullying is suicide's quiet little secret, as some victims of bullying suffer such humiliation and loss of self-esteem they become violent toward themselves. Estimates based on suicide statistics compiled by the Centers of Disease Control and Prevention (CDC) place the number of suicides by children under age 19 that are bully-related in the triple digits.

Garrett (2006, 8) notes, "Technology has made brutality—particularly the emotional kind—much easier to inflict. Through e-mails, blogs, Internet bulletin boards and Instant Messaging, cyber bullies can cast their wrath instantly—and anonymously. These tactics have far-reaching impacts on the juvenile community."

A leading researcher on bullying is Dan Olweus (pronounced Ol-VEY-us), whose Bullying Prevention Program was developed in Norway and has since been replicated in the United States. According to the U.S. Web site for the *Olweus Bullying Prevention Program* (2011), this comprehensive, school-wide program is designed for use in elementary, middle or junior high schools and attempts to restructure the existing school environment to reduce opportunities and rewards for bullying. The program has proven highly successful in Norway and has demonstrated similarly positive results in the United States:

- In the 1990s in South Carolina, after one year of implementation, researchers found large, significant decreases in boys' and girls' reports of bullying others; large, significant decreases in boys' reports of being bullied; and decreases in boys' reports of social isolation (Limber 2004).
- An evaluation of the program in 12 elementary schools in the Philadelphia area found significant reductions in self-reported bullying and victimization and significant decreases in adults' observations of bullying in the cafeteria and on the playground (Black 2003).
- The Chula Vista (California) Police Department implemented the program in 2003 in collaboration with three local elementary schools and found a 21 percent decrease in reports of being bullied after 1 year and a 14 percent decrease after 2 years; and an 8 percent decrease in reports of bullying others after 1 year and a 17 percent decrease after 2 years. Furthermore, after one year, students were more likely to perceive that adults at school tried to stop bullying and parents believed administrators had done more to stop bullying (Pagliocca, Limber, and Hashima 2007).

IN THE NEWS | "Bullying of Jamey Addressed Just Once, Middle School Incident Resulted in Discipline"
by Sandra Tan, *The Buffalo News*, October 5, 2011

The Williamsville School District appears to have only one documented case of bullying involving Jamey Rodemeyer, police say. The incident apparently happened when he was a student at Heim Middle School, and disciplinary action was promptly taken.

In an update of the investigation into the Sept. 18 suicide of the 14-year-old Williamsville North High School freshman, Amherst Police Chief John C. Askey said Wednesday that a single documented incident of harassment occurred when Jamey was in seventh grade.

He may have been referring to an incident that Jamey himself recounted in a separate YouTube video six months ago when he was an eighth-grader.

Describing himself as "14 and gay," Jamey said his class participated in an activity in which students offered their opinions in response to various questions.

In one instance, the question was, "Should gay marriage be legal in all 50 states?"

"A kid was making fun of me because I was gay," Jamey said. "I didn't really care. He called me disgusting because being gay is disgusting."

The student teacher leading the class took action, calling the guidance office and the vice principal, he said. That student wound up with a detention. Jamey said he subsequently went on to defend gay marriage in his class but later left the room in tears.

"I kind of got upset because of the lives that have been lost because of gay bullying, and I ran out of the room crying,' he said.

He ended his two-minute video by giving thanks to his pop star idol, Lady Gaga, and referring to her anthem song, "Born This Way."

"Lady Gaga, I want to make a difference," he said. "You are the reason why I am alive. You're the reason why I was born. I was born this way."

It's clear that Jamey lived a lot of his life online, Askey said.

For that reason, Amherst police have turned over Jamey's computer and cell phone to the Erie County Regional Computer Forensic Laboratory to see if there's a pattern of bullying that ultimately may warrant charges of aggravated harassment and hate crimes in the coming weeks.

"Jamey can't talk to us anymore," Askey said. "Hopefully, his computer can."

Meanwhile, the chief said, police have determined that many recent allegations of bullying directed toward Jamey and later his 16-year-old sister, Alyssa, do not yet rise to the level of criminality. . . .

While single incidents at school or online may not rise to the level of "unlawful behavior," investigators want to determine whether there was a pattern of conduct online and/or at school that could lead to criminal charges, Askey said.

Having evidence collected from Jamey's electronic devices will help with that, Askey said. He added that it appears that hateful comments on [Jamey's] online accounts began appearing in late 2010 after he "declared his sexual orientation."

The police currently are focusing on a limited group of Jamey's peers as possible culprits.

"We're looking at less than a half-dozen people over the span of his time at Heim and North High School," he said.

Most recently, Alyssa and others at Williamsville North reported that at a homecoming dance Sept. 22, a juvenile student in a small group of other students stated that she was glad Jamey was dead, touching off a brief altercation in the school parking lot.

Police said that while there's credible evidence that the incident occurred, the statement was not made in a direct confrontation with Alyssa and could not be considered a crime. School officials previously said a student has been suspended in connection with the incident. . . .

The police chief said it's apparent that Jamey, who at various points identified himself as either bisexual or gay, looked for support online through accounts such as Facebook, Formspring, Tumblr, Twitter and YouTube. But they also made him a target for hateful comments.

"Acts motivated by hate deserve extra attention from the police," Askey said.

Askey said he hopes to have at least some preliminary information on the case back from the computer forensic lab within a week or so. He also said the Rodemeyer family has been very understanding of the Police Department's efforts over the last two weeks.

"I know the public wants—and the Rodemeyer family wants—this done right," he said. "They want us to do this correctly, not quickly."

IN THE NEWS | "Police Close Rodemeyer Case with No Arrests"
by Sandra Tan, *The Buffalo News*, November 22, 2011

In September and early October, Amherst Police Chief John Askey committed to investing long hours of police time and extensive evidence gathering to see if any criminal charges—perhaps even for hate crimes—might be warranted in the case of 14-year-old Jamey Rodemeyer.

Jamey, a Williamsville North High School freshman, killed himself less than two weeks into a new school year after years of complaining in online videos and posts about being bullied on the Web and in school over his sexual orientation.

But on Tuesday, after an exhaustive effort, Askey announced he was closing Jamey's case without arrests or charges because, in this case, what is wrong is not the same as what is criminally prosecutable.

Askey admitted to being disappointed at being unable to send a stronger message that bullying and harassment is intolerable.

"I would have liked to have arrested someone for this," he said of a case that has gained national attention, but "[w]e can't make a case when the proof necessary to prosecute it isn't there."

Police investigated a total of seven bullying incidents involving Jamey, the chief said, two of which occurred at Heim Middle School and five at Williamsville North.

But no charges will be brought forward because all of the alleged perpetrators were juvenile classmates, either 14 or 15 years old, who could not be held criminally accountable for what would be considered violations— not even misdemeanors—had they been adults.

In addition, Askey said:

- The statute of limitations has expired regarding two incidents that occurred when Jamey was in sixth and seventh grade at Heim Middle School.
- In a few incidents, evidence was lacking that a reported offense was actually committed, or information was received second- or third-hand and the actual perpetrator could not be identified.
- In all of the five incidents that occurred at North High School, neither Jamey nor his friends reported the bullying incidents to school administrators or his parents. The incidents were reported to police after Jamey died. And of the incidents that were reported, none involved actual threats.
- Jamey is not alive to attest to any of the incidents involved, which most frequently involved subjecting the boy to gay slurs. Jamey had identified himself as bisexual and gay over the course of the last year prior to his death. "In most cases, you need a victim and a complaint," Askey said.
- A targeted forensic analysis of Jamey's computer showed no pattern of "an ongoing course of conduct" of online abuse by the classmates reputed to have been harassing him. There

was no evidence of a repeated pattern of cyberbullying by anyone in the days most immediately leading up to his death. In only two or three of the seven known bullying incidents involving Jamey in middle school and high school was the same student clearly responsible. The other incidents involved other students, Askey said.

- Hate crime charges are not possible in this case because there is no prosecutable crime to which hate crime laws could be applied. Also, the motives behind the gay slurs used by kids to antagonize and harass Jamey were not clear-cut. Many kids are subjected to such slurs for many reasons.

Askey said the decision to close Jamey's case was made after consulting with Erie County District Attorney Frank A. Sedita III and the Erie County Attorney's Office, which handles Family Court cases.

Sedita, who was briefed on the case and even went to Amherst Police Headquarters a few weeks ago to review the evidence, said Tuesday that he supported Askey's decision.

"Being charitable," he said, "the evidence, at best, was very thin." He added, "It's not a crime to be an obnoxious, teenage idiot."

Jamey's parents were informed of the decision not to prosecute before the information was made public, as was Williamsville School Superintendent Scott Martzloff. Tracy and Timothy Rodemeyer were unavailable to comment late Tuesday, but Askey described them as understanding.

"They weren't expecting some kind of smoking gun," Askey said. "They knew it would be kind of difficult."

Although the Williamsville Central School District has received a lot of attention because Jamey was a North High freshman at the time of his death, Askey and other school and legal officials said the reasons behind Jamey's death appear far broader than a simple matter of bullying by classmates.

"The source of the most stress in Jamey's life wasn't the school," Askey said.

Jamey blogged about experiencing a variety of personal problems in his life outside of school in the weeks leading up to his death.

Earlier Tuesday, Superintendent Martzloff said the school district's own investigation regarding Jamey's case is ongoing.

Whether any additional students will be held accountable for their actions is an open question, though Martzloff said he was interested to hear the findings of the police investigation first.

Source: http://www.buffalonews.com/topics/school-bullying/article644397.ece. Sandra Tan, "Police Close Rodemeyer Case with No Arrests," *Buffalo News*, November 22, 2011. Reprinted by permission.

Although intervention against bullies is desirable from the standpoint of the victims, it is also beneficial to the aggressive students, who are much more likely than other students to increase their antisocial behaviors. Research has found that bullying can be an early warning sign of later criminal behavior (Fox et al. 2003). In one study, approximately 60 percent of the boys whom researchers classified as bullies in grades six through nine had been convicted of at least one crime by age 24, compared with 23 percent of the boys not classified as either bullies or victims. Furthermore, 40 percent of the boys classified as bullies had three or more convictions by age 24, compared with 10 percent of those who were neither bullies nor victims of bullying (Olweus, Limber, and Mihalic 1999).

Being bullied can also lead its victims to turn their anger and frustration outward. Consider the following excerpt from a 15-year-old boy's journal: "I hate being laughed at. But they won't laugh after they're scraping parts of their parents, sisters, brothers and friends from the wall of my hate." These are the words of Kip Kinkel, who later killed his parents and then went on a shooting spree in his high school in Springfield, Oregon, killing two students and wounding two dozen more.

School Shootings

It ranks as one of the worst nightmares a parent can imagine—the shooting of their child by another child while at school. Such shootings, although rare, capture intense media coverage, which can lead the public to believe these events are more pervasive than they actually are.

The School Shooter   Following traditional law enforcement protocol, many have tried to profile the shooters and victims involved in school violence, searching for a pattern that may help predict or prevent similar events in the future ("Targeted School Violence" 2008). To date, none have succeeded, and several experts contend this is a good thing because profiles tend to foster a blind reliance on a certain laundry list of traits or behaviors rather than encouraging an awareness of individual signals that may indicate a potential shooting incident (Caster 2008). All school personnel, including SROs, should be trained to look for disturbing writings, comments and postings on Web sites. Most school shooters are not drug abusers and do not have an extensive juvenile record. They may, however, know a lot about firearms and may use high-quality weapons and train frequently (Caster 2008, 79).

Early Warning Signs   School violence almost never occurs without warning. Although use of profiles and checklists is strongly discouraged, early warning signs of violent behavior have been recognized that, when presented in combination, might aid in identifying and referring children who may need help. Among these are having low tolerance for frustration, poor coping skills, signs of depression, alienation, lack of empathy, an exaggerated sense of entitlement, an attitude of superiority, anger management problems, intolerance, lack of trust, rigid and opinionated convictions and negative role models (O'Toole 2000, 18–21).

The Safe School Initiative was a study conducted in 2002 by the U.S. Secret Service in collaboration with the U.S. Department of Education of

Programs in Practice: The South Euclid (Ohio) School Bullying Project

Following is a detailed description of how the South Euclid (Ohio) Police Department addressed bullying in their schools using the survey, analysis, response and assessment (SARA) model. The South Euclid School Bullying Project is a 2001 Herman Goldstein Award winner for excellence in problem-oriented policing.

Scanning Unchecked disorderly behavior of students led the school resource officer (SRO) to review school data regarding referrals to the principal's office. He found that the high school reported thousands of referrals a year for bullying, and the junior high school had recently experienced a 30 percent increase in referrals for bullying. Police data showed that juvenile complaints about disturbances, bullying and assaults after school hours had increased 90 percent in the past 10 years.

Analysis All junior high and high school students were surveyed. Interviews and focus groups were also conducted with students—identified as victims or offenders—teachers and guidance counselors. Finally, the South Euclid Police Department purchased a geographic information system to complete crime and incident mapping of hotspots within the schools. The main findings pointed to four principal areas of concern: the environmental design of school areas, teachers' knowledge of and response to the problem, parents' attitudes and responses and students' perspectives and behaviors.

Environmental design findings revealed that locations in the school with less supervision or denser population (primarily the hallways, cafeteria and gymnasium) were more likely to have higher rates of bullying; students avoided certain places at school for fear of being bullied (e.g., hallways near lockers of students who were not their friends or who were not in their classes), and a vast majority of students reported witnessing bullying or being bullied during class.

Teacher issues revealed that although bullying occurred frequently, teachers and students infrequently intervened. And when students were asked what would happen if they told a teacher about an incident of bullying, more than 30 percent said "nothing." Finally, students said they wouldn't tell teachers about bullying because they were afraid of retaliation, expected the teacher to "do nothing" or were afraid the teacher wouldn't believe or support them, especially if the bully was popular or well liked by the teacher.

Parent issues revealed that students who reported being physically disciplined at home were more likely to report that they had been bullied. More than one third of parents who had talked to their children about bullying had instructed them to fight back.

Students said they would not tell a parent if they were bullied because they believed their parents would overreact.

Student issues revealed that students reporting they engaged in bullying typically perceived their own behavior as playful or a normal part of growing up. They said everyone gets picked on but some "don't know how to take it," "take things too seriously" or "just don't know how to fight back." Victims of bullying did not perceive this behavior as fun or normal, yet victims viewed bullies as popular. Students were more likely to seek adult help for someone else who was bullied than for themselves. Students with lower grade point averages were significantly more likely to physically hurt someone else. Students who were secure in a peer group were more likely to intervene in bullying and less fearful of retaliation. Students suggested that involvement in school activities helped them to form a niche where they felt safe, supported and free from victimization.

Response The SRO, collaborating with a social worker and university researchers, coordinated a Response Planning Team to respond to each of the areas identified in the analysis. Environmental changes involved modifying the school bell times and increasing teacher supervision of hotspot areas. Counselors and social workers conducted teacher training courses in conflict resolution and bullying prevention. Parent education included mailings with information about bullying, an explanation of the new school policy and discussion about what they could do at home to address the problems. Finally, student education focused on classroom discussions with homeroom teachers and students and assemblies conducted by the SRO. The Ohio Department of Education also contributed by opening a new training center for at-risk students to provide a nontraditional setting for specialized help.

Assessment The results from the various responses were dramatic. School suspensions decreased 40 percent. Bullying incidents dropped 60 percent in the hallways and 80 percent in the gym area. Follow-up surveys indicated positive attitudinal changes among students about bullying, and more students felt confident teachers would take action. The overall results suggested that the school environments were safer and that early intervention was helping at-risk students succeed in school.

SOURCE: Adapted from "The South Euclid School Bullying Project." 2001. In *Excellence in Problem-Oriented Policing: The 2001 Herman Goldstein Award Winners*, pp. 55–62. Washington, DC: National Institute of Justice, Community Oriented Policing Services and the Police Executive Research Forum.

school shooting incidents and other school-based attacks. The following are among the attacker characteristics identified in that study ("Targeted School Violence" 2008, 1):

- Although all of the attackers were boys, they varied considerably in demographics, background and other characteristics and came from a variety of family situations.

- Many attackers felt bullied, persecuted or injured before the attack.
- A history of having been the subject of a mental health evaluation, diagnosed with a mental disorder or involved in substance abuse did not appear to be prevalent among attackers. However, most attackers showed some history of suicidal attempts or thoughts or a history of feeling extreme depression or desperation.
- More than half of the attackers demonstrated some interest in violence, through movies, video games, books and other media. However, there was no one common type of interest in violence indicated. Instead, the attackers' interest in violent themes took various forms. The largest group of attackers exhibited an interest in violence in their own writings, such as poems, essays or journal entries.
- Most attackers had no history of prior violent or criminal behavior.
- Most attackers were known to have had difficulty coping with significant losses or personal failures.

Nearly all of the attackers studied had planned their attack in advance, and revenge was the motive cited most often ("Targeted School Violence" 2008).

Threat Assessment   Because incidents of targeted school violence are rarely sudden, spontaneous acts, there is often an opportunity to discover and interrupt the attack during the planning phase. Some attackers' intentions become known because of threats they make. However, not all threats are created equal—some herald a clear and present danger; others represent little cause for concern (O'Toole 2000).

A *direct threat* identifies a specific act against a specific target and is delivered in a straightforward manner, clearly and explicitly; for example, "I am going to put a bomb in Lucy's locker." An *indirect threat* is vague and ambiguous; for example, "If I wanted to, I could blow up this school." A *veiled threat* strongly implies but does not explicitly threaten violence; for example, "We would all be better off if this school were destroyed." A *conditional threat* warns that a violent act will occur unless certain demands are met; for example, "If you don't go out with me, I'm going to blow up this school."

A four-pronged assessment approach may be used to determine the likelihood of a student becoming a school shooter based on the "totality of the circumstances" known about a student (O'Toole 2000).

 The four-pronged threat assessment approach examines the student's personality, family dynamics, school dynamics and the student's role in those dynamics and social dynamics.

This model provides a framework to evaluate a student to determine whether he or she has the motivation, means and intent to carry out a threat.

The Police Response to School Shooters   In 1999, after the catastrophe at Columbine, law enforcement agencies across the nation responded to school shooters by calling in highly trained and heavily armed special weapons and tactics (SWAT) teams. However, this is no longer the recommended tactic. When dealing with an active school shooter, "First responders no longer hold and contain, waiting for SWAT teams to arrive. Instead, they run to the gunfire and attempt to force surrender" (Scanlon 2008, 43).

Brownsville police officers stand in front of Cummings Middle School in Brownsville, Texas, after police shot and killed an armed eighth-grader who brandished a weapon in the main hallway of the school. The 15-year-old, whose name police and district officials didn't immediately release, was taken to a local hospital and pronounced dead.

 The role of the first responder in a school shooting situation is to pursue and engage the shooter.

In light of this change in philosophy, Caster (2008, 79) stresses that active shooter training cannot be limited to situations where three or four more officers respond and form a team: "Good, solid training must be given to the officer inside the school so an adequate response can be successfully completed without waiting for more officers."

In Search of Safer Schools

A common measure to reduce school violence is automatic suspensions for weapons violations. The problem with school suspensions is that the suspended student might fall behind in assignments and that the student might also commit crimes while on suspension. Other common measures include revising disciplinary codes, designating schools as drug-free zones and conducting conflict resolution and mediation programs.

 An effective approach to school security includes crisis planning, security technology and school/law enforcement/community partnerships.

Crisis Planning Every agency and institution affected or involved during an episode of school violence must decide, in advance, how they plan to respond, knowing that no two situations will be exactly the same and even the best-laid plans will require on-the-spot, last-minute adjustments. For police, the first step is generally to obtain blueprints or floor plans and to conduct walk-throughs of local schools. Law enforcement should know the layouts of every school in its jurisdiction.

Some departments stage mock disasters to test their emergency preparedness for acts of school violence and to identify areas that need improving. Such drills frequently highlight the importance of collaboration and communication with other agencies for an effective response.

Schools must also necessarily participate in crisis planning. Most, if not all, schools have preparedness plans for emergencies such as fires, tornados, hurricanes or earthquakes. Many, however, have neglected to devise a response plan for school violence, thus remaining unsecure and unprepared for such crises. Some school systems in the United States have adopted a lockdown procedure as a standard response to the threat of an active shooter.

Security Technology   A second requirement to achieve safer schools involves implementing security technology, such as weapons screening programs, entry control systems and video cameras. Recognizing that a significant proportion of school violence is perpetrated by those who neither attend nor work at the school, many districts are implementing entry control systems, such as photo ID cards, to make it easier to spot outsiders.

Video cameras are also being installed as a way to curb school violence. Most cameras are not actively monitored but, rather, tape on a continuous loop and are reviewed only when an incident is reported. When a high school in Washington State became beset by bullying problems, school officials gathered as much data as they could using surveillance, police incident reports and student surveys. The lunchroom was identified as the center of bullying and harassment.

The city of Hollywood, Florida, uses digital surveillance technology for school security (Sanchez 2007). The first school selected for the new technology was South Broward High School, which implemented wireless remote surveillance technology with 60 security cameras controlled from a single access point inside the camera room. School administrators and SROs have welcomed the ability to view footage from the cameras from their office computers or laptops.

Although many other schools have found positive benefits in using video cameras and other security devices, technology cannot replace personnel. Technology works best when balanced with human resources.

Partnerships   Partnerships are a vital component in an effective response to school violence. Although partnerships to address the issue of school violence can take many forms and involve numerous entities, one of the most effective approaches has been to station officers directly on school campuses as SROs.

Demand for SROs has increased dramatically, which can be understood by looking at the School Safety Pyramid developed by the Center for the Prevention of School Violence. Illustrated in Figure 8.1, the pyramid reflects the importance of the community policing concept in school safety, discussed shortly.

The community sits at the pyramid's base because the school environment often mirrors what is happening in the community. Community problems can disrupt the school environment and contribute to crime and violence in that environment. The school resource officer rests on the pyramid's next level because the SRO is an integral connection between the school and the community.

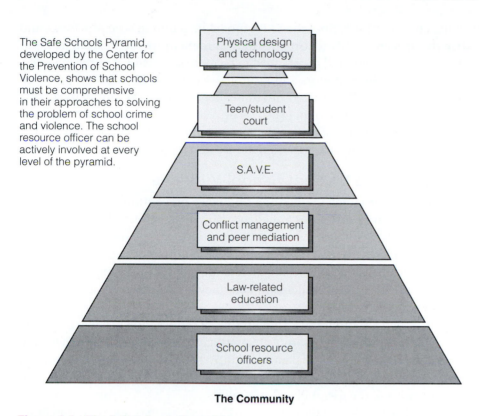

The Safe Schools Pyramid, developed by the Center for the Prevention of School Violence, shows that schools must be comprehensive in their approaches to solving the problem of school crime and violence. The school resource officer can be actively involved at every level of the pyramid.

Physical design and technology

Teen/student court

S.A.V.E.

Conflict management and peer mediation

Law-related education

School resource officers

The Community

Figure 8.1   The Safe Schools Pyramid

Copyright © Center for the Prevention of School Violence. Permission to reproduce contents of the Center's site will be granted under the condition that source credit is given to the Center, and the purpose of reproduction is educational.

Many schools take a break during the summer months, a period that can be used for law enforcement personnel and school administrators to address some safety and security issues. Police and school staff may take advantage of this time to:

- Discuss the law enforcement–school partnership. A memorandum of agreement should be in place defining the roles and responsibilities of both and should be reviewed annually.
- Evaluate the school's physical security. Are the grounds, particularly near entrances, well lit? Do the entrances lock securely? Does vegetation obscure windows or hide doors? Are surveillance cameras operating as they should?
- Fine-tune crisis plans considering natural disasters, bus accidents, bomb threats, hostage situations, suicide and school shootings.
- Train for trouble. (Garrett 2008, 6)

A school walk-through is also recommended—for SROs and for every officer assigned to the beats in which schools are located, to familiarize themselves with the layout (Webb 2008). Hard-copy maps or blueprints of every school in the district should also be stored and available to the on-duty supervisor.

The South Euclid School Bullying Project using problem solving was discussed earlier in the chapter. *School-Based Partnerships: A Problem Solving Strategy*

(Uchida et al., n.d.) describes the SARA model in action in several schools and police departments. This report stresses, "Students provided excellent input regarding the problems and they tended to be more successful at retrieving information. School administrators and faculty assisted in policy change, provided program support and organized programs beneficial to the problem-solving effort. School support personnel (i.e., security staff, cafeteria workers, and the like) were key sources of information concerning problem identification such as locations, offenders and victims, and response development."

Other Efforts to Prevent School Violence

Some schools have supplemented their violence prevention efforts with programs, policies and procedures aimed at problematic student behavior. Intervention and behavior modification programs have proved successful in some jurisdictions. Increased staff presence in identified problem areas, such as the lunchroom, and a Big Brothers/Big Sisters mentoring program pairing high school and middle school students to help prevent bullying of freshmen have also proven to be effective.

Youth leadership programs can help thwart school violence when school-age students are provided with tools to assist authorities in the early detection of violence-prone students (Eckenrode 2007, 130). The desired outcome is a population of adolescents who, through acquired self-leadership skills, will reject violence and the use of illegal substances.

Many policies and procedures focus on the possession of weapons and other contraband on school property. And although it seems to make good sense that schools, in fulfilling their duty to maintain a safe learning environment, should restrict what students are allowed to carry on campus, policies and procedures aimed at achieving the goal of safety are not without controversy.

 Some schools have adopted controversial measures such as zero-tolerance policies or school security procedures known as lockdowns.

Zero-Tolerance Policies   Zero-tolerance policies mandating predetermined consequences or punishments, such as suspension or expulsion for specific

At Issue: Do Zero-Tolerance Policies Make Zero Sense?

In May 2001, an 18-year-old high school honor student in Ft. Myers, Florida, was arrested and sent to jail on a felony charge of possession of a weapon on school property after a kitchen knife was seen on the floor of her car, which was parked in the school lot. Her explanation was that she had moved some possessions over the preceding weekend and had simply overlooked the knife, which had fallen out of its box. Despite this honest mistake and the student's academic standing, she was kept from attending her high school graduation ceremony and made to endure the humiliation of arrest and spending time behind bars.

Incidents such as this have led some authors and researchers to refer to "the dark side of zero tolerance"—the overzealous and often inappropriately strict punishments handed out under the pretense of keeping schools safe. But what are the costs to kids of these policies? In this case, did this zero-tolerance policy truly affect school safety? Should a student with no prior offenses, who offers an explanation such as the one described, be treated the same as a student who knowingly brings a weapon into a school and keeps it, for example, in a locker? Should the type of weapon matter—for example, a kitchen knife versus a firearm? What about "weapons" made from items commonly found in school, such as rubber bands and paper clips?

offenses, have become a popular disciplinary choice. Critics of these policies caution school administrators to use them with discretion and common sense to avoid a net-widening effect.

Proactive Lockdowns   Another controversial effort aimed at preventing school violence is the planned but unannounced lockdown. Some schools use a **lockdown** not as a reactive response to a crisis, but rather as a proactive step to avoid a crisis. During a lockdown, students are held in classrooms while police and K-9s search the campus for contraband or any danger to a safe educational environment. Numerous legal issues must be considered if planning a lockdown, and collaboration with the district attorney's office is required (Guy 2001, 8).

Although some criticize lockdowns as being frightening or intimidating to students, and some students complain they feel threatened when their day is interrupted by the police, this approach has not been challenged before school boards or in court. Furthermore, beyond curbing the possession of drugs and weapons in the public schools, these lockdowns emphasize the partnership between law enforcement and the school, providing visible evidence that government agencies are collaborating to prevent drug abuse and violence in schools and to provide a safe educational environment for students and teachers.

Although proactive lockdowns may be effective in locating and securing weapons that might be used in incidents of school violence, they are employed very infrequently in very few schools. Zero-tolerance policies fall dangerously short in their effectiveness if students believe any prohibited items they bring to school will go unnoticed. In fact, many weapons are discovered only after they have been used in a violent episode. Metal detectors, again, are used relatively infrequently, especially in smaller schools and in smaller communities, despite statistics showing these jurisdictions also are vulnerable to fatal school violence.

So even though these efforts are seen as luxuries for schools able to afford the fiscal and human resources needed to implement them, they cannot be relied on alone and are no substitute for the power of partnerships between students, teachers, officers, parents and other members of a community.

Partnerships and Community Policing

The need for cooperative efforts when dealing with juveniles cannot be stressed enough. Law enforcement must draw upon the expertise of psychologists, psychiatrists and social workers. Police also need the assistance of parents, schools, churches, community organizations and businesses. Such collaboration is at the heart of community policing. The thrust of the *community policing* philosophy is toward proactive, problem-oriented policing, seeking causes to crime and allocating resources to attack those causes through partnerships.

Traditionally law enforcement has been *separate* from the community and *reactive*, responding to incidents as they occur. During the past few decades, however, the emphasis has shifted to viewing law enforcement—indeed, the entire juvenile justice system—as part of the community, reliant upon collaborative efforts to deal with our nation's youths.

Besides police personnel, other participants vital in a community's effort to address school violence in particular and youth violence in general include parent group leaders, such as PTA officers; business leaders; violence prevention group representatives; youth workers and volunteers; family resource center staff; recreational and cultural organizations staff; mental health and child welfare personnel; physicians and nurses; media representatives; other criminal justice professionals, such as lawyers, judges and probation officers; clergy and other representatives from the faith community; and local officials, such as school board members.

Police officers need to be aware of the referral resources available in the community, including the names of the resource agencies as well as addresses, phone numbers and contact persons. Among the possible referral resources for the juvenile justice system are:

- Child welfare and child protection services
- Church youth programs
- Crisis centers
- Detox centers
- Drop-in centers or shelters for youths
- Guardian *ad litem* programs
- Human services councils
- Juvenile probation services
- School resources, including chemical dependency counselors, general counselors, nurses, school psychologists and social workers
- Support groups such as Al-Anon, Emotions Anonymous and Suicide Help Line
- Victim/witness services
- YMCA or YWCA programs
- Youth Service Bureaus

Ideally law enforcement officers would serve on community boards and task forces that promote services for youths.

Spotlight on Fight Crime: Invest in Kids

Fight Crime: Invest in Kids is a national, bipartisan, nonprofit anti-crime organization of more than 5,000 police chiefs, sheriffs, prosecutors, attorneys general and other law enforcement leaders and violence survivors.

Our national office is located in Washington, D.C. We also operate state offices in California, Illinois, Maine, Michigan, Montana, New York, Ohio, Oregon, Pennsylvania, Tennessee and Washington.

Our members include the top law enforcement leaders in the country, including presidents of many state and national law enforcement associations. Among our crime survivor members are the parents of children killed at Columbine and other school shooting sites, survivors of the Oklahoma City bombing, and many others whose tragic encounters with crime are well known.

Fight Crime: Invest in Kids takes a hard-nosed look at crime prevention strategies, informs the public and policymakers about those findings, and urges investment in programs proven effective by research. Our organization focuses on high quality early education programs, prevention of child abuse and neglect, after-school programs for children and teens, and interventions to get troubled kids back on track.

We do not fund or operate any direct service programs for children. Funding for Fight Crime: Invest in Kids comes from foundations, corporations and individuals. Fight Crime: Invest in Kids accepts no funds from federal, state or local government agencies.

SOURCE: http://www.fightcrime.org/state/usa/about-us

Police as Mentors to At-Risk Youths

Police who are committed to a mentoring relationship have an enormous impact on youths who are at risk of becoming chronic offenders. Carefully selected and trained police personnel can be the conduit for restoring youthful lives to productive relationships with families, schools and the community.

The Juvenile Mentoring Program (JUMP) of the Office of Juvenile Justice and Delinquency Prevention (OJJDP) supports one-to-one mentoring projects for youths at risk of failing in school, dropping out of school or becoming involved in delinquent behavior, including gang activity and substance abuse. The OJJDP defines mentoring as a one-to-one supportive relationship between a responsible adult 18 or older (mentor) and an at-risk juvenile (mentee), which takes place on a regular basis, one to two hours per week for an average of at least one year. The three principal program goals for JUMP are (1) to reduce juvenile delinquency and gang participation by at-risk youths, (2) to improve academic performance of at-risk youths and (3) to reduce the school dropout rate for at-risk youths. The OJJDP awards dozens of JUMP grants to communities throughout the nation each year.

 Summary

- Youths' attitudes toward law and law enforcement are tremendously influenced by personal contacts with law enforcement officers. Positive interactions are crucial to delinquency prevention.
- The primary responsibility of police officers assigned to child neglect or abuse cases is the immediate protection of the child.
- Challenges in investigating crimes against children include the need to protect the child from further harm, the possibility of parental involvement, the difficulty of interviewing children, credibility concerns and the need to collaborate with other agencies.
- The majority of police dispositions involve status offenses (violating curfew, truancy, loitering, underage smoking and drinking of alcoholic beverages and running away).
- In the disposition of status offenders, how police resolve matters often depends on the officers' discretion, the specific offense and the resources available.
- Police officers have considerable discretionary power when dealing with juveniles.
- The four-pronged threat assessment approach examines the student's personality, family dynamics, school dynamics and the student's role in those dynamics and social dynamics.
- The role of the first responder in a school shooting situation is to pursue and engage the shooter.
- An effective approach to school security includes crisis planning, security technology and school/law enforcement/community partnerships.
- Some schools have adopted controversial measures such as zero-tolerance policies or school security procedures known as lockdowns.

Discussion Questions

1. What restrictions are placed on minors owning firearms in your state?

2. Do you believe police should make unofficial referrals, such as to community service agencies? What problems would police face when referring youths to community service agencies?

3. Do the police display a helping attitude toward youths when they make their referrals?

4. Do you believe the social standing, race and age of juveniles influence the referral procedure?

5. Which do you think is more effective, street justice by police or processing juveniles through the court system? Why?

6. Should the police be in the schools as a crime prevention method? Why or why not?

7. Joe, a 13-year-old White male, has been apprehended by a police officer for stealing a bicycle. Joe took the bicycle from the school grounds shortly after a program at the school by the police on "Bicycle Theft Prevention." Joe admits to taking the bicycle, but says he only intended to "go for a ride" and was going to return the bicycle later that day. Joe has no prior police contacts that the officer is aware of. The bicycle has been missing for only an hour and is unharmed. What should the officer do in handling the incident? Do you think the bicycle theft prevention program is worthwhile? Why or why not?

8. Have there been any instances of school shootings in your state?

9. Are there SROs in the schools in your city?

10. How important do you believe partnerships are in addressing school crime and violence?

References

Black, Sally. 2003. "An Ongoing Evaluation of the Bullying Prevention Program in Philadelphia Schools: Student Survey and Student Observation Data." Paper presented at the annual Centers for Disease Control and Prevention Safety in Numbers Conference, Atlanta, GA.

Caster, Richard. 2008 (April). "Ten Things Police Chiefs Need to Know about School Shooting." *Law and Order* 56 (4): 77–80.

Crime in the United States 2010. 2011. Washington, DC: U.S. Department of Justice, Federal Bureau of Investigation.

Dunworth, Terence. 2000 (November). *National Evaluation of the Youth Firearms Violence Initiative.* Washington, DC: National Institute of Justice Research in Brief. (NCJ 184482)

Eckenrode, Lex T. 2007 (October). "Can Youth Leadership Programs Thwart School Violence?" *The Police Chief* 74 (10): 130–146.

Fox, James Alan, Delbert S. Elliott, R. Gil Kerlikowske, Sanford A. Newman, and William Christeson. 2003. "Bullying Prevention *Is* Crime Prevention: A Report by Fight Crime: Invest in Kids." Washington, DC: Fight Crime, Invest in Kids.

Garrett, Ronnie. 2006 (November). "Internet 'Burn Books.'" *Law Enforcement Technology* 33 (11): 8.

———. 2008 (June). "School's Out for Summer." *Law Enforcement Technology* 35 (6): 6.

Guide for Preventing and Responding to School Violence, 2nd ed. 2009. Alexandria, VA: International Association of Chiefs of Police.

Guy, Joe D. 2001. "Lock Down." *Community Links* (September): 7–8.

Limber, Susan P. 2004. "Implementation of the Olweus Bullying Prevention Program: Lessons Learned from the Field." In *Bullying in American Schools: A Social-Ecological Perspective on Prevention and Intervention*, edited by Dorothy L. Espelage and Susan M. Swearer, 351–363. Mahwah, NJ: Erlbaum.

Mowatt, Robert M., and Linda Chezem. 2001 (June). *An Implementation Guide for Juvenile Holdover Programs.* Washington, DC: National Highway Traffic Safety Administration, Office of Juvenile Justice and Delinquency Prevention and the American Probation and Parole Association. (DOT HS 809260, NCJ 193986)

Noonan, James H., and Malissa C. Vavra. 2007 (October). *Crime in Schools and Colleges*, Washington DC: Federal Bureau of Investigation.

Olweus Bullying Prevention Program. 2011. Hazelden Foundation. Accessed November 11, 2011. http://www.olweus.org/public/bullying_prevention_program.page.

Olweus, Dan, Susan Limber, and Sharon F Mihalic. 1999. *Bullying Prevention Program: Blueprints for Violence Prevention, Book Nine.* (Delbert S. Elliott, Series Editor). Boulder: Center for the Study and Prevention of Violence, Institute of Behavioral Science, University of Colorado.

O'Toole, Mary Ellen. 2000. *The School Shooter: A Threat Assessment Perspective.* Washington, DC: Federal Bureau of Investigation.

Pagliocca, Pauline M., Susan P. Limber, and P. Y. Hashima. 2007. "Evaluation Report for the Chula Vista Olweus Bullying Prevention Program." Unpublished report prepared for the Chula Vista, CA, Police Department.

Petrocelli, Joseph. 2007. "School Vandalism." *Police* (October): 32–35.

Robers, Simone, Jijun Zhang, and Jennifer Truman. 2010 (November). *Indicators of School Crime and Safety: 2010* (NCES 2011-002/NCJ 230812). Washington, DC: National Center for Education Statistics,

U.S. Department of Education, and Bureau of Justice Statistics, Office of Justice Programs, U.S. Department of Justice.

Sanchez, Tomas. 2007 (August). "School Watch Digital Surveillance Technology for School Safety." *The Police Chief* 74 (8): 110–112.

Scanlon, James. 2008. "Blueprint of a Bloodbath." *Law Enforcement Technology* (June): 40–47.

"The South Euclid School Bullying Project." 2001. In *Excellence in Problem-Oriented Policing: The 2001 Herman Goldstein Award Winners*, pp. 55–62. Washington, DC: National Institute of Justice, Community Oriented Policing Services and the Police Executive Research Forum.

Straub, Frank G. 2008 (June). "Commissioner Frank Straub Testifies on Reducing Gang and Youth Violence." *Subject to Debate* 22 (6): 1, 4–5.

"Targeted School Violence." 2008 (November). Fact Sheet FS-SC19. From *The Final Report and Findings of the Safe School Initiative: Implications for the Prevention of School Attacks in the United States*. Washington, DC: U.S. Secret Service and U.S. Department of Education.

Uchida, Craig D., Shellie Solomon, Charles M. Katz, and Cynthia E Pappas. n.d. *School-Based Partnerships: A Problem-Solving Strategy*. Washington, DC: Office of Community Oriented Policing Services.

Webb, David. 2008 (June). "School Walk-Throughs." *Law and Order* 56 (6): 84–86.

Pretrial Services and Diversion

> " Justice delayed is justice denied. "
>
> —**William Gladstone**

Youths who enter the juvenile justice system must proceed through various pretrial stages before their case has a chance of appearing before the court. In fact, for many juveniles, formal court processing never occurs, as they are diverted into various alternative programs based on their needs and offense history. Here, an 8-year-old boy accused of hitting his school principal with a wood pole appears with his attorney at a juvenile detention hearing in front of the court commissioner. The youth told police he brought the pole for protection from other students, but he did not explain why he attacked the principal.

© AP Images/Journal Times, Mark Hertzberg

DO YOU KNOW?

- What the primary duty of the juvenile prosecutor is?
- What the possible results of an intake hearing might be?
- What the four principles of effective intervention are?
- What the results of effective diversion criteria should be?
- What forms diversion from juvenile court may take?
- What specialized courts are available for diverted youths?

- What the two most common criteria for participating in drug court are?
- What the four cornerstones of the Blueprint for Change are?
- Who is eligible to participate in juvenile gun court?
- What the three core principles of the balanced and restorative justice (BARJ) model are?
- What the three main components of restorative justice are?
- What the four models of restorative justice are?

CAN YOU DEFINE?

comorbidity

deep end strategy

detention hearing

diversion

dynamic risk factor

family courts

intake

meta-analysis

net widening

petition

public defender

static risk factor

CHAPTER OUTLINE

Introduction

Having just examined in the previous chapter the role of the police in dealing with juveniles, it should come as no surprise that many young offenders enter the juvenile justice system through contact with a law enforcement officer. This chapter focuses on the decision points that occur *pretrial* in delinquency case processing, including custody, detention, intake and, very commonly, diversion. Figure 9.1 illustrates the stages a delinquency case typically passes through before it reaches the court for formal processing.

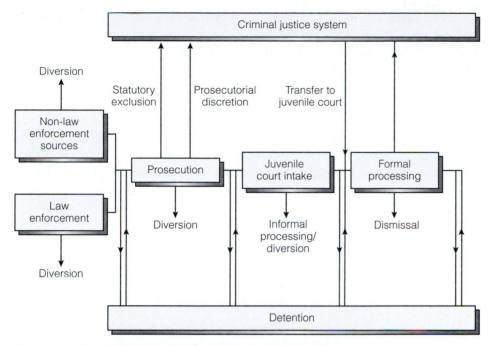

Figure 9.1   Pretrial Stages of Delinquency Case Processing

SOURCE: Adapted from Howard N. Snyder and Melissa Sickmund. 2006 (March). *Juvenile Offenders and Victims 2006 National Report*, p. 105. Washington, DC: U.S. Department of Justice, Office of Justice Programs, Office of Juvenile Justice and Delinquency Prevention.

Note that this figure is the first half of the flowchart that was presented in Chapter 1, and as was true with Figure 1.5, states and communities may vary somewhat for this generalized process. The organization of this chapter will roughly follow the flow outlined in Figure 9.1 and the steps that lead up to formal processing of a delinquent in juvenile court.

Custody

As mentioned previously, most youth enter the juvenile justice system when they are taken into custody by police. Children can be taken into custody by court order, by lawful arrest, if there are reasonable grounds to believe that the child is suffering from illness or injury, that the child is in immediate danger from the surroundings or that the child has run away. It is important to recognize that the taking of a child into custody is not necessarily an *arrest*.

After children are taken into custody, law enforcement evaluates the situation by talking with the victim(s), the offender and the offender's parents or guardians and by reviewing any prior record the offender may have with the juvenile justice system. With this information, the officer decides on a course of action: release the juvenile to the parents, guardians or custodians; refer the juvenile to the prosecutor or intake division for processing into the system; or divert the juvenile to another agency such as a shelter care facility or to a medical facility if needed. This decision is to be made with all reasonable speed and without first taking the child elsewhere. Also, the parents, guardians or custodians and the court must promptly be given a written notice stating the reason the child was taken into custody.

Of all juvenile arrests made in 2010, approximately one fifth (22.6 percent) percent were handled within the police department and were resolved with juveniles being released to their parents or guardians, two thirds (67.7 percent) were referred to juvenile court and nearly 8 percent (7.9%) were referred to criminal court (*Crime in the United States 2010,* 2011; numbers don't total 100% because of rounding and estimates).

Sometimes, however, a juvenile must be temporarily detained while a parent or guardian is located or while other facets of a case are immediately tended to. In these situations, detention can be used. Note in Figure 9.1 (and also in Figure 1.5) that detention is always an option, at any stage of delinquency case processing.

Detention

One in five youths is detained between the referral to court and case disposition (Snyder and Sickmund 2006, 105). Section 14 of the Uniform Juvenile Court Act (UJCA) deals with the detention of juveniles:

> A child taken into custody shall not be detained or placed in shelter care prior to the hearing on the petition unless his detention or care is required to protect the person or property of others or of the child or because the child may abscond or be removed from the jurisdiction of the court or because he has no parent, guardian, or custodian or other person able to provide supervision and care for him and return him to the court when required, or an order for his detention or shelter care has been made by the court pursuant to this Act.

The National Juvenile Detention Association (NJDA) provides the following definition: "Juvenile detention, as part of the juvenile justice continuum, is a process that includes the temporary and safe custody of juveniles whose alleged conduct is subject to court jurisdiction who require a restricted environment for their own and the community's protection while pending legal action. Juvenile detention may range from the least restrictive community-based supervision to the most restrictive form of secure care" (NJDA 2007).

The UJCA provides in Section 16 that a delinquent can be detained only in:

- A licensed foster home or a home approved by the court.
- A facility operated by a licensed child welfare agency.
- A detention home or center for delinquent children that is under the direction or supervision of the court or other public authority or of a private agency approved by the court.
- Any other suitable place or facility designated or operated by the court.

Section 16 further specifies that delinquents may be kept in a jail or other adult detention facility only if one of the preceding is not available, the detention is in a room separate from adults and it appears that public safety and protection reasonably require detention. The act requires that the person in charge of a jail inform the court immediately if a person under age 18 is received at the jail. The act further stipulates that deprived or unruly children "shall not be detained in a jail or other facility intended or used for the detention of adults charged with criminal offenses or of children alleged to be delinquent." The intent of this section is to protect children from the harm of exposing them to criminals and the "degrading effect of jails, lockups and the like."

Detention is a process, not a place, and detention practices should be guided by the following principles (Griffin and Torbet 2002, 57):

- Secure detention and detention alternatives are essential components of the juvenile justice system, integral to a complete continuum of local supervision and custody options for court-involved youth.
- Detention options must be short-term and appropriate to the level of risk posed by the youth.
- Detention services must be designed to safeguard the community or ensure the juvenile's appearance at subsequent hearings.
- Detention services must be consistent with the goals of the juvenile justice system—community protection, offender accountability and practical rehabilitation.

The NJDA (2007) lists the following critical components of juvenile detention:

- *Screening*—to ensure detention is the appropriate decision
- *Assessment*—to determine proper placement, supervision and custody level
- *Policies*—to promote the safety, security and well-being of juveniles and staff
- *Services*—to address the immediate educational, mental, physical, emotional and social needs of detained juveniles

Section 17 of the UJCA states that if a child is brought before the court or delivered to a detention or shelter care facility, an investigation must be made immediately as to whether detention is needed. If the child is not released, a petition must be filed promptly with the court. In addition an informal **detention hearing** should be held within a period defined by state statute, typically ranging from 24 to 72 hours, to determine whether detention is required. A written notice of the time, place and purpose of the hearing is given to the child and, if possible, to the parents or guardians. Before the hearing begins, the court must inform the people involved of their right to counsel—court-appointed if they cannot afford to pay private counsel—and of the child's right to remain silent during the hearing.

Initial detention decisions are often made by either a prosecutor or an intake officer.

Intake

Intake is the initial phase of the juvenile court process. **Intake** is the stage at which someone must decide whether a referral merits a petition, that is, whether the matter described in the complaint against the juvenile should become the subject of formal court action. According to Griffin and Torbet (2002, 34), "Intake may be the most crucial case processing point in the juvenile justice system because so much follows from that decision. Intake authority is entrusted to prosecutors in some jurisdictions—either in all cases or in those involving allegations of serious crimes—and to juvenile court intake or juvenile probation departments in others."

Who Should Decide: The Juvenile Prosecutor or Intake Officer?

Some debate has centered on which agency should have intake authority—the prosecutor's office or an intake officer in the juvenile probation department.

The Juvenile Prosecutor   The juvenile prosecutor wears multiple hats and must enforce the law, represent the state and protect the safety of the community and keep the best interest of the juvenile in mind. The National District Attorneys Association (NDAA) Prosecution Standards—Juvenile Justice, standard 92.1(b) states,

 "The primary duty of the prosecutor is to seek justice while fully and faithfully representing the interests of the state."

The NDAA takes the stance that the prosecutor should have the exclusive right to make juvenile intake decisions and screen facts obtained from the police and other sources to determine whether those facts are legally sufficient for prosecution.

The Intake Officer   In some jurisdictions, the intake officer decides whether a case should move ahead for court processing. This officer is usually a probation officer or designated court personnel, not a lawyer. The intake process of the juvenile justice system requires the development of employee screening practices, certification standards and caseload guidelines. Caseworkers should be certified to practice on the basis of education, training and experience.

In matters handled by intake, the biggest disparity from state to state is in how abused, neglected and dependent children are helped. Regarding juvenile offenders, the intake officer may release the youth to the parents with a warning or reprimand. Or the officer may release the youth on the condition that the youth enroll in a community diversion program or be placed on probation and be under the supervision of a juvenile court officer.

If the intake officer determines that the case should move ahead for court processing, the officer will recommend that a **petition** (charge) be filed and will refer the case to the juvenile court prosecutor. In addition, if a petition is recommended, the intake officer determines whether the youth should be detained pending further court action or be released to the custody of the parents pending the hearing. When juveniles are detained, this decision is reviewed by a judge or court administrator at a detention hearing.

The Intake Hearing

At the intake stage of the referral, the decision is made whether to adjust, settle or terminate the matter. Referrals are also made to other interests out of concern for the child's health, welfare and safety. This process in most states is called the intake hearing. The purpose of this proceeding is not to adjudicate the affirmation (guilty) or denial (not guilty) of juveniles in the matter, but to determine whether the matter requires the court's attention. Thus, the intake unit serves in an advisory capacity.

The person handling the juvenile offender at this stage—whether it is a prosecutor or an intake officer—must ask two basic questions:

1. From a review of the complaint and the evidence, is it clear that the complaint against the juvenile is *legally sufficient*? If not, the case should be dismissed.
2. If the complaint is legally sufficient, does a background investigation of legal and social factors—including interviews with the juvenile as well as parents, victims and others—indicate that the case should be formally processed? If not, diversion is the likely alternative.

 The intake hearing may result in dismissal, diversion, referral to juvenile court for adjudication or transfer to adult court.

Youths released at intake with no further processing should be followed up with after any referral to a community agency by either the police or the intake unit. Such follow-up promotes closer cooperation between the agencies involved and ensures that a youth does not "fall through the cracks," should the dismissal prove to have not been the most appropriate decision.

Regardless of who performs the intake function, the decision-making process is roughly the same and covers the same points of assessment.

Assessment

One of the most important functions during intake is an accurate assessment of each youth. Assessment is the engine that drives good diversion decisions and good programs. Young et al. (2006, 135) studied implementation practices and dissemination of new assessment technologies in juvenile justice and concluded, "Assessment in juvenile justice exemplifies the 'science-practice gap' that has spurred a growing national interest in technology transfer." They describe the evolution of assessment instruments through four generations, beginning with the first generation that involved the professional judgment and intuition of the individual conducting the assessment. Second-generation assessments involved standardized assessments using actuarial methods, focusing on static risk factors such as age at first arrest and age of first alcohol or drug use. Third-generation assessments were more comprehensive, using static and dynamic risk and need factors. (Recall the definition of a risk factor from Chapter 4. A **static risk factor** is one that cannot be changed, such as an offender's delinquency record. A **dynamic risk factor**, in contrast, is one that can be changed, such as an offender's addiction to drugs.) The fourth generation of assessment involves a series of specialized instruments for particular needs.

Assessment instruments are of two basic types: generic (or generalized) and locally developed (or specialized). Miller and Lin (2007, 552) studied the issues raised by applying a generic actuarial juvenile risk instrument (the Model Risk Assessment Instrument) to delinquency cases in New York City and found that a generic instrument is less predictive than is a locally developed risk assessment tool.

An example of a locally developed assessment tool is the Positive Achievement Change Tool (PACT), an evidence-based assessment tool linked to a case management system, developed by Florida's Department of Juvenile Justice. This innovative tool is designed to improve information gathering, standardize the risk classification process and more accurately determine the individualized risk and needs of young offenders (Olson 2007). This Web-based, automated tool is synchronized with the department's existing information system, thereby alleviating paperwork overload. According to Olson (18), a key element of the new assessment tool is motivational interviewing (MI): "In recent years MI has gained increasing relevance in juvenile justice as the evidence piled up that behavioral change most frequently occurs when the motivation for change comes from within."

Some jurisdictions have developed juvenile assessment centers (JACs) to address service fragmentation among agencies providing services to youth involved with the juvenile justice system. A study by McReynolds et al. (2008, 330) found that 30 percent of youths undergoing Orange County (Florida) JAC intake met criteria for one or another probable psychiatric disorder, with girls having higher rates of many disorders. Discussing the benefits of JACs, McReynolds et al. conclude, "This type of setting, where a range of assessments can be efficiently conducted, offers particular opportunities to determine service needs for young and first-time offenders at an early point in the juvenile justice intake process" (330).

However, because many jurisdictions lack the resources and expertise to develop their own locale-specific assessment instruments, many rely on generic instruments. Some of these are better assessment tools than others. One such tool gaining popularity and scientific acceptance is the Youthful Level of Service Inventory (Y-LSI), an assessment instrument that predicts risk of failure (risk classification) and identifies specific areas of treatment needs, with the goal being to treat the criminogenic needs that place a juvenile at risk of offending, thus lowering recidivism. Administration of the Y-LSI involves a face-to-face interview during which 42 questions are asked of the juvenile offender, the items spanning eight risk domains: prior and current offenses/adjudications, family circumstances and parenting, education and employment, peer relations, substance abuse, leisure and recreational activities, personality and behavior, and attitudes and orientations (Flores, Travis, and Latessa 2004, 5). Evaluation of the Y-LSI shows this assessment tool can be significantly accurate in predicting case outcomes for both male and female juveniles and across ethnicities, if the scores are normed for specific offender populations (Flores, Travis, and Latessa 2004). Unfortunately, many departments fail to take this extra step and, thus, compromise the optimal capacity of this instrument.

As analysis of the Y-LSI and other assessment tools reveals that juvenile offender case outcomes benefit when assessment results are integrated with service provision. Tjaden and Martinez (2007, 76) explain, "An integrated assessment (or client management) system refers to a relatively new concept in the classification and management of juvenile offender cases. In an integrated model, systematic assessment of a youth's criminogenic needs (or risk factors) provides the basis for all future client management activities including:

- Determining the level of risk and supervision needed.
- Developing a service plan and treatment interventions.
- Measuring the youth's progress.
- Adjusting the service plan to reflect changes in the youth's behavior or lack thereof."

A Critical Need: Assessing Mental Health Issues in Juvenile Offenders

Shufelt and Cocozza (2006, 2) compared mental health prevalence findings from recent juvenile justice studies and found a range of 67.2 percent to 72.6 percent with a positive diagnosis. Other studies have found even higher rates of mental health issues among juvenile detainees: "Nationally, research shows that up to 75 percent of youths in detention centers demonstrate diagnosable mental health disorders" (Hanger 2008, 36). Williams et al. (2008, 25) explain, "Mental health screening is a brief process administered by nonclinical staff using a standardized tool. It is a triage process that is carried out with every youth soon after intake in pretrial detention during an initial probation intake interview or upon entrance into juvenile justice placement."

Clark (2008, 8) reports on surveys completed by more than 500 juvenile detention administrators of 49 states, representing three quarters of all juvenile detention facilities, which found that:

- Two thirds of juvenile detention facilities hold youths who are waiting for community mental health treatment.
- Two thirds of these juveniles have attempted suicide or attacked others.
- Juvenile detention facilities spend an estimated $100 million each year to house youths who are waiting for community mental health services.

The Northwestern Juvenile Project (Teplin et al. 2006), which involved a random sample of more than 1,800 juvenile detainees ages 10 to 18, studied psychiatric disorders of youths in detention by using a widely accepted and reliable measurement tool, the Diagnostic Interview Schedule for Children (DISC) Version 2.3. The longitudinal study looked at gender, race and ethnicity and age for six categories of disorders: (1) affective (major depressive episode, dysthymia, manic episode); (2) psychosis; (3) anxiety (panic, separation anxiety, overanxious, generalized anxiety, obsessive-compulsive disorders); (4) attention deficit/hyperactivity disorder (ADHD); (5) disruptive behavior (oppositional-defiant and conduct disorders); and (6) substance abuse. The study found that nearly 66 percent of males and nearly 75 percent of females met the diagnostic criteria for one or more of the disorders identified (Teplin et al. 2006). Furthermore, many of the juveniles met the criteria for multiple disorders (known as **comorbidity**, when two or more diagnoses occur together in the same individual). Finally, the study revealed that a significant number of juvenile offenders—more than 20 percent of males and nearly 30 percent of females—who had any type of substance abuse disorder also had a major mental disorder (Abram et al. 2003; Teplin et al. 2006).

A mental health evaluation is a crucial step in assessing a juvenile offender and determining the most effective disposition for that individual, and this step most often occurs while a youth is in detention.

Tjaden and Martinez suggest that such an integrated system keeps the focus on youth outcomes and provides clearer direction about how one should intervene with at-risk youths: "Research provides ample evidence that certain interventions are more effective than others in addressing recidivism. Punitive sanctions, in and of themselves, are not particularly effective in changing a youth's behavior and, in some cases, may even increase recidivism. By the same token, not all forms of treatment are effective."

Principles of Effective Interventions

A growing body of research has provided evidence that certain features of interventions make them more effective than others are at reducing juvenile recidivism (Burns et al. 2003; Latessa, Cullen, and Gendreau 2002). Awareness of these principles of effective intervention can help during the intake phase when assessing offenders and determining how best to process them. These principles are introduced briefly here, although they are equally relevant and pertinent at just about every stage between and including intake and corrections.

Any treatment or intervention used with juveniles should be evidence based, not merely a continuation of "this is how we've always done it." The "lowest" form of evidence is anecdotal, that derived from personal experience working in the field. Such evidence is generally not very scientific but it makes us feel good because it holds a high degree of familiarity. In contrast, the "highest" form of evidence is empirical evidence gathered from controlled studies. Such evidence holds up to the rigors of statistical analysis but does not always make us feel good because it often suggests a change is needed in how an agency performs.

One way researchers determine which interventions are effective is by conducting a **meta-analysis**, or a "study of studies," to derive a quantitative review of a body of literature. Meta-analysis, now the favored approach by most criminal justice researchers, has identified some major risk/need factors that, when assessed at intake, should influence how a delinquency case is processed (Latessa and Lovins 2010):

1. Antisocial/procriminal attitudes, values, beliefs and cognitive-emotional states (rage, anger, defiance and criminal identity)
2. Procriminal associates and isolation from prosocial others
3. Temperamental and antisocial personality pattern conducive to criminal activity including weak socialization, impulsivity, adventurous, pleasure seeking, restless, aggressive, egocentrism, below-average verbal intelligence, a taste for risk and weak problem-solving, lack of coping and self-regulation skills
4. A history of antisocial behavior evident from a young age, in a variety of settings and involving a number and variety of different acts—early onset is a powerful predictor. By age 12, as many as 40 percent of later serious offenders have committed their first criminal act; by age 14, as many as 85 percent have committed their first criminal act
5. Family factors that include criminality and a variety of psychological problems in the family of origin, including low levels of affection, caring and cohesiveness, poor parental supervision and discipline practices, and outright neglect and abuse
6. Low levels of personal educational, vocational or financial achievement
7. Low levels of involvement in prosocial leisure activities
8. Abuse of alcohol or drugs

These risk/need factors drive delinquent behavior and should be the focus of intervention options and measurement of progress.

 Principles of effective intervention include:

- Risk Principle—target higher-risk offender (WHO)
- Need Principle—target criminogenic risk/need factors (WHAT)
- Treatment Principle—use behavioral approaches (HOW)
- Fidelity Principle—implement program as designed (HOW WELL)

Evidence shows that when these principles are adhered to, the outcome for delinquency cases is greatly improved. These principles are important to consider when making diversion decisions.

Diversion from Formal Juvenile Court

The juvenile court was established to prevent children from being treated as criminals and to let them "grow out of delinquency." This is the same rationale in the twenty-first century that considers diversion from the juvenile court as a viable option for some youths. **Diversion** is "the process of channeling a referred juvenile *from* formal juvenile court processing *to* an alternative forum for resolution of the matter and/or a community-based agency for help" (Griffin and Torbet 2002, 49). Table 9.1 contains the legal variables involved in the diversion decision-making process from the perspectives of both county attorneys and court-designated workers. The similarities and differences between the two groups are interesting. Prior record was the only legal variable that was very important to both groups.

Table 9.2 presents the extra-legal variables influencing the diversion decision-making process. County attorneys found the child's attitude toward the offense and toward treatment as more important than did court-designated workers. Neither indicated that the local political environment was very important. Diversion serves several purposes, including avoiding stigma of being

Table 9.1 Test of Significance for Differences in Juvenile Court Practitioners' Perceptions on the Effects of Legal Variables: Prior Record, Severity of Crime, Severity of Injury/Damage and Premeditated Action

	County Attorneys (n = 48)		Court-Designated Workers (n = 52)		
	%	f	%	f	Chi-Square
Prior record[a]					
Important			3.8	2	4.31
Somewhat important	10.4	5	9.6	5	
Very important	89.6	43	88.3	45	
Severity of crime					
Not important	2.0	1	13.4	7	7.08*
Important	12.5	6	23.0	12	
Somewhat important	14.5	7	15.3	8	
Very important	70.8	34	48.0	25	
Severity of injury/damage					
Not important	2.0	1	9.6	5	5.81
Important	10.4	5	23.0	12	
Somewhat important	20.8	10	15.3	8	
Very important	66.6	32	51.9	27	
Premeditated action					
Not important	2.0	1	21.1	11	16.84**
Important	6.2	3	13.4	7	
Somewhat important	16.6	8	26.9	14	
Very important	75.0	36	38.4	20	

[a] The specific question asked was, "How important is prior record in making diversion decision? Not important, important, somewhat important or very important?"
*$P < .05$.
**$P < .001$.

SOURCE: Roberto Hugh Potter and Suman Kakar. 2002 (February). "The Diversion Decision-Making Process from the Juvenile Court Practitioners' Perspective." *Journal of Contemporary Criminal Justice* 18 (1): 31. Copyright © 2002 Sage Publications. Reprinted by permission of SAGE Publications.

Table 9.2 Test of Significance for Differences in Juvenile Court Practitioners' Perceptions on the Effects of Extra-Legal Variables: Child's Appearance, Child's Attitude toward Offense and Treatment and Local Political Environment

	County Attorneys (n = 48)		Court-Designated Workers (n = 52)		
	%	f	%	F	Chi-Square
Child's appearance[a]					
Not important	58.3	28	67.3	35	3.97
Important	27.0	13	15.3	8	
Somewhat important	14.5	7	9.6	5	
Very important			7.6	4	
Child's attitude toward offense[b]					
Not important	4.1	2	13.4	8	21.41**
Important	12.5	6	40.3	21	
Somewhat important	16.6	8	11.5	6	
Very important	66.6	32	32.6	17	
Child's attitude toward treatment[c]					
Not important			13.4	8	16.74**
Important	14.5	7	32.6	17	
Somewhat important	22.9	11	5.7	3	
Very important	58.3	28	46.1	24	
Local political environment[d]					
Not important	81.2	39	82.6	43	2.74
Important	8.3	4	7.6	4	
Somewhat important	10.4	5	4.0	2	
Very important			7.6	3	

[a] The specific question asked was, "How important is the child's appearance in making diversion decision? Not important, important, somewhat important or very important?"
[b] The specific question asked was, "How important is the child's attitude toward offense in making diversion decision? Not important, important, somewhat important or very important?"
[c] The specific question asked was, "How important is the child's attitude toward treatment in making diversion decision? Not important, important, somewhat important or very important?"
[d] The specific question asked was, "How important is the local political environment in making diversion decision? Not important, important, somewhat important or very important?"
**$P < .001$.

SOURCE: Roberto Hugh Potter and Suman Kakar. 2002 (February). "The Diversion Decision-Making Process from the Juvenile Court Practitioners' Perspective." *Journal of Contemporary Criminal Justice* 18 (1): 32. Copyright © 2002 Sage Publications. Reprinted by permission of SAGE Publications.

labeled delinquent, involving the community and the victim and reducing court loads.

Although criteria for diversion vary from jurisdiction to jurisdiction, they should all be based on specific guidelines. Furthermore, every diversion arrangement should be stated in a clear, complete, written agreement and have a definite, limited duration (Griffin and Torbet 2002, 50).

 Effective diversion criteria should result in the diversion of most minor offenders who have no serious prior involvement with the court and who, along with their families, accept services and sanctions voluntarily.

One of the most common forms of diversion is being ordered to do community service. Degelman, Doggett and Medina (2006) have developed a guide to making community service more meaningful: *Giving Back: Introducing Community Service Learning—Improving Mandated Community Service for Juveniles*. The Preface of this guide states,

> Educators have long known the value of community service. Beyond its value to the community, they know that school-based community service can provide young people with the knowledge, skills and attitudes they need to assume the most important role in our society—that of active citizens.
>
> Community service, as mandated by the courts, plays a prominent role in our juvenile justice system as well. Today, many juvenile justice professionals regard it as an opportunity for rehabilitation. They believe that mandated community service can help juvenile justice respondents understand the impact of their actions on others; give back to the communities they have harmed; learn critical-thinking, citizenship and problem solving skills; develop a personal stake in the well-being of their communities; and raise awareness of their own self worth.
>
> Perhaps most important, many juvenile justice professionals, particularly in youth courts, have seen a possible correlation between effective community service, heightened civic awareness and reduced recidivism rates. (Degelman, Doggett, and Medina 2006, 3)

 Diversion may include community service, restitution, letters of apology, participation in prosocial activities, mentoring or tutoring programs, work programs, educational programs, skill-development programs, counseling programs or referral to a specialized court to meet individual needs.

An in-depth description of these various options is beyond the scope of this text. However, the growing popularity of specialized courts does merit brief discussion.

Diversion to Specialized Courts

Informed by a growing recognition that many youths who come in contact with the juvenile justice system face challenges better addressed outside the formal court system (e.g., drug abuse, mental health issues, etc.), many jurisdictions have developed specialized courts to handle cases with mitigating circumstances that lend themselves to an option shy of full, formal court processing. The stipulation set forth in these courts, however, is that if youth do not abide by the conditions set forth in specialized court rulings, their cases will be referred to the more stringent and formal juvenile court. Thus, these specialized courts offer youth an opportunity to avoid formal processing.

 Specialized courts include teen courts, drug courts, mental health courts, traffic courts and gun courts.

Teen Court

An innovative alternative to the traditional juvenile court is the teen court, also called peer, student or youth court. Teen courts are intervention programs, not courts within the judicial branch of government; therefore, their processes and procedures are significantly less formal and not held to the traditional due process requirements of regular courtrooms (Fisher 2006). However, their sanctions are recognized as valid by the court; consequently, youths who fail to abide by sanctions imposed by teen courts may face formal charges in juvenile court.

Teen courts are juvenile diversion programs used primarily for first-time offenders in misdemeanor, nonviolent cases. Cases handled in teen court may include shoplifting/theft, alcohol possession, criminal mischief, vandalism/property damage and traffic offenses. Teen courts are also used for school disciplinary issues. Figure 9.2 shows the points at which juvenile offenders can be diverted to teen court.

The courtroom models used in teen courts are generally divided into four types: adult judge, youth judge, youth tribunal and peer jury. Youth volunteer roles in teen court hearings commonly include the defense attorney (youth advocate), prosecuting attorney (community advocate), clerk, bailiff, juror and sometimes judge. Table 9.3 presents courtroom models used by teen and youth courts in the United States.

Teen courts are voluntary and most are *postadjudicatory*, meaning they require youth to admit to the charge and plead guilty before the case will

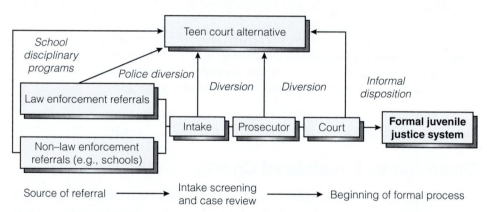

Figure 9.2   Points at Which Juvenile Offenders Can Be Diverted to Teen Court

SOURCE: The Urban Institute. Evaluation of Teen Courts Project. Reprinted by permission. https://www.ncjrs.gov/pdffiles1/ojjdp/183472.pdf

Table 9.3   Courtroom Models Used by U.S. Teen and Youth Courts

	Adult Judge Model	*Youth Judge Model*	*Tribunal Model*	*Peer Jury Model*
Who performs the role of judge in the courtroom?	Adult	Youth	3 Youth	Adult (sometimes no judge)
Are teen attorneys included in the process?	Yes	Yes	Yes	No
What is the role of the teen jury during court?	Listen to attorney presentations, recommend sentence to judge	Listen to attorney presentations, recommend sentence to judge	Usually no jury	Question defendant, recommend or order sentence

SOURCE: Jeffrey A. Butts, Janeen Buck, and Mark B. Coggeshall. 2002 (April). *The Impact of Teen Court on Young Offenders*, p. 7. Washington, DC: Urban Institute Justice Policy Center. Reprinted by permission.

be accepted. Less than 10 percent of teen courts are structured to determine guilt or innocence (Norris, Twill, and Kim 2011). In addition, parental consent is generally required for participation. The typical teen court process is shown in Figure 9.3. Figure 9.4 illustrates sanctions imposed by teen courts.

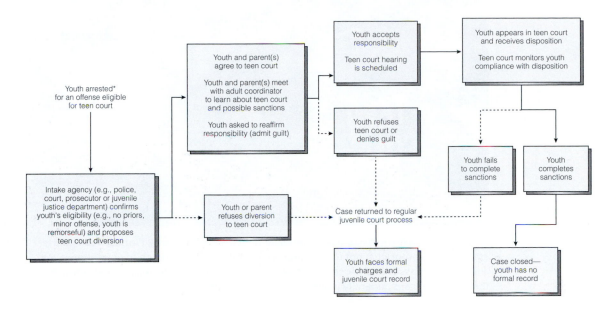

*Not all teen court cases are prompted by an arrest. Some teen courts accept school referrals for truancy, fighting and other rule violations. Others accept traffic violations. This report primarily addresses teen courts that handle delinquencies or violations of the criminal law.

Figure 9.3   Typical Teen Court Process

SOURCE: Jeffrey A. Butts, Janeen Buck, and Mark B. Coggeshall. 2002 (April). *The Impact of Teen Court on Young Offenders*, p. 5. Washington, DC: Urban Institute Justice Policy Center. Reprinted by permission.

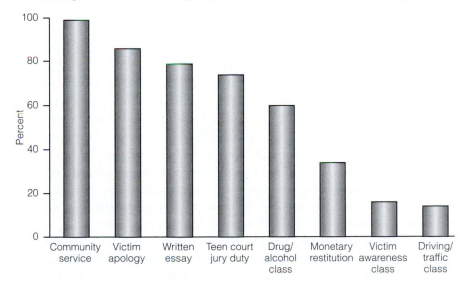

Percentage of teen courts reporting they impose selected sanctions "often" or "very often"

Figure 9.4   Sanctions Imposed by Teen Courts

SOURCE: Jeffrey A. Butts and Janeen Buck. 2000 (October). *Teen Courts: A Focus on Research*, p. 6. Washington, DC: OJJDP Juvenile Justice Research Bulletin.

© Jeff Greenberg/PhotoEdit

A male bailiff swears in a female defendant in teen court in Miami, Florida. Teen courts are diversion programs, not formal courts within the judicial branch of government. As such, the processes and procedures they follow are substantially less formal, although their sanctions are generally deemed valid by the court.

Teen courts provide an effective intervention in jurisdictions where the enforcement of misdemeanor charges is given low priority because of heavy caseloads of more serious offenses. In a collaborative report by the U.S. Department of Justice (DOJ) and the American Bar Association (ABA) titled *Youth Cases for Youth Court: Desktop Guide* (Fisher 2006), it is noted that youth courts turn peer pressure into a positive tool by letting offenders know, through other teens, that their behavior was wrong.

Teen courts have existed in the United States for at least five decades but began to spread rapidly across the nation during the 1990s (Norris, Twill, and Kim 2011). The growth and acceptance of teen courts are exemplified by the establishment of the National Association of Youth Courts in 2007. *Youth Courts: An Empirical Update and Analysis of Future Organizational and Research Needs* (2008) reports that in 2008 some 1,250 youth courts were in operation across the country, with the average court handling about 100 cases per year. One study estimated that teen courts handle approximately 12 percent of the informal caseload nationwide involving juveniles (Butts, Hoffman, and Buck 1999).

An estimated 86 percent of the youth accepted into teen court successfully completed their sentence. The average youth court reported over 1,730 hours of completed community service. Furthermore, the typical youth court serving 100 offenders per year operated on a budget of less than $30,000.

Despite their popularity and a widely held belief that such interventions can reduce juvenile recidivism while saving money for resource-strapped court systems, many of the assumptions about teen courts remain untested and a dearth of empirical evidence exists regarding their effectiveness (Norris, Twill, and Kim 2011). Among the few studies that have been published, conflicting results are noted.

Programs in Practice: Teen Courts

At 4:00 P.M., a youth bailiff for the Anchorage Youth Court [AYC] steps into a waiting area on the third floor of the Anchorage courthouse and, reading from a docket sheet, calls out "Case Number 687432." A 15-year-old girl named Angela stands and begins to move toward the thick courtroom door, along with her mother and father.

Waiting in the courtroom are two teenage defense attorneys (both female) that Angela and her parents met 45 minutes before in the basement offices of the Anchorage Youth Court. Two young men in their mid-teens are sitting at a table near the front of the courtroom. They will be serving as the prosecuting attorneys for Angela's hearing, and they are currently reading through a case file that describes the incident in which Angela has admitted to being involved. An adult legal advisor sits at the side of the courtroom, near a chair used for witness testimony during daytime hearings in the criminal court. During the youth court hearing, the adult legal advisor will be quiet unless the young people in charge of the courtroom direct a question to him or seek his advice about procedural matters.

Angela's parents take their places on one of the five or six long, wooden, church-style pews at the rear of the courtroom that provide seating for spectators. During youth court, however, there are no spectators. The proceedings of the AYC are confidential and closed to the public. Visitors, such as journalists and researchers, are allowed to watch youth court hearings only if permission is granted by the court, and only if Angela and her parents agree, which they do. . . .

The youth volunteers study Angela as she enters the courtroom. . . . She exchanges nervous glances with her parents as the youth attorneys direct her to come forward to sit near them. Her parents sit directly behind Angela in the spectator area.

The judges' bench at the front of the courtroom is elevated. The jury box on the right side of the courtroom will not be used. The Anchorage Youth Court uses the "youth tribunal" model for its courtroom. All cases are heard by a panel of three judges, and they alone will deliberate on the presentations by the youth attorneys before choosing the most appropriate disposition for Angela. Each pair of attorneys sits at one of two tables designated for this purpose. A speaker's podium is placed between the tables. Anyone standing at the podium will be looking directly at the judges.

For several minutes after Angela enters the courtroom, everyone sits quietly. The attorneys continue to look through their papers, occasionally whispering instructions to each other—"I'll say this part . . . why don't you say that?" . . .

[Eventually] the adult legal advisor looks at each pair of attorneys and silently raises his eyebrows, as if to say, "O.K., ready?" The attorneys nod and the legal advisor leaves the courtroom. . . .

The program director, Sharon Leon, suddenly comes in and hands the defense attorneys a document that must be related to the case. Ms. Leon is normally working in the downstairs AYC office at this time, getting youth and parents ready for court and ensuring that the youth volunteers are prepared. Her appearance in the courtroom suggests that some detail about the case must have been nearly missed, but she is just in time. She smiles at Angela and Angela's parents as she leaves the quiet courtroom and closes the door behind her. Other than this brief appearance by the program director and the silent presence of the adult legal advisor, the entire courtroom is managed by teenagers.

Moments later, the door behind the judges' bench opens and the adult legal advisor comes back in. The youth bailiff stands and announces in a clear, loud voice, "All rise," and everyone in the courtroom stands. The three youth judges enter and immediately take their places behind the bench. The chief judge motions for the participants and spectators to take their seats. No one speaks. The chief judge sits in the middle chair, the only high-backed chair. . . .

The bailiff announces the case, reading the case number and charges aloud. The chief judge asks Angela to verify her name, and then asks Angela and her parents to confirm that they have voluntarily consented to have visitors in the courtroom this evening. The chief judge asks the visiting researchers to identify themselves—and the adult legal advisor later chastises the researchers because they fail to stand when addressing the bench. It is a mistake nobody makes twice in Anchorage Youth Court. Everyone addresses the judges while standing; everyone calls the judges "Your honors." Most importantly, nobody in Anchorage Youth Court speaks without permission from the bench.

Angela's mother learns this during the hearing. She disagrees with something said by one of the prosecuting attorneys, and being one of the few adults in the room, she feels free to interrupt and correct the young man. She barely gets a syllable out before the chief judge cuts her off—"M'am! I'm very sorry, but you have not been recognized by the court. You'll have an opportunity to talk in a few minutes, but for now, I'd ask you to take your seat."

Angela's mother complies, but she seems very surprised. The visiting researchers are surprised. Angela, on the other hand, tries to hide just the slightest smile. The youth volunteers barely notice any of this. It's just an average night in Anchorage Youth Court, and the judges are managing their courtroom, just as they always do.

The three judges in Anchorage Youth Court on this particular evening appear to be 16 or 17 years old. Two are female and one is male. Dressed in black judicial robes, they study the defendant from behind their raised bench as the hearing begins. They start the process by asking the defendant if she has actually read the agreement she signed. Prompted by her youth attorneys to stand and address the judges, 15-year-old Angela indicates that she signed it knowingly and voluntarily. One of the judges announces that Angela has admitted responsibility for a charge of misdemeanor shoplifting, a violation of Alaska statute 11.46.220. The judge looks at the two teenagers that are serving as prosecutors for the case and says, "We're ready for your opening statement."

To read how this case proceeded and what the final disposition was, go to http://www.urban.org/UploadedPDF/410457.pdf and read pages 18–19.

SOURCE: The preceding extract was taken from Jeffrey A. Butts, Janeen Buck, and Mark B. Coggeshall. 2002 (April). *The Impact of Teen Court on Young Offenders*, pp. 14–19. Washington, DC: The Urban Institute, Research Report. http://www.urban.org/UploadedPDF/410457.pdf

The National Youth Court Center has set forth guidelines for communities considering implementing teen courts in *Youth Court: A Community Solution for Embracing At-Risk Youth* (Pearson and Jurich 2005). Some teen courts address young people with substance abuse problems. In other jurisdictions separate juvenile drug courts have been established.

Juvenile Drug Courts

"Reclaiming Futures" (2007) reports that the majority of youths in the juvenile justice system were under the influence at the time of their offense. Consequently, the juvenile justice system has become the default agency for providing drug and alcohol treatment services. As the juvenile courts have become increasingly overwhelmed with complex and difficult caseloads and diminishing resources, one approach that has emerged as a solution to the crowded court dockets is the drug court.

The first drug court was established in 1989 in Miami, Florida, to deal with adult drug offenders and had the dual expectations of reducing substance abuse and the related criminal behavior while freeing up the criminal court and corrections to handle other more serious nondrug-related cases (Myers 2007). The popularity of drug courts, combined with promising research results, led to the application of drug court principles in juvenile drug cases. The philosophy behind the creation of juvenile drug courts is that children and adolescents are different from adults and that the root causes of drug use among young people are found in developmental and family-based risk factors (Myers 2007).

A typical juvenile drug court offers delinquents who meet certain eligibility criteria the option of participating in the drug court rather than in a traditional case processing.

 The two most common criteria for participating in a drug court are having a substance abuse problem and not having committed a violent offense.

Juvenile Drug Courts: Strategies in Practice (2003) lists 16 strategies that can be used in a juvenile drug court, summarized in Table 9.4. Participants who successfully complete a drug court program may be rewarded by dismissed charges, shortened sentences or reduced penalties.

Only 10 to 20 percent of juveniles enrolled in drug courts have used anything other than alcohol or marijuana, leading researchers to suggest that drug courts need to better distinguish adolescents who are substance abusers, or are likely to become drug dependent, from the larger majority of youths who have experimented with alcohol or other drugs but will not develop long-term problems as a result (Myers 2007).

Given the limited research showing that the drug court model has not proven as effective for juveniles as for adults, the Office of Juvenile Justice and Delinquency Prevention (OJJDP) has partnered with the Substance Abuse and Mental Health Services Administration's (SAMHSA) Center for Substance Abuse Treatment (CSAT) in an effort to improve youth drug court results through the implementation of best practices for adolescent treatment (*National Drug Control Strategy* 2011). Working with several existing juvenile drug courts and more traditional juvenile courts, the OJJDP/CSAT partnership has focused on improving assessment capacities through the use of the Screening, Brief Intervention, and Referrals to Treatment (SBIRT) program, which enables the courts

Table 9.4   The Strategies Used in Juvenile Drug Courts

1.	Engage all stakeholders in creating an interdisciplinary, coordinated and systemic approach to working with youth and their families.
2.	Develop and maintain an interdisciplinary, nonadversarial work team.
3.	Define a target population and eligibility criteria that are aligned with the program's goals and objectives.
4.	Schedule frequent judicial reviews and be sensitive to the effect that court proceedings can have on youth and their families.
5.	Establish a system for program monitoring and evaluation to maintain quality of service, assess program impact and contribute to knowledge in the field.
6.	Build partnerships with community organizations to expand the range of opportunities available to youth and their families.
7.	Tailor interventions to the complex and varied needs of youth and their families.
8.	Tailor treatment to the developmental needs of adolescents.
9.	Design treatment to address the unique needs of each gender.
10.	Create policies and procedures that are responsive to cultural differences and train personnel to be culturally competent.
11.	Maintain a focus on the strengths of youth and their families during program planning and in every interaction between the court and those it serves.
12.	Recognize and engage the family as a valued partner in all components of the program.
13.	Coordinate with the school system to ensure that each participant enrolls in and attends an educational program that is appropriate to his or her needs.
14.	Design drug testing to be frequent, random and observed. Document testing policies and procedures in writing.
15.	Respond to compliance and noncompliance with incentives and sanctions that are designed to reinforce or modify the behavior of youth and their families.
16.	Establish a confidentiality policy and procedures that guard the privacy of the youth while allowing the drug court team to access key information.

SOURCE: *Juvenile Drug Courts: Strategies in Practice*, p. 10. 2003 (March). Washington, DC: Bureau of Justice Assistance. (NCJ 197866)

to use a brief, non-intensive intervention to help identify the most appropriate referrals and admissions criteria for youth involved in the juvenile justice system (*National Drug Control Strategy* 2011).

Juvenile Mental Health Courts

Frequently youths who have a substance abuse problem also have mental health issues. Skowyra and Cocozza (2006, 1) contend, "It is now well established that the majority of youths involved with the juvenile justice system have mental health disorders." Some studies have found that as many as three fourths of all juvenile detainees have some type of diagnosable mental health issue. Indeed, it appears that many youth are placed into the juvenile justice system specifically as a way to access mental health services that would otherwise be unavailable to them in the community (Skowyra and Powell 2006). These are among the major reasons behind the development of mental health courts, specialized courts that use a separate docket, combined with a team approach and regular judicial supervision, to respond to individuals with mental illnesses who come in contact with the justice system (Council of State Governments 2005).

The first adult mental health court opened in 1997 in Broward County, Florida, and has since expanded to address the mental health needs of juvenile offenders as well (Cocozza and Shufelt 2006). The first juvenile mental health court—the Court for the Individualized Treatment of Adolescents (CITA)—opened in 2001 in Santa Clara County, California. CITA accepts youths who were under age 14 at the time of their offense and have a serious mental illness, including brain disorders (schizophrenia, severe anxiety, bipolar disorder and severe ADHD) or severe head injury that has contributed to their offending. The court also accepts youths with certain developmental disabilities such as mental retardation and autism (Cocozza and Shufelt 2006).

Diversion to such courts of juveniles with mental health needs holds many benefits for the youths themselves, the justice system and the community at large, including (Skowyra and Powell 2006):

- Reducing recidivism.
- Providing more effective and appropriate treatment.
- Decreasing overcrowded detention facilities.
- Facilitating the further development of community-based mental health services.

Skowyra and Cocozza (2006) propose a Blueprint for Change, providing a conceptual and practical framework for juvenile justice and mental health systems to use when developing strategies and policies aimed at improving mental health services for youths involved with the juvenile justice system. The model is based on four cornerstones that reflect those areas where the most critical improvements are necessary to enhance the delivery of mental health services to youths involved with the juvenile justice system.

 The four cornerstones of the Blueprint for Change model are collaboration, identification, diversion and treatment.

Juvenile Gun Courts

Throughout the nation, juvenile and **family courts** (courts with broad jurisdiction over family matters) have been criticized for not providing appropriate sanctions and program services for young offenders involved in gun crimes. Some states have instituted juvenile gun courts and targeted interventions that expose youths charged with gun offenses to the ramifications of such acts.

Gun courts are short-term, early intervention programs with an intensive education focus including a wide range of court personnel and law enforcement officials—judges, probation officers, prosecutors, defense counsel and police—working with community members. A major goal of gun court is to effectively deliver to juveniles the message that gun violence hurts victims, families and entire communities; guns cannot protect juveniles; being involved in gun violence will negatively affect their entire lives; and there are adults who can and will help them find nonviolent ways to solve problems.

A gun court is a type of problem-solving court that intervenes with youths who have committed gun offenses that have not resulted in serious physical injury. Most gun courts include several principal elements including

1. Early intervention.
2. Shorter, intensive programming (often a single 2- to 4-hour session).

3. An intensive educational focus to show youths the harm that can come from unlawful gun use and the immediate response that will result when youths are involved with guns.

4. The inclusion of a wide range of court personnel and law enforcement officials working together with community members. ("Gun Court" 2007)

 First-time, nonviolent gun offenders age 17 and younger are sometimes eligible to participate in juvenile gun court programs.

Juvenile Traffic Court

Minors charged with traffic offenses may appear in juvenile traffic court with a parent or guardian. The juvenile is entitled to a trial if the citation is contested. If a minor admits the citation or is found by the judge or hearing officer to have committed the violation, the minor can be ordered to pay a fine, have driving privileges suspended or restricted, be required to do a certain number of hours of community service or be placed on probation (*Juvenile Justice Handbook* 2008, 7).

Balanced and Restorative Justice

In addition to specialized courts, diversion can also be provided through various models of restorative justice, often through some form of conferencing. *Bringing Balance to Juvenile Justice* (2002, 1–2) notes,

> Since its inception in the late 1800s, the juvenile justice system has been an amalgam of contradictions and competing concerns. On some level, society believes that crime should result in punishment and that children must experience swift, certain and negative consequences for their crimes to deter them from future delinquency. Society also wants rehabilitation of wayward youths, but it wants to be protected from them while the rehabilitation takes place. The needs of crime victims must be central to the justice system. They need compensation for damages, contrition from offenders and a sense of justice restored. …
>
> [If the punishment model and the therapeutic intervention model] coexist in a jurisdiction, they are in constant conflict. If either one exists by itself, it fails to serve all stakeholders in the system.
>
> There is a better approach. Balanced consideration of community protection, offender accountability and competency development brings clarity and reason to juvenile justice issues. This comprehensive philosophy speaks to every aspect of delinquency, punishment, treatment and prevention. These three principles, fully implemented, create a juvenile justice system that truly operates in the best interest of the child and the community.

 "Ensuring community safety, insisting on offender accountability to victims and equipping offenders in the system with skills so they are able to pursue noncriminal paths after release are the core principles of the balanced and restorative justice (BARJ) model" (*Bringing Balance to Juvenile Justice* 2002, 2).

As Bazemore and Umbreit (2001, 1) explain, "Restorative justice is a framework for juvenile justice reform that seeks to engage victims, offenders and their families, other citizens and community groups both as clients of juvenile justice services and as resources in an effective response to youth crime. … Reconciling the needs of victims and offenders with the needs of the community is the under-lying goal of restorative justice. Unlike retributive justice, which is primarily concerned with punishing crime, restorative justice focuses on repairing the injury that crime inflicts."

 The three main components of restorative justice are the offender, the victim and the community, including juvenile justice professionals.

In the balanced and restorative justice format offenders, victims, community members and juvenile justice professionals have new roles as they seek to sanction offenders through accountability, rehabilitate them through competency development and enhance community safety. These new roles are briefly summarized in Table 9.5.

 Four models of restorative justice may also be a means of diversion: victim–offender mediation, community reparative boards, family group conferencing and circle sentencing.

Table 9.5 New Roles in the Balanced and Restorative Justice Model

	Sanctioning through Accountability	*Rehabilitation through Competency Development*	*Enhancement of Community Safety*
Juvenile Offender	Must accept responsibility for behavior and actively work to restore loss to victims (if victims wish) and the community and face victims or victim representatives (if victims wish) and community members	Actively participates as a resource in service roles that improve quality of life in the community and provide new experiences, skills and self-esteem as a productive resource for positive action	Becomes involved in constructive competency building and restorative activities in a balanced program while under adult supervision; develops internal controls and new peer and organizational commitments; and helps others escape offending patterns of behavior
Victim	Actively participates in all stages of the restorative process (if victim wishes and is able), documents psychological and financial impact of crime, participates in mediation voluntarily and helps determine sanctions for juvenile offender	Provides input into the rehabilitative process, suggests community service options for juvenile offenders and participates in victim panels or victim-awareness training for staff and juvenile offenders (if victim wishes)	Provides input regarding continuing safety concerns, fear and needed controls on juvenile offenders and encourages protective support for other victims
Community Member	Participates as volunteer mediator/facilitator and community panel member; develops community service and compensated work opportunities for juvenile offenders with reparative obligations; and assists victims and supports juvenile offenders in completing obligations	Develops new opportunities for youth to make productive contributions, build competency and establish a sense of belonging	Provides guardianship of juvenile offenders, mentoring and input to juvenile justice systems regarding safety concerns; addresses underlying community problems that contribute to delinquency; and provides "natural surveillance"
Juvenile Justice Professional	Facilitates mediation, ensures that restoration occurs (by providing ways for juvenile offenders to earn funds for restitution), develops creative/restorative community service options, engages community members in the process and educates community on its role	Develops new roles for young offenders that allow them to practice and demonstrate competency; assesses and builds on youth and community strengths; and develops community partnerships	Develops range of incentives and consequences to ensure juvenile offender compliance with supervision objectives; assists school and family in their efforts to control and maintain juvenile offenders in the community; and develops prevention capacity of local organizations

Adapted from Gordon Bazemore and C. Washington. 1995. "Charting the Future for the Juvenile Justice System: Reinventing Mission and Management. *Spectrum: Journal of State Government* 68 (2): 51–66.

SOURCE: Shay Bilchik. 1998 (December). *Guide for Implementing the Balanced and Restorative Justice Model*, p. 41. Washington, DC: Office of Juvenile Justice and Delinquency Prevention.

Victim–Offender Mediation

Victim–offender mediation originated in the mid-1970s. Eligibility varies, but it is primarily used with first-time property offenders. Referrals are made by the court, the police and other entities. A mediator, victim and offender meet in a neutral setting such as a church or community center. Parents also may be involved. The primary outcome sought is to allow the victim to relay the impact of the crime to the offender, expressing feelings and needs while the offender has increased awareness of the harm of the offense, gains empathy with the victim and agrees on a reparative plan. For example:

> The victim was a middle-aged woman. The offender, a 14-year-old neighbor of the victim, had broken into the victim's home and stolen a VCR. The mediation session took place in the basement of the victim's church.
>
> In the presence of a mediator, the victim and offender talked for two hours. At times, their conversation was heated and emotional. When they finished, the mediator felt that they had heard each other's stories and learned something important about the impact of the crime and about each other.
>
> The participants agreed that the offender would pay $200 in restitution to cover the cost of damages to the victim's home resulting from the break-in and would also reimburse the victim for the cost of the stolen VCR (estimated at $150). They also worked out a payment schedule.
>
> During the session, the offender made several apologies to the victim and agreed to complete community service hours working in a food bank sponsored by the victim's church. The victim said that she felt less angry and fearful after learning more about the offender and the details of the crime. (Bazemore and Umbreit 2001, 9)

Community Reparative Boards

Reparative boards typically consist of a small group of citizens who have received intensive training and who then conduct public, face-to-face meetings with offenders ordered by the court to participate in the process. The target group is nonviolent offenders assigned to the board. During the board meeting, board members discuss with the offender the offense and its negative consequences. The board then develops a set of proposed sanctions that they discuss with the offender. The board also monitors compliance and submits a compliance report to the court. Following is an example of a community reparative board session:

> The reparative board convened to consider the case of a 17-year-old who had been caught driving with an open can of beer in his father's pickup truck. The youth had been sentenced by a judge to reparative probation, and it was the board's responsibility to decide what form the probation should take. For about 30 minutes, the citizen members of the board asked the youth several simple, straightforward questions. The board members then went to another room to deliberate on an appropriate sanction for the youth. The youth awaited the board's decision nervously, because he did not know whether to expect something tougher or much easier than regular probation.

> When the board returned, the chairperson explained the four conditions of the offender's probation contract: (1) begin work to pay off his traffic tickets, (2) complete a state police defensive driving course, (3) undergo an alcohol assessment and (4) write a three-page paper on how alcohol had negatively affected his life. The youth signed the contract, and the chairperson adjourned the meeting. (Bazemore and Umbreit 2001, 4)

Family Group Conferencing

Family group conferencing originated in New Zealand. Referrals are usually by police and school officials. Family group conferencing involves those most affected by a youth's crime, usually the victim, offender and family, friends and key supporters of the victim and offender. These individuals are brought together by a trained facilitator to discuss how they and others have been harmed by the offense and how that harm might be repaired. Such conferences typically take place in a social welfare office, school, community building or police facility. The primary outcomes sought are to clarify the facts of a case and to denounce crime while affirming and supporting the offender and restoring the victim's loss.

Eligibility criteria for such a conference usually include being no older than age 14 and being a first-time offender committing a nonviolent offence with no pending charges and admitting guilt. Consider the following example of a family group conferencing session:

> A family conferencing group convened in a local school to consider a case in which a student had injured a teacher and broken the teacher's glasses in an altercation. Group members included the offender, his mother and grandfather, the victim, the police officer who made the arrest and about 10 other interested parties, including two of the offender's teachers and two friends of the victim.
>
> The conferencing process began with comments by the offender, his mother and grandfather, the victim and the arresting officer. Each spoke about the offense and its impact. The youth justice coordinator next asked for input from the other group members and then asked all participants what they thought the offender should do to pay back the victim and the community for the damage caused by his crime. In the remaining 30 minutes of the hour-long conference, the group suggested that the offender should make restitution to the victim for his medical expenses and the cost of new glasses and that the offender should also perform community service work on the school grounds. (Bazemore and Umbreit 2001, 5)

Circle Sentencing

Circle sentencing is a modernized version of the traditional sanctioning and healing practices of aboriginal peoples in Canada and American Indians in the United States. According to Bazemore and Umbreit (2001, 6), "Circle sentencing is a holistic reintegrative strategy designed not only to address the criminal and delinquent behavior of offenders but also to consider the needs of victims, families and communities." The circle usually includes victims, offenders, family and friends of both, justice and social service personnel and interested community residents.

The target group is offenders who admit guilt and express willingness to change. The primary outcomes sought are to increase community strength and capacity to resolve disputes and prevent crime, develop reparative and rehabilitative plans, address victim concerns and public safety issues, assign victim and offender support group responsibilities and identify resources. Bazemore and Umbreit (2001, 7) provide the following example of a circle sentencing session:

> The victim was a middle-aged man whose parked car had been badly damaged when the offender, a 16-year-old, crashed into it while joyriding in another vehicle. The offender had also damaged a police vehicle.
>
> In the circle, the victim talked about the emotional shock of seeing what had happened to his car and his costs to repair it (he was uninsured). Then, an elder leader of the First Nations community where the circle sentencing session was being held (and an uncle of the offender) expressed his disappointment and anger with the boy. The elder observed that this incident, along with several prior offenses by the boy, had brought shame to his family. The elder also noted that in the old days, the boy would have been required to pay the victim's family substantial compensation as a result of such behavior. After the elder finished, a feather (the "talking piece") was passed to the next person in the circle, a young man who spoke about the contributions the offender had made to the community, the kindness he had shown toward elders and his willingness to help others with home repairs.
>
> Having heard all this, the judge asked the Crown Council (Canadian prosecutor) and the **public defender** [lawyer who works for the defense of indigent offenders] who were also sitting in the circle to make statements and then asked if anyone else in the circle wanted to speak. The Royal Canadian Mounted Police officer, whose vehicle had also been damaged, then took the feather and spoke on the offender's behalf. The officer proposed to the judge that in lieu of statutorily required jail time for the offense, the offender be allowed to meet with him on a regular basis for counseling and community service. After asking the victim and the prosecutor if either had any objections, the judge accepted this proposal. The judge also ordered restitution to the victim and asked the young adult who had spoken on the offender's behalf to serve as a mentor for the offender.

Considerations When Using a Restorative Justice Approach

Studies of the four models of restorative justice just discussed have found that each model had strengths and weakness and that different approaches will work best in different situations (Bazemore and Umbreit 2001). It is recommended that when using diversion programs such as those just discussed, the programs will be more successful if they have a participatory rather than an adjudicatory focus (Griffin and Torbet 2002). The differences between these two approaches are summarized in Table 9.6.

In many instances success is also more likely using a strength-based approach rather than a problem-centered approach. The features of these two approaches are summarized in Table 9.7.

Table 9.6   Types of Alternative Dispute Resolution Programs

Adjudicatory	Participatory
Intent is to assert a moral or legal message and impose a solution	Intent is to preserve and enhance ongoing relationships
Facilitator/panel makes and imposes all decisions	Parties arrive at mutually acceptable agreement with aid of facilitator
Facilitator/panel assesses facts and culpability in determining appropriate remedy	Less fact-finding; parties define issues, engage in search for solutions
Focus is on the immediate conflict and the issues raised in the complaint	Focus is ongoing relationships among neighbors, family members, etc.
Teaches accountability for offenses	Teaches conflict-resolution and problem-solving techniques
The more formal the process and the more serious the problem presented, the more formal the resulting agreement	The more participatory and inclusive the process, the less formal the resulting agreement

Adapted from National Council of Juvenile and Family Court Judges. 1989. *Court-Appointed Alternative Dispute Resolution: A Better Way to Resolve Minor Delinquency, Status Offense and Abuse/Neglect Cases.* Reno, NV: NCJFCJ.

SOURCE: Patrick Griffin and Patricia Torbet, eds. 2002 (June). *Desktop Guide to Good Juvenile Probation Practice*, p. 51. Pittsburgh, PA: National Center for Juvenile Justice. Reprinted by permission.

Table 9.7   Problem-Centered Approach versus Strength-Based Approach

Problem-Centered	Strength-Based
Approaches clients with attention to their failure, dysfunction and deficits with an eye to fixing their flaws	Approaches clients with a greater concern for their strengths, competencies and possibilities, seeking not only to fix what is wrong but to nurture what is best
Assumes an "expert" role in naming clients' problems and then instructing clients how to fix them	Assumes clients to be competent and "expert" on their life and situation. Helps clients discover how strengths and resources can be applied to negotiate third-party concerns and mandates while also furthering their wants and concerns
Sanction-focused: client "takes the punishment" without taking responsibility or earning redemption	Incentive-focused: holds youth accountable while furthering their prosocial interests, skills or passions
Route to solution: fix the problem	Route to solution: strengthen connection to clients' competencies, past successes, positive interests and wants
Goals are obedience and compliance	Initial goals are obedience and compliance; final goals are behavior change and growth
No direct strategies are used for building motivation. Relies on coercion and "pushing from without"	Employs specific principles and strategies for building client motivation to change. Uses sanctions to stabilize out-of-control behavior but works to raise motivation that comes from within
Court has nonnegotiable mandates, and probation officer determines both the goals and the means for reaching those goals	Court has nonnegotiable mandates but beyond these, clients are partners in the process of setting personalized goals. Probation officer helps them focus on what they want to change, maintains the focus and works to increase positive options

SOURCE: Patrick Griffin and Patricia Torbet, eds. 2002 (June). *Desktop Guide to Good Juvenile Probation Practice*, p. 97. Pittsburgh, PA: National Center for Juvenile Justice. Reprinted by permission.

Net Widening

Whatever form of pretrial service and diversion is used, juvenile justice officials must be careful not to "widen the net" for those entering the juvenile justice system. **Net widening** refers to involving youths in a diversion program who, without such opportunities, probably would not be involved in *any* type of intervention. Net widening diverts resources away from those youth most in need of intervention and treatment and, consequently, diminishes public safety.

Research conducted during the past four decades has consistently demonstrated that nearly 70 percent of youths who are arrested once are never arrested again: "In other words, by doing nothing the state can achieve a 70 percent success rate—meaning no subsequent arrests—with first-time offenders. ... By reducing net widening, research shows that systems can improve their effectiveness and better promote public safety. To shorten the net and improve public safety, juvenile justice systems and affiliated community-based agencies need to adopt a deep end strategy" (*Widening the Net in Juvenile Justice* 2001, 5). A **deep end strategy** would target youths with the highest likelihood of continuing their delinquent careers without comprehensive interventions.

The Importance of Timely Case Processing

Whether the decision at intake is to use diversion or to refer to juvenile court, timely case processing is critical. Siegel and Halemba (2006, 1) contend, "Timely intervention (informal or formal) is critical in attempting to disrupt the development of a youth's delinquent 'career' before her/his behavior becomes more engrained and chronic. It also makes considerable intuitive sense to try to intervene before a youth is again referred on a subsequent law violation." They further assert, "There is little question that unnecessary delays in case processing may increase the likelihood of a juvenile's subsequent involvement with the court as well as the likelihood that the juvenile's law-violating behavior will continue to escalate." Siegel and Halemba (7) suggest the following time standards for processing informal/diverted cases:

- Filing of police report/referral: 75 percent of cases completed in 7 days; 98 percent in 10 days
- Intake screening: 75 percent completed in 7 days; 98 percent in 15 days
- Develop diversion plan: 75 percent in 3 days; 98 percent in 10 days
- Initiate diversion plan: 75 percent in 4 days; 98 percent in 25 days
- Total days to implementation: 75 percent in 21 days; 98 percent in 60 days

Ideally these times would be even shorter.

 **Summary**

- "The primary duty of the prosecutor is to seek justice while fully and faithfully representing the interests of the state" (NDAA).
- The intake hearing may result in dismissal, diversion, referral to juvenile court for adjudication or transfer to adult court.

- Principles of effective intervention include:
  - Risk Principle—target higher-risk offender (WHO)
  - Need Principle—target criminogenic risk/need factors (WHAT)
  - Treatment Principle—use behavioral approaches (HOW)
  - Fidelity Principle—implement program as designed (HOW WELL)
- Effective diversion criteria should result in the diversion of most minor offenders who have no serious prior involvement with the court and who, along with their families, accept services and sanctions voluntarily.
- Diversion may include community service, restitution, letters of apology, participation in prosocial activities, mentoring or tutoring programs, work programs, educational programs, skill-development programs, counseling programs or referral to a specialized court to meet individual needs.
- Specialized courts include teen courts, drug courts, mental health courts, traffic courts and gun courts.
- The two most common criteria for participating in a drug court are having a substance abuse problem and not having committed a violent offense.
- The four cornerstones of the Blueprint for Change model are collaboration, identification, diversion and treatment.
- First-time, nonviolent gun offenders age 17 and younger are sometimes eligible to participate in juvenile gun court programs.
- "Ensuring community safety, insisting on offender accountability to victims and equipping offenders in the system with skills so they are able to pursue noncriminal paths after release are the core principles of the balanced and restorative justice (BARJ) model" (*Bringing Balance to Juvenile Justice* 2002, 2).
- The three main components of restorative justice are the offender, the victim and the community, including juvenile justice professionals.
- Four models of restorative justice may also be a means of diversion: victim–offender mediation, community reparative boards, family group conferencing and circle sentencing.

Discussion Questions

1. Should there be a separate justice system for juveniles, or should all juveniles be dealt with in the adult system?
2. Is diversion being too soft on youths who commit status offenses?
3. Is restorative justice compatible with the juvenile justice system?
4. What form of restorative justice do you find most appealing?
5. What benefits, if any, do specialized courts offer to the juvenile justice system? Do such courts address any of the principles of effective intervention?
6. How can the juvenile prosecutor fulfill both the role of protecting society and acting in the best interest of the child?
7. Have you seen any instances of net widening in your community?
8. What alternatives for diversion are available in your community?
9. Which of the pretrial services do you believe are most important?
10. Why can juveniles be detained before they have a trial?

References

Abram, Karen M., Linda A. Teplin, Gary M. McClelland, and Mina K. Dulcan. 2003 (November). "Comorbid Psychiatric Disorders in Youth in Juvenile Detention." *Archives of General Psychiatry* 60 (11): 1097–1108.

Bazemore, Gordon, and Mark Umbreit. 2001 (February). *A Comparison of Four Restorative Conferencing Models.* Washington, DC: OJJDP Juvenile Justice Bulletin. (NCJ 184738)

Bringing Balance to Juvenile Justice. 2002. Alexandria, VA: American Prosecutors Research Institute.

Burns, Barbara J., James C. Howell, Janet K. Wiig, Leena K. Augimeri, Brandon C. Welsh, Rolf Loeber, and David

Petechuk. 2003 (March). *Treatment, Services, and Intervention Programs for Child Delinquents.* Washington, DC: Office of Juvenile Justice and Delinquency Prevention, Bulletin Series. (NCJ 193410)

Butts, Jeffrey A., Janeen Buck, and Mark B. Coggeshall. 2002 (April). *The Impact of Teen Court on Young Offenders*, pp. 14–19. Washington, DC: The Urban Institute, Research Report. http://www.urban.org/UploadedPDF/410457.pdf

Butts, Jeffrey A., Dean Hoffman, and Janeen Buck. 1999 (October). *Teen Courts in the United States: A Profile of Current Programs* (OJJDP Fact Sheet FS-99118). Washington, DC: Office of Juvenile Justice and Delinquency Prevention.

Clark, Pam. 2008 (February). "Juvenile Justice Faces Mental Health Issues." *Corrections Today* 70 (1): 8–13.

Cocozza, Joseph J., and Jennie L. Shufelt. 2006 (June). *Juvenile Mental Health Courts: An Emerging Strategy.* Research and Program Brief. Delmar, NY: National Center for Mental Health and Juvenile Justice.

Council of State Governments. 2005. *A Guide to Mental Health Court Design and Implementation.* New York: Council of State Governments.

Crime in the United States 2010. 2011. Washington, DC: U.S. Department of Justice, Federal Bureau of Investigation.

Degelman, Charles, Keri Doggett, and Gregorio Medina. 2006. *Giving Back: Introducing Community Service Learning—Improving Mandated Community Service for Juvenile Offenders.* Chicago: Constitutional Rights Foundation.

Fisher, Margaret E. 2006. *Youth Cases for Youth Courts: Desktop Guide.* Chicago: American Bar Association.

Flores, Anthony W., Lawrence F. Travis III, and Edward J. Latessa. 2004 (February). *Case Classification for Juvenile Corrections: An Assessment of the Youth Level of Service/Case Management Inventory (YLS/CMI), Final Report.* Unpublished report, funded by the U.S. Department of Justice. Document 204005, Award # 98-JB-VX-0108. Made available online by the National Criminal Justice Reference Service (NCJRS) at http://www.ncjrs.gov/pdffiles1/nij/grants/204005.pdf.

Griffin, Patrick, and Patricia Torbet. 2002 (June). *Desktop Guide to Good Juvenile Probation Practice.* Pittsburgh, PA: National Center for Juvenile Justice.

"Gun Court." 2007. Washington, DC: OJJDP Model Programs Guide.

Hanger, JauNae M. 2008 (February). "Indiana Addresses Mental Health in Juvenile Detention Centers." *Corrections Today* 70 (1): 36–38.

Juvenile Drug Courts: Strategies in Practice. 2003 (March). Washington, DC: Bureau of Justice Assistance. (NCJ 197866)

Juvenile Justice Handbook 2008. 2008. Newcastle, CA: Placer County Peer Court Board of Directors.

Latessa, Edward L., Francis T. Cullen, and Paul Gendreau. 2002 (September). "Beyond Correctional Quackery—Professionalism and the Possibility of Effective Treatment." *Federal Probation* 66 (2): 43–49.

Latessa, Edward J., and Brian Lovins. 2010. "The Role of Offender Risk Assessment: A Policy Maker Guide." *Victims and Offenders* 5 (3): 203–219.

McReynolds, Larkin S., Gail A. Wasserman, Robert E. DeComo, Reni John, Joseph M. Keating, and Scott Nolen. 2008 (April). "Psychiatric Disorder in a Juvenile Assessment Center." *Crime & Delinquency* 54 (2): 313–334.

Miller, Joel, and Jeffrey Lin. 2007 (October). "Applying a Generic Juvenile Risk Assessment Instrument to a Local Context." *Crime & Delinquency* 530 (4): 552–580.

Myers, David L. 2007. "Assessing the Implementation and Effectiveness of Juvenile Drug Courts." *Criminal Justice Research Reports* 19 (3): 89–90.

National Drug Control Strategy, 2011. 2011. Washington, DC: Office of National Drug Control Policy. (NCJ 234320)

National Juvenile Detention Association (NJDA). 2007. "Definition of Juvenile Detention." Richmond, KY: National Partnership for Juvenile Services.

Norris, Michael, Sarah Twill, and Chigon Kim. 2011 (March). "Smells Like Teen Spirit: Evaluating a Midwestern Teen Court." *Crime and Delinquency* 57 (2): 199–221.

Olson, Darryl. 2007. "Florida Makes PACT with State's Youthful Offenders." *Juvenile and Family Justice Today* (Winter): 16–19.

Pearson, Sarah S., and Sonia Jurich. 2005. *Youth Court: A Community Solution for Embracing At-Risk Youth.* Washington, DC: American Youth Policy Forum.

"Reclaiming Futures Initiative Seeks to Improve Delivery of Services to Juvenile Delinquents." 2007. *Juvenile Justice Update* 13 (3): 9–10.

Shufelt, Jennie L., and Joseph J. Cocozza. 2006 (June). *Youth with Mental Health Disorders in the Juvenile Justice System: Results from a Multi-State Prevalence Study.* Delmar, NY: National Center for Mental Health and Juvenile Justice.

Siegel, Gene, and Gregg Halemba. 2006 (July). *The Importance of Timely Case Processing in Non-Detained Juvenile Delinquency Cases.* Washington, DC: National Center for Juvenile Justice.

Skowyra, Kathleen, and Joseph J. Cocozza. 2006 (June). *A Blueprint for Change: Improving the System Response to Youth with Mental Health Needs Involved with the Juvenile Justice System.* Research Program and Brief. Delmar, NY: National Center for Mental Health and Juvenile Justice.

Skowyra, Kathleen, and Susan Davidson Powell. 2006 (June). *Juvenile Diversion: Programs for Justice-Involved Youth with Mental Health Disorders.* Research and Program Brief. Delmar, NY: National Center for Mental Health and Juvenile Justice.

Snyder, Howard N., and Melissa Sickmund. 2006 (March). *Juvenile Offenders and Victims: 2006 National Report.* Washington, DC: U.S. Department of Justice,

Office of Justice Programs, Office of Juvenile Justice and Delinquency Prevention.

Teplin, Linda A., Karen M. Abram, Gary M. McClelland, Amy A. Mericle, Mina K. Dulcan, and Jason J. Washburn. 2006 (April). *Psychiatric Disorders of Youth in Detention*. Juvenile Justice Bulletin.

Tjaden, Claus D., and Orlando L. Martinez. 2007 (February). "Integrating Assessment Results with Service Provision." *Corrections Today* 69 (1): 76–78.

Widening the Net in Juvenile Justice and the Dangers of Prevention and Early Intervention. 2001 (August). San Francisco: Center on Juvenile and Criminal Justice. Accessed November 23, 2011. http://cjcj.org/files/widening.pdf.

Williams, Valerli, Thomas Grisso, Melissa Valentine, and Nicole Remsburg. 2008 (February). "Mental Health Screening: Pennsylvania's Experience in Juvenile Detention." *Corrections Today* 70 (1): 24–27.

Young, Douglas, Karl Moline, Jill Farrell, and David Bierie. 2006 (January). "Best Implementation Practices: Disseminating New Assessment Technologies in a Juvenile Justice Agency." *Crime & Delinquency* 52 (1): 135–158.

Youth Courts: An Empirical Update and Analysis of Future Organizational and Research Needs. 2008. Washington, DC: Hamilton Fish Institute on School and Community Violence.

The Juvenile Court

> " The first idea that should be grasped concerning the juvenile court is that it came into the world to prevent children from being treated as criminals. "
>
> —Miriam Van Waters

The juvenile court as an American institution has existed for more than 100 years, and its original aim was to offer youthful offenders individualized justice and treatment rather than punishment. States today vary considerably in how they define the purposes of their juvenile courts, with some continuing to adhere to the traditional child welfare philosophy and others shifting to a more punitive, "get tough" approach. Here a handcuffed teen stands before a juvenile judge at a preliminary hearing.

EQUAL JUSTICE UNDER LAW

© Joel Gordon

DO YOU KNOW?

- What three classifications of children are under juvenile court jurisdiction?
- What two factors determine whether the juvenile court has jurisdiction?
- What the possible bases for the declaration of wardship are?
- What the three types of juvenile courts are?
- Who is part of the juvenile courtroom work group?
- What two actions juvenile courts may take on behalf of children in need?

- What two kinds of intervention for abused children are available?
- What the juvenile court process typically involves?
- Who can certify a juvenile as an adult?
- What mechanisms have been created to transfer juveniles to criminal court?
- What a major concern when transferring a juvenile to criminal court is?
- What the results of transferring a juvenile to adult court may be?

CAN YOU DEFINE?

adjudicated

bifurcated hearing

blended sentence

certification

coercive intervention

competent

concurrent jurisdiction

decertification

guardian ad litem (GAL)

jurisdiction

justice model

juvenile court

reverse waiver

statutory exclusion

therapeutic intervention

venue

waiver

welfare model

CHAPTER OUTLINE

Introduction

In the United States justice for juveniles is administered by a separate system with its own juvenile court. The **juvenile court** has jurisdiction over minors (those below the age of majority) alleged to be delinquent, status offenders and dependents or those in need of decisions by the court. Many of the concepts and terms provided in this chapter were briefly introduced in Chapter 1.

A review of that chapter will provide an overview of the juvenile court and place it within the context of the juvenile justice system.

Basic Philosophy and Purpose of Juvenile Court

A philosophy underlying the juvenile court is that of *parens patriae*, a concept previously discussed. The aim of the first juvenile court was to offer youthful offenders individualized justice and treatment rather than punishment. Recall, however, that today there exists not one, but at least 51 different juvenile justice systems. According to the National Center for Juvenile Justice (Snyder and Sickmund 2006, 97), there is considerable variation in the way the states define the purposes of their juvenile courts—not just in their assumptions and underlying philosophies, but also in the approaches they take to the task. Some continue to adhere to the traditional child welfare philosophy, but others have been heavily influenced by shifts occurring in the broader criminal justice community to "get tough" on offenders.

Differences in Purpose Clauses

Many juvenile court purpose clauses have been substantially and repeatedly amended over the years, reflecting philosophical or rhetorical changes in how states approach juvenile delinquency. Most state juvenile court purpose clauses fall into one or more of five thematic categories (Snyder and Sickmund 2006, 98):

- Balanced and restorative justice (BARJ) clauses—At least 16 state purpose clauses incorporate the language of the BARJ movement, which advocates that juvenile courts give balanced attention to three primary interests: public safety, individual offender accountability to victims and the community and skill development to help offenders live law-abiding and productive lives.
- Standard Juvenile Court Act clauses—Seventeen states have purpose clauses modeled after the Standard Juvenile Court Act, first issued in 1925 and revised many times, the declared purpose of which is that "each child coming within the jurisdiction of the court shall receive … the care, guidance and control that will conduce to his welfare and the best interest of the state, and that when he is removed from the control of his parents the court shall secure for him care as nearly as possible equivalent to that which they should have given him."
- Legislative guide clauses—Twelve states use all or most of a more elaborate, multipart purpose clause contained in the *Legislative Guide for Drafting Family and Juvenile Court Acts*, a publication issued by the Children's Bureau in the late 1960s. This guide states four purposes: (1) "to provide for the care, protection and wholesome mental and physical development of children" involved with the juvenile court; (2) "to remove from children committing delinquent acts the consequences of criminal behavior and to substitute therefore a program of supervision, care and rehabilitation"; (3) to remove a child from the home "only when necessary for his welfare or in the interests of public safety"; and (4) to ensure all parties "their constitutional and other legal rights."
- Clauses that emphasize punishment, deterrence, accountability or public safety— At least six states' purpose clauses can be loosely characterized as "tough" in that they veer away from the traditional rehabilitative slant to stress community protection, offender accountability and crime reduction through deterrence or outright punishment, either predominantly or exclusively. This is often a matter of interpretation, however. Texas and Wyoming,

for example, have primarily adopted the multipurpose language of the *Legislative Guide* but have inserted two additional purpose points—the "protection of the public and public safety" and the promotion of "the concept of punishment for criminal acts"—into their list, giving their purpose clauses a decidedly more punitive edge.

■ Clauses with traditional child welfare emphasis—At least four states, plus the District of Columbia, have statutory language emphasizing the promotion of the welfare and best interests of the juvenile as the sole or primary purpose of the juvenile court system. For example, one state says only that accused juveniles should be "treated, not as criminals, but as children in need of aid, encouragement and guidance." Another declares that it intends to institute "all reasonable means and methods that can be established by a humane and enlightened state, solicitous of the welfare of its children, for the prevention of delinquency and for the care and rehabilitation of juvenile delinquents."

The Welfare Model versus the Justice Model

Traditionally, juvenile courts followed the **welfare model**. As states experienced the wave of increasing juvenile violence during the late 1950s and early 1960s, many responded by viewing juveniles not as having problems, but as being problems. These states called for a **justice model** whereby youths would be held accountable and, in some instances, punished. The call for an increasingly punitive juvenile justice system was pushed further still during the 1980s and 1990s, as a new wave of juvenile violence swept through the country. Today, however, despite all of the rhetoric about "getting tough" on youth, most juvenile courts still operate much as they did before the 1980s.

Although this position is contrary to the social welfare philosophy of the traditional juvenile court, it is not necessarily contrary to the way that juvenile

At Issue: What Is the Mission of the Juvenile Court?

Juvenile justice in the United States is at a crossroads of sorts, adrift without a clear sense of purpose or mission. Many are calling for a return to the basics, as when the juvenile court was first established, with a clear focus on rehabilitating children and giving youthful offenders a second chance. Others, however, argue that the "get tough" approach that has permeated the juvenile justice system over the past several decades and increasingly blurred the lines between the juvenile and criminal justice systems has been responsible for reversing the trend of rising juvenile violence and needs to be continued for the protection of society.

The *Federal Advisory Committee on Juvenile Justice Annual Recommendations Report to the President and Congress of the United States* (2007, 3) has an opinion on what the mission of the juvenile court should be:

> Since the Juvenile Justice and Delinquency Prevention (JJDP) Act as was first enacted more than 30 yeas ago, the juvenile justice landscape has changed considerably. The basic premises of the original act remain—to support

state and local programs that prevent juvenile delinquent behavior, to offer core protections to youths in the juvenile justice system and to protect the safety of the community....

One of the first questions that needs to be answered is, "What is the mission of the juvenile justice system? Should it focus on rehabilitation with a goal of reducing future criminal behavior in youths?" There are some who perceive the rehabilitative approach as too soft because it does not provide punitive consequences believed to reduce criminal behavior. However, research by criminologists over the past several years has shown that punitive consequences do not, in fact, reduce criminal behavior and in some cases actually increase it.

Herein lies the challenge to juvenile court: How does the court hold youth accountable for their criminal actions and *punish* them while at the same time maintaining a core belief that adolescents can change their ways and be *rehabilitated*?

court judges have traditionally handled delinquent cases. Treating and caring for youthful criminals, rather than punishing them, is too contrary to our experience and too counterintuitive to be accepted by judges or the general public. A philosophy that denies moral guilt and punishment and views criminals as innocent, hapless victims of bad social environments may be written into law, but this does not mean that it will be followed in practice. Law violators, young and old, should be punished for their crimes. Children understand punishment, and they understand fairness.

Jurisdiction of the Juvenile Court

The **jurisdiction** of the juvenile court refers to the types of cases it is empowered to hear. In almost every state, the juvenile court's jurisdiction extends to three classifications of children: (1) those who are neglected, dependent or abused because those charged with their custody and control mistreat them or fail to provide proper care; (2) those who are incorrigible, ungovernable or status offenders; and (3) those who violate laws, ordinances and codes classified as penal or criminal.

> The jurisdiction of the juvenile court includes children who are neglected or abused, who are unruly or commit status offenses and who are charged with committing serious crimes.

The juvenile court system has been criticized for its "one-pot" jurisdictional approach, in which neglected and abused children, status offenders and youths who commit serious crimes are put into the same "pot." Historically, all three kinds of children were thought to be the products or victims of bad family and social environments. As a result, it was thought, they should be subject, as wards of the court, to the same kind of solicitous, helpful care. The common declaration of status was that of wardship.

The importance of differentiating between criminal and noncriminal conduct committed by juveniles and the limitation on the state's power under *parens patriae* were established more than 100 years ago in *People ex rel. O'Connell v. Turner* (1870). In this case Daniel O'Connell was committed to the Chicago Reform School by an Illinois law that permitted the confinement of "misfortunate youngsters." The Illinois supreme court's decision was that the state's power of *parens patriae* could not exceed that of the parents except to punish crime. The court ordered Daniel to be released from the reform school.

Factors Determining Jurisdiction

State statutes define who is under the juvenile court's jurisdiction. In most states two factors determine the jurisdiction of the court.

> Jurisdiction of the juvenile court is determined by the offender's age and conduct.

The limit for the exercise of the juvenile court's jurisdiction is determined by establishing a maximum age below which children are deemed subject to the improvement process of the court. A *child* is generally defined as a person under the maximum age that establishes the court's jurisdiction. Age 17 is accepted in two thirds of the states and in the District of Columbia (see Table 1.1 in Chapter 1). Many states have lowered their juvenile court age cap in response to acts of violence committed by children younger than the established jurisdictional age. For example, a bill was passed in Texas to reduce from 14 to 10 the age at which youths can be tried in adult criminal court. The bill was motivated by the school shooting in Jonesboro, Arkansas, in which four students and a teacher were killed by two boys, ages 11 and 13.

Seventeen states have established a minimum age below which the court does not have jurisdiction, as shown in Table 10.1. States not listed in the table rely on case law or common law in determining the youngest age at which children come under the jurisdiction of the juvenile court. The rationale behind setting such a minimum age is that very young children are presumed to be incapable of criminal intent and, as such, should not be subject to prosecution and punishment the way older, more culpable individuals are. For instance, hitting (assault) and taking things that don't belong to them (theft) are very common behaviors among toddlers, but our system of justice does not attach any criminal intent to these acts given the extremely young age of the actors, and most would consider it ridiculous to bring such cases before a court. At some point, however, society seeks to begin holding children accountable for their actions, and their crimes.

Several states have moved to raise the upper limit of jurisdictional age to 18, an expansion in juvenile court jurisdiction driven by recent research that shows the human brain is not fully developed until the early to mid-20s. The last part of the brain to develop, the prefrontal cortex (PFC), is that region responsible for higher-order "executive-level" thinking, such as planning and future

Table 10.1 Lowest Age for Original Juvenile Court Jurisdiction in Delinquency Matters (Updated: June 3, 2010)

Age 6	Age 7	Age 8	Age 10	
North Carolina	Maryland	Arizona	Arkansas	Pennsylvania
	Massachusetts		Colorado	South Dakota
	New York		Kansas	Texas
	North Dakota		Louisiana	Vermont
			Minnesota	Wisconsin
			Mississippi	

No Specified Lowest Age				
Alabama	Georgia	Maine	New Jersey	Tennessee
Alaska	Hawaii	Michigan	New Mexico	Utah
California	Idaho	Missouri	Ohio	Virginia
Connecticut	Illinois	Montana	Oklahoma	Washington
Delaware	Indiana	Nebraska	Oregon	West Virginia
DC	Iowa	Nevada	Rhode Island	Wyoming
Florida	Kentucky	New Hampshire	South Carolina	

© 2010 National Center for Juvenile Justice

SOURCE: National Center for Juvenile Justice. http://www.ncjj.org/Topic/Delinquency-Jurisdiction.aspx. Reprinted by permission.

orientation, assessing and managing risk and reward and controlling impulses. Indeed, these new studies merely confirm what parents of teenagers have always known—that adolescents often act first and think later.

Extended jurisdiction mechanisms allow the juvenile court to maintain authority even after a youth has aged beyond the upper age of original jurisdiction, if it is determined the continued provision of sanctions and services is in the best interests of the juvenile and the public. As of June 2010, 34 states and the District of Columbia had statutes that extended juvenile court jurisdiction in delinquency cases until the offender's 21st birthday.

The issue of jurisdiction and age was first questioned in 1905 by the Pennsylvania Supreme Court. Frank Fisher was **adjudicated** (judged) a delinquent in the Philadelphia Juvenile Court. On appeal his lawyer challenged the constitutionality of the legislation establishing the court, urging in particular that Fisher was denied due process in the manner in which he was taken into custody and that he was denied his constitutional right to a jury trial for a felony. The Pennsylvania supreme court upheld a lower court's sanction. The court found that due process, or lack of it, simply was not at issue because its guarantee applied only to criminal cases. The state could, on the other hand, place a child within its protection without any process at all if it saw fit to do so. Recall from Chapter 2 that in *Commonwealth v. Fisher* (1905) the court stated, "To save a child … the legislature surely may provide for the salvation of such a child … by bringing it into the courts of the state without any process at all, for the purpose of subjecting it to the state's guardianship and protection." The court further stated, "The natural parent needs no process to temporarily deprive his child of its liberty by confining it to his own home, to save it and to shield it from the consequences of persistence in a career of waywardness; nor is the state, when compelled as *parens patriae*, to take the place of the father for the same purpose, required to adopt any process as a means of placing its hands upon a child to lead it into one of its courts." Similarly, the court argued, a jury trial could hardly be necessary to determine whether a child deserved to be saved.

In addition to the jurisdictional age, *conduct* determines the juvenile court's jurisdiction. Although the definition of delinquency varies from state to state, the violation of a state law or local ordinance (an act that would be a crime if committed by an adult) is the main category. Youths who violate federal laws or laws from other states or who commit status offenses are considered delinquent and subject to juvenile court jurisdiction.

Other Cases within Juvenile Court Jurisdiction

In addition to having jurisdiction over children who are in need of protection, who commit status offenses or who commit serious crimes, some juvenile courts have authority to handle other issues, such as adoptions, matters of paternity and guardianship. The court's jurisdiction is further extended by provisions in many states that it may exercise its authority over adults in certain cases involving children. Thus in many states the juvenile court may require a parent to contribute to child support, or it may charge and try adults with contributing to the delinquency, neglect, abuse or dependency of a child.

In the News

The state's authority to take children from their families when it deems such measures to be in the best interest of the children is an awesome power. One of the largest child custody cases to date occurred in Texas in April 2008, when the state removed more than 400 children from the Yearning for Zion Ranch, a settlement of the Fundamentalist Church of Jesus Christ of Latter Day Saints (FLDS), in Eldorado, Texas, under allegations the polygamist sect was allowing physical and sexual abuse of the children and, specifically, sanctioning marriages for underage girls. The Texas Supreme Court later ruled that the categorical removal from the ranch and placement into foster care of all of the children by child protective services (CPS) was an overreach of state authority because the state was unable to demonstrate evidence that more than several girls may, in fact, have been abused. The CPS investigation that followed confirmed 12 girls as victims of sexual abuse and neglect based on evidence these girls had been married at ages ranging from 12 to 15.

SOURCE: From *Eldorado Investigation*. A Report from the Texas Department of Family and Protective Services, December 22, 2008.

Although the substantive justice system for juveniles is administered by a specialized court, a great deal of variation exists in juvenile law between different jurisdictions. Before a court with juvenile jurisdiction may declare a youth a ward of the state, it must be convinced that a basis for that wardship exists.

 The possible bases for a declaration of wardship include demonstrating that the child is abused or neglected or has committed a status offense or a criminal act.

Offenses Excluded from Juvenile Court Jurisdiction

Not all offenses committed by young people are within juvenile court jurisdiction. There are no firm assurances that a case will be heard in the juvenile court. The juvenile judge is given discretion to waive jurisdiction in a case and to transfer it to a criminal court if the circumstances and conduct dictate, as will be discussed later.

In some states delinquency is not exclusively within the scope of the juvenile court. Jurisdiction in juvenile court may be concurrent with criminal court jurisdiction—that is, it happens at the same time or may occur in either. Often this **concurrent jurisdiction** is limited by law to cases being handled by either court. Furthermore, certain offenses, such as murder, manslaughter or rape, may be entirely excluded from juvenile court jurisdiction. In states with such laws, children charged with these offenses are automatically tried in criminal court.

Several states have excluded specified offenses from juvenile court jurisdiction. Colorado statutes, for example, state,

> Juvenile court does not have jurisdiction over: children 14 or older charged with crimes of violence classified as Class 1 felonies; children 16 or older who within the previous two years have been adjudicated delinquent for commission of a felony and are now charged with a Class 2 or Class 3 felony or any nonclassified felony punishable by death or life imprisonment.

Several other states exclude youths who have had previous problems with the law.

Venue and Transfer

The geographic location of a trial, called its **venue**, is established by constitutional or statutory provisions. Usually proceedings take place in the county where the juvenile lives. If a proceeding involving a juvenile begins in a different county, the court may ask that the proceedings be transferred to the county where the juvenile lives. Likewise, transfer can be made if the child's residence changes before proceedings begin.

Types of Juvenile Courts

Only in isolated cases have completely separate courts for juveniles been established. Where they have been, it has been primarily in larger cities. Boston, for example, has a specialized court for handling juvenile matters, but its jurisdiction is less than citywide. Elsewhere throughout the country, juvenile court jurisdiction resides in a variety of courts: municipal, county, district, superior or probate. Some are multiple-judge courts; others are served by a single judge.

 Juvenile courts are separated into three types: independent and separate courts, part of a family court and a unit within a trial court.

Characteristics of the Juvenile Court

As early as 1920, Evelina Belden of the U.S. Children's Bureau listed the following as the essential characteristics of the juvenile court:

- Separate hearings for children's cases
- Informal or chancery procedure
- Regular probation service
- Separate detention of children
- Special court and probation records
- Provisions for mental and physical examinations

In addition to the emphasis on informality, other defining characteristics of juvenile court include a focus on the best interest of the child and confidentiality.

In the United States, juvenile courts vary from one jurisdiction to another, manifesting all stages of the system's complex development. Its philosophy, structure and functions are still evolving. Rarely is the court distinct and highly specialized. In rural counties, juvenile court is largely rudimentary. Usually it is part of a court with wider jurisdiction than simply juvenile cases. In Minnesota, for example, juvenile court is a part of the probate court. Judges hold sessions for juveniles at irregular intervals or when the hearings can be held in clusters.

Juvenile Court Personnel

As with the criminal court, various participants are essential to the workings of the juvenile courtroom.

 The juvenile courtroom work group consists of judges, hearing officers, prosecutors, defense attorneys and probation officers.

The *judge* is the central authority in the juvenile court system. However, in many jurisdictions, assignment to the juvenile court is not a highly sought after position, with many judges viewing it as a dead-end assignment. Even judges fully committed to the welfare of juveniles may seek rotation to another assignment to further their careers.

A *hearing officer*, also called a *referee* or *commissioner*, may assist the judge. The hearing officer enters findings and recommendations the judge must confirm to make an order.

In most jurisdictions, the *prosecutor* is the dominant figure in intake processing and is typically responsible for negotiating the disposition of all but the most serious juvenile delinquency cases (Neubauer 2008). Similar to the commonly perceived status of juvenile judges, appointment to be a juvenile prosecutor is not a highly desirable position. Usually juvenile prosecutors are assistant district attorneys right out of law school who hope to be promoted to felony court where they can practice "real law" and convict "real criminals" (Neubauer 2008).

Defense attorneys have a secondary role in juvenile court because of the court's informality. Many juveniles have no representation because juvenile prosecutors have heavy caseloads and tend to prosecute only the most serious cases. In some cases the juvenile court judge appoints a **guardian ad litem (GAL)** to represent youths and their best interests. Although most often an attorney, the GAL can be anyone who is concerned about the youths' best interests.

Probation officers have been a key part of juvenile court since its beginning. They are involved from the early stages of the process on. The probation officer, rather than a judge or prosecutor, usually is the first court official to have contact with the child. In addition, the probation officer often recommends an informal disposition, and in more serious cases, the probation officer's recommendations, along with those of social workers, most often become the court's order.

Court Actions for Neglected and Abused Children

Two distinct kinds of court action may result for neglected or abused children.

 Court action on behalf of neglected and abused children may be noncriminal or criminal.

Court action on behalf of neglected, abused or dependent children may be *noncriminal.* The court seeks to identify whether the child is in danger and, if so, what is needed for the child's protection. The parents may lose custody of the child, be required to pay child support or be ordered to make adjustments in care, custody and control. A second option is *criminal* prosecution of the parents on charges that they have committed a harmful act against the child or have failed to discharge their responsibility, thus placing the child in active danger. This action does not involve the child's status. The scope of the court's position in these referrals is based on the juvenile court's responsibility for the child's welfare under the philosophy of *in loco parentis*, Latin for "in the place of the parent."

Cases of neglect or abuse begin with filing an initial pleading with a court by a CPS caseworker and supervisor, often after consulting with the agency's lawyer (Jones 2006b). Most states allow only CPS to initiate child protection proceedings, but some states allow other public officials and even private citizens to do so.

The petition is usually captioned "*In re* John Doe," meaning it is brought regarding him. The state or county is the petitioner, and the parents, caretakers or child may be referred to as respondents, not defendants. The petition does not charge them with maltreatment.

The first event following the filing of a petition is the initial hearing, also known as a preliminary protective hearing, detention hearing, emergency removal hearing or temporary custody hearing. This hearing is the most critical stage in the court process (Jones 2006b). At this hearing, the judge determines if reasonable efforts have been made to ensure the child's safety, assesses the child's safety and makes a placement decision. Some courts use pretrial conferences, also called settlement conferences, in child maltreatment cases. These conferences allow parents, their attorneys and the child's advocates to come to an agreement before the scheduled adjudication, often saving time and money. Many states are using mediation as a way to settle cases. If a conference is not settled by agreement or through mediation, it goes to adjudication, also called a fact-finding hearing. CPS has the burden of proving the maltreatment alleged in the petition. At the conclusion of adjudication, if the finding is in favor of CPS, the judge enters an order stating specific problems that must be resolved before the child can return home. At the disposition hearing the court decides whether the child needs the court's help and, if so, what services should be provided. Placement is the most important decision made at the dispositional hearing: the child is left with or returned to the parents (under CPS supervision), kept in an existing placement or moved to a new placement. A case plan is also developed.

The next stage is usually a review hearing to evaluate the progress made in completing the case plan. The review hearing report by CPS should state whether the case plan is on target; whether the child's physical, emotional and mental health needs are being met; whether progress has been made toward achieving the case plan's objectives; what reasonable efforts have been made to achieve reunification; whether the child should be returned home and why or why not; what remains to be accomplished before reunification can be offered; what timetable has been established for returning the child home; and whether and how the case plan should be modified.

The final stage of the process is the permanency hearing, which should be held no later than 12 months after a placement other than with the family has occurred. Options include returning the child home; returning the child by a specific date (no longer than three months after the permanency hearing); terminating parental rights; granting legal guardianship; or permanently placing the child with a relative, foster parent or other nonrelative (Jones 2006b). The following are commonly considered grounds for termination of parental rights:

- A child of any age has been in foster care for 15 of the most recent 22 months unless exceptions apply.
- The child is an abandoned infant.
- The parent has committed, aided or attempted the murder or voluntary manslaughter of a sibling of the child.
- The parent has committed a felony assault resulting in serious bodily injury to the child or a sibling of the child.

The National Committee for Prevention of Child Abuse describes two kinds of intervention for deprived children: coercive and therapeutic.

Coercive intervention is out-of-home placement, detainment or mandated therapy or counseling. **Therapeutic intervention** is a recommendation of an appropriate treatment program. Coercive intervention should be used with children only when necessary, either to protect society or to impose an effective treatment plan for the children.

In some states juvenile court is referred to as dependency court. Krinsky (2006, 16) states, "Decisions made in our nation's dependency courts play a critical role in the lives of more than half a million children currently in foster care, often profoundly altering their future." Noting that one in four foster youths reported never attending their own court hearing, Krinsky critically contends, "Courts should be organized to enable children and families to participate in a meaningful way in their own court proceedings." The reason: "Youths are in the best position to provide accurate and compelling insights into their wishes, needs and progress. Putting a human face to the discussion of these issues and experiences forces all concerned to see the system through their eyes." The National Council of Juvenile and Family Court Judges (NCJFCJ Staff Report 2006, 17) echoes, "Ensuring that children are both seen *and* heard in courtrooms is a fundamental goal of the NCJFCJ's Victims Act Model Court Project."

Jones (2006a, 20) notes, "Children under the abuse and neglect jurisdiction of the juvenile court have great needs and face daunting challenges.... Foster youths need and deserve the opportunity to participate as partners with the court in making decisions that have enormous impact on their lives." However, he notes that many judges have well-intentioned concerns about youth participation in court proceedings, believing that the court process is too complex for them to effectively participate. Another concern is that children will miss valuable school time. An additional concern is that information discussed in court may be disturbing and upsetting to children. Jones (2006a) suggests the following techniques judges can use for creating a child-friendly court:

- Help children understand, in simple terms, the purpose of the hearing, what issues might be discussed, what type of information might be helpful for them to share and what issues are appropriate to raise in court.
- Review the court report with the youth for any inaccuracies, clarifications or additions.
- Explain your role as a judge and the issues you can address. Also educate youths about their rights.
- Provide information about how children can advocate for themselves if they have concerns about the legal or social services they are receiving.
- Provide a list of legal terms and definitions that may be used in the hearing.
- Describe the roles of adults who take part in the hearing, including attorneys and family members. Explain what these individuals say or do at the hearing.
- Discuss how long the hearing will last and the time frames for future hearings.
- Ensure that youths have therapeutic and relational support both before and after the hearing to deal in healthy ways with any strong reactions or emotions that surface as the result of the hearing.

Table 10.2 Supreme Court Decisions Affecting Juvenile Court

Case	Year	Holding
Kent v. United States	1966	Established that juvenile transfers to adult court must consider due process and fair play, the child must be represented by an attorney and the attorney must have access to the juvenile records of child
In re Gault	1967	Required that the due process clause of the Fourteenth Amendment apply to proceedings in state juvenile courts, including the right of notice, the right to counsel, the right against self-incrimination and the right to confront witnesses
In re Winship	1970	Established proof beyond a reasonable doubt as the standard for juvenile adjudication proceedings, eliminating lesser standards such as a preponderance of the evidence, clear and convincing proof and reasonable proof
McKeiver v. Pennsylvania	1971	Established that a jury trial is not a required part of due process in the adjudication of a youth as a delinquent by a juvenile court
Breed v. Jones	1975	Established that a juvenile cannot be adjudicated in juvenile court and then tried for the same offense in an adult court (double jeopardy)
Oklahoma Publishing Co. v. District Court	1977	The press may report juvenile court proceedings under certain circumstances
Smith v. Daily Mail Publishing Co.	1979	As long as the information is lawfully obtained, the state cannot restrict the press from publishing a juvenile offender's name unless the restriction serves a substantial state interest
Eddings v. Oklahoma	1982	Defendant's youthful age should be considered a mitigating factor in deciding whether to apply the death penalty
Schall v. Martin	1984	Established that preventive detention fulfills a legitimate state interest of protecting society and juveniles by detaining those who might be dangerous to society or to themselves
Thompson v. Oklahoma	1988	Minimum age for death penalty is set at 16
Stanford v. Kentucky	1989	Minimum age for death penalty is set at 16
Roper v. Simmons	2005	Minimum age for death penalty is set at 18

Youths who are status offenders, delinquents and serious, violent offenders also have the right to be heard during any of the stages in the juvenile justice process. Other important Supreme Court cases presented in Chapter 2 have a direct bearing on juvenile court proceedings, as shown in Table 10.2, and should be kept in mind when looking at the juvenile court and how it differs from criminal court.

The Juvenile Court Process for Delinquency Cases

Changes in the juvenile court interrelate with such factors as industrialization, urbanization, population shifts, the use of natural resources, the rapid development of technology and the acceleration of transportation and communication. All have influenced the family and neighborhood, forcing communities to find new or additional sources of social control. This has given considerable impetus to taking a broader look at the juvenile court process, another version of which is illustrated in Figure 10.1.

Custody, detention and intake were discussed in previous chapters. As noted, the juvenile court process is most often initiated by law enforcement, with police agencies referring roughly two thirds of all arrested youths to a court with juvenile justice jurisdiction and diverting the other one third. The court, in turn, may also choose to divert juveniles out of the formal justice system to receive treatment or services from other agencies. In fact, most cases

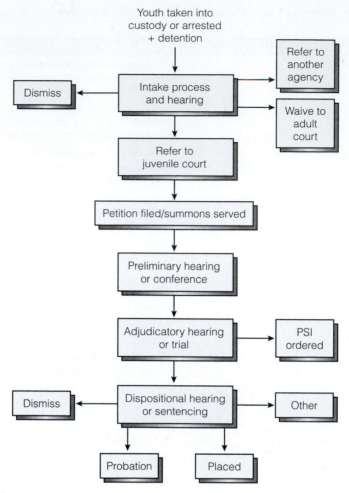

Figure 10.1 The Juvenile Court Process
© Cengage Learning 2013

that enter juvenile court are eventually diverted. Prosecutors, likewise, may file some juvenile cases—usually those involving serious, violent crimes or juveniles with extensive criminal histories—directly to criminal court. In 2008 juvenile courts processed more than 1.6 million delinquency cases, an increase from the 1.15 million cases processed in 1985 but a decrease from a peak of 1.88 million cases processed in 1997 (Table 10.3).

Research has found that first-time court appearance during high school increases the chances of dropping out of high school independent of involvement in delinquency (Sweeten 2006).

 The juvenile court process usually involves the filing of a petition, a detention hearing, an adjudication hearing and a disposition hearing.

The Petition

If the decision is made to file charges against a juvenile, the district attorney files a petition, stating the name, age and address of the minor; what parts of the code sections the minor broke; if the charges are misdemeanors or felonies;

Table 10.3   National Estimates of Juvenile Court Processing for Delinquency Cases—1985, 1997, 2008

	1985	1997	2008
TOTAL delinquency cases processed by juvenile court	1,155,100	1,881,300	1,653,300
Not petitioned	625,900	824,500	729,000
Petitioned	529,200	1,056,900	924,400
Nonadjudicated (probation, other, dismissed)	188,600	397,000	351,600
Adjudicated	333,400	647,700	563,900
Waived to criminal court	7,200	12,200	8,900
Youth Age			
15 and under	707,300	1,100,500	871,300
16	258,800	441,100	421,300
17 and older	188,900	339,700	360,700
Gender			
Male	932,300	1,433,600	1,203,600
Female	222,800	447,700	449,700
Race			
White	843,000	1,276,100	1,043,600
Non-White	312,100	605,200	609,700

SOURCE: Adapted from Charles Puzzanchera and W. Kang. 2011. *Easy Access to Juvenile Court Statistics: 1985–2008*. Accessed November 28, 2011. http://www.ojjdp.gov/ojstatbb/ezajcs/asp/process.asp

the names and address of the parents or guardians; a short statement that says what happened; and whether the minor is in custody or has been released.

The Detention Hearing

After the petition is filed, a detention hearing is held to decide if the minor should be placed in secure custody, as described in Chapter 9. The juvenile can contest the detention decision if the court determines the juvenile should be confined. Valid reasons for detaining a juvenile include that the minor disobeyed a court order, poses a high risk of running away if the court releases the juvenile, needs protection because the home is not a safe environment or the youth has mental or physical problems that warrant the system keeping the juvenile in detention. Approximately 20 percent of all delinquency cases involve detaining a youth between referral to court and the case disposition (Snyder and Sickmund 2006).

Care must be taken when placing a juvenile in detention, and well-constructed policies must be implemented to specify where to detain youths. Inappropriate detention environments can pose significant risks to juveniles. According to one study, "Youth are 19 times more likely to commit suicide in jail than youth in the general population and 36 times more likely to commit suicide in an adult jail than in a juvenile detention facility" ("New Study Details the Dangers" 2008, 11). Furthermore, the study documented evidence that such youths are also more likely to be physically and sexually assaulted.

Although many well-intentioned policies aim to keep youth under age 18 physically separated from adult prisoners, and rightfully so, this sometimes results in the youth being placed in segregation or isolation, leading to exacerbated problems related to depression, anxiety and other mental disorders as well as increasing the risk of suicide. In addition, many detention facilities do not provide any educational services, which, for youths detained for any substantial length of time, can place them at even greater disadvantages for later success.

Just as timely processing of informal/diverted cases is important, so too is timely processing of formal/nondetained cases. Siegel and Halemba (2006, 12) give as an example of timely disposition of juvenile cases the expedited docket used in Tulsa, Oklahoma:

> The Tulsa County Juvenile Court established its special Arraignment Docket in March 2006 to reduce the number of non-detained juveniles who "fall through the cracks." Historically in Tulsa, as in many other places, there have been difficulties with tracking juveniles who are arrested for crimes but not detained. Before the creation of the Arraignment Docket, juveniles arrested and released were not given specific dates for their initial court hearings.... Referred juveniles and their parents would often wait months due to unavailable court dockets and time taken by the District Attorney's office to make filing decisions.

> [Now] when a juvenile is arrested and a decision is made to not detain the youth, the police officer provides notice to the juvenile and parents of an initial semi-formal hearing date. The Arraignment Docket for non-detained juveniles begins at 9 A.M. Mondays through Thursdays. If a juvenile is arrested on a weekday, the arresting officer selects a court date that is one week from the day of arrest. If a juvenile is arrested on a weekend, the court date is set the second Tuesday after the arrest date. The seven- to eleven-day period from point of arrest to the arraignment hearing allows juvenile bureau staff to complete necessary background work to determine if the case should be diverted or otherwise handled informally or to forward the case to the District Attorney's Office for petition filing consideration.

The Adjudication Hearing

At the adjudication hearing (comparable to the trial in the adult system) the youth is questioned about the offense described in the petition. The juvenile's lawyer can cross-examine witnesses, object to evidence, present witnesses and evidence and argue the case to the court. If the evidence is insufficient, the judge may dismiss the case. If enough evidence exists that the child is delinquent, a court date is set for the disposition hearing. Being adjudicated a delinquent is comparable to being convicted in criminal court. It is a formal legal finding of responsibility.

Most juvenile justice professionals recommend a **bifurcated hearing**, which means keeping the adjudication hearing separate from the dispositional hearing.

The Dispositional Hearing

At the dispositional hearing, the judge has to balance how to protect the community, how to fix the harm done and what is in the best interest of the minor. Juvenile courts commonly rely on the juvenile assessment contained in the

© Joel Gordon

Being adjudicated a delinquent is comparable to being convicted in criminal court. It is a formal legal finding of responsibility. Here a female delinquent stands with her attorney before the juvenile judge during an adjudication hearing.

investigative report and accompanying dispositional recommendations provided by probation officers, with judges following these recommendations more than 90 percent of the time. Griffin and Torbet (2002, 68) suggest the following disposition recommendations checklist:

- What risks does the juvenile pose to the community?
- What is the juvenile's attitude toward the victim and the offense?
- What factors and circumstances contributed to the juvenile's offending?
- What skills does the juvenile need to acquire?
- What are the juvenile's (and the juvenile's family's) strengths, resources and receptiveness to intervention?

Based on the investigative report, the judge may place the youth on probation or in a foster home, release the child to the parents, commit the child to an institution, make the child a ward of the court or order one of the diversionary options discussed in Chapter 9. Serious juvenile offenders may be committed to mental institutions, reformatories, prisons or county and state schools for delinquents.

The most common sentence given to juvenile offenders is probation. Of all youths adjudicated delinquent in 2008, 57 percent were placed on formal probation, 28 percent were placed in residential facilities and 15 percent received other dispositions, such as community service, restitution or referral to an outside agency (Puzzanchera and Kang 2011). Specific correctional sanctions are the topic of Chapter 11.

Transferring Juveniles to Criminal Court

Despite the rehabilitative ideal on which it was founded, the juvenile court has always recognized the need for a safety valve to move the tough cases—serious, violent or chronic youthful offenders—to the jurisdiction of the criminal court (Bishop and Frazier 2000; Forst, Fagan, and Vivona 1989). Because it was acknowledged that the bulk of cases involving youth were best served within the juvenile justice system, transfer was historically justified only for those exceptional cases in which the sanctions deemed appropriate exceeded the maximum sanctioning capacities of the juvenile court (Kupchik 2006; Redding and Howell 2000; Zimring 2000). As such, transfer was intended to be reserved for those relatively few cases that involved serious, violent offenders who posed a substantial threat to public safety or chronic offenders who seemed impervious to rehabilitation, having failed to reform after previous treatment attempts (Bishop and Frazier 2000; Steinberg and Cauffman 2000). Transfer was also a way to preserve the political credibility of the juvenile justice system because society expected more severe sanctions be placed on dangerous or repeat offenders, despite their age (Dawson 2000). Today every state has a provision of some sort allowing juveniles who meet specific criteria to be tried in criminal court and face adult sanctions. Some states call this process **certification**, with a juvenile being *certified* as an adult and, as such, eligible to face the same criminal consequences as someone of legal age.

 In some states the court makes the decision to certify a juvenile as an adult. In other states this is done by the prosecutor.

Most often the criteria for such transfers include (1) the youth's age and criminal sophistication, with older juveniles, such as those approaching the age of majority, facing an increased likelihood of transfer, (2) whether the youth can be adequately treated or rehabilitated before the juvenile court's jurisdiction's expires, (3) the youth's previous delinquency history, (4) the success of the court's previous attempts to rehabilitate the youth and (5) the severity of the alleged offense and amount of harm caused.

The rising rate of juvenile violent crime, a trend that began during the mid-1980s and peaked in 1994, fed a public fear and the demand that legislators "do something" to get tough on youthful predators. As a result, during the mid-1990s, 46 states passed legislation making it easier to transfer juvenile offenders to adult court.

Despite the allowance of such transfers, analysis of delinquency case processing data shows that a relatively small percentage of all juveniles arrested and formally placed into the justice system are transferred to adult criminal court. Of the estimated 1.65 million delinquency cases brought before the juvenile court in 2008, only 8,900 (0.54 percent) were waived to criminal court (Puzzanchera and Kang 2011).

Primary Transfer Mechanisms

The authority to order juvenile transfer has historically rested with the judicial branch. Starting in the 1970s, the nature of transfer began to change considerably, with new mechanisms created that vested waiver authority in the executive and legislative branches as well. Thus, for the past 30 years, the primary transfer methods have been judicial waiver, prosecutorial waiver or discretion and legislative waiver, also called statutory exclusion (Bishop and Frazier 2000; Feld 2000; Kupchik 2006; McGowan et al. 2007; Zimring 2000).

 Juveniles may be transferred to criminal court via three basic mechanisms: judicial waiver, prosecutorial discretion and statutory exclusion.

In addition to these three transfer mechanisms, many states also have reverse waiver or decertification provisions, "once an adult/always an adult" laws and blended sentencing statutes (Griffin et al. 2011). Table 10.4 summarizes the mechanisms states use to transfer juveniles to criminal court, as of the end of the 2009 legislative session.

Judicial Waiver   Judicial **waiver** is a transfer mechanism whereby the juvenile court judge is allowed the discretion to make an individual determination about whether a juvenile who meets statutory criteria should be tried in juvenile court or, instead, be waived to criminal court. Judicial waiver, alternately known as *remanding* or *binding over for criminal prosecution*, is the most common transfer provision, with 46 states allowing for this transfer mechanism as of the end of the 2009 legislative session (Griffin et al. 2011). Judicial waiver may be discretionary, presumptive or mandatory; the prevalence of their use is shown in Table 10.4.

Discretionary judicial waiver is the original transfer mechanism, in which a juvenile court judge makes an individualized, offender-based sorting decision to move a case to the jurisdiction of the criminal court (Kupchik 2006). This is the traditional "safety valve" transfer mechanism that allows the most serious, violent or chronic offenders—those for whom the minimum sanctions deemed appropriate exceed the maximum capacities of the juvenile justice system—to receive more proportionate handling in the criminal justice system (Bishop and Frazier 2000; Dawson 2000; Forst, Fagan, and Vivona 1989).

In *presumptive judicial waiver*, the transfer decision remains in the hands of the juvenile court judge but is weighted in favor of transfer, with the burden of proof shifting to the youthful respondent, who is required to provide persuasive evidence that the case belongs in juvenile, not criminal, court (Dawson 2000; Griffin 2003). In this transfer scheme, the legislature sets statutory criteria pertaining to the offense, the offender's age or the offender's prior record (Griffin 2003). Absent the requisite evidence, the judge will *presume*, theoretically, that the case should be waived.

Mandatory judicial waiver functions like statutory exclusion, explained shortly, by removing the juvenile court judge's discretion to make transfer decisions and requiring that offenders who meet certain criteria be waived directly to criminal court (Griffin 2003). Fifteen states had mandatory waiver provisions as of the end of the 2009 legislative session (Griffin et al. 2011).

Table 10.4 Mechanisms Used to Transfer Juveniles to Adult Court

Most States Have Multiple Ways to Impose Adult Sanctions on Juveniles

State	Judicial Waiver			Prosecutorial Discretion	Statutory Exclusion	Reverse Waiver	Once an Adult Always an Adult	Blended Sentencing	
	Discretionary	Presumptive	Mandatory					Juvenile	Criminal
Total States	**45**	**15**	**15**	**15**	**29**	**24**	**34**	**14**	**18**
Alabama	•				•		•		
Alaska	•	•			•			•	
Arizona	•			•	•	•	•		
Arkansas	•			•		•		•	•
California	•	•		•	•	•	•		•
Colorado	•	•		•				•	•
Connecticut			•			•		•	
Delaware	•		•		•	•	•		
Dist. of Columbia	•	•			•		•		
Florida	•			•	•				•
Georgia	•		•	•	•	•			
Hawaii	•						•		
Idaho	•				•				•
Illinois	•	•	•		•		•	•	
Indiana	•		•		•		•		
Iowa	•				•	•	•		
Kansas	•	•					•	•	
Kentucky	•		•			•			•
Louisiana	•		•	•	•				
Maine	•	•					•		
Maryland	•				•	•	•		
Massachusetts					•			•	•
Michigan	•			•			•	•	•
Minnesota	•	•			•		•	•	
Mississippi	•				•	•	•		
Missouri	•						•		•
Montana				•	•	•			
Nebraska				•		•			•
Nevada	•	•			•		•		
New Hampshire	•	•					•		
New Jersey	•	•	•						
New Mexico					•			•	•
New York					•	•			
North Carolina	•		•				•		
North Dakota	•	•	•				•		
Ohio	•		•				•	•	
Oklahoma	•			•	•	•	•		•
Oregon	•				•	•	•		

Pennsylvania	•	•			•	•	•		
Rhode Island	•	•	•				•	•	
South Carolina	•		•		•				
South Dakota	•				•	•	•		
Tennessee	•					•	•		
Texas	•						•	•	
Utah	•	•			•		•		
Vermont	•			•	•	•			•
Virginia	•		•	•		•	•		•
Washington	•				•		•		
West Virginia	•		•						•
Wisconsin	•				•	•	•		•
Wyoming	•			•		•			

SOURCE: Patrick Griffin, Sean Addie, Benjamin Adams, and Kathy Firestine. 2011 (September). *Trying Juveniles as Adults: An Analysis of State Transfer Laws and Reporting*, p. 3. Washington, DC: Office of Juvenile Justice and Delinquency Prevention, Juvenile Offenders and Victims National Report Series Bulletin. (NCJ 232434) https://www.ncjrs.gov/pdffiles1/ojjdp/232434.pdf.

Table 10.5 shows the characteristics of judicially waived delinquency cases in 1994 and 2007 and how the likelihood of judicial waiver among petitioned delinquency cases was lower in 2007 than in 1994—the year violent juvenile crime peaked—across all offense categories and demographic groups.

Prosecutorial Discretion   *Prosecutorial discretion*, also referred to as *prosecutorial waiver* or *direct file*, places the transfer decision in the hands of the prosecutor. Although the legislature grants this transfer authority and sets predetermined eligibility criteria, the end decision of whether to waive a youth falls to the prosecutor, without the requirement of any judicial oversight or input (Dawson 2000; Kupchik 2006). This transfer mechanism is seen as a natural extension of the prosecutor's authority to decide which cases to charge by expanding their discretion to include whether to charge a youth as a juvenile or an adult (McCarthy 1993). Fifteen states have direct file laws (Griffin et al. 2011).

Statutory Exclusion   Another common way juveniles are transferred to criminal court is through **statutory exclusion**, also called *legislative waiver*, a mechanism that describes instances where a state has passed legislation specifically banning certain youthful offenders from being tried as juveniles, effectively bypassing the juvenile court entirely and sending certain qualifying offenders directly to criminal court (Feld 2000; Griffin 2003; McGowan et al. 2007). In these transfer schemes, the state legislature designates which juvenile offenses and offenders to waive to criminal court, with transfer criteria generally based on the seriousness of the offense, the offender's age and the offender's prior record (Dawson 2000). Unlike judicial waiver, legislative waiver is devoid of individualized offender assessment; juveniles who meet the criteria on paper are transferred (Dawson 2000; Feld 2000; McCarthy 1993). Some states have mandatory criminal court requirements for 14-, 15- and 16-year-olds for certain

Table 10.5 Characteristics of Delinquency Cases Judicially Waived (1994 and 2007)

Offense/demographic	Profile of judicially waived delinquency cases		Percentage of petitioned cases judicially waived to criminal court	
	1994	2007	1994	2007
Total Cases Waived	**13,100**	**8,500**	**13,100**	**8,500**
Most Serious Offense	**100%**	**100%**		
Person	42	48	2.6%	1.7%
Property	37	27	1.1	0.7
Drugs	12	13	2.1	1.0
Public order	9	11	0.6	0.3
Gender	**100%**	**100%**		
Male	95	90	1.7	1.1
Female	5	10	0.4	0.4
Age at Time of Referral	**100%**	**100%**		
15 or younger	13	142	0.3	0.2
16 or older	87	88	3.0	1.7
Race/Ethnicity	**100%**	**100%**		
White	53	59	1.2	0.9
Black	44	37	1.8	1.0

NOTE: These data on cases judicially waived from juvenile court to criminal court do not include cases filed directly in criminal court via other transfer mechanisms.

SOURCE: Analysis by Griffin et al. Patrick Griffin, Sean Addie, Benjamin Adams, and Kathy Firestine. 2011 (September). *Trying Juveniles as Adults: An Analysis of State Transfer Laws and Reporting*, p. 10. Washington, DC: Office of Juvenile Justice and Delinquency Prevention, Juvenile Offenders and Victims National Report Series Bulletin) of *Juvenile Court Statistics 2007*, by Charles Puzzanchera, Benjamin Adams, and Melissa Sickmund. 2010. Pittsburgh, PA: National Center for Juvenile Justice.

serious, violent offenses, such as murder and rape. These policies effectively tie judges' hands and remove all judicial discretion in determining whether a young offender would be better handled in the juvenile system. The largest number of juvenile transfers to criminal court results from statutory exclusion provisions, which currently exist in 29 states (Griffin et al. 2011). Table 10.6 shows the states that had statutory exclusion laws at the end of the 2009 legislative session and which offenses the laws applied to.

Reverse Waiver or Decertification   Just as the juvenile court has recognized the need for a "safety valve" to transfer particularly difficult cases to criminal court, the reciprocal need exists for a "fail safe" to return to juvenile court jurisdiction those cases improperly or unjustly transferred to criminal court. One basic type of fail-safe mechanism is **reverse waiver**, also called **decertification** (Bishop and Frazier 2000; Griffin, 2003). This provision is often present in jurisdictions where direct file or statutory exclusion laws are used to give the criminal court exclusive jurisdiction over juveniles who commit specified serious crimes, such as murder. Reverse waiver corrects instances where the net widening effects of prosecutorial or legislative waiver have transferred a juvenile case that, in the criminal court judge's opinion, would be better handled

Table 10.6   Many States Exclude Certain Serious Offenses from Juvenile Court Jurisdiction

State	Any criminal offense	Certain felonies	Capital crimes	Murder	Certain person offenses	Certain property offenses	Certain drug offenses	Certain weapon offenses
Alabama		16	16				16	
Alaska					16	16		
Arizona		15		15	15			
California				14	14			
Delaware		15						
Florida				16	NS	16	16	
Georgia				13	13			
Idaho				14	14	14	14	
Illinois		15		13	15			15
Indiana		16		16	16		16	16
Iowa		16					16	16
Louisiana				15	15			
Maryland			14	16	16			16
Massachusetts				14				
Minnesota				16				
Mississippi		13	13					
Montana				17	17	17	17	17
Nevada	16*	NS		NS	16			
New Mexico				15				
New York				13	13	14		14
Oklahoma				13				
Oregon				15	15			
Pennsylvania				NS	15			
South Carolina		16						
South Dakota		16						
Utah		16		16				
Vermont				14	14	14		
Washington				16	16	16		
Wisconsin				10	10			

* In Nevada, the exclusion applies to any juvenile with a previous felony adjudication, regardless of the current offense charged, if the current offense involves the use or threatened use of a firearm.

NOTES: An entry in the column below an offense category means that there is at least one offense in that category that is excluded from juvenile court jurisdiction. The number indicates the youngest possible age at which a juvenile accused of an offense in that category is subject to exclusion. "NS" means no age restriction is specified for an offense in that category. Table information is as of the end of the 2009 legislative session.

Patrick Griffin, Sean Addie, Benjamin Adams, and Kathy Firestine. 2011 (September). *Trying Juveniles as Adults: An Analysis of State Transfer Laws and Reporting*, p. 6. Washington, DC: Office of Juvenile Justice and Delinquency Prevention, Juvenile Offenders and Victims National Report Series Bulletin. (NCJ 232434).

by the juvenile court (Bishop and Frazier 2000). For example, New York statutes specify that juvenile court jurisdiction:

> Excludes children 13 or older charged with second-degree murder and children 14 or older charged with second-degree murder, felony murder, kidnapping in the first degree, arson in the first or second degree, assault in

the first degree, manslaughter in the first degree, rape in the first degree, sodomy in the first degree, aggravated sexual abuse, burglary in the first or second degree, robbery in the first or second degree, attempted murder, or attempted kidnapping in the first degree, unless such case is transferred to the juvenile court from the criminal court.

To decertify a case, the burden of proof is usually on the juvenile and defense council to show that there are mitigating circumstances and that the case is more appropriate for juvenile court processing. However, this process is rarely invoked. Older juveniles and those with a great number of risk factors are more likely to remain in the adult criminal justice system.

Once an Adult/Always an Adult   Thirty-four states have laws that require juveniles who have been convicted in criminal court to be automatically treated as an adult for any further crimes committed (see Table 10.4). In other words, a criminal conviction renders a juvenile an "adult" forever, and all subsequent, post-transfer offenses will be processed in the adult criminal justice system (Griffin et al. 2011). However, several states have exception clauses to these "once an adult/always an adult" laws. For example, Iowa, California and Oregon require that the juvenile involved be at least 16; and Maryland, Michigan, Minnesota and Texas laws state that the "once an adult/always an adult" rule applies only to post-transfer felonies (Griffin et al. 2011).

Blended Sentencing   Blended sentences have become increasingly popular alternatives to transfer, focusing not on the trial forum, as is the case with the preceding types of transfer mechanisms, but, instead, on the correctional system (Griffin 2003). A **blended sentence** allows courts to "blend" juvenile and adult sanctions and effectively extend their jurisdiction beyond the traditional age boundary that demarcates juveniles and adults (Redding and Howell 2000).

The two main types of blended sentences are juvenile and criminal blended sentences, with inclusive and exclusive subdivisions within each category (Redding and Howell 2000). Juvenile blended sentences originate in the juvenile court. Under a juvenile-inclusive model, the court is permitted to impose *both* a juvenile *and* an adult sentence, with the adult sanction being invoked only if the offender fails to satisfactorily complete the juvenile portion of the sentence (Griffin 2003; Redding 2003; Redding and Howell 2000). In a juvenile-exclusive model, the juvenile court imposes *either* a juvenile *or* an adult sentence.

In a criminal blended sentencing scheme, original jurisdiction lies with the criminal court. Criminal-inclusive models allow the criminal court to impose *both* a juvenile *and* an adult sentence, with the adult sanction suspended if the offender satisfactorily completes the juvenile portion of the sentence (Griffin 2003; Redding 2003; Redding and Howell 2000). In a criminal-exclusive model, the criminal court imposes *either* a juvenile *or* an adult sentence.

Minnesota was the first state to use a blended sentence for youths who committed violent, but not extremely violent or murderous, crimes. In Minnesota, if youths comply with the juvenile sentence, which usually includes longer, more intense supervision than a typical juvenile sentence, the criminal (adult) portion of the sentence is suspended and the youth will be released after serving the juvenile sentence without the stigma of a criminal record. If, however, the youth does not successfully adhere to the terms of the juvenile disposition, the criminal (adult) portion of the sanction is invoked. As of the end of the 2009 legislative session, 26 states had either a juvenile or criminal blended sentencing structure in place, with some states having both (Griffin et al. 2011).

Critics of blended sentencing contend that this is a return to "getting soft" on juvenile crime. In reality, however, blended sentencing exposes youthful offenders to the possibility of receiving harsh criminal penalties and, in this regard, is similar in gravity to the outright transfer of juveniles to criminal court. Consequently, juveniles facing a court that uses blended sentencing are given the same due process protections afforded adult criminal defendants, including the right to be tried by a jury (Snyder and Sickmund 2006).

The Issues of Competency and Culpability

Two issues that are receiving increased attention of late are those concerning juvenile competency and culpability, two distinctly different constructs that are commonly confused, even by those supposedly well versed in criminal law: "Adjudicative competence refers to the ability of an individual to function effectively as a defendant in a criminal or delinquency proceeding. In contrast, determinations of culpability focus on the defendant's blameworthiness in engaging in the criminal conduct and on whether and to what extent he will be held responsible" (Scott and Steinberg 2008, 152).

As discussed in previous chapters, emerging brain research has revealed that the parts of the human brain responsible for "executive functions" such as risk and consequence analysis, future planning and impulse control—behaviors all heavily connected to delinquency and criminal conduct—are still developing well into a person's early 20s. These findings have led many juvenile justice scholars to argue that young law violators, by virtue of their inherent developmental immaturity, simply lack the same degree of blameworthiness, or culpability, that adult offenders do. This is not to say that juveniles should not be held responsible for their actions, but it does challenge the practice of transferring youth to an adult system and holding them to the same standards of criminal blameworthiness to which offenders in their 20s, 30s and beyond are held.

Although transfer to criminal court is relatively infrequent, when it does occur, juveniles go through the same procedures and have the same constitutional rights as adults tried in a criminal court. This also means being held to the same competency standards as adults. However, a criminal proceeding meets due process requirements *only* when the defendant is legally **competent** to stand trial, including the ability to assist counsel and to participate in the process and make decisions about his or her rights. Under law a person's competence is conceptualized as a specific functional ability. The word *competent* is usually followed by the phrase "to …" rather than presented as a general attribute of a person. An adult who is deemed incompetent to stand trial for a specific offense may still be presumed competent to function as a custodial parent or to manage financial affairs. For the adult, specific incompetence must be proved case by case.

Conversely minors are presumed incompetent for most purposes, without any concern for whether they have the capacity to make required decisions in a practical sense. Juveniles who are deemed legally competent for one purpose are often considered generally incompetent in other decision-making contexts. For example, persons under legal age are generally prohibited from executing contracts, consenting to most medical treatment and procedures, marrying, voting and so on. In many states, persons under age 16 are not allowed to drive. Youths under age 18 are ineligible to join the military. Persons under age 21 are not allowed to drink alcohol legally. Yet some states are willing to transfer to criminal court and try as adults 14-year-olds charged with serious violent crimes. Thus the concept of competency for such youthful offenders necessarily becomes an issue.

In general, there has been little recognition that youths in criminal court may be incompetent because of developmental immaturity. In addition, until now, little meaningful data have been available regarding the capacities of adolescents relevant for adjudicative competence. However, basic research on cognitive and psychosocial development suggests that some youths will manifest deficits in legally relevant abilities similar to deficits seen in adults with mental disability, but for reasons of immaturity rather than mental disorder. In addition, many youths involved in the criminal justice system are of below-average intelligence and are more likely to comply with requests by authority figures. Nonetheless, competency standards for juveniles facing transfer remain relatively low, essentially requiring a "yes" to the question, "Did the juveniles appreciate the nature of their act?"

 A major concern when transferring a juvenile to criminal court is that the juvenile may not be competent to stand trial there.

Consequences of Transferring Juveniles to Adult Court

Waiver or certification is of paramount importance because it may result in far more severe consequences to the juvenile than would have occurred had the youth remained under juvenile court jurisdiction. Furthermore, when waiver occurs certain procedural guidelines apply. For example, no statements made by the child before the transfer may be used against him or her in the criminal proceedings after the transfer. In this regard, such delinquency cases are handled in basically the same way as those involving adult offenders.

Without a doubt, some juveniles need to be treated as adults and transferred to the criminal courts for handling. However, the proliferation of transfer laws since the 1980s has occurred amid a concerning lack of empirical data as to the efficacy of such mechanisms in achieving their purported goals (Bishop and Frazier 2000; Fass and Pi 2002; Zimring and Fagan 2000). Only during the past decade and a half have studies been done to determine the impacts transfer has on the particular juveniles involved and on the criminal justice system and society in general. Although the research is still very patchy in many areas, a picture is beginning to emerge regarding the overall effectiveness of juvenile transfer policy, and many jurisdictions are now seriously reconsidering their transfer policies in the wake of mounting evidence that such practices are falling short of their intended effects (Steiner, Hemmens, and Bell 2006). In fact, the Centers for Disease Control and Prevention (CDC) has taken an official stance in recommending juveniles not be transferred to criminal court (Shepherd 2007, 7).

Data show that youth transferred to and convicted in criminal court have a high likelihood of being incarcerated (Applegate, Davis, and Cullen 2009; Bishop and Frazier 2000). Results are mixed, however, regarding the length of sentences received by transferred youth versus those retained in the juvenile justice system. According to some sources, transferred youth generally serve longer terms than they would have had they been retained (Bishop and Frazier 2000; Forst, Fagan, and Vivona 1989; Redding 2003). In contrast, Feld (2000, 119) asserts, "Despite the legislative desire to increase the sentences imposed on juveniles tried as adults, many youths receive shorter sentences as adults than juvenile court judges could have imposed on them as delinquents."

Regardless of whether transferred juveniles serve longer or shorter prison terms than retained juveniles, the fact that they are incarcerated as adults often carries substantial negative consequences. Most (44) states allow courts to sentence transferred juveniles to adult facilities, commonly medium- or maximum-security institutions that are ill-equipped to meet the social, educational and other age-related needs of these young offenders (Bishop and Frazier 2000; Redding 2003). For many of the juveniles held in these adult prisons, daily life consists of violence and victimization (Forst, Fagan, and Vivona 1989), where young offenders are exposed to far greater risk of physical abuse, sexual assault and suicide than they would face in a juvenile facility (Bishop and Frazier 2000; Feld 2000; McGowan et al. 2007; Redding 2003). In these settings, young offenders are at risk of learning "social rules and norms that [legitimate] domination, exploitation and retaliation" (Bishop and Frazier 2000, 263), and they are likely to be socialized into true career criminals by older, more experienced inmates (Redding 2003).

Most youths prosecuted in criminal court and imprisoned as adults will return to society at a relatively young age, regardless of the sentence received (Corriero 2006), so this prisonization effect must be addressed and mitigated if transfer policy is to retain a high degree of utility. This is not to imply that incarceration should never be used with juveniles. Without question, there are serious, violent youth for whom public safety demands a lengthy and secure prison term (Corriero 2006; Feld 1981). However, policymakers must remain cognizant of the pitfalls associated with locking up young offenders, away from prosocial contacts but in daily contact with negative role models from whom they may learn a great deal of antisocial behavior.

Policymakers have generated strong rhetoric around the claim that tougher transfer laws better serve the crime control goal of deterrence because the risk of severe consequences discourages youth from offending (Bishop and Frazier 2000; McGowan et al. 2007; Redding 2003; Steiner, Hemmens, and Bell 2006). Limited evidence exists that the threat of such sanctions curbs adolescent offending when youths know they have "aged up" to criminal court jurisdiction (Glassner et al. 1983), and a small handful of studies have concluded that transfer laws have a modest deterrent effect (Redding 2003; Steiner, Hemmens, and Bell 2006). However, the bulk of the literature reveals a lack of empirical evidence to support a general deterrent effect from juvenile transfer policies (Bishop and Frazier 2000; McGowan et al. 2007; Singer and McDowall 1988; Steiner, Hemmens, and Bell 2006).

Recidivism is often used as a metric with which to measure the specific deterrent effect of an intervention, and an inverse relationship is hypothesized. A low level of re-offending may be attributed to a high level of specific deterrence, although this is overly simplistic and myriad other factors, such as rehabilitation or natural desistance, may be at play. Evidence shows that most adolescent-limited (AL) offenders—and AL offenders constitute the vast majority of juvenile offenders—will naturally "age out" of criminal activity after one or two contacts and by age 18, regardless of any intervention provided by the justice system (Feld 2000; Redding 2003; Redding and Howell 2000). Thus, although policymakers may wish to credit the deterrent effect of a particular crime control policy for a decline in criminal offending, in many cases desistance is more likely the result of simple maturation.

Nonetheless, legislators have passed juvenile transfer laws with the expectation that such reform will lower the rate of juvenile offending through the mechanism of deterrence. However, several large-scale comparative studies have found evidence that juveniles tried in criminal court for violent person offenses have *higher* post-release recidivism rates and re-offend more quickly than do those retained in juvenile court for similar offenses (Bishop and Frazier 2000; Redding 2003; Redding and Howell 2000; Steinberg and Cauffman 2000; Steiner, Hemmens, and Bell 2006). Another study found that the higher recidivism rates seen among juveniles transferred for violent offenses were magnified when the criminal disposition included incarceration (McGowan et al. 2007). This evidence casts significant doubt on the claim that juvenile transfer policy can effectively deter serious crime by youth and, instead, suggests that the result of transfer may be diminished community protection over time (Redding 2003).

 Evidence shows that transferring juveniles to adult court results in higher rates of conviction, greater likelihood of incarceration and greater risk of the youths being victimized. Furthermore, transfer to criminal court has been found to have little deterrent effect on youthful offenders and has been shown to actually increase juvenile recidivism.

Some studies have focused on how transfers negatively affect the maturation process of juveniles in mid-adolescence to late adolescence and interfere with their abilities to accomplish vital developmental tasks, thereby heightening their risk of failure once released from the justice system:

> During this period (and into early adulthood), individuals normally make substantial progress in acquiring and coordinating skills in several areas that are essential to making the transition to the conventional roles that are part of self-sufficient adulthood. First, they acquire basic educational and vocational skills that enable them to function in the workplace as productive members of society. They also acquire the social skills necessary to establish stable intimate relationships and cooperate in groups. Finally, they begin to learn to behave responsibly without external supervision and to set meaningful personal goals for themselves. (Scott and Steinberg 2008, 58)

The *Federal Advisory Committee on Juvenile Justice (FACJJ) Annual Recommendations Report to the President and Congress of the United States* (2007, 5) states, "FACJJ believes that the majority of juvenile offenders should be handled by the juvenile justice system, not the criminal justice system. This belief supports a recommendation by the National Council of Juvenile and Family Court Judges that the decision about whether to transfer a juvenile charged with a serious crime to criminal court should be made by a juvenile delinquency court judge after an individual hearing with a youth who is represented by qualified council."

A study of how the public views juvenile transfers to criminal court found that public support of such policies rests on several factors, including offense and offender characteristics, views on the appropriate aims of juvenile sentencing, perceptions of juvenile maturity and expectations about the results of transferring juvenile cases to the adult criminal justice system (Applegate, Davis, and Cullen 2009). The study concluded that citizens want juvenile transfer used sparingly and selectively, as it is currently used, and that support is greatest when the public believes that the adult system can provide effective rehabilitation as well as punishment.

Juveniles and Capital Punishment

The death penalty has always been one of the most contentious issues in discussions about American justice. Capital punishment as applied to youthful offenders has, until recently, been handled in very different ways by the individual states, with some states allowing the execution of persons who were as young as 16 at the time of their offense and other states banning the death penalty for any offender, regardless of age.

The American Bar Association took an official stance against executing juveniles when it adopted the following policy statement in August 1983: "BE IT RESOLVED, That the American Bar Association opposes, in principle, the imposition of capital punishment upon any person for any offense committed while under the age of eighteen (18)." Nonetheless, more than 200 juvenile death sentences were handed down between 1973 and 2005, with the last execution for an offense committed as a juvenile occurring in 2003, when Oklahoma put to death 32-year-old Scott Allen Hain, who was 17 at the time of his crime. Previous editions of this text discussed the minimum ages authorized by the various states in which capital sentencing was used and presented data on how many juveniles were currently on death row. This has changed, however, in the wake of *Roper v. Simmons* (2005).

Before this case, the Supreme Court had upheld the constitutionality of capital punishment for juvenile defendants age 16 and older at the time of their crime. In *Thompson v. Oklahoma* (1988) the Court ruled that our society's standards of decency did *not* permit the execution of any offender under the age of 16 at the time of the crime. In *Stanford v. Kentucky* (1989) the Court held that execution for crimes committed at ages 16 and older did not necessarily violate the Eighth Amendment prohibition against "cruel and unusual punishment." For 15 years following *Stanford*, 19 states permitted the sentencing to death of defendants convicted of capital crimes committed while they were 16 or 17 years old. Five states allowed capital punishment for defendants aged 17 or older, and 14 states set age 16 as the minimum age for death penalty eligibility. The remaining 21 death penalty jurisdictions had expressly set a minimum age of 18 for imposition of the capital sentences.

Then came *Roper*, which effectively made moot the issue of the juvenile death penalty. Although some still advocate the appropriateness of this sanction, the Court has determined the practice of sentencing juveniles to death to be unconstitutional. This case began in 1993 when 17-year-old Christopher Simmons, a White male with no prior criminal record or history of violence, kidnapped neighbor Shirley Crook during a burglary at her Missouri home, hogtied her and then pushed her off a bridge into the river below. The coroner ruled she died by drowning. According to reports, Simmons had bragged to friends that he could get away with the murder because of his age. The trial jury, however, disagreed and sentenced Simmons to death.

On appeal, Simmons's new lawyer argued that the jury, at sentencing, should have been informed of the numerous mitigating circumstances involving his client—that Simmons had a long family history of abuse, had a below-average IQ, suffered from alcohol and drug abuse and had been diagnosed with a personality disorder—which, when considered collectively, would most likely have led the jury to choose a sentence of life in prison without parole (LWOP) instead of the death penalty.

After several appeals, the case had worked its way before the Supreme Court. In 2005 a tightly divided Court ruled 5–4 to overturn the capital sentence, declaring the execution of those who committed crimes as juveniles to be in violation of the Eighth and Fourteenth Amendments and an affront to society's evolving standards of decency. In reaching their decision, the Court cited public opinion polls that showed a steady decline in support for capital punishment for juvenile offenders and noted that even in those states that allowed capital punishment of juveniles, very few actually imposed this ultimate punishment. In a lengthy opinion, Justice Kennedy, writing for the majority, stated in part,

> Capital punishment must be limited to those offenders who commit "a narrow category of the most serious crimes" and whose extreme culpability makes them "the most deserving of execution." ... In any capital case a defendant has wide latitude to raise as a mitigating factor "any aspect of [his or her] character or record and any of the circumstances of the offense that the defendant proffers as a basis for a sentence less than death." ...
>
> The death penalty may not be imposed on certain classes of offenders, such as juveniles under 16, the insane, and the mentally retarded, no matter how heinous the crime.…
>
> The reality that juveniles still struggle to define their identity means it is less supportable to conclude that even a heinous crime committed by a juvenile is evidence of irretrievably depraved character. From a moral standpoint it would be misguided to equate the failings of a minor with those of an adult, for a greater possibility exists that a minor's character deficiencies will be reformed. Indeed, "The relevance of youth as a mitigating factor derives from the fact that the signature qualities of youth are transient; as individuals mature, the impetuousness and recklessness that may dominate in younger years can subside." ...
>
> Once the diminished culpability of juveniles is recognized, it is evident that the penological justifications for the death penalty apply to them with lesser force than to adults.…

When a juvenile offender commits a heinous crime, the state can exact forfeiture of some of the most basic liberties, but the state cannot extinguish his life and his potential to attain a mature understanding of his own humanity.

Drawing the line at 18 years of age is subject, of course, to the objections always raised against categorical rules. The qualities that distinguish juveniles from adults do not disappear when an individual turns 18. By the same token, some under 18 have already attained a level of maturity some adults will never reach. For the reasons we have discussed, however, a line must be drawn. The plurality opinion in *Thompson* drew the line at 16. In the intervening years the *Thompson* plurality's conclusion that offenders under 16 may not be executed has not been challenged. The logic of *Thompson* extends to those who are under 18. The age of 18 is the point where society draws the line for many purposes between childhood and adulthood. It is, we conclude, the age at which the line for death eligibility ought to rest. (*Roper v. Simmons* 2005)

A Debate: Juveniles and the Death Penalty

Roper v. Simmons categorically prohibits capital punishment for offenders who commit crimes before age 18. This decision has caused an avalanche of debate. Consider both sides of the argument and the pros and cons associated with such a categorical ruling.

"It is difficult even for expert psychologists to differentiate between the juvenile offender whose crime reflects unfortunate yet transient immaturity, and the rare juvenile offender whose crime reflects irreparable corruption.... As we understand it, this difficulty underlies the rule forbidding psychiatrists from diagnosing any patient under 18 as having antisocial personality disorder, a disorder also referred to as psychopathy or sociopathy, and which is characterized by callousness, cynicism, and contempt for the feelings, rights, and suffering of others.... If trained psychiatrists with the advantage of clinical testing and observation refrain, despite diagnostic expertise, from assessing any juvenile under 18 as having antisocial personality disorder, we conclude that States should refrain from asking jurors to issue a far graver condemnation—that a juvenile offender merits the death penalty" (Justice Kennedy, excerpt from the opinion written for *Roper v. Simmons* 2005).

"Some victim advocacy groups [wonder] what's so magical about a person's 18th birthday to make them eligible for a death sentence while killers just months younger are not. 'The idea that a male who is 17 years and 364 days old doesn't know better than a male who is 18 years old is absurd,' said ... a Texas lawyer who filed a brief with the high court on behalf of the victims rights group Justice For All. 'Taking a human life is a bit more than voting or consuming alcohol or going to X-rated movies'" (Tisch 2005).

Proponents of the juvenile death penalty argue:

- The death penalty provides a much-needed deterrent to violent youth in our society.
- Setting any one age as the "cutoff" for exclusion from execution is too artificial, considering the wide variety of individual offender differences on both sides of that line.
- The culpability of juvenile offenders should be determined on a case-by-case basis, factoring in the nature of the crime and the developmental maturity level of the individual juvenile.
- Lawmakers in each state, not the federal judiciary, should determine whether juveniles should be executed for capital crimes.

Those who oppose the juvenile death penalty, and who support the Court's decision in *Roper v. Simmons*, point to:

- A growing body of scientific research supporting the conclusion that juveniles are developmentally immature, particularly in regard to brain development and the ability to control impulses and plan appropriately for consequences of actions, and that therefore youthful offenders should not be held to the same culpability standards as adult offenders.
- Data indicating a vast majority of juveniles on death row have histories of being abused, suffer from a host of mental illnesses and were addicted to drugs at the time of their offense.
- International opposition to the practice, with the execution of juveniles expressly forbidden in the United Nations Convention on the Rights of the Child, the Geneva Convention Relative to the Protection of Civilian Persons in Time of War, the International Covenant on Civil and Political Rights and the American Convention on Human Rights.
- The company we keep—Iran, Pakistan, the Democratic Republic of Congo (DRC) and China are the only other countries to have allowed execution of juveniles since 2000. Although Pakistan and China have since officially abolished the practice, Iran executed at least seven juvenile offenders during 2008. And with the exception of Somalia, the United States is the only other member of the United Nations that has not ratified the UN Convention on the Rights of the Child.

The Court's ruling in *Roper v. Simmons* took 72 offenders off death row, converting their sentences to LWOP, and dashed prosecutors' hopes of seeking the death penalty for teen sniper Lee Boyd Malvo in those states where he had yet to stand trial for his involvement in the Washington, DC–area Beltway murders. Malvo is currently serving multiple LWOP sentences.

Juvenile Delinquency Guidelines for Improving Juvenile Court Practices

The NCJFCJ has developed guidelines with the dual goals of improving both delinquency case processing and outcomes (*Juvenile Delinquency Guidelines* 2005). The guidelines identify preferred practices from intake to case closure and articulate 16 key principles that should frame the entire court process:

1. Juvenile delinquency court judges should engage in judicial leadership and encourage system collaboration.
2. Juvenile delinquency systems must have adequate staff, facilities and program resources.
3. Juvenile delinquency courts and juvenile abuse and neglect courts should have integrated one family–one judge case assignments.
4. Juvenile delinquency court judges should have the same status as the highest level of trial court in the state and should have multiple-year or permanent assignments.
5. All members of the juvenile delinquency court shall treat youths, families, crime victims, witnesses and others with respect, dignity, courtesy and cultural understanding.
6. Juvenile delinquency court judges should ensure their systems divert cases to alternative systems whenever possible and appropriate.
7. Youths charged in the formal juvenile delinquency court must have qualified and adequately compensated legal representation.
8. Juvenile delinquency court judges should ensure crime victims have access to all phases of the juvenile delinquency court process and receive all services to which they are entitled by law.
9. Juvenile delinquency courts should render timely and just decisions, and trials should conclude without continuances.
10. Juvenile delinquency system staff should engage parents and families at all stages of the juvenile delinquency court process to encourage family members to participate fully in the development and implementation of the youth's intervention plan.
11. The juvenile delinquency court should engage the school and other community support systems as stakeholders in each individual youth's case.
12. Juvenile delinquency court judges should ensure court dispositions are individualized and include graduated responses, both sanctions and incentives (discussed in Chapter 11).
13. Juvenile delinquency court judges should ensure effective post-disposition review is provided to each delinquent youth as long as the youth is involved in any component of the juvenile justice system.
14. Juvenile delinquency court judges should hold their systems and the systems of other juvenile delinquency court stakeholders accountable.

15. Juvenile delinquency court judges should ensure the court has an information system that can generate the data necessary to evaluate performance, facilitate information sharing with appropriate agencies and manage operations information.

16. The juvenile delinquency court judge is responsible to ensure that the judiciary, court staff and all system participants are both individually trained and trained across systems and roles.

The Annie E. Casey Foundation's *2008 KIDS COUNT Data Book* (2008) also makes recommendations for ensuring that the juvenile court system is effective, including reducing reliance on secure confinement, keeping youths out of the system, reducing racial disparities, increasing reliance on effective community-based services and implementing developmentally appropriate policies and interventions. This final recommendation is intended as harsh criticism of current policies and practices that push juveniles into the criminal justice system, particularly in light of growing research evidence that shows juveniles tried and punished as adults have higher recidivism rates than do youths retained in the juvenile justice system (*2008 KIDS COUNT Data Book* 2008, 15).

 ## Summary

- The jurisdiction of the juvenile court includes children who are neglected or abused, who are unruly or commit status offenses and who are charged with committing serious crimes.
- Jurisdiction of the juvenile court is determined by the offender's age and conduct.
- The possible bases for a declaration of wardship include demonstrating that the child is abused or neglected or has committed a status offense or a criminal act.
- Juvenile courts are separated into three types: independent and separate courts, part of a family court and a unit within a trial court.
- The juvenile courtroom work group consists of judges, hearing officers, prosecutors, defense attorneys and probation officers.
- Court action on behalf of neglected and abused children may be noncriminal or criminal.
- The National Committee for Prevention of Child Abuse describes two kinds of intervention for deprived children: coercive and therapeutic.
- The juvenile court process usually involves the filing of a petition, a detention hearing, an adjudication hearing and a disposition hearing.
- In some states the court makes the decision to certify a juvenile as an adult. In other states this is done by the prosecutor.
- Juveniles may be transferred to criminal court via three basic mechanisms: judicial waiver, prosecutorial discretion and statutory exclusion.
- A major concern when transferring a juvenile to criminal court is that the juvenile may not be competent to stand trial there.
- Evidence shows that transferring juveniles to adult court results in higher rates of conviction, greater likelihood of incarceration and greater risk of the youth being victimized. Furthermore, transfer to criminal court has been found to have little deterrent effect on youthful offenders and has been shown to actually increase juvenile recidivism.

Discussion Questions

1. Should the juvenile court have two separate courts for civil and criminal matters?

2. Should there be a separate justice system for juveniles, or should all juveniles be dealt with in the adult system?

3. What is the purpose statement of the juvenile court in your area?

4. What criteria are used in decisions to waive juvenile court jurisdiction?

5. Who can certify a juvenile as an adult in your state?

6. Should juveniles be subject to the death penalty?

7. Do you think most juveniles are competent to stand trial in criminal court?

8. Does your state have the death penalty? If so, can juveniles under age 18 be executed?

9. Who has jurisdiction over maltreated youths in your community?

10. What are the major differences between juvenile court and adult criminal court?

References

Applegate, Brandon K., Robin King Davis, and Francis T. Cullen. 2009 (January). "Reconsidering Child Saving: The Extent and Correlates of Public Support for Excluding Youths from the Juvenile Court." *Crime & Delinquency* 55 (1): 51–77.

Belden, Evelina. 1920. *Courts in the United States Hearing Children's Cases: Results of a Questionnaire Study Covering the Year 1918.* U.S. Department of Labor, Children's Bureau. Dependent, Defective and Delinquent Classes Series No. 8, Bureau Publication No. 65. Washington, DC: U.S. Government Printing Office.

Bishop, Donna, and Charles Frazier. 2000. "Consequences of Transfer." In *The Changing Borders of Juvenile Justice,* edited by Jeffrey Fagan and Franklin E. Zimring, 227–276. Chicago: University of Chicago Press.

Corriero, Michael A. 2006. *Judging Children as Children: A Proposal for a Juvenile Justice System.* Philadelphia: Temple University Press.

Dawson, Robert O. 2000. "Judicial Waiver in Theory and Practice." In *The Changing Borders of Juvenile Justice,* edited by Jeffrey Fagan and Franklin E. Zimring, 45–82. Chicago: University of Chicago Press.

Fass, Simon M., and Chung-Ron Pi. 2002 (November). "Getting Tough on Juvenile Crime: An Analysis of Costs and Benefits." *Journal of Research in Crime and Delinquency* 39 (4): 363–399.

Federal Advisory Committee on Juvenile Justice. 2007 (August). *Federal Advisory Committee on Juvenile Justice Annual Recommendations Report to the President and Congress of the United States.* http://www.facjj.org/annualreports/ccFACJJ%20Report%20508.pdf

Feld, Barry C. 1981 (October). "Legislative Policies toward the Serious Juvenile Offender: On the Virtues of Automatic Adulthood." *Crime & Delinquency* 27 (4): 497–512.

———. 2000. "Legislative Exclusion of Offenses from Juvenile Court Jurisdiction: A History and Critique." In *The Changing Borders of Juvenile Justice,* edited by Jeffrey Fagan and Franklin E. Zimring, 83–144. Chicago: University of Chicago Press.

Forst, Martin, Jeffrey Fagan, and T. Scott Vivona. 1989. "Youth in Prisons and Training Schools: Perceptions and Consequences of the Treatment-Custody Dichotomy." *Juvenile and Family Court Journal* 40: 1–14.

Glassner, Barry, Margret Ksander, Bruce Berg, and Bruce D. Johnson. 1983 (December). "A Note on the Deterrent Effect of Juvenile versus Adult Jurisdiction." *Social Problems* 31 (2): 219–221.

Griffin, Patrick. 2003. *Trying and Sentencing Juveniles as Adults: An Analysis of State Transfer and Blended Sentencing Laws.* Pittsburgh, PA: National Center for Juvenile Justice.

Griffin, Patrick, Sean Addie, Benjamin Adams, and Kathy Firestine. 2011 (September). *Trying Juveniles as Adults: An Analysis of State Transfer Laws and Reporting.* Washington, DC: Office of Juvenile Justice and Delinquency Prevention, Juvenile Offenders and Victims National Report Series Bulletin. (NCJ 232434)

Griffin, Patrick, and Patricia Torbet. 2002 (June). *Desktop Guide to Good Juvenile Probation Practice.* Pittsburgh, PA: National Center for Juvenile Justice.

Jones, William G. 2006a. "Making Youth a Meaningful Part of the Court Process." *Juvenile and Family Justice Today* (Fall): 20.

———. 2006b. *Working with the Courts in Child Protection.* User Manual Series. Washington, DC: Child Welfare Information Gateway.

Juvenile Delinquency Guidelines: Improving Court Practice in Juvenile Delinquency Cases. 2005 (Summer). Reno, NV: National Council of Juvenile and Family Court Judges.

Krinsky, Miriam Aroni. 2006. "The Effect of Youth Presence in Dependency Court Proceedings." *Juvenile and Family Justice Today* (Fall): 16–17.

Kupchik, Aaron. 2006. *Judging Juveniles: Prosecuting Adolescents in Adult and Juvenile Courts.* New York: New York University Press.

McCarthy, Francis B. 1993. "The Serious Offender and Juvenile Court Reform: The Case for Prosecutorial Waiver of Juvenile Court Jurisdiction." *St. Louis University Law Journal* 38: 629–671.

McGowan, Angela, Robert Hahn, Akiva Liberman, Alex Crosby, Minday Fullilove, Robert Johnson, Eve Moscicki, LeShawndra Price, Susan Snyder, Farris

Tuma, et al. 2007. "Effects on Violence of Laws and Policies Facilitating the Transfer of Juveniles from the Juvenile Justice System to the Adult Justice System: A Systematic Review." *American Journal of Preventive Medicine* 32: S7–S28.

National Council of Juvenile and Family Court Judges (NCJFCJ) Staff Report. 2006. "NCJFCJ Model Courts Advocate Giving Children a Voice." *Juvenile Justice Today* (Fall): 17.

Neubauer, David W. 2008. *America's Courts and the Criminal Justice System*. 9th ed. Belmont, CA: Wadsworth.

"New Study Details the Dangers of Holding Youth in Adult Jails." 2008. *Juvenile Justice Update* (February/March): 11–12.

Puzzanchera, Charles, and W. Kang. 2011. *Easy Access to Juvenile Court Statistics: 1985–2008*. Accessed November 28, 2011. http://www.ojjdp.gov/ojstatbb/ezajcs/asp/process.asp

Redding, Richard E. 2003 (April). "The Effects of Adjudicating and Sentencing Juveniles as Adults: Research and Policy Implications." *Youth Violence and Juvenile Justice* 1 (2): 128–155.

Redding, Richard E., and James C. Howell. 2000. "Blended Sentencing in American Juvenile Courts." In *The Changing Borders of Juvenile Justice*, edited by Jeffrey Fagan and Franklin E. Zimring, 145–180. Chicago: University of Chicago Press.

Scott, Elizabeth S., and Laurence Steinberg. 2008. *Rethinking Juvenile Justice*. Cambridge, MA: Harvard University Press.

Shepherd, Robert E. 2007. "CDC Task Force Recommends against Transferring Juveniles to Adult Courts." *Juvenile Justice Update* (June/July): 7–8.

Siegel, Gene, and Gregg Halemba. 2006 (July). *The Importance of Timely Case Processing in Non-Detained Juvenile Delinquency Cases*. Pittsburgh, PA: National Center for Juvenile Justice (NCJJ).

Singer, Simon I., and David McDowall. 1988. "Criminalizing Delinquency: The Deterrent Effects of the New York Juvenile Offender Law." *Law and Society Review* 22 (3): 521–535.

Snyder, Howard N., and Melissa Sickmund. 2006 (March). *Juvenile Offenders and Victims: 2006 National Report*. Washington, DC: U.S. Department of Justice, Office of Justice Programs, Office of Juvenile Justice and Delinquency Prevention.

Steinberg, Laurence, and Elizabeth Cauffman. 2000. "A Developmental Perspective on Jurisdictional Boundary." In *The Changing Borders of Juvenile Justice*, edited by Jeffrey Fagan and Franklin E. Zimring, 379–406. Chicago: University of Chicago Press.

Steiner, Benjamin, Craig Hemmens, and Valerie Bell. 2006 (March). "Legislative Waiver Reconsidered: General Deterrent Effects of Statutory Exclusion Laws Enacted Post-1979." *Justice Quarterly* 23 (1): 34–59.

Sweeten, Gary. 2006 (December). "Who Will Graduate? Disruption of High School Education by Arrest and Court Involvement." *Justice Quarterly* 23 (4): 462–480.

Tisch, Chris. 2005. "18 Is Threshold for Death Penalty." *St. Petersburg Times*, March 2.

2008 KIDS COUNT Data Book. 2008. Baltimore, MD: Annie E. Casey Foundation.

Zimring, Franklin E. 2000. "The Punitive Necessity of Waiver." In *The Changing Borders of Juvenile Justice*, edited by Jeffrey Fagan and Franklin E. Zimring, 207–226. Chicago: University of Chicago Press.

Zimring, Franklin E., and Jeffrey Fagan, Jeffrey. 2000. "Transfer Policy and Law Reform." In *The Changing Borders of Juvenile Justice*, edited by Jeffrey Fagan and Franklin E. Zimring, 407–424. Chicago: University of Chicago Press.

Cases Cited

Commonwealth v. Fisher, 213 Pa. 48, 62 A. 198, 199, 200 (1905)

Eddings v. Oklahoma, 455 U.S. 104 (1982)

People ex rel. O'Connell v. Turner, 55 Ill. 280, 8 Am. Rep. 645 (1870)

Roper v. Simmons, 543 U.S. 551 (2005)

Stanford v. Kentucky, 492 U.S. 361 (1989)

Thompson v. Oklahoma, 487 U.S. 815 (1988)

Juvenile Corrections

> "It is in the juvenile justice system that we will succeed or fail in reducing corrections populations.... If we do not address juvenile corrections fully, these children will end up as tomorrow's clients in the adult system.
>
> **—John J. Wilson**

Juvenile corrections serves the dual function of holding youthful offenders accountable for their behavior and providing them with the educational, vocational, personal and social skills needed to successfully return to the community as productive, self-regulated, law-abiding adults. Sometimes public safety requires juvenile offenders be removed from the community and securely confined. Here two female offenders spend time in their cell during lockdown.

© Joel Gordon

 DO YOU KNOW?

- What four components are typically included in a modern, comprehensive graduated sanctions system?
- What the most common disposition of the juvenile court is?
- What the formal goals of probation are?
- What the two main functions of a probation officer traditionally have been?
- What common intermediate sanctions are?
- How public and private correctional institutions differ?

- Whether juvenile institutions are similar to adult institutions in social organization and culture?
- What the six performance-based standards goals for corrections are?
- What most effective youthful offender programs include?
- What the weakest element in the juvenile justice system process often is?
- What two key components of effective aftercare are?

CAN YOU DEFINE?

aftercare

boot camp

criminogenic need principle

deterrence

graduated sanctions

incapacitation

intensive supervision probation (ISP)

intermediate sanctions

ombuds

parole

probation

reentry

rehabilitation

responsivity principle

retribution

risk principle

shock incarceration

CHAPTER OUTLINE

Introduction

After a youth has been processed by the court and adjudicated delinquent, some form of government response is expected and warranted. This is the role of juvenile corrections. In 2008, of the 1.6 million cases presented to the juvenile court for processing, more than one third (563,900 cases) were adjudicated and turned over to the correctional component of the juvenile justice system, with the majority of youthful offenders (57.3%) receiving probation (Puzzanchera and Kang 2011). Nearly 30 percent were placed in residential facilities, and the remainder (14.7%) received another disposition.

The various correctional alternatives available reflect the need for the system to accommodate a variety of offenders whose delinquent acts range in degree of seriousness and chronicity. As with any other area of criminal or juvenile justice, differing viewpoints exist regarding how to best handle offenders once they enter the "corrections" stage of the process. These differences in perspective often rest on how one regards the purpose or function of corrections, and this chapter begins by briefly examining the various goals of corrections.

Goals of Corrections

Historically corrections has served several goals:

- Retribution
- Incapacitation
- Deterrence
- Rehabilitation

These goals are not mutually exclusive, nor are they equally attainable or effective. They are, however, the primary philosophies on which the various correctional alternatives are based.

Retribution

Retribution, also called *just desserts*, is the punishment of offenders for crimes they committed. This punishment does not try to reduce crime, alter an offender's behavior or make a community safer—the only purpose is to get revenge or "even the scales of justice" by imposing a harm on someone who brought harm to another or to society. This is punishment for the sake of punishment. This correctional philosophy is rarely, if ever, used to justify the handling of juvenile offenders today, although a degree of retributive intent is evident in "get tough" measures aimed at the most serious and violent youthful offenders.

Incapacitation

Incapacitation refers to locking up offenders or removing their ability to move freely in society and, thus, eliminate their abilities to commit crime. This correctional goal is reserved for only the most dangerous or high-risk juvenile offenders because incarceration is a relatively expensive sanction.

Deterrence

Deterrence, previously discussed in Chapters 2 and 3, aims to prevent crime and delinquency by showing offenders that the costs and consequences of aberrant behavior outweigh the benefits. Deterrence theory states that the decision to commit a crime is based on a cost–benefit calculation. If a person believes the legal costs of committing a crime are greater than the benefits, crime will be deterred. When a person believes the benefits outweigh the costs, a crime will be committed. Deterrence theory suggests that sanctions be tailored to be just severe enough to exceed the gain offered by crime. Overly severe sanctions are unjust; sanctions that are not severe enough will not deter.

Rehabilitation

Rehabilitation provides the philosophical foundation for our juvenile justice system and describes intervention efforts that seek to modify the factors that cause offenders to engage in crime and delinquency. Morrell (2007, 87) notes, "Rehabilitation is the ideological juxtaposition to retribution. It is positive, progressive and actually attempts to address offenders' needs.... Recent evidence demonstrates that these efforts are cost-effective and long lasting." Two surveys funded by the MacArthur Foundation show strong public backing for the rehabilitation of youthful offenders and a greater willingness of taxpayers to pay for rehabilitating them: "More than 70 percent of the public agree that incarcerating youthful offenders without rehabilitation is the same as giving up on them. Nine out of 10 people surveyed believe that almost all youths who commit crimes have the potential to change." According to the president of the foundation: "Momentum is gathering across the nation to replace harsh, ineffective measures with programs that address the welfare of young people while preserving safe communities" (*Rehabilitating Juvenile Offenders* 2008, 1).

The Concept of Graduated Sanctions

Promising Sanctioning Programs in a Graduated System (2003, 1) explains, "A graduated sanctions system is a set of integrated intervention strategies designed to operate in unison to enhance accountability, ensure public safety and reduce recidivism by preventing future delinquent behavior. The term **graduated sanctions** [emphasis added] implies that the penalties for delinquent activity should move from limited interventions to more restrictive (i.e., graduated) penalties according to the severity and nature of the delinquent act. In other words, youths who commit serious and violent offenses should receive more severe sentences than youth who commit less serious offenses." A graduated continuum of increasingly severe sanctions adheres to an underlying philosophy that youths should be dealt with in the least restrictive environment necessary to achieve the desired goals. Although the administration of sanctions that "match" an offense in severity appears to be common sense, some jurisdictions have not always handled juvenile offenders so rationally.

Griffin and Torbet (2002, 77) list the essential features of a good graduated sanctions system:

- *Certainty*: It responds to every infraction.
- *Speed*: The response is swift.
- *Consistency*: Similar infractions receive similar responses.
- *Economy*: The response chosen is the minimum likely to produce the desired result.
- *Proportionality*: The level of response should equal the level of the offense.
- *Progressiveness*: Continued noncompliance results in increasingly severe responses.
- *Neutrality*: Responses are objective, impartial reactions to the offense.

Griffin and Torbet (2002, 77) also contend, "Incentives—rewards for compliance—may be an even more useful tool for changing behavior than sanctions. Incentives for compliance should be delivered with the same consistency, immediacy and certainty as sanctions for noncompliance."

According to *Promising Sanctioning Programs in a Graduated System* (2003, 2), "A modern comprehensive juvenile justice system must include programs less restrictive than confinement but more intensive than probation. But such a system should not simply be a hodgepodge of alternative programs. It must embody a correctional philosophy that can deal with youths who commit serious and violent offenses, 'one time and you're out youths,' and everyone in between." In other words, a juvenile justice system that offers a continuum of care must include a wide range of sanctions designed to increase offender accountability so a sanction can be matched to the seriousness of the offense.

 A modern, comprehensive graduated sanctions continuum set includes four components for targeted populations: (1) informal sanctions within the community for first-time, nonviolent offenders, (2) intermediate sanctions (including probation) within the community for more serious offenders, (3) secure confinement programs for the most violent offenders and (4) reentry/aftercare programs that provide high levels of social control and treatment services.

Informal sanctions are usually diversion mechanisms that hold youths accountable for their behavior by avoiding formal court processing. These sanctions are typically appropriate for most first-time offenders, status offenders and some minor repeat offenders. Such sanctions include community service, informal hearings, family group conferences, mediation, mentoring, special courts and restitution. Diversion programs were discussed in Chapter 9. This chapter focuses on the other three components of graduated sanctions: probation and intermediate sanctions, secure confinement and aftercare/reentry.

Standard Probation

Probation has been called the "workhorse of the juvenile justice system" and falls at the least restrictive end of the continuum of intermediate sanctions, allowing youths who are adjudicated delinquent to serve their sentences in the community under correctional supervision. As mentioned at the beginning of the chapter, of all the petitioned cases in which a youth was adjudicated delinquent in 2008, more than half (57.3%) received probation.

 Probation is the most common disposition of the juvenile or family court.

After the dispositional hearing, if the court orders that a youngster be placed on probation, certain procedures and commitments must be satisfied. An order must give the probation officer authority for controlled supervision of the youth within the community. The terms of the probation are described in the order.

An important responsibility of the probation officer is helping the court establish the conditions for probation. Two kinds of probationary conditions are usually established: mandatory and discretionary. Most mandatory conditions specify that probationers (1) may not commit a new delinquent act,

(2) must report as directed to their probation officer and (3) must obey all court orders. The discretionary conditions are more extensive, as illustrated by the discretionary conditions set forth in New Jersey Juvenile Statutes:

- Pay a fine.
- Make restitution.
- Perform community service.
- Participate in a work program.
- Participate in programs emphasizing self-reliance, such as intensive outdoor programs that teach survival skills, including but not limited to camping, hiking and other appropriate activities.
- Participate in a program of academic or vocational education or counseling, which may require attendance after school, evenings and weekends.
- Be placed in a suitable residential or nonresidential program for the treatment of alcohol or narcotic abuse.
- Be placed in a nonresidential program operated by a public or private agency that provides intensive services to juveniles for specified hours, which may include education, counseling to the juvenile and the juvenile's family if appropriate, vocational counseling, work or other services.
- Be placed with any private group home with which the Department of Corrections has entered into a purchase of service contract.

© Joel Gordon

Juvenile restitution programs hold offenders accountable while making restoration for some of the harm done to both the victim and community. Although offenders traditionally pay restitution money directly to their victims, some offenders are unable to pay because of family circumstances, age or inability to find employment. Consequently, some courts have created a payback restitution work fund that allows juveniles to earn money by participating in community service projects. Victims then receive restitution payments directly from the fund. Here, a corrections officer supervises juveniles as they take a water break while participating in the LEARN Juvenile Pay-Back restitution program in Orange County, Florida.

The New Jersey statute also allows the court to set conditions for the probationer's parents and to revoke the juvenile's driver's license as a condition of probation. Conditions may include such matters as cooperating with the program of supervision, meeting family responsibilities, maintaining steady employment or engaging in or refraining from engaging in a specific employment or occupation, pursuing prescribed educational or vocational training, undergoing medical or psychiatric treatment, maintaining residence in a prescribed area or in a prescribed facility, refraining from consorting with certain types of people or frequenting certain types of places, making restitution or reparation, paying fines, submitting to search and seizure or submitting to drug tests.

Several constraints govern the setting of probation conditions. The conditions must be doable, must not unreasonably restrict constitutional rights, must be consistent with law and public policy and must be specific and understandable. If the youth does *not* meet the conditions, probation can be revoked. This is normally accomplished by the probation officer reporting the violation of conditions to the juvenile court. A violation of probation leads to a revocation hearing, where evidence and supportive information are presented to a juvenile judge. (Such hearings are also called *surrender hearings* or *violation hearings*.) If the court decides to revoke the probation, the youth can be institutionalized or other penalties may be applied.

Probation originated with John Augustus (1784–1859), a prosperous Boston shoemaker and the first probation officer. He was the first to use the word *probation* in its modern sense, from Latin meaning a period of proving or trial (Griffin and Torbet 2002). Several aspects of the system used by Augustus remain a basic part of modern probation. He thoroughly investigated each person he considered helping. He considered the person's character, age and likely future influences. Augustus supervised each defendant and kept careful case records that he submitted to the court.

Griffin and Torbet (2002, 1) state, "We envision the role of juvenile probation as that of a catalyst for developing safe communities and healthy youths and families. We believe we can fulfill this role by:

- Holding offenders accountable.
- Building and maintaining community-based partnerships.
- Implementing results-based and outcome-driven services and practices.
- Advocating for and addressing the needs of victims, offenders, families and communities.
- Obtaining and sustaining sufficient resources.
- Promoting growth and development of all juvenile probation professionals."

Griffin and Torbet reject the "closed, passive, negative and unsystematic approach that has too often characterized traditional juvenile probation practices," and emphasize that protecting the public is a primary responsibility of juvenile probation (2002, 2). In addition, probation is a guidance program to help juveniles overcome problems that may lead to further delinquency and to supervise them. It functions as an alternative to a correctional facility and operates much like adult probation.

 The formal goals of probation are to protect the public by supervising and controlling juvenile conduct, to hold juveniles accountable for their actions and to improve the delinquents' behavior through rehabilitation.

There is ample variation in the structure of probation throughout the country, and some departments emphasize control more whereas others focus more on the rehabilitation aspect. Because probation is the disposition given to so many offenders, and these juveniles' conduct and needs run a wide gamut, there are myriad demands and responsibilities placed on the probation officers to whom these youth are assigned.

The Probation Officer

Probation officers are in the unique position of serving both the court and the correctional areas of juvenile justice. Although they work in a correctional capacity, probation officers are officers of the court. In many states probation officers determine if there is sufficient evidence to move forward with a formal petition or whether the case can and should be handled informally.

Informal probation can be a crucial time in a juvenile's life. If it succeeds, the youngster may avoid further juvenile court processing and its potentially serious consequences. If informal probation efforts fail, the usual recourse is for the probation officer to request a petition be filed to make the case official.

Filing Petitions and Court Hearings
Recall from Chapter 10 the three phases of the juvenile court system that youths usually go through after a petition is filed. The probation officer may play an important role in each phase. During the first phase, the detention hearing, the judge may determine with the assistance of a probation officer whether a child's behavior is a threat to the public or to himself or herself. If so, the judge will order preventive detention of the youth. During the second phase, the adjudication hearing or trial, the judge will usually order a social investigation, presentence investigation (PSI) or predisposition report. The probation officer is responsible for investigating and assessing the child's home, school, physical and psychological situation. The *predisposition* or *presentence investigation report* has the objective of satisfying the goal of the juvenile court, which is to provide services.

Other Services
In addition to assessing the needs of probationers, devising a case plan or contract and supervising compliance with that contract, probation officers can also serve as mature role models. They can provide family counseling, crisis intervention and mediation. Mediation can be used to divert cases at intake, settle cases by community groups or by the probation officer and settle disputes between a juvenile and the school or family.

 The probation officer has traditionally been responsible for two key functions: (1) personally supervising and counseling youths who are on probation and (2) serving as a link to other community services.

Although counseling skills are considered important, the role of probation officers has shifted to that of social service "brokers." In many jurisdictions, probation officers link "clients" with available resources within the community, such as vocational rehabilitation centers, vocational schools, mental health centers, employment services, church groups and other community groups, such as Girl Scouts, Boy Scouts and Explorers.

In 1987 the National Center for Juvenile Justice (NCJJ) established the Juvenile Probation Officer Initiative (JPOI) to increase professionalism in juvenile probation. The JPOI has developed *The Desktop Guide to Good Juvenile Probation Practice,* a reference book written by and for juvenile probation officers (Griffin and Torbet 2002). The demanding, challenging, multifaceted role of the juvenile probation officer is illustrated in Table 11.1.

Table 11.1   The Multifaceted Role of the Juvenile Probation Officer

Role	Description
Cop	Enforces judge's orders
Prosecutor	Assists D.A., conducts revocations
Father confessor	Establishes helpful, trustful relationship with juvenile
Rat	Informs court of juvenile's behavior/circumstances
Teacher	Develops skills in juvenile
Friend	Develops positive relations with juvenile
Surrogate parent	Admonishes, scolds juvenile
Counselor	Addresses needs
Ambassador	Intervenes on behalf of juvenile
Problem solver	Helps juvenile deal with court and community issues
Crisis manager	Deals with juvenile's precipitated crises (usually at 2 A.M.)
Hand holder	Consoles juvenile
Public speaker	Educates public re: tasks
P.R. person	Wins friends, influences people on behalf of probation
Community resource specialist	Service broker
Transportation officer	Gets juvenile to where he or she has to go in a pinch
Recreational therapist	Gets juvenile to use leisure time well
Employment counselor	Gets youth a job
Judge's advisor	Court service officer
Financial advisor	Monitors payment, sets pay plan
Paper pusher	Fills out myriad forms
Sounding board	Listens to irate parents, youths, police, teachers, etc.
Punching bag	Person to blame when anything goes wrong, youth commits new crime
Expert clinician	Offers or refers to appropriate treatment
Family counselor/marriage therapist	Keeps peace in juvenile's family
Psychiatrist	Answers question: Why does the juvenile do it?
Banker	Provides cab fare money when juvenile needs it
Tracker	Finds youth
Truant officer	Gets youth to school
Lawyer	Tells defense lawyer/prosecutor what juvenile law says
Sex educator	Facts of life, AIDS and child support
Emergency foster parent	In a pinch
Family wrecker	Files petitions for abuse/neglect
Bureaucrat	Helps juvenile justice system function
Lobbyist	For juvenile, for department
Program developer	For youth, for department

(continued)

Table 11.1   The Multifaceted Role of the Juvenile Probation Officer (*continued*)

Role	Description
Grant writer	For youth, for department
Board member	Serves on myriad committees
Agency liaison	With community groups
Trainer	For volunteer, students
Public information officer	"Tell me what you know about probation"
Court officer/bailiff	In a pinch
Custodian	Keeps office clean
Victim advocate	Deals with juvenile's victim

SOURCE: Adapted from Juvenile Probation Officer Initiative (JPOI) Working Group. 1993 (May). *Desktop Guide to Good Juvenile Probation Practice*, 119–120. Washington, DC: Office of Juvenile Justice and Delinquency Prevention.

Challenges Facing Probation

Courts often attribute juveniles' troubles to something that is wrong with the youths or with their social milieu. The courts seldom recognize that a juvenile's problems may be the result of the juvenile justice system's ineffective delivery of guidance and control services. In many cases probation officers simply do not have the training, skills or resources to provide probationers with the kinds of assistance they might require. A problem commonly encountered at the dispositional stage is a lack of viable options to help or treat a youngster. Another inhibiting factor is time constraints brought about by unmanageably high caseloads in some jurisdictions. Even if probation officers possessed the skills necessary to offer psychotherapy, vocational guidance and school counseling with diverse types of youths, caseloads dictate that they would not have the time to exercise these skills.

Problems such as illegal drug use, street gangs, school violence and abused, homeless and runaway youths have strained the resources of the juvenile justice system. Given that probation departments are the single largest component of juvenile corrections, these departments especially feel the strain. One proposed solution is privatization. Another solution is to implement school-based probation programs.

School-Based Probation

According to the Juvenile Sanctions Center (JSC), *School-Based Probation: An Approach Worth Considering* (2003), placing juvenile probation officers in schools rather than in central offices goes a long way toward increasing the contacts between officers and the youths they are monitoring, leading to more immediate and effective responses to problems: "School-based probation (SBP) changes the very nature of probation by physically moving probation officers from the 'fortress' of traditional central or district offices into middle, junior and high school buildings where youths on probation spend the majority of their day."

According to the JSC document, "School-based probation represents an important shift in the delivery of probation services for in-school probations, and departments across the country are embracing this approach. More importantly, two evaluations of Pennsylvania's SBP program have documented several important benefits, including more contact, better monitoring, a focus on school success and a fit with balanced and restorative justice framework."

Intermediate Sanctions

Intermediate sanctions hold youths accountable for their actions through interventions that are more restrictive and intensive than standard probation yet that fall short of secure long-term incarceration. Although intended to provide swift, certain punishment while avoiding the expense and negative effects of institutionalization, intermediate sanctions unfortunately often fall short of these lofty goals because of limited financial and human resources and because the processing of cases can become slowed by procedural issues. Intermediate sanctions are appropriate for youths who fail to respond to informal sanctions by re-offending and for some violent or drug-involved offenders who need supervision, structure and monitoring but not necessarily institutionalization.

 Common forms of intermediate sanctions are intensive supervision probation, nonsecure juvenile residential facilities, nonresidential day treatment alternatives, electronic monitoring, house arrest, training schools and boot camps.

Intensive Supervision Probation (ISP)

Intensive supervision probation (ISP) is highly structured probation intended to provide a higher level of control over an offender and, thus, increased public safety without the added cost incurred with residential placement or incarceration. Intensive supervision programs differ from routine or standard probation in that contact between the probation officer or caseworker and the juvenile offender is more frequent, caseloads are smaller and strict compliance is required. Furthermore, ISPs usually include:

- Greater reliance placed on unannounced spot checks; these may occur in a variety of settings including home, school, known hangouts and job sites.
- Considerable attention directed at increasing the number and kinds of collateral contacts made by corrections staff with family members, friends, staff from other agencies and concerned residents in the community.
- Greater use of curfew, including both more rigid enforcement and lowering the hour at which curfew goes into effect. Other measures for imposing control include home detention and electronic monitoring.
- Surveillance expanded to ensure 24/7 coverage.

Other components of intensive supervision are clear, graduated sanctions with immediate consequences for violations; restitution and community service; parent involvement; youth skill development; and individualized and offense-specific treatment.

To determine whether a probationer needs intensive supervision, the probation officer should have a classification procedure. Because intensive supervision is extremely time-consuming, it should be reserved for those probationers at greatest risk of violating their probation.

The National Institute of Corrections (NIC) Classification Project has been adopted by many juvenile court jurisdictions. NIC research suggests that an assessment of the following variables appears to be universally predictive of future delinquent behavior:

- Age at first adjudication
- Prior delinquent behavior (combined measure of number and severity of priors)
- Number of prior commitments to juvenile facilities
- Drug or chemical abuse
- Alcohol abuse
- Family relationships problems
- School problems
- Peer relationships problems

The NIC calls for a reassessment every six months. After the assessment is completed, a case plan must arrange services so the youth, the family and the community all are served. The National Council on Crime and Delinquency (NCCD) has a case planning strategy that involves two main components:

1. Analysis, including identification of problems, strengths and resources.
2. Problem prioritization based upon
   - Strength—Is the problem an important force in the delinquent's behavior?
   - Alterability—Can the problem be modified or circumvented?
   - Speed—Can the changes be achieved rapidly?
   - Interdependence—Will solving the problem help resolve other problems?

This case plan is next reduced to a contract between the probation department, the juvenile offender and the family. The probation officer then presents this contract to the juvenile and the parents and reaches agreement on it, after which the probation officer monitors compliance with the contract.

Brank et al. (2008, 193) studied the effects of using a team approach to service delivery in an ISP that focused on improving parent-child relationships and teaching youths how to choose better peers. The posttest showed that the experimental and control youths were not significantly different on key family or peer relationship measures. Yet, despite the null results, other valuable findings were gleaned from the research:

First, intensive family interventions will take an enormous commitment of time and resources. A phasing in of different components will be useful in that the service providers and probation officers can become acclimated to each new component one at a time.

Second, general questions about family relationships may illicit false perceptions, or at least incomplete perceptions from the youths.

Third, legislators and policy makers should give careful consideration when implementing parental involvement programs in their statutes. The results from the current project imply that a simple inclusion of such language in the statutes (without the focused, intensive programs to back them up) will likely not result in the intended impact or any impact at all. (Brank et al. 2008, 217)

Nonsecure Juvenile Residential Facilities

Court dispositions are often compromises among deterrence, incapacitation, retribution and rehabilitation, and community-based residential programs are designed to improve the structure and supervision of youths who have been adjudicated delinquent. These facilities, while providing a higher level of supervision, are also more costly to operate than traditional probation or even ISP programs. Community-based residential correctional programs, such as foster care and group homes, try to normalize social contacts, reduce the stigma of being institutionalized and provide opportunities for jobs and schooling.

Data from the Juvenile Residential Facility Census (JRFC), a biannual survey developed by the Office of Juvenile Justice and Delinquency Prevention (OJJDP) to collect information about facilities that house juvenile offenders, show that in 2008, 2,860 juvenile facilities were operating throughout the nation, 2,458 of which held 81,015 offenders younger than 21 on the census date (Hockenberry, Sickmund, and Sladky 2011). The five major categories of nonsecure residential programs are shelters, group homes, foster homes, foster group homes and other types of nonsecure facilities.

A *shelter* is a nonsecure residential facility where juveniles may be temporarily assigned, often in place of detention or returning home, after they are taken into custody or after adjudication while they await more permanent placement. Shelters usually house status offenders and are not intended for treatment or punishment.

A *group home* is a nonsecure facility with a professional corrections staff that provides counseling, education, job training and family-style living. The staff is small because the residence generally holds a maximum of 12 to 15 youths. Group home living provides support and some structure in a basically nonrestrictive setting, with the opportunity for close but controlled interaction with the staff. The youths in the home attend school in the community and participate in community activities. The objective is to facilitate reintegrating young offenders into society.

Group homes are used extensively in almost all states. Some are operated by private agencies under contract to the juvenile court. Others are operated directly by probation departments or some other governmental unit. Some, called boarding homes, deserve special mention. These homes often accommodate as few as three or four youths, so they can be found in an apartment or flat in an urban setting. They are sometimes called "Mom and Pop" operations because the adults serve as parent substitutes. The adults are usually paraprofessionals whose strengths are personal warmth and an ability to relate to young people.

A *foster home* is intended to be family-like, as much as possible a substitute for a natural family setting. Small and nonsecure, foster homes are used at any of several stages in the juvenile justice process. In jurisdictions where a juvenile shelter is not available, foster homes may be used when law enforcement authorities take a juvenile into custody.

Foster care is used less for misbehaving and delinquent children than it is for children whose parents have neglected, abused or abandoned them. Social service agencies usually handle placement in and funding of foster care programs. The police and courts coordinate their efforts through these agencies.

Programs in Practice

The Colorado Boys Ranch (CBR) Youth Connect is a private, non-sectarian, nonprofit organization providing residential mental health services, education and prevocational and vocational training for males 10 to 21 years old. Its mission is to achieve excellence in providing troubled youths with the means to become hopeful, productive citizens. All treatment is customized and designed to fit the unique mental health needs of each client. All treatment begins where the youth is cognitively and emotionally challenged and proceeds at his pace (empowerment). Treatment offers the typical skills training (assertiveness, stress reduction, sensitivity, relationships training and the like), but CBR Youth Connect also provides "real-life" learning opportunities including banking programs, college credits, horsemanship programs, small animals therapy and horticulture.

Among Youth Connect's most important components is its planned aftercare and discharge, a stage that is considered at the time of admission. This individualized planning incorporates a continuum of care based on individual needs and also focuses on the coordination of health care professionals and organizations, including the primary aftercare agency and persons providing or directing the services; the primary educational resources and recommendations; recommendations and arrangements for transition care and treatment; and appropriate prescribed medications, psychotherapy recommendations and job training and community recreation. Aftercare and discharge plans are made collaboratively by youths, family, clinicians, referral sources, mental health centers and placement facilities. "We wrap a support system around the youth and family with the goal of restoring unity and giving them resources to move forward in life" (CBR Youth Connect, n.d.).

SOURCE: *CBR Youth Connect.* 28071 Hwy 109, P.O. Box 681, La Junta, CO 81050. http://www.cbryouthconnect.org.

A *foster group home* is a blend of group home and foster home. Foster group homes are run by single families, rather than professional staffs. They are non-secure facilities usually acceptable to neighborhood environments that can give troubled youths a family-neighborhood type relationship. Foster group homes can be found in various parts of the United States.

Other nonsecure facilities include correctional farms, ranches and camps for youths, which are usually located in rural areas. These facilities are alternatives to confinement or regimented programs. The programs with an outdoor or rural setting encourage self-development, provide opportunities for reform and secure classification and placement of juveniles according to their capabilities. Close contact with staff and residents instills good work habits.

Nonresidential Day Treatment Alternatives

Many state and local governments are turning to nonresidential day treatment for delinquent juveniles because it appears to be effective and is less costly than residential care: "Day treatment facilities (also known as day reporting centers) are highly structured, community-based, post-adjudication, nonresidential programs for serious juvenile offenders. The goal of day treatment is to provide both intensive supervision to ensure community safety and a wide range of services to the offender to prevent future delinquent behavior" (*Promising Sanctioning Programs* 2003, 4). Day treatment programs tend to succeed because they can focus on the family unit and the youth's behavior in the family and the community. These programs are also effective from a legal standpoint in states that require that youths be treated in the least restrictive environment possible.

Nonresidential day treatment corrections programs can take a variety of forms, such as community supervision, family crisis counseling, proctor programs and service-oriented programs, including recreational programs, counseling, alternative schools, employment training programs and homemaking and financial planning classes. Other alternatives might include evening and weekend reporting centers, school programs and specialized treatment facilities.

Such programs can provide education, tutoring, counseling, community service, vocational training and social or recreational events.

A variety of alternative education programs have been developed to serve vulnerable youths, including children with disabilities and those who drop out or are "pushed" out of traditional K–12 schools (or are at risk of either). The term *alternative education* refers to all educational programs that fall outside the traditional K–12 school system. The programs can be physically located in many different places, and sometimes the location is what makes the program "alternative" (e.g., in a juvenile justice center).

Alternative education program settings include (in order of distance from traditional classrooms in regular K–12 schools): resource rooms (separate room/teacher provides additional services such as study skills, guidance, anger management, small group/individual instruction); a school-within-a-school; and, finally, pull-out programs, which can be run from a storefront, community center or former school and can include schools/programs within the juvenile justice system (detention, corrections, etc.) or a homeless services system (emergency and transitional shelters). These programs may be administered by any one of a variety of organizations including community-based organizations (CBOs), school districts, adult education divisions, state departments of juvenile justice, charter schools and, in the case of Job Corps, contractors to the U.S. Department of Labor.

The type and quality of alternative education programs vary. Most offer high school or General Educational Development (GED) diplomas. These programs can differ from traditional schools by having flexible hours and schedules, open admission and exit policies and individualized instruction, often connected to employment. Alternative schools serve the dual purpose of reinforcing the message that students are accountable for their offenses and removing disruptive students from the mainstream.

Electronic Monitoring and Home Detention

Electronic monitoring (EM) requires offenders to wear bracelets or ankle cuffs that tell probation officers where the juveniles are. EM has been tried with some success in numerous jurisdictions and is sometimes a key component in intensive probation and parole programs. Electronic monitoring can be used to impose curfew, home detention (more restrictive than curfew, the offender must be home except when at work or at treatment) or home incarceration (the offender must be at home almost all the time).

Use of EM has grown considerably. Electronic monitoring is a supervision tool that can satisfy punishment, public safety and treatment objectives by providing cost-effective community supervision for offenders selected according to specific program criteria; promoting public safety through active surveillance; and increasing the confidence of legislative, judicial and releasing authorities in intensive supervision probation or parole program designs as a viable sentencing option.

Electronic monitoring is frequently used in conjunction with home incarceration (house arrest). Youths under such sentences are allowed to leave their homes for specific reasons, such as meeting with their probation officer, attending a treatment program or going to the doctor. The two general types of home

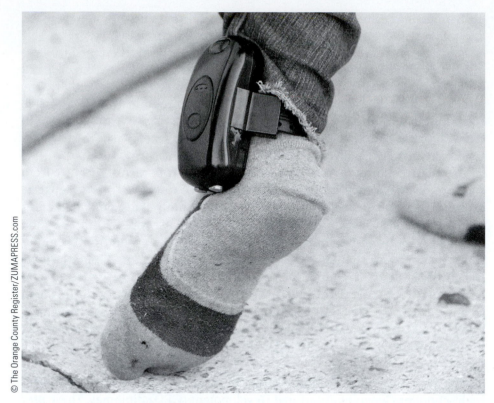

An ankle bracelet worn by a teen who is under house arrest for violating probation. The bracelet will alert probation officials if she leaves her home.

confinement are pretrial and post-adjudication. Pretrial programs use home confinement as an alternative to detention to ensure that juveniles appear in court. Post-adjudication programs use home confinement as a more severe sanction than intensive supervision but less restrictive than incarceration.

Training Schools

Training schools exist in every state except Massachusetts, which abolished them in the 1970s. They vary greatly in size, staff, service programs, ages and types of residents. Some training schools resemble adult prisons, with the same distinguishing problems of gang-oriented activity, homosexual terrorism and victimization, which often lead to progressive difficulties or suicide.

Most legislation requires training schools to provide both safe custody and rehabilitative treatment. A 1983 federal court case, however, rejected the idea of a constitutional right to treatment and training: "We therefore agree … that, although rehabilitative training is no doubt desirable and sound as policy and perhaps of state law, plaintiffs have no constitutional right to rehabilitative training" (*Santana v. Collazo* 1983). Treatment was discussed in Chapter 9.

Boot Camps

Juvenile boot camps are fundamentally the same as those for adults. Also known as **shock incarceration**, a **boot camp** stresses military discipline, physical fitness and strict obedience to orders, as well as educational and vocational training and drug treatment when appropriate. Most boot camps are designed for young, nonviolent, first-time offenders as a means of punishment and rehabilitation without long-term incarceration. Furthermore, offender consent is required for placement in shock incarceration.

Many offenders entering a boot camp lack basic life skills, are in poor physical condition, have quit school and have had frequent encounters with the justice system. Their self-esteem is low, and they are seen as losers. Young offenders' false sense of pride must be stripped away before positive changes can be made. This is a primary function of boot camps, just as it is in a military boot camp. The camps are intended to provide a foundation of discipline, responsibility and self-esteem to be built on.

Earlier editions of this text reported that more than a dozen states and the federal system were operating at least one boot camp each. The presentation of boot camps was discussed in a more promising light, for when they were first implemented in the early 1980s, there were high hopes that these "get tough" facilities could help turn delinquent kids around and put them on track for a more disciplined, law-abiding way of life. However, after several decades of implementation and numerous studies examining how boot camp graduates fared following release, a growing body of contradictory evidence has accumulated. Although some programs were well structured and achieved success in reducing offender recidivism, more than a handful were found to not only *not* reduce juvenile offending but to actually exacerbate delinquency and criminality in those who passed through them. Furthermore, investigations of several facilities revealed how prevalent abuse of youth can be in these settings. In fact, the death of a 14-year-old at one of Florida's boot camps in 2006 led to a statewide moratorium on the use of such facilities. To date, results remain mixed, with some studies showing positive effects, others negative and others nil. Currently, there are no state- or federally operated boot camps; those few still in existence are privately run.

Indeed, there has been a shift away from the militarized style of boot camps, toward a paradigm that emphasizes cognitive restructuring and greater attention to educational and vocational programming. Such a shift does seem to enhance the effectiveness of this correctional alternative for youthful offenders.

Although boot camps, training schools and other residential facilities are certainly "custodial," in the sense that offenders live there, if only briefly, and are not free to leave at will, these intermediate sanctions are generally used only for relatively short periods (such as boot camps) or are nonsecure, meaning the offenders are not kept locked in (as with foster homes and the like). Recall that such intermediate sanctions are also typically reserved for first-time, nonviolent offenders. For a small percentage of juveniles, such intermediate sanctions are judged an inappropriate alternative for the severity of their offense or their extensive criminal history, and these youths are placed in long-term secure correctional institutions.

Institutionalization: Long-Term Secure Confinement

Juvenile offenders are placed in a variety of correctional institutions, with varying levels of security and programming. Although secure institutions are necessary for chronic, serious and violent offenders, and offer a heightened degree of community protection, these facilities must also address the rehabilitative

Table 11.2 Respondents' Views on What Is and What Should Be the Main Emphasis in Juvenile Prisons and the Amount of Importance Placed on Each (in percentages)

A. Main Emphasis of Juvenile Prisons

Goals of Imprisonment	Is	Should Be
Rehabilitation: Do you think the main emphasis in juvenile prison is [should be] to try and rehabilitate the adolescent so that he might return to society as a productive citizen?	29.4	63.3
Punishment: Do you think the main emphasis in juvenile prison is [should be] to punish the adolescent convicted of a crime?	16.8	18.7
Protection: Do you think the main emphasis in juvenile prison is [should be] to protect society from future crime he might commit?	17.6	11.2
Not sure	36.1	6.7

B. Importance of Goals of Juvenile Institutions

Goals of Imprisonment	Very Important	Important	A Little Important	Not Very Important
Rehabilitation	64.5	30.0	4.3	1.1
Punishment	42.5	52.1	4.3	1.1
Protection	43.2	47.0	8.4	1.3

SOURCE: Melissa M. Moon, Jody L. Sundt, Francis T. Cullen, and John Paul Wright. 2008 (January). "Is Child Saving Dead? Public Support for Juvenile Rehabilitation." *Crime & Delinquency* 46 (1): 26. Copyright © 2008 Sage Publications. Reprinted by permission of SAGE Publications.

and treatment aspects incumbent on correctional entities that service juvenile offenders. Table 11.2 summarizes respondents' views on what the emphasis should be, and is, in juvenile prisons.

Public versus Private Institutions

An investigation of the characteristics of inmates of public long-term juvenile institutions shows a pattern not unlike that of America's jails and prisons. The disadvantaged and the poor make up a large percentage of the population. In addition, disproportionate minority confinement (DMC) is common. Public facilities hold the majority of delinquent offenders and, thus, drive the trend for delinquency populations. Private facilities, in contrast, drive the trend for status offender populations (Snyder and Sickmund 2006, 199). Whereas the private institutions of an earlier period were products of philanthropic or religious impulse, the newer ones result from a more economic, entrepreneurial drive. From the earliest days, private institutions attracted more youths from affluent backgrounds than did public institutions. Many newer private institutions have chosen to emphasize their mental health and drug treatment programs. In this way they can capitalize on young people from families who have medical insurance or who can pay their children's confinement and treatment costs. Private institutions may offer greater diversity in programs and structures than public institutions. They also may have very strict rules.

 Compared with public correctional institutions, private correctional institutions confine more Whites, more girls and more status offenders. The inmates are younger, and their stays are usually longer.

Social Structure within Correctional Institutions

Correctional institutions—whether high- or low-security, locked or unlocked, public or private, sexually integrated or segregated—often have an elaborate informal social organization and culture. The social organization includes a prestige hierarchy among inmates and a variety of inmate social roles. The inmate culture includes a complex of norms that indicate how inmates should relate to one another, to staff members and to the institutional regimen.

 The sociopolitical climate that exists in juvenile correctional institutions is the same as that found in adult institutions.

Despite the diverse ideologies and strategies pursued by correctional institutions, to a great extent they all generate an underlife that includes an informal social organization and an inmate code. While they are confined, youths are immersed in a culture that defines the institution, its staff and many of its programs in negative terms.

Challenges Facing Juvenile Correctional Facilities

Major challenges in juvenile correctional facilities include overcrowding, violence, sexual assault, the problem of gangs and the specific needs of female offenders.

Overcrowding   Facility crowding affects a substantial proportion of youths in custody. Public facilities are more likely than private facilities to suffer from overcrowding. Although the national population of juvenile offenders in custody declined overall between 2006 and 2008, some facilities continued to experience significant bed shortages: "Twenty-five percent (25%) of facilities said that the number of residents they held on the 2008 census date put them at or over the capacity of their standard beds or that they relied on some makeshift beds. These facilities held more than 17,291 residents, the vast majority of whom were offenders younger than 21" (Hockenberry, Sickmund, and Sladky 2011, 6). Overcrowding can cause significant deterioration in the conditions of confinement, making it difficult for a facility to provide adequate and effective treatment, educational programming, medical and mental health services and recreational opportunities. Furthermore, crowding increases the tension level within the facility, raising the likelihood of violence and assaults and creating an unsafe environment for both juvenile residents and staff (Roush 2008a).

Violence and Assaults   When a population of violent youth are confined in the same space, often alongside youth who have committed less serious offenses, a valid concern is the potential for violence and assault among the residents. Sedlak and McPherson (2010, 4) report, "Nearly one-fifth of the less serious career offenders (status offenders, technical parole violators, and youth who report no offense) are placed in living units with youth who have killed someone, and about one-fourth reside with felony sex offenders.... Extensive mixing of youth who have dramatically different offense histories raises concern about the safety of the less serious offenders." Additional data indicate that nearly 20 percent of youth in custody are classified with some form of assault as their most serious current offense, and these "person offenders" are often housed with "property offenders" or other youth who have no history of assault against others (Sedlak and Bruce 2010).

One survey found that more than one third of youths in custody (38 percent) reported a fear of being attacked by someone, the majority of whom said they feared attack by another resident. Other youths were fearful that a staff member would physically attack them (Sedlak and McPherson 2010).

Limited research suggests that younger inmates tend to assault others more than older inmates (Vivian, Grimes, and Vasquez 2007, 17). Such violence also tends to be more respected and even promoted by some staffs' failure to address or punish aggression by juvenile inmates. Some studies have found that inmates assault others to achieve higher status, reassure peers of their competence in the correctional environment and for defensive purposes. Most documented assaults in 2006 involved juveniles assaulting juveniles (46 percent), followed by mutually instigated fights (29 percent) and staff assaulted by juveniles (24 percent) (Vivian, Grimes, and Vasquez 2007). Actual assault cases tended to involve juveniles with higher numbers of referrals to separation, those who had two or more prior assault offenses and those with mental instabilities. Contextual factors that predicted escalation of an incident into an injury assault included placing youth in housing units that were either in the top quartile of separation rates or in the top quartile of assault rates (Vivian, Grimes, and Vasquez 2007).

Stickrath and Wallis (2007) describe the Ohio Department of Youth Services (DYS) plan for reducing aggression in juvenile facilities through a curriculum designed to build the skills needed to provide youths with behaviorally and emotionally appropriate alternatives to "fight or flight." The plan relies on in-service and preservice training of employees as well as multiple levels of staff in conflict resolution, defined as "a spectrum of processes that use communication skills and creative and analytic thinking to prevent, manage and peacefully resolve conflict." These conflict resolution skills are then taught to youths, providing a common language for understanding conflict, expressing emotions (especially anger), interpreting nonverbal and verbal communication and engaging in problem solving to develop solutions.

Sexual Assault Data gathered between June 2008 and April 2009 as part of the first National Survey of Youth in Custody (NSYC) indicate that an estimated 12.1 percent of adjudicated youth held in state-operated or large non-state facilities experienced one or more incidents of sexual victimization during the past 12 months or since admission, if less than 12 months (Beck, Harrison, and Guerino 2010). Approximately 2.6 percent reported an incident involving another youth, 10.3 percent reported being sexually assaulted by facility staff, and 0.8 percent reported being victimized by both another youth and facility staff (Beck, Harrison, and Guerino 2010). Of those youth victimized by another youth, one fifth (20 percent) reported they had been physically injured during the assault, and 5 percent said they had sought medical attention for their injuries. Among those youth assaulted by staff, 5 percent reported being physically injured, and fewer than 1 percent had sought medical attention following the assault (Beck, Harrison, and Guerino 2010). Interestingly, roughly 95 percent of the youth who reported staff sexual misconduct said they had been victimized by a female staff member (Beck, Harrison, and Guerino 2010).

Roush (2008b, 32) suggests that three factors seem to play a role in all such occurrences: (1) an insufficient number of staff to provide adequate supervision,

(2) an inadequate amount of relevant training to prepare workers to supervise competently and (3) the inability to screen out those adults who want to work with troubled and vulnerable youths for the wrong reasons.

Asbridge (2007, 80) stresses, "Sexual assault—both youth-on-youth and staff-on-youth—in juvenile correctional settings is a problem that cannot be ignored." Asbridge (84) suggests the following strategies to address this situation: examine existing mechanisms for youths to report sexual assault by staff or other youths; talk frequently with staff and youths under their care; critically evaluate existing procedures for investigating juvenile complaints; ensure procedures are in place to provide the appropriate medical care for sexual assault victims; assess the supervision schemes used at the facility; and ensure a strong network of policies and procedures built around best practices.

The dual relationships that staff in juvenile facilities have with youthful inmates, in which a professional relationship co-occurs with a social one, can be a highly troublesome issue (Roush 2008b, 33). To prevent a dangerous interaction, agencies should strengthen appropriate formal structures such as good policies and procedures, and good recruitment, selection and orientation of new staff; zero-tolerance disciplinary procedures; and informal structures such as good, clear definitions of misconduct, training on expected practices and good supervision of staff (Roush 2008b). The institution might insist on uniforms, or at least a dress code, for staff; forbid profanity (staff may use the profane language of the streets to relate to offenders); and strengthen resident privacy. Two universal policies should be part of every institutional policy and procedure manual: (1) sexual contact between staff and youths is always forbidden and illegal, and anyone violating this policy will be fired and prosecuted; and (2) any person who fails to report known or suspected incidences of child sexual abuse will be fired and prosecuted (Roush 2008b).

The Prison Rape Elimination Act (PREA) of 2003 requires "the training of correctional staff sufficient to ensure that they understand and appreciate the significance of prison rape and the necessity of its eradication." PREA policies address the issue of prison rape from the perspective of staff and youths in custody, with a focus on raising staff awareness of "red flags" indicative of sexual misconduct, institutional culture and the importance of professionalism to create an atmosphere where youths feel comfortable reporting incidents of sexual misconduct to staff (Pihl-Buckley 2008, 44). It is vital for staff to recognize and understand that a professional dress code and appearance, as well as use of respectful language, significantly affects their impact as role models for youths.

Gangs   Data from the Survey of Youth in Residential Placement (SYRP) reveal that the majority (60 percent) of youth in custodial facilities report a gang presence and that, on average, youth in residential placement are housed in units where 19 percent of residents claim membership to a gang in the facility (Sedlak and McPherson 2010).

Although juvenile gangs are not a ubiquitous problem for every correctional facility, and some administrations have done an admirable job of separating gang members at intake and promptly quelling any type of offender organization that suggests gang activity, for some institutions, gangs have a strong foothold and have proven extremely difficult to eradicate. In these facilities, gangs are responsible for causing numerous other problems, such as bullying, gambling, extortion of food and the imposition of other "taxes" on nongang-affiliated inmates. Some youth report they fear leaving their cells for treatment and education programs because of intimidation or assault risks posed by gang members. Furthermore, "SYRP reveals that the presence of gangs in a facility is significantly related to the percentage of youth who say they have been offered contraband … and to the percentage of youth who are in living units characterized by poor youth-staff relations" (Sedlak and McPherson 2010, 8).

Juvenile Females in Corrections   Girls involved in the juvenile justice system bring unique challenges not as commonly found among the male offender population, such as higher rates of depression, lower self-esteem and a greater tendency to attempt suicide; more acute substance abuse treatment needs; and extraordinarily high levels of abuse and trauma. There is long-standing recognition in the research literature that many adolescent female delinquents have a history of sexual trauma or abuse. Scholars have also begun to recognize that there may be gender-based responsivity differences (the responsivity principle is explained shortly) and that treatments that work well for males may not necessarily work well for females. "Juvenile justice systems need to develop specific programs for girls that focus on building relationships and addressing victimization and improving self-esteem. Adolescent girls have multiple and unique programming needs, including health care, education, mental health treatment, mutual support and mentoring opportunities, prenatal care and parenting skills, substance abuse prevention and treatment, job training and family support-strengthening services" (*Mental Health and Adolescent Girls* 2003, 1–2).

Morton (2007, 6) offers six guiding principles to ensure that correctional agencies provide gender-responsive management, supervision and treatment services for women and girls:

1. Acknowledge that being female makes a difference.
2. Create an environment based on safety, respect and dignity.
3. Develop policies, practices and programs incorporating the fact that women are relationship-oriented.
4. Address substance abuse, trauma and mental health issues in a comprehensive, integrated and culturally relevant manner.
5. Provide women an opportunity to improve their socioeconomic status.
6. Establish a system of community supervision and reentry with comprehensive, collaborative services.

Improving Conditions of Confinement

In 1980 Congress enacted the Civil Rights of Institutionalized Persons Act (CRIPA) to help eradicate unlawful conditions of confinement for juveniles held in correctional facilities. Through CRIPA the Department of Justice is authorized to bring action against state or local governments for violating the civil rights of any person institutionalized in a publicly operated facility.

Another way to improve confinement conditions and to protect the rights of youths in custody is to establish **ombuds** programs. Ombuds can monitor conditions, investigate complaints, report findings, propose changes, advocate for improvements and help expose and reduce deficiencies in juvenile detention and correctional facilities.

Perhaps most important is setting standards, with particular emphasis on those performance-based standards with proven records of success or those otherwise identified as meeting "best practices" criteria.

 The performance-based standards goals for corrections cover security, order, safety, programming, justice and health/mental health.

- *Security:* To protect public safety and provide a safe environment for youths and staff. Security is essential for effective learning and treatment.
- *Order:* To establish clear expectations of behavior and an accompanying system of accountability for youths and staff that promotes mutual respect, self-discipline and order.
- *Safety:* To engage in management practices that promote the safety and well-being of staff and youths.
- *Programming:* To provide meaningful opportunities for youths to improve their educational and vocational competence, address underlying behavioral problems and prepare for responsible lives in the community.
- *Justice:* To operate the facility in a manner that is consistent with principles of fairness and that provides ways to ensure and protect the legal rights of youths and their families.
- *Health/Mental Health:* To identify and effectively respond to youths' physical and mental health problems and related behavioral problems throughout the course of confinement by using professionally appropriate diagnostic, treatment and prevention methods.

Achieving Effective Correctional Programs for Youth

Many youthful offender programs use a point system of rewards and consequences operating on four levels and in four areas: security, school, work and therapy. Positive behavioral interventions and support (PBIS) are long-term problem-solving strategies to reduce inappropriate behavior, teach more appropriate behavior and provide support. PBIS emerged in the early 1980s as an alternative to traditional behavioral approaches for students with severe disabilities who engaged in extreme forms of self-injury and aggression. Since then PBIS has evolved into an approach used with a wide range of students, with and without disabilities.

 Most effective youthful offender programs include in-depth evaluation, screening and assessment; daily scheduling; point system discipline; positive behavioral support therapy; and education, including literacy, GED preparation and computer literacy.

Caldwell, Vitacco and Van Rybrock (2006, 148) examined the costs and benefits of an intensive treatment program for violent juvenile delinquent boys compared with the typical treatment provided in a secured juvenile corrections facility: "Outcome data indicated the initial costs of the intensive treatment program were more than offset by improved treatment progress and lowered recidivism. These results are consistent with those from other research that has found a beneficial impact from treating serious and violent offenders, and this study also illustrates the importance of considering longer-term outcomes in assessing the costs and benefits of treatment programs."

Their research found that the treatment group's total time incarcerated was significantly shorter and that youths in the matched comparison group averaged more than twice the number of total charged offenses in the follow-up period and more than three times the number of violent offenses. Finally, although the study had a daily bed cost more than double that of the usual correctional program, the shorter treatment time and lowered recidivism rates resulted in criminal justice costs substantially lower than usual: "In total, the mean-per-youth cost for the comparison group was over $216,000, whereas the figure for the youths receiving the intensive treatment program was $173,000, meaning the net treatment group costs averaged 20 percent less than the comparison group" (148).

A NIC training program called *Youthful Offenders in Adult Corrections: A Systemic Approach Using Effective Interventions* is based on three primary principles that have emerged from research: risk, need and responsivity (Shomaker and Gornik 2002, 123): "The **risk principle** embodies the assumption that criminal behavior can be predicted for individual offenders on the basis of certain factors. Some factors, such as criminal history, are static and unchangeable. Others, such as substance abuse, anti-social attitudes and anti-social associates, are dynamic and changeable. With proper assessment of these factors, researchers and practitioners have demonstrated that it is possible to classify offenders according to their relative likelihood of committing new offenses with as much as 80 percent accuracy." Recall the dynamic and static risk factors introduced in Chapter 9 in the discussion on effective treatment interventions.

The **criminogenic need principle** is explained thusly: "Most offenders have myriad needs. However, certain needs are directly linked to crime. Criminogenic needs constitute dynamic risk factors or attributes that, when changed, influence the probability of recidivism. Non-criminogenic needs also may be dynamic and changeable, but they are not directly associated with new offense behavior" (Shomaker and Gornik 2002). "The **responsivity principle** refers to the delivery of treatment programs in a manner that is consistent with the ability and learning style of an offender."

To summarize, the NIC training program applies the risk principle to identify *who* should receive treatment, the criminogenic need principle to focus on *what* should be treated and the responsivity principle to determine *how* treatment should be delivered.

The Importance of Education

In addition to intensive treatment for mental health issues, substance abuse problems and behavior problems, education is critically important within juvenile correctional facilities. Research evidence has shown that increased educational attainment plays a significant role in reducing juvenile recidivism: "The majority of students are at least two grade levels behind peers of the same age, and many have dramatic gaps between their chronological age and expected skills and knowledge" (Conlon et al. 2008, 49). Individualized education programs (IEPs), as applied to youth in confinement facilities, are now governed by three pieces of federal legislation: the No Child Left Behind (NCLB) Act of 2001, the Individuals with Disabilities Education Improvement Act (IDEA) of 2004 and the Family Educational Rights and Privacy Act (FERPA) of 1974.

All personnel working in juvenile correctional facilities should know the provisions of these three pieces of legislation (Brooks 2008, 28).

Brooks (2008, 46) points out, "Confinement education programs are unique education programs—certainly different from the public school systems the lawmakers had in mind. This uniqueness requires innovative solutions and broad interpretations of the guiding principles of the legislation governing the delivery of educational services in confinement settings." However, given the many educational and psychological challenges facing incarcerated students, retaining juvenile justice teachers is difficult: "Maintaining a qualified teacher work force is one of the most significant challenges in correctional education. One of the greatest frustrations of teachers in this situation is lack of resources, including outdated textbooks and the need for more supplies and materials. In addition, they want to implement a sound, consistent behavior management system to reward students for good behavior and for making amends for unacceptable behavior, perhaps based on a point system. Finally, they want to be involved in the change process, wanting more input and involvement in the education program" (O'Rourke, Catrett, and Houchins 2008, 42–43). Table 11.3 outlines characteristics of successful education programs in secure facilities.

Juveniles Sentenced to Adult Institutions

Meyer (2008, 19) contends, "Our country's biggest law and order issue is not what is happening on the streets of our cities but, instead, what is not happening in our prisons. The counseling, educational and vocational services absent in many adult prisons are far more abundant in juvenile facilities." Research by Kupchik (2007, 247) found that relative to adult facilities, juvenile facilities are generally smaller, have much lower inmate-to-staff ratios and place greater emphasis (in their official guidelines) on treatment, counseling, education and mentoring of inmates. Yet, every year, many juveniles are sentenced to serve time in adult facilities. Youthful offenders housed in adult jails and prisons are

Table 11.3 Characteristics of Successful Education Programs in Secure Facilities

- Administrators regard education as a vital part of the rehabilitation process.
- Programs help students develop competencies in basic reading, writing and math skills, along with thinking and decision-making skills and character development traits, such as responsibility and honesty.
- Student/teacher ratios reflect the needs of the students.
- Academic achievement is reinforced through incremental incentives.
- Teachers are competent, committed and trained in current research and teaching methods, rather than relying on old model drill and workbook exercises.
- Instruction involves multiple strategies appropriate to each learner's interests and needs.
- Youths are assessed for learning disabilities and provided with special education in full compliance with federal law.
- When appropriate, parents, community organizations and volunteers are involved in the academic program.
- Opportunities exist for on-the-job training, work experience and mentorships.
- Partnerships are developed with potential employers.
- Students are scheduled for jobs and further education before reentry into the community.

SOURCE: *Abandoned in the Back Row: New Lessons in Education and Delinquency Prevention*, 30–31. 2001. Washington, DC: Coalition for Juvenile Justice.

more likely to commit suicide, to be sexually assaulted, to be beaten by staff and to be attacked with a weapon compared with youthful offenders housed in juvenile facilities.

Whether incarcerated in a juvenile or adult facility, most youths at some point are eligible for release, often through parole or, as it is now commonly called, reentry or aftercare.

Reentry

Historically, the term **parole** has been used to describe the planned, supervised early release from institutionalization authorized by the correctional facility. Recently, **reentry** has gained prominence in the field as the preferred term used to describe the process of transitioning youthful offenders from secure custody back into the community. Alternately, **aftercare**—the supervision of youths for a limited time after they are released from a correctional facility but while they are still under the control of the facility or the juvenile court—can also apply to this process previously called *parole*. All three terms are used interchangeably. However, the entities responsible for overseeing this process generally still go by the names *parole agencies* and *parole officers*.

Parole is unlike probation in both authority and concept. Probation can be granted only by the juvenile court and is subject to the court's stipulations. It provides the individual with freedom and continuity within the community. Parole, on the other hand, is a release from confinement issued by the correctional facility or a board on a recommendation by the correctional facility. Parole or reentry follows some period of incarceration, whereas probation is an alternative to incarceration. Each state has its own procedures for parole, as do federal corrections. In Minnesota, for example, the Department of Corrections parole agents supervise juveniles sentenced to a correctional facility. The release of a juvenile from a correctional institution is the responsibility of a juvenile hearing officer, who uses a scale incorporating both the offense's severity and the delinquent's history.

After returning to the community, the youth is supervised by a parole officer or by a probation officer given that responsibility. The juvenile is required to abide by a set of rules, which, if violated, can return the youth to a locked or secure facility. The conditions under which a typical juvenile parole agreement is granted include obeying all federal, state and local laws and ordinances; obtaining approval before purchasing or using any motor vehicle, borrowing money, going into debt, doing any credit or installment buying, changing residence, changing employment, changing vocational or school programs or getting married; obtaining permission before leaving the state for any reason; keeping in close contact with the supervising agent; not possessing or using narcotics or other drugs except those prescribed by a physician; and not purchasing or otherwise obtaining any type of firearm or dangerous weapon.

The parole officer makes regular contacts and visits to the youth's residence, school or place of employment. One objective is to involve the family, school and community in helping the youth rehabilitate and integrate back into the community. This is also the goal of probation officers.

Unfortunately, the release and community return aspect of offender care is often poorly executed, with many jurisdictions failing to consider what will happen to these youth once they go back to the environments from which they came.

Reentry/aftercare is often the weakest element in the juvenile justice process.

Barriers to successful reentry identified by researchers include lack of housing and educational options, limited interpersonal and life skills and education, substance abuse or mental health problems and lack of community support. The school is a crucial institution in aftercare for many offenders.

Planning for Reentry

The *Report of the Re-Entry Policy Council* (2005, xxi–xxiii) sets forth specific details on promoting the safe, successful return of offenders to the community. Although the report focuses on adults, it includes considerations for juveniles incarcerated in adult facilities, and the principles are equally applicable to juvenile correctional facilities. The basic premise is that planning for reentry/aftercare should begin as soon as a person is incarcerated and continue through the person's release into the community. Indeed, "The role of correctional institutions in preparing for reentry begins at intake when a case plan is built based on a validated assessment instrument in conjunction with parole" (Gibson and Duncan 2008, 58).

© Joel Gordon

After juvenile offenders are released from a correctional facility, they continue to receive support and supervision from probation or parole officers. A crucial part of a reentry plan is helping offenders find employment. Here a juvenile probation officer works with a client and his mother during a mock interview, as they discuss and prepare for the types of questions the youth is likely to encounter during a job interview.

A significant element in the reentry plan is the development of an individualized programming plan that details the specific treatment needs of the offender during incarceration, including physical and mental health care, substance abuse treatment, cognitive-behavioral therapy to develop positive behaviors and attitudes, education and vocational training and work experience. The plan also includes managing the key transition period including finding housing, providing continuity of care, creating employment opportunities and preparing family members, victims and the community. The report states that successful reentry planning should ensure that community corrections officers have a range of options available to them to reinforce positive behavior and to address, swiftly and certainly, failure to comply with conditions of release (*Report of the Re-Entry Policy Council* 2005).

Two key components of aftercare are that offenders receive both services and supervision and that offenders receive intensive intervention while they are incarcerated, during their transition to the community and when they are under community supervision (a continuity of treatment) (Gies 2003, 1).

 Two key components of aftercare are (1) services and supervision and (2) intensive intervention while incarcerated, during transition into the community and while under community supervision.

Many juveniles being released from confinement and requiring aftercare come from dysfunctional or abusive homes and must be provided with alternative living arrangements. The types of aftercare that can help youths to transition back into the community include home visits before release, a continuation of the treatment program and services within the community, identification of community support systems, availability of 24-hour supervision and a gradual phasing-out of services and supervision based on the youth's response, not on a predetermined schedule. Unfortunately, in many jurisdictions, aftercare is an afterthought.

Table 11.4 summarizes the best and most promising transition practices for youths in custody.

Principles of Intensive Aftercare Programs (IAPs)

More than a decade ago, researchers Altschuler and Armstrong (1994) described the Intensive Aftercare Program (IAP) model designed to make the process of transitioning confined youth back into the community more successful. The IAP model is based on five underlying principles:

1. Preparing youth for progressively increased responsibility and freedom in the community
2. Facilitating youth–community interaction and involvement
3. Working with both the offender and community support systems on qualities needed for constructive interaction and the youth's successful return to the community
4. Developing new resources and supports where needed
5. Monitoring and testing the youth's and the community's ability to work productively together (*Intensive Aftercare Program*, n.d.)

Recently, efforts have been made to adapt the traditional IAP model for use with girls in the juvenile justice system, incorporating the comprehensive,

Table 11.4   Best and Promising Transition Practices for Youths in Custody

- Staff awareness of and familiarity with all county, state, local and private programs that receive and/or send youths to/from jail, detention centers or long-term correctional facilities

- To the extent possible, individualized preplacement planning prior to the transfer of youths from jails or detention centers to the community or long-term correctional facilities

- Immediate transfer of youth's educational records from public and private educational programs to detention centers or from other programs to detention or long-term correctional facilities

- In short-term detention centers, an extensive diagnostic system for the educational, vocational and social, emotional and behavioral assessment of youths

- In long-term correctional facilities, a range of specific educational programs (e.g., vocational and job-related skills, social skills, independent living skills and law-related education); support services (e.g., work experience and placement, alcohol and drug abuse counseling, anger management, vocational counseling, health education and training for parenthood); and external resources (e.g., speakers, tutors, mentors, vocational trainers and counselors, drug abuse counselors, employers and volunteers)

- Access to a resource center, which contains a variety of materials related to transition and support

- Special funds earmarked for transition and support services

- Regular interagency meetings, cooperative in-service training activities and crossover correctional and community school visits to ensure awareness of youths and agency transition needs

- A process for the immediate identification, evaluation and placement of youths with disabilities

- Individualized education program developed for each student with disabilities

- Individual transition plan developed for all students, which includes the student's educational and vocational interests, abilities and preferences

- A transition planning team formed immediately upon student entry into a long-term correctional facility to design and implement the individual transition plan

- Community-based transition system for maintaining student placement and communication after release from a long-term correctional facility

- Immediate transfer of youth's educational records from detention centers and long-term correctional facilities to community schools or other programs

- Coordination with probation or parole to ensure a continuum of services and care is provided in the community

- Coordination between educational program and justice system personnel to ensure that they advocate for youths with disabilities, cultivate family involvement, maintain communications with other agencies and place students in supportive classroom settings

- A system for periodic evaluations of the transition program and all its components

SOURCE: National Center on Education, Disability and Juvenile Justice, 2002, pp. 179–180.

theoretically grounded approach to reentry with compatible "best practices" for female juvenile offenders that emphasize individualized treatment plans and consistent relationships throughout the treatment process (Ryder 2008, 54). Gender-specific services for girls and young women should be designed to meet female offenders' unique needs, value the female perspective, celebrate the female experience and empower young women to reach their full potential.

Promising Aftercare Programs

Gies (2003, 8–24) describes six promising aftercare programs and compares the program characteristics as well as types of services and supervision options after release (see Table 11.5). Note that with one exception, all the programs facilitate transitional structure, use assessment and classification, develop individualized case planning, use rewards and sanctions, link to community treatment services and combine intensive supervision and treatment.

Table 11.5 Comparison of Six Promising Aftercare Programs

	Intensive Aftercare Program	Thomas O'Farrell Youth Center	Bethesda Day Treatment Center	Florida Environmental Institute	Project CRAFT	GROWTH
General Program Information						
Location	Colorado/Nevada/Virginia	Maryland	Pennsylvania	Florida	Florida/Maryland/North Dakota/Tennessee	Alabama
Funding	IAP grant, state funds	Maryland Department of Juvenile Services	Formula grant, private (nonprofit)	Florida Department of Juvenile Justice	CRAFT grant, state funds	Boys & Girls Clubs of South Alabama
Gender	Male	Male	Male/Female	Male	Male/Female	Female
Age	12–18	13–18	10–18	15–18	16–21	13–17
Risk of recidivism	High	High	High	High	High	High
Average length of program	*Colorado:* 10 months incarceration, 8 months aftercare / *Nevada:* 8 months incarceration, 8 months aftercare / *Virginia:* 7 months incarceration, 6 months aftercare	8 months incarceration, 9 months aftercare	6–12 months	9 months incarceration, 9 months aftercare	2–12 months	18 weeks intensive treatment (residential or day treatment), minimum of 6 months aftercare
Program Characteristics						
Facilitates transitional structure	Yes	Yes	Yes	Yes	Yes	Yes
Uses assessment and classification	Yes	Yes	Yes	No	Yes	Yes
Develops individualized case planning	Yes	No	Yes	Yes	Yes	Yes
Uses rewards and sanctions	Yes	Yes	Yes	Yes	No	Yes
Links to community treatment services	Yes	Yes	Yes	Yes	Yes	Yes
Combines intensive supervision and treatment	Yes	Yes	Yes	Yes	Yes	Yes

Types of Services and Supervision Options after Release

Treatment services	• Education • Employment • Vocational training • Mental health counseling • Life skills training • Drug/alcohol treatment	• Education • Vocational counseling • Crisis intervention • Mentoring • Family services • Transportation	• Individual, group and family counseling • Drug/alcohol treatment • Education • Life skills development	• Education • Employment • Vocational skills • Family assistance	• Employment • Drug/alcohol treatment • Housing services • Family services • Vocational training • Financial assistance	• Female-specific life skills • Community service • Education • Functional family therapy • Adventure therapy • Trauma recovery • Substance abuse • Parenting teen
Supervision options	• Staff contact (1–5/week) • Curfew • Urinalysis • House arrest • Electronic monitoring • Paging • Monthly court review • Day treatment (NV) • Furlough (NV) • Group home (VA)	• Staff contact (12/month) • Coordination with probation staff • Surveillance	• Intensive supervision program • Search and rescue • 24-hour crisis hotline • Treatment detention accountability	• Staff contact (4/week) • Curfew • Required job attendance • Frequent calls	• Coordination with parole and probation officers • Community work service • Traditional probation and parole	• Staff contact (weekly empowerment meetings)

SOURCE: Steve V. Gies. 2003 (September). *Aftercare Services*, pp. 23–24. Washington, DC: OJJDP Juvenile Justice Bulletin. (NCJ 201800)

Summary

- A modern, comprehensive graduated sanctions continuum set includes four components for targeted populations: (1) informal sanctions within the community for first-time, nonviolent offenders, (2) intermediate sanctions (including probation) within the community for more serious offenders, (3) secure confinement programs for the most violent offenders and (4) reentry/aftercare programs that provide high levels of social control and treatment services.
- Probation is the most common disposition of the juvenile or family court.
- The formal goals of probation are to protect the public by supervising and controlling juvenile conduct, to hold juveniles accountable for their actions and to improve the delinquents' behavior through rehabilitation.
- The probation officer has traditionally been responsible for two key functions: (1) personally supervising and counseling youths who are on probation and (2) serving as a link to other community services.
- Common forms of intermediate sanctions are intensive supervision probation, nonsecure juvenile residential facilities, nonresidential day treatment alternatives, electronic monitoring, house arrest, training schools and boot camps.
- Compared with public correctional institutions, private correctional institutions confine more Whites, more girls and more status offenders. The inmates are younger, and their stays are usually longer.
- The sociopolitical climate that exists in juvenile correctional institutions is the same as that found in adult institutions.
- The performance-based standards goals for corrections cover security, order, safety, programming, justice and health/mental health.
- Most effective youthful offender programs include in-depth evaluation, screening and assessment; daily scheduling; point system discipline; positive behavioral support therapy; and education, including literacy, GED preparation and computer literacy.
- Reentry/aftercare is often the weakest element in the juvenile justice process.
- Two key components of aftercare are (1) services and supervision and (2) intensive intervention while incarcerated, during transition into the community and while under community supervision.

Discussion Questions

1. How effective is probation in juvenile justice? What, if any, changes should be made in the juvenile probation process?

2. Should parents, custodians or guardians of youths be actively involved in a youth's rehabilitation? Why or why not?

3. Is community corrections worthwhile? Does it work? What would you do to improve it?

4. Is there a difference in attitude between a youth who has been confined and one who has been directed by programs in community corrections? What makes the difference?

5. Do community corrections give judges more options in sentencing youths? Is this an advantage or disadvantage?

6. Should violent offenders be subject to community corrections or directed to a secure facility? Why?

7. What are some potential alternatives to secure detention? What problems may be involved in expanding alternative programs?

8. Do you support a conservative or a liberal approach to treating juveniles? Why? Why do you think society is inclined to a "get tough on juveniles" attitude?

9. What would constitute an effective reentry/aftercare program in your community?

10. What resources are available while youths are under the control of the juvenile justice system and when they return to the community?

References

Altschuler, D. M., and T. L. Armstrong. 1994. *Intensive Aftercare for High-Risk Juveniles: A Community Care Model.* Washington, DC: Office of Juvenile Justice and Delinquency Prevention.

Asbridge, Caleb S. 2007 (October). "Sexual Assault in Juvenile Corrections: A Preventable Tragedy." *Corrections Today* 69 (5): 80–85.

Beck, Allen J., Paige M. Harrison, and Paul Guerino. 2010 (January). *Sexual Victimization in Juvenile Facilities Reported by Youth, 2008–2009.* Washington, DC: Bureau of Justice Statistics, Special Report. (NCJ 228416)

Brank, Eve, Jodi Lane, Susan Turner, Terry Fain, and Amber Sehgal. 2008 (April). "An Experimental Juvenile Probation Program: Effects on Parent and Peer Relationships." *Crime & Delinquency* 54 (2): 193–224.

Brooks, Carol Cramer. 2008 (February). "The Challenge of Following Education Legislation in Confinement Education Programs." *Corrections Today* 70 (1): 28–30, 46.

Caldwell, Michael F., Michael Vitacco, and Gregory J. Van Rybrock. 2006 (May). "Are Violent Delinquents Worth Treating? A Cost-Benefit Analysis." *Journal of Research in Crime and Delinquency* 43 (2): 148–168.

CBR Youth Connect. n.d. 28071 Hwy 109, P.O. Box 681, La Junta, CO 81050. http://www.cbryouthconnect.org

Conlon, Bill, Scott Harris, Jeffrey Nagel, Mike Hillman, and Rick Hanson. 2008 (February). "Education: Don't Leave Prison without It." *Corrections Today* 70 (1): 48–52.

Gibson, Steve, and Karen Duncan. 2008 (February). "A Multifaceted Approach from Intake to Discharge." *Corrections Today* 70 (1): 58–59.

Gies, Steve V. 2003 (September). *Aftercare Services.* Juvenile Justice Bulletin, Washington, DC: Office of Juvenile Justice and Delinquency Prevention. (NCJ 201800)

Griffin, Patrick, and Patricia Torbet. 2002 (June). *Desktop Guide to Good Juvenile Probation Practice.* Washington, DC: National Center for Juvenile Justice.

Hockenberry, Sarah, Melissa Sickmund, and Anthony Sladky. 2011 (July). *Juvenile Residential Facility Census, 2008: Selected Findings.* National Report Series. Washington, DC: Office of Juvenile Justice and Delinquency Prevention. (NCJ 231683)

Intensive Aftercare Program (IAP). n.d. Sacramento, CA: The Center for Delinquency & Crime Policy Studies (CDCPS), California State University.

Juvenile Sanctions Center. 2003. *School-Based Probation: An Approach Worth Considering.* 2003. Reno, NV: National Council of Juvenile and Family Court Judges, Juvenile Sanctions Center. http://www.ncjfcj.org/content/view/513/331/

Kupchik, Aaron. 2007 (June). "The Correctional Experiences of Youth in Adult and Juvenile Prisons." *Justice Quarterly* 24 (2): 247–270.

Mental Health and Adolescent Girls in the Justice System. 2003. Fact Sheet from the National Mental Health Association. http://www.nmha.org/children/justjuv/girlsjj.cfm

Meyer, Edward. 2008 (February). "Get Tough on Crime, Not Kids." *Corrections Today* 70 (1): 19.

Morrell, Barbara. 2007. "Rehabilitative Approaches to Corrections Bolstered by Knowledge of Effective Treatment Principles and Firm Public Support." *Criminal Justice Research Reports* (July/August): 87–88.

Morton, Joann Brown. 2007 (August). "Providing Gender-Responsive Services for Women and Girls." *Corrections Today* 69 (4): 6, 12.

O'Rourke, Tom, Jack Catrett, and David Houchins. 2008 (February). "Teacher Retention in the Georgia DJJ: A Plan That Works." *Corrections Today* 70 (1): 40–43.

Pihl-Buckley, Heidi. 2008 (February). "Tailoring the Prison Rape Elimination Act to a Juvenile Setting." *Corrections Today* 70 (1): 44–47.

Promising Sanctioning Programs in a Graduated System. 2003. Reno, NV: Juvenile Sanctioning Center.

Puzzanchera, Charles, and W. Kang. 2011. *Easy Access to Juvenile Court Statistics: 1985–2008.* Accessed November 28, 2011. http://www.ojjdp.gov/ojstatbb/ezajcs/asp/process.asp

Rehabilitating Juvenile Offenders. 2005–2008. Chicago: MacArthur Foundation.

Report of the Re-Entry Policy Council: Charting the Safe and Successful Return of Prisoners to the Community. 2005 (January). New York: Council of State Governments, Reentry Policy Council.

Roush, David W. 2008a. "Helpful Juvenile Detention." *Reaching Today's Youth* 3 (3): 63–68. Accessed January 30, 2012, from *CYC-Online* 110 (April). http://www.cyc-net.org/cyc-online/cycol-0408-roush.html

———. 2008b (February). "Sexual Misconduct in Juvenile Justice Facilities: Implications for Work Force Training." *Corrections Today* 70 (1): 32–35.

Ryder, Judith. 2008. "Revamping the Altschuler and Armstrong Intensive Aftercare Program for Use with Girls in the Juvenile Justice System." *Criminal Justice Research Review* (March/April): 54–57.

Sedlak, Andrea J., and Carol Bruce. 2010 (December). *Youth's Characteristics and Backgrounds: Findings from the Survey of Youth in Residential Placement.* Washington, DC: Office of Juvenile Justice and Delinquency Prevention. (NCJ 227730)

Sedlak, Andrea J., and Karla S. McPherson. 2010 (May). *Conditions of Confinement: Findings from the Survey of Youth in Residential Placement.* Washington, DC: Office of Juvenile Justice and Delinquency Prevention. (NCJ 227729)

Shomaker, Nancy, and Mark Gornik. 2002 (October). "Youthful Offenders in Adult Corrections: A Systemic Approach Using Effective Interventions." *Corrections Today* 64 (6): 112–123.

Snyder, Howard N., and Melissa Sickmund. 2006. *Juvenile Offenders and Victims: 2006 National Report.* Washington, DC: U.S. Department of Justice, Office of Justice Programs, Office of Juvenile Justice and Delinquency Prevention.

Stickrath, Thomas J., and Sarah Wallis. 2007 (June). "Reducing Aggression in Juvenile Facilities: Ohio's Plan." *Corrections Today* 69 (3): 70–71.

Vivian, John P., Jennifer N. Grimes, and Stella Vasquez. 2007. "Assaults in Juvenile Correctional Facilities: An Exploratory Study." *Journal of Crime and Justice* 30 (1): 17–34.

Case Cited

Santana v. Collazo, 714 F.2d 1172, 1177 (1st Cir. 1983)

Preventing Delinquency and Recidivism

12

> " The truism that an ounce of prevention is worth a pound of cure surely applies to delinquency. If we are to check...violent crime by juveniles, we must go beyond treating symptoms, however diligently, to examine causes. Nor must we be so preoccupied with what is wrong with a minority of our youth that our tunnel vision blinds us to what is right with the majority. "
>
> **—Office of Juvenile Justice and Delinquency Prevention**

Positive interactions between officers and youths can go a long way toward preventing delinquency and recidivism. It is vital that juveniles perceive authority figures as caring advocates, rather than heavy-handed adversaries, which can often be a challenging task.

© Bob Daemmrich/PhotoEdit

DO YOU KNOW?

- What approach to the delinquency problem emerged during the late 1960s?
- What three approaches to juvenile crime prevention are?
- What the three general levels of prevention are?
- What an effective prevention approach must address?
- How the numerator and denominator approaches to prevention differ?

- What the two-pronged public health model for prevention consists of?
- What the Blueprints for Violence Prevention Initiative is?
- What strategy has proved effective in reducing gun violence? What strategies have proved ineffective?
- What antigang programs can be implemented?
- What the purpose of drug testing in the school is?

CAN YOU DEFINE?

corrective prevention

denominator
    approach

desistance

gateway drugs

mechanical
    prevention

numerator approach

polydrug use

primary prevention

protective factors

punitive prevention

recidivism

risk factors

secondary prevention

tertiary prevention

CHAPTER OUTLINE

Introduction

Defining Prevention

Defining and Measuring
    Recidivism and
    Desistance

Classifying Prevention
    Approaches

Prevention versus Control

*Three Levels of Delinquency
    Prevention*

Prevention as an Attack on
    Causes

*Which Youth to Target: The
    Numerator and Denominator
    Approaches*

*Prevention and the Public Health
    Model*

What Works in Preventing
    Delinquency and Violence?

Blueprints for Violence
    Prevention Initiative

*Midwestern Prevention Project
    (MPP)*

*Big Brothers Big Sisters of America
    (BBBS)*

Functional Family Therapy (FFT)

LifeSkills® Training (LST)

Multisystemic Therapy (MST)

Nurse–Family Partnership (NFP)

*Multidimensional Treatment
    Foster Care (MTFC)*

*Olweus Bullying Prevention
    Program (OBPP)*

*Promoting Alternative THinking
    Strategies (PATHS)*

The Incredible Years Series (IYS)

*Project Toward No Drug Abuse
    (Project TND)*

Truancy and Dropout
    Prevention

Communities In Schools (CIS)

*Alternative to Suspension
    Program (ASP)*

Alternative Schools

*Safe Schools/Healthy Students
    (SSHS) Program*

Project H.E.L.P.: High
    Expectations Learning
    Program

Preventing Delinquency
    through Improved Child
    Protection Services (CPS)

Violence Prevention

Reducing Gun Violence

Gang Prevention

Drug Use Prevention Programs

DARE

*The National Commission on
    Drug-Free Schools*

Parents: The Anti-Drug

*A Reality-Based Approach to Drug
    Education*

Drug Testing in Schools

Mentoring

Teens, Crime and the
    Community (TCC)

A Caution Regarding Net
    Widening in Prevention
    Efforts

Introduction

Common sense says it is better to prevent a problem than to react to it once it arises. The health care fields have embraced this preventive approach by advocating that it is better to prevent disease and other health issues before they occur than to try and treat or cure them after the fact. This same philosophy is true for juvenile delinquency as well as for child neglect and abuse. Traditionally our society's approach to youthful offending has been reactive, and juvenile courts and diversion programs have responded with a wide range of services focused on punishment, control or rehabilitation. However, "Attempting to reduce crime by focusing only on law enforcement and corrections is like providing expensive ambulances at the bottom of a cliff to pick up the youngster who falls off, rather than building a fence at the top of the cliff to keep them from falling in the first place" (Mendel 2000).

In 1967 the President's Commission on Law Enforcement and the Administration of Justice advocated, "In the last analysis, the most promising and so the most important method of dealing with crime is by preventing it—by ameliorating the conditions of life that drive people to commit crime and that undermine the restraining rules and institutions erected by society against antisocial conduct." Subsequently this prevention emphasis was written into federal law in the Juvenile Delinquency Prevention Acts of 1972 and 1974 and the Juvenile Justice Amendments of 1977.

 During the late 1960s a new approach for dealing with delinquency emerged—a focus on the prevention of crime.

Each municipality, county and state is unique in its particular crime problems. Each is also unique in how it approaches crime and how it disposes of those who commit crime. What constitutes delinquency is subject to varied interpretations across places, times and social groupings. A youth's behavior may be viewed as "delinquent" by police, as "acting out" by mental health professionals, as "sin" by members of the clergy and as "just plain mischief" by those who view some misbehavior as a normal part of growing up. The National Crime Prevention Council (NCPC) Web site states:

> Many adults do not think well of teenagers. In individual teenagers, they see rebellion, mood swings and tempers. In groups of young people, they see threats (even when none are made), malice (even when they're just talking outside the local convenience store) and gangs (even in kids just walking around the mall). But the great majority of teens are sources of strength, not trouble, to their communities. They are, by and large, intensely interested in the adult world and eager to help. Even among those who get into trouble, the first brush with the juvenile justice system is usually the last.

In dealing with youth, it is critical to remember that adolescence is a developmental period often characterized by risk-taking, acting before thinking, impulsivity and challenging of adult authority. These are *normative* behaviors for teens in their search for self and separation from parents. Even "good" kids will likely experience some, if not all, of these behaviors during adolescence. For those in juvenile justice, it is crucial to know the difference between a youth who is on a path to delinquency and crime and one who is simply on the path to normal adulthood, with all of its "fits and starts."

Defining Prevention

Recall from Chapter 1 that there exists not one, but at least 51 different juvenile justice systems in this country. In fact, at a recent conference, a juvenile court judge from Pennsylvania noted that there are 60 counties in her state and, thus, 60 juvenile justice systems in that state. Juvenile justice is truly a local process, and with this extent of individualization comes inevitable variation in language and definitions. For example, an online search of various state statutes and juvenile justice departments revealed the following definitions of delinquency prevention:

- "Prevention" [is] the creation of conditions, opportunities and experiences that encourage and develop healthy, self-sufficient children and that occur before the onset of problems (Arizona State Senate 2002).
- Prevention: Efforts that help prevent a youth from entering the juvenile justice system as a delinquent (Florida Department of Juvenile Justice 2008).
- Delinquency Prevention: Programs to prevent or reduce the incidence of delinquent acts and directed to youth at risk of becoming delinquent to prevent them from entering the juvenile justice system or to intervene with first-time and nonserious offenders to keep them out of the juvenile justice system. This program area excludes programs targeted at youth already adjudicated delinquent, on probation and in corrections and those programs designed specifically to prevent gang-related or substance abuse activities undertaken as part of other program areas (Illinois Department of Human Services, n.d.).
- *Prevention* is a process of intervention designed to alter the circumstances associated with problem behaviors. Effective prevention practices decrease problem behaviors and subsequent difficulties children and adolescents experience in school and in the community. Prevention includes a wide range of activities that address the needs of an equally wide range of children and youth (National Center on Education, Disability and Juvenile Justice, n.d.).

As these examples illustrate, *prevention* is a broadly defined term, open to wide interpretation. The common thread is that prevention encompasses any and all measures taken *before* delinquent behavior occurs.

Defining and Measuring Recidivism and Desistance

Before moving on to the classification of prevention approaches, it is important to understand what is meant by **recidivism**—repeated offending or a return to crime after being caught, convicted and "corrected"—and how it is measured, because prevention efforts seek not only to keep delinquency from occurring in the first place, they also aim to stop a recurrence of delinquent behavior. Recidivism is a central concept when assessing the effectiveness of a prevention program because policymakers and practitioners want to know what impact a program or sanction has on criminality. Does the intervention keep offenders from returning to delinquency? When a person reaches a permanent state of non-offending, it is called **desistance**. Desistance is the ultimate goal of all prevention and correctional intervention efforts. Thus, offenders who are processed through the justice system face two paths upon release: They will either desist from further delinquency or they will recidivate.

Measuring recidivism is not always easy, Recall the discussion in Chapter 1 regarding how delinquency is measured and the challenges criminologists encounter when trying to reach an accurate count of delinquent offenses. A variety of data sources exist—official reports, victimization surveys and offender self-reports—yet they rarely, if ever, produce the same results regarding number of offenses. Similar challenges are faced when attempting to measure recidivism. Official arrest records do not reflect the true number of crimes committed—only those that come to the attention of law enforcement. Victimization surveys and self-reports are imperfect measures as well. Further questions arise regarding whether recidivism rates should be determined by counting arrests, convictions or a return to confinement; whether it matters if the offenders repeat the criminal act for which they first were sanctioned or if they engaged in a different type of crime; and how to handle the passage of time, specifically, when to start the recidivism clock ticking and what event will cause it to stop:

> The timing of recidivism is key not only to its measurement but also to understanding the processes underlying the effects of sanctions and interventions with respect to the propensity of the individual to commit crime. Recidivism is delineated by starting and stopping events. The starting event can be the entry into a program or the release from prison. Other criminal justice events such as starting probation or the beginning of parole also qualify as starting events. The stopping event is typically a criminal justice action such as an arrest or revocation of supervision.
>
> Recidivism refers to both the *type* of stopping event (such as the arrest) and the *amount of time* between the starting and stopping criminal justice events (such as between entering a program and rearrest). Sometimes researchers report only statistics on the stopping event, such as the percentage of people arrested. Other times, researchers report the average amount of time from starting and stopping event(s).
>
> The "at-risk" environment must be considered when measuring recidivism. The level of risk for someone released from prison may depend on the level of post-release supervision. For example, it may depend on whether drug testing is conducted. Studies have shown that the higher the at-risk environment, the more likely someone will recidivate. ("Measuring Recidivism" 2008)

Classifying Prevention Approaches

Several approaches to classifying prevention efforts have been set forth. Following are two ways to classify prevention efforts.

Prevention versus Control

Technically prevention is a measure taken *before* a delinquent act occurs to forestall the act; control is a measure taken *after* a delinquent act occurs. In reality, prevention can also serve the purpose of control when the concept of recidivism is involved. Thus, crime *prevention* can be thought of as efforts to thwart crime from occurring in the first place; crime *control* can be conceptualized as measures to deal with and contain criminal behavior once it has already occurred.

In this context, three kinds of prevention are relevant for juvenile justice.

 Prevention can be corrective, punitive or mechanical.

- **Corrective prevention** focuses on eliminating conditions that lead to or cause criminal behavior.
- **Punitive prevention** relies on the threat of punishment to forestall criminal acts.
- **Mechanical prevention** is directed toward "target hardening," making it difficult or impossible to commit particular offenses. Locks on doors, bars on windows, alarms, security guards and many other options are available to protect possible targets of criminal acts.

Another way to classify prevention efforts is by level. These levels encompass the three methods just discussed.

Three Levels of Delinquency Prevention

The first line of defense against all forms of juvenile crime is prevention, whether *primary* (directed at the population as a whole), *secondary* (aimed at a specific at-risk population) or *tertiary* (targeted at an offending population to prevent repetition of the behaviors).

 Prevention may be primary, secondary or tertiary.

Primary Prevention   **Primary prevention** modifies and changes crime-causing conditions in the overall physical and social conditions that lead to crime. Corrective and mechanical prevention fit into this level. Primary prevention efforts are usually directed toward **risk factors**, those characteristics or variables that increase an individual's likelihood of committing delinquent acts, with no distinction made between those who have committed a crime and those who have not. Fitting into the primary prevention category are programs that provide after-school activities and mentoring, including boys and girls clubs, Big Brothers Big Sisters and youth foundations.

An example of primary prevention is the community crime prevention program in Seattle, Washington. This program focused on preventing residential burglaries, specifically crimes of opportunity by juveniles who entered homes through unlocked doors and windows during the day when residents were away. Prevention efforts were aimed at contributing environmental factors. Certain neighborhoods and types of housing were identified as being vulnerable to burglaries using demographics, criminal incidents and physical characteristics statistics. The community then gave citizens home security checklists. Citizens in target areas used these checklists to protect their homes against relatively easy entry by burglars. This program was directed at making crime more difficult rather than at attacking individual motivations to commit crime. Such deterrence programs effectively increase the risks to potential burglars, thus decreasing the opportunities for burglary.

As noted by the American Psychological Association (APA) (n.d., 55–56) in its discussion of primary prevention programs: "Prevention programs directed early in life can reduce factors that increase risk for antisocial behavior and clinical dysfunction in childhood and adolescence." Among the most promising primary prevention programs are those that include family counseling for pregnant women and for new mothers in the home, with continued visits during the first few years of the child's life. The APA (55) reports that in a 20-year follow-up study, of one home visitor program, positive effects were seen for both the at-risk child and mother.

Preschool programs also hold promise if they include activities that develop intellectual, emotional and social skills and introduce children to responsible decision making. According to the APA (n.d., 56), "Primary prevention programs of the type that promote social and cognitive skills seem to have the greatest impact on attitudes about violent behavior among children and youth. Skills that aid children in learning alternatives to violent behaviors include social perspective-taking, alternative solution generation, self-esteem enhancement, peer negotiation skills, problem-solving skills training and anger management."

Secondary Prevention   **Secondary prevention** seeks early identification and intervention into the lives of individuals or groups found in crime-causing circumstances. It focuses on changing the behavior of those likely to become delinquent. Punitive prevention fits into this level. The APA (n.d., 56) notes, "Secondary prevention programs that focus on improving individual affective, cognitive and behavioral skills or on modifying the learning conditions for aggression offer promise of interrupting the path toward violence for high-risk or predelinquent youth. ... Programs that attempt to work with and modify the family system of a high-risk child have great potential to prevent development of aggressive and violent behavior."

Tertiary Prevention   **Tertiary prevention**, the third level, is aimed at preventing recidivism—that is, it focuses on preventing further delinquent acts by youths already identified as delinquent. Tertiary prevention is also called treatment or rehabilitation.

Prevention as an Attack on Causes

Of the three levels of prevention, primary and secondary prevention most closely approach the essence of *prevention*, in that they seek to preclude delinquent acts *before* they occur. Tertiary prevention is really remediation aimed at forestalling future acts after an initial act has been committed and detected.

Primary and secondary prevention activities are effective only if they address the underlying causes of delinquency. To prevent a behavior from occurring, those factors that stimulate the behavior must be removed or mitigated. Conditions that stimulate delinquent acts and those that lack constraints to inhibit those acts are both potential causes of delinquency.

 Effective prevention approaches must address both the conditions and the lack of constraints that cause delinquency.

Using a proactive approach to alter the environments that produce delinquency, an ecological analogy can be made, as stated by one police chief: "We have to stop swatting at the mosquitoes and start looking to the swamps that produce them." With delinquents, as with mosquitoes, it is much harder to get rid of this year's swarm than to prevent next year's from hatching. This approach is consistent with the public health model introduced in Chapter 6.

Which Youth to Target: The Numerator and Denominator Approaches

The public health model focuses the scarce resources of the juvenile justice system on those at greatest risk—young Black males living in areas of poverty with high crime rates and drug dealing. Applying a mathematical analogy, consider the number of at-risk youths compared with the total number of youths in a population; the at-risk youths would be the *numerator* and the total number of youths would be the *denominator*.

Many crime and delinquency researchers suggest dealing with the denominator for best results. Focusing efforts only on juvenile offenders (i.e., taking a numerator approach) is unlikely to reduce youth crime, just as focusing only on those who are unemployed will not lower unemployment rates (because there is a vast pool of the "potentially unemployed"). The relative ineffectiveness of the numerator approach, and the contrasting effectiveness of the denominator approach, is seen in medicine. For example, a numerator approach in polio and tuberculosis would have had little impact on prevalence, but denominator approaches such as mass vaccination and screening have almost eradicated these diseases. Such an approach can also be effective in delinquency prevention.

 The **numerator approach** focuses on individuals and symptoms, whereas the **denominator approach** focuses on the entire group and causes.

One reason the denominator approach is ignored is because it tends to generate turf fights. It is also sometimes *easier* (albeit less effective) to act to improve an existing problem than to focus on a broader approach to prevent problems in the future. The denominator approach is consistent with the public health model.

Prevention and the Public Health Model

For more than a decade, juvenile justice has been shifting back toward a public health model in attempting to understand the causes of delinquency and tailor approaches to its prevention. Effective crime and delinquency prevention based on the public health model uses a two-pronged strategy involving risk and protective factors.

 The public health model's two-pronged juvenile crime prevention strategy reduces known risk factors and promotes protective factors.

Recall the discussion in Chapter 4 pertaining to risk and protective factors. As a brief review, risk factors are conditions, characteristics or variables that increase the likelihood that a child will become delinquent, whereas **protective factors** (which are often the opposite of corresponding risk factors) are strengths or assets that help reduce the negative impacts of risk factors by providing positive ways for an individual to respond to risks and avoid delinquency. Among the commonly identified protective factors are individual characteristics such as having a resilient temperament and positive social orientation; bonding with family and having positive relationships with other adults, teachers and peers; monitoring and supervision; positive discipline methods; and having healthy values and high standards. However, the Office of Juvenile Justice and Delinquency Prevention (OJJDP 2009) is very clear on one point: "It should be noted that risk and protective factors are neither causes nor cures. Rather, risk and protective factors are statistical predictors that … have a strong theoretical base."

What Works in Preventing Delinquency and Violence?

With many programs now having several decades of experience behind them, and the road ahead appearing more challenging than ever for those involved in handling juvenile delinquency and crime, the question has become, "What works?" The evidence, thus far, is mixed.

Research has begun to reveal that many popular anticrime programs simply do not work and that vast amounts of money continue to be spent on programs that, although they may enjoy widespread public and policy support, do not demonstrate any evidence of having positive impacts on juvenile delinquency and violence. A team of criminologists, led by Lawrence W. Sherman, reviewed more than 500 scientific evaluations of crime-prevention programs funded by the Justice Department, with a special focus on factors relating to juvenile crime and program effects on youth violence, and concluded that the following programs do *not* work (Sherman et al. 1998, 7): gun buyback programs; military-style correctional boot camps; "scared straight" programs; shock probation/parole; residential programs for juvenile offenders using challenging experiences in rural settings; short-term nonresidential training for at-risk youth; summer jobs or subsidized work programs for at-risk youth; the DARE program; drug prevention classes focused on fear and other emotional appeals, including self-esteem; counseling and peer counseling of students in schools; home detention with electronic monitoring; and arrests of juveniles for minor offenses. Although this study was conducted more than a decade ago, no new data have become available to refute or reverse these conclusions.

The news is not all bad, however. Programs that consistently demonstrate positive effects on youths at risk of developing delinquent behavior include those that strengthen the institutions of family and school in the youth's life, such as family therapy and parent training about delinquent and at-risk preadolescents; training or coaching in thinking skills for high-risk youth; clarifying and communicating norms about behavior through rules, reinforcement of positive behavior and schoolwide initiatives (such as antibullying campaigns); providing social competency skills curriculums; providing frequent home visits to infants aged 0 to 2 in high-risk homes by trained nurses to help prevent child neglect and abuse; and rehabilitation programs for juvenile offenders that apply treatments appropriate to their risk factors (Sherman et al. 1998, 7–8).

In trying to answer the question "What works?" most research has led to the conclusion that punishment alone, in the absence of some form of human intervention or services, is unlikely to have much of an effect on recidivism. Evidence has also shown that although treatment is more effective than punishment in reducing recidivism, not all treatment programs are equally effective. Furthermore, what works for one offender might not work for another. The constellation of individual offender characteristics will drive treatment needs.

It is critical to target offenders with the highest probability of recidivism and to provide the most intensive treatment to the highest-risk offenders. Interestingly, intensive treatment directed at low-risk offenders can actually increase recidivism.

Evidence has also shown that targeting for change in criminogenic needs, as opposed to noncriminogenic needs, can have a much greater effect in reducing recidivism. This means programs that focus on changing antisocial attitudes, distancing offenders from antisocial friends, treating substance abuse and helping offenders control impulsive behavior are far more effective in preventing further offending than are those that try to build up an offender's self-esteem, creative abilities (art therapy) or physical conditioning, all of which are noncriminogenic needs.

The most effective interventions are cognitive and behavioral in nature: They focus on current factors that influence offender behavior; they are action-oriented, and offender behavior is appropriately reinforced. Most effective behavioral interventions involve structured social learning where new skills and behaviors are modeled, cognitive-behavioral approaches that target criminogenic risk factors and family-based approaches that train family members on appropriate techniques. Two of the most effective programs are Functional Family Therapy (FFT) and Multisystemic Therapy (MST) (discussed shortly).

Cognitive-behavioral treatment (CBT) and intervention has been shown to be particularly effective in changing the behavior that drives delinquency. CBT is based on the principles that antisocial, distorted, unproductive, irrational thinking causes antisocial and unproductive behavior; that thinking can be influenced; and that we can change how we feel and behave by changing what we think. A meta-analysis of CBT found that, on average, this intervention reduced recidivism by 25 percent, but in those programs with the most effective configuration recidivism was reduced by more than 50 percent (Landenberger and Lipsey 2005).

In between the "what works" and "what doesn't work" categories are a multitude of programs that may hold promise but that have not yet produced enough evidence for researchers to know, one way or the other, if they are effective in preventing or reducing delinquency.

As already mentioned, when considering strategies to prevent or reduce juvenile offending, one must necessarily look at the issue of recidivism and tertiary prevention efforts. It is hoped, presumably, that juvenile justice's handling of delinquency is effective to the degree that once children come into the system and receive some type of treatment, punishment or both, the response will be sufficient to turn the youths around and put them on a path of prosocial, law-abiding behavior, such that these individuals will never again cross paths with either the juvenile or criminal justice systems. The reality, however, is that some youths pass through the system only to go back to their old ways and offend again. In some cases, their experience in the justice system exacerbates their antisocial tendencies or other underlying issues, and these youth actually return to the streets worse than when they entered the system. As more programs have been evaluated and scientifically scrutinized for effectiveness in reducing recidivism, we have begun to see a clearer picture of what constitutes effective intervention. The principles of effective intervention, discussed in depth in Chapter 9, are worth considering again here in the context of tertiary prevention.

The current belief is that a dual approach—working to reduce risk factors while building the skills and competencies that improve resiliency—holds the most promise for effective delinquency prevention (Federal Advisory Committee on Juvenile Justice 2007, 4). To this end, the OJJDP has, since 1996, actively sought and funded programs that show empirical evidence of effectively preventing youth crime and delinquency. This effort is known as the Blueprints for Violence Prevention Initiative.

Blueprints for Violence Prevention Initiative

Launched by the Center for the Study and Prevention of Violence (CSPV) at the University of Colorado at Boulder, the Blueprints Initiative set out to identify effective violence prevention programs across the country so that communities could begin replicating successful programs locally.

 The Blueprints for Violence Prevention Initiative is the OJJDP's comprehensive effort to provide communities with a set of programs whose effectiveness has been scientifically demonstrated.

As of year-end 2011, more than 900 programs have been reviewed using rigorous selection criteria. Of these, 11 model programs, or Blueprints, have been identified as being exemplary in their effects of reducing adolescent violent crime, aggression, delinquency, substance abuse, predelinquent childhood aggression and conduct disorders. Another 19 programs are identified as promising.

This section briefly discusses some of the Blueprints programs that show the strongest empirical evidence of thwarting youthful offending, whether it is in keeping predelinquent behavior from evolving into actual delinquency or in serving as an intermediate intervention program to help reduce recidivism in youths who have already come into contact with the juvenile justice system. For a more complete description of these programs and the risk and protective factors each targets, access the "Prevention" tab on the OJJDP's Model Programs Guide (MPG) Web site or go to the Blueprints for Violence Prevention Web site. For more information, visit the Criminal Justice Companion Web site at cengagebrain.com, then access the web links for this chapter.

Midwestern Prevention Project (MPP)

The Midwestern Prevention Project (MPP) is a comprehensive, community-based, multifaceted program for adolescent drug abuse prevention that targets the entire population of middle-school students, ages 10 to 12. The ultimate goal of MPP is to prevent or reduce the onset and prevalence of use of **gateway drugs** (alcohol, tobacco and marijuana) by (1) helping youths recognize the tremendous social pressures to use drugs and (2) providing skills in how to avoid drug use.

MPP employs a system of well-coordinated, communitywide strategies, including mass media programming, a school program, continuing school boosters, a parent education and organization program, community organization and training and local policy change regarding tobacco, alcohol and other drugs. These components are introduced to the community in sequence at a rate of one a year, with the mass media component occurring throughout all the years.

The central component for the MPP drug prevention program is the school, where active social learning techniques are taught (modeling, role playing and discussion, with student peer leaders assisting teachers). The parental program consists of a parent–principal committee that reviews both school drug policy and parent–child communications training. The three other components—mass media coverage and programming, community organization and local health policy change—are used to send a consistent message supporting a norm of nondrug use. All components involve regular meetings of respective deliverers (e.g., community leaders for organization) to review and refine programs.

Big Brothers Big Sisters of America (BBBS)

Big Brothers Big Sisters (BBBS), an exemplary mentoring program, is a federation of more than 420 agencies that serve children and adolescents between the ages of 6 and 16, a significant number of whom are from disadvantaged single-parent households. The BBBS program seeks not to ameliorate specific problems but rather to provide a widespread foundation of support in all aspects of young people's lives through a professionally sustained one-on-one relationship between a youth and a caring adult.

In the community-based traditional program, the volunteer mentor commits substantial time to the youth, meeting for about four hours, two to four times a month, for at least one year. During this time together, the mentor and youth engage in developmentally appropriate activities such as walking; grocery shopping; watching television; visiting a library; washing the car; playing catch; attending a play, movie, school activity or sporting event; or just hanging out and sharing thoughts. BBBS has also added a school-based program in which volunteers meet with their Little Brother or Little Sister for an hour each week for such activities as playing educational games, working on homework or crafts or just talking.

Although individual agencies occasionally customize their programs to fit specific needs, the integrity of the program is protected through a national infrastructure that oversees recruitment, screening, matching and supervision in a regulated process whereby adults who are most likely to be successful mentors are selected and matched to adolescents who share a common belief system. Staff supervision and support are critical to ensuring that mentor and mentee meet regularly to build positive relationships.

An 18-month study of eight BBBS affiliates found that when compared with a control group on a waiting list for a match, youths in the mentoring program were 46 percent less likely to start using drugs, 27 percent less likely to start drinking and 32 percent less likely to hit someone. Mentored youths skipped half as many days of school as control youths, had better attitudes toward and performance in school and had improved peer and family relationships.

Functional Family Therapy (FFT)

Functional Family Therapy (FFT) is a family-based prevention and intervention program for dysfunctional youths ages 11 to 18 that has been applied successfully in a variety of multiethnic, multicultural contexts to treat a range of high-risk youths and their families. It integrates several elements (established clinical theory, empirically supported principles and extensive clinical experience) into a clear, comprehensive clinical model that allows flexible, culturally sensitive and effective intervention across a variety of complex and multidimensional problems.

The specific phases of the FFT model are engagement/motivation, behavior change and generalization. The engagement/motivation phase aims to reduce the intense negativity often characteristic of high-risk families. The goal of the behavior change phase is to reduce or eliminate problem behaviors and related family interaction dynamics by teaching skills such as effective family communication, proficient parenting, problem solving and conflict management. The generalization phase seeks to increase the family's capacity to access multisystemic community resources and proactively avoid relapse.

FFT ranges from an average of 8 to 12 one-hour sessions for mild cases to 30 or more sessions of direct service for families in more difficult situations. Sessions are generally spread over a three-month period and can be conducted in clinical settings as an outpatient therapy or as a home-based model. In addition to being a model Blueprint program, FFT is also endorsed by the National Institutes of Health panel of experts, the Substance Abuse and Mental Health Services Administration (SAMSHA) and the National Institute on Drug Abuse as being highly effective in reducing aggression, delinquency and substance abuse.

LifeSkills® Training (LST)

LifeSkills Training (LST) is a classroom-based tobacco, alcohol and drug abuse prevention program for upper-elementary and junior high school students that targets individuals who have not yet initiated substance use. The program is designed to prevent the early stages of substance use by reducing risk factors associated with substance abuse, particularly occasional or experimental use. Recognizing that the most common approaches to substance abuse prevention for the past two decades have involved either presenting information about the dangers of drug use or using classroom discussion and classroom activities to enrich youths' personal and social development—approaches that have generally neglected to address the risk factors for substance abuse among youths and, therefore, have been largely ineffective—the LST curriculum is based on understanding the causes of tobacco, alcohol and drug use and targets the psychosocial factors associated with the onset of drug involvement.

The LST approach is based on the latest scientific evidence, teaching general personal and social skills in combination with drug resistance skills and normative education. Its prevention curriculum specifically provides students with the necessary skills to resist social pressures to drink alcohol, smoke cigarettes and use drugs; helps them develop greater self-esteem, self-mastery and self-confidence; increases knowledge of the immediate consequences of substance abuse; gives students tools to cope effectively with social anxiety; and enhances cognitive and behavioral competency to prevent and reduce a variety of health risk behaviors.

LST has been found to cut alcohol, tobacco and marijuana use among young adolescents by 44 percent. Long-term results of the program reveal a 66 percent reduction in regular (weekly) **polydrug use** (use of multiple types of drugs at once), a 25 percent reduction in pack-a-day smoking and a decrease in the use of inhalants, narcotics and hallucinogens. Long-term follow-up data reveal that reductions can last through 12th grade.

Multisystemic Therapy (MST)

Multisystemic Therapy (MST) addresses the multiple aspects of serious antisocial behavior in adolescents across key settings within which youths live, work and play, and typically uses a home-based model of service delivery to reduce barriers that keep families from accessing services. Therapists have small caseloads of four to six families; work as a team; are available 24 hours a day, 7 days a week; and provide services at times convenient to the family. The average treatment involves about 60 hours of contact during a four-month period.

MST therapists focus on empowering parents and improving parental effectiveness by identifying strengths and developing natural support systems (e.g., extended family, neighbors, friends, church members) and removing barriers (e.g., parental substance abuse, high stress, poor relationships between partners). Specific treatment techniques used to facilitate these gains are integrated from those therapies that have the most empirical support, including behavioral, cognitive-behavioral and the pragmatic family therapies. In this family–therapist collaboration, the family takes the lead in setting treatment goals, with the therapist facilitating this effort.

Numerous studies of the MST approach with violent and chronic juvenile offenders showed this program produced 25 percent to 70 percent decreases in long-term rates of rearrest and 47 percent to 64 percent decreases in long-term rates of days in out-of-home placements. A recent meta-analysis that included most of these studies (Curtis, Ronan, and Borduin 2004) indicated that the average MST effect size for both arrests and days incarcerated was 0.55, with efficacy studies having stronger effects than effectiveness studies. (Efficacy studies are controlled experimental research trials, whereas effectiveness studies use real-world clinicians and clients.)

In addition to being a model Blueprint program, MST is also endorsed by the National Institutes of Health panel of experts, the SAMSHA and the National Institute on Drug Abuse as being highly effective in reducing aggression, delinquency and substance abuse.

Nurse–Family Partnership (NFP)

The most serious and chronic offenders often show signs of antisocial behavior as early as the preschool years. Three risk factors associated with early development of antisocial behavior can be modified: (1) adverse maternal health-related behaviors during pregnancy, (2) child abuse and neglect and (3) troubled maternal life course. The Nurse–Family Partnership (NFP), already discussed in depth in Chapter 5, has been shown to have positive outcomes on obstetrical health, psychosocial functioning and other health-related behaviors of mothers, which ultimately benefits their children. The program also has reduced rates of child abuse and neglect by helping young parents learn effective parenting skills and deal with a range of issues such as depression, anger, impulsiveness and substance abuse. One study found that participating in the program was associated with a 79 percent reduction in state-verified cases of child abuse and neglect among mothers who were poor and unmarried. In their second year of life, nurse-visited children had 56 percent fewer visits to emergency rooms for injuries and ingestions than did children who were not visited. Moreover, a 15-year follow-up study of one sample found that the program reduced arrests among the mothers, resulted in 54 percent fewer arrests and 69 percent fewer convictions among the 15-year-old adolescents and resulted in 58 percent fewer sexual partners among the 15-year-olds.

When the program focuses on low-income women, program costs are recovered by the time the first child reaches age 4. The RAND Corporation estimated that once the child reaches age 15, cost savings are four times the original investment because of reductions in crime, welfare expenditures and health care costs and as a result of taxes paid by working parents.

Multidimensional Treatment Foster Care (MTFC)

Multidimensional Treatment Foster Care (MTFC) is a behavioral treatment alternative to residential placement for youth ages 11 to 18 who display chronic antisocial behavior or emotional disturbance or are delinquent. MTFC is a multifaceted intervention used across multiple settings and based on social learning theory, a model that describes the mechanisms by which individuals learn to behave in social contexts and the daily interactions that influence both prosocial and antisocial patterns of behavior. Intervention activities include:

- Behavioral parent training and support for MTFC foster parents.
- Family therapy for biological parents (or other aftercare resources).
- Skills training for youth.
- Supportive therapy for youth.
- School-based behavioral interventions and academic support.
- Psychiatric consultation and medication management, when needed.

Three components of the intervention work in unison to treat the youth: MTFC parents, the family and the treatment team. Evaluation results of MTFC are overwhelmingly positive and show that this program is feasible and is, when compared with alternative residential treatment models, more cost-effective and leads to better outcomes for children and families.

Olweus Bullying Prevention Program (OBPP)

The Olweus Bullying Prevention Program (OBPP) was developed, refined and systematically evaluated in Bergen, Norway, after three young Norwegian boys committed suicide following severe bullying by peers. The original project, which took place from 1983 to 1985, involved 2,500 youths in 42 schools throughout the city. Because bullying is such a prevalent problem, the program has been replicated throughout Norway and in other countries, including the United States.

OBPP is a universal intervention developed to promote the reduction and prevention of bullying behavior and victimization problems. The program, geared toward youths ages 6 to 14, is based on an ecological model and incorporates interventions aimed at a variety of levels within a child's environment: the individual children who are bullying and being bullied, the families, the teachers and students within the classroom, the school as a whole and the community. The principal venue for the program is the school; school staff have the primary responsibility for introducing and implementing the program and are provided ongoing support by OBPP project staff.

Adult awareness and behavior is crucial to the success of the OBPP, and two conditions must be met for the program to achieve its intended goals. First, the adults at school and, to some degree, at home must be made aware of the extent of bully–victim problems in the given school. Second, the adults must actively engage in changing the situation. Without adults' acknowledgment of schools' existing bully–victim problems and a clear commitment by a majority of the school staff to participate actively in the antibullying efforts, the program is likely to have limited, if any, success. These principles have been translated into numerous specific measures, or interventions, that are used at the school, class and individual levels.

The program has been implemented and assessed in a variety of cultures (e.g., Bergen, Norway; the southeastern United States; Sheffield, England; and Schleswig–Holstein, Germany) and school contexts (elementary and middle schools). The U.S. evaluation of the OBPP has produced somewhat modest but still positive findings. For example, a study of middle-school students revealed significant decreases in students' self-reports of bullying in the intervention schools, when compared with control schools. The program also appeared to slow the natural rate of increase in students' engagement in several other anti-social behaviors. There were, however, no effects on victimization, bullying of teachers, group delinquency, theft, substance abuse or attitudes toward bullying. Furthermore, no program effects were found by year 2.

Promoting Alternative THinking Strategies (PATHS)

The Promoting Alternative THinking Strategies (PATHS) is a conflict resolution/interpersonal skills curriculum that promotes emotional and social competencies and reduces aggression and behavior problems in elementary school-aged children (ages 5–10), while enhancing the educational process within the classroom. This school-based intervention, based on the affective-behavioral-cognitive-dynamic (ABCD) model of development, includes lessons in self-control, emotional understanding, self-esteem and interpersonal problem-solving skills. A basic premise of PATHS is that a child's coping mechanisms, as reflected in his or her behavior and internal regulation, are a function of emotional awareness, affective-cognitive control and behavioral skills and social-cognitive understanding.

To this end, the PATHS curriculum contains numerous lessons that build protective factors by helping children identify and label feelings, express feelings, assess the intensity of feelings and manage feelings; understand the difference between feelings and behaviors; learn how to delay gratification and control impulses; reduce stress; read and interpret social cues; understand the perspectives of others; use steps for problem solving and decision making; achieve a positive attitude toward life; gain self-awareness; and learn effective verbal and nonverbal communication skills.

Although the curriculum is designed for use by educators and counselors and concentrates primarily on school and classroom settings, it also includes information and activities for use with parents. Ideally, the program should be initiated at the start of schooling and continued through sixth grade. Teachers generally receive training in a 2- to 3-day workshop and in biweekly meetings with the curriculum consultant.

Studies have compared classrooms receiving the intervention with matched controls using populations of normally adjusted students, behaviorally at-risk students and deaf students. Compared with the control groups, youths in the PATHS program have done significantly better in recognizing and understanding emotions, understanding social problems, developing effective alternative solutions and decreasing frequency of aggressive/violent solutions. Teachers reported significant improvements in children's self-control, emotional understanding, ability to tolerate frustration and use of conflict resolution strategies. Among special-needs youths, teachers reported decreases in internalized symptoms (sadness, anxiety and withdrawal) and externalized symptoms (aggressive and disruptive behavior).

The Incredible Years Series (IYS)

Youth on a trajectory of lifelong persistent antisocial behavior are often recognizable quite early in life. Young aggressive children may have already established a pattern of social difficulty in preschool that continues and becomes fairly stable by middle school. Many children with conduct problems (defined as high rates of aggression, defiance and oppositional and impulsive behaviors) have been asked to leave four or five schools by age 6, and by the time they enter middle school, their negative reputations and their rejection by peers and parents may be well established. Early intervention is crucial in reducing aggressive behavior and negative reputations before they develop into permanent, stable patterns.

The Incredible Years Series (IYS) targets children between the ages of 2 and 10 who exhibit or are at risk for conduct problems. The series, based on the social learning model, emphasizes the importance of the family and teachers in a child's socialization process and features three comprehensive, multifaceted and developmentally based curricula for parents, teachers and children. A basic premise of IYS is that negative reinforcement develops and maintains children's deviant behaviors and parents' and teachers' critical or coercive behaviors, sustaining a cycle of dysfunctional socialization that must be stopped. Therefore, the first step is to change parents' or teachers' behaviors so that the children's social interactions can be altered. If parents and teachers can learn to deal effectively with children's misbehavior and to model positive and appropriate problem-solving and discipline strategies, children can develop social competence and reduce aggressive behavior at home and at school. To achieve this goal, trained facilitators use interactive presentations, videotape modeling and role-playing techniques to encourage group discussion, problem solving and sharing of ideas.

In six randomized trials, the parent training component of IYS has been shown to reduce conduct problems and improve parenting interactions; these improvements have been sustained as long as three years after the intervention. The cycle of aggression appears to have been halted for approximately two thirds of families whose children have conduct disorders and who have been treated in clinics. In two randomized trials, the teacher training component has been shown to improve children's behavior in the classroom (improvements include less hyperactivity, antisocial behavior and aggression and more social and academic competence) and teachers' classroom management skills. The child training component resulted in significantly improved social skills and positive conflict management strategies with peers, in addition to reduced child behavior problems at home and school. Preliminary results of the classroom-based curriculum suggest it is effective in reducing overall classroom aggression and increasing children's social competence.

Project Toward No Drug Abuse (Project TND)

This school-based initiative is an interactive program designed to help high school youths (ages 14–19) resist substance use. The curriculum consists of 12 40- to 50-minute lessons conducted over a four-week period that include motivational activities, social skills training and decision-making components delivered through a variety of means, such as group discussions, role-playing exercises, videos, games and student worksheets. The program delivers detailed information to students about the social and health consequences of drug use, instruction on cognitive motivation enhancement activities to avoid drug use and correction of cognitive misperceptions. It addresses topics such as active listening skills, effective communication skills, stress management, coping skills, tobacco cessation techniques and self-control—all to counteract risk factors for drug abuse relevant to older teens. The program can be used in a self-instruction format or run by a health educator. Evaluation results show that TND can significantly reduce hard drug and alcohol use among high school students.

The preceding model programs all aim to prevent delinquency by reducing the negative impacts of risk factors while building an arsenal of protective factors for youths to draw upon when navigating the often-tumultuous waters of adolescence. Other exemplary and effective prevention programs can be found on the OJJDP Model Programs Guide Web site. For more information, visit the Criminal Justice Companion Web site at cengagebrain.com, then access the web links for this chapter.

Truancy and Dropout Prevention

Another area showing effective delinquency prevention benefits pertains to truancy and efforts to keep children in school. Truancy, as discussed in Chapter 4, is a risk factor for serious juvenile delinquency as well as a host of other complications in adult life. Truants are more likely to drop out of school, setting such individuals on a path of diminished opportunities for future employment and other economic challenges. Truancy has also been linked to increased risk of substance abuse and teen pregnancy. Thus the reasons to prevent truancy and keep kids in school are many.

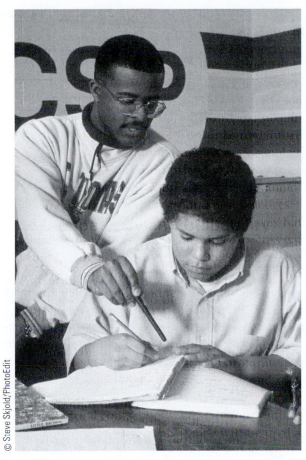

Academic failure and low bonding with teachers are reasons why students may choose to drop out of school. For those youths struggling with coursework, tutoring can provide the necessary academic assistance as well as a positive relationship with a caring adult.

An effective truancy prevention response requires a partnership approach, as illustrated in Figure 12.1.

It is no mystery that some youths are truant because they simply do not enjoy school or would rather hang out with their friends, and the communication between the school and the parents is lacking to the extent that the truancy is able to continue unchecked. Such administrative or system failures should be relatively easy to resolve once they are identified and made a priority by school officials. More challenging, from a practitioner's perspective, are those cases where the truancy stems from family or individual student factors, as these cases often require a therapeutic intervention beyond that needed to simply fix lax record-keeping or other supervisory loopholes. It is documented that some youths are absent from school because of personal mental health or substance abuse issues (sometimes in combination) or because family health or financial concerns put pressure on the student to either stay home to care for family members or go to a job to bring in essential funds to keep the family financially afloat.

The National Center for School Engagement (NCSE), a national leader in applying research to help communities prevent and reduce truancy, has worked with the OJJDP to evaluate various anti-truancy programs across the country. Their *Toolkit for*

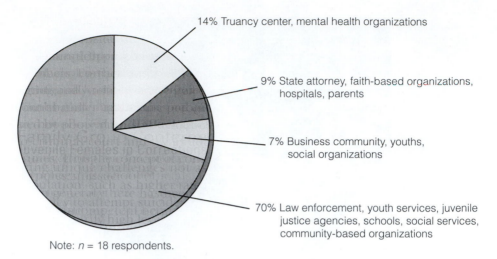

Note: *n* = 18 respondents.

Figure 12.1 Partners Identified as Necessary to Reduce Truancy

SOURCE: Myriam L. Baker, Jane Nady Sigmon, and Elaine Nugent. 2001 (September). *Truancy Reduction: Keeping Students in School*, p. 12. Washington, DC: OJJDP Juvenile Justice Bulletin. (NCJ 188947)

Creating Your Own Truancy Reduction Program is a compendium of approaches taken by various jurisdictions. For more information, visit the Criminal Justice Companion Web site at cengagebrain.com, then access the web links for this chapter. Their most recently available assessment of best practices in truancy prevention identified the following components of successful programs (Dimock 2005):

■ *Collaboration*—Truancy programs that include a broad-based collaborative as part of their approach are stronger and may last longer.

■ *Family involvement*—Involving parents/guardians and other family members is critical and entails more than simply inviting their attendance at a school or court meeting. True participation means actively engaging the entire family, seeking their advice and experiences as "experts" in the lives of their children.

■ *Comprehensive approach*—Effective programs focus simultaneously on both prevention and intervention and address the myriad reasons youth fail to attend school (personal, academic, school climate and family-related issues). An effective truancy program may need to help a family receive counseling, arrange for transportation solutions, negotiate schedules and extracurricular activities or advocate for families to receive financial aid to remove the pressure for children to choose work over school.

■ *Use of meaningful sanctions and incentives*—Traditionally, sanctions for truancy have mirrored the punitive response given to other misbehavior: detention, suspension, petition to juvenile court, denial of privileges and so on. Sanctions must be used judiciously, as these actions often are in direct conflict with the goal of keeping students in school (e.g., suspension). More effective is the use of meaningful incentives, which tend to be recognition-based but may also include special experiences (attending a sporting event or concert) or monetary rewards.

■ *Supportive context*—This element is crucial to developing a sustainable and effective truancy program, for those that have support are much more likely to survive than are those acting in isolation or fighting against a system that does not value its mission. A "context" can be an umbrella agency, a neighborhood, a collection of laws and policies or a political entity. Stakeholders to involve in this context, beyond the obvious educators, include law enforcement, mental health workers, mentors and social service providers.

- *Ongoing evaluation*—Programs must measure their impact in an effort to optimize delivery of services and identify where improvements or modifications are needed.

Communities In Schools (CIS)

The Communities In Schools (CIS) network is a web of local, state and national partnerships working together to bring at-risk youths four basics that every child needs and deserves: a personal one-on-one relationship with a caring adult, a safe place to learn and grow, a marketable skill to use upon graduation and a chance to give back to peers and community. CIS treats the student and his or her family in a holistic manner, bringing together in one place a support system of caring adults who ensure that the student has access to the resources that can help him or her build self-worth and the skills needed to embark on a more productive and constructive life.

Alternative to Suspension Program (ASP)

The Alternative to Suspension Program (ASP) addresses the problem of suspended students and how, instead of staying home under parental supervision during such suspensions, such students often tend to hang out at the mall, loiter at local convenience stores or engage in criminal activity such as breaking into homes and cars. To counter such unsupervised suspensions, many communities have implemented ASP, bringing together parents, schools and law enforcement in an effort to keep suspended students off the streets and away from criminal activity.

Alternative Schools

Alternative education programs are being used to reach at-risk youths. Such programs are based on the belief that failure in school increases the likelihood that youths will commit delinquent acts. The school is considered an appropriate vehicle to help children meet their early developmental needs in six major roles: learner, individual, producer, citizen, consumer and family member. Helping children recognize and prepare for these roles should prevent problems, including delinquency, in later life. Alternative schools commonly include such prevention programs as:

- *Job/career programs* that help youths define their career interests, provide vocational training and teach youths how to look for a job and other employment services.
- *Advocacy programs* in which youths, their families and school staff members monitor and pressure for needed changes in youth services.

Safe Schools/Healthy Students (SSHS) Program

The Safe Schools/Healthy Students (SSHS) program supports urban, rural, suburban and tribal school district efforts to link prevention activities with community-based services and thereby strengthen local approaches to violence prevention and child development. Plans are required to address six elements: (1) a safe school environment, (2) violence, alcohol and drug abuse prevention and early intervention programs, (3) school and community mental health prevention and treatment intervention services, (4) early childhood psychosocial and emotional development services, (5) education reform and (6) safe school policies.

Project H.E.L.P.: High Expectations Learning Program

Project H.E.L.P.'s program mission is to ensure all students have the opportunities they need to work to their full academic and social potentials. This year-round educational program offers an extra 200 hours of supplemental classroom instruction per year to underachieving elementary school students. This supplemental instruction is offered within the context of a five-week summer term and a nine-month school year extension. To ensure a powerful transition into the regular school year, Project H.E.L.P. provides teacher continuity; the student's teacher during the summer term is also the student's teacher during the school year.

According to the program's Web site, "The key component in the success of Project H.E.L.P. has always been parental involvement. From the beginning, Project H.E.L.P. has set high standards for parent participation, and the prerequisite for enrollment in Project H.E.L.P. is a clear understanding of the role parents will need to play if they wish their children to be a part of

© AP Images/Jae C. Hong

An 18-year-old high school dropout holds her 4-month-old son as she talks to two "chasers" from Learning Works! Charter School, in Pasadena, California. The school was founded in 2008 to serve Pasadena's highest risk youth—gangbangers, teen mothers, parolees—with one goal in mind: to get them to graduate high school. The school employs former dropouts as chasers, whose job it is to round up the students and counter every excuse they use to not attend school. Chasers bring students to school, take them to Planned Parenthood appointments or to see parents in jail, drive them to court hearings and even pick them up from juvenile hall and police stations.

the project." The parental performance standards include (1) attendance at weekly parent–teacher conferences during the summer term and monthly conferences during the school year extension, (2) setting aside time each evening to monitor homework and provide assistance and encouragement as needed, (3) attending parent seminars that offer encouragement, support and strategies to implement at home to enhance their child's prospects for academic programs and (4) financial support through tuition, which typically covers 15 to 20 percent of program costs, with financial aid available to parents who demonstrate a need for tuition assistance.

Preventing Delinquency through Improved Child Protection Services (CPS)

One potentially powerful prevention effort, frequently overlooked, is to reduce the incidence of child neglect and abuse. Evidence clearly shows that a disproportionate number of neglected and abused children become delinquents, so preventing child neglect and abuse serves a dual function: "If the public remains silent about child neglect and abuse, then the supportive services these children need will not reach them. The children who survive may produce another generation to perpetuate the cycle of violence" (Ennis 2000, 95).

Although it is never recommended that a child be left in a family where abuse and neglect is actively occurring, there is a strong movement to preserve families and keep the custodial turnover of dependents to a minimum. What this means, of course, is that treatment and intervention services must be delivered efficiently and effectively to parents. In these cases, the need for collaborative efforts and the link between juvenile justice and child welfare are very clear.

For example, when a drug-dependent child is born and placed outside its biological family, the court must try to learn whether the mother is willing and able to undergo drug treatment, with the goal being eventual reunification of the family. If spousal abuse is the issue, and with recognition that child abuse often co-occurs in such environments, the system should act to obtain abuse treatment for the offending parent such that the child may safely stay with its family: "Child abuse is present in 30 to 70 percent of families in which there is spousal abuse, and the severity of the child abuse generally parallels the severity of the abuse to the spouse" (Graves 2002, 137).

Violence Prevention

The OJJDP identifies six principles for preventing delinquent conduct and reducing serious, violent and chronic delinquency:

1. Strengthen families to instill moral values and provide guidance and support to children
2. Support core social institutions such as schools, religious institutions and other community organizations to alleviate risk factors for youths
3. Promote delinquency prevention strategies that reduce the impact of risk factors and enhance the influence of protective factors for youths at the greatest risk of delinquency

4. Intervene immediately when delinquent behavior occurs
5. Institute a broad spectrum of graduated sanctions that provide accountability and a continuum of services to respond appropriately to the individual needs of an offender
6. Identify and control the small segment of serious, violent and chronic juvenile offenders

Many delinquency prevention efforts are unsuccessful because of their negative approach—attempting to keep juveniles from misbehaving. What has proved to work more effectively are positive approaches that emphasize opportunities for healthy social, physical and mental development. Table 12.1 presents several education, legal/regulatory change and environmental modification strategies to prevent youth violence.

In structuring violence prevention programs, communities and agencies must be mindful that different racial/ethnic groups experience different types of violence at different rates, and each calls for different prevention strategies.

Reducing Gun Violence

The political right resists any new gun-control legislation as unnecessary, suggesting more enforcement of existing laws. In opposition, the left advocates the policies of all other developed countries that have a virtual ban on handgun possession with tight registration and control over a limited number of long guns. Considering the strong pro-gun sentiment in this country, it seems unlikely that laws will be passed that take handguns out of the hands of citizens. As long as guns are a part of our society, they will invariably be used by some youths for violent purposes.

 A program known to work to reduce gun violence is having uniformed police patrols in gun crime hotspots. Gun buyback programs and criminal history checks do not appear to work.

Table 12.1   Strategies to Prevent Youth Violence

Education	Legal/Regulatory Change	Environmental Modification
Adult mentoring	Regulate use of and access to weapons:	Modify the social environment:
Conflict resolution	▪ Weaponless schools	▪ Home visitation
Training in social skills	▪ Control of concealed weapons	▪ Preschool programs such as Head Start
Firearm safety	▪ Restrictive licensing	▪ Therapeutic activities
Parenting centers	▪ Appropriate sale of guns	▪ Recreational activities
Peer education	Regulate use of and access to alcohol:	▪ Work/academic experiences
Public information and education campaigns	▪ Appropriate sale of alcohol	Modify the physical environment:
	▪ Prohibition or control of alcohol sales at events	▪ Make risk areas visible
	▪ Training of servers	▪ Increase use of an area
	Other types of regulations:	▪ Limit building entrances and exits
	▪ Appropriate punishment in schools	
	▪ Dress codes	

SOURCE: *The Prevention of Youth Violence: A Framework for Community Action.* 1992. Atlanta, GA: U.S. Department of Health and Human Services, Centers for Disease Control, National Center for Environmental Health and Injury Control, Division of Injury Control, Office of the Assistant Director for Minority Health. Accessed February 7, 2012. http://wonder.cdc.gov/wonder/prevguid/p0000026/p0000026. asp#head003003000000000.

Gang Prevention

Closely related to the general youth violence issue in this country is the concern about gangs. Preventing gangs and gang-related violence will undoubtedly have an impact on the overall level of juvenile violence. The National School Safety Center suggests several prevention and intervention strategies.

Behavior codes should be established and enforced firmly and consistently. Such behavior codes may include a dress code, a ban on the showing of gang colors and a ban on using gang hand signals. Friendliness and cooperation should be promoted and rewarded.

Graffiti removal should be done immediately. Graffiti is unattractive, and it allows gangs to advertise turf and authority. A Los Angeles school administrator suggests that graffiti be photographed before removal so the police can better investigate the vandalism. Evidence, such as paint cans and paint brushes, should be turned over to the police. In addition students might design and paint their own murals in locations where graffiti is likely to appear.

Conflict prevention strategies can also be effective. Teachers should be trained to recognize gang members and to deal with them in a nonconfrontational way. All gang members should be made known to staff. Teachers should try to build self-esteem and promote academic success for all students, including gang members. School-based programs can combine gang and drug prevention efforts.

Crisis management should be an integral part of the administration's plan for dealing with any gang activity that might occur. A working relationship should be established with the police department, and a plan for managing a crisis should be developed. The plan should include procedures for communicating with the authorities, parents and the public.

Community involvement can also be extremely effective in reducing or even preventing gang activity. Parents and the general public can be made aware of gangs operating in the community, as well as heavy metal and punk bands that promote violence or inappropriate behavior. Parents and community members can be encouraged to apply pressure to radio and television stations and bookstores to ban material that promotes the use of alcohol or drugs, promiscuity or devil worship.

 Antigang programs include establishing behavior codes, removing graffiti, implementing conflict prevention strategies, developing a plan for crisis management and fostering community involvement.

The OJJDP's Gang Reduction Program (GRP) (*Best Practices to Address Community Gang Problems* 2008, 4) identifies two types of prevention in its integrated approach to targeting gangs:

■ *Primary prevention*—targets the entire population in high-crime and high-risk communities. The key component is a one-stop resource center that makes services accessible and visible to community members. Services include prenatal and infant care, after-school activities, truancy and dropout prevention, tutoring, mentoring and job programs. Other primary prevention initiatives include conducting workshops and training sessions to increase neighborhood and community awareness about gangs.

- *Secondary prevention*—identifies children ages 7 to 14 at high risk for join-ing gangs and, drawing on the resources of schools, community-based organizations and faith-based groups, intervenes with appropriate services before early problem behaviors turn into serious delinquency and gang involvement.

To optimize effectiveness, primary and secondary service providers must understand the gang culture and have experience working with at-risk youths and their families (*Best Practices* 2008, 26).

The National Crime Prevention Council's (NCPC) *Effective Strategy: Provide Positive Alternative to Gang Activity* (2003) suggests, "By providing positive alter-natives to violent gang activities and tracking interact[ions] with gang members, community groups can combat gang violence successfully." A challenge to this approach is overcoming the fear of gang activity, which can make some indi-viduals and groups reluctant to get involved. Another challenge is to gain the gang members' trust by listening to them and designing services that respond to their needs.

According to the NCPC, "Strategies to deter youth gang membership include education, counseling and alternative activities, such as recreation and job training." Respondents to surveys in several major cities with serious youth gang violence reported that providing positive alternatives for gang members was the most effective strategy, with community organization being next most effective. Suppression strategies were considered to be less effective except in conjunction with other approaches.

Drug Use Prevention Programs

Because of the known link between drug abuse and delinquency, many pro-grams focus on drug abuse prevention. The Office of National Drug Control Policy (2009, 7) states, "When it comes to alcohol and drugs, young people are especially vulnerable, in part because of the significant health and social

---

Highlights from the Field—Prevention Activities

Richmond, VA Through meetings with community representa-tives, project staff learned of a need for a number of programs that ultimately led to the funding of more than 50 programs. For example, community members identified the need for longer after-school hours and options for summer activities. The project expanded its partnership with Boys and Girls Clubs and entered into a partnership with the faith-based Richmond Outreach Cen-ter to provide additional activities and longer hours. A viable One-Stop Office has been a key part of integrating services to cli-ents. The ability of the Office of the Attorney General to reach out to all partners and successfully communicate the overall goals of the project has contributed to successfully integrating services for clients.

Miami-Dade, FL The main prevention efforts were a direct response to a student survey that asked students what would keep

them from getting involved in gang activities. The response was "something to do or a job." The project designed an on-the-job training program that has been a main draw for students. The greatest success of the on-the-job training component of the proj-ect was the resulting level of pride and commitment that the youth showed while participating in the program. This component pro-vides long-term effects and knowledge that the youth can use for career advancement and entrepreneurship.

Houston, TX Gang awareness presentations resulted in more calls from residents to report suspected gang-related crime according to reports from police.

SOURCE: *Best Practices to Address Community Gang Prob-lems: OJJDP's Comprehensive Gang Model*, p. 27. 2008 (June). Washington, DC: U.S. Department of Justice, Office of Juve-nile Justice and Delinquency Prevention. (NCJ 222799)

consequences of early drug use and drug-using behavior. Consequently, youth should be provided with an array of prevention activities—from an evidence-based substance abuse prevention curriculum to random drug testing—to shield them from drug-related harms."

DARE

Drug Abuse Resistance Education (DARE) is perhaps the best-known and most recognized drug prevention program in the country. Although the program enjoys great popularity—schools love DARE, students and families love DARE, police departments love DARE—most of the research to date does not support the finding that DARE effectively reduces long-term drug use among students. Nonetheless, what the program has been able to do is forge positive relationships between youth and members of law enforcement, which supporters of the program advocate has a positive impact on juvenile behavior. The hope, although unsubstantiated through data at present, is that these prosocial bonds will serve as a protective factor for youth.

The National Commission on Drug-Free Schools

A comprehensive drug education and prevention program should have eight key elements:

1. Student survey, school needs assessment and resource identification
2. Leadership training of key school officials and staff with authority to develop policies and programs
3. School policies that are clear, consistent and fair, with responses to violations that include alternatives to suspension
4. Training for the entire staff on the school's alcohol and drug policies and policy implementation throughout
5. Assistance programs/support for students from preschool through grade 12, including tutoring, mentoring and other academic activities; support groups (e.g., Alcoholics Anonymous and Children of Alcoholics); peer counseling; extracurricular activities (e.g., sports, drama, journalism); vocational programs (e.g., work-study and apprenticeship); social activities (including drug-free proms and graduation activities); alternative programs (e.g., Upward Bound and Outward Bound); and community service projects
6. Training for parents, including the effects of drug use, abuse and dependency on users, their families and other people; ways to identify drug problems and refer people for treatment; available resources to diagnose and treat people with drug problems; laws and school policies on drugs, including alcohol and tobacco; the influence of parents' attitudes and behavior toward drugs including alcohol and tobacco and of parents' expectations of graduation and academic performance of their children; the importance of establishing appropriate family rules, monitoring behavior of children, imposing appropriate punishments and reinforcing positive behavior; ways to improve skills in communication and conflict management; the importance of networking with other parents and knowing their children's friends and their families
7. Curriculum for preschool through grade 12, including information about all types of drugs, including medicines; the relationship of drugs to suicide, AIDS, drug-affected babies, pregnancy, violence and other health and

safety issues; the social consequences of drug abuse; respect for the laws and values of society, including discussions of right and wrong; the importance of honesty, hard work, achievement, citizenship, compassion, patriotism and other civic and personal values; promotion of healthy, safe and responsible attitudes and behavior; ways to build resistance to influences that encourage drug use, such as peer pressure, advertising and other media appeals (refusal skills); ways to develop critical-thinking, problem-solving, decision-making, persuasion and interpersonal skills; strategies to get parents, family members and the community involved in preventing drug use; and information on contacting responsible adults when young people need help and on intervention and referral services

8. Collaboration with community services to provide student assistance programs; employee assistance programs for school staff; latchkey child care; medical care, including treatment for alcohol and other drug abuse; nutrition information and counseling; mental health care; social welfare services; probation services; and continuing education for dropouts and pushouts

Curricula should be developmentally oriented, age-appropriate, up-to-date and accurate. Individual components work best as part of a comprehensive curriculum program. When presented in isolation, components such as information about drugs can exacerbate the problem.

Parents: The Anti-Drug

The Office of National Drug Control Policy (ONDCP) through its National Youth Anti-Drug Media Campaign launched new national advertising targeting parents and other adult caregivers, reminding them that they are an important influence in their children's lives and that they can make a difference in their children's decision making. The campaign—called "Parents: The Anti-Drug"—focuses on five basic values: truth, love, honesty, communication and trust. The advertising sends consistent messages in all media—print, billboards, radio and television— to reassure parents that they can positively affect their children's decisions regarding drugs by spending time with them; listening to them genuinely; asking them what they think; giving them clear, consistent rules to follow; praising and rewarding them for good behavior; telling them they are loved; encouraging them to participate in extracurricular activities; and being involved in their lives. For more information, visit the Criminal Justice Companion Web site at cengagebrain.com, then access the web links for this chapter.

A Reality-Based Approach to Drug Education

It is reality that many teenagers experiment with drugs. Most conventional school-based drug education equates *any* use of illegal drugs with dangerous behavior when, in fact, experimenting with drugs seems to be a normal part of growing up for many youths. Drug use should not be equated with drug abuse. Students who experiment with drugs know others who have done so, with few ill effects and without becoming drug addicts. In fact, some suggest that taking an alarmist approach and overstating claims that any drug use sets a youth on an irrevocable course toward delinquency and a life of disadvantage can backfire and cause the source to lose credibility in the eyes of the juvenile, as youth often know of people who have experimented with drugs and then gone on to lead productive adult lives.

Drug Testing in Schools

In June 2002 the U.S. Supreme Court broadened the authority of public schools to test students for illegal drugs. Voting 5 to 4, the Court ruled to allow random drug tests for all middle- and high-school students participating in competitive extracurricular activities (*Board of Education of Independent School District No. 92 of Pottawatomie County et al. v. Earls et al.* 2002). Justice Thomas commented, "We find that testing students who participate in extracurricular activities is a reasonably effective means of addressing the school district's legitimate concerns in preventing, deterring and detecting drug use. This ruling expands the scope of school drug testing, which previously was allowed only for student athletes."

 The purpose of drug testing in the school is to prevent drug dependence and to help drug-dependent students become drug-free.

Mentoring

Mentoring is one of the oldest forms of prevention. The mentoring movement began at the end of the nineteenth century, when adults called the Friendly Visitors served as role models for poor children. During the 1970s mentoring found its way into corporate America as a means for the ambitious employee to find success on the corporate ladder. Most recently mentoring has returned to its roots, focusing on disadvantaged youths and providing support and advocacy to children in need. Under the Juvenile Justice and Delinquency Prevention (JJDP) Act, the OJJDP is authorized to fund mentoring efforts.

Research has shown that youth who experience a mentoring relationship reap a variety of positive benefits, including better attendance and attitude toward school, diminished drug and alcohol use, improved social attitudes and relationships, more trusting relationships and better communication with parents and a better chance of going on to higher education. The BBBS program discussed earlier is one of the most effective mentoring programs currently in use throughout the country.

Teens, Crime and the Community (TCC)

The National Crime Prevention Council (NCPC) has consistently advocated for involving young people in bettering their communities. One program, Teens, Crime and the Community (TCC), is a nationwide effort sponsored by the NCPC and Street Law, Inc., and implemented at the local level to reduce the incidence of teen victimization and engage teens as crime prevention resources in their schools and communities. Participating teens tackle critical issues facing American society today, including violent crime, shoplifting, child abuse, rape, hate crime and substance abuse. More importantly, TCC empowers youths with the skills and knowledge to make a difference in addressing these problems.

A Caution Regarding Net Widening in Prevention Efforts

Net widening is a serious issue because it depletes system resources and impedes proper intervention with appropriate youths. Instead of improving public safety, some early intervention and prevention strategies promote net widening by shifting resources from youths most in need to youths least in need. Macallair and Roche (2001, 3–4) state:

Many argue that the juvenile justice system should focus on first-time or low-level offenders who are more malleable to rehabilitation. Under this argument net widening is a good thing because it allows the system to target youths early before they become serious delinquents. However, this argument is not supported by research.

For the past 40 years criminal justice research repeatedly shows that almost 70 percent of youth who are arrested once are never arrested again. In other words, by doing nothing the state can achieve a 70 percent success rate—meaning no subsequent arrests—with first-time offenders.

Most youth who come in contact with the juvenile justice system are considered "low-risk" because the reality is most youth are not on a life-course trajectory for persistent offending. By treating these first-time, low-risk offenders overly harshly, we waste precious resources that should be directed to the more serious and violent offenders, and we risk criminalizing these youth and actually pushing them in a direction of delinquency instead of steering them away from it.

This realization is one of the new realities facing those in juvenile justice and serves as the part of the impetus for system reform, as will be discussed in the next and final chapter.

 **Summary**

- During the late 1960s a new approach for dealing with delinquency emerged—a focus on the prevention of crime.
- Prevention can be corrective, punitive or mechanical. Corrective prevention focuses on eliminating conditions that lead to or cause criminal behavior. Punitive prevention relies on the threat of punishment to forestall criminal acts. Mechanical prevention is directed toward "target hardening," making it difficult or impossible to commit particular offenses. Locks on doors, bars on windows, alarms, security guards and many other options are available to protect possible targets of criminal acts.
- Prevention may be primary, secondary or tertiary.
- Effective prevention approaches must address both the conditions and the lack of constraints that cause delinquency.
- The numerator approach to prevention focuses on individuals and symptoms, whereas the denominator approach focuses on the entire group and causes.
- The public health model's two-pronged juvenile crime prevention strategy reduces known risk factors and promotes protective factors.
- The Blueprints for Violence Prevention Initiative is the OJJDP's comprehensive effort to provide communities with a set of programs whose effectiveness has been scientifically demonstrated.
- A program known to work to reduce gun violence is having uniformed police patrols in gun crime hotspots. Gun buyback programs and criminal history checks do not appear to work.
- Antigang programs include establishing behavior codes, removing graffiti, implementing conflict prevention strategies, developing a plan for crisis management and fostering community involvement.
- The purpose of drug testing in the school is to prevent drug dependence and to help drug-dependent students become drug-free.

Discussion Questions

1. Do you support the numerator or the denominator approach to juvenile crime prevention? Be prepared to defend your choice.

2. Do delinquency prevention programs succeed? Do the programs deter delinquency?

3. What prevention programs are available in your area? Is there a specific target area?

4. Are all three levels of delinquency prevention applied in your area? Which one best suits your area? Why?

5. If social responses treat youths' behavior as delinquent in prevention strategies, does this cause a labeling effect? How would you handle a program so that labeling was not a factor?

6. At what types of delinquency should programs be directed? Violent youths? Status offenders? Antisocial and criminal activity in general? Gang activity?

7. List the assumptions you think are basic to effective delinquency prevention programs. To what extent do you think each assumption is justified?

8. What are some contemporary attempts to prevent delinquency? Why are they effective or ineffective?

9. What programs exist in your area to prevent child neglect and abuse?

10. What programs to prevent child neglect and abuse do you think have the most promise?

References

American Psychological Association. n.d. *Violence & Youth: Psychology's Response*, Vol. 1. Summary Report of the American Psychological Association Commission on Violence and Youth. Washington, DC: American Psychological Association.

Arizona State Senate. 2002. Arizona Statute 8-201. http://www.azleg.gov/ars/8/00201.htm.

Best Practices to Address Community Gang Problems: OJJDP's Comprehensive Gang Model. 2008 (June). Washington, DC: U.S. Department of Justice, Office of Juvenile Justice and Delinquency Prevention. (NCJ 222799)

Curtis, Nicola M., Kevin R. Ronan, and Charles M. Borduin. 2004. "Multisystemic Treatment: A Meta-Analysis of Outcome Studies." *Journal of Family Psychology* 18 (3): 411–419.

Dimock, Kaki. 2005 (July). *Truancy Prevention in Action: Best Practices and Model Truancy Programs*. Denver, CO: National Center for School Engagement.

Effective Strategy: Provide Positive Alternatives to Gang Activity. 2003. Washington, DC: National Crime Prevention Council. http://www.ncpc.org.

Ennis, Charles. 2000 (June). "Twelve Clues That Could Save a Child." *Law and Order* 48 (6): 92–95.

Federal Advisory Committee on Juvenile Justice. 2007 (August). *Annual Report 2007*. Washington, DC: U.S. Department of Justice, Office of Juvenile Justice and Delinquency Prevention. (NCJ 219500)

Florida Department of Juvenile Justice. 2008. Florida Statute CH 985.03. http://www.djj.state.fl.us/parents/glossary.html.

Graves, Alexander. 2002 (July). "Child Abuse and Domestic Violence." *Law and Order* 50 (7): 137–141.

Illinois Department of Human Services. n.d. http://www.dhs.state.il.us/page.aspx?item=34334.

Landenberger, Nana A., and Mark W. Lipsey. 2005 (December). "The Positive Effects of Cognitive Behavioral Programs for Offenders: A Meta-Analysis of Factors Associated with Effective Treatment." *Journal of Experimental Criminology* 1 (4): 451–476.

Macallair, Daniel, and Tim Roche. 2001. *Widening the Net in Juvenile Justice and the Dangers of Prevention and Early Intervention*. San Francisco, CA: Justice Policy Institute. (NCJ 192131)

"Measuring Recidivism." 2008 (February 20). Washington, DC: National Institute of Justice. http://nij.gov/nij/topics/corrections/recidivism/measuring.htm.

Mendel, Richard A. 2000. *Less Hype, More Help: Reducing Juvenile Crime, What Works and What Doesn't*. Washington, DC: American Policy Forum.

National Center on Education, Disability and Juvenile Justice. n.d. http://www.edjj.org/focus/prevention/phcsc.html.

National Crime Prevention Council. http://www.ncpc.org

Office of Juvenile Justice and Delinquency Prevention. 2009. *Model Programs Guide, Version 2.5*. Washington, DC. Created under Cooperative Agreement #2004-JF-FX-K101. http://www.ojjdp.gov/mpg/

Office of National Drug Control Policy. 2009. *National Drug Control Strategy: 2009 Annual Report*. Washington, DC: Office of National Drug Control Policy, The White House. (NCJ 225358)

Sherman, Lawrence W., Denise C. Gottfredson, Doris L. MacKenzie, John Eck, Peter Reuter, and Shawn D. Bushway. 1998 (July). *Preventing Crime: What Works, What Doesn't, What's Promising*. Washington, DC: U.S. Department of Justice, National Institute of Justice Research in Brief. (NCJ 171676)

Case Cited

Board of Education of Independent School District No. 92 of Pottawatomie County et al. v. Earls et al., 536 U.S. 822 (2002)

Juvenile Justice at a Crossroads:

The Continuing Call for Reform

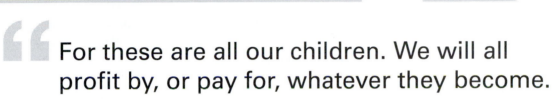

> " For these are all our children. We will all profit by, or pay for, whatever they become. "
>
> —**James Baldwin**

The unfortunate reality is that many youths are victims before they become victimizers—victims of abuse, neglect, prenatal drug exposure, dysfunctional families, poor parenting, poverty, lead exposure, intergenerational gang involvement, learning disabilities, mental illness—the list of risk factors is extensive. Juvenile justice is not just about working with the youths who have reached delinquency but is also about working with children before they make the transformation from victim to victimizer. The challenge today is getting involved with at-risk youth at the earliest stage possible.

© Steve Liss/Time & Life Pictures/Getty Images

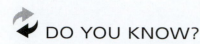

DO YOU KNOW?

- What factors are encouraging policymakers to seek reform in the juvenile justice system?
- What nine tenets have been set forth by *A Blueprint for Juvenile Justice Reform*?
- What the National Partnership for Juvenile Services (NPJS) is and what its focus is?

- What work in the juvenile justice field offers and whether more practitioners are needed?
- What trends indicate that America is moving toward reform in the juvenile justice system?

CHAPTER OUTLINE

Introduction

More than 110 years have passed since the first juvenile court ushered in a separate justice system for juveniles, based on an ideology that children were different from adults in crucial ways—biologically, emotionally, psychologically—and deserved a different, more rehabilitative-oriented approach to their wrongdoings. The stage for toughened juvenile sanctions began to be set during the 1970s, when the rehabilitative model came under attack, for both juvenile and adult offenders. Although we now understand that the collapse of this model was due, in large part, to poorly implemented programs and faulty research assessments, policymakers at the time (and the public as a whole) had lost faith in the concept of treatment and rehabilitation.

Then, in the late 1980s and early 1990s, with violent juvenile crimes increasing at an alarming rate, policymakers were faced with a series of difficult decisions. Many believed that "getting tough" on juvenile delinquency was the correct response and that treating delinquent kids more harshly would send a powerful message to youthful offenders and ultimately make us a safer nation. This reaction was spurred somewhat by criminal justice scholars who predicted (wrongly, in retrospect) that our country was on the brink of being overrun by juvenile "superpredators" unless we acted quickly and decisively to crack down on youthful offenders, for the level of juvenile violence was increasing and the *type* of violence being committed was qualitatively different from previous years. John DiIulio, a well-respected and highly credible researcher, author and political scientist who is often credited with coining the term *juvenile superpredator,* has admitted that his prophecy never came to pass. Nonetheless, many in our juvenile justice system, and society as a whole, had accepted this shift toward a more punitive approach in dealing with juvenile delinquency as a way to ensure public safety. Even as statistics were beginning to show levels of violent juvenile crime were dropping in the latter part of the 1990s, the public still believed a generation of out-of-control youth posed an ever-present and growing threat of victimization. And although there was a lot of heated rhetoric, there was also a serious problem in that policymakers had limited options to draw on with regard to juvenile justice. They began exercising options that those in the *criminal* justice system were advocating. Juvenile transfers to criminal court increased, tougher juvenile sentencing laws were passed and the general boundaries between the juvenile and adult system grew increasingly blurred.

Today, with the benefit of hindsight and several decades of research data, we are beginning to see more clearly the implications of this policy shift to get tough on delinquency, and it has brought us to a crossroads—how do we maintain a system of justice on diminishing financial resources? The reality is that the rhetoric of the 1980s and 1990s led policy makers to respond in ways that appeared to emphasize accountability and punishment of juvenile offenders over rehabilitation but that, for the most part, were not broadly implemented. And today, states are no longer asking if they *should* be more punitive but whether they can afford to be punitive. Many states have closed their juvenile justice institutions as cost-saving mechanisms, and a considerable number of institutions for females, specifically, have been shuttered. A large number of states have, in recent years, made it more difficult to incarcerate young people, not because of an ideological shift that juveniles should not be placed in secure institutions but out of financial necessity.

The juvenile justice system was born from a call for reform, so it has forever found itself under the microscope, and today there exists a continued belief among some practitioners and scholars that change is needed. Some have asked if there is even a need for a separate juvenile justice system today. Should all offenders, regardless of age, be dealt with in one justice system? Or is there a valid reason to sustain a separate justice system for youth? Scott and Steinberg (2008b, 282) contend,

> For a generation, there has been no clearly articulated rationale for maintaining a separate justice system for juvenile offenders or for dealing with them more leniently than adults. It is reasonable to assume that this conceptual void contributed to the seeming ease with which punitive reforms transformed the juvenile justice system in a relatively short period of time.... What is needed, and what this book [and a growing body of empirical evidence] begins to provide is a new justification for policies that treat juveniles differently from adults and in so doing, protect the community and promote societal welfare.

As you have learned throughout this text, new data concerning human development, coupled with research on the impacts and effectiveness of various treatments and correctional interventions, provides the justification sought to maintain a distinctly separate system to handle youthful offenders and supports the contention that reform is needed and overdue in the juvenile justice system.

 Among the factors encouraging policymakers to seek reform are falling crime rates, state budget crises, new research on brain development in adolescents and evidence-based programs amenable to replication.

To help guide juvenile justice through this period of transition, numerous advisory committees, work groups and other initiatives have emerged, each with suggestions for reform. Although the various entities differ slightly in what they identify specifically for reform, considerable overlap also exists, as you will notice.

Federal Advisory Committee on Juvenile Justice

The Federal Advisory Committee on Juvenile Justice (FACJJ) is a consultative body established in 2004 by the Office of Juvenile Justice and Delinquency Prevention (OJJDP) to oversee the provision required by the Juvenile Justice and Delinquency Prevention (JJDP) Act. Composed of 56 appointed representatives of the nation's state and territorial advisory groups, the committee brings a breadth and wealth of experience, knowledge and leadership in the field in its mission to advise the president and Congress on matters related to juvenile justice, evaluate the progress and accomplishments of juvenile justice activities and projects and advise the OJJDP administrator on the work of OJJDP.

The results and suggestions contained in the most recent *Annual Report* by the FACJJ (2010) echo those of the past several years and identify specific challenges to juvenile justice, including the lack of support and resources devoted to delinquency prevention programs; the number of youths who have mental health, substance abuse and co-occurring disorders; the disproportionate number of minority youth in contact with the juvenile justice system; the inappropriate use of secure pretrial detention for juvenile offenders; the consequences of transferring juveniles to adult criminal court; the lack of access to effective legal counsel for many youths involved in the juvenile justice system; and the need to develop and finance effective reentry programs for juvenile offenders. Amid these myriad challenges, the primary concern expressed by the FACJJ in its *2010 Annual Report* is the same as it was in 2009: the reauthorization of the JJDP Act.

The FACJJ's *Annual Report 2010*, a 49-page document, is a comprehensive assessment of what is working in various local jurisdictions and what some recommended steps are for improving the delivery and effectiveness of juvenile justice services in communities throughout the country. It is available online on the FACJJ's Web site. For more information, visit the Criminal Justice Companion Web site at cengagebrain.com, then access the web links for this chapter.

A Blueprint for Juvenile Justice Reform

Another group actively working to address the reform needs of juvenile justice is the Youth Transition Funders Group (YTFG). The Juvenile Justice Work Group of the YTFG consists of regional and national grant makers working across fields of justice, education, foster care and mental health to support policies and programs that treat youth like youth: "We aim to help governments and nonprofits preserve public safety and improve young people's chances to become successful and productive adults" (Peterson 2005). According to YTFG, "Today in America, more than three million young adults, ages 14 to 24, are neither in school nor employed. The [YTFG] is composed of foundations dedicated to improving the lives of these disconnected youths who are transiting out of foster care, entangled in the juvenile justice system or at risk of dropping out of school" (Peterson, 15). The work group's *A Blueprint for Juvenile Justice Reform* sets forth nine basic tenets that lay the groundwork for juvenile justice reform across the nation.

A Blueprint for Juvenile Justice Reform sets forth nine basic tenets that lay the groundwork for juvenile justice reform across the nation: reduce institutionalization; reduce racial disparity; ensure access to quality counsel; create a range of community-based alternatives; recognize and serve youths with specialized needs; create smaller rehabilitative institutions; improve aftercare and reentry; maximize youth, family and community participation; and keep youths out of adult prisons.

Reduce Institutionalization

The best systems for reducing institutionalization are those that offer community-based alternatives using tools such as risk assessment and sentencing guidelines to distinguish between youths who pose risks to public safety and those who would be better served in less-restrictive settings. For example, the 12-year-old Annie E. Casey Foundation's Juvenile Detention Alternatives Initiative (JDAI) has decreased average daily populations in secure detention by 31 to 66 percent, while improving indicators of public safety.

Reduce Racial Disparity

Young people of color are significantly overrepresented in the justice and foster care systems and among struggling students. Indeed, racial disparity is a vexing issue in the juvenile justice system and no one has been able to fully understand the causes of such disparity. Some jurisdictions have reduced racial disparity by analyzing data by race and ethnicity to detect disparate treatment, using objective screening instruments and coordinating with police to influence who comes into the juvenile justice system. These jurisdictions have also changed hiring practices so staff are more representative of youths in the system and have developed culturally competent programming and used mechanisms to divert those of color from secure confinement, although no studies thus far have shown any measurable results to indicate these efforts can effectively reduce disparity.

Ensure Access to Quality Counsel

Across the country, youths often face court hearings without the assistance of competent counsel—some appointed five minutes before the case is heard. Given their vulnerability, youths' access to competent counsel is essential. Suggested reforms include early assignment of counsel with specialized training on adolescent development, mental health and special education and cross-system

© Joel Gordon

A public defender consults with her young client as he waits for his disposition hearing to begin. Juvenile defense attorneys must possess not only all of the legal knowledge and courtroom skills that a criminal defense attorney who represents adult defendants has, but must also understand child and adolescent development to communicate effectively with their young clients and must be able to evaluate the client's level of maturity and competency and its relevance to the delinquency case.

representation if adolescents are involved in multiple systems. In addition, all jurisdictions must honor their constitutional obligation to provide counsel to indigent youths.

Create a Range of Community-Based Alternatives

Community-based programs include a range of approaches from probation to intensive supervision, home confinement, alternative education, family preservation, restitution, community service and day and evening reporting centers with opportunities for recreation, education and counseling. According to the *Blueprint* (Peterson 2005, 8),

> Three evidence-based programs are scientifically proven to prevent crime, even among youths with the highest risk of re-offending. Functional Family Therapy, Multidimensional Treatment Foster Care and Multisystemic Therapy (MST) all focus on the family. None involve incarceration. All deliver results. Evaluations of MST for serious juvenile offenders demonstrate reductions of 25 to 70 percent in long-term rates of rearrest, reductions of 47 to

64 percent in out-of-home placements, improvements in family functioning and decreased mental health problems, all at a lower cost than other juvenile justice services.

Recognize and Serve Youths with Specialized Needs

Youths with special mental health needs present the juvenile justice system with unique problems and challenges. The problem of youths with mental illness was introduced in Chapter 9. In some jurisdictions, juveniles with mental health disorders can receive treatment, whereas in other areas of the country such services are unavailable. And although mental health services for anyone are sometimes difficult to obtain, for youths involved in the juvenile justice system, such treatment may be especially hard to obtain. Hunsicker (2007, 60) points out, "The juvenile justice system is facing the trend experienced by the adult criminal justice system—the criminalization of mental illness. Youth facilities have become substitute mental health hospitals, while also facing the pressure of economic constraints, difficulties recruiting and retaining qualified staff and the possible shift in focus from a treatment and rehabilitation model to one of custody and control."

Create Smaller Rehabilitative Institutions

Evidence supports treating youths like youths, not adults. This can be translated into smaller, more home-like facilities. Small rehabilitation centers can give youths the care and interaction needed to integrate back into society. Such facilities can be run by youth specialists to provide developmentally appropriate individual and group programming, with families participating in the rehabilitation to ensure youths successfully transition back into society.

The Missouri model provides an example. No facility contains more than 40 youths, all served by an ethnically diverse staff trained in youth development. The goal is to help youths transition into their communities as productive citizens. This model has proven "extremely successful." Seventy percent of youths released in 1999 avoided recommitment to any correctional program three years later, compared with a 45 to 75 percent rearrest rate nationally. This model has been replicated in several jurisdictions.

Improve Aftercare and Reentry

This is closely related to the preceding discussion. Nearly 100,000 youths are released from institutions yearly. Critical to their success is having community agencies and schools equipped and trained to handle them on their return. As noted in Chapter 11 and again here: "The best reentry programs begin while a youth is still confined. They require coordination between multiple government agencies and nonprofit providers, not only to develop new services, but to help youths better access existing services" (Peterson 2005, 9). Young people need to be placed into programs where they can develop skills and begin to accept adult roles, such as preparing for the transition from school to the workforce.

In 2004 the John D. and Catherine T. MacArthur Foundation selected Pennsylvania as the first site of its Model Systems Project, a multiyear, multimillion-dollar effort to produce replicable, systemwide juvenile justice reform. Pennsylvania's promising approach to aftercare, beginning when a youth is first sentenced and extending after release from confinement, has become a model program.

Maximize Youth, Family and Community Participation

True reform addresses not just the juvenile justice system, but engages those who youths encounter daily. Reforming the juvenile justice system will take a total community effort, involving all stakeholders, including the youths themselves.

Keep Youths Out of Adult Prisons

This goal was a mainstay of the Juvenile Delinquency and Control Act of 1974. The hazards associated with incarcerating youths in adult prisons were discussed in Chapter 11. However, during the 1990s, 49 states changed their laws to increase the number of minors being tried as adults. The *Blueprint* reports (Peterson 2005, 10) that about 210,000 minors nationwide are now being prosecuted in adult courts and sent to adult prisons each year despite studies showing that youths held in adult facilities are eight times more likely to commit suicide, five times more likely to report being a victim of rape, twice as likely to report being beaten by staff and 50 percent more likely to be attacked with a weapon. In addition, youths sent to adult court also return to crime at a higher rate.

Another influential publication is the fall 2008 issue of *The Future of Children: Juvenile Justice*.

The Future of Children

In introducing *The Future of Children: Juvenile Justice*, Steinberg (2008, 3) states, "American juvenile justice policy is in a period of transition.... State legislatures across the country have reconsidered punitive statutes they enacted with enthusiasm not so many years go. What we may be seeing now is a pendulum that has reached its apex and is slowly beginning to swing back toward more moderate policies, as politicians and the public come to regret the high economic costs and ineffectiveness of the punitive reforms and the harshness of the sanction." Indicators of this shift are noted in various ways—the Supreme Court abolishing the juvenile death penalty (*Roper v. Simmons* 2005), several states having repealed or considering repealing statutes imposing sentences of life without parole (LWOP) on juvenile murderers, the scaling back of automatic juvenile transfer laws, a trend in states increasing the age to 18 for juvenile court jurisdiction and expanded procedural protection by authorizing findings of incompetence to stand trial on the basis of developmental immaturity.

Steinberg (2008, 4) asserts, "The scientific study of adolescent development has burgeoned in the past two decades, but its findings have not yet influenced juvenile justice policy nearly as much as they should." Indeed there exists a lag time of 10 to 15 years between the discovery and documentation of scientific evidence, such as that found by brain research, and the implementation of that data into public policy form (Culotta 2009).

Steinberg (2008, 7) reminds us that most young offenders will desist from crime as they mature psychologically, merely in the course of normal development: "To protect society in the long run and to promote social welfare, the response to juveniles' antisocial behavior must not imperil their development into productive adulthood." Following are brief summaries of some of the articles in this issue of *The Future of Children: Juvenile Justice*, each of which nicely encapsulates a key issue in the big picture of juvenile justice reform.

Adolescent Development and the Regulation of Youth Crime

Scott and Steinberg (2008a) emphasize the developmental perspective so vital to juvenile justice reform, noting that lawmakers and the public, until recently, have acted as if the differences between adolescents and adults were immaterial in matters dealing with youth crime policies. Fortunately, legislators and the public appear to be reconsidering the appropriateness, or perhaps inappropriateness, of a justice system that ignores age and immaturity when calculating criminal punishment: "A substantial body of new scientific knowledge about adolescence and about criminal activity during this important developmental period provides the building blocks for a new legal regime superior to today's policy. Under the developmental model, adolescent offenders constitute an intermediate legal category of persons who are neither children … nor adults" (16).

Improving Professional Judgments of Risk and Amenability in Juvenile Justice

Mulvey and Iselin (2008) address the issue of improving professional judgment of risk and amenability in juvenile justice, noting that the juvenile justice system has been slow to adopt structured methods for assessing risk and amenability to treatment: "Juvenile justice professionals must make well-reasoned judgments about two key issues: the risk of future harm to the community posed by an adolescent and how likely the adolescent is to benefit from intervention" (37).

Mulvey and Iselin (2008) point out that adolescents should be held responsible for antisocial acts but their responsibility mitigated by their diminished decision-making capacity, their susceptibility to peer influence and their unformed characters. Mulvey and Iselin conclude that most adolescent crime is the product of developmental immaturity, attested to by research showing that few adolescent offenders grow into adult criminals.

Mulvey and Iselin (2008, 35) examine and recommend three ways to integrate structured judgment into the juvenile justice system: First, more reliance on actuarial methods of detention and intake would promote more efficient and equitable screening of cases for court involvement. Second, probation officers using structured decision making could provide more consistent and valid guidance for the court when formulating dispositions. Third, implementing structured data systems to chart adolescents' progress in placement could allow judges to oversee service providers more effectively. However, it is important to keep in mind that actuarial justice is the antithesis of individualized justice, which is the paradigm the juvenile justice was premised on. Thus actuarial approaches deprive the juvenile justice system of its emphasis on individualized treatment.

Disproportionate Minority Contact

Disproportionate minority contact (DMC) is addressed by Piquero (2008), who explains that the traditional research approach to DMC has been a comparative research endeavor to come up with an index figure. For example, if the youth population in a given jurisdiction was about 3 percent minority and 12 percent of juveniles in custody were minority, the index would be 4.0. States with an index greater than 1.0 were required to implement a plan to reduce this proportionality: "Asking how much minority overrepresentation in the juvenile justice system is due to differences in processing and how much to differences in offending no longer seems a helpful way to frame the discussion" (61). He says both processes contribute to the problem.

Piquero suggests that what started out as an issue of disproportionate minority *confinement* has broadened into DMC, affecting all points in the juvenile justice system. He recommends that researchers should move to other concerns, such as understanding the mechanisms that contribute both to differential involvement in crime and to differential treatment by decision makers and study the effect of various interventions to reduce disparities in both arenas and at different points in the process.

Juvenile Crime and Criminal Justice: Resolving Border Disputes

The controversy about whether juveniles should be processed in juvenile or adult court is discussed by Fagan, who suggests that between 20 and 26 percent of all juvenile offenders younger than 18 are prosecuted in adult court because their states' jurisdictional boundary is either 16 or 17: "Sending an adolescent offender to the criminal court is a serious and consequential step. It is an irreversible decision that exposes young lawbreakers to harsh and sometimes toxic forms of punishment that, as the empirical evidence shows, have the perverse effect of increasing criminal activity" (2008, 83). The impact of juvenile transfer to adult court was discussed in Chapter 10.

Prevention and Intervention Programs for Juvenile Offenders

Greenwood (2008) describes prevention and intervention programs for juvenile offenders: "Cost-effectiveness and cost-benefit studies make it possible to compare the efficiency of programs that produce similar results, allowing policy-makers to achieve the largest possible crime-prevention effect for a given level of funding" (188). Greenwood (186) notes, "Fairly strong evidence now demonstrates the effectiveness of a dozen or so 'proven' delinquency-prevention program models and generalized strategies." Adding credibility to the argument is that different reviews conducted by different groups of investigators have led to mostly the same five conclusions:

1. Family-based programs, such as functional family therapy, multisystemic therapy or multidimensional treatment foster care, are consistently more effective than are programs focusing on treating individual juveniles alone.
2. In institutional settings, treatments that follow basic principles of cognitive-behavioral therapy are usually superior to other approaches.
3. Excessively harsh or punitive programs have either no effects or negative effects.
4. Incarceration is expensive and yields little benefit other than short-term incapacitation.
5. Even the best evidence-based programs must be implemented correctly to be effective.

This final point is critical. Most programs need to be adapted to fit the local jurisdiction, but the basic principles and processes should remain fairly intact. In addition, the impact of the intervention should be systematically assessed.

The National Partnership for Juvenile Services

Throughout this text the importance of partnerships and collaboration has been emphasized because juveniles do not live in a vacuum. As the poet John Donne wrote, "No man is an island. Do not ask for whom the bell tolls. It tolls for thee." These words ring true in the twenty-first century. Several juvenile justice organizations have realized they could accomplish more by working in partnership than by working alone or competing with one another for limited resources. The shift in federal funding priorities following September 11, 2011, prompted five nonprofit juvenile justice organizations to find an approach to minimize duplication and maximize resources, resulting in the creation of the National Partnership for Juvenile Services (NPJS) in the late 1990s. This coalition is made up of the National Juvenile Detention Association (NJDA), the National Association of Juvenile Correctional Agencies (NAJCA), the Juvenile Justice Trainers Association, (JJTA), the Council for Educators of At-Risk and Delinquent Youth (CEARDY) and the National Association for Children of Incarcerated Parents (NACIP): "Each of the individual organizations represents different disciplines of the juvenile justice continuum; however, all of the organizations are formally united under one operational structure" (Jones 2008, 120).

 The National Partnership for Juvenile Services (NPJS) is a nonprofit collaboration of five juvenile justice advocacy groups committed to improving the nation's juvenile justice system by providing specific, results-oriented training and technical assistance.

Jones (2008) explains that collectively, each organization brings expertise and excellence in designing, developing and delivering:

- Best practices in staff training and professional development.
- Community-based prevention and intervention programs.
- Educational services for at-risk and delinquent youths.
- Safe and humane treatment of confined youths.
- Sound systemic approaches to operating an effective and efficient juvenile justice system while ensuring the safety of the surrounding communities.

Since its inception, the NPJS has made significant contributions to the juvenile justice system by providing more than 300,000 hours of training and technical assistance nationwide (Jones 2008, 121). Such support should make a career in juvenile justice more appealing.

A Career in Juvenile Justice

For those who enjoy working with youths and families, the juvenile justice system can provide challenging and satisfying employment. With a growing priority placed on the high rates of juvenile delinquency and serious, violent offenses committed by youths, the juvenile justice system is expanding and should be a significant employer of personnel in the years ahead (Harr and Hess 2010, 34).

Work in the juvenile justice field is very challenging and rewarding, and the need for juvenile justice practitioners is growing.

Howe, Clawson and Larivee (2007, 35) point out, "Juvenile justice workers fulfill a dual role: a public safety and accountability role, which involves the management of youths' behavior, and a rehabilitation and youth development role, which involves mentoring and coaching youths in prosocial skill development. This duality is a source of frustration as well as opportunity among the juvenile justice workers." They (34) also observe

- The juvenile justice workforce comprises approximately 300,000 workers.
- Workers remain in the field because they enjoy working with children and families, and they want to help children achieve meaningful outcomes.
- Workers leave the field because of long hours, insufficient support from supervisors, low pay, lack of a career ladder and high stress.
- Workers perceive they are managing more high-need children than in the past, such as those with substance abuse or mental health disorders, and that they are not trained to manage this population.

Howe, Clawson and Larivee (2007) point out a "marketing crisis" in juvenile justice, citing data from a Brookings Institute survey in which 86 percent of students pursuing bachelor of arts and social work degrees said they were "not too seriously" or "not seriously at all" considering working in juvenile justice.

© AP Images/Jay LaPrete

A licensed social worker teaches a problem-solving seminar to youthful offenders in the revocation unit at Scioto Juvenile Correctional Facility in Columbus, Ohio.

When asked how informed they were about career opportunities in juvenile justice, 73 percent were "not too informed" or "not informed at all."

The Juvenile Justice Officer

The juvenile justice officer must operate within a system that handles a broad range of offenders and victims. A significant challenge facing juvenile justice is that the system must deal effectively with a wide range of youth from extremely diverse circumstances—from children and youths who are abused and neglected, to those who commit status offenses and other minor offenses, to those who commit vicious, violent, predatory crimes.

In many departments, juvenile work is considered a promotion after three to five years as a patrol officer. In addition, increasing numbers of departments have school resource officers (SROs) who work within local schools. In the accepted SRO model, SROs engage in three types of activities: law enforcement, teaching and mentoring (Finn 2006, 1). The emphasis devoted to each duty varies considerably from school to school: "Interest has grown in placing sworn law enforcement personnel in schools to improve school safety and relations between officers and young people" (Finn, 2). Finn's research found four main benefits of an SRO program: reducing the workload of patrol officers, improving the image of officers among juveniles, creating and maintaining better relationships with the schools and enhancing the agency's reputation in the community.

In addition to jobs with police agencies, careers in juvenile justice include group home child care workers and counselors, as well as intake officers and child care workers in juvenile detention facilities or correctional facilities, such as juvenile probation and so on. Those interested in working with juveniles might consider volunteering with a youth group to gain experience and to confirm that this is, indeed, an area of special interest. One initiative that has a place for everyone is the NPJS.

The Role of Social Workers and Social Services

Social workers are involved in community supervision programs for troubled youths and their families, in juvenile court-sponsored, community-based diversion programs and in school-based counseling programs. Social work functions in all aspects of the juvenile justice system.

Usually a combination of approaches is most effective. Social work can provide a range of services that may include, but by no means be limited to, direct counseling with the juvenile. The broader role of social work within the context of juvenile facilities may include advocacy and brokerage on behalf of juveniles in their relations with family members, social agencies, school officials and potential employers. Social work tries by a variety of means to ease juveniles' passage through the most difficult stage of life and to prevent institutionalized youths from becoming brutal, embittered adults.

Where Juvenile Justice Stands Today

Juvenile justice stands at a crossroads, with those in the field and those about to enter it holding tremendous sway over the policies and practices that will shape how we deal with juvenile offenders—youths who either will be guided and encouraged to become productive, self-monitoring, law-abiding adults or who will become the next generation of criminals. For the vast majority of youths who have contact with the system, a positive outcome is entirely within reason because America is beginning to act on the research of the past several decades.

 Collectively, the nation has begun to do all of the following: put the brakes on criminalization and turn away from failed approaches, recognize the limits of incarceration and invest in proven alternatives (Griffin 2008, 1–2).

What is important to acknowledge is that every juvenile in "the system" comes from somewhere—somewhere where things didn't work right. These youths are often victimized—abused, neglected, bullied, exposed to violence, unsupervised and left to raise themselves in an increasingly troubled and morally challenged society. They often come into the world with multiple strikes already against them—born to young, single and uneducated or undereducated mothers; exposed to a variety of drugs while still developing in the womb; stunted by a life of poverty and lack of early childhood stimulation. They may be trapped by intergenerational gang involvement or suffering from an undiagnosed mental illness. Every one of these circumstances and situations is an opportunity for "the system" to intervene and take notice of that child before the child makes the transition from *having* a problem to *being* a problem, before the child transforms from victim to victimizer. Juvenile justice is not just about working with the youths who have reached the stage of delinquency but is also about working with children *before* they make that transformation.

The challenge facing the juvenile justice system today is whether it will be a conductor or a custodian of the lives of the young people in its care: "Conductors just move juveniles through the system, but custodians guide, develop and take care of their juvenile charges" (Bayliss 2007, 106). "What this country needs is more people … who are interested in lighting candles, and fewer who blow them out" (Knight 2008, 63).

 ## Summary

- Among the factors encouraging policymakers to seek reform are falling crime rates, state budget crises, new research on brain development in adolescents and evidence-based programs amenable to replication.
- *A Blueprint for Juvenile Justice Reform* sets forth nine basic tenets that lay the groundwork for juvenile justice reform across the nation: reduce institutionalization; reduce racial disparity; ensure access to quality counsel; create a range of community-based alternatives; recognize and serve youths with specialized needs; create smaller rehabilitative institutions; improve aftercare and reentry; maximize youth, family and community participation; and keep youths out of adult prisons.
- The National Partnership for Juvenile Services (NPJS) is a nonprofit collaboration of five juvenile justice advocacy groups committed to improving the nation's juvenile justice system by providing specific, results-oriented training and technical assistance.
- Work in the juvenile justice field is very challenging and rewarding, and the need for juvenile practitioners is growing.
- Collectively, the nation has begun to do all of the following: put the brakes on criminalization and turn away from failed approaches, recognize the limits of incarceration and invest in proven alternatives.

Discussion Questions

1. Which aspect of the juvenile justice system do you think is most in need of reform?
2. What should the criteria be for transferring violent juveniles to adult court?
3. What are evidence-based programs? Can you give an example?
4. What do you think are the major reasons for disproportionate minority contact?
5. Has your state made any reforms in its treatment of juveniles in the past few years?
6. What should be done about juveniles who were sentenced to adult criminal facilities before any reforms occurred?
7. Of the nine tenets of *A Blueprint for Juvenile Justice Reform*, which three do you think are most important?
8. How far should the pendulum swing between punitive and rehabilitative approaches to juvenile crime?
9. Should there be a bigger push for other aspects of services to juveniles or is the one-pot approach working?
10. Would you consider a career in the juvenile justice field? Why or why not?

References

Bayliss, Bridget. 2007 (April). "Juvenile Justice Professionals Discuss the Future of America's Youths." *Corrections Today* 69 (2): 106–107.

Culotta, Vincent. 2009. "Juvenile Waivers to Adult Court: New Issues, Growing Concerns and Potential Solutions." Orlando, FL: Seminar D-7 presented at the 36th National Conference on Juvenile Justice, March 13.

Fagan, Jeffrey. 2008 (Fall). "Resolving Border Disputes." *The Future of Children: Juvenile Justice* 18 (2): 81–118.

Federal Advisory Committee on Juvenile Justice (FACJJ). 2010 (November). *Annual Report 2010.* Washington, DC: U.S. Department of Justice, Office of Juvenile Justice and Delinquency Prevention. (NCJ 231620)

Finn, Peter. 2006 (August). "School Resource Officer Programs: Finding the Funding, Reaping the Benefits." *FBI Law Enforcement Bulletin* 75 (8): 1–7.

Greenwood, Peter. 2008 (Fall). "Prevention and Intervention for Juvenile Offenders." *The Future of Children: Juvenile Justice* 18 (2): 185–210.

Griffin, Patrick. 2008 (November). *Models for Change 2008 Update: Gathering Force.* Pittsburgh, PA: National Center for Juvenile Justice.

Harr, J. Scott, and Kären M. Hess. 2010. *Careers in Criminal Investigation and Related Fields: From Internships to Promotion.* Belmont, CA: Wadsworth.

Howe, Meghan, Elyse Clawson, and John Larivee. 2007 (February). "The 21st-Century Juvenile Justice Work Force." *Corrections Today* 69 (1): 34–39.

Hunsicker, Leslee. 2007 (October). "Mental Illness among Juvenile Offenders—Identification and Treatment." *Corrections Today* 69 (5): 60–63.

Jones, Michael A. 2008 (October). "National Partnership for Juvenile Services: Welcome to the Path Less Traveled." *Corrections Today* 70 (5): 120–121.

Knight, Melissa. 2008 (April). "Beyond Buzzwords: Making Partnerships Work for the Benefit of Youths." *Corrections Today* 70 (2): 58–63.

Mulvey, Edward P., and Anne-Marie R. Iselin. 2008 (Fall). "Improving Professional Judgments of Risk and Amenability in Juvenile Justice." *The Future of Children: Juvenile Justice* 18 (2): 35–58.

Peterson, Julie. 2005 (Spring). *A Blueprint for Juvenile Justice Reform.* Chicago: Youth Transition Funders Group.

Piquero, Alex F. 2008 (Fall). "Disproportionate Minority Contact." *The Future of Children: Juvenile Justice* 18 (2): 59–80.

Scott, Elizabeth S., and Laurence Steinberg. 2008a (Fall). "Adolescent Development and the Regulation of Youth Crime." *The Future of Children: Juvenile Justice* 18 (2): 15–34.

———. 2008b. *Rethinking Juvenile Justice.* Cambridge MA: Harvard University Press.

Steinberg, Laurence. 2008 (Fall). "Introducing the Issue." *The Future of Children: Juvenile Justice* 18 (2): 3–14.

Case Cited

Roper v. Simmons, 543 U.S. 551 (2005)

Job Description: School Resource Officer (SRO)

A School Resource Officer (SRO):

- Is directly responsible to the Flint Police Division, Juvenile Bureau. However, is readily available to school administrators in time of need or emergency school–police matters.
- Patrols school area when called upon or as deemed necessary by the School Resource Officer.
- Contributes helpful information to the Regional Counseling Team.
- Assists Community School Director to mitigate antisocial behavior by investigating delinquent or criminal acts that take place during evening Community School Programs.
- Serves as a resource person or counselor for all youths, school administration and staff and members of the community with school–police related problems. Also is a resource person or counselor for those youths who have personal problems in their homes.
- Acts as resource person and serves on committees that provide services for youths.
- Gives presentations on police-related subjects to students in the classroom and to business and community organizations.
- Serves as a resource person to the Police School Cadet Program when called upon.
- Supervises and prepares necessary records and reports as requested by the Flint Police Division and Flint Community Schools.
- Assists with crowd control at school athletic events.
- Serves as a resource person for other police personnel.
- Refers youths into Probate Court or District Court when necessary.
- Performs other related duties as assigned or as appropriate.
- Suppresses by enforcement of the law any and all illegal threats, such as drugs and acts of violence, that endanger the children's educational program and improves community relations with police, schools and the general public.

SOURCE: Flint, Michigan, Police Department.

Glossary

The numbers following the definitions refer to the chapters in which the terms are defined.

adjudicated—roughly equivalent to being judged in criminal court, it is a formal legal finding of responsibility, with a juvenile being cleared or declared a delinquent, status offender or dependent. (1, 10)

adult supremacy—subordination of children to the absolute and arbitrary authority of parents and, in many instances, teachers; characterized by force and violence, including physical punishment; children are denied legal identity and treated as objects. (4)

aftercare—the supervision of youths for a limited time after they are released from a correctional facility but while they are still under the control of the facility or the juvenile court; can also apply to the process previously called *parole*. (11)

anomie—normlessness, detachment and an ambiguity in understanding relationships within the state and society. (3)

anomie theory—holds that people who believe in and strive for the American Dream (that is, through hard work anyone can become rich) but fall short of achieving it experience a strain that can manifest as crime, caused by the frustration felt by people in the lower socioeconomic levels of an affluent society that denies them legal access to social status and material goods; also called *strain theory*. (3)

anticipated strain—an individual's expectation that current stresses will continue into the future or that new stresses will be experienced. (5)

antisocial personality disorder (APD)—a disorder that exists in individuals age 18 or older who show evidence of a conduct disorder before age 15 as well as a pattern of irresponsible and antisocial behavior since age 15. (4)

attention deficit hyperactivity disorder (ADHD)—a common childhood disruptive behavior disorder characterized by heightened motor activity, short attention span, distractibility, impulsiveness and lack of self-control; often accompanied by a learning disability. (4)

beyond a reasonable doubt—less than absolute certainty, but more than high probability; the degree of proof required for guilt in a juvenile court proceeding. (8)

bifurcated hearing—a two-part hearing in which the adjudication occurs separately from the disposition. (10)

binge drinking—the consumption of large quantities of alcohol within a short period; a common amount used in the United States is five drinks for adult males and four drinks for adult females within a 2- to 3-hour time span. (6)

blended sentence—allows courts to "blend" juvenile and adult sanctions and effectively extend their jurisdiction beyond the traditional age boundary that demarcates juveniles and adults. (10)

boot camp—a correctional alternative that stresses military discipline, physical fitness and strict obedience to orders, as well as educational and vocational training and drug treatment when appropriate; also called *shock incarceration*. (11)

Bridewell—the first correctional institution to control youthful beggars and vagrants, the goal of which was to make wayward youths earn their keep, to reform them by compulsory work and discipline and to deter others from vagrancy and idleness. (2)

certification—a process in which a juvenile is legally designated an adult and, as such, eligible to face the same criminal consequences as someone of legal age; a procedure whereby a juvenile court waives jurisdiction and transfers the case to the adult criminal court. (10)

child savers—wealthy, civic-minded reformers of the mid- to late 1800s who believed that children's environments could make them "bad" and who tried to "save" unfortunate children by placing them in houses of refuge and reform schools. (2)

chronic juvenile offender—a youth who has a record of five or more separate charges of delinquency, regardless of the offenses' gravity. (6)

civil gang injunction (CGI)—a court-issued order designed to disrupt a gang's routine activities by prohibiting specific gangs or gang members from gathering in a particular public location and engaging in nuisance behaviors such as loitering, playing loud music, cursing and using certain hand gestures. (7)

classical view of criminality—holds that humans have free will and are responsible for their own actions. (3)

coercive intervention—out-of-home placement, detainment or mandated therapy or counseling. (10)

comorbidity—multiple disorders (when two or more diagnoses occur together in the same individual). (9)

competent—a legal status regarding an individual's functional ability to stand trial. (10)

concordance—similarity in trait possession, as in heredity studies where identical twins were more likely to both have criminal records than were fraternal twins. (3)

concurrent jurisdiction—when both the juvenile and criminal court have authority over a case. (10)

conduct disorder (CD)—a serious childhood psychiatric condition that manifests itself in aggression, lying, stealing and other chronic breaches of socially acceptable behavior; two major subtypes are childhood-onset type and adolescent-onset type. (4)

conflict theory—suggests that laws are established to keep the dominant class in power. (3)

consensus theory—contends that individuals within a society agree on basic values, on what is inherently right and wrong. (3)

contagion—a way to explain the spread of violence, equating it with the spread of infectious diseases. (6)

corporal punishment—inflicting bodily pain or harm. (2)

corrective prevention—focuses on eliminating conditions that lead to or cause criminal behavior; is a type of primary prevention. (12)

crew—a group of taggers. (7)

criminogenic need principle—"certain needs are directly linked to crime; criminogenic needs constitute dynamic risk factors or attributes that, when changed, influence the probability of recidivism." (11)

critical theory—combines the classical free will and positivist determinism views of crime, suggesting that humans are both self-determined and society-determined; assumes humans create the institutions and structures that ultimately dominate and constrain them; includes labeling theory, conflict theory and radical theory. (3)

dark figure of crime—the unknown true number of crimes, which may be substantially greater than official data indicate. (1)

decertification—the court may transfer a case from criminal court back to juvenile court; also known as *reverse waiver*. (10)

decriminalization—legislation to make status offenses noncriminal acts. (2)

deep end strategy—targets youths with the highest likelihood of continuing their delinquent careers without comprehensive interventions. (9)

delinquent—a youth who commits an act that would be a crime were it to be committed by an adult; the term is intended to avoid stigmatizing youth as criminals. (1, 6)

denominator approach—the view that prevention efforts should target the whole population of youths, not just the delinquents; focuses on the entire group and causes. (12)

dependency—the legal status of children over whom a juvenile court has assumed jurisdiction because the court has found their care to fall short of legal standards of proper care by parents, guardians or custodians. (5)

deserts—punishment as a kind of justified revenge— the offending individual gets what is coming; the concept of *lex talionis*, or an eye for an eye; also called *just deserts*. (2)

desistance—a permanent state of non-offending; the ultimate goal of all prevention and correctional intervention efforts. (12)

detention—the period during which a youth is taken into custody by police or probation before a petition is filed. (8)

detention hearing—an informal hearing held in juvenile court within a period defined by state statute, typically ranging from 24 to 72 hours, to determine whether a child held in custody shall remain in custody for the best interests of the child and the public. (9)

determinism—the view that human behavior is the product of multiple environmental and cultural influences rather than a single factor. (3)

deterrence—uses punishment or the threat of other sanctions, either formal or informal, to prevent future lawbreaking by showing there are consequences to aberrant behavior. (2, 3, 11)

developmental pathway—model to describe how "stages of behavior unfold over time in an orderly fashion"; for example, disruptive and delinquent behavior in boys typically occurs in an orderly, progressive manner. (4)

deviance—behavior that departs from the social norm. (6)

differential association theory—states that a person becomes delinquent because of an excess of definitions favorable to violation of law over definitions unfavorable to violation of law. (3)

discrimination—refers to unfair, differential treatment of a particular group of youths, for example, Hispanics. (1)

disparity—refers to a difference, but not necessarily involving discrimination. (1)

diversion—a filtering process that removes a youth from formal juvenile court jurisdiction and places them on an alternative path that allows the case to proceed with adjudication. (1, 9)

double jeopardy—being tried for the same offense twice. (2)

due process—a difficult-to-define term; the Due Process Clause of the U.S. Constitution requires that no person shall be deprived of life, liberty or property without due process of law, *or* carrying out the course of formal legal proceedings regularly and in accordance with established rules and principles, as provided for by the Fourteenth Amendment, with the result that no person is deprived of life, liberty or property unjustly. (2)

dynamic risk factor—one that can be changed, such as an offender's addiction to drugs; compare with *static risk factor*. (9)

ecological model—a sociological model used to compare the growth of a city and its attendant crime problems to growth in nature. (3)

emotional/behavioral disorder (EBD)—condition in which youths have one or more of the following behavior patterns: severely aggressive or impulsive behavior; severely withdrawn or anxious behaviors, pervasive unhappiness, depression or wide mood swings; or severely disordered thought processes that show up in unusual behavior patterns, atypical communication styles and distorted interpersonal relationships; often co-occurs with autism, Asperger's syndrome and/or ADHD. (4)

expressive violence—violence used as a way to vent emotions, such as anger, frustration or fear; compare to *instrumental violence*. (6)

extrafamilial sexual abuse—sexual abuse by a friend or stranger, a nonfamily member; compare with *intrafamilial sexual abuse*. (5)

family courts—courts with broad jurisdiction over family matters, such as neglect, delinquency, paternity, support and noncriminal matters and behavior. (9)

fetal alcohol spectrum disorder (FASD)—the leading known preventable cause of mental retardation in the western world, caused when a pregnant woman drinks large amounts of alcohol over a long period during a pregnancy; consequences to the child include lifelong mental and physical deficits. (4)

functionalism—the view that crime and deviance serve several "greater" purposes for society, such as promoting social solidarity and clarifying and maintaining social boundaries. (3)

gang—an group of people that have a common name or common identifying sign or symbol, form an ongoing allegiance for a common purpose and engage in unlawful or criminal activity. (7)

gateway drugs—drugs such as alcohol, tobacco and marijuana, the use of which, some have theorized, may lead people to try "harder," more dangerous drugs. (12)

general deterrence—deterrence that occurs when a sanction influences others' behavior and turns them away from delinquency by demonstrating the consequences of aberrant conduct. (3)

graduated sanctions—penalties for delinquent activity that move from limited interventions to more restrictive penalties according to the severity and nature of the delinquent act. (11)

graffiti—gang communication in the form of wall writings; proclaims the status of the gang, delineates the boundaries of their turf and offers a challenge to rivals. (7)

guardian ad litem (GAL)—an individual appointed by the juvenile court to represent a youth and protect the best interests of that child during the juvenile justice process. (10)

heritability—a concept key to the biosocial theory of criminality that reflects the degree to which genetic factors influence traits or behaviors; it exists at a group level and refers to the proportion of variance, across an entire population, in a trait. (3)

horizontal prosecution—an organizational structure strategy whereby individual assistant prosecutors or a small group of assistant prosecutors are responsible for certain phases of the adjudication of criminal complaints; compare with *vertical prosecution*. (7)

incapacitation—a consequence for criminal activity advocated by classical theory that involves institutionalization or imprisonment as a way to render an offender incapable of committing further crime. (3,11)

instrumental violence—violence used to obtain material possessions, for example, forcefully robbing another youth to take a team jacket; compare with *expressive violence*. (6)

intake—the initial phase of the juvenile court process, at which someone must decide whether a referral merits a petition, that is, whether the matter described in the complaint against the juvenile should become the subject of formal court action. (9)

intensive supervision probation (ISP)—highly structured probation intended to provide a higher level of control over an offender and, thus, increased public safety without the added cost incurred with residential placement or incarceration. (11)

intermediate sanctions—hold youths accountable for their actions through interventions that are more restrictive and intensive than standard probation yet which fall short of secure long-term incarceration. (11)

intrafamilial sexual abuse—sexual abuse by a parent or other family member; compare with *extrafamilial sexual abuse*. (5)

jurisdiction—refers to the types of cases a court is empowered to hear. (10)

just deserts—see *deserts*. (2)

justice model—the judicial process wherein young people who come into conflict with the law are held responsible and accountable for their behavior. (2, 10)

juvenile—a youth who is at or below the upper age of original jurisdiction in their resident state. (1)

juvenile court—a court having jurisdiction over children who are neglected or abused, youths who are unruly or commit status offenses and juveniles who are charged with committing serious crimes. (10)

labeling theory—calls attention to the interplay between social control and personal identity and suggests that official efforts to control crime may actually increase it, for when individuals are labeled as delinquents, others may treat them as such. (3)

lockdown—a proactive step to avoiding a crisis, during which time high school students are held in classrooms while police and K-9s search the campus for contraband or any danger to a safe educational environment. (8)

maltreatment—an act or omission by a parent or other caregiver that results in harm or serious risk of harm to a child; includes neglect, medical neglect, physical abuse, sexual abuse and psychological maltreatment. (5)

marginalization—the sense that an individual or specific demographic group (e.g., females, Hispanics) feels inferior or subordinate to mainstream society, socially disenfranchised and excluded from full participation in that society. (7)

maximalist alarmist perspective—holds that the problem of child and sexual abuse is reaching epidemic proportions; "dire consequences will follow unless drastic steps are taken . . . to mobilize people and resources to combat this growing crisis." (5)

mechanical prevention—efforts directed toward "target hardening" to make it difficult or impossible to commit particular offenses. (12)

medical model—model of individual diagnosis and individual treatment, an underlying philosophy of which was that delinquency was a preventable and treatable condition; in cases where prevention failed and delinquent behavior occurred, the condition could be treated and cured. (2)

meta-analysis—a "study of studies" that provides a quantitative review of a body of literature; now the favored approach by most criminal justice researchers. (9)

minimalist skeptical perspective—the opposite of the maximal alarmist perspective; asserts that estimates of child and sexual abuse are "grossly inflated for either a well-intentioned reason or perhaps for a self-serving purpose." (5)

moniker—a gang member's street name. (7)

natural law—the rules of conduct that are the same everywhere because they are basic to human behavior. (3)

neglect—inattention to the basic needs of a child, including appropriate supervision, adequate clothing and proper nutrition. (5)

net widening—a phenomenon in which youths who would have been simply released or directed away from the formal system were instead referred to other programs and agencies, a result in opposition of diversion's original purpose, which was to lessen the states' power to control juveniles. (2, 9)

numerator approach—the view that the focus of prevention efforts should be on those youths who are at greatest risk; focuses on individuals and symptoms. (12)

ombuds—individuals whose role is to improve conditions of confinement for juveniles and protect the rights of youths in custody; responsibilities include monitoring conditions, investigating complaints, reporting findings, proposing changes, advocating for improvements and helping expose and reduce deficiencies in juvenile detention and correctional facilities. (11)

one-pot approach—lumps children and youths who are abused and neglected, those who commit status offenses and those who commit serious, violent crimes into the same judicial "pot." (1)

osteogenesis imperfecta (OI)—a condition characterized by bones that break easily and can be mistaken for child abuse. (5)

parens patriae—literally "parent of the country"; the legal provision through which the state may assume ultimate parental responsibility for the custody, care and protection of children within its jurisdiction; the right of the government to take care of minors and others who cannot legally take care of themselves. (1)

parental efficacy—examines how parental support and control of youth are associated with delinquency. (4)

parole—the planned, supervised early release from institutionalization authorized by the correctional facility. (11)

petition—the formal process for bringing a matter before the juvenile court; a document alleging that a juvenile is a delinquent, status offender or dependent, and asking the court to assume jurisdiction; the same as a formal complaint in the adult criminal process. (9)

petitioned—formally charged. (1)

polydrug use—the use of multiple drugs at once. (12)

poor laws—established the appointment of overseers to indenture poor and neglected children into servitude. (2)

positivist view of criminality—the belief that humans are shaped by their society and are the products of environmental and cultural influences. (3)

preventive detention—the confinement of an accused juvenile delinquent prior to trial if there is a substantial probability that they will not appear in court on the return date or if there is a serious risk that they may pose a danger to themselves or to others. (2)

primary deviance—the original act defined as deviant by others. (3)

primary prevention—modifies and changes crime-causing conditions in the overall physical and social conditions that lead to crime, usually by directing efforts toward risk factors; corrective and mechanical prevention fit into this level. (12)

probation—the most common disposition of the juvenile or family court, under which an offender is subject to supervision by the court and required to adhere to specific court-ordered conditions for a specific time. (11)

protective factor—behavior and circumstance related to individual characteristics, family, school, peers and the community that may keep youths from becoming victims or offenders; strength or asset that helps reduce the negative impacts of risk factors by providing positive ways for an individual to respond to risks and avoid delinquency; often the opposite of an identified risk factor. (4, 12)

psychopath—one who is virtually lacking in conscience, displaying remarkable emotional blandness, particularly about actions that profoundly shock "normal" people; cares not between right and wrong. (4)

public defender—a lawyer who works for the defense of indigent offenders and is reimbursed for services by a public agency. (9)

pulling levers—a deterrence strategy in which targeted gang members are arrested for the slightest infraction, even jaywalking. (7)

punitive prevention—relies on the threat of punishment to forestall criminal acts. (12)

radial concept—the view that growth and development do not occur in isolation but instead involve a complex interaction of family, school and community, with the family being the first and most vital influence; as children grow, the school becomes an important influence, and as youths approach adolescence, the influence of parents and teachers wanes and that of peers becomes stronger; all of this occurs within the broader community in which children live. (4)

radical theory—has its roots in the conflict between those in power and the powerless and is the belief that "crime is a product of the political economy that, in capitalist societies, encourages an individualistic competition among and between wealthy people and poor people (the intra- and interclass struggle) and the practice of taking advantage of other people (exploitation)." (3)

rave—an all-night party with loud techno music, dancing, drinking and doing drugs. (6)

recidivism—repeated offending or a return to crime after being caught, convicted and "corrected." (6, 12)

reentry—the preferred term to describe transitioning youthful offenders from secure custody back into the community. (11)

rehabilitation—intervention efforts that seek to modify the factors that cause offenders to engage in crime and delinquency. (11)

representing—a manner of dressing that uses an imaginary line drawn vertically through the body and shows gang allegiance or opposition. (7)

responsivity principle—interventions are most effective when the delivery of treatment programs is in a manner consistent with the offender's ability and learning style. (11)

restorative justice—focuses on repairing the harm done to victims and to the community and stresses that offenders must contribute to the repair; alternately referred to as *reparative justice*. (1)

retribution—punishment of offenders for crimes they committed, the only purpose of which is to get revenge or "even the scales of justice"; punishment for the sake of punishment; also called *just desserts*. (11)

retributive justice—seeks revenge or recompense for unlawful behavior (*lex talionis*). (1)

reverse waiver—when the criminal court transfers a case to the juvenile court; also known as *decertification*. (10)

risk factor—a condition, characteristic or variable that increases the likelihood that a child will become delinquent. (4, 12)

risk principle—"embodies the assumption that criminal behavior can be predicted for individual offenders on the basis of certain factors." (11)

routine activity theory—states that crime is the result of a conscious choice made possible when three factors intersect: (1) availability of a suitable target, (2) absence of a capable guardian and (3) presence of a motivated offender. (3)

runaway—a child who "leaves home without permission and stays away overnight, or a child 14 years old or younger (or older and mentally incompetent) who is away from home and chooses not to return when supposed to and stays away overnight; or a child 15 years old or older who is away from home and chooses not to return and stays away two nights." (5)

school resource officer (SRO)—a career law enforcement officer, with sworn authority, deployed in community-oriented policing and assigned by the employing police department or agency to work in collaboration with school and community-based organizations. (8)

secondary deviance—an act that results because society has labeled the offender a deviant, the offender has accepted the criminal label and, consequently, the offender has committed other crimes. (3)

secondary prevention—seeks early identification and intervention into the lives of individuals or groups found in crime-causing circumstances and focuses on changing the behavior of those likely to become delinquent; punitive prevention fits into this level. (12)

serious child delinquent—youth between the ages of 7 and 12 who has committed one or more acts of homicide, aggravated assault, robbery, rape or serious arson. (6)

serious juvenile offender—a juvenile who has been convicted of a Part I offense as defined by the FBI Uniform Crime Reports, excluding auto theft, petty theft/larceny or distribution of a controlled dangerous substance. (6)

shock incarceration—a correctional alternative that stresses military discipline, physical fitness and strict obedience to orders, as well as educational and vocational training and drug treatment when appropriate; also called *boot camp*. (11)

social contract—a philosophy whereby free, independent individuals agree to form a community and to give up a portion of their individual freedom to benefit the security of the group. (3)

social disorganization theory—states that urban areas produce delinquency directly by weakening community controls and generating a subculture of delinquency passed on from one generation to the next. (3)

social ecology theory—states that ecological conditions predict delinquency and that gang membership is a normal response to social conditions. (3)

specific deterrence—deterrence aimed at a particular offender, such as sentencing a juvenile shoplifter to probation or community service, where the sanction is intended to dissuade that juvenile from further delinquency. (3)

static risk factor—one that cannot be changed, such as an offender's delinquency record; compare with *dynamic risk factor*. (9)

station adjustment—occurs when a juvenile offender is handled by the police within the department and released. (8)

status offense—an offense by a juvenile that would not be a crime if committed by an adult, for example, truancy, running away, curfew violation or smoking cigarettes. (1)

statutory exclusion—a mechanism of juvenile transfer to criminal court where a state has passed legislation specifically banning certain youthful offenders from being tried as juveniles, effectively bypassing the juvenile court entirely and sending certain qualifying offenders directly to criminal court; also called *legislative waiver*. (10)

stereotypical kidnapping—occurs when a stranger or slight acquaintance perpetrates a nonfamily abduction in which the child is detained overnight, transported at least 50 miles, held for ransom, abducted with intent to keep the child permanently, or killed. (5)

strain theory—see *anomie theory*. (3)

street gang—a group of individuals who meet over time, have identifiable leadership, claim control over a specific territory in the community and engage in criminal behavior, either individually or collectively; they frequently create an atmosphere of fear and intimidation in a community. (7)

tagging—a type of graffiti that mimics gang graffiti, but often those doing the tagging are not members of gangs or involved in criminal activity (other than vandalism). (7)

taken into custody—language of the Juvenile Court Act referring to the physical apprehension by a police action of a child engaged in delinquency; equivalent to *arrested* for adults. (8)

temporary custody without hearing—refers to a period usually of 48 hours under conditions in which authorities are justified in placing a child in protective custody. (8)

teratogens—agents that interfere with the normal development of a fetus. (4)

tertiary prevention—the third level of prevention, aimed at preventing recidivism; focuses on preventing further delinquent acts by youths already identified as delinquents; also called *treatment* or *rehabilitation*. (12)

therapeutic intervention—recommendation of an appropriate treatment program. (10)

thrownaway—a child who is asked or told to leave home by a parent or other household adult, and no adequate alternative care is arranged for the child by a household adult and the child is out of the household overnight; or a child who is away from home is prevented from returning home by a parent or other household adult, and no adequate alternative care is arranged for the child by a household adult and the child is out of the household overnight. (5)

truancy—loosely defined as habitual unexcused absence from school; considered a status offense because, although compulsory attendance laws vary from state to state, every state requires children between certain ages to be in school during the academic year absent a valid excuse. (4)

turf—a gang's territorial boundaries. (7)

Uniform Crime Reports (UCR)—the FBI's annual statistical summary titled *Crime in the United States*, intended to collect offense information for the Part I offenses of murder and nonnegligent manslaughter, forcible rape, robbery, aggravated assault, burglary, larceny-theft, motor vehicle theft and arson. (1)

venue—the geographic location of a trial, established by constitutional or statutory provisions. (10)

vertical prosecution—one assistant prosecutor or small group of assistant prosecutors handles the criminal complaint from start to finish through the entire court process; compare with *horizontal prosecution*. (7)

vicarious strain—real-life strain or stress experienced by others around an individual who is experiencing stress. (5)

violent juvenile offender—a youth who has been convicted of a violent Part I offense, one against a person rather than property, and who has a prior adjudication of such an offense; or a youth convicted of murder. (6)

waiver—transfer mechanism whereby the juvenile court judge is allowed the discretion to make an individual determination about whether a juvenile who meets statutory criteria should be tried in juvenile court or, instead, be waived to criminal court. (10)

welfare model—the approach traditionally used by juvenile courts following its underlying *parens patriae* philosophy focusing on the "best interests of the child." (10)

youth gang—term often used interchangeably with *street gang* and, in the context of juvenile justice, is preferred as it helps avoid any confusion between this type of gang and the adult criminal street gang. (7)

youthful offenders—persons adjudicated in a criminal court who may be above the statutory age limit for juveniles but below a specified upper age limit for special correctional commitment. (2)

Author Index

Subject Index